Baja
California

Mexico's
Baja California

Where to go—
from locals
who know!

Acknowledgements

Editorial:

David J. Brackney, Lead Writer
Kristine Miller, Editor
Michael Lugenbuehl, Contributing Writer

Design & Illustration:

Barbara Stanfield, Interior Design/Production
Virginia Matijevac, Illustrator
Michael Lee, Graphic Support

Principal Photographers:

David J. Brackney
Todd Masinter

Cartography:

Donald Olivares, Lead Cartographer
John Skinner, Field Charting
Anna Davila, Cartographer
William R. Scharf and James Kendall, Cartographic Support

Project Management:

John Austerman, Doug Halpin, Grant Henkins and Stephanie Jones

Opening Photo Credits:

Todd Masinter
Cover Photo: *Land's End, Cabo San Lucas*
Opening Photo: *Playas de Tijuana*
Title Page Photo: *Curios for sale, Cabo San Lucas*

David J. Brackney
Introduction Photo: Palapas *on the sand, La Paz*

Complete Photo Credits On Page 544

Although information presented in this publication has been carefully researched and was as accurate as possible at press time, the Automobile Club of Southern California is not repsonsible for any changes or errors that may occur. Readers should keep in mind that travel conditions in Baja California change rapidly. The Automobile Club is not responsible for the performance of any agency or service mentioned in this publication. It is wise to verify information immediately before your visit.

ISBN: 1-56413-506-3

Printed in the United States of America

Information Products, A327
3333 Fairview Road, Costa Mesa, California 92626

Table of Contents

Getting to know Baja California

Daylight gives way to twilight as a well-worn jeep careens down a dusty desert road and the lights of a seaside camp pull into view, 50 miles from the nearest pavement. A mission belfry rises to meet the new day's sun above the date palms in a red rock canyon. Lovers cuddle on a wrought iron park bench while the orange glow fades across the western rim of La Paz Bay.

Baja California evokes a thousand images, each with its own set of followers—RV nomads, surfers, yachties, off-road warriors, sport anglers, eco-tourists—the list goes on and on. In the end, though, the land and lifestyle together are an incredible equalizer. "Baja," as it is usually known for short, has a sense of place like few other destinations. No one stays a stranger long and motorists inevitably wave as they cross paths on lonely desert roads. Some are unmoved by Baja, visiting once and dismissing it as a vast, backward wasteland. For others, though, it strikes a chord deep inside and becomes the focus of their lives, bringing them back year after year.

Baja is part of Mexico yet remains a land unto itself, not unlike Alaska or Hawaii in relation to the United States. All but cut off from the mainland, this rugged peninsula is unknown to most Mexicans, stretching 800 miles below the U.S. border and with a deep blue sea separating it from the rest of Mexico. As such, it has developed a unique culture, a blending of Mexican and North American with a healthy dose of frontier spirit.

WHAT'S IN A NAME

The northern state of the Baja California peninsula is officially known as Baja California, although many people call it Baja California Norte. The official name of the southern state is Baja California Sur. Throughout this book, "Baja California" (or simply "Baja") refers to the entire peninsula.

Still, it's impossible to describe Baja or its people in broad terms. The northwest, with its booming cities, modern freeways and English signage, lies well within the orbit of Southern California. Tens of thousands cross the border every day at Tijuana, Mexico's fourth-largest city and home of the busiest border crossing in the world. In the far south, the resort towns of Los Cabos attract visitors from

BAJA CALIFORNIA

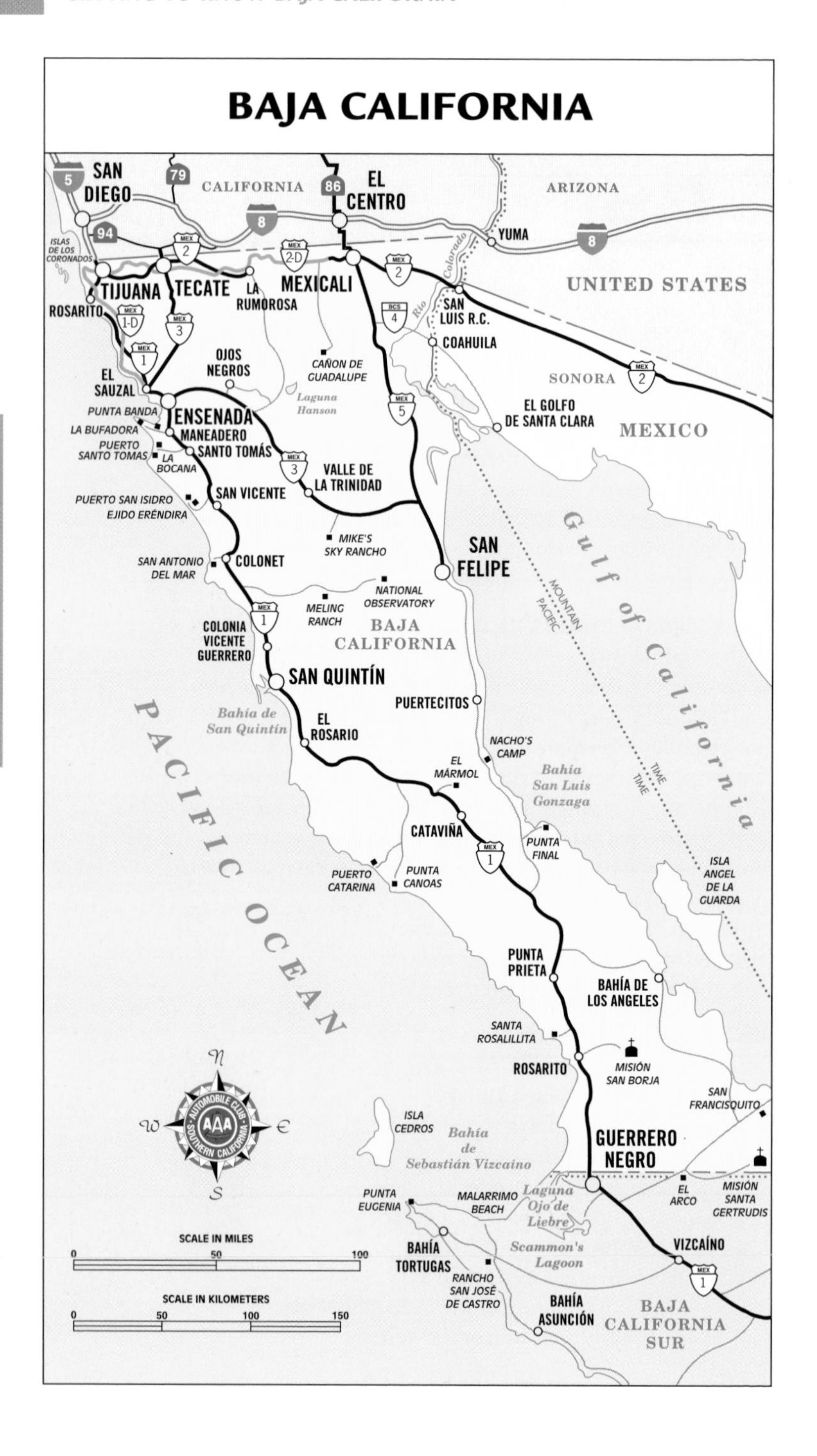

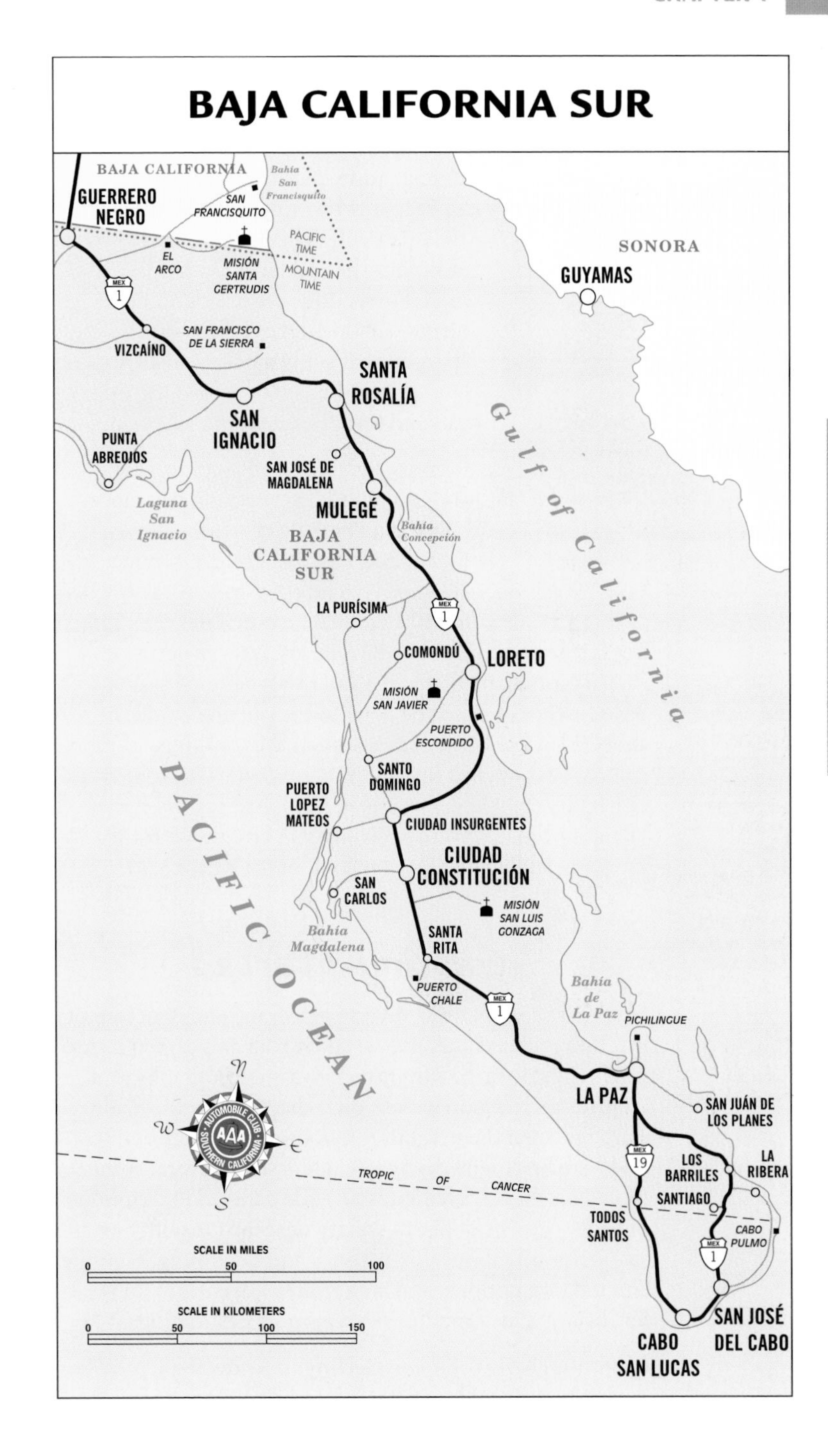
BAJA CALIFORNIA SUR
BAJA CALIFORNIA
GUERRERO NEGRO
SAN FRANCISQUITO
Bahía San Francisquito
PACIFIC TIME
MOUNTAIN TIME
EL ARCO
MISIÓN SANTA GERTRUDIS
SONORA
GUYAMAS
VIZCAÍNO
SAN FRANCISCO DE LA SIERRA
SANTA ROSALÍA
SAN IGNACIO
PUNTA ABREOJOS
SAN JOSÉ DE MAGDALENA
MULEGÉ
Laguna San Ignacio
Bahía Concepción
BAJA CALIFORNIA SUR
Gulf of California
LA PURÍSIMA
COMONDÚ
LORETO
MISIÓN SAN JAVIER
PUERTO ESCONDIDO
SANTO DOMINGO
PUERTO LOPEZ MATEOS
CIUDAD INSURGENTES
CIUDAD CONSTITUCIÓN
SAN CARLOS
MISIÓN SAN LUIS CONZAGA
Bahía Magdalena
SANTA RITA
PUERTO CHALE
PACIFIC OCEAN
Bahía de La Paz
PICHILINGUE
LA PAZ
SAN JUÁN DE LOS PLANES
LOS BARRILES
LA RIBERA
TROPIC OF CANCER
SANTIAGO
TODOS SANTOS
CABO PULMO
SAN JOSÉ DEL CABO
CABO SAN LUCAS
AUTOMOBILE CLUB SOUTHERN CALIFORNIA AAA
N
W
E
S
SCALE IN MILES
0 50 100
SCALE IN KILOMETERS
0 50 100 150

One face of Baja: an elderly ranch hand at San Borja

around the world who may pay several hundred dollars a night for a hotel room.

In between, though, Baja remains an almost empty place. From Ensenada to La Paz, only two towns have more than 15,000 people. This is the land that travelers call "the real Baja," with gnarled cacti, horrendous dirt roads and turquoise waters that lap against deserted shorelines. It is *not* a place most families have in mind when they load the minivan and set off on a week's vacation.

Even so, Baja's days of isolation are gone for good. Every year a few more RVs make the long drive down the most famous of Baja roads, Mexico Highway 1. The 1059-mile route opened in 1973 and ushered in a new era, linking the border with Cabo San Lucas. A ferry network, international airports and a microwave phone system have further opened the door to the outside world. In short, Baja California has assumed the trappings of modern civilization, but its soul remains somewhere far from city lights or the nearest paved road. Just say the word "Baja" to those who've heard its call, and watch for the knowing smile and far-away look in their eyes.

For quick reference, maps on pages 10 and 11 show major cities and other destinations with the roads connecting them. Heavy lines indicate major highways, lighter lines show side routes. An index of place names begins on page 529.

Getting Started

Baja California is a big, diverse place, and the structure of this book reflects that. We've taken Baja and carved it into **nine regions**, each with its own distinct geography and culture. Each region gets its own chapter, and those nine chapters form the heart of this volume. Built around travel on the major highways, the chapters share several common elements. **Travelogues** provide detailed descriptions of each segment of highway; **city descriptions** offer extensive write-ups about things to see and do, dining, nightlife and lodging options; and **side routes** leave the main road for distant and sometimes very remote destinations.

First though, this chapter, **Getting to Know Baja**, provides the big picture with general information on geography, climate, history and other aspects of Baja. Next comes **Tourist Regulations and Travel Tips**, a must-read before any trip to Baja, covering legal issues, travel conditions, tourist assistance and more. Then there's **GreatestHits**, which has the inside pitch on some of Baja's top attractions. Most of these two-page essays provide a virtual tour of the destinations, including a map and directions on how to reach them.

Chapters toward the back of this volume cover **special events and holidays** (of which there are many in Baja), offer a few **itinerary inspirations**, list AAA-inspected **lodgings and campgrounds**, and provide an **appendix** full of information on transportation, recreation, speaking Spanish, etc. Dozens of detailed maps, plus an exhaustive **alphabetical index** and a separate **index for side trips,** will help you quickly find what you're looking for.

Bahía Concepción, one of Baja's GreatestHits

Finally, as you flip through this book, take notice of the informative notes in the margins. Some are practical information and trivia, others are boxed and highlighted with savvy travel tips, such as a hazardous road condition or how you should pay for a mariachi song in downtown Tijuana.

In, Out and Around Baja

A lack of good roads, airports and other infrastructure kept mankind at bay for a long, long time in Baja California, and while that's changing now, getting around can still be one of the region's biggest challenges. Unless you're flying straight to Baja Sur or staying right along the border, you'll be spending a lot of time on the road. This book reflects that, with its detailed travelogues and side route descriptions, which offer the best way to reach many towns and attractions.

Here's an overview of major transit forms:

AIR

Air travel has helped make Baja California a major tourist destination, especially southern Baja, where **Loreto, La Paz** and **Los Cabos** have international airports. All three have daily flights from California, mainland Mexico and **Tijuana**. Tijuana, for its part, has the largest airport in Baja California, with daily service not only to southern Baja, but the rest of Mexico as well. Moreover, airfares out of Tijuana are often considerably lower than nearby Southern California. Farther east, **Mexicali** has daily service to mainland Mexico as well, but no direct flights within Baja. Elsewhere,

It's about a two-hour flight from Southern California to La Paz or Los Cabos.

Highway 1 north of Cataviña

Central Baja's sole airport is at **Guerrero Negro**, which has service to Hermosillo, Sonora.

AUTOMOBILE

Unless your interests lie off-road, nearly all of your driving will be along Baja's five major intercity highways. Best known by far is **Mexico Highway 1**, the 1059-mile transpeninsular route, which opened in 1973 and paved the way for development throughout much of Baja. The other main highways include these:

SHOWING THE WAY

Besides the maps in this book, the Auto Club's Baja California road map is another valuable travel aid. It's available free to AAA members at offices throughout California and Arizona, and at some other AAA offices around the United States. The book and map are also sold at some retail outlets in Baja and elsewhere.

Mexico Highway 2 parallels the border from Tijuana to Mexicali before continuing east to Sonora. **Mexico Highway 3** runs a zigzag from Tecate to Ensenada and across the peninsula to Mexico Highway 5 near San Felipe. **Mexico Highway 5** runs due south from Mexicali to San Felipe on the Gulf of California. **Mexico Highway 19** hugs the Pacific coastline between Cabo San Lucas and Todos Santos, then angles inland to meet Mexico Highway 1 south of La Paz.

For details on automobile travel in Baja, see *Tourist Regulations and Travel Tips*, Chapter 2, and *Appendix*, Chapter 16. For details on other forms of transit, see *Appendix*.

BUS

Millions of Mexicans use the bus as their primary means of transit, and Baja California is no exception. Bus service is one of the cheapest means to get around Baja, and offers a close-up look at the people and their culture. Buses depart Tijuana several times a day for La Paz, stopping in major towns along the way. Connecting service is available to Cabo San Lucas. Buses also link Tijuana to Mexicali, with connecting service available to mainland cities.

FERRY

One of Baja's most enjoyable travel experiences is the Baja California Ferry, which offers service from mainland Mexico to the ports of **La Paz** and **Santa Rosalía.** Many travelers drive down Highway 1 before loading their vehicle aboard the ferry and returning north via the mainland. Sailing times range from eight to 18 hours, depending on the route; sleeping quarters are available on overnight trips.

Geography

Check the map and at first glance you might think that Baja California was as large as *Alta California,* its neighbor across the U.S. border. It is, after all, about the same length as *Alta California,* more than 800 miles from north to south, making it one of the world's longest peninsulas. It's even longer if you drive Mexico Highway 1, which runs more than 1000 miles from Tijuana to Cabo San Lucas. In fact, however, Baja is only about one-third the size of its northern counterpart, which reflects its narrow, highly irregular form.

At its widest (along the U.S. border), Baja is nearly 150 miles across, but it narrows to less than 30 miles in the desert north of La Paz. Along the way, innumerable bays and coves break up the coastlines—the Pacific Ocean on the west and the Gulf of California on the east. Those bodies of water play key roles in nearly all aspects of Baja California life, including climate, plant life, culture and economy. Although it is a part of Mexico, Baja is all but cut off from the rest of Mexico, mainly by the Gulf of California, also known as the Sea of Cortez. In the extreme north, the Colorado River separates Baja from the Mexican state of Sonora and a sliver of the U.S. state of Arizona.

Oasis at Cañon de Guadalupe, southwest of Mexicali

Besides the coastlines, perhaps the most outstanding feature of Baja's landscape is the chain of rugged mountains that runs virtually unbroken down the peninsula. All told, there are nine ranges, subdivided into different *sierras,* starting with the Sierra Juárez at the California border and ending with the Sierra de la Laguna, which plunges seaward at Land's End. Those mountains transcend three broad geographical zones, each with different topography, climates and life forms.

The far north, often called the California Zone, reaches about 200 miles below the border and is basically an extension of Southern California. It is an uneven landscape in the west, with brush-covered hills that rise sharply from the ocean, dissected by canyons, valleys and a few broad coastal plains. Farther inland, the terrain gradually rises toward the northern mountains, which resemble

Baja California is the fourth-longest peninsula in the world.

California's Sierra Nevada, with rolling foothills and gentle slopes to the west and steep drop-offs to the east. Baja's highest peaks are here, crowned by Picacho del Diablo, which rises 10,154 feet west of San Felipe and bears a strong likeness to California's highest point, Mt. Whitney.

Beyond the mountains lie the lowlands of the Sonoran Desert, a very hot and mostly barren region with terrain and plant life much like that southeast California. Amid this desert is the Mexicali Valley, a southern extension of California's Imperial Valley and the most productive farming region in Baja California. Waters from the Colorado River have been diverted to irrigate the rich alluvial soil of the valley, left there by the river over many centuries.

Picacho del Diablo, Baja California's highest peak

Central Baja, which extends from El Rosario to La Paz, is entirely desert. The central desert, as it's widely known, is a scenic and diverse place with a fantastic range of landscapes. One might best describe the terrain as barren mountains and mesas separated by rocky valleys and sandy plains. On the east flank, abrupt slopes rise from the Gulf of California, while the Pacific side is less rugged. Two major lowlands along the west coast contrast with the rugged landscape elsewhere in this region. One is the Vizcaíno Desert, a vast, sandy plain near Guerrero Negro with little plant life except saltbrush and scattered yucca válida. Farther south there's the Santo Domingo Valley (Magdalena Plain), a major farming region centered around Ciudad Constitución.

Baja California Sur is the least populous of Mexico's 31 states.

Another hallmark of this region is its history of volcanic activity, evidenced by a series of extensive lava flows that begin near San Ignacio and spread southward for more than 100 miles. Las Tres Vírgenes, three large volcanic cones, are in this area as well and are a major landmark southeast of San Ignacio. Farther south, there's the Sierra de la Giganta, a

Tropic of Cancer monument near Santiago

Government

The Baja California peninsula is comprised of two states, Baja California and Baja California Sur, separated by the 28th parallel.

State Capitals

Baja California: Mexicali · Baja California Sur: La Paz

Municipal Divisions

Mexican states, including Baja California and Baja California Sur, are divided into *municipios*, which are roughly equivalent to American counties. Baja California has five *municipios*, which bear the names of its largest cities, including Tijuana, Ensenada, Rosarito, Tecate and Mexicali. Baja California Sur is home to five *municipios* as well: Mulegé, Loreto, Comondú, La Paz and Los Cabos.

Size

Baja California: 27,648 square miles
Baja California Sur: 28,369 square miles

Total: 56,017 square miles, about one-third the size of the U.S. state of California.

High Points

Baja California: Picacho del Diablo, 10,154 feet
Baja California Sur: Picacho de la Laguna, 7,100 feet

Population

*Baja California: 2.5 million · *Baja California Sur: 420,000

Largest City: Tijuana

*Based on 2000 census preliminary results. The actual population for the state of Baja California is believed to be much larger than the official number.

rugged mountain range of volcanic origin extending from Santa Rosalía almost to La Paz.

No place in Baja California is more than 90 miles from the sea.

The southernmost portion of Baja picks up from the central desert near La Paz and runs clear to Cabo San Lucas. The major feature here is the Sierra de la Laguna, the highest mountain range in Baja California Sur, which slopes up from both coasts to heights of more than 7000 feet. The Tropic of Cancer cuts a path across this region, passing just south of Todos Santos on the Pacific coast, crossing the mountains and through the town of Santiago before heading out to sea near Cabo Pulmo.

Part desert and part semi-arid, this part of Baja gets a bit more rainfall on average than the central desert, but still lies beyond reach of most major weather systems. And with its excellent beaches and superlative scenery, it's no surprise that this region is home to Baja's largest and most luxurious resorts.

Climate

See *Appendix*, Chapter 16, for a complete temperature and precipitation chart.

Think of one word that describes Baja California and you may respond with "desert." It's a fitting answer, since nearly two-thirds of the region meets the definition of desert, receiving less than 10 inches of precipitation a year. Still, Baja boasts a wide range of climates, even within its deserts, not surprising for a peninsula that ranges from more than 32 degrees to less than 23 degrees in latitude. Yet latitude is just one of several factors that affect the region's climate. The Pacific Ocean, Gulf of California and elevation changes are all major players, and a few miles' travel can mean a big difference in temperature and precipitation.

Wine grapes thrive in the inland climate of the Guadalupe Valley.

From north to south, Baja falls into three broad climatic zones. The far north has a climate much like that of Southern California, where elevation and distance from the ocean are the primary influences. The region is semiarid and temperate in the west, with the mildest weather along the coast and a rainy season between November and March. Cooled by the south-flowing California Current, the Pacific keeps things mild along the coastline nearly all the time, and makes for foggy, overcast conditions during much of late spring and early summer. Summer temperatures in Ensenada and San Quintín average in the 70s by day and 60s by night, while winter highs average in the upper 60s with nighttime lows in the upper 40s—about the same as San Diego.

Farther inland across the north, the weather shows more extremes throughout the year. Case in point is the Guadalupe Valley near Ensenada, where summer days climb to the 80s or 90s, while winter nights may dip to near freezing, a combination that makes this the biggest wine-producing region in Baja. Still farther inland, the northern mountains have the coolest weather in all of Baja. Conditions at higher elevations resemble those of Southern California's mountains, with mild days and cool nights in the summer, and freezing temperatures with occasional heavy snowfalls in the winter. Farther east are the arid lowlands of the Sonoran Desert, which includes the Mexicali Valley and northern Gulf of California coast. It is the hottest, driest region in all of Baja, with summer days that average well above 100 degrees, winters that are mild and sunny, and average annual rainfall of less than 3 inches.

BAJA BRRR!

Astronomers stationed at the National Autonomous University of Mexico's observatory, 9000 feet above sea level in the Sierra San Pedro Mártir, sometimes work in nighttime temperatures as low as -20 Celsius, or -4 Fahrenheit.

Farther south, the next major climatic zone is the Central Desert, which extends from about El Rosario in the north to Bahía Magdalena in the south. (On the gulf coast, the Central Desert meets the Sonoran Desert around Bahía de los Angeles.) Perhaps the leading hallmark of this region is its erratic rainfall. Violent thunderstorms may bring several inches of rain all at once, but then a year may pass with hardly a drop of moisture.

Baja at its driest: crossing the lakebed of Laguna Salada

Winter is the most agreeable time of year across much of this region, with brilliant sunshine, warm temperatures and very little rain. Winters can be cool, though, in the higher mountains and along the coastlines. On the Pacific coast, the prevailing wind is from the northwest most of the year, while on the gulf coast steady northeast winds blow on most days between November and March; either one may send you scrambling for a jacket. Summers, meanwhile, are mild along the west coast as far south as the Vizcaíno Peninsula, but the remainder of this zone swelters beneath oppressive summer heat. Inland areas such as San Ignacio have a drier heat than along the gulf coast, where the humid air can make towns like Loreto hard to bear during the hottest months.

The southernmost climatic zone runs from Bahía Magdalena to Cabo San Lucas, and has a distinct tropical feel to it. Part desert and part semiarid, this zone is balmy throughout the year and receives the most rain between

Driving in Loreto after a late-summer chubasco

late summer and mid-autumn. It comes mostly in the form of downpours known as *chubascos*—heavy squalls that move onshore from the gulf and drench the terrain, sometimes flooding towns and normally dry riverbeds. Every several years, a hurricane will join the mix, bringing driving rains to the region and occasionally moving farther north along the gulf. Like the Central Desert, rainfall may vary widely from one year to the next, but on average La Paz gets 6 inches per year, while Cabo San Lucas receives 8 inches and San Antonio (in the foothills of the Sierra de la Laguna) gets 16 inches.

Baja California's wettest region is the Sierra de la Laguna, where some areas receive up to 35 inches of precipitation a year.

The most comfortable weather in this zone comes between November and May, with highs in the 70s or 80s, lows in the 50s or 60s, low humidity and very little rainfall. Summers are quite hot, with average highs around 100 degrees in La Paz and Los Cabos. The west coast is a bit milder, as the Pacific Ocean comes into play, keeping summer readings five or 10 degrees cooler than other areas in this southernmost quarter of Baja.

Flora and Fauna

Entire volumes have been devoted to the flora and fauna of Baja California, and no wonder, since the 800-mile-long peninsula enjoys a rich variety of both. Space doesn't allow an extensive review of them here, but it is important to note that many species exist in this region that are found nowhere else in the world. That is most apparent in central and southern Baja, which are largely removed from any other large landmass.

Quaking aspen on an autumn day in the Sierra de San Pedro Mártir

Starting with plant life, the far north is again similar to Southern California. The coastal area is home to chaparral, grasses, scattered oaks and seasonal wildflowers that will make Southern Californians feel right at home. Beyond the coasts, the northern mountains have the least likely vegetation in Baja, with forests of pine and fir that blanket the upper slopes—again resembling similar terrain north of the border.

Beyond the mountains, the Sonoran Desert looks a lot like textbook Baja, with its low-lying shrubs, and scattered growths of cardón cacti, mesquite and ocotillo. Some parts of this super-arid region are almost devoid of vegetation. A different landscape is found in the Mexicali Valley, where cotton, grains, and fruit and truck crops thrive across huge tracts of irrigated desert. The same goes for the coastal plain around San Quintín, where water from an underground aquifer has helped create a major vegetable-growing district.

Farther south, the Central Desert harbors the plants for which Baja is most famous, including several species that grow naturally nowhere else on earth. The best known is the giant cardón cactus—often confused with the saguaro of Arizona and Sonora. Two more plants unique to this region are the yucca válida, a smaller cousin of California's Joshua tree; and the cirio, a tall, column-shaped oddball that grows only in Baja and Sonora. Other species have cousins in the American Southwest or mainland Mexico, including agave, cholla, pitahaya (organ pipe) and barrel cacti, along with fan palm, ocotillo, palo verde and elephant tree.

Central desert foliage: a cardón cactus, cirio tree and an elephant tree

The two main lowlands of central Baja, both near the Pacific coast, are studies in contrast. The Vizcaíno Desert near Guerrero Negro is the most barren region in all of Baja—a vast, sandy plain where saltbrush and scattered yucca válida are the main plant life, getting most of their moisture from the fog. Elsewhere, a visit to central Baja's oasis towns could make you think that date palms were native species as well. They aren't, but they've been thriving in these parts for hundreds of years now, planted mostly by Jesuit missionaries during Baja's colonial days. The same holds true for citrus, olive and banana trees, which have their roots in the mission era as well.

In southern Baja, the foliage grows denser and new species join the mix, given the proximity of the Tropic of Cancer and increases in rainfall. Botanists classify the region as tropical desert and tropical thorn forest, depending on rainfall and elevation. At lower elevations, the cacti of the Central Desert still abound but share the terrain with

Wild burros supervise a vehicle repair along the East Cape, 1998.

acacias, sumac, mesquite and other low-lying trees. Meanwhile, a forest of oaks and piñon pines thrives on the higher slopes of the Sierra de la Laguna, where tropical storms provide reliable rainfall in the summer and early fall.

Baja's fauna, meanwhile are as diverse as the land and surrounding waters, and sometimes are the biggest attraction for visitors. Depending on where you go, and when, Baja may seem to be devoid of interesting wildlife or a prolific haven for all sorts of exotic species.

Few land-based animals would be considered exotic, but thanks to the peninsula's isolation, more than two dozen native species exist here and nowhere else on Earth. You're more likely to see most of these creatures after dark, when the weather cools and they emerge from their daytime lairs for feeding. Among the land mammals found throughout most of Baja are coyotes, mule deer, bobcats, raccoons, and various breeds of rabbits and foxes. Common rodents include several varieties of squirrels, gophers, mice, and in the desert, several subspecies of the kangaroo rat. Among reptiles, Baja supports about 30 varieties of lizards, a like number of snakes, and a few varieties of turtles, frogs and toads.

Lucky travelers may also spy an occasional bighorn sheep or peninsular pronghorn antelope, both endangered species that once roamed the peninsula in large numbers.

Poisonous Creature Alert

Major poisonous species in Baja include rattlesnakes, scorpions and tarantulas. Fortunately, none are aggressive toward humans unless defending themselves, and the wounds they inflict are seldom fatal. However, it pays to take sensible precautions wherever you go. Desert hikers should use sturdy, high-top boots and avoid areas where snakes may be hiding. Campers should zip shut their tents at night to keep animals out. And wherever you spend the night in the desert, shake out your footwear in the morning to avoid any surprises.

A dead rattler near Meling Ranch

More likely you'll encounter a wild burro, descended from the beasts of burden that the early Spaniards imported and have adapted well to Baja's dry, rugged interior.

With 3000 miles of coastline and a vast, empty interior, Baja also supports a tremendous variety of bird life. The islands, bays and wetlands are huge habitats for marine birds and waterfowl, far more than we can list here. A few of the notable coastal birds you'll likely see are brown pelicans, petrels, cormorants, boobies, egrets and terns.

The desert, meanwhile, is home to various sparrows, hummingbirds, wrens and other small birds, including the fleet-footed roadrunner. Several good-sized birds of prey patrol the desert skies, including falcons, hawks and owls. More common is the turkey vulture, the oversized raptor that you'll see feeding on road kill or peering down from the crooked limb of a cardón cactus.

Perhaps the most famous of Baja's fauna hails from the sea—the California gray whales, which travel this way to mate and bear their young. Migrating from the Arctic, the whales reach the lagoons of Baja California Sur starting in late-December, while the final stragglers are usually gone by early April. During their stay, the whales attract visitors from around the world, who can view them up close like nowhere else, sometimes within touching distance.

Turkey vultures stand watch near Loreto.

The grays are not the only whales known to Baja. Orcas, humpbacks, sperm whales and blue whales (the largest creatures on earth) also ply the gulf and Pacific waters. Other marine mammals common to both coasts include California sea lions, harbor seals, and white sided and bottlenose dolphins.

See *GreatestHits,* Chapter 3, for more on the California gray whale.

Otherwise, the sea life along the Pacific and gulf coasts are quite different. The Pacific waters are usually cooler, thanks to the southward flow of the California Current, and support most of the same fish and other marine life as *Alta California.* Seabass, kelp bass, cod, barracuda, mackerel and various tuna all thrive in the Pacific from the Vizcaíno Peninsula on northward. Farther south, more warm water species begin to appear, including sailfish, marlin, dorado and other big game fish.

The gulf, for its part, harbors a tremendous variety of sea life, including nearly 900 identified species of fish. It's the coast most travelers head for when they're angling for game fish or diving to see a gallery of colorful tropical species. The seas off the Cape, where the Pacific and gulf merge, produce the grandest variety of all, with a large number of species from both bodies of water.

See *GreatestHits,* Chapter 3, and various city listings under *Outdoor Fun* for more on Baja sea life.

Economy

Tijuana has for many years had Mexico's lowest unemployment rate, around 1 percent.

Free trade has become a way of life in the past decade between the United States and Mexico, but it's nothing new in Baja California, which has a long tradition of cashing in on its proximity to the United States. While Baja does not rely completely on its huge neighbor, Americans and their dollars have helped the Baja states achieve the highest living standard in Mexico, creating thousands of jobs in manufacturing, farming, tourism and other industries. In the north, factories assemble all manner of goods for export to the United States and other lands, while in the south, the luxury resorts of Los Cabos earn most of their livelihood from American guests. Elsewhere, the region's farms turn out rich harvests of fruits and vegetables, much of it bound for U.S. store shelves.

Cuauhtémoc Brewery, Tecate's largest employer

Manufacturing is a big business along the border, led by Tijuana, where factories turn out electronic components, clothing and auto parts, many earmarked for shipment to the United States. Among those factories are hundreds of *maquiladoras,* those so-called "in-bond plants" that assemble foreign-produced components into finished consumer goods for reshipment abroad. Mexicali is another center of *maquiladoras* and other manufacturing, although it still is better known as the hub of Baja's largest agricultural region. Elsewhere in the north, Ensenada earns its keep largely from the sea, with a good-sized fishing fleet, several canneries and the largest port on Baja's Pacific coast. Tecate, meanwhile, is growing as a *maquiladora* town, but its largest employer remains the brewery that makes the town's namesake beer.

***Maquiladora* employment in Baja California increased by 16 percent in 1999 alone, reaching almost a quarter-million workers.**

Farther south, commercial activity is fairly sparse before you reach La Paz, but there are some notable exceptions.

One is Guerrero Negro in central Baja, home of the largest salt evaporating operation in the world; another is the Santo Domingo Valley, centered around Ciudad Constitución, where irrigation has created the largest agricultural district in Baja Sur. La Paz is the primary port for shipping the valley's farm products.

Tourism Los Cabos-style: Westin Regina Golf & Beach Resort—Los Cabos

In the end, however, tourism remains Baja California's leading moneymaker, generating revenue and jobs throughout the peninsula. Most tourists spend only a few hours in Baja, but leave billions of dollars in their wake, mainly in the border towns and south to Ensenada. Beyond Ensenada, the main tourist action is along the gulf coast. La Paz and Los Cabos are the biggest destinations, but San Felipe, Bahía de los Angeles, Mulegé and Loreto have all earned loyal followings as well. Fishing has always been the biggest draw to the gulf, but so are its lovely beaches, diving, nightlife and a climate that is best described as "endless summer."

History

From prolific cave paintings to early tools and arrowheads, evidence abounds that human beings were afoot in Baja California thousands of years before the first Europeans showed up. No one's sure when the first humans arrived, but by most accounts it was at least 8000 years ago and perhaps thousands of years before that. By the time the Spaniards arrived, some 50,000 Indians were believed to be living in Baja, belonging to numerous tribes and four main linguistic groups: the Yumans, Guaicura, Huchiti and the Pericu.

It was Spanish explorer Hernán Cortés who established the first settlement in Baja California. Cortés, who had conquered central Mexico in 1521, was attracted here by rumors of great wealth, and in 1535 he landed at the site of the modern-day Pichilingue, north of La Paz. Cortés hoped to found a permanent colony, but shortages of food and other supplies doomed his party's efforts, and it was abandoned after just two years.

Signpost from early locals—Cueva La Pintada in central Baja's Sierra San Francisco

More than 150 years would pass before the first permanent settlement was established, although Baja received sporadic visits in the meantime. In 1542 Juán Rodríguez Cabrillo explored the entire west coast of Baja on his way up the Pacific coast of North America. In 1602 Sebastián Vizcaíno made a more detailed exploration of the west coast and produced the first detailed maps of the shoreline. Meanwhile, several small settlements came and went, while pirates used Cabo San Lucas as a base from which to ambush Spanish galleons crossing the Pacific from Manila.

Finally, on October 15, 1697, Jesuit Padre Juán María Salvatierra landed on Baja's east coast and founded a mission at Loreto, which became the first permanent European settlement in the Californias. The Jesuits would forever change the face of Baja, bringing Christianity, modern agriculture and fine arts to the Indians, while building a network of 23 missions. They also studied the flora and fauna, made elaborate maps and prepared ethnological reports on the native peoples. Fourteen of the missions took firm root, and a few of them remain standing to this day.

It was a mixed legacy, however, for while the Jesuits brought modern civilization to Baja, they also brought diseases that killed off thousands of Indians, who lacked immunities to them. What's more, the priests were often heavy-handed in their attempts to convert the Indians, many of whom rose up in revolt. In time the Jesuits' political and economic order began to unravel while diseases continued their frightful toll, eventually reducing the Indian population of southern Baja by more than 90 percent. Finally, as the Jesuits were preparing to move north, the Spanish crown expelled them from Baja in 1768.

Loreto was settled 72 years before Padre Serra founded his mission at San Diego, the oldest city in Alta California.

Later that same year, 13 padres of the Franciscan Brotherhood landed at Loreto, under the leadership of Padre Junípero Serra. A quick appraisal convinced Serra that their work lay far to the north in Alta California, and the Franciscans founded only one mission in Baja. With the

Franciscans heading north, the Dominican Order took charge in Baja and founded nine more missions, all from El Rosario northward.

The Dominicans maintained control of Baja's missions for more than 60 years, although their influence was perhaps dubious, since diseases had killed most of the Indians and Spain was losing interest in the region. During those years, Mexico won its independence from Spain, following an 11-year war that ended in 1821. Then, in 1832 the Mexican government ordered the secularization of Baja's missions and their conversion to parish churches. The only exceptions were the missions in the far north, which the Dominicans retained control of until 1846, since they were the sole links between Baja and the more prosperous Alta California.

Misión San Ignacio, completed in 1786

Baja was largely forgotten until the 1846-48 Mexican-American War, which brought lasting change to both the Californias. Only a few minor battles took place in Baja, but the war ended with Mexico losing more than half its territory to the United States. In the Treaty of Guadalupe Hidalgo, Mexico gave up possession of Alta California, while retaining control of Baja California, with the border drawn one league below the southern edge of San Diego Bay.

Baja did not fade quietly from the scene, however, as renegade U.S. soldier William Walker led a band of mercenaries in seizing control of La Paz in 1853. Walker proclaimed himself "President of Lower California," but was soon forced to flee under the threat of Mexican counterattack. After Walker's aborted takeover (and a failed attempt to seize the state of Sonora) the balance of the 19th century was a comparatively subdued time in Baja, but not completely uneventful. Whalers hunted the gray whales to near-extinction at Scammon's Lagoon, the French launched a huge copper-mining venture at Santa Rosalía, and Tijuana and Ensenada emerged as fledgling towns in the far north.

Stability would prevail until the Mexican Revolution, which brought armed conflict along the border. In 1911, Ricardo Flores Magón led an anti-government uprising that became known as the Tijuana Revolution. Insurgents (known as "*Magonistas*") seized control of the city, but the rebellion soon foundered when Mexican troops arrived and the rebels fled north across the border. Thereafter, a succession of politically appointed governors maintained an uneasy peace over the region.

As the 1920s unfolded, Baja received more attention from its northern neighbor, starting with U.S. Prohibition, which brought thousands of Americans south in search of legal alcohol. Tijuana became a major getaway for drinking, gambling and other guilty pleasures, while a paved road put Rosarito and Ensenada within reach of weekend tourists. The boom fizzled, however, with the repeal of Prohibition in 1933 followed by a government decree in 1938 that outlawed gambling in Mexico.

Early Auto Club research trip near Rosarito Beach, sometime in the 1920s. The Auto Club's oldest Baja map dates to 1924.

Soon enough, however, the Americans would be back. World War II brought a huge influx of military men to San Diego, and northern Baja became a natural destination for sailors and marines on leave. After the war, more gringos headed south as a paved road reached from the border to San Felipe in 1951. The following year, the northern half of Baja officially became a state of Mexico, with an elected government in the state capital, Mexicali. Baja California Sur followed suit in 1974, with its state capital in La Paz.

Less than a year earlier, workers in late 1973 completed construction of Mexico Highway 1, which arguably has had the greatest impact of any event on Baja California in the last 50 years. The 1059-mile highway became the first paved route between the border and Cabo San Lucas, bringing thousands of tourists south each year and encouraging development throughout the peninsula. Some feared that Highway 1 would bring the end of the wild old Baja, bringing rampant growth and development throughout the peninsula. Those fears may yet come to pass, but apart from the big cities, the scenic grandeur and sense of isolation remain largely unspoiled.

Still, Baja has developed far faster in recent decades than the rest of Mexico, with the most growth in the extreme north and south. Along the border, Tijuana has mushroomed to become the fourth-largest city in Mexico, with nearly 2 million people and more arriving every week to take jobs in the huge *maquiladora* assembly plants. Rosarito and Ensenada have developed rapidly as well, while Mexicali has grown to 800,000 people living amid one of the most productive farming areas in Mexico. A thousand miles to the south, the twin towns of San José del Cabo and Cabo San Lucas have grown from tiny fishing villages to become one of the largest resort areas in the country.

Most of Baja's backcountry remains pristine, thanks to roads like this.

In between, though, most of Baja remains an untamed place where the rugged terrain and desert climate have helped hold development at bay. Those very attributes have brought visitors from around the world, seeking a frontier spirit and seclusion that have largely disappeared elsewhere. How well business and government leaders manage that growth without destroying the virtues that created it is the biggest question facing Baja California as a new century unfolds.

Tourist Regulations & Travel Tips

Your travels in Baja California will go much more smoothly if you have some background on Mexican laws and customs before you cross the border. If you're not already a seasoned Baja traveler, this chapter will help make you one, covering Mexican and U.S. regulations, tourist assistance and what to expect on the road. For additional information, including road signs, supply lists, Spanish vocabulary and more, see *Appendix,* Chapter 16.

Calexico border crossing, across from downtown Mexicali

Baja California has six border crossings for entering and leaving Mexico, two each in Tijuana and Mexicali, and one each in Tecate and Algodónes. From west to east they are as follows:

- San Ysidro, just north of downtown Tijuana; open 24 hours.
- Otay Mesa, six miles east of San Ysidro and near the Tijuana airport; open 6 a.m. to 10 p.m.
- Tecate, open 6 a.m. to midnight.
- Calexico, adjacent to downtown Mexicali; open 24 hours.

- Calexico East, six miles east of downtown Mexicali; open 6 a.m. to 10 p.m.
- Algodónes, at the extreme northeast corner of Baja California and 10 miles west of Yuma, Arizona; open 6 a.m. to 8 p.m.

Tourist Regulations

Mexican tourist regulations have been a moving target of sorts over the past couple of years, leaving many visitors confused over what documentation is required and what fees they may have to pay. The biggest change has been the 1999 introduction of a fee on tourist cards, which the Mexican government formerly issued free of charge. However, the majority of Baja tourists face no fees or paperwork for their cross-border visits. This includes all those making short visits to border towns or resort cities in northern Baja. Business travelers and minors not accompanied by both parents continue to face additional (but not unmanageable) requirements. Current regulations as of our publication deadline are as follows:

Tourist Cards—Foreign nationals traveling into the interior of Baja California or planning visits of 72 hours or longer in the border region are required to obtain a tourist card. They are available free of charge on both sides of the border, but a 170-peso fee (about 18 U.S. dollars) must be paid before leaving Mexico. For visitors arriving by land, the tourist card allows multiple entries for a period of 180 days. The fee can be paid at any Mexican bank, where your card will be stamped to certify it. Travelers overstaying the time limit on the card will be subject to a fine.

The following travelers do *not* have to obtain a tourist card:

- Those traveling no farther south than Maneadero (10 miles south of Ensenada) on Mexico Highway 1 and staying for less than 72 hours.
- Those traveling no farther south than San Felipe on Mexico Highway 5 and staying for less than 72 hours.
- Those arriving by sea and staying for less than 72 hours.
- Mexicans living abroad.

Tourist cards are available at many venues, including the border, the Mexican Immigration office near the north entrance of Ensenada, and Mexican consulates in the United States. They may be available at offices of the Automobile Club of Southern California, other AAA offices and many travel agencies. Supplies can be erratic at those places, however, so it's a good idea to phone ahead. If you're flying to Baja, tourist cards are available through airlines, at the airport, or sometimes through the travel agency booking the flight.

BE PREPARED

Mexico tends to be erratic in its enforcement of tourist regulations, so don't be complacent. Several visits may pass without being asked to present any documents, but one day an official will ask for your stamped tourist card and citizenship papers. Take no chances and make sure you're in compliance.

If you're driving to Baja, your tourist card should be validated at the border or before traveling south of Maneadero or San Felipe. Officials may require you to pay the 170-peso fee before validating your card, but they may also allow you to pay later. Even if you're allowed to pay later, it's a good idea to make payment as soon as possible to avoid potential difficulties with authorities. If you are flying to Baja, your card will be validated at the airport where you enter the country.

To have your tourist card validated, you will need to provide proof of citizenship. The original document used to provide proof of citizenship must be carried into Mexico with the tourist card. Copies are not acceptable.

U.S.-born citizens will need *one* of the following:

- A valid (unexpired) U.S. passport.
- A birth certificate issued by a federal, state, county or city agency in whose jurisdiction the holder was born. A photocopy is not acceptable unless it has been certified by the issuing authority.

Naturalized U.S. citizens will need *one* of the following:

- A valid (unexpired) U.S. passport.
- The *original* Certificate of Naturalization *or* Certificate of Citizenship, *or* Report of Birth Abroad, *or* a Consular Report of Birth (form FS-240), *or* Certification of Birth (form DS-1350 or FS-240).

A voter registration card, record of birth, baptismal certificate or notification of birth issued by hospitals, churches, etc. are not acceptable as citizenship documents.

Canadian citizens will need *one* of the following:

- A valid (unexpired) passport.
- A birth certificate issued in Canada.

U.S. residents who are citizens of other nations must have a resident alien card and a passport. Citizens of other nations who are not living in the United States should contact a Mexican Consulate for specific requirements.

Minors—Any minor (under age 18) traveling to Mexico must have a tourist card and proof of citizenship, as

Tourist Cards, Regulations and More

For the latest on Mexican tourist regulations or how to obtain a tourist card, a good information source is the Mexican Government Tourism Office in Los Angeles. It is located on the fifth floor of the Mexican Consulate building at 2401 W. Sixth Street, 90057; phone (213) 351-2069. It is open Monday through Friday, 9 a.m. to 5 p.m. (The consulate in Los Angeles is open Monday through Friday from 7 a.m. to 1 p.m.) Other Mexican consulates can provide information as well. In California they are located in Calexico, Fresno, Oxnard, Sacramento, San Bernardino, San Diego, San Francisco, San Jose and Santa Ana. The Mexican government has consulates in other U.S. cities along the border or with large Mexican populations.

described in the section above. In addition, minors traveling alone, traveling with anyone other than their parents or legal guardians, *or* traveling with only one parent or guardian must provide further documentation. This includes a completed and notarized copy of a form granting permission for the minor to enter Mexico. These forms are available at any notary public or at the Mexican Government Tourist Office. A photocopy of a parent's identification, such as a drivers license, is recommended as well. You should present these documents when applying for a tourist card.

Mexican travel regulations and fees are subject to change. Call a Mexican consulate or other government agency to verify current requirements.

If a child's parents are divorced or separated, the signed letter must be accompanied by the divorce or separation papers. If one parent is deceased, the death certificate must accompany the form in lieu of the deceased's signature; the surviving parent must still sign the form. If a child is under legal guardianship, the guardian(s) must sign the form and provide guardianship papers and, when applicable, death certificates for both parents.

Business Travel—Non-Mexican citizens who wish to do business of any kind in Mexico must obtain a business form, known as an FMN, by applying personally at a Mexican consulate or at any port of entry. The form is good for 30 days and costs 170 pesos or its equivalent in dollars. To request an extension or if you plan to conduct business for more than 30 days, you must obtain an FM3 work permit. You must have a valid passport, a letter from the company stating the business to be conducted in Mexico, proof of the company's validity, and two photographs. The fee for an FM3 is 1362 pesos or its equivalent in dollars. Any person traveling on business without this form is subject to a fine.

AUTOMOBILE REQUIREMENTS

No special permits are required for vehicles traveling in Baja California. While driving, however, you must carry acceptable proof of vehicle ownership and a valid driver's license at all times, along with a tourist card in areas where one is required. Auto permits, officially known as Temporary Vehicle Import Permits, are not required in Baja, *except* for vehicles being shipped to mainland Mexico aboard the Baja California ferries.

Calexico border crossing, 1950

Temporary Vehicle Import Permits—If you are traveling to the mainland you must obtain a Temporary Vehicle Import Permit for your passenger car, light truck, motorhome or motorcycle. Other persons age 18 or older may drive the vehicle in question as long as the permit holder is in the vehicle. Only one permit can be issued per person. Permits are issued for 180 days and can be renewed at any customs office if you wish to stay longer in Mexico. At the end of your stay, you can return with your vehicle at any border crossing.

It is illegal for a foreign citizen to sell a motor vehicle anywhere in Mexico.

To obtain a permit, you will have to provide the following documents:

1) Proof of citizenship, which can include a birth certificate, a valid passport or resident alien card.

2) The vehicle title or original current registration.

3) A bill of sale under the name of the vehicle holder. If you are buying a vehicle on credit and have not paid off the loan, you must obtain written notarized permission from the lien holder.

You do not need a Temporary Vehicle Import Permit to drive to El Golfo de Santa Clara, Sonora. A permit is required for driving south of Sonoíta, Sonora, on Mexico Highway 2.

You can obtain a Temporary Vehicle Import Permit at any Mexican port of entry, although Tijuana is usually not a good bet due to heavy congestion. They are usually available at the Mexican Immigration Authority (INM) office, where you should also be able to obtain a tourist card. After presenting the documents above, you must complete the following steps:

1) Fill out a Tourist Card Form (FMT or FME).

2) Fill out a Temporary Import Permit form.

3) Fill out a Vehicle Return Promise Agreement form.

4) Go to a Mexican Army Bank (Banjercito).

5) At the bank you will post a vehicle security deposit, either by credit card or bond. (Visa, MasterCard, American Express and Diners Club are all acceptable.)

6) Pay a permit fee of $16.50 USD or its equivalent in pesos.

Before leaving Mexico, you must go to a Mexican Army Bank and turn in the Temporary Vehicle Import Permit, along with the Vehicle Return Promise Agreement form. After that, your vehicle security deposit or bond agreement will be returned, depending upon which method you used. Failure to follow these steps will result in a large fine upon your next entry into Mexico.

Only one permit can be issued per person. For example, one person may not enter mainland Mexico or board a ferry with both a motorhome and a motorcycle, even if he or she owns both vehicles. One of the vehicles must be registered to another person in the party, or a second person can obtain a permit for the extra vehicle by presenting notarized permission from the owner. Under no circumstances can more permits be obtained than there are qualified drivers (18 years or older) in the party. *If your vehicle is found in mainland Mexico beyond the authorized time, or without appropriate documents, authorities may confiscate it immediately.*

BANK HOURS

BANCO

Banco del Ejercito offices in Baja California observe the following schedule: San Ysidro, Monday-Friday 8 a.m.-10 p.m., Saturday 8 a.m.-6 p.m., Sunday noon-4 p.m.; Otay Mesa, daily 10 a.m.-6 p.m., Tecate, daily 8 a.m.- 4 p.m., Mexicali, 24 hours a day.

Insurance—Mexican authorities only recognize insurance policies issued by Mexico-licensed companies, which means you must purchase a separate policy before crossing the border. Mexican law does not require drivers to have auto insurance, but it behooves you to purchase coverage before entering the country. Under Mexican law, if you're involved in an accident and cannot produce a valid policy, you may be detained by authorities, no matter how minor the accident, until an investigation is complete. In the event of an accident, you should file a report with the Mexican insurance company before returning to the United States.

If you're an AAA member, you can obtain Mexican insurance at any

COVERING EVERY BASE

The Auto Club offers other forms of travel insurance. A comprehensive travel plan is available providing medical insurance, coverage for nonrefundable travel expenses in the event of delay or cancellation, and insuring baggage and personal possessions. Air passenger insurance is available too, covering scheduled or charter flights.

office of the Automobile Club of Southern California. Policies are written by the day, with a discount for more than 30 days' coverage, and are issued immediately upon application. If you're a member, call an Automobile Club district office to determine what information (vehicle ID number, accessories on the vehicle, etc.) you'll need to provide to ensure you get the right policy.

In addition, several Mexican-licensed insurance brokers have offices near the border in San Ysidro and Calexico, selling policies to walk-in (or even drive-through) customers. Single-day policies are available in Tijuana and Mexicali as well, offering coverage effective only within their city limits. However, those policies often do not cover medical payments or the driver's person and property. Inquire before signing anything. Finally, if you'll be spending more than three weeks in Baja, consider buying an annual insurance policy. After about three weeks, an annual policy will cost about the same as a per-day policy, and after about 26 days the price is actually less. Plus, an annual policy delivers more services.

OTHER REQUIREMENTS

Baggage Inspections—Baggage is subject to inspection by Mexican officials at border crossings or at airports upon your arrival in the country. While driving in Baja, particularly in rural areas, you'll face occasional baggage and vehicle inspections at police or military roadblocks. For details, see the Highway Travel section of this chapter.

Cameras—Tourists may take one still camera and one digital or video camera, and a total of 12 rolls of film or videocassettes, plus all the necessary equipment to use the cameras. Tripods are allowed in most areas, but a special permit is required to use them in historic sites. Photography may not be for commercial purposes.

Citizens Band Radios—Mexico allows the use of citizens band radios by tourists. Three channels—9, 10 and 11—have been designated for visitor use. Channel 9 is for emergencies; Channel 10 can be used for communications among tourists; Channel 11 is reserved for directions and information. Permits are not required for CB radios. Any linear amplifier or other device increasing the transmission power by more than five watts is prohibited.

Firearms—It is against the law to bring guns into Mexico, except during hunting season for the express purpose of hunting and when accompanied by the appropriate documents. For details on these procedures, see Hunting in the *Appendix*, Chapter 16.

Pets—It's a good idea to leave dogs and other pets at home before traveling to Baja California, due to the various inspections and other requirements you'll face when returning to the United States. Pets taken out of the United States and returned are subject to the same requirements as those entering for the first time. If your pet fails an inspection or does not have the proper certification, it may be denied reentry into the country. If you do bring an animal to Mexico, it must have both a veterinarian's vaccination certificate for rabies and the Official Interstate and International Health Certificate for Dogs and Cats (form 77-043). If the pet is out of the United States for more than 30 days, you must present the rabies certificate upon your return.

Many hotel operators in Baja do not allow pets in their guestrooms.

Trailers—A trailer measuring more than eight feet in width and 40 feet in length requires a special permit, available at the Federal Highway Police Road Office in Tijuana or Mexicali. Permits cost about $15 and are issued at the discretion of the officials, since road conditions in much of Baja make trailer travel prohibitive.

RETURNING TO THE UNITED STATES

You should always carry proof of citizenship when traveling to Mexico. Odds are you won't need it, but you may be asked to present it to U.S. officials when you return to the United States. A passport or copy of your birth certificate or Certificate of Naturalization should suffice.

Not more than 100 cigars and 200 cigarettes (one carton) may be included in a $400 duty exemption.

U.S. Customs Regulations

Duty Exemptions—Residents of the United States may bring back articles worth up to $400 in retail value without paying duty, providing they are for personal use and accompany them at the time of return. This $400 exemption may be used only once in a 30-day period. Returning tourists need not be absent from the United States for any minimum time to qualify for the exemption. While customs inspectors are trained to estimate the retail value of goods, it's a good idea to hold onto your sales receipts or other evidence of purchase in case any doubts arise.

U.S. Customs station, Tijuana, 1926

There are certain restrictions, and U.S. Customs offices at border crossings have a number of pamphlets detailing regulations. They also have information for business travelers and persons returning with specialized products.

YOUR WEB SOURCE

A wealth of information on U.S. Customs regulations and entry requirements is available on the agency's web site, www.customs.gov/travel.

Sending Gifts—While in Mexico, you may send gifts worth up to $100 in fair retail value to persons in the United States without paying duty or taxes. You may send as many gifts as you like, provided the total value of gift packages or shipments received by one person in one day does not exceed $100. The words "Unsolicited Gifts" and the value in large letters should be written on the outside of the package. Alcoholic beverages and tobacco products are not included in this privilege, nor are perfumes valued at more than $5. You need not include these gifts in your customs declaration or as part of your customs exemption when you return to the United States. However, any gifts accompanying you upon your return must be declared and included within your exemption.

Adults 21 or older may bring back duty-free one liter of liquor per visit. Shipping alcoholic beverages by mail is prohibited.

Prohibited Items—Along with narcotics and dangerous drugs, many agricultural products and other goods are prohibited from entry into the United States. Most fresh fruits and vegetables are prohibited or require an import permit. Most canned or processed items are admissible. Fresh meats, meat byproducts (ham, sausage, etc.), poultry items and eggs are generally prohibited as well, but canned meats are admissible. In addition, meats, produce and birds taken from the United States to Mexico may not be allowed to reenter. Failure to declare all agricultural items can result in delays and fines of up to $1000. Some other prohibited items include drug paraphernalia; switchblade knives; anabolic steroids; "date rape" drugs; Cuban cigars; and pirated videos, music, books and computer programs.

Prescription Drugs—Many Americans purchase prescription medications in Mexico for personal use, usually at substantial savings compared to the United States. You may import them legally if you observe the following regulations: You must declare the medications to the U.S. Customs agent at the border. They have to be approved by the Food and Drug Administration (FDA) for use in the United States. A physician's written prescription must accompany the medication. The quantity is limited to a three-month personal supply. The FDA prohibits the entry of fraudulent prescription and non-prescription drugs and medical devices. These may include unorthodox "cures" for cancer, AIDS and multiple sclerosis, even if they are approved for use in Mexico.

Registering Your Valuables—When taking a lot of expensive foreign-made items such as cameras, binoculars, laptop computers, etc., into Mexico, consider registering these articles with U.S. Customs before crossing the border, unless you still have the original purchase receipts. So doing will remove any suspicions that you bought the merchandise in Mexico, in which case you could face duties. Only articles having a manufacturer's serial number may be registered.

Travel Tips

CURRENCY

Mexico uses the same symbol ($) to denote pesos as the United States uses for dollars.

If you went shopping in Tijuana or Ensenada and didn't know better, you might conclude the U.S. dollar was the official currency of Baja California. The venerable greenback is universally accepted—even preferred—by merchants along the border and in the resort towns of the Cape Region. However, the Mexican peso remains the official currency throughout Baja, and you'll want to carry pesos if you are traveling south of Ensenada or north of La Paz. A peso is worth 100 centavos, and you can expect to receive coins in denominations of 10, 20 and 50 centavos. Other coins include 1, 2, 5, 10 and 20 pesos, while bills come in denominations of 10, 20, 50, 100, 200 and 500 pesos.

As this book went to press, a U.S. dollar bought about 9.5 pesos, which meant an individual peso was worth slightly more than 10 U.S. cents. However, the exchange rate can vary from one day to the next, and not every place charges the same rate. You can exchange your money in the following ways:

Banks—If you're exchanging dollars for pesos, your best exchange rate will come at a Mexican bank, taking your money to the teller window or using the ATM. Mexican ATMs generally work the same as their U.S. counterparts, although you may need to know some basic Spanish to make your way through a transaction. Bear in mind that many smaller towns do not have banks.

Exchange Houses—Known as *casas de cambio* in Spanish, exchange houses are your best bet after banks to get a good rate of exchange. However, they sometimes charge a commission, especially if you want to exchange traveler's checks. On the U.S. side of the border, San Ysidro and

DON'T COUNT ON IT

Don't rely too much on traveler's checks. They may be useful in Baja's large cities or resort towns, but elsewhere most businesses won't accept them and there may not be any banks. When cashing traveler's checks, be prepared to present your passport, or a tourist visa and a photo I.D.

Calexico both have a number of exchange houses, and all of them charge about the same rate. Tijuana, Mexicali and Ensenada all have exchange houses, although your dollars will be accepted almost anywhere in those cities. In southern Baja, La Paz, San José del Cabo and Cabo San Lucas have exchange houses as well.

U.S. credit cards, including Visa, MasterCard and American Express, are another way to get a good exchange rate, since you'll be receiving the so-called interbank rate. Credit cards are widely accepted at hotels, restaurants and other tourist establishments along the border and in major resort cities. However, some businesses charge a fee for using a credit card, which sometimes more than offsets any exchange rate savings. Inquire before paying. Also, credit cards are not widely accepted in many small towns, especially in central Baja.

Many businesses in non-tourist areas accept dollars, but you're likely to receive your change in pesos, and at a poor rate of exchange. *As a rule, if you're paying with dollars, try to receive your change in dollars, and if you're paying in pesos, try to receive your change in pesos.* And, before traveling in central Baja, try to have enough pesos in cash to cover several days' needs. Carry some smaller denomination bills, since many establishments in this area keep very little cash on hand.

Prices throughout this publication are listed in dollar equivalents as they were quoted at press time.

With exchange rates forever in flux, it's especially important to have a clear understanding about prices, whether in dollars or pesos, before paying for anything. Sales tax throughout Baja is 10 percent. It is usually included in the base price of goods and services, but occasionally appears added to the bill. Some areas, most notably Los Cabos, may tack on an additional service charge.

FACILITIES AND SERVICES

Shopping For Supplies—As a rule, you'll want to pack the supplies that you'll need before crossing the border, but you'll find plenty of places to shop in Baja if you need to obtain or replenish supplies. All but the smallest of towns will have a general store or market selling groceries and a limited selection of other merchandise. However, only in major cities and towns can you expect to find a truly wide selection of goods. That goes for clothing, sporting goods, hardware and fuel for camp stoves. Across northern Baja, all of the larger towns have U.S.-style supermarkets, including **Tijuana, Rosarito, Mexicali, Tecate** and **Ensenada**. In Baja Sur you'll find supermarkets in **Ciudad Constitución, La Paz** and **Cabo San Lucas**. By and large, prices average about the same as in the United States.

Tourist Facilities—Visit the northern border cities or southern resort towns and you'll find lodging, dining and shopping on a par with that in the United States or Canada. In smaller towns, though, it's a much different story. In remote parts of the peninsula, some communities have very few retail businesses, and little or nothing in terms of lodging, dining or auto repair facilities. However, Baja locals are famous for their generosity and willingness to help strangers in an emergency. A humble, respectful attitude will work wonders in your time of need.

Many residents in northern Baja use post office boxes in San Ysidro and Calexico to ensure the safe, rapid delivery of their mail.

Postal Service—Postal service extends throughout Baja California, but your letter may take two or three weeks in transit—even when mailed from a town with scheduled air service. And, experience has taught us, some letters and packages never arrive at all. If you are sending a letter or parcel from the United States and want to ensure its safe and prompt arrival, use a courier service. At a minimum, send things by registered mail; it won't speed the delivery but it will ensure that your letter or package arrives safely.

Telephone Numbers—Local phone numbers in Baja (and most of Mexico) used to have only five or six digits, in contrast to the United States, where seven digits has long been the standard. However, Mexico has updated its numbering system, and all local numbers in Baja have converted to seven digits. Telephone numbers printed in this book include the international code 01152, the one-digit area code (shown in parentheses), and the local number. The only exceptions are U.S. contacts for some businesses operating in Baja.

As is common in Mexico, this book lists phone numbers with a hyphen between the last two pairs of numbers (e.g. 172-30-30).

The following guidelines apply for phone calls within Mexico (including Baja) and between Mexico and the United States:

- For local phone calls, dial the seven-digit number, just as you would in the United States. For instance, if you were in Ensenada and wished to call the local state tourism office, you'd dial 172-30-00.
- For long-distance phone calls within Mexico, dial 01, followed by the area code and the phone number. To reach Ensenada's state tourism office from Cabo San Lucas, you'd dial 01 (6) 172-30-00.
- On calls from the United States to Mexico, dial 01152, followed by the area code and the phone number. (Do not dial "1" before 01152.) To reach

Ensenada's state tourism office from the United States, then, you would dial 01152 (6) 172-30-00.

- To call the United States or Canada from Mexico, dial 001 followed by the area code and the phone number.

Public Phone Service—Public telephones in Mexico, though commonplace, have long been infamous for their lack of reliability. That situation is changing, spurred in large part by the influx of foreign investment in the country's phone system. As a result, coin-operated phones have all but disappeared, replaced by phones that accept prepaid calling cards. These cards are sold at businesses throughout Baja California in denominations of 30, 50 and 100 pesos. You can use them for either local or long-distance calls.

A recent trend in tourist areas has been the spread of public telephones designed for international phone calls. These phones, complete with signage and instructions in English, allow you to make collect calls to another country or charge those calls to a credit card. We've found them to be reliable but also notoriously expensive, usually charg-

Why Not Try Smoke Signals?

We had heard several horror stories about the bills racked up by those special Baja phones designed specifically for collect or credit-card calls to the United States and Canada, so we decided to find out for ourselves. From the pictured phone, in San José del Cabo, we called an operator to find out the rates for calls to Los Angeles and Dayton, Ohio. The verdict? For either city the minimum charge was $40.45 USD—good for a call of up to five minutes, billed to your credit card or the party unlucky enough to accept charges.

Using this phone will be hazardous to your bank account.

Put another way, on Nickel Sundays in the U.S. you could talk from 8:01 in the morning till 9:30 at night for the same price ... although we doubt your living room enjoys the same tropical charm as Boulevard Mijares in this peaceful seaside town. Fortunately, gabby types who must talk longer will be rewarded with a lower rate. While the per-minute cost works out to $8.09 for the first five minutes, the charge for additional minutes drops to a paltry $4.99. Again, all figures are U.S. dollars.

ing several dollars per minute. Avoid them except for the most dire of emergencies.

Cell phones—Cellular service has been up and running in Baja California for several years now, but don't expect full coverage or to rely on one in case of an emergency. Coverage remains limited to the major cities near the border, with localized service elsewhere. Besides the border region, the San Felipe and San Quintín areas generally have coverage in northern Baja. In the south, Ciudad Constitución and the territory between La Paz and Cabo San Lucas have service as well. Even in these areas, rugged terrain can result in erratic reception.

Using a cell phone in Baja may also mean an unpleasant surprise at billing time, since you may face some expensive roaming charges. For example, Verizon Wireless in late 2000 announced a plan allowing its Southern California customers to place and receive cellular calls in Baja at a rate of 60 cents per minute, plus long distance charges. Whatever provider you use, before traveling to Baja with your phone inquire to make sure they allow roaming outside the United States and find out what the charges are.

And, if you spend more than a few days in Baja in a given year, consider opening an account with a local cellular provider. Baja Celular has been serving the peninsula since 1990 and has offices in 17 cities and towns, including 14 in Tijuana alone. It can be reached in the United States via its web site, www.bajacelular.com.mx. A newer provider is Telcel, which has offices in Tijuana, Mexicali, La Paz and Cabo San Lucas. It can be reached in the United States at (800) 483-5235.

Other Communications—Telephone and telegraph terminals are located in most Baja towns. In cases of emergency, you can send messages via government radio, which also has terminals in most communities. In smaller towns, it's not uncommon for local businesses, such as a general store or *farmacia,* to have a fax machine that, for a fee, you can use to send documents.

TIME ZONES

The northern state of Baja California observes Pacific Time, the same time as the U.S. state of California. Baja California Sur, the southern state, observes Mountain Time, which means its clocks are one hour ahead of California's throughout the year. Both states observe daylight-saving time from the first Sunday in April until the last Sunday in October.

HEALTH CONDITIONS AND MEDICAL EMERGENCIES

Depending on who you talk to, Baja California is a breeding ground for all sorts of exotic diseases where the food and drink are unfit for human consumption, or a modern place with good health and hygiene standards and high-quality medical care. Like most things, the truth lies somewhere in between, but on the whole, health conditions in Baja are good compared to the rest of Mexico, and in some cases approach those of the first world. That's especially true in the resort areas, which have been playing host to foreign travelers for many decades, and if you're like most visitors, you'll probably come and go without any major ailments. But even while using common sense and taking all the right precautions, you may still fall prey to some sort of sickness or injury.

No doubt the greatest fear most tourists have is of the drinking water or contaminated food, which can lay low the healthiest of individuals. Probably the best way to avoid the intestinal disturbance known as *turista* or "Montezuma's revenge" is to go easy on the food, beverages and exercise, and to get plenty of rest.No one is immune to the effects of too much alcohol and spicy food on top of overexertion under the Baja sun. Avoiding tap water is a good idea, and in Baja that isn't hard to do, since most hotels and even the smallest of markets sell bottled water. Other beverages such as beer, soda and juices are omnipresent as well, and trying them is part of the Baja experience.

Many Mexicans contract an illness similar to "Montezuma's Revenge" when they visit the United States.

As for dining out, stick to established restaurants, and avoid sidewalk or street-side food stands whenever possible. And if your instincts tell you a restaurant may have sub-par health standards, go somewhere else. The same holds true if your food doesn't taste right for whatever reason. It's far better to miss a meal than be laid low for several days by a bout of food poisoning. Also, take care when choosing dairy products, and be sure the fresh fruits and vegetables you buy have been washed or peeled before eating them. If you do come down with *turista,* several remedies will help ease the effects. Two of the best known are Pepto-Bismol and Lomotil, which are available in *farmacias* throughout Baja.

Of course, *turista* is not the only threat to travelers' body and health. Sunstroke, heat exhaustion, dehydration and sunburn are of particular concern in the deserts of Baja. Then there are wounds inflicted by scorpions, rattlesnakes, stingrays, jellyfish and other poisonous creatures, which will require immediate first aid and proper medical attention.

If you're traveling beyond border towns or resort areas, it behooves you to carry a first aid kit and know how to use it.

Should you require medical care, you'll find good doctors and dentists in all the larger cities and towns, along with well-equipped hospitals, clinics and pharmacies. Small towns may have clinics with limited facilities. The local Red Cross (*Cruz Roja*) can also be helpful. In case of emergency, you can also summon help via a government radio network, which is available in most communities.

One agency that provides cross-border help is the Binational Emergency Medical Committee, located in Chula Vista, California. This voluntary group works with both Mexican and American authorities to help travelers stranded due to accident, illness, legal difficulty or lack of money. They can be reached 24 hours at (619) 425-5080. The group requests a $25 per-person annual fee, which entitles the holder to a bilingual "Lifesaver" card, telling authorities to call the committee in case of emergency. It also enters your name in a database with your vital personal and medical data. The group also lends assistance to non-card holders.

In addition, emergency critical-care air transport services operate throughout Baja California with in-flight doctors and nurses. These services can be quite expensive, from under $2000 to $15,000 or more, depending on the length of flight and type of aircraft, although many U.S. health insurance policies will reimburse the cost. The following companies offer 24-hour emergency air service:

- Aeromedevac, located in San Diego, can be reached toll-free in the United States at (800) 832-5087 or toll free from Mexico at 011 (800) 832-5087.

- Critical Air Medicine, also in San Diego, may be contacted toll-free within the United States at (800) 247-8326, toll free within Mexico at 001 (800) 010-0268, or by calling collect from Mexico at (858) 571-0482.

- Transmedic, located in Ensenada, can be reached toll free in Mexico at 01 (800) 026-33-42 or toll free from the United States at (877) 269-7296. Toll-required numbers are 01152 (6) 178-14-00 and 178-28-91. Its street address in Ensenada is Avenida Ruiz 842, Interior 3.

Other companies offer emergency evacuation service from anywhere in Mexico or elsewhere in North America to members who pay an annual fee, usually around $120 per year. Some will deliver members directly to their hometown hospitals. Two companies offering memberships are these:

- Medical Air Services Association, (800) 643-9023. Their mailing address is 1250 South Lake Blvd., South Lake, Texas 76092.
- SkyMed International, (800) 475-9633. Their mailing address is 4435 N. Saddleback Trail, Scottsdale, AZ 85251.

OTHER EMERGENCIES

Baja California authorities have made considerable strides in recent times to help tourists seek help in emergencies. That's especially true in the northern state (from the border south to the 28th parallel), where the government has established a series of three-digit hotlines to call in the event of a crime, auto accident or other emergency. A summary:

- **078** Established in 2000, this number is operated by the state Secretariat of Tourism and is designed to aid tourists needing various types of assistance. Visitors can report crimes, accidents, or alleged abuses by police. Other types of assistance, such as directions for lost travelers, are also available. During tourist office hours (Monday through Friday 8 a.m. to 5 p.m., and Saturday and Sunday 10 a.m. to 3 p.m.), the hotline is staffed by bilingual personnel. During other hours you can leave a recorded message. The number is supposed to be effective statewide, including cities and rural areas.
- **061** Operated by the state Attorney General, this service is available 24 hours a day for reporting crimes and other emergencies involving civil authorities. Not all personnel may speak English, however. *This is not a general information number and should be used for emergencies only.*
- **Other Numbers** Throughout the state of Baja California, the following numbers provide emergency assistance: police 060, fire 068, Red Cross (medical) 066. However, many operators may not speak English.

Baja California Sur does not have any statewide emergency numbers, but you may find help through the State Tourism Office in La Paz, which has experience dealing with travelers needing assistance. The address and phone are listed at the end of this chapter. Throughout Baja, you may find help in smaller towns through the local *delegado*, an elected official who oversees all emergencies and civil or legal disputes. He can be found at the *delegación municipal* or *subdelegación*. In more isolated areas, authority is usually vested in an appointed citizen who reports to the nearest *delegado*.

Legal Difficulties—If you're in trouble with the law, your first step should be to contact your nation's consulate or consular agency. These offices do not provide legal advice, but they can explain the basics of Mexican law and help put you in contact with an attorney. More than a dozen countries operate consulates in Tijuana, including the United States and Canada. In southern Baja, you can find assistance through the U.S. Consular Agency in Cabo San Lucas, or the Canadian Consular Agency in San José del Cabo. You may also find assistance through the nearest state tourism office, where personnel can act as interpreters. Address and phone information for all of these offices appears at the end of this chapter.

If you believe you've received inappropriate treatment by Mexican police, tourism officials recommend you take the following steps: (1) Observe or ask for as many of the following as possible—the officer's name (most officers wear a name tag), badge number, department (city, state, federal) and car number. (2) If there is a fine, go to the nearest police station to pay it and ask for a receipt. Traffic tickets received in Tijuana may be paid by mail from the United States. (3) Write out the complaint and mail it to the attorney general.

HIGHWAY TRAVEL

Driving in Baja California is not a dangerous endeavor—at least for those who obey the laws, stay alert and use common sense at all times. Defensive driving skills, like those you learned in driver's training, are even more important in Baja or anywhere else where you're unfamiliar with the rules of the road. Driving in major cities, such as Tijuana, Ensenada and Mexicali, is a separate issue that we've addressed in their respective sections of this book. However, highway driving deserves attention in its own right.

You may find roadside cattle almost anywhere, including this center median in San José del Cabo.

By and large, Baja's paved roads are well signed, and maintenance has improved somewhat over the years.

See *Appendix*, Chapter 16, for a chart of Mexican road signs and Mexico Highway 1 Distance Table.

Four-lane highways are beginning to appear, such as Highway 1-D between Tijuana and Ensenada, and the new Highway 2 toll road between Tijuana and Mexicali. On the whole, though, conditions remain behind those of the United States, with mostly narrow two-lane roads and some sections in disrepair. Bad weather, heavy trucks and other factors take a heavy toll on the pavement, and lengthy stretches may be marred by potholes. No one stretch stays in bad shape for a long time, and repair crews are a common site along the major highways. If often seems, though, that as soon as crews repair the road in one place, new potholes appear somewhere else as an endless cycle continues. Also, workers sometimes take their time painting a new center stripe after repaving a road, which may leave you guessing where the center of the road is.

Baja roads are also quite narrow by U.S. standards, ranging from about 19 to 25 feet wide along the major two-lane routes. Shoulders are nonexistent along many stretches, and turnouts are rare. In many areas the pavement has a rounded crown and rests on a raised roadbed, which makes careful steering important, since vehicles tend to drift to the right. Heavy winds are another hazard, especially if you have a trailer, camper or motorhome. Heavy winds can also mean drifting sand, which sometimes finds its way onto a highway and may narrow a road to only one lane. Another danger lurks on hilly or winding sections of highway, where drivers of large trucks and buses sometimes like to straddle the center line.

Bearing all that in mind, your maximum speeds will be lower in Baja than on comparable U.S. highways. On level terrain, you'll do well to limit your speed to 50 to 60 mph, while 20 to 30 mph is a safe maximum in hilly or mountainous areas. Also, nighttime driving is ill-advised under nearly all circumstances. Cattle and other livestock often wander onto the asphalt at night for warmth, and have caused many serious accidents as a result. If you can't avoid driving at night, slow way down and pay extra attention to the road in front of you *and* the shoulders as well.

Roadblocks—If you drive Baja's main highways for any length of time, you'll encounter roadblocks of armed police or soldiers who search vehicles for arms or drugs. Most inspections amount to a few questions and a wave-through. Sometimes, however, officials will make a more thorough inspection of a vehicle and luggage. Even then, they seldom last more than a few minutes. Your best bet is to cooperate fully and maintain a friendly, respectful attitude. Odds are you'll be treated the same way in return. Some knowledge of Spanish helps, although there's almost

Mexico's Silent Testaments to Crash Victims

Mexicans are renown for preserving the memories of their dead—a truth apparent to anyone who has walked amid the magnificent gravestones of their cemeteries, been in Mexico for November 2 Day of the Dead observances ... or driven the nation's highways.

So it is in Baja California, where shrines of all size and description line the roadways, marking the spots where auto accidents claimed someone's life. Usually placed by loved ones of the deceased, they can range from a simple cross to elaborate structures the size of a small mausoleum. Often they resemble a doghouse in size and shape, complete with the slanted roof.

Inside or out, an inscription will bear the victim's name, date of birth and death, and perhaps a short epitaph. Religious icons are typical—a crucifix, cross or image of the Virgin of Guadalupe, Mexico's patron saint. Old or new, shrines are usually well maintained, and few show signs of serious disrepair. Often they are bedecked with flowers, photos of the deceased or accompanied by votive lights that burn in silent remembrance.

Shrine north of San Felipe remembers a family who died in a crash.

Along straight, flat expanses of road, one may drive for many miles without seeing a single shrine. On more dangerous stretches—narrow, winding passages with sheer drop-offs—several may appear within a short distance, often in clusters. Sometimes the guardrail may remain torn away where a vehicle left the road, its crumpled, rusting carcass lying hundreds of feet below the pavement.

By no means are these markers limited to highways, but can be found wherever someone died. In his 1941 classic *The Log from the Sea of Cortez,* Steinbeck wrote of a humble seaside shrine placed where a fisherman had emerged sick and weak from his boat and succumbed before he could make his way home. A little cross and a flickering candle inside a can marked the spot, and the author waxed philosophically on its significance:

> "It seems good to mark and to remember for a little while the place where a man died. This is his one whole lonely act in all his life. In every other thing, even in his birth, he is bound close to others, but the moment of his dying is his own."

Whatever inspires those who place them, roadside memorials bear poignant testimony to the perils of careless driving—tangible and more blunt than any classroom lecture or a hundred conventional highway signs.

always at least one person at each roadblock who speaks fluent English. If you do believe you have received unfair treatment, report the matter to the U.S. Consulate in Tijuana or to the nearest tourist assistance office.

SAFETY TIPS

It isn't the Wild West and reports of crime are often exaggerated, but Baja California is not immune to the perils of the society at large. That's the case not only in tourist centers, but in remote areas as well, where travelers sometimes fall prey to crime. That's no reason to not visit Baja, or to travel with fear as your constant companion. Common sense will be your greatest ally while traveling in Baja or anywhere else, and if you take the same precautions you would in a large U.S. city, you should be all right. A few pointers for safe travel follow:

- **Lock your vehicle at all times.**
- **Avoid night driving whenever possible. When driving after dark, park only in well-lighted areas.**
- **Don't park alone when camping overnight. Always look for other vehicles or people.**
- **Carry as much cash as necessary, but no more.**
- **Don't carry all of your money in one wallet or purse.**
- **Keep a list of all travelers checks and credit card numbers.**
- **Never leave valuables in your vehicle at night or in your hotel room during the day.**

GASOLINE

You can buy any brand of gasoline you want in Mexico, as long as it's Pemex, the state-owned petroleum monopoly whose full name is Petróleos Mexicanos. For many years that was a dubious prospect, since the quality of Pemex gas sagged well behind that of U.S. brands. However Pemex has come a long way in the last five to 10 years, with improved formulation, higher octane ratings, and the phase-out of leaded fuels. In fact, much of Pemex gasoline is refined in the United States.

Big, colorful signs accompany most—but not all—Pemex stations

So Many Miles, So Little Gas

The longest section of paved road without a Pemex station in Baja is a 200-mile stretch of Highway 1 between El Rosario and Villa Jesus María. A station in Cataviña occasionally opens, and roving vendors sometimes sell gas from cans in this area. But neither supply is reliable, and roving vendors charge huge markups. The next longest stretch without gas is the 84 miles on Highway 1 between Mulegé and Loreto.

Chances are your main concern with gasoline in Baja will be availability. That's usually not a problem in the bigger cities and towns, but shortages can occur in small towns, along remote stretches of highway, or in resort areas during holiday periods. A telltale sign a station is out of fuel is if the attendants have draped the hoses over the tops of the pumps. To avoid running out, keep your tank at least half-full at all times, and top it off before driving across remote regions. The government controls the retail price of gas, which means you should pay the same rate at all Pemex stations within a certain geographical area.

Pemex fuel prices in the border region at press time: Magna, 5 pesos per liter ($1.93 per gallon); Premium, 5.6 pesos per liter ($2.16 per gallon); diesel, 4.14 pesos per liter ($1.59 per gallon).

Most Pemex stations are clearly flagged with their red, white and green signage, but there are exceptions. In smaller towns off the main highways, the "station" may be a single pump sitting in front of a mini-market, or a tanker truck with a hose attached parked in a driveway. And, in some far-flung towns that don't have Pemex stations, you may find gas pumped out of metal drums at prices far above the government-set rate.

Pemex gas comes in three varieties—the regular-grade Magna, super-grade Premium and Diesel. Magna is sold in green pumps and carries an 87 octane rating, while Premium is sold in red pumps and has a 93 octane rating. Diesel is sold from pumps plainly marked "Diesel." Magna is sold at all Pemex stations and in many areas is the only gas available. Premium is readily available in the border region and in the far south, but is hard to find between Ensenada and La Paz. Diesel is available at most stations that sell Premium and many others as well. In port towns, you'll often find it for sale at the local docking facilities.

The Auto Club's *Baja California* map indicates which towns sell gasoline and diesel throughout the peninsula.

While Pemex has improved the quality of its gasoline, it's still erratic, with octane ratings two or three points less than the posted numbers. That's especially true in central and southern Baja, where gasoline is shipped from mainland Mexico. Pinging and preignition may occur and possibly could cause engine damage. However, many Pemex stations and auto parts stores sell octane boosters and other additives, which may ease the problem if not eliminate it altogether. If you're buying gas in remote areas, especially if it's pumped from a drum, consider using a chamois cloth or other filter while filling your tank.

Finally, it's hard to discuss Pemex stations without a word about integrity. While Mexicans are by and large an honest lot, Pemex stations have a long-standing reputation as bastions for shady, underhanded dealings. We've seen and heard of many schemes to separate customers from their money by unscrupulous means. Some employees will "forget" to reset the pump before dispensing fuel. Others may try to shortchange you, hoping you won't notice that missing 100-peso bill. On other occasions, you may find that it mysteriously takes 24 gallons to fill your 20-gallon gas tank. Remember, too, that Pemex stations only accept cash, and if you're not paying in pesos, you're sure to take a heavy hit on the exchange rate. With all that in mind, be sure to count your change, make sure the pump is set at zero before fueling, and pay in pesos whenever possible.

If you believe you've been treated unfairly by a Pemex station, your first step is to take the matter to the manager. If you don't get satisfaction there, you may not get your money back, but you can take other actions against the station. One is to report the station to the Green Angels the next time you encounter one of their trucks. Another, if you speak Spanish, is to contact the Mexican Consumer Protection Agency (PROFECO), which has offices in most large cities. You can also lodge a complaint in English through the agency's web site, www.profeco.gob.mx. PROFECO handles all types of consumer complaints.

Do bear in mind that the majority of Pemex stations and their employees are honest and deserve to be treated as such. Show them the same courtesy and respect that you would anyone else, and you may keep a good employee from fulfilling your worst expectations.

Emergency Road Service and Auto Repairs

See *Appendix*, Chapter 16, for a list of recommended vehicle and personal supplies.

Preparing Your Vehicle—Before traveling in Mexico, your vehicle should be in top mechanical condition. Tires, including spares, should be inspected for tread wear and proper inflation, and all fluid levels should be checked. Brakes, batteries, shock absorbers, filters, pumps and radiators all warrant special attention. The wise traveler will carry extra belts, filters, hoses and gaskets, as well as the tools needed to install them.

Auto Repairs and Dealers—Where there's a town in Baja, you're almost sure to find a mechanic of some sort, but that's no guarantee you'll get your vehicle fixed right or in a short period of time. The level of service varies widely, depending on where you are and what kind of vehicle you're driving. If you break down in a major city while driving a common make and model, odds are you'll find a dealer or garage that can repair your vehicle in fairly short order. It's another story though, if you're stranded in a remote area far from a major highway. You may find a mechanic who's a wizard at salvaging parts from junk cars and repairing older vehicles, but he may be mystified by modern drive trains with their fuel injection, computers, anti-smog systems and other equipment. In that case, you may need a tow to the nearest major town.

Fixing a dangling exhaust pipe in Bahía Tortugas during a 1999 Auto Club research trip

Many times your biggest problem will be finding the right part, especially if your vehicle is not a common model or make. Most vehicles in Mexico are products of the Big Three U.S. makers (Ford, GM, and the former Chrysler Corporation), Volkswagen or Nissan, and you'll find dealers in Baja that sell and service all of those. Cities with auto dealers in Baja include Tijuana, Mexicali, Ensenada, Ciudad Constitución and La Paz. Toyotas are also common and have a fairly good parts network, thanks to Baja's *frontera* (border) status, which allows the sale of used vehicles from the United States without high import duties.

Parts for other makes can be extremely scarce, and you may face a long wait for the right component to arrive, unless a mechanic can make a temporary repair that lets you return home with your vehicle. Carrying extra parts is all the more important if you're driving to Baja in such a vehicle, even if you're staying on the main highways. Sometimes dealers may not have the right part in stock, so a major repair may take several days. In 2000, an Auto Club research team was stranded in La Paz for more than a week while its 1996 Ford Bronco sat at the local Ford dealership waiting for a new transaxle to arrive.

Green Angels—The Green Angels *(Angeles Verdes)* are a familiar sight in Baja, patrolling the roads in their bright green trucks and providing free emergency service to motorists. Founded in 1960, this government-sponsored group covers the major highways of Baja, and are supposed to pass any given point at least twice a day. Their staff are mechanics (sometimes bilingual) who carry limited spare parts, gasoline (provided at cost) and a first aid kit. They can also tow your vehicle for a short distance and radio for emergency medical assistance.

BACKCOUNTRY TRAVEL

See *Appendix,* Chapter 16, for a complete list of recommended off-road supplies.

When Mexico Highway 1 opened in 1973, many off-road "purists" bemoaned the day, saying it marked the death knell for the vast and untamed wilderness known as Baja California. Baja has certainly grown since then, but the old hands were premature in their predictions of runaway growth and over-development. That much is clear to all those who have traveled off the pavement at all. A rugged, unspoiled frontier is still there, a timeless land of open spaces, virgin beaches, lonely ranchos and roads that are little better than mule trails. Baja's back roads are not for the faint of spirit or those with low thresholds of discomfort. But with the proper vehicle, equipment and mindset, they offer one of the premier outdoor experiences in North America.

Baja roads take their toll—tire damage south of Puertecitos during a 1995 research trip

Many dirt roads get plenty of traffic and periodic maintenance, but others are seldom-used tracks that can be downright grueling. Even "good" roads may have their bad stretches, and any unpaved route is only as good as its worst spot. Among the many obstacles you'll encounter are jarring washboard sections, hazardous arroyo crossings, deep sand, precarious curves, steep grades and jagged rocks that can puncture even the sturdiest of tires.

Such roads require a heavy-duty, high-clearance rig, preferably with four-wheel drive. It should be equipped with oversize tires, extra low gears, and protective steel pans beneath the engine, transmission and gas tank. Dual rear tires are not advisable because they do not easily fall into existing road tracks. As important as the proper vehicle is the driver who proceeds slowly and cautiously. Speeding on any unpaved road is an invitation for a serious accident.

A journey to Baja's remote reaches requires careful planning and preparation. Before leaving the pavement, let someone know where you are going and when you plan to return. You may also consider caravaning with two or more vehicles. Plan to be as self-sufficient as possible as facilities are extremely scarce. Take enough extra gasoline to extend your range by at least 50 miles, stored outside the vehicle if possible. Take at least five gallons of drinking water per person and a two-weeks' supply of non-perishable food. A good first-aid kit is essential as well. Also, take a supply of plastic bags to protect cameras and other valuable items from the ever-present Baja dust.

There are few road signs in Baja's remote areas—largely because the locals assume that anyone driving the back roads knows where to go. That means you're likely to reach many junctions with no signs showing the way. Often, though, you'll find that both branches leaving a fork soon rejoin one another. If you reach an unsigned junction, a good rule is to choose the road that appears more heavily traveled. Odds are it will be the correct route, and if it's not it will likely lead to a ranch or other outpost where you can obtain directions. And be sure to take along the Auto Club's *Baja California* map and carefully check all junctions against those indicated on the map. Bear in mind, however, that odometers often vary and the mileage yours shows may disagree slightly with those on the map.

When you read the Auto Club map, you'll soon realize that there are literally hundreds of potential side routes in Baja. Many are seldom traveled and it's impossible to list them all, but this volume includes write-ups to more than 40 of Baja's most popular side routes. Most leave the pavement far behind as they journey to some of the remotest and most scenic corners of the peninsula.

Camping Out—In the broadest of terms, there are two basic approaches to camping in Baja. One is sticking to the major highways and staying in established campgrounds, which often have the same amenities as their U.S. counterparts. Nightly fees can vary widely, from around $3 for a plot of dirt in a campground with no hookups or other services, on up to $15 or more for a paved site with full hookups in a large, established RV park.

Be sure to pack out whatever trash you cannot burn while camping off-road.

The other approach is for those who travel off-road extensively, which almost surely will mean camping out at some point—perhaps many miles from the nearest settlement of any kind. If you're heading off-road to camp, bear in mind that high winds are common, nighttime temperatures can be quite cool in the mountains and desert, and potentially dangerous creatures like rattlesnakes and scorpions thrive in most of Baja's backcountry.

If you're heading off road, be sure to bring a tent, warm sleeping bag, suitable clothing, and several days of food supplies. Camping off-road is allowed almost anywhere, but avoid arroyos and low-lying areas, where flash floods can strike with little warning. Wood for campfires can be hard to find in the desert, but the shells of dead cacti provide an abundant and easy-to-ignite source of fuel.

TOURISM OFFICES

If you are new in town and (God forbid) forgot your guidebook, a good place to get advice on where to go, what to do, and where to sleep and eat is the local tourism office. You'll find them in all of Baja's larger cities and resort areas, staffed with personnel who know the locale and should be able to answer your questions. They should know which hotels have vacancies and they may be able to help you book a room. They'll also have the lowdown on new attractions and current road conditions.

SMALL TOWN ASSISTANCE

In smaller towns that don't have a tourism office, you'll often find a hotel, restaurant or other business with information on the local scene. Some have done this so long they've become de facto tourism offices.

Some are run by the state tourism secretariat (Secture), while others are run by the city or a convention and visitors bureau. State- and city-run offices are a good place to seek help if you've had an accident, or difficulties with a local business or police. At least one person on staff should speak fluent English. The following tourism offices operate in Baja:

Ensenada

Dialing 078 in the state of Baja California should put you in touch with the nearest state tourism office.

STATE TOURISM OFFICE *Blvd Costero (Lázaro Cárdenas) at Calle las Rocas, next to the other state government buildings. 01152 (6) 172-30-00 or 172-30-22. Open Mon-Fri 8 am-5 pm, Sat-Sun 10 am-3 pm.*

TOURISM AND CONVENTION BUREAU (COMITÉ DE TURISMO Y CONVENCIÓNES) *On Blvd Costero (Lázaro Cárdenas) near the west entrance to the city. 01152 (6) 178-24-11, 178-36-75. Open Mon-Fri 9 am-7 pm, weekend hours vary by season.*

La Paz

STATE TOURISM OFFICE
Tourist Wharf office: *Paseo Alvaro Obregón at 16 de Sep-*

tiembre. 01152 (1) 124-59-39. Open Mon-Fri 8 am-10 pm, Sat-Sun noon-midnight.
Main Office: *Near the north entrance to town, Km 5.5, across from the Crowne Plaza Resort. 01152 (1) 124-01-03. Open Mon-Fri 8 am-3 pm.*

Loreto

MUNICIPAL TOURISM OFFICE *On Plaza Cívica in the Municipal Hall. 01152 (1) 135-04-11. Open Mon-Fri 8 am-3 pm.*

Mexicali

STATE TOURISM OFFICE *Calzada Juárez 1, in front of the Benito Juárez monument. (877) 700-2092; 01152 (6) 566-12-77, 566-11-16. Open Mon-Fri 8 am-5 pm, Sat-Sun 10 am-3 pm.*

TOURISM AND CONVENTION BUREAU (COMITÉ DE TURISMO Y CONVENCIÓNES) *Corner of Calzada López Mateos and Calle Camelias. 01152 (6) 557-23-76, 557-25-61. Open Mon-Fri 9 am-7 pm.*

Rosarito Beach

TOURISM AND CONVENTION BUREAU (COMITÉ DE TURISMO Y CONVENCIÓNES) *In Oceana Plaza on Blvd Juárez in southern part of town. 01152 (6) 612-03-96 (800) 962-2252. Open Mon-Fri 8 am-5 pm, Sat 10 am-1 pm.*

STATE TOURISM OFFICE *In Plaza Villa Floresta on Blvd Juárez near northern entrance to town. 01152 (6) 612-02-00. Open Mon-Fri 8 am-5 pm, Sat-Sun 10 am-3 pm.*

San Felipe

STATE TOURISM OFFICE *Corner of Ave Mar de Cortez and Calle Manzanillo. 01152 (6) 577-11-55, 577-18-65. Open Mon-Fri 8 am-5 pm, Sat-Sun 10 am-3 pm.*

San Quintín

STATE TOURISM OFFICE *West side of Hwy 1 at Km 178.3, Colonia Vicente Guerrero. 01152 (6) 166-27-28. Open daily 8 am-3 pm.*

Tecate

STATE TOURISM OFFICE
Main office: *On the south side of Parque Hidalgo. 01152 (6) 654-10-95. Open Mon-Fri 8 am-5 pm, Sat-Sun 10 am-3 pm.*

Border crossing office: *Just south of pedestrian border crossing. No phone. Open Mon-Fri 8 am-5 pm, Sat 10 am-1 pm.*

Tijuana

STATE TOURISM OFFICE
Avenida Revolución office: *Corner of Ave Revolución and Calle 1. 01152 (6) 688-05-55. Open Mon-Sat 8 am-5 pm, Sun 10 am-5 pm.*
Main office: *Fourth floor of Edificio Nacional Financiera, corner of Paseo de los Héroes and José María Velazco, Zona Río. 01152 (6) 634-63-30, 634-68-73. Open Mon-Fri 8 am-3 pm and 5-7 pm, Sat 9 am-1 pm.*

TOURISM AND CONVENTION BUREAU (Comité de Turismo y Convenciónes) *Paseo de los Héroes 9565, across from the Tijuana Cultural Center. 01152 (6) 684-05-37. Open Mon-Fri 9 am-6 pm. Second branch near San Ysidro border crossing, across from taxi stands.*

CONSULATES AND CONSULAR AGENCIES

U.S. State Department website www.usembassy-mexico.gov/Tijuana.html lists consular services offered in Tijuana.

Consulates and consular agencies offer assistance to foreign nationals in a variety of emergency situations. For individuals in trouble with Mexican law, they can provide guidance and attorney referrals, but no legal assistance. Citizens can also report any inappropriate treatment they receive by Mexican police. (Questionnaires concerning police mistreatment are available at the U.S. Consulate in Tijuana.)

Around 20 countries operate consulates in the Tijuana area. In addition, the United States and Canada have consular agents representing them in the Los Cabos area. The U.S. and Canadian governments operate the following offices in Baja California:

Tijuana

UNITED STATES CONSULATE *Near the Caliente Racetrack at Calle Tapachula 96. Open Mon-Fri, 8 am-4:30 pm. 01152 (6) 681-74-00. After-hour emergencies, phone (619) 692-2154. Send written complaints to PO Box 439039, San Ysidro, CA 92143.*

CANADIAN CONSULATE *At Germán Gedovious 10411-101 (in the Zona Río between Paseo de los Héroes and Ave Sánchez Taboada). 01152 (6) 684-04-61. Open Mon-Fri, 9 am-1 pm. After-hour emergencies, call 01 (800) 706-2900.*

Los Cabos

UNITED STATES CONSULAR AGENCY *In downtown Cabo San Lucas, Plaza Nautica, interior C-4 (near Banco Bital). Open Mon-Fri 9 am-3 pm. 01152 (1) 143-35-66. After-hour emergencies, phone (619) 692-2154.*

CANADIAN CONSULAR AGENCY *In San José del Cabo, in Plaza José Green on Blvd Mijares. 01152 (1) 142-43-33. Open Mon-Fri 9 am-1 pm. After-hour emergencies, call 01 (800) 706-29-00.*

GreatestHits™

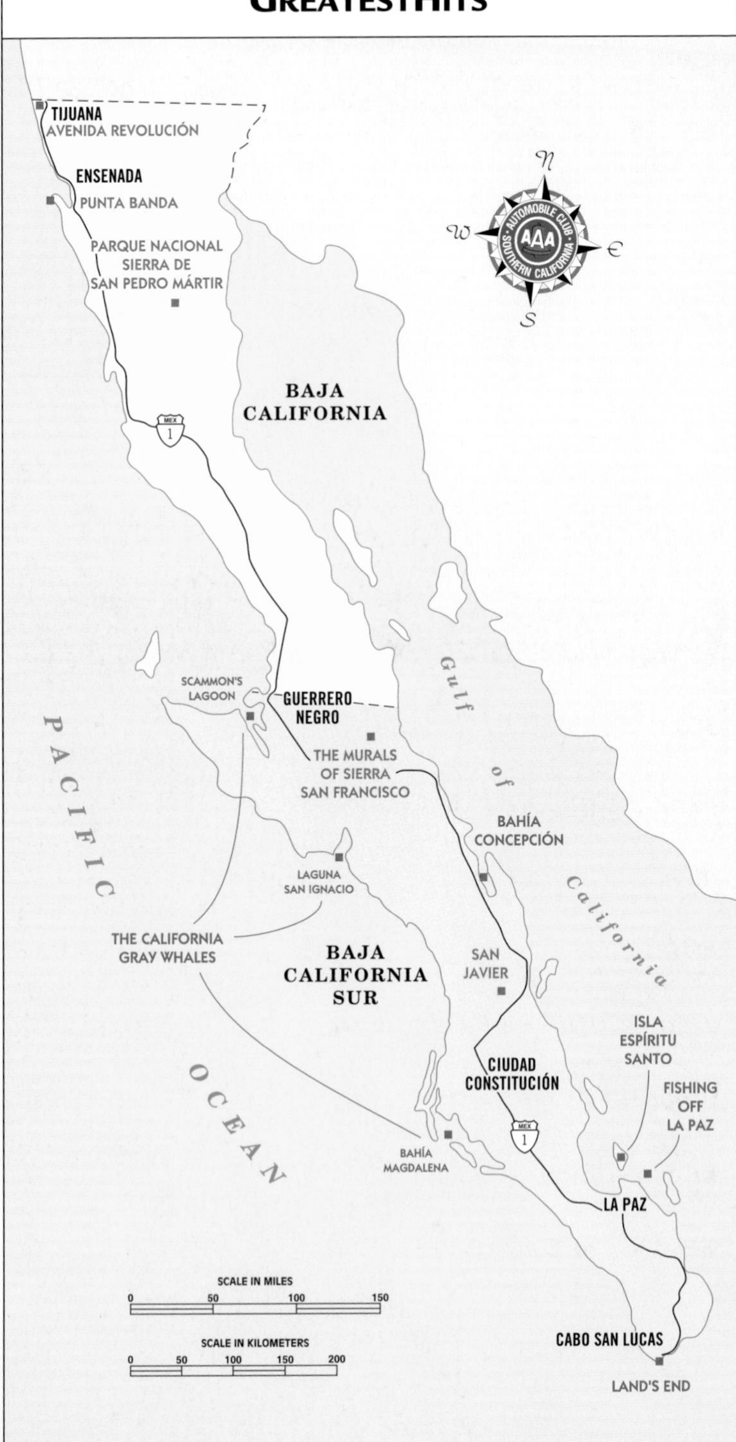
TIJUANA
AVENIDA REVOLUCIÓN
ENSENADA
PUNTA BANDA
PARQUE NACIONAL
SIERRA DE
SAN PEDRO MÁRTIR
AUTOMOBILE CLUB
AAA
SOUTHERN CALIFORNIA
BAJA
CALIFORNIA
MEX
1
SCAMMON'S
LAGOON
GUERRERO
NEGRO
THE MURALS
OF SIERRA
SAN FRANCISCO
PACIFIC
Gulf of California
BAHÍA
CONCEPCIÓN
LAGUNA
SAN IGNACIO
THE CALIFORNIA
GRAY WHALES
BAJA
CALIFORNIA
SUR
SAN
JAVIER
ISLA
ESPÍRITU
SANTO
CIUDAD
CONSTITUCIÓN
FISHING
OFF
LA PAZ
OCEAN
BAHÍA
MAGDALENA
LA PAZ
SCALE IN MILES
0 50 100 150
SCALE IN KILOMETERS
0 50 100 150 200
CABO SAN LUCAS
LAND'S END

BAJA CALIFORNIA'S GreatestHits™

We've compiled our top picks of what we consider "must see" attractions in Baja California. They're called "GreatestHits" because they represent some of the best the peninsula has to offer. Each one contributes solidly to the Baja experience, be it historical significance, striking beauty, uniqueness, or just enduring popularity.

Tijuana's Avenida Revolución

How Long? *An hour or two will cover the nine blocks, but give yourself a half-day if you plan to shop at length and see the nearby attractions.*

In Brief

"La Revo," as locals irreverently call this famous avenue, embodies every cliché of a Mexican border town. This is *not* the modern-day Tijuana of high-tech factories, gleaming office towers and tree-lined parkways. No, this is the Tijuana of rowdy nightclubs, gaudy gift shops, painted burros, and loud-mouthed shills stationed in front of seedy strip joints.

See *The Northern Triangle,* Chapter 4, for details on crossing the border, getting around in Tijuana, and restaurants on Avenida Revolución.

Love it, loathe it, or laugh out loud at it, but Avenida Revolución is an essential part of the Baja experience. For many tourists, this wacky, colorful nine-block strip is all they'll ever see of Baja, or the rest of Mexico for that matter. For the rest of us, it's still a great place to buy an Indian blanket or order a decent plate of *tacos al pastor*.

The Details

La Revo is about many things—eating, drinking, bargain-priced prescription drugs, mariachis crooning at your street-side table. In the end, though, shopping is the great equalizer, and almost no one leaves without some kind of keepsake. Nowhere in Baja will you find so many shops selling so many goods within such a small area. It's all here, from the shoddy and lowbrow to the tasteful and exquisite, be it clothing, arts, ceramics, handcrafts, leather or whatever else. No matter what you're looking for, it's best to bide your time and inspect all the wares before you buy. Walk the entire avenue, checking your impulses and taking mental notes as you go. You'll end up with a more discerning eye and a working knowledge of how much things should cost.

In general, you'll get better prices from sidewalk vendors, but better quality (and usually better value) from established merchants. Besides the conventional shops, you'll find a few large

bazaar areas with rows of open-air craft stalls. Most notable is **Bazaar de Mexico**, at the corner of Calle 7, with several dozen stalls selling quality handmade goods from around the country. Wherever you go, some savvy bargaining may fetch you a nice-sized discount off the quoted price. La Revo is legendary for haggling, and you can often bring the price down through patience and a willingness to walk away.

The state tourism office at the corner of Revolución and Calle 1 is a good source of information on "La Revo" and the rest of Tijuana.

Besides shopping, clubs and restaurants, there's plenty more to see and do in the neighborhood, including a few worthwhile venues just off the avenue. One is the **Museo de Cera (Tijuana Wax Museum)** on Calle 1, with an eclectic collection of personalities from past and present, including Bill Clinton, John Lennon, Mother Theresa and Ayatollah Khomeini, to name but a very few. An hour or less should cover them all, and admission is just $1.25. Near the south end of the avenue there's **L.A. Cetto Winery**, on Callejón Johnson, which offers tours and tasting daily, plus a cool respite from the noisy street scene. Then there's **Nuestra Señora de Guadalupe**, the twin-towered church on Calle 2, whose airy sanctuary is another inviting place to unwind.

TO DRIVE OR NOT TO DRIVE

Unless you plan a major shopping spree, you're probably better off parking in San Ysidro and crossing the border on foot. You'll avoid traffic and parking headaches, or the grueling border backups heading home. It's only a half-mile from the border to La Revo; taxi rides average $5 per carload.

Wherever you are, enjoy the moment and take in the sights, sounds, aromas and bizarre contrasts that make this an avenue like no other. There's the faded grandeur of the **Palacio Frontón**, the old jai-alai palace whose Moorish roofline stands high above Calle 8. There's the chaotic mixture of disco, rock, hip-hop and old-time marimba music with the din of revving engines, squealing tires and blaring horns on the street. And there's the shiny new Lexus from San Diego sitting at a stoplight next to some wizened old Chevy sedan packed to the gills for a family outing. It's all part of the Baja experience.

For details on the Museo de Cera and L.A. Cetto Winery, see *The Northern Triangle*, Chapter 4.

■ *Ave Revolución runs north-to-south, starting about ½ mile southwest of the San Ysidro border crossing. The main tourist strip is between calles 1 and 10.*

Punta Banda

How Long? *Give yourself an hour each way for the drive from Ensenada—time enough to stop and enjoy the views. Plan on another hour at* ***La Bufadora****, longer if you plan to eat.*

Punta Banda is also an excellent diving and kayaking area. For more information, see *The Northern Triangle,* Chapter 4.

In Brief

For gringos and locals alike, this is one of the most popular side trips in all of Baja California, and with good reason. It features beautiful scenery, a good paved road, and one of the most amazing natural phenomena in Baja, within an hour's drive of downtown Ensenada. This side route leads through city and countryside to the rugged peninsula known as Punta Banda and the journey's end at La Bufadora. Spanish for "the Snorter," La Bufadora is a natural sea geyser that throws huge columns of spray into the sky, earning bilingual oohs and ahs from throngs of onlookers. The drive is a highlight in its own right, scaling the northeast flank of Punta Banda, which rises almost 1000 feet above the Pacific and forms the southern shore of Bahía de Todos Santos.

The Details

Heading south from Ensenada, follow Highway 1 about 10 miles to the suburb of Maneadero, where a well-marked turnoff leads to Punta Banda. Leaving the city behind, the two-lane route heads southwest through several miles of farmland, with dozens of food stands lining the two-lane road. Beyond this fertile plain, the road climbs quickly onto the peninsula, and suddenly you'll be hundreds of feet above the ocean with a commanding 180-degree view. Find a place to pull over and soak in the panorama, gazing across the enormous Bahía de Todos Santos, with Ensenada spread along its eastern shore. To the north, the view on good days extends clear to Los Coronados Islands, near the international border. Looking seaward, you may catch a glimpse of the Todos Santos Islands beyond the mouth of the bay. Resuming your drive, the road crests near the tip of Punta Banda before turning south and dropping steeply toward **La Bufadora.**

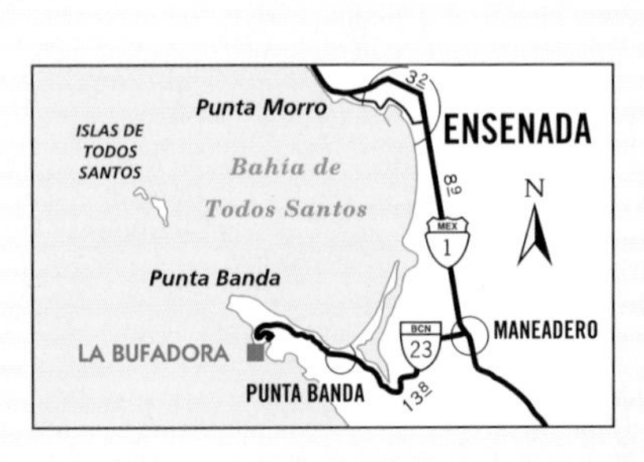

Tucked in a narrow cove at the base of rocky cliffs, La Bufadora is the focal point of a bustling tourist zone that has seen a major upgrade in recent years. Paved parking lots, new restrooms and a small botanical garden have all helped make it more visitor-friendly, while food stands and souvenir shops line a paved walkway that leads toward the star attraction. It's just a few steps from the nearest parking lot to La Bufadora, but with luck you should hear it beforehand. There's the enormous *whoosh* of air and water blown skyward, followed by a shower of spray raining down and roars of approval from the crowd. So it goes on good days, when this natural geyser blasts nearly 100 feet in the air. La Bufadora nearly always produces some spray, but works best on an incoming tide with some kind of a swell running.

During a large swell, you can see the waves crashing along the Todos Santos Islands' shoreline.

There are two main decks for viewing the action, one just above the blowhole and another farther up the cliffs. Enjoy the show wherever it suits you, but use caution on the lower deck, where you just might get splashed on a big day. If all that sea air makes you hungry, there's plenty to eat at all those food stands. Fish tacos and deep-fried *churros* (tube-shaped pastries) are the local specialties, plus there are three sit-down restaurants nearby if you want something more substantial.

WHALE OF A VIEW

From the heights of Punta Banda, a sharp eye during the winter may spot a pod of gray whales, swimming beneath the cliffs on their way south to the calving lagoons of Baja Sur.

Summer weekends can be extremely crowded here and unless you arrive early, you'll end up parking in one of the makeshift dirt lots. You may also wish you had fewer people and less commotion to enjoy these surroundings. Try instead to visit on a weekday or during the non-summer months, when you'll have the place largely to yourself.

Unless it's raining, fall and winter generally have clearer weather (and better views) than other times of the year.

■ *Located southwest of Ensenada along BCN 23. From Hwy 1, take the La Bufadora turnoff in Maneadero, 10 miles south of downtown Ensenada. It's another 14 miles to the road's end. La Bufadora is open daily from dawn to dusk. Parking is $1.*

Parque Nacional Sierra de San Pedro Mártir

How Long? *Give yourself at least two days and two nights to enjoy the park, not including the drive.*

In Brief

There's a place in Baja California, less than 40 miles from the Sea of Cortez, where cool breezes blow through stately pines, snowdrifts linger until late spring and aspens turn bright yellow with autumn's first frost. It's among the least-visited national parks in Mexico but offers some of its finest scenery, with superb hiking and secluded camping amid a vast, unspoiled wilderness.

April through October are the best months to visit here.

Parque Nacional Sierra de San Pedro Mártir is a world unto itself, an alpine oasis between the Pacific coast foothills and sun-baked Colorado Desert. On clear days you can see the Pacific and Sea of Cortez at the same time, while billions of stars shine down at night with incredible brilliance. It's home to Mexico's largest telescope, and the highest peak in Baja—10,154-foot Picacho del Diablo. All manner of wildlife thrive undisturbed here—bighorn sheep ply the rugged east slope, while mule deer, bobcat and mountain lion roam the verdant forests.

This trip is not for everyone, however, with its 50 mile-plus drive up an unpaved road that's best left to high-clearance off-road vehicles, and there are no restaurants, stores or lodging of any kind. If it is for you, then you'll enjoy Baja's premier high-mountain setting, with 170,000 acres of virgin woodlands, spectacular vistas and inspiring tranquillity.

The Details

From Highway 1, allow three hours to reach the center of the park, following the graded dirt road through more than 30 miles of rolling foothills beyond the Meling Ranch turnoff, then climbing steeply, with several narrow and rough stretches near the park entrance. You'll know you're nearing the entrance (48

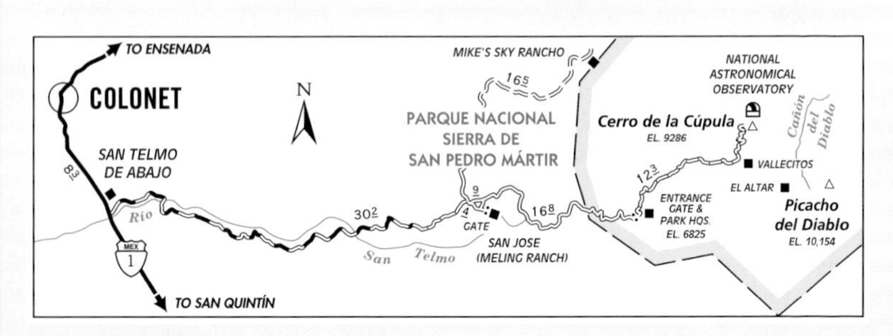

miles from Highway 1) when the mid-altitude brushland suddenly gives way to a pines, cedars, firs and other alpine flora. At 6825 feet, the entry gate is staffed year round by rangers, who'll have you sign in and give you a guide map to the park. Another eight miles leads to **Vallecitos** ("Little Valleys"), a series of open meadows about 8000 feet high, and the major camping area of the park. Campsites equipped with tables, stoves and pit toilets dot the woods along the east and south sides of the valley.

Look north from Vallecitos and you'll see the **National Astronomical Observatory**, perched atop **Cerro de la Cúpula**, a rounded 9286-foot summit. A locked gate usually blocks the road leading to the domed white structure, unless it's a Saturday between April and October, when astronomers from the National Autonomous University of Mexico (UNAM) hold tours in Spanish. They usually start at 11 a.m. and last about an hour, showcasing the main telescope with its 83-inch reflector. Astronomers from around the world have studied the heavens here, and no wonder. Far removed from city lights and seldom marred by haze or clouds, the site is said to be among the finest on earth for viewing stars.

The nearest food and lodging of any kind to San Pedro Mártir are at Meling Ranch, a rustic tourist retreat 18 miles from the entry gate.

The views on earth are no less grand, and numerous rails lead to the best viewpoints, several along the east face of the sierra. Among the finest is **El Altar**, a lookout at 9500 feet, the destination of a three-mile trail starting near Vallecitos. From the top you'll look down on the desert and Sea of Cortez, almost two vertical miles below, and on many days you'll see the Pacific on the western horizon. To the south stands the jagged massif of **Picacho del Diablo**, rising high above the yawning gorge known as **Cañón del Diablo.**

DETAILS, DETAILS

For trails and other highlights, refer to "Parque Nacional San Pedro Mártir, Topographic Map and Visitor's Guide to Baja's Highest Mountains," sold at map stores in Southern California and northern Baja. Order by calling Map Centre in San Diego, (888) 849-6277; or Map World, in Encinitas, CA, (800) 246-6277.

Whichever trail you choose, odds are you'll have perfect solitude, since fewer than 5000 people visit the park annually. That also means the normal hiking precautions are even more important here: Don't hike alone, and be sure to let a ranger know your plans before setting out.

For more specific directions to San Pedro Mártir and Meling Ranch, see *South of Ensenada*, Chapter 6.

■ *The turnoff to the park from Hwy 1 is 84 miles south of Ensenada (8 miles south of Colonet) and about 34 miles north of San Quintín. No admission is charged, but the park accepts donations.*

The California Gray Whales

How Long? *The typical boat trip lasts about three hours. Depending where you're staying, the entire outing will last a half-day or full day.*

In Brief

Scattered clouds skid across the horizon and a hint of rainbow spans the western sky as a February day breaks across a Baja California lagoon. A fleet of small motorboats bounce across the green waters—the search is on for the California gray whales, which migrate to the Pacific coast lagoons of Baja California Sur each winter. These inlets mark the end of the whales' southern migration, the first leg of a 10,000-mile round trip from the Arctic.

Some gray whales used to winter in California's San Diego Bay, before heavy shipping traffic forced them farther south.

Meanwhile, visitors from around the world arrive to see the same specie that humans once hunted to near-extinction. The gray whales are perhaps the most famous of all Baja fauna, and a visit to their calving lagoons is among the greatest eco-tourism adventures found anywhere. The first whales arrive in late December, while the final stragglers usually depart by early April. On a fortuitous outing, you may see dozens of the finned mammals—a few of which may approach within touching distance. And, you'll see fellow travelers erupt in laughter and tears as they pat one on the head.

The Details

Gray whales migrate to three main lagoons on the Pacific coast of Baja California Sur, each with its own unique selling points. Northernmost is **Scammon's Lagoon** and its smaller neighbor **Estero San José**. Just west of Guerrero Negro, these are the busiest calving grounds, and more than half the pregnant females give birth here. Though closest to the U.S. border, they're still a 10 to 12-hour drive from San Diego. Next south is **Laguna San Ignacio**, southwest of the town of San Ignacio, which has the most pristine setting of any lagoon, and a reputation for the friendliest whales. The grays seem more inclined to approach boats here than elsewhere. Then there's **Bahía Magdalena**, west of Ciudad Constitución. The season is slightly shorter here (starting in mid-January), but the bay lies within reach of daylong tours from Loreto and La Paz.

It's a long way from the border to all three venues, so make the most of your experience. While you can view the whales from land, a boat's the only way to get a close-up look, although there's still no guarantee that you'll get one. Boats are forbidden by law to come within 100 meters of the whales, but there's nothing to stop the whales from approaching the boats, and they often do just that, sometimes within hand's reach. You need to join a guided tour, however, since only boats with government permits may enter the lagoons during calving season.

Choppy conditions are possible in all three lagoons. If you're prone to seasickness, take appropriate measures beforehand.

Tours embark in all three lagoons, and with luck you might join one without reservations. Far better to book a tour in advance, however, as well as lodging reservations, since both may sell out weeks ahead. And on trip day, bring a jacket, sunscreen, binoculars, and several rolls of film.

WHALE LINGO AT A GLANCE

On any whale-watching trip, you'll likely hear the following terms, and with luck you'll see examples of them.

- Breaching: A whale leaps from the water, returning with a huge splash.
- Spyhopping: A whale pops its head out of the water and looks about.
- Tail Fluke: The flat edge of a whale's tail, which usually leaves the water as a whale dives.
- Flukeprint: A boil-like patch of smooth water created by a tail fluke—a telltale sign that a whale is nearby.

By the way—you'll only see female adults and their newborn calves in any of the lagoons. Male adults remain at sea, where they engage in courtship and mating with females that aren't bearing young that year. After a 13-month gestation, those females will give birth as the cycle of life begins anew.

Gray whale calves average 16 feet long at birth. Female adults typically grow to 46 feet while males average about 43 feet.

- *Tours originate in Guerrero Negro (Scammon's Lagoon), San Ignacio (Laguna San Ignacio), Loreto, Puerto Lopez Mateos, Puerto San Carlos and La Paz (Bahía Magdalena). See specific chapters for more information on the lagoons and tour operator listings. Prices range from about $30 for a non-narrated boat ride to $140 for an all-inclusive daylong excursion.*

The Murals of Sierra de San Francisco

How Long? *Viewing the more accessible murals takes two days and one night. Viewing all of the major paintings requires three days and two nights.*

In Brief

Hundreds of ancient Indian paintings adorn cave and rock walls across the badlands of central Baja California, but none rival the grandeur of those in a secluded corner of the Sierra de San Francisco. Hidden beneath rock overhangs, they remained unknown to outsiders until writer-explorer Erle Stanley Gardner discovered them in 1962 in the depths of a remote gorge known as Cañon San Pablo. The significance of these murals wasn't lost on Gardner, nor on UNESCO, which in 1993 declared them a World Heritage Site. Requiring a grueling drive on a perilous mountain road, a mule ride down a rocky trail, a boulder-scrambling hike and at least one night camping out, a trip here isn't for everyone. But those who take this journey will see some of Mexico's greatest artistic and historic treasures, amid the rugged beauty of Baja's central sierra.

The definitive book on this topic, *The Cave Paintings of Baja California*, by Harry W. Crosby (Sunbelt Publications, 1997), is widely available in Baja

For more information on San Ignacio, see *San Ignacio & Down the Gulf*, Chapter 8.

The Details

You need government permission and a licensed guide to visit the murals, which can be arranged in San Ignacio, the closest town to the sierra. At the Museo de San Ignacio, you'll complete a brief application and pay a small fee at least one day before departure. The staff will also hire your guide, for whom you must provide food during the trip. You'll also need camping gear, food for yourself and adequate drinking water.

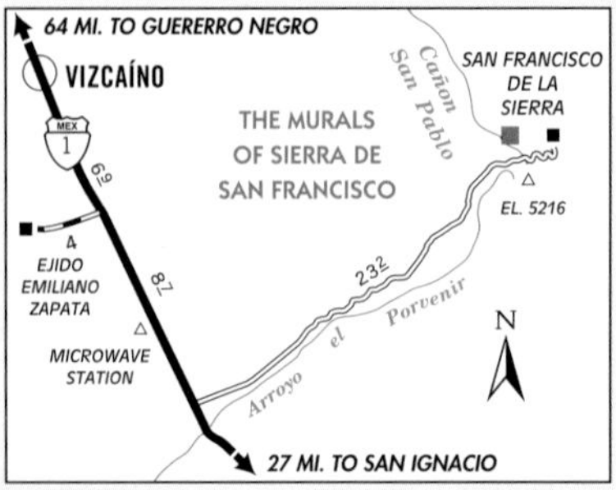

This trip requires an early start, leaving San Ignacio by dawn and taking Highway 1 north to the lonely, 23-mile road leading to San Francisco de la Sierra. Only the sturdiest high-clearance vehicles should attempt this road, which climbs a canyon wall and narrows to one lane in spots with sharp rocks, blind curves and harrowing drop-offs. It takes more than an hour to reach **San Francisco de la Sierra,** a tiny, hardscrabble village where you'll meet your guide and embark on the mule ride. (For a nominal price, you can have breakfast first.) Expect a

Several streams with potable water usually run through the canyon, but may dry to a trickle during droughts. Inquire ahead of time.

four-hour ride to the floor of **Cañon San Pablo**, a cavernous red-rock barranca that resembles a miniature Grand Canyon. The trail crosses a high, arid plateau before descending a steep, cacti-laced trail leading to the depths of the canyon.

With its lush palm oasis, the canyon floor makes a good lunch stop before heading to the mural sites. You'll ride another hour down the arroyo and then continue a short way on foot until your guide points up to **Cueva de las Flechas (Cave of the Arrows).** It's a short hike up to the site, not a cave per se, but a rock overhang that proved a durable canvas for native artists. Painting in red and black, they depicted several larger-than-life animals and humans, including two persons impaled by arrows. This barely hints, though, at what lies just ahead—the massive **Cueva La Pintada (the Painted Cave).** A short scramble leads to an observation deck that provides an intimate view of the entire mural. The painting spans nearly 500 feet beneath a 30-foot-high ledge, where you'll marvel at enormous red, beige and black frescoes of deer, bighorn sheep, birds and humans with outstretched arms. It is by far the largest mural in Baja, and the place where most people turn back.

The maximum weight allowed for mule riders is 110 kilograms (242 pounds). Heavier visitors must walk.

¿NO HABLAS ESPAÑOL?

Most of the licensed guides living in the Sierra de San Francisco speak little or no English. For information on English-speaking guides (at additional cost) contact Ecoturismo Kuyima, located directly across from the mission in San Ignacio. the phone number is 01152 (1) 154-00-70.

Plan ahead should you desire an extra day in the canyon to see other paintings, most notably **El Cacariso**—widely considered Baja's single most beautiful mural. Either way, plan on your way out to see **Cueva del Ratón (the Mouse's Cave),** within a half-hour's walk from San Francisco de la Sierra. It touts an impressive montage of rabbits, deer, sheep, humans, and a mountain lion said to resemble a mouse.

Flash photography is not allowed at any of these paintings. Consider a minimum film speed of ISO 200 for a hand-held camera.

- *San Francisco de la Sierra is located 23 miles east of Highway 1 in central Baja. The turnoff is 27 miles northwest of San Ignacio. Two people will pay about $50 apiece per night for mules and a guide.*

Cañon San Pablo is also known to local ranchers as Cañon Santa Teresa.

Bahía Concepción

How Long? *Some people camp along the shoreline for months at a time, but you can explore a good deal of the bay in one to two days.*

In Brief

See *Lodging and Campgrounds,* Chapter 15, under Bahía Concepción and Mulegé for a list of area accommodations.

Some say it's the most beautiful body of water in Mexico, and who's to say otherwise? A 25-mile-long bay about halfway down the Sea of Cortez, Bahía Concepción is one of, if not *the* greatest of, scenic treasures in Baja California. Every bend in the road offers another postcard view—desert-meets-the-South-Seas panoramas where brown and beige mountains rise abruptly from mangroves and aquamarine waters. Barren islets dot the shallows off the scalloped western shoreline, while the massive headland known as Punta Concepción guards the bay from the open sea.

During the cooler months, the bay is a favored haunt for vagabonds from across North America and beyond. Sailboats from distant ports rest at anchor in turquoise coves, while trailers and motorhomes fill beachside campgrounds. Still, the shoreline has remained largely undeveloped, only increasing the bay's appeal as an outdoor playground. The waters are warm, lovely and lucid, teeming with sea life and birds that have enhanced its status as a center for eco-tourism. In short, outdoor-lovers will find that Bahía Concepción possesses all the virtues that make Baja a special place—only more so.

The Details

Water temperatures in Bahía Concepción range from the low 60s in winter to the mid-80s in late summer.

For many travelers, it's enough to admire the bay from Highway 1, pulling off to soak in the vistas and take a few snapshots from one of the numerous turnoffs. For the rest of us, Bahía Concepción is full of opportunities for exploring and recreation. Diving, boating, fishing, windsurfing and other diversions are all excellent at one place or another.

To explore the bay, though, there's no better choice than a **kayak.** In fact, Bahía Concepción has few peers in Baja or anywhere else for paddlers. Its sheltered waters miss the worst of winter's northeast winds, and the pocket coves, islets and crescent beaches cry out for a closer look. The exploration goes on beneath the surface, and **snorkeling** is the perfect companion as you paddle along the shallows. You'll find kayaks for rent in **Mulegé,** and several spots along the west shore. Perhaps the last word on kayak exploration here is **EcoMundo,** at the south end of Playa Concepción. Along with kayaks, snorkeling gear and wet suits for rent, you'll find a small restaurant, bookstore, campsites, and a friendly bilingual staff that emphasizes eco-tourism and education.

Meanwhile, the remote east shore presents a worthy off-road challenge, if you have the right vehicle and mindset. It's a long haul, 36 miles on a dirt road that's extremely rough toward the end, to reach the tip of the rugged **Punta Concepción**. Leaving Highway 1 from an unmarked junction 37 miles south of Mulegé, the road hugs the south end of the bay before turning up the east shore. You'll pass lonely fish camps, virgin beaches and millions of cardón cacti with the blue bay as a backdrop before you reach the waters of the open gulf.

If you want to hang your hat along the bay, a chain of lovely campgrounds dot the west shore between **Playa Santispac** and **San Buenaventura.** Plan your stay here, if you can, April through June, or early October through mid-November. During the winter the best sites are often filled for weeks on end, while during the summer you'll face the sun's worst wrath with no shade beyond the nearest *palapa*. Of course, you'll also have the shoreline all to yourself.

"TOP OF THE WORLD"

That's the feeling you'll have from Estación Microóndas Tiburónes ("Sharks Microwave Station"), atop a promontory hundreds of feet above the mouth of the bay. Your gulf view extends more than 50 miles up and down the coastline. The mile-long cobblestone road leaves Highway 1 near Kilometer 124.

The closest commercial airport to Bahía Concepción is in Loreto, about 70 miles south of the most popular beaches.

■ *South of Mulegé along the Gulf of California. Mexico Hwy 1 follows the west shore of the bay for more than 20 miles. For information on EcoMundo and other outfitters, see* San Ignacio and Down the Gulf, *Chapter 8.*

San Javier

How Long? *Allow at least a half-day—90 minutes each way for the drive, plus a couple of hours to explore the mission and town.*

In Brief

As you climb into the rugged mountains west of Loreto, you may marvel at the Jesuits' resolve to build a mission in such a hard-to-reach area. You'll also marvel at the stupendous canyon and coastal views, and the picturesque valley that harbors the second-oldest mission in Baja California. Misión San Javier remains a well-preserved masterpiece of its era and may well have the grandest setting of any mission in the Californias. It makes for one of the most outstanding side trips in Baja California.

For more details on the route to San Javier and other nearby roads, see *San Ignacio & Down The Gulf,* Chapter 8.

The Details

Less than two years after Jesuit priests established their first Baja mission, Nuestra Señora de Loreto, they ventured into the Sierra de la Giganta, where in March 1699 they founded **Misión San Francisco Javier**. Groundbreaking on the present-day church came in 1744, with completion in 1759. It remains a working parish for the village of San Javier and surrounding farms and ranches.

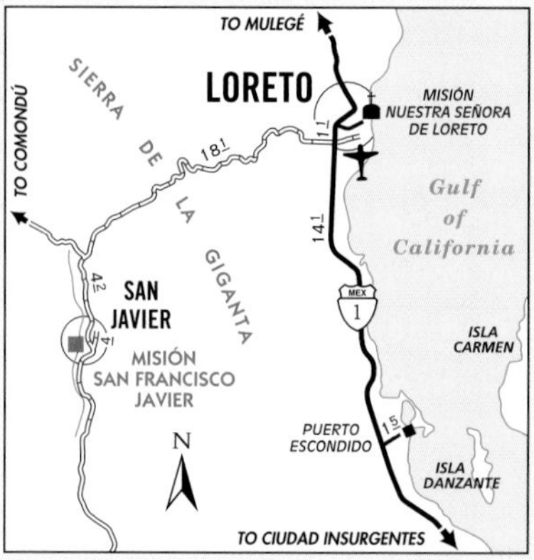

As is often the case in Baja, getting there is one of the great highlights of this trip. Leaving Highway 1, a graded-dirt road winds through several miles of low hills before climbing through a steep red-rock canyon that leads into the **Sierra de la Giganta**. Take time along the way to stop and take in the breathtaking view. This is classic Baja, with an eternal sun lording over the yawning gorge, with thousands of palms and fruit trees at its floor. Beyond the canyon lies the Sea of Cortez, with the desert peaks of Isla del Carmen rising offshore. Back on the road you'll leave those vistas behind as the road drops into the deep valley that is home to San Javier.

San Javier has no real dining options. If you're spending more than a half-day here, consider bringing your own food.

The entrance to town is marked by a long, divided parkway, which ends at the front gate of the mission. Sunflowers, fruit trees, and thatched-roof homes line this dusty main drag, while barking dogs and cackling roosters provide the usual small-town soundtrack. Aside from the church, the parkway is the prime focal point in this village of fewer than 500, taking the place of the traditional Mexican *zocalo* or main square.

The church remains among the most beautiful of Spanish missions in North America, graced by a single belfry where three ancient bells (two date to 1761) still call the locals to mass. Built of stone blocks from the nearby Arroyo de Santo Domingo, the building derives its splendor from its outstanding preservation and simple Moorish design. Enjoy the grandeur from a pew in the dimly lit sanctuary, then peruse the outside grounds and the superlative exterior handiwork. Many churches are more ornate, but the stonework and lava rock ornamentation of San Javier are without peers in Baja.

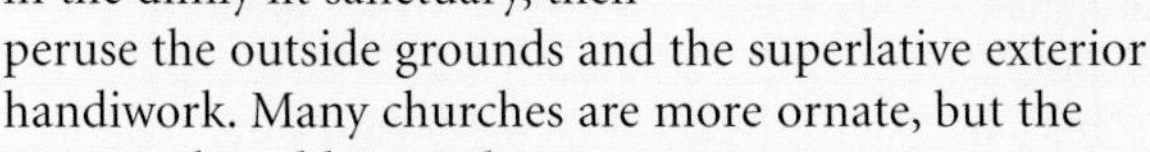

YOUR BEST PHOTO OP

Like other spots along the Gulf of California, your best photo moments along the road to San Javier come in late afternoon. You'll have the sun behind you and the color tones will be their richest. Just allow enough time to get back to Highway 1 before dark.

A passenger car can make this drive, and you'll likely see one or more old taxis out of Loreto ferrying visitors to and from the town. However, you probably won't want to take your own sedan on this road, with its numerous dips, gourd-size rocks and a shallow stream that must be forded in several spots. A pickup or SUV with sturdy tires and ample clearance should do fine; four-wheel drive is not necessary, except after the occasional heavy rainstorms.

Taxi trips and guided tours to San Javier can be arranged through most hotels and any travel agency in Loreto. Prices typically run $40-50 per person.

■ *San Javier is located 23 miles west of Mexico Hwy 1 in the Sierra de la Giganta. The turnoff from Hwy 1 is 1.1 miles south of the entrance to Loreto. The mission is open most days from 7 am to 6 pm.*

Fishing Off La Paz

How Long? *Plan on the equivalent of a full day—seven or eight hours from your pre-dawn departure until your mid-afternoon return to La Paz.*

In Brief

The quintessential La Paz experience is shoving off a remote beach in the pre-dawn darkness and heading offshore to fish the Gulf of California. For many gringos, this was the original La Paz attraction, rooted decades before the completion of Highway 1. It's still a major draw, luring thousands of *turistas* each year to the cobalt waters of the gulf, where they hook all the big-game species known to Baja. The fishing isn't what it was, say, 40 years ago, but it's still darn good, and within easy reach of southern Baja's largest city.

Avoid outfitters who would take you to Bahía de La Paz, which has been fairly well fished out.

La Paz is just one of several great fishing locales in Baja California, but we couldn't make them all "greatest hits." We chose it because it's an ideal place for first-time anglers: The fishing is excellent, there's airline service from the United States, and there are enough other diversions to enjoy if you tire of fishing

The Details

La Paz is best known for its mid-sized fish—tuna, dorado, wahoo and rooster fish, among others—although the catch varies by season. Larger, so-called billfish (marlin, sailfish) thrive here as well, but aren't the main attraction, like at Cabo San Lucas. Your boat will probably be a *panga,* an open-deck motor launch that averages 22-26 feet long and is the workhorse of Baja's sportfishing fleet. *Pangas* can usually carry up to three anglers plus a captain/guide, although two anglers will be more comfortable.

Step one, though, is booking your excursion. You can usually book one day in advance, although during busy times (e.g. late spring) it's better to do so before leaving home. La Paz has several reputable fishing services from which to choose, and most hotels and travel agencies also book trips. Prices may vary, but the average is around $180 a day per boat—$90 apiece for two anglers. The sum should include bait, tackle, license and transportation. A box lunch runs a few dollars extra, and it's customary to tip your captain/guide for good service.

On trip day, you can probably arrange for pick-up at your hotel, but do plan on an early start. Fishing starts around dawn, and you may travel some ways to reach your boat. Nowadays the best action is about an hour's drive southeast of town in **Canal de Cerralvo** and nearby **Bahía de la Ventana. Canal de San Lorenzo**, north of town, is another good spot. Space doesn't allow us to describe fishing techniques, but several good books are available. Perhaps the best is *The Baja Catch*, by Gene Kira and Neil Kelly (Apples & Oranges Publishers, Valley Center, California). It's the most comprehensive volume we know of on Baja fishing.

If you're alone (or have an odd number in your group), your outfitter can probably find another angler who'd like to share the cost of a boat.

With any luck, you'll face a pleasant dilemma during your outing: what to do with your fish. "Catch and release" is one option, and will benefit future anglers. Otherwise, it's normal to give some of your fish to your guide, who can sell them or feed his family with them. If you're traveling by air, bring an ice chest to take home some of your fish. Most outfitters will freeze and hold fish until you're ready to leave. Meanwhile, you can enjoy your catch right away—take a few fillets to your favorite restaurant and have the kitchen staff fix them for dinner. They'll usually cook them to order with all the trimmings.

FISHING CHECKLIST

Don't forget to bring sunscreen, sunglasses, a broad-brimmed hat, lip balm, waterproof sandals and seasick pills. A Spanish-English dictionary is a good idea too, since few guides speak fluent English. In winter, bring a light jacket or sweatshirt. Even in La Paz, early mornings in winter can be cool.

See *Appendix*, Chapter 16, for details on fishing regulations and a comprehensive fishing quality chart.

■ *For a list of outfitters, their addresses and phone numbers, see* La Paz & Environs, *Chapter 10.*

Isla Espíritu Santo

***How Long?** The typical outing lasts a day, but tours of several days are available.*

In Brief

There are other Baja islands with excellent diving, superlative kayaking and breathtaking scenery, but few combine those virtues so effectively, and within easy reach of a major city, as Isla Espíritu Santo and its neighboring islands. They make for an aquatic nirvana with their calm clear waters, pristine shoreline and bounty of interesting sea life. These desert isles are visual wonders by land too, with gnarled cacti, sagebrush and granite headlands that form a stunning contrast with the teal and turquoise seas. All this lies an hour's boat ride from La Paz, with ideal weather during most of the year. Small wonder, then, that Isla Espíritu Santo (Holy Spirit Island), and nearby Isla Partida (Departure Island) and Los Islotes (the Islets) have attracted outdoor enthusiasts from around the world.

Water temperatures around these islands range from the upper 60s in winter to the upper 80s in late summer.

Inclement weather, in the form of high winds or late-summer *chubascos* (rainsqualls) may force the cancellation of an occasional outing.

The Details

Odds are you'll want a one-day outing for your first trip to these islands, which should provide a good overview. You can usually book one day in advance through any of several outfitters in La Paz, or through most hotels or travel agencies. Each trip is slightly different, but nearly all include snorkeling at the sea lion colony off **Los Islotes**, and somewhere along the shore of **Espíritu Santo**. Some trips also include kayaking as an option.

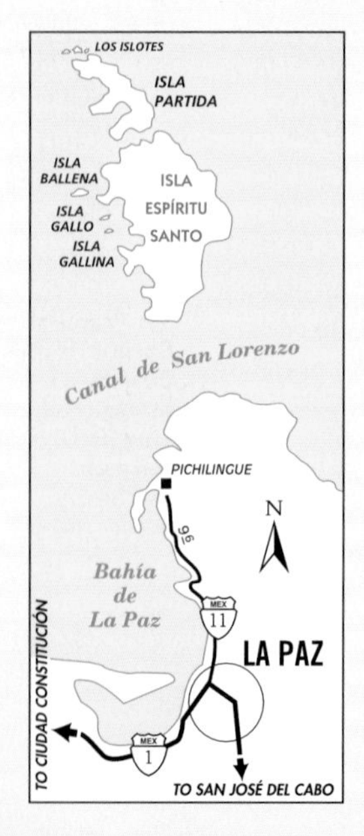

Your boat will probably set out between 8 and 9 a.m., skirting the desert headlands and scalloped beaches north of town before crossing **Canal de San Lorenzo** toward Espíritu Santo. Look about, and with any luck you'll spot some of the local sea life: graceful dolphins, a leaping manta ray, and perhaps a huge (but harmless) whale shark. It's a long ride, though, so consider traveling on a full-sized dive boat—faster and far roomier than your standard *panga,* the trusty (but sometimes cramped) workhorse of Baja's water recreation fleet.

Nearly all boats head first to **Los Islotes**, a clump of rocks off the northern tip of **Isla Partida** where the sea lions have grown

accustomed to human visitors. Diving, leaping, zipping about like whiskered torpedoes, these friendly beasts are a surefire hit for your first plunge of the day. Just give a wide berth to the bulls, which are far bigger than the females and juveniles, and often territorial. They're seldom aggressive (unless provoked) but have their ways to make sure you stay clear of the rocky shoreline.

Scuba gear is available for rent on most of these outings.

Lest you wear out your welcome, you'll head south for lunch, stopping in one of the sheltered coves along Espíritu Santo. *Pangas* pull right up on the beach, while on larger craft you'll enjoy your midday meal on board. Afterward, you should be primed for more snorkeling at one of several spots along the west side of the island, where a full-on rainbow of tropical fish awaits. Angelfish, parrot fish, Moorish idols, eel-like coronet fish and thousands of five-stripe sergeant majors are among the dazzlers you'll surely see amid the shallows. If you're planning to kayak, odds are you'll find these waters very agreeable: warm and clear, with soaring headlands that shield paddlers from the afternoon sea breeze. If your tour is like most, you'll have a couple of hours for exploring after lunch—time enough for diving and paddling before returning to La Paz.

WORTH TAKING ALONG

Besides the usual beach gear, the following items should prove especially useful on this trip: underwater camera, binoculars and a plastic fish-identification card (available from most outfitters). Between November and April, bring a light jacket.

It's customary to give a small tip to your dive master and boat pilot.

■ *Along the northeast edge of Bahía de la Paz. Daylong tours run $80-100, including lunch and snorkeling gear. Boats depart daily from the beach along the* malecón *in La Paz and from the port of Pichilingue. For a list of outfitters, see* La Paz & Environs, *Chapter 10.*

See *La Paz & Environs*, Chapter 10, for more on diving and kayaking in this area.

Land's End

How Long? *A boat tour to El Arco lasts less than an hour. Add another one to two hours if you arrange for a drop-off at Lover's Beach.*

In Brief

It is Baja's best-known landmark, a chain of granite headlands ending with a poignant arch rock where the Sea of Cortez meets the Pacific Ocean. Land's End is an icon known to millions, including many who've never been to Baja. Its image has graced the big screen, the covers of travel books and untold thousands of postcards. "Finisterra" to the locals, this landmass is the marquee attraction of Baja's biggest resort, Cabo San Lucas. Cabo may or may not suit your taste as resorts go, but if you're in the area, include a trip to Land's End, here at the southernmost tip of the Baja California peninsula.

See *The Cape Region*, Chapter 11, for more on Land's End.

Bring a waterproof bag to keep your camera and other valuables dry while wading ashore at Lover's Beach.

The Details

Famed for the arch rock known as **El Arco**, Land's End in fact comprises the entire chain of rocks jutting south from Cabo San Lucas, sculpted by wind and sea into a myriad of strange formations. The lone flat spot is **Lover's Beach**, a well-trod plot of sand that fronts the Gulf on one side and the Pacific on the other.

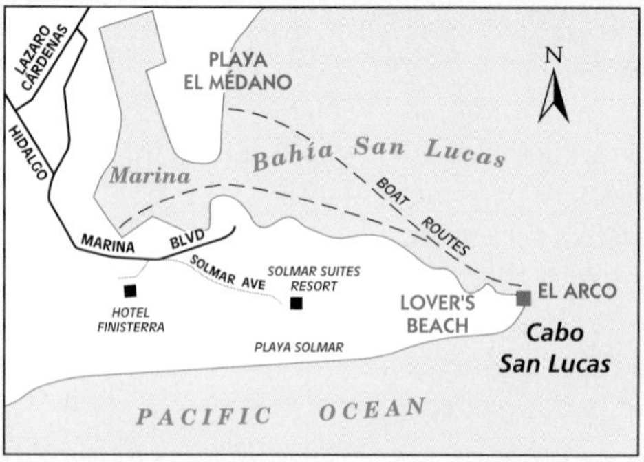

You can view Land's End from any elevated place in town or from along the sand at **Playa El Médano**, but for a close-up look you'll need some sort of boat. Any fishing cruiser or party boat will pass the rocky promontory on its way out to sea, which may suit you just fine. If not, catch a ride on a water taxi, the nimble little boats that make the milk run between the marina and El Arco. For less than $10, they'll take you around the arch rock and drop you off at Lover's Beach, where you can stroll from "coast to coast" in less than three minutes.

Having a Spanish-speaker in your group will help ensure your boat picks you up from Lover's Beach at the desired time.

It's a short "taxi" ride to El Arco, about 45 minutes for the round trip, but unless you're really rushed, plan to get off at Lover's Beach. Be sure, though, to arrange for the same boat to pick you up later on. Then take the short walk to

the Pacific side of the beach, but stay out of the shore break, with its powerful undertow that can overwhelm the best of swimmers. In marked contrast, the calm waters on the gulf side are ideal for swimming and snorkeling. These aren't the crystal-like depths like you'll encounter farther up the gulf, but with your mask and snorkel, you'll still find a superb assortment of finned creatures within a few yards of the shoreline.

See front cover for photo of El Arco.

Another way to reach Land's End is to rent a kayak at Playa El Médano and paddle across the bay. You'll have time to do all the exploring you want, but stay alert for other craft in these busy waters, and avoid the often-rough seas on the Pacific side. You can also reach Lover's Beach overland by climbing your way over a rough, rocky saddle from nearby Playa Solmar, in front of the Solmar Suites Resort. It's a suitable trip if you're in good shape and travel with a partner, although at low tide you can sometimes make it along the sand. The overland route is free, but the water taxi ride, at around $7 for the round-trip, is among the best bargains going in Cabo.

FREE ENTERPRISE AT THE CAPE

Where the tourists go, so do the vendors. Blown glass, woodcarvings, jewelry and onyx are among the goodies you'll find for sale on the sand at Lover's Beach. For a small fee, a wizened old man will plunk an iguana on your shoulder to make for a most unusual photo op.

Even at Cabo, the ocean can be chilly in winter. Water temperatures on the Pacific side may dip to 60 degrees.

- *Boats traveling to Land's End depart the Cabo San Lucas marina daily from 9 am to 4:30 pm. The round-trip fare is $6-10.*

Eating in Baja

In Brief

It's one of Baja California's great unsolved mysteries: the endless parade of tourists who cross the border, then head straight to the nearest Golden Arches or 31 Flavors sign when their stomachs start to growl. Understand, we bear no grudge against gringo-style food or its purveyors in foreign lands, but what's the point of international travel, anyhow?

"LA CUENTA, POR FAVOR"

You'll wait a long time for your check in a Baja restaurant if you don't speak up and ask for it. It is considered rude in Mexico for a server to present the check before the diner has requested it.

Baja is a wonderful place for gastronomic adventures, with many unique experiences that go far beyond the conventions of fish tacos, combo plates or bargain lobster dinners—many distinctly non-Mexican *and* non-American. We can't list them all here, and you may find someplace that becomes your own favorite. But the ones below (listed north to south) still earn our nod as "GreatestHits" of Baja dining.

A 15 percent tip is normal for good service in Mexico.

Flour and corn tortillas share equal billing in Baja restaurants, as opposed to central and southern Mexico, where flour tortillas are rare.

Mexicali

The most Chinese city in all of Mexico, this border metropolis boasts somewhere around 100 Chinese restaurants. Most specialize in Cantonese cuisine and are easy to spot, with their enormous red, yellow and green signboards. A few notables include **Restaurant Dragón**, **Alley 19** and the palatial **La Misión Dragón**.

Tijuana

Savvy travelers know there's life far beyond Avenida Revolución, like in the Zona Río, where you'll find **La Espadaña, La Fogata**, **Cien Años** and **Guadalajara Grill**. Near the Caliente Racetrack is **Los Arcos**, one of the top seafood spots in town. If you must stay on "La Revo," try **Restaurant Caesars**, which invented Caesar salad in 1930 and still serves it today.

Rosarito

Dining alone brings thousands of tourists every weekend to **Puerto Nuevo**, 11 miles south of downtown. More than 30 restaurants crowd the narrow streets of Lobster Village, the "downtown" of this seaside settlement. A few good ones include **El Galeón**, **Puerto Nuevo #1** and **#2**, the **Lobster House**, **Miramar**, **Sandra's** and **Ortega's**.

Ensenada

The bayside town is full of great restaurants, including the award-winning **El Rey Sol**, one of the oldest French restaurants in Mexico. Another standout is **La Embotelladora Vieja**, with its Mediterranean menu and Baja's longest wine list. Down the road, the phalanx of **walk-up food stands at Punta Banda** make it the undisputed *churro* capital of Baja.

Mulegé

A Baja legend lives on at the **Hotel Serenidad**, which hosts "Fiesta Night" on Saturdays, complete with roast pig, a huge buffet, mariachis and folkloric dancers. Other local restaurants have followed suit with their own fiesta nights.

Los Cabos

With many dozens of restaurants, there's no way to name all the good ones here, but all of these deserve mention: In San José del Cabo, **Damiana** and **Tequila Restaurante Garden** earn praise for their refined cuisine and atmospheres. **Tacos Rossy**, in marked contrast, is hardly refined but may be the best taco stand in southern Baja. In Cabo San Lucas, **Misiónes de Kino** and **Mocambo de los Cabos** are two spots where the menu trumps pretension, while **Sancho Panza** offers an enticing combination of live jazz, art and Mediterranean food. On the Corridor, **Arrecifes Restaurant**, in the Westin Regina Golf & Beach Resort—Los Cabos, may have the best view of the gulf in Baja to go with its diverse international menu. In Todos Santos, **Café Santa Fé** has earned followers all across southern Baja with its renowned Italian cuisine.

Restaurants geared toward the local crowd (as opposed to toursits) usually fill up in mid-afternoon, when most Mexicans eat the day's main meal.

For a more complete list of food Spanish food terms, see *Appendix*, Chapter 16.

Elsewhere

Here and there, sometimes in the least likely places, are restaurants that merit special note. A fine example is **Mama Espinosa's** with its famous lobster omelets and burritos in El Rosario. Farther south in Guerrero Negro, there's **Malarrimo**, the top seafood restaurant in central Baja. Elsewhere, in the village of Santiago, **Palomar** is one of the most pleasant *al fresco* eating spots in the land. And, this list would not be complete without mention of **Las Cazuelas**, at the Hotel La Pinta in Cataviña, home of the best *flan* we've tried in Baja California.

- *See individual city listings under* Dining *and* Nightlife *for more details.*

Chapter 4

The Northern Triangle

At the westernmost tip of the U.S.-Mexico border, a simple concrete marker straddles the fence atop a bluff overlooking the Pacific Ocean. An engraved inscription recounts the history of the border region. It's one place where you can shake hands with someone standing in the other country. Within an hour's drive of that marker live more than half the people in Baja, and most visitors will never stray beyond this small area.

Baja's northwest corner is the most populous area not just in Baja California, but along the entire U.S.-Mexico frontier. For good or ill, this land of painted burros, lobster restaurants, tourist cantinas and ceramic Tweety statues is the Baja California that most foreign tourists know. It's a place where cross-border distinctions often blur—where dollars

Vineyards in the Guadalupe Valley, between Tecate and Ensenada

are preferred to pesos, English signage is everywhere, and football fans from both countries crowd sports bars to cheer on their beloved San Diego Chargers.

Like much of Baja California, the northwest corner is a breed apart from the rest of Mexico but distinctly non-American. As the gull flies, it runs about 60 miles down the coast, past the fast-growing resort of Rosarito Beach and miles of beachfront developments to the picturesque seaport of Ensenada. From there it charts a northeast course along Mexico Highway 3 to the unlikely border town of Tecate. Some 25 miles inland, Tecate is an oddball among border towns, with a slow-paced atmosphere that feels far removed from the United States. That's slowly changing, however, as more multinational firms open factories here, while Tijuana continues expanding ever-eastward.

Long the biggest city in Baja, Tijuana has grown into a border colossus of close to 2 million people, most of whom came here from somewhere else in Mexico. Tourism is a major moneymaker and a big reason why the San Ysidro border gate is the busiest in the world, with more than 30 million crossings a year. But Tijuana depends far less on tourists than it once did, as other industries have come to dominate the economy.

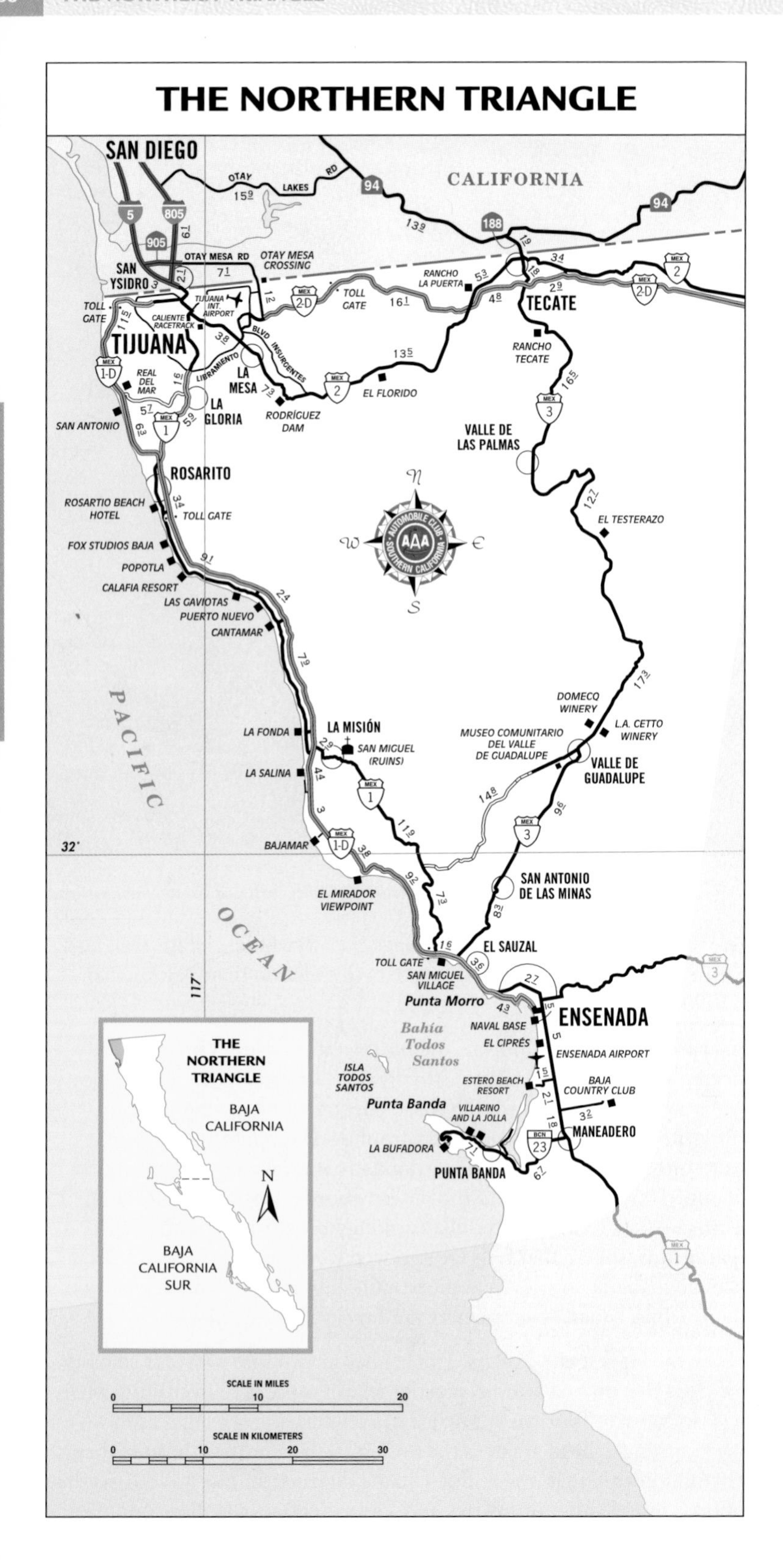
THE NORTHERN TRIANGLE
SAN DIEGO
CALIFORNIA
OTAY LAKES RD
OTAY MESA RD
OTAY MESA CROSSING
SAN YSIDRO
TOLL GATE
TIJUANA INT. AIRPORT
CALIENTE RACETRACK
TIJUANA
BLVD INSURGENTES
LIBRAMIENTO
LA MESA
REAL DEL MAR
LA GLORIA
SAN ANTONIO
RODRÍGUEZ DAM
EL FLORIDO
RANCHO LA PUERTA
TOLL GATE
TECATE
RANCHO TECATE
VALLE DE LAS PALMAS
ROSARITO
ROSARTIO BEACH HOTEL
TOLL GATE
FOX STUDIOS BAJA
POPOTLA
CALAFIA RESORT
LAS GAVIOTAS
PUERTO NUEVO
CANTAMAR
EL TESTERAZO
PACIFIC
LA FONDA
LA MISIÓN
SAN MIGUEL (RUINS)
LA SALINA
DOMECQ WINERY
L.A. CETTO WINERY
MUSEO COMUNITARIO DEL VALLE DE GUADALUPE
VALLE DE GUADALUPE
BAJAMAR
EL MIRADOR VIEWPOINT
SAN ANTONIO DE LAS MINAS
OCEAN
EL SAUZAL
TOLL GATE
SAN MIGUEL VILLAGE
Punta Morro
ENSENADA
NAVAL BASE
EL CIPRÉS
ENSENADA AIRPORT
Bahía Todos Santos
ISLA TODOS SANTOS
ESTERO BEACH RESORT
BAJA COUNTRY CLUB
Punta Banda
VILLARINO AND LA JOLLA
MANEADERO
LA BUFADORA
PUNTA BANDA
32°
117°
THE NORTHERN TRIANGLE
BAJA CALIFORNIA
BAJA CALIFORNIA SUR
N
SCALE IN MILES
0 10 20
SCALE IN KILOMETERS
0 10 20 30

Manufacturing is huge, propelled by cross-border trade and sprawling foreign-owned plants that assemble components into all sorts of finished products.

Tijuana has for many years had the lowest unemployment rate in Mexico.

Farther south, Americans and their greenbacks are still the biggest income source, yielding windfalls for Rosarito Beach and Ensenada. Thousands gather here on weekends for dining, shopping, outdoor fun, and carousing that lasts long past midnight. Hotels may sell out weeks ahead of major tourist events, while the restaurants of Puerto Nuevo's Lobster Village may serve well over 1000 seafood dinners in a single weekend. Elsewhere, the uninitiated will find a surprise or two, like the scenic rural drive between Ensenada and Tecate, where the lush vineyards of the Guadalupe Valley comprise the largest wine-producing region in Mexico.

As its growth has paralleled nearby Southern California's, this part of Baja has emerged as one of the world's major gateway regions. For Mexicans it offers the sweet promise of a better life, whether here or across the border in the U.S. Americans head here on their way to a myriad of adventures—whether a shopping spree in Tijuana, or a three-week odyssey into the most desolate reaches of the Baja California peninsula.

Experience ...

- Gawking shamelessly at the shiny office buildings and towering traffic circle monuments while strolling along Tijuana's Paseo de los Héroes.
- Wading in with the locals, shopping bag in hand, seeking the best bargain on tropical fruits, piñatas and homemade candies at Tijuana's sprawling Mercado Hidalgo.
- A pair of mariachi trumpets reverberating loud and true off the sawdust-covered floor of Ensenada's cozy Hussong's Cantina.
- Frantic foot-clomping across a hardwood stage as a troupe of folkloric dancers show their moves at the Rosarito Beach Hotel.
- The guilty pleasure of a bag of hot, sugar-drenched *churros* washed down with fresh coconut milk while waiting for the next salt-spray geyser at La Bufadora.

Tijuana

Traffic circle along Paseo de los Héroes in the Zona Río

Approached from the north, Tijuana presents one of the most imposing sights in Baja California. Countless descriptions apply to the largest city of Baja, yet somehow can't capture the whole—thriving, squalid, modern, third-world, seamy, refined .... In short, this city is full of enigmas and contradictions—praised and loathed, sought out and avoided, and forever misunderstood by observers on both sides of the border.

Tijuana is farther away from the nation's capital, Mexico City, than any other city in Mexico.

For Mexicans, a suitable nickname for Tijuana might be the City of Hope. For legions of *tijuanenses,* this city represents their last and best chance of success in their homeland before migrating to the United States. In fact, thousands commute to day jobs in neighboring San Diego. Others end up employed here following failed attempts at illegal entry into the United States.

For many non-Mexicans, their image of Tijuana is one of colorful craft stalls, boisterous nightclubs, festively decorated restaurants, bullrings and other trappings typical of a border town. This is the tourist's Tijuana, and in its own way is part of the cross-border experience. Yet in the big picture, it's only a speck amid a huge metropolis that spills across hills and canyons for many miles in all directions.

It marks a staggering transformation for a city that grew from around 60,000 souls in 1950 to about 1.7 million today. As such, the term "border town" is hardly justified anymore, as Tijuana is the fourth-largest city in all of Mexico, and its fortunes are no longer tied exclusively to tourism.

In retrospect, Tijuana's rise to fame seems inevitable. The city's history dates to 1888, when a short-lived gold rush near Ensenada fueled U.S. interest in the border region, and a year later Tijuana was founded. In the ensuing years, billing itself as the ideal weekend or vacation getaway, Tijuana grew in tandem with Southern California. Tijuana was also the scene of fighting during the Mexican Revolution in 1911, when federal troops routed the insurgent forces of Ricardo Flores Magón, which had seized control of the city. Following the revolution, the U.S. Prohibition in the 1920s generated cross-border fortunes as thousands of Americans came south looking not only for legal booze, but gambling and furtive calls to the city's bordellos.

After Prohibition's repeal in 1933, many carousers headed back north, and then in 1935 Mexico outlawed gambling, sending the city into a mild depression. The Mexican government responded by declaring Baja a duty-free zone, which helped restore cross-border commerce. By then, though, Tijuana had gained an image of a crass, tawdry town that pandered to visitors' basest instincts, a reputation—with some justification—that shapes thinking to this day.

Minaret at the old Casino de Agua Caliente

Tijuana still claims to the title of "world's most-visited city," and while the allure of sin lingers in places, more genteel pursuits have emerged as major attractions. On weekends, thousands flock to the restaurants, shops and artisans' markets of the old downtown and the upstart Zona Río. Saving money in one form or another is perhaps the biggest attraction, with hundreds of discount auto body shops, duty-free liquor stores, medical offices, and *farmacias* offering prescription drugs at a fraction of their U.S. cost. Of course, other attractions exist, such as historical sites, museums, sporting events and one of the finest cultural centers in Mexico.

While tourist dollars have helped Tijuana establish one of the country's highest standards of living, the economic base has broadened substantially. An important center for manufacturing, trade, and service industries, Tijuana has prospered greatly from the arrival of *maquiladora* plants. Owned by multinational companies based in the United States, Europe and Asia, these plants assemble imported components into finished goods before exporting them, with duty charged only on the value added by labor.

More television sets are assembled in Tijuana than anyplace else in the world.

Hundreds of *maquiladoras* have sprung up since the 1970s, giving rise to a large industrial district on the city's eastern flank. High-rise hotels and gleaming office buildings have sprouted elsewhere, lending a cosmopolitan touch that many visitors hardly expect. The upshot is that if you have never been to Tijuana—or haven't been there for some time—the city will likely astound you on any number of fronts.

Getting Around

To drive, or not to drive. That is the biggest question that you'll face before crossing the border, and influences all other decisions about getting around in Tijuana. You may well need your own vehicle if you're traveling beyond Tijuana or planning a major shopping spree. On the other hand, if you're not going beyond downtown, you may want to leave your wheels behind.

One example of how Mexican driving laws are different: Turning right on a red light is illegal.

There is no pat answer, but as a general rule you're better off not driving in Tijuana if at all possible. Border backups are the most obvious drawback, topping two hours at the San Ysidro crossing on summer weekend afternoons and an hour plus at Otay Mesa (see Crossing the Border in Tijuana). Moreover, unfamiliar signage, more aggressive driving, potholes and other hazards can unnerve those who don't drive here regularly. Insurance is another concern, since U.S. policies are invalid in Mexico, and without a Mexican policy you could be liable for any damage or injuries resulting from an accident.

TRY THE TROLLEY

You need not drive to San Ysidro at all if you take the San Diego Trolley, which links the border with downtown San Diego and points north. One-way rates range from $1 to $2, depending on distance traveled, with service between 5 a.m. and 1 a.m.

Having said that, thousands of Americans drive in Tijuana every day without incident, and the city becomes less intimidating with practice. If you do drive, be alert all times—a moment's inattention or indecision invites some sort of mishap. Among the hazards: inconspicuous traffic lights, hard-to-see stop signs, numerous one-way streets, and jaywalkers who casually step in front of speeding autos.

When approaching or returning from the border, be on the lookout for undocumented immigrants or other persons crossing the freeways.

Then there are traffic circles *(glorietas)*, known for their stately monuments but daunting for American drivers who are unfamiliar with them. When entering a traffic circle, bear right and follow the flow of traffic counterclockwise. With patience and persistence, after a few encounters you should become comfortable with them.

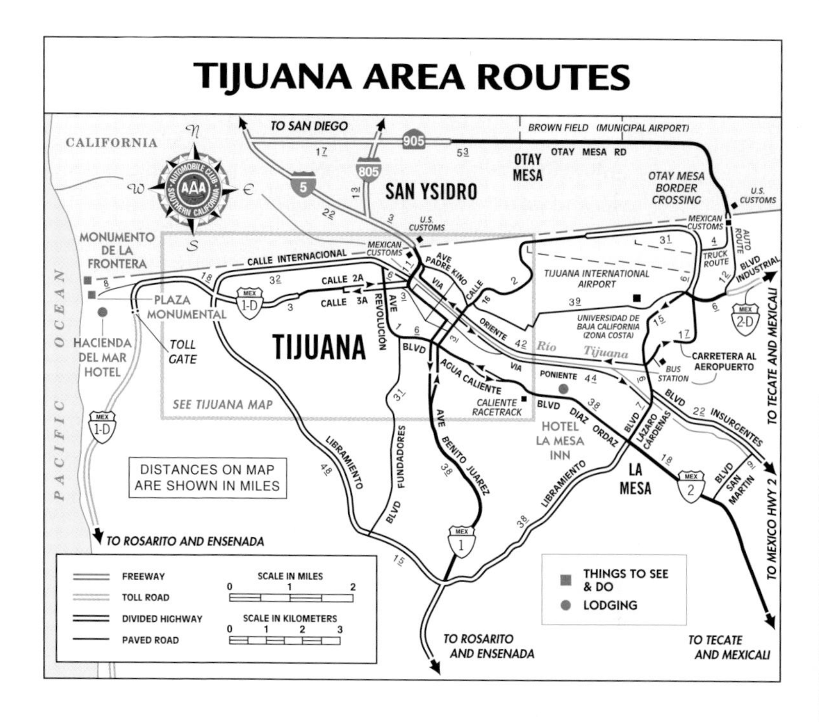

For those who'd rather not drive, most of Tijuana's major attractions lie within a few miles of the border crossings, many within walking distance, and buses and taxis are good alternatives to driving. Moreover, several San Ysidro parking lots are within a few steps of the border and open around the clock, charging about $2 per hour to $6-8 for 24 hours. Most lots provide security, but it's wise to inquire before paying to park.

Cuauhtémoc presides over a frenzied traffic circle, Paseo de los Héroes.

BUS

One of the least expensive, most convenient ways to get between San Ysidro and downtown Tijuana is on the big, bright red Mexicoach buses. They run daily, with departures every 20 to 30 minutes, charging $1 each way. Delays can occur, but Mexicoach buses use designated lanes at the San Ysidro crossing and avoid the worst of border backups.

The first bus leaves San Ysidro at 7:30 a.m., while the last bus leaves Tijuana at 9 p.m. Pickup and drop-off points in San Ysidro are at the Preferred, 5 Star and Border Station parking lots, all on the west side of I-5. The Mexicoach terminal in Tijuana is on Avenida Revolución between calles 6 and 7.

TAXIS

Cabbies abound in the main tourist areas, fares are reasonable, and nearly all drivers speak at least some English. Walk across the border at San Ysidro or stroll down Avenida Revolución and you'll hear the steady refrain, "*¿Taxi? ¿Taxi?*" While they can be annoying at times, once hired, cabbies are generally courteous and can offer some pointers about major attractions. Like most of Baja, the typical Tijuana taxi is an older U.S.-built sedan seating four or five passengers.

One thing you won't find in Tijuana (or most Baja cities) are taximeters to record your fare. Instead, you'll pay a fixed price, which should be agreed upon before getting in the cab. While bargaining may net you a small savings, most rides to major attractions have fixed fares, mostly in the $4-10 range. Plan on paying about $5 per carload for a ride between the San Ysidro border crossing and Avenida Revolución, the downtown bullring, the Caliente Racetrack or the Zona Río. To the Tijuana airport or Bullring-by-the-Sea, the going rate is about $8-10 per carload. Whatever your destination, don't pay the fare until you arrive.

> **BETTER LATE THAN NEVER**
>
> It's never too late to buy a trinket in Tijuana, with long rows of souvenir stalls lining the approaches to the San Ysidro and Otay Mesa border crossings. Dozens of vendors stroll amid waiting cars, selling all sorts of mostly lowbrow keepsakes.

In addition, *taxis de ruta* (route taxis) follow preset routes and will pick up passengers anywhere along the way. Fares are very low, about 50 cents per person, but expect crowded conditions on board these rattly old workhorses, usually three-seat station wagons.

WALKING

With literally hundreds of gift shops, craft stalls, restaurants and clubs crammed into a few square blocks, downtown Tijuana is a pedestrian's paradise. Some of Tijuana's prime tourist destinations are less than a mile from the San Ysidro border crossing, including Avenida Revolución and its many attractions. A foot route from the San Ysidro border passes through Plaza Viva Tijuana and Mercado de Artesenías to reach the north end of Revolución. Plaza Pueblo Amigo is even closer. You should, however, avoid walking between the border and major tourist areas after dark, since street crime can be a problem.

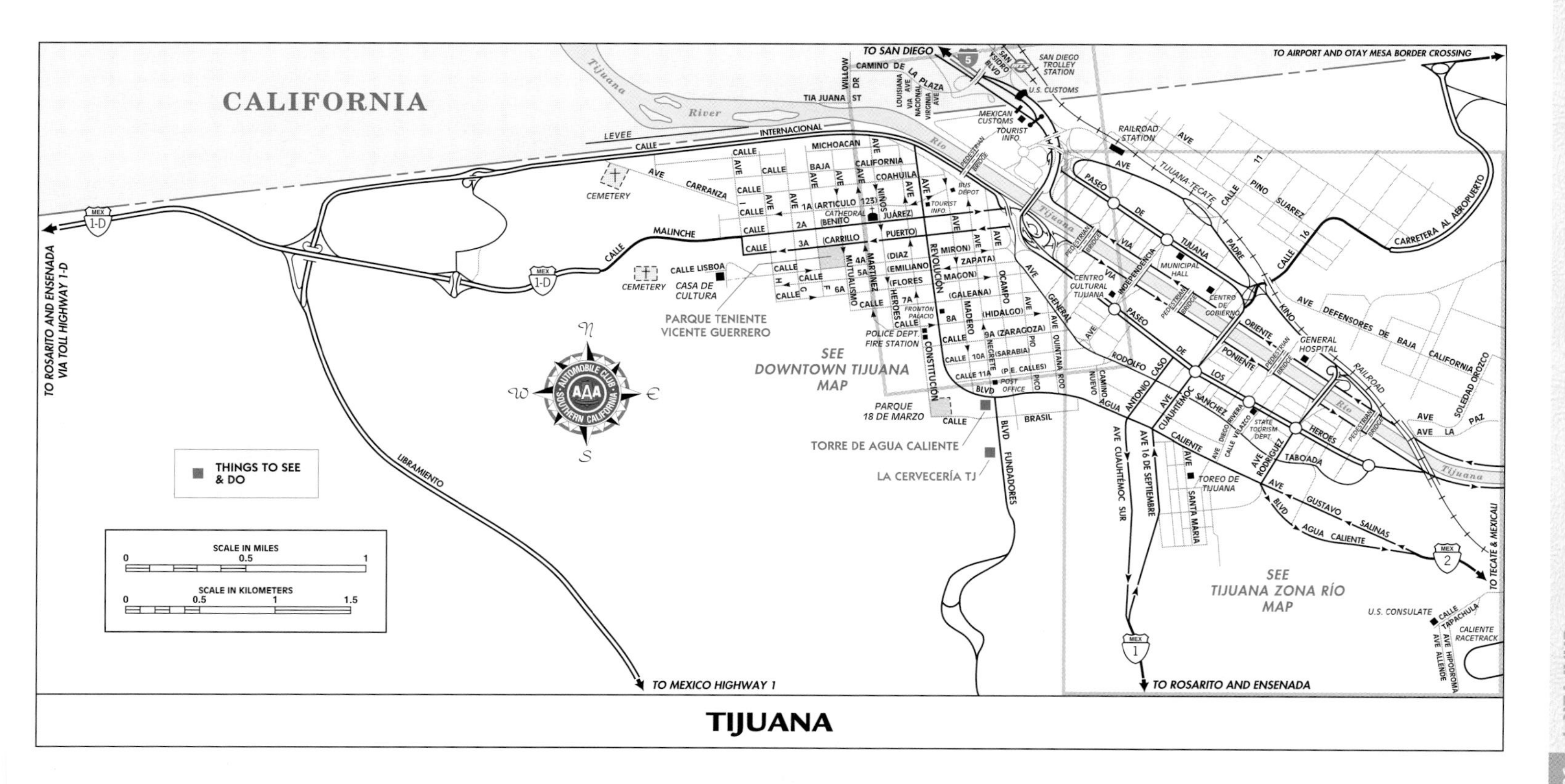
CALIFORNIA
TO SAN DIEGO
TO AIRPORT AND OTAY MESA BORDER CROSSING
TO ROSARITO AND ENSENADA VIA TOLL HIGHWAY 1-D
TO MEXICO HIGHWAY 1
TO ROSARITO AND ENSENADA
TO TECATE & MEXICALI
SAN DIEGO TROLLEY STATION
U.S. CUSTOMS
MEXICAN CUSTOMS
TOURIST INFO.
RAILROAD STATION
BUS DEPOT
CATHEDRAL
MUNICIPAL HALL
CENTRO DE GOBIERNO
CENTRO CULTURAL TIJUANA
GENERAL HOSPITAL
STATE TOURISM DEPT.
TOREO DE TIJUANA
U.S. CONSULATE
CALIENTE RACETRACK
FRONTÓN PALACIO
POLICE DEPT. FIRE STATION
POST OFFICE
PARQUE 18 DE MARZO
TORRE DE AGUA CALIENTE
LA CERVECERÍA TJ
PARQUE TENIENTE VICENTE GUERRERO
CALLE LISBOA
CASA DE CULTURA
CEMETERY
Tijuana River
SEE DOWNTOWN TIJUANA MAP
SEE TIJUANA ZONA RÍO MAP
AVE REVOLUCIÓN
CALLE CONSTITUCIÓN
BLVD FUNDADORES
PASEO DE TIJUANA
PASEO DE LOS HEROES
VIA INDEPENDENCIA
AVE CUAUHTÉMOC SUR
AVE 16 DE SEPTIEMBRE
BLVD AGUA CALIENTE
BLVD GUSTAVO SALINAS
LIBRAMIENTO
CALLE MALINCHE
CARRETERA AL AEROPUERTO
AVE DEFENSORES DE BAJA CALIFORNIA
THINGS TO SEE & DO
SCALE IN MILES
0
0.5
1
SCALE IN KILOMETERS
0
0.5
1
1.5
AUTOMOBILE CLUB · SOUTHERN CALIFORNIA
AAA
TIJUANA

Crossing the Border in Tijuana

It's a long way from Tijuana to the U.S. border, at least on weekend afternoons—two hours by auto at the San Ysidro crossing, and an hour or more at Otay Mesa. Even crossing the border on foot can take a while, as those who've stood in line for a half-hour or more can attest. Without a doubt, crossing the border is the biggest headache most people face on their visit to Tijuana, and will likely influence where, when and how you cross the international boundary.

Entering Mexico is usually the easy part, with delays that seldom last more than a few minutes, and most travelers pass through with no inspection. Heading north is another matter, however, as everyone must stop at U.S. Customs. Your own inspection may last just a few seconds, but with thousands of people crossing the border every hour (at least during busy periods), it translates into long, tedious waits.

Passing Mexican Customs on foot at the San Ysidro crossing

The worst delays happen on weekends and grow progressively worse as the day goes on, peaking in late afternoon or early evening. Weekday mornings and afternoons are backup-prone, too, when thousands of motorists commute to and from cross-border jobs. Car-pool lanes at San Ysidro can speed the process on weekdays, but they're only open to vehicles with four or more persons. Conversely, late-night hours and midday hours (10 a.m. to 3 p.m.) on weekdays have fairly short waits.

Of Tijuana's two border crossings, San Ysidro's lines are invariably longer, no surprise given its proximity to downtown Tijuana as well as major San Diego freeways. Open 24 hours, it is the world's busiest international gateway. Interstates 5 and 805 lead from San Diego directly to the San Ysidro gate, located within a few blocks of both downtown Tijuana and the Zona Río.

The Otay Mesa crossing is six miles east of San Ysidro, just south of Otay Mesa Road and just east of the Tijuana International Airport. It is open daily from 6 a.m. to 10 p.m. To reach the crossing from San Diego, take SR 905 east from either I-5 or I-805 until it turns into Otay Mesa Road. Continue east for about four miles and follow the signs to the border.

Returning to the United States, the Otay Mesa crossing is a good alternative on the weekends, when border waits at San Ysidro can be especially grueling. From Tijuana, a bypass road loops around the southern and eastern part of the city to Otay Mesa. Approached from Highway 1-D (the toll road) south of Tijuana, exit at the La Gloria turnoff, then follow the highway north to the bypass, named Libramiento. Follow the "La Mesa-Tecate-Mexicali" signs, then bear right onto the bypass and follow the signs marked "Aeropuerto."

Like many Mexican roads, the bypass route's name changes several times between Highway 1-D and Otay Mesa. Nearing the airport, signs in Spanish point the way to the border crossing. Otay Mesa handles all the commercial truck traffic crossing the border, and there are separate lanes for heavy vehicles *(Vehículos Pesados)* and light vehicles *(Vehículos Ligeros)*, which include cars, light trucks and RVs.

If you're entering Mexico, you'll have a shorter wait at either crossing, but you still must stop and wait for one of two lights to flash. A green light sends you on your way, while a red light requires you stop for inspection. If you are stopped, the process is usually quick, although officials may search your vehicle and luggage and inquire about where you're going in Mexico. Firearms are usually the main contraband that inspectors are looking for, and are illegal in Mexico without a special hunting permit. Transporting firearms into Mexico without the required permits can result in your immediate arrest and incarceration.

Things To See & Do

Firearms are illegal in Mexico. If you are caught bringing one into the country, you will go to jail.

Gone for good are the days of Tijuana as the one-dimensional border town that lived or died by the tourist trade, but this is still a great place to buy an Indian blanket, catch a bullfight, or sing along with mariachis in a garishly decorated restaurant. All that and much more beckons within a mile or two of the border, which helps explain why this city remains Baja California's leading tourist destination.

The old downtown, a few blocks southwest of the San Ysidro crossing, has always been the center of action and is still a good place to begin your explorations. The main drag is Avenida Revolución, a raucous 10-block strip known to generations of U.S. tourists, with a vast assortment of restaurants, clubs and shops of all description. By night it

Piñatas, Mercado Miguel Hidalgo

rattles and hums till well past midnight as knots of youthful revelers make their way from one watering hole to the next. By day it is a shopper's paradise, with all the clothing, arts and crafts, liquors, prescription drugs and other goods for which border towns are famous.

Come inside! Everything for free!
—Curio salesman, Avenida Revolución

While Revolución is the best-known strip, more shopping abounds nearby, along with some worthwhile (if unexpected) attractions. One of those is L.A. Cetto Winery, which offers tours and tasting in its modern facility near the south edge of downtown. If wine-tasting somehow

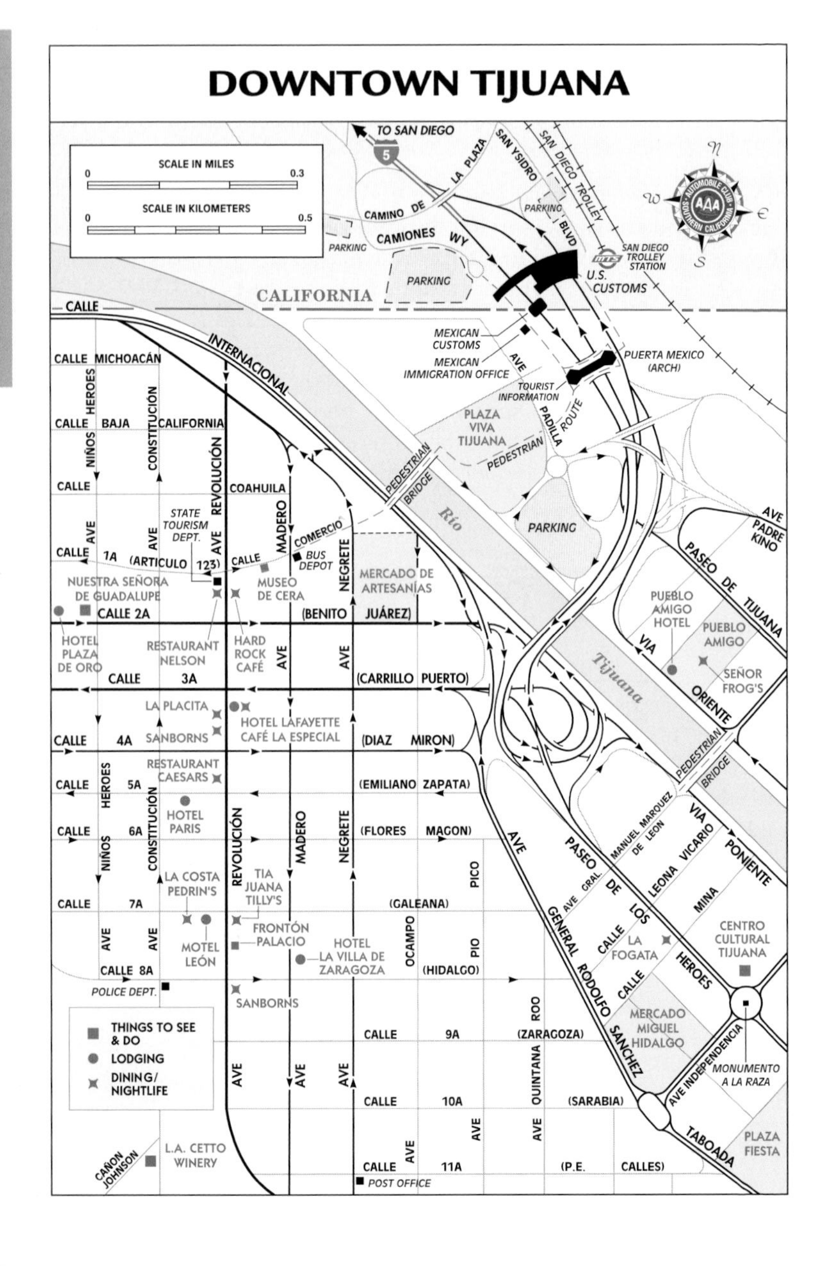

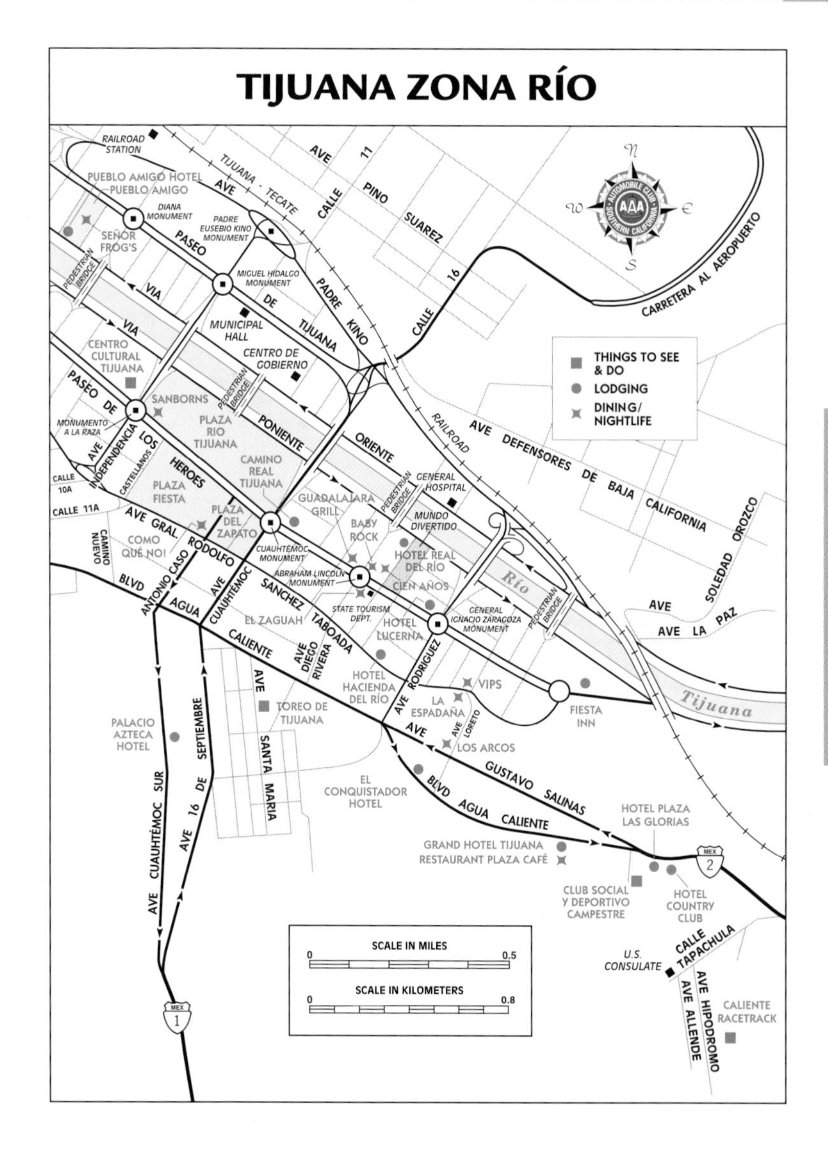

seems un-Mexican, then try a cold one nearby at La Cervecería TJ, the home of TJ Beer. Opened in early 2000, it is the city's only brewery and serves its suds inside an attached cantina. Meanwhile, at the north end of downtown is the Museo de Cera, home to several dozen wax figures depicting famous personalities from past and present. Though hardly the biggest of its genre, the museum certainly merits a visit, and the cost of admission is unbeatable.

When you need a breather, a couple of good rest stops await nearby. Nuestra Señora de

DOLLARS AND SENSE

Dollars are universally accepted for sales transactions in Tijuana, although you may receive your change in pesos. If so, make sure you get the correct amount back; a few unscrupulous vendors will try to short-change unsuspecting customers.

Entrance gate to Caliente Racetrack

Guadalupe, a landmark church with soaring twin towers, offers a quiet refuge from the downtown street scene. Another is Parque Teniente Vicente Guerrero, a good-sized green space that is a magnet for tourists and locals.

Tijuana presents a distinctly cosmopolitan face in the Zona Río, with its broad, tree-lined boulevards, modern office buildings and stately statues that rise from traffic circles. Shopping is superb, including a bustling open-air marketplace (Mercado Miguel Hidalgo), the city's largest shopping mall (Plaza Río Tijuana) and many other venues. Several topflight restaurants and nightclubs also dot this upscale district, which is a magnet for the city's middle- and upper-classes. The crown jewel is the Centro Cultural Tijuana, a hard-to-miss modern complex where exhibits by top Mexican artists, a performing arts center and a brand-new museum on the history of Baja California are highlights.

Farther southeast is Tijuana's classic Caliente Racetrack, where fleet-footed greyhounds race nightly on an oval track. Just a chip shot away is the Tijuana Country Club, where reasonable greens fees attract golfers from both sides of the border to the verdant 18-hole course.

In other ways the sporting scene is distinctly Latin, such as the *charreadas*, Mexican-style rodeos that take place at several *charro* rings scattered about the city. Then there are bullfights, which bring some of the world's top matadors to two main bullrings. One is Toreo de Tijuana, a short drive east of downtown on the way to the Caliente Racetrack. The other is Plaza Monumental, better known as Bullring-by-the-Sea, which overlooks the Pacific.

In the shadow of the bullring is another landmark that merits a visit—a simple concrete cairn marking the western terminus of the Mexico-U.S. border. A few steps west,

¡Hola Amigo! *No Offense Intended*

For some gringos, the word *amigo* sounds like an insincere come-on when it comes from a fast-barking border town salesman. After all, this guy isn't my friend, he just wants a piece of my wallet, right? Not so fast. *Amigo* is one of those words that transcends its literal translation to English. To the Mexican, *amigo* can signify not only "friend," but any fellow to whom he is speaking, not unlike the American words "buddy" or "pal."

the metal border fence descends a shallow bluff and crosses a narrow beach as the 2000-mile border ends in the crashing Pacific surf.

Top Attractions

See GreatestHits, **Chapter 3, for more on Avenida Revolución.**

AVENIDA REVOLUCIÓN

Shopping, dining, nightlife and the legendary painted burros are all part of the scene along this nine-block tourist strip, perhaps the most famous street of any Mexican border town. For many tourists, their Mexican journey begins and ends with a walk down this street, past countless gift shops, craft stalls, nightclubs, strip joints, restaurants of all description and the famed Frontón Palacio, where professional jai-alai players competed for many years. *½ mile southwest of the San Ysidro border crossing.*

ENTER AT YOUR OWN RISK

Take extra precautions before entering the seedy neighborhood known as the Zona Norte, along Avenida Revolución north of Calle 1—if you enter it at all. Drug-dealing and prostitution are rampant, creating an environment conducive to street crime.

CENTRO CULTURAL TIJUANA

(Tijuana Cultural Center) One of Mexico's largest, most impressive cultural centers is found in Tijuana. The country's artistic heritage is preserved and promoted through galleries, murals, gift shops and a 1000-seat performing arts center, among other attractions. Recent additions include an IMAX Theater and the Museo de los Californias (Museum of the Californias), a historical tour de force that opened in early 2000. *Corner of Paseo de los Héroes and Ave Independencia in the Zona Río. 01152 (6) 687-96-50, 684-11-32. Open Tue-Sun 10 am-8 pm, closed Mon. Museum admission $2, IMAX movies $3.*

Centro Cultural Tijuana

LA CERVECERÍA TJ (TJ Brewery)

The home of TJ Beer, this microbrewery began production in early 2000. A lavish cantina, paneled with wood imported from the Czech Republic, serves beer and finger food. While tours are usually available on a walk-in basis, calling ahead is recommended. *Blvd Fundadores 2951, south of Calle Brasil. 01152 (6) 638-86-62, 638-86-63. Open Mon-Wed 1-10 pm, Thu-Sat 1 pm-midnight, Sun 10 am-5 pm.*

L.A. Cetto's main winery is in the Guadalupe Valley, northeast of Ensenada.

L.A. CETTO WINERY

It's a ways from the vineyards of the Guadalupe Valley, but the winery has built a good-sized aging and tasting complex amid downtown. Tours and tasting are available, and a large gift shop sells wine, brandy and a variety of souvenirs. *Corner of Callejón Johnson and Ave Constitución Sur. 01152 (6) 685-30-31, 5-16-44. Open Mon-Fri 10 am-6:30 pm, Sat 10 am-5 pm; closed Sun. Last tours start ½ hour before closing. Winetasting $2.*

MONUMENTO DE LA FRONTERA (Border Monument)

The western terminus of the Mexico-U.S. border is marked by a simple, pyramid-shaped monument straddling the international frontier next to the Pacific Ocean. Bilingual plaques tell the border's history, and you can look through the fence at Border Field State Park on the U.S. side. Local activists have used a portion of fence to make a political statement, listing the names of undocumented immigrants who have died while trying to enter the United States. *At Playas de Tijuana, just north of Bullring-by-the-Sea.*

Border fence at Playas de Tijuana includes the names of Mexicans who died while trying to enter U.S.

MUSEO DE CERA (Tijuana Wax Museum)

John F. Kennedy, Mahatma Gandhi, Pancho Villa and Marilyn Monroe are a sample of the many personalities depicted by wax figures at this small downtown museum. By and large, the figures of Mexican personalities appear more lifelike than do those from elsewhere. *On Calle 1 between Ave Revolución and Ave Madero. 01152 (6) 688-24-78. Open Mon-Fri 10 am-7 pm, Sat-Sun 10 am-8 pm. Admission $1.25. Ages 5 and under free.*

NUESTRA SEÑORA DE GUADALUPE

The twin towers of this church, a classic example of Mexican cathedral architecture, rise majestically above the old downtown. The cavernous sanctuary, which hosts mass daily, offers a respite from the hub-hub of the downtown scene. *Corner of Calle 2 and Ave Niños Héroes. Open dawn to dusk.*

PARQUE TENIENTE VICENTE GUERRERO

This pleasant park is the closest thing Tijuana has to a *zócalo* and makes a pleasant spot for visitors who want a breather. The park is named for Lt. Vicente Guerrero, who successfully led federal troops against the revolutionary forces of Ricardo Flores Magón in 1911 during the Mexican Revolution. *Calle 3 at Ave F.*

SHOPPING

Many Baja towns offer superlative shopping, but Tijuana remains in a class by itself in terms of variety, selection and quantity of goods. Several large shopping districts within a short distance of the border sell arts, handcrafts and clothing from throughout Mexico, along with a huge selection liquor, groceries and household goods, all at prices well below those in the United States. In some ways, shopping here is little different than the U.S.—dollars are universally accepted, and virtually all shopkeepers in the major tourist zones speak at least some English.

By far the best-known shopping area is downtown, mainly **Avenida Revolución** (see separate listing), with its colorful blocks brimming with gift shops, craft stalls, street vendors and much more. One block west is **Avenida Constitución,** the main downtown block for locals. Rather than souvenirs, Constitución offers better deals on liquor, food and household goods. Close by is the **Mercado de Artesanías (Artisans' Market)**, on Calle 2 between avenidas Negrete and Ocampo, with a huge variety of clothing, arts and crafts sold at dozens of open-air booths. Yet another large shopping area is **Plaza Viva Tijuana,** on the pedestrian route between downtown and the San Ysidro border crossing.

Farther east, the Zona Río has several great destinations, though most tourists never make it this way. **Mercado Miguel Hidalgo**, a square block fronting Avenida Independencia between Paseo de los Héroes and Avenida Sánchez Taboada, provides an authentic, open-air market experience, with dozens of stalls selling produce, prepared foods, household goods and the best selection of piñatas in town. Nearby is Tijuana's leading shopping mall, **Plaza Río Tijuana**, spread along Paseo de los Héroes between Independencia and Avenida Cuauhtémoc. Across from the mall is **Plaza del Zapato** (Shoe Plaza), with more than 30 footwear shops, and the adjacent **Plaza Fiesta**, a colonial-style center with assorted restaurants, bars and shops. Still more shopping in this zone is at **Pueblo Amigo**, between Paseo de Tijuana and Via Oriente, about a half-mile southeast of the border crossing.

Auto body and paint shop

Tijuana also specializes in **automobile services**, with many shops offering bargains on auto painting, body work and seat covers. The major district is downtown, bordered by calles 3 and 8, and avenidas Ocampo and Pío Pico. Nearly all the shops have an English-speaking manager and experience with cross-border customers.

TORRE DE AGUA CALIENTE (Agua Caliente Tower)

This onetime lighthouse took on new life in its new location several miles from the coast, at the southern edge of downtown. With fancy belfries and elaborate tile work on the facade, it has become one of the best-known symbols of the city. *South end of Ave Revolución and west end of Blvd Agua Caliente.*

ZONA RÍO MONUMENTS

Drive the main boulevards of this district and you'll view some of the biggest monuments in Baja, straddling the major traffic circles. Several of the best examples are on Paseo de los Héroes, including the **Monumento a la Raza** (at Avenida Independencia), Aztec emperor **Cuauhtémoc** (at Avenida Cuauhtémoc Norte) and **General Ignacio Zaragoza** (at Avenida Rodríguez). Others include Mexican independence leader **Miguel Hidalgo** (Paseo de Tijuana at Avenida Independencia), early Baja missionary **Padre Eusebio Kino** (Avenida Independencia at Avenida Padre Kino), and **Diana**, the huntress of Greek mythology fame (Paseo de Tijuana at Avenida Márquez de León). Surely the least expected is at the intersection of Paseo de los Héroes and Avenida Diego Rivera—**Abraham Lincoln**, a gift presented by U.S. President Jimmy Carter on behalf of the American people.

VIVA LA KITSCH

The days of velvet Elvis paintings, that enduring symbol of lowbrow border culture, live on at Mercado de Artesanías, where a rendering of The King fetches $45, frame included. Other stars of yore available include James Dean, Marilyn Monroe and John Wayne.

Spectator Sports

Bullfight tickets are available at bullrings the same day as the fight, but reservations are advisable for optimum seating.

BULLFIGHTS

Top matadors from Mexico and around the world perform at two cavernous bullrings, El Toreo, on Boulevard Agua Caliente near downtown, and Plaza Monumental (Bullring-by-the-Sea), where the border fence meets the Pacific at Playas de Tijuana. The season runs from May into November, with July and August being the most popular months. Bullfights take place on selected Sundays, always at 4:30 p.m. Tickets range from $13 to $41, with the shaded side of the ring costing more. Tickets are available at the bullrings, from Mexicoach in downtown Tijuana, and through Five Star Tours, which offers bus trips from San Diego.

Plaza Monumental (Bullring-by-the-Sea) *6 miles west of downtown off Hwy 1-D. 01152 (6) 680-18-08.*

Toreo de Tijuana *2 miles east of downtown on Blvd Agua Caliente. 01152 (6) 686-15-10.*

Five Star Tours *Inside the Santa Fe depot in downtown San Diego. (619) 232-5049.*

Mexicoach *Ave Revolución between calles 6 and 7. 01152 (6) 685-14-70.*

Bullring-by-the-Sea

CHARREADAS

Ornate costumes, festive music and a distinctly south-of-the-border flavor highlight *charreadas,* equestrian events that inspired the development of American-style rodeo. *Charreadas* take place throughout the year at several *charro* rings located around the city, usually on Saturdays or Sundays, although the schedule is not fixed. Admission is usually free or a nominal charge. One of the largest, best-known rings is the 3000-seat **Cortijo San José**, at the corner of Avenida del Agua and Paseo Ensenada in Playas de Tijuana, phone 01152 (6) 630-18-25. For more information on other locations and dates for upcoming *charreadas,* contact the Tijuana Tourism Board, phone (888) 775-24-17, 01152 (6) 684-28-54, or the state Secretariat of Tourism at 01152 (6) 688-05-55.

DOG RACING

The greyhounds run nightly at Caliente Racetrack in their relentless pursuit of the mechanical rabbit, while frenzied fans cheer their favorite canines on in hopes of a big payday. Caliente is the only greyhound track in Baja, and also the flagship for a chain of betting parlors that offer wagering on U.S. horseracing, boxing and professional team sports.

Caliente Racetrack *3 miles east of downtown along Blvd Agua Caliente. (619) 231-1910, 01152 (6) 681-80-88. Greyhounds run Mon-Fri at 7:45 pm, and Sat-Sun at 2 and 7:45 pm. General admission free. Turf Club Restaurant open daily 9 am-7 pm.*

Outdoor Fun

GOLF

Affordable greens fees and proximity to the border have made the Tijuana Country Club (Club Social y Deportivo Campestre) a favorite with many golfers from Southern California. The club's 18-hole course is adjacent to the Grand Hotel Tijuana.

Club Social y Deportivo Campestre (Semi-private) 18 holes; 6233 yards; par 72; 120 slope; 70.2 rating. Rates: $30-40. *On Blvd Agua Caliente next to the Grand Hotel Tijuana. (800) 217-1165, 01152 (6) 681-78-55.*

Adios, Jai-Alai

It remains one of the best-known buildings in Tijuana, its distinctive Moorish form rising high above Avenida Revolución, where it has been a landmark since 1947. But aside from an occasional concert, all's quiet these days at the Frontón Palacio, as it has been since late 1997, when the final jai alai game was played at the downtown arena.

The statue remains, but jai-alai is gone from the Frontón.

A fast-moving, two-man court game using a ball and scoop-shaped wicker basket attached to the wrist, jai alai was a nightly fixture for decades at the 380-seat Frontón. Betting on players was legal, and the sport enjoyed a loyal following from both sides of the border before declining attendance during the 1980s and '90s led to its departure. While jai alai may be gone, the Frontón itself remains in good repair, and you can still bet on the horses, your favorite U.S. sports team or the next championship bout at the Caliente betting parlor, located at the south entrance of the building.

Nightlife

Welcome to Baja's original party town, one that earned its carousing credentials decades before Rosarito or Cabo San Lucas even appeared on the map. That freewheeling reputation dates to the late 1800s, but took off in the 1920s when Prohibition swept the United States, sending "thirsty" Americans south in search of legal booze. Tijuana cashed in big-time, although its reputation took a seedy turn, as in 1926 when American author Ring Lardner described this as "a city of about 50 buildings, of which three ain't saloons."

HIRE A SONG

Mariachis who gather at the corner of Revolución and Calle 1 will perform for $10 a song or $220 per hour, and will accompany you to the restaurant, bar or other venue of your choice.

Much has changed since Lardner made his wry observation, but for many gringos the image lingers of a town for busting loose and leaving one's cares across the border. It's not hard to see why—just take a nighttime stroll down Avenida Revolución past the blocks of drink and dance clubs where boisterous Americans carry on till well past midnight. Another hot spot is the Zona Río, a more highbrow version of "La Revo," favored by middle- and upper-class Mexicans dressed to boogie. Somewhat more casual is the night scene at Pueblo Amigo, a tourist-geared plaza with several drink and dance spots mixed in among restaurants, shops and hotels. It's only a half-mile from the San Ysidro crossing.

There's something for every taste—rowdy dance clubs, bawdy stage shows, high-tech discos, sports bars, and quite a few romantic drinking and dining spots. The appeal runs across the board, although it's mainly younger gringos who head this way after dark. High school and college students, sailors and Marines and other youthful types flock here on weekends, lured in no small part by a legal drinking age of 18.

Expect a dress code prohibiting shorts, jeans or sneakers at any nightspots in the Zona Río.

The younger crowd has proved a windfall for some local clubs, but a mixed blessing for the city as a whole, as it tries to shake its sinful reputation of decades past. Civic leaders have made continued efforts to clean up Tijuana's image, and have tried, with mixed results, to force all-night establishments to close by 3 a.m. in an effort to curb binge drinking by U.S. teens. We haven't listed those clubs here, instead naming a few that offer something more than cheap alcohol for under-21-year-olds.

BABY ROCK

There's nothing subtle about this Zona Río fixture, with its gaudy exterior in the shape of a massive boulder, or the high-decibel soundtrack inside. In true Mexican fashion, the action doesn't heat up till around midnight, when it busts loose with techno-dance, disco and rock tunes, backed by fancy pyrotechnics and a steady supply of well drinks. *Corner of Paseo de los Héroes and Diego Rivera. 01152 (6) 634-24-04. Full bar.*

COMO QUÉ NO!

It's a long way from the collegiate binge-drinking scene to this spacious, well-groomed restaurant/nightclub in the

Zona Río. It's more grown-up but still a fun place, with dancing to live and recorded salsa, disco, rock, jazz, etc. Wednesday (Ladies Night) and Saturday nights generally draw the biggest American crowds, ranging from 20-somethings on up to 40s. For a more subdued experience, the piano bar next door is open nightly except Sunday. *Corner of Ave Sánchez Taboada and Calle Antonio Caso in the Zona Río. 01152 (6) 684-27-88. Full bar; full menu till 10 pm; cover charge Fri-Sat; live music schedule varies.*

GUADALAJARA GRILL

Not a nightclub or dance club per se, but a great place for eating, drinking and music with a fun mix of tourists and locals. The loud yellow exterior sets the tone for the lively (but not unruly) spirit inside. The mariachis arrive at 9 every night, so consider showing up early for dinner or dessert, or to pull up a stool at one of the two good-sized bars. *Corner of Paseo de los Héroes and Ave Diego Rivera in the Zona Río. 01152 (6) 634-30-65. Full bar; full menu till midnight.*

SANBORNS

There's nothing terribly complicated here, just a good place to ease back, nurse a drink and let your mind drift inside a softly lit, thoroughly middle-class cocktail lounge. Should the urge for a midnight snack strike, an adjacent coffee shop is open late. *Downtown on Ave Revolución at the corner of Calle 8. 01152 (6) 688-14-33. Zona Río in Plaza Río Tijuana shopping center on Paseo de los Héroes. 01152 (6) 684-89-99. Full bar; full menu served in adjacent restaurant.*

SEÑOR FROG'S

This is *not* a place you go to for a profound cross-cultural experience, but Grupo Anderson's makes few pretensions otherwise at any of its Mexican tourist-town clubs. Love it or hate it, Anderson's formula works, wooing herds of gringos and quite a few Mexicans for its international food, potent libations, and loud dance music at this cavernous restaurant/club. *Plaza Pueblo Amigo, ½ mile southeast of San Ysidro border crossing. 01152 (6) 682-49-62. Full bar; full menu until midnight.*

TIA JUANA TILLY'S

A downtown fixture since 1947, this is a time-honored place to enjoy a late-evening supper or nightcap while the club-hopping crowd parades up and down *La Revo*. It's one of the best people-watching spots in town and the place to go for live marimba tunes. *Corner of Ave Revolución and Calle 7, next to the Frontón Palacio. 01152 (6) 685-60-24.*

Dining

In a city of around 1.7 million next to the world's busiest border crossing, you would expect to find a grand variety of restaurants, and Tijuana delivers in a big way. From the humblest taco stand to the most elegant of establishments, Baja's largest city has something for every budget and palate.

There is no one cuisine that personifies this city, the way Chinese does in Mexicali or seafood in Ensenada (although Tijuana claims to be the birthplace of Caesar salad). What you will find is a vast assortment of Mexican eateries, which serve regional dishes from all over the country. Steak and seafood are the norm at the upscale restaurants, some with cuisine and ambiance that would compete with the finest establishments across the border. Ethnic restaurants run the gamut—Chinese, Spanish, pizza, French, and gringo-style coffee shops among the main ones. And, for those who just can't subsist without a taste of home, Tijuana has the most fast-food franchises of any city in Baja.

Dining at its simplest: corn for sale at Mercado Hidalgo

Still, many travelers never look beyond downtown (as in Avenida Revolución), and while this neighborhood has many good restaurants, they're a small fraction of what this city has to offer. Beyond dowtown, the Zona Río and Boulevard Agua Caliente both beckon the savvy traveler (as opposed to tourist) who is willing to look beyond the usual offerings. Some of Tijuana's finest restaurants are in these neighborhoods southeast of the San Ysidro border gate.

The vitals on some well-known restaurants follow and make a good starting list, but many more will merit a look in this booming border city.

Favorites

CAFÉ LA ESPECIAL — Mexican

Walk down the steps, adjust your eyes to the flashy paint job and pull up one of the lacquered chairs (no two are alike) inside this quintessential Tijuana establishment. There's no pretense of "the real Mexico" here, but it's hard to knock a place that agreeably melds the cross-border cultures. Part of the Revolución scene since 1952, La Especial attracts a healthy cross-section of visitors and locals

Hail Caesar (Salad)!

With its modest size and unassuming appearance, you would never guess that Restaurant Caesars has a well-earned place in gastronomic history. If the name didn't tip you off, then the tagline will: "Home of the famous Caesars Salad since 1930." Lore has it that the Caesars salad sprung from necessity, cobbled together from assorted ingredients to feed a pack of diners who unexpectedly waltzed through the doors late one night. The original recipe calls not for raw eggs but eggs boiled for one minute, combined with mustard, Worcestershire sauce, Parmesan cheese, vinegar, oil and ground pepper. Caesars does a credible job of making its namesake dish, prepared from scratch at your table.

seeking good service and fairly priced Mexican favorites. *Ave Revolución between calles 3 and 4, downstairs from the Hotel Lafayette. 01152 (6) 685-66-54. Open daily 9 am-10:30 pm. $3.25-12.*

LA ESPADAÑA **Mexican**

One of Tijuana's loveliest restaurants, inside and out, La Espadaña ("the Bell Gable") exudes a timeless colonial feel in a city with no deep sense of history. There's no letdown in the food or service at this fairly priced establishment. Quality is apparent in the ingredients and preparation of the broad-ranging Mexican menu, while the servers are attentive but not obtrusive. *Corner of Ave Sánchez Taboada and Ave Loreto in the Zona Río (across from Vips). 01152 (6) 634-14-88, 634-14-89. Open daily 7:30 am-11 pm, Sundays to 10 pm. $4-13.*

LA FOGATA **Steakhouse**

A great selection of steaks joins seafood, poultry and a pack of Mexican standbys served in classy surroundings, across from the Tijuana Cultural Center. The *carne asada a la tampiqueña*—one of Mexico's most popular steak combination meals—is one of the best we've had anyplace in the country. *Corner of Paseo de los Héroes and Calle Mina in the Zona Río. 01152 (6) 684-22-50. Open daily, Sun-Thu 7 am-midnight; Fri-Sat 7 am-1 am. $7.50-22.*

LOS ARCOS **Seafood**

They pack 'em in on weekends with middle- to upper-class Mexicans and savvy gringos at Los Arcos, which offers an amazing selection of seafood dishes, including 13 ways to prepare shrimp. The maritime motif is a winner, too, with splashy murals and mounted fish all over the walls, and fishnet hanging from the ceiling. *In Colonia Aviación: Blvd Salinas 1000, 1½ blks west of Grand Hotel Tijuana (twin towers). 01152 (6) 68631-71. Open Tue-Sun 8 am-mid-*

night; closed Mon. In Colonia La Mesa: Blvd Díaz Ordaz 4200, north of Calle Benton near Las Brisas shopping center. $6.50-20.

RESTAURANT NELSON — **Mexican**

The plain-Jane but clean surroundings echo those of countless Mexican diners at this establishment, a few blocks from U.S. Customs. If you're hoofing it back to the border, this may be your last chance for some dependable, back-to-basics *antojitos*. The $1.30 Coronas are the cheapest we've found on Revolución. *Corner of Ave Revolución and Calle 1, next to Tourism Office. 01152 (6) 685-77-50. Open daily 8:30 am-11 pm. $2.30-5.*

RESTAURANT PLAZA CAFÉ — **Varied Menu**

Sunday brunch may force you to rethink any lingering notions of Tijuana being a seedy, uncouth border town. The food is good all week, but Sunday mornings stand out at this polished, well-run restaurant. The buffet has something to suit all comers, including omelets, crepes and tortillas made before your eyes. *Grand Hotel Tijuana (Twin Towers), Blvd Agua Caliente 4500. 01152 (6) 681-70-00, ext 4199. Open daily 7 am-1 am. $4.70-14.50, Sunday brunch $11.50.*

SANBORNS — **Mexican/American**

With a name like that and the soft-edged feel of an American-style coffee shop, you'd never know this is a Mexican-owned chain and a familiar landmark nationwide. If your group can't settle on what to eat, this is the place, with everything from tacos and chicken *mole* to burgers and hot turkey sandwiches. Breakfasts are reliably good as well, and the enchiladas are the best of any Mexican restaurant chain. *Locations citywide, including 2 on Ave Revolución (between calles 3 and 4 and at the corner of Calle 8) and 2 in Plaza Río Tijuana on Paseo de los Héroes. Open daily 7 am-1 or 1:30 am, depending on location. $3-10.*

Others

CIEN AÑOS — **Mexican/Steaks**

$8-14. *Calle José María Velazco, ½ blk north of Paseo de los Héroes in the Zona Río. 01152 (6) 634-30-39, 634-72-62.*

COMO QUÉ NO! — **Varied Menu**

$5.50-13. No shorts, caps or tennis shoes. *Corner of Ave Sánchez Taboada and Calle Antonio Caso in the Zona Río. 01152 (6) 684-27-88.*

EL ZAGUAH — **Steak/Seafood**

$5-13.50. *Corner of Paseo de los Héroes and Ave Diego Rivera in the Zona Río. 01152 (6) 634-67-81.*

GUADALAJARA GRILL — **Varied Menu**
$7-12. *Corner of Paseo de los Héroes and Ave Diego Rivera in the Zona Río. 01152 (6) 634-30-65.*

HARD ROCK CAFÉ — **American**
$8-15.50. *Ave Revolución just south of Calle 1. 01152 (6) 685-02-06.*

LA COSTA PEDRIN'S — **Seafood**
$8-27. *Calle 7 between Ave Revolución and Ave Constitución. 01152 (6) 685-31-24, 685-84-94.*

LA PLACITA — **Mexican/American**
$3.50-25. *Ave Revolución between Calle 3 and Calle 4. 01152 (6) 688-27-04.*

RESTAURANT CAESARS — **Mexican**
$4-12. *Ave Revolución between calles 4 and 5. 01152 (6) 638-45-62.*

TIA JUANA TILLY'S — **Mexican**
$7.50-15. *Corner of Ave Revolución and Calle 7, next to the Frontón Palacio. 01152 (6) 685-60-24.*

VIPS — **Coffee Shop**
$4.50-8.50. *Corner of Ave Sánchez Taboada and Ave Loreto in the Zona Río. 01152 (6) 684-28-11.*

Lodging

It's Baja's biggest city and home to the world's busiest border crossing, yet Tijuana is the last place that many people would think of to spend the night. Most gringos make day-trips here, but if you're looking for a truly international experience, then Tijuana responds with hotels in a broad range of price and comfort levels.

For information on lodging in nearby San Diego, see the AAA *Southern California-Las Vegas TourBook*.

A resort town this is not, but as a booming manufacturing and international trade center, Tijuana is full of business-class hotels attracting a steady clientele. Many tourists never see the larger, better-managed properties, which are well-removed from downtown's noise and commotion, with secured parking and all the amenities of a modern, first-world hotel. The best picks are in the Zona Río and along Boulevard Agua Caliente, southeast of the San Ysidro border crossing. Several less prestigious but still comfortable properties can be in those and other neighborhoods within a few miles of the border.

Because few tourists stay overnight, hotel rates in Tijuana hardly change throughout the year, weekday and weekend alike. At times, though, you might get a better price with some polite but firm negotiating, or by asking, "Is that the best rate you can offer?" Besides its AAA-rated hotels (see *Lodging & Campgrounds*, Chapter 15), Tijuana has many nonrated properties that run the gamut in price and appointments.

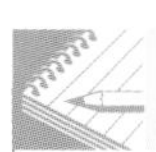

TRAVELOGUE

Tijuana to Rosarito via Old Highway 1

(16 mi., 24 km.; 0:30 hrs.)

Tijuana and Rosarito are growing together to form a single border/coastal metropolis, as you'll discover on this first leg of the toll-free road from the U.S. border to Ensenada. Leaving the border at San Ysidro, the route cuts through a modern maze of interchanges before heading southeast along the broad boulevard Paseo de los Héroes, famous for its traffic circles replete with stately monuments. Do not follow signs pointing to the "Rosarito-Ensenada Scenic Road," which is the same as the toll road. Two short blocks before the Cuauhtémoc monument is Calle Antonio Caso, where a large sign points the way south to Ensenada. After one block Antonio Caso becomes Cuauhtémoc Sur, a one-way boulevard that leads south from the urban core.

Eventually Cuauhtémoc Sur joins a four-lane divided road that winds through rolling hills with teeming commercial zones and residential areas. Just beyond the southern sprawl of Tijuana, you'll reach the northern outskirts of Rosarito, crossing the Highway 1 toll road before entering the main part of town.

00.0 Tijuana (U.S. border crossing).

01.5 Corner of Paseo de los Héroes and Antonio Caso, where a large sign points south to Ensenada. Turn right here.

01.9 Corner of Cuauhtémoc Sur and Boulevard Agua Caliente (see Highway 2 Travelogue). Ahead to the left are the downtown bullring and the Caliente Racetrack. The road to Rosarito Beach continues straight ahead.

05.7 Interchange with Libramiento, a bypass that skirts the southern part of Tijuana.

10.6 Highway 1 enters the *municipio* of Rosarito.

16.1 Rosarito Beach near its southern edge, in front of the Rosarito Beach Hotel.

Rosarito

Rosarito Beach Hotel pier

Given its proximity to the border and scenic location between the ocean and ambling coastal foothills, it's really no wonder that Rosarito became one of the leading resort towns in northern Baja California. Also known as Rosarito Beach or Playas de Rosarito, this spread-out town still has a fair amount of open space and a climate like that of nearby San Diego, factors which have endeared it to Southern Californians for decades.

Although Rosarito is spread out and still has some open spaces, the urban "core" centers around a four-mile-long corridor of strip malls, restaurants, hotels and gift shops. Boulevard Juárez between the Highway 1 toll road and the sea is this main drag, although you'd never know it in a town that's notorious for its lack of useful street signs. Nevertheless, finding your way around is not an ordeal, given that most major tourist venues in town are on or very close to Juárez.

However, Rosarito has spread far beyond the urban core as more and more Americans head this way to retire, vacation, party, or just indulge in a Saturday night lobster dinner. No surprise, then, that in 1996 Rosarito became its own *municipio,* stretching from the southern edge of Playas de Tijuana to La Misión, 25 miles south of downtown. Where miles of headlands and beachfront once sat undisturbed, the coastline is rapidly evolving into a solid stretch of development, and more than 100,000 now live in the *municipio.*

Compare that to the 1927 opening of the Rosarito Beach Hotel, which made a name for this otherwise sleepy hamlet. Celebrities flew in from across the border, seeking seclusion and legal libations during this era of U.S. Prohibition. It wasn't until 1930 that a paved highway reached from the border, which brought with it a small stream of overland tourists. Rosarito was on its way to greater acclaim and prosperity, although it remained a village into the 1960s. The rapid growth has continued ever since.

Flag vendor at Puerto Nuevo

Rosarito scored a major publicity and economic coup with the making of the 1997 film *Titanic*. Fox Studios built a huge production lot overlooking the sea south of downtown, and a 90-percent scale model of the ill-fated ship remained a fixture there for months. The windfall has been long-lasting, as the Fox production lot remains in use, while restaurants and shops continue to sell *Titanic*-related memorabilia.

The influx of people and foreign capital has created thousands of jobs and brought a higher standard of living for those lucky enough to live here. At the same time, local leaders face a dilemma known to attractive locales worldwide—to preserve the remaining open space and tranquillity fundamental to maintaining this locale's essential character.

Getting Around

Unless you're content to stroll along Boulevard Juárez, you're going to need some sort of vehicle to get around. The main tourist strip is a little more than a mile long, from Quinta Plaza to the Rosarito Beach Hotel, but the region extends more than 20 miles south, to the point where the Highway 1 free road turns inland, just beyond La Fonda.

Driving in Rosarito presents a number of potential hazards, like any other Baja town. Potholes and inconspicuous stop signs are the main perils along Boulevard Juárez. Navigating can also be a headache, since street signs are often hard to spot, if they exist at all. Even the locals are frequently unfamiliar with street names, and when providing directions refer instead to landmarks such as large hotels, shopping centers or the police station. South of town, your main worry along the free road is cars pulling on and off the pavement at the countless restaurants, shops and other roadside businesses. They're not a major

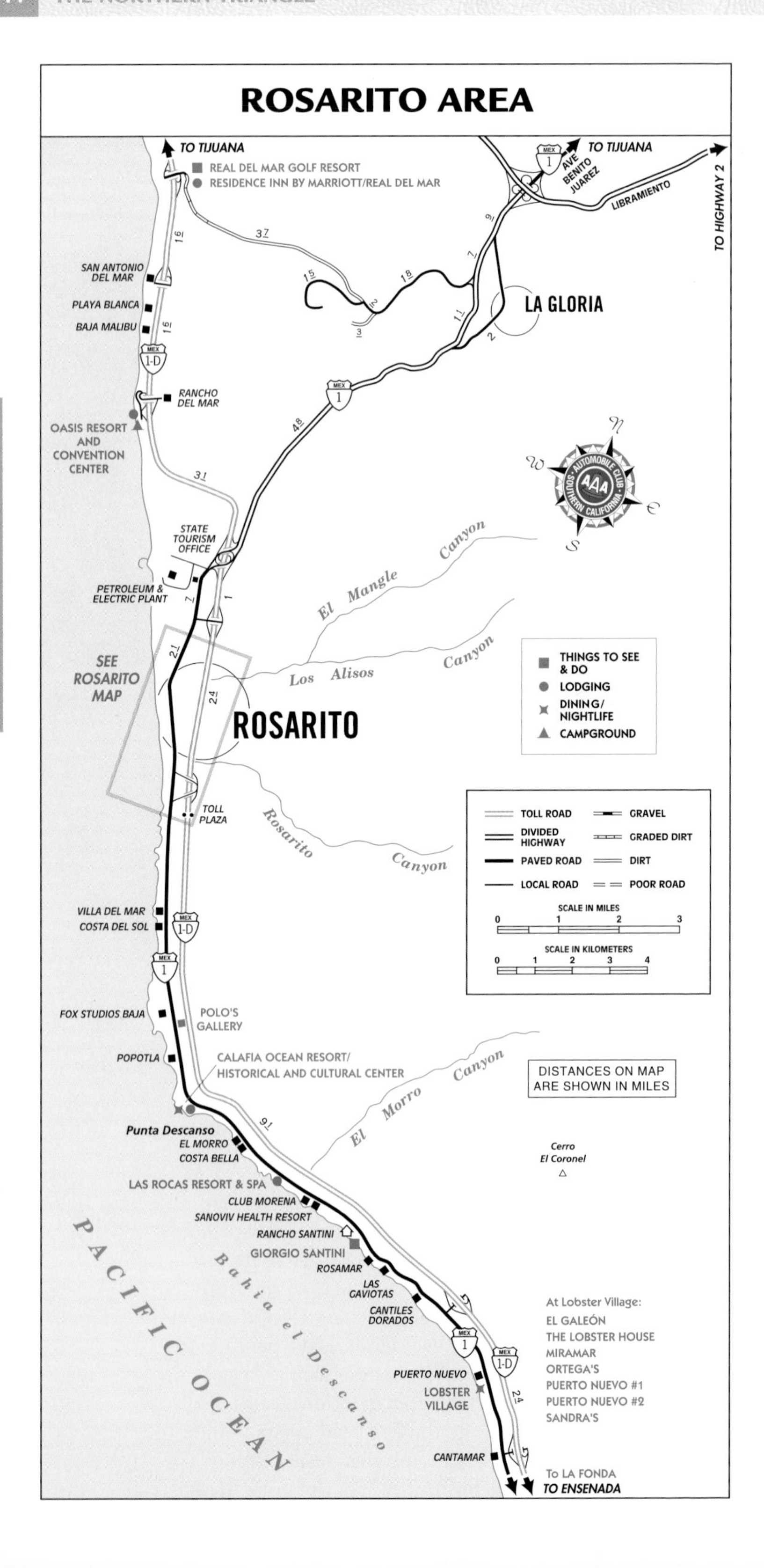
ROSARITO AREA
TO TIJUANA
REAL DEL MAR GOLF RESORT
RESIDENCE INN BY MARRIOTT/REAL DEL MAR
TO TIJUANA
AVE BENITO JUAREZ
LIBRAMIENTO
TO HIGHWAY 2
LA GLORIA
SAN ANTONIO DEL MAR
PLAYA BLANCA
BAJA MALIBU
RANCHO DEL MAR
OASIS RESORT AND CONVENTION CENTER
STATE TOURISM OFFICE
PETROLEUM & ELECTRIC PLANT
El Mangle Canyon
Los Alisos Canyon
SEE ROSARITO MAP
ROSARITO
TOLL PLAZA
Rosarito Canyon
THINGS TO SEE & DO
LODGING
DINING/ NIGHTLIFE
CAMPGROUND
TOLL ROAD
GRAVEL
DIVIDED HIGHWAY
GRADED DIRT
PAVED ROAD
DIRT
LOCAL ROAD
POOR ROAD
SCALE IN MILES
SCALE IN KILOMETERS
VILLA DEL MAR
COSTA DEL SOL
FOX STUDIOS BAJA
POLO'S GALLERY
POPOTLA
CALAFIA OCEAN RESORT/ HISTORICAL AND CULTURAL CENTER
El Morro Canyon
DISTANCES ON MAP ARE SHOWN IN MILES
Punta Descanso
EL MORRO
COSTA BELLA
Cerro El Coronel
LAS ROCAS RESORT & SPA
CLUB MORENA
SANOVIV HEALTH RESORT
RANCHO SANTINI
GIORGIO SANTINI
ROSAMAR
LAS GAVIOTAS
CANTILES DORADOS
PACIFIC OCEAN
Bahia el Descanso
At Lobster Village:
EL GALEÓN
THE LOBSTER HOUSE
MIRAMAR
ORTEGA'S
PUERTO NUEVO #1
PUERTO NUEVO #2
SANDRA'S
PUERTO NUEVO
LOBSTER VILLAGE
CANTAMAR
To LA FONDA
TO ENSENADA
AUTOMOBILE CLUB SOUTHERN CALIFORNIA AAA

hazard, as long as you're alert.

If you plan to stay in town or simply want to avoid driving, taxi and bus service are both viable alternatives, with service between Rosarito and the border, and to nearby destinations.

Looking down on Boulevard Juárez, Rosarito's main drag

BUS SERVICE

Unless you have a large group, this is the most affordable option. The primary bus service for tourists is Mexicoach, which charges $6 for a round-trip ticket between its downtown Tijuana depot (Avenida Revolución between Calle 6 and Calle 7) and the Rosarito Beach Hotel. Mexicoach runs four round trips daily, the first bus leaving Tijuana at 11 a.m. and the last bus departing Rosarito at 8 p.m.

ROUTE TAXIS

Service from Boulevard Juárez to Tijuana or Lobster Village costs only $1 or less, but route taxis are also the slowest and least comfortable means of transit.

TAXI CABS

Early-morning to late-night taxi service typically costs $20 per carload from Rosarito to the San Ysidro border crossing, and $10 to downtown Tijuana. To Lobster Village, 11 miles south of town, a round-trip fare runs about $30 per carload, including an hour's waiting time, or $15 one way. Taxis patrol the length of Boulevard Juárez in town, although the main pick-up and drop-off point is across from the Rosarito Beach Hotel. Rosarito taxi cabs are typically big 1980s-vintage Ford and Chevy station wagons, replete with a third seat, and handling six or seven passengers comfortably.

Things To See & Do

In the 1920s CEOs and Hollywood stars were among those drawn to Rosarito, as much for its lovely seaside location as an escape from U.S. Prohibition. Much has changed since then, and today Rosarito's beach, and a host of new attractions and diversions woo tourists from across the border.

The prime attractions extend well beyond Boulevard Juárez, but the main thoroughfare is still a good place to

Stained glass above Rosarito Beach Hotel entrance

begin your explorations. Near the south end of Juárez is the town's original landmark, the Rosarito Beach Hotel, which opened in 1927. Still a major draw, the hotel has kept up with the times, with new rooms, a spa, and a pier that opened in 2000. The lobby features lavish murals and lovely wood paneling, and above the main entryway a famous stained glass piece of a smiling girl. Next door to the hotel is the Kuyima Museum, named for the region's indigenous people. A collection of Indian artifacts and historic photos of the town and visiting celebrities trace the area's history.

Juárez also rivals the best shopping in northern Baja, with its terrific assortment of galleries, shops and stalls. Mercado de Artesanías (Artisans' Market) alone has close to 200 art and craft stalls selling wares from all over Mexico. Locally made ceramics predominate, as you'll discover driving south of town past vendors lining the road.

Shopping and all else took a back seat for a while during 1996 and 1997, when a near life-size model of the most famous ship to ever hit an iceberg came to town. Rosarito was filming headquarters for *Titanic*, and Fox Studios built a huge production lot south of town to film the most expensive (and biggest money-making) of all time. The model is gone now, but the studio remains.

Seaside vista at Calafia

Other props from the film have moved a short ways south to Calafia, a seaside resort that boasts a dining room lined with wood paneling that once lined the model ship's hallways. Photos, paintings and blueprints of the doomed ship can also be found here, but Calafia has more to it than that, including Japanese-style gardens, replicas of early missions, and a treasure trove of old photos and artifacts from early 20th-century Baja.

On a clear day, Calafia is one of several spots south of Rosarito with outstanding coastal views. During the winter you may spot a pod of gray whales migrating down the coastline. Year round, you'll spy any swells moving in from the open Pacific to break along this coastline. When the surf's up, a long string of point breaks, reef breaks and beach breaks spring to life, bringing surfers south from Southern California in their pursuit of uncrowded waves.

Elsewhere, the sea views provide the backdrop for the fairways at Real del Mar, a golf course on the coastal hills north of town. Southern Californians are again the main devotees, drawn by a lovely setting and (relatively) affordable green fees. Perhaps this locale's most inclusive sport is horseback riding, along the shore and elsewhere nearby.

The beach in town, for its part, is more than five miles long and perhaps the best one between Tijuana and Ensenada. Several more strands dot the shoreline farther south, offering more seclusion. Contamination is an ongoing problem along this fast-growing coast, however, and you'd be well advised to confer with locals if you have doubts about the cleanliness of the water.

DISASTER BEGETS DISASTER

Motorists passing the Fox Studios lot in the summer of 2000 could see the form of another ill-fated ship where the *Titanic* once stood—the battleship *Arizona*, which was re-created for the making of the movie *Pearl Harbor*.

Top Attractions

CALAFIA HISTORICAL AND CULTURAL CENTER

This lovely seaside retreat, replete with hotel, restaurants and nightclub, offers an interesting hodgepodge of things to look at, including replicas of the Spanish missions at San Diego and Loreto, Japanese-style gardens, and a large model of Columbus' vessel the *Santa María* that overlooks the ocean. There's a good collection of relics from the old Agua Caliente Casino in Tijuana, such as wine bottles, a tea set and fountain. More recent additions include models, photos and paintings of the *Titanic. 5 miles south of town on the free road to Ensenada. 01152 (6) 612-15-81.*

The model of the *Titanic* used for the making of the movie measured 750 feet in length, 90 percent the size of the actual ship.

ROSARITO BEACH HOTEL

Opened in 1927, the town's oldest hotel merits a visit even if you don't plan to spend the night. The ornate main lobby is one of the loveliest in Baja, with 20-foot-high ceilings, elaborate woodwork and 1930s-era murals of missions, volcanoes and tropical beaches. Out

WHERE THE STARS HAVE SLEPT

Famous guests of the Rosarito Beach Hotel have included Hollywood stars such as Clark Gable, Orson Wells, Rita Hayworth, Marilyn Monroe and Bill Paxton, *Titanic* director James Cameron, and Mexican film legend María Felix.

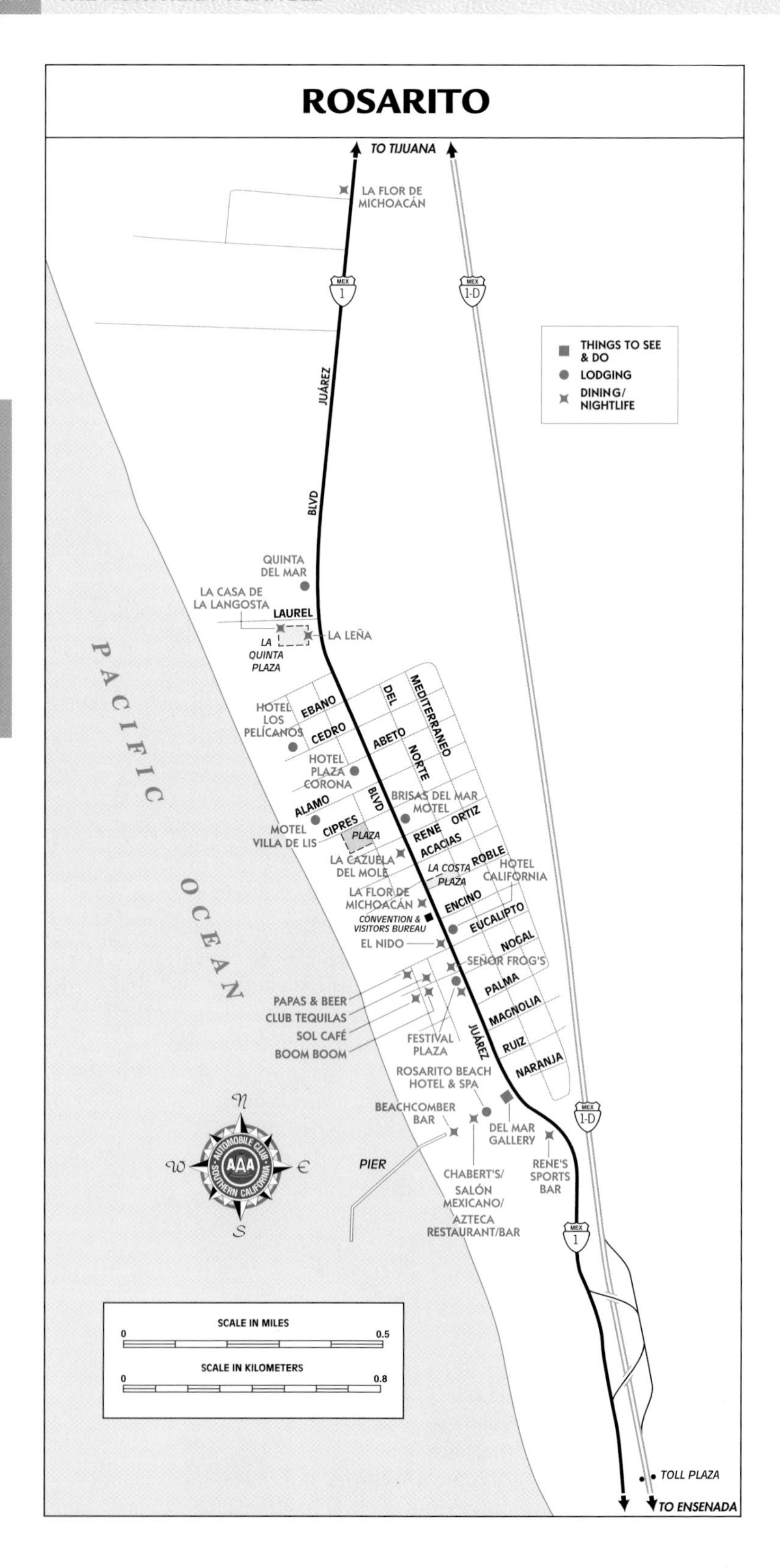
ROSARITO
TO TIJUANA
LA FLOR DE MICHOACÁN
JUÁREZ
BLVD
THINGS TO SEE & DO
LODGING
DINING/ NIGHTLIFE
QUINTA DEL MAR
LA CASA DE LA LANGOSTA
LAUREL
LA LEÑA
LA QUINTA PLAZA
PACIFIC OCEAN
HOTEL LOS PELÍCANOS
EBANO
CEDRO
DEL
MEDITERRANEO
ABETO
NORTE
HOTEL PLAZA CORONA
ALAMO
BLVD
BRISAS DEL MAR MOTEL
MOTEL VILLA DE LIS
CIPRES
PLAZA
RENE
ORTIZ
ACACIAS
LA CAZUELA DEL MOLE
LA COSTA PLAZA
ROBLE
HOTEL CALIFORNIA
LA FLOR DE MICHOACÁN
ENCINO
CONVENTION & VISITORS BUREAU
EUCALIPTO
EL NIDO
NOGAL
SEÑOR FROG'S
PALMA
PAPAS & BEER
CLUB TEQUILAS
SOL CAFÉ
BOOM BOOM
MAGNOLIA
FESTIVAL PLAZA
JUÁREZ
RUIZ
NARANJA
ROSARITO BEACH HOTEL & SPA
BEACHCOMBER BAR
DEL MAR GALLERY
PIER
CHABERT'S/ SALÓN MEXICANO/ AZTECA RESTAURANT/BAR
RENE'S SPORTS BAR
AUTOMOBILE CLUB SOUTHERN CALIFORNIA
AAA
SCALE IN MILES
0
0.5
SCALE IN KILOMETERS
0
0.8
TOLL PLAZA
TO ENSENADA

Not Your Everyday Art

You normally don't think of Rosarito as an artist colony, but there are several interesting galleries full of works that break the usual Mexican mold. A few worth checking out are **Del Mar Gallery**, on Boulevard Juárez in front of the Rosarito Beach Hotel; **Giorgio Santini**, on the west side of the Highway 1 free road at kilometer 40; and **Polo's Gallery**, just south of the Fox Studios lot on the east side of the Highway 1 free road.

the back door is the hotel's newest attraction, which opened in early 2000—the first pleasure pier along Baja's Pacific Coast. The hotel's best-known icon, however, remains the stained-glass piece above the arched entryway, which features a smiling *señorita* with an inscription that translates: "Through these doors pass the most beautiful women in the world." *On Blvd Juárez near the south end of town. 01152 (6) 612-01-44.*

SHOPPING

If you can tell a tourist town by the number of places to shop, then Rosarito is among the leading tourist destinations in Baja California, with its huge assortment of gift shops, open-air stalls and galleries. Boulevard Juárez is the biggest shopping zone, with a terrific selection of souvenir shops, plus many liquor stores and *farmacias* aimed at cross-border visitors. If you're souvenir hunting, a good place to begin is the **Mercado de Artesanías** (Artisans Market), on the west side of Juárez south of Calle Acacias. Its nearly 200 shops run the gamut from tacky figurines and low-brow T-shirts to lovely regional handcrafts from all over the country.

Shoppers browsing through Mercado de Artesanías

Farther south, a string of pottery shops stretches for several miles along the Highway 1 free road, with thousands of figures lining the roadway. There's something for every taste and budget, from ceramic Tweety birds and Teletubbies on up to regal busts of Mexican heroes and multi-tiered fountains costing hundreds of dollars. In their midst, you'll find a good selection of other curios. Lobster Village at Puerto Nuevo has still more shops selling all sorts of wares.

Outdoor Fun

GOLF

The first golf course south of Tijuana is Real Del Mar, the centerpiece of an upscale resort overlooking the Pacific north of downtown Rosarito. Hotel/golf packages are a big attraction for many guests at this scenic venue.

Real del Mar (Semi-private) 18 holes; 5949 yards; par 72; 120 slope; 68.1 rating. Rates: $59-69. *5 miles north of downtown. (800) 803-6038, 01152 (6) 631-36-75.*

Horses for rent at south edge of town

HORSEBACK RIDING

A sunset trot along the sandy shoreline is a time-honored activity in Rosarito. There's no fixed place to rent a horse, but free-lance wranglers ply their trade along Boulevard Juárez near the north and south ends of town. Expect to pay around $7 per half-hour and $14 per hour, although you may get a better deal on weekdays or during the winter months. Groups of eight or more may also negotiate a better rate.

SURFING

Southern California surfers have long headed this way in search of quality waves without the crowds so common along their own coast. Nearly two dozen named spots dot the coast between Baja Malibu (north of town near Real del Mar) and La Salina, where the Highway 1 free road turns inland. You'll find ridable waves year-round, but conditions are generally best in the winter, when an assortment of beach breaks, reef breaks and point breaks come to life.

Surfers will find similar water temperatures to Southern California, ranging from the low- to mid-50s in winter to around 70 degrees in late summer.

Inner Reef Surf Shop, located at kilometer 34.5, has surfboards, wet suits and other equipment for rent. Surfboards with a leash rent for $2 per hour or $20 per day, body boards rent for $1.50 per hour or $10 per day, while wet suits rent for $10 per day. Inquire at the shop or with locals for details on specific breaks. Inquire as well about water conditions, since pollution is a problem along this coastline.

Inner Reef Surf Shop *At Km 34.5 on the free road to Ensenada. 01152 (6) 615-08-41.*

Nightlife

¿Quién es más loca?

For many years it was a two-way battle between Tijuana and Cabo San Lucas, with Ensenada placing runner-up for honors as Baja California's wildest party town. That was before a wave of new nightclubs opened in Rosarito Beach, and before a 1999 *Playboy* article declared this town a "Super Hot Spot" for the college crowd to whoop it up on spring break.

Festival Plaza entrance

These days the seaside town feels something akin to a cool-weather Cabo, with throngs of under-21-year-olds and their high-spirited elders prowling from one neon-laced club to the next. The center of action is near the south end of town amid a few square blocks between Boulevard Juárez and the ocean. Head that way, and your eyes and ears should do the rest, as all these nightspots seem to have flamboyant facades and noise levels that rival a jumbo jet on takeoff.

For those of you who have mellowed with age or overindulgence, we're not trying to scare you off. There is a kinder, gentler side to the Rosarito night scene. It's just not so conspicuous, and in some cases you may need to leave the bright city lights behind. But if your goal is a soothing nightcap to accompany some meaningful dialogue next to the crashing surf, you will not be let down.

As for which town is *más loca* today, we won't make that call, but for the young and restless, it *is* clear that Rosarito Beach has joined the short list of biggest players in Baja.

The list of nightspots here is not exhaustive but represents a cross section of what's available in Rosarito. Our inclusion of certain establishments does *not* represent an endorsement of the behavior they may encourage.

Favorites

BEACHCOMBER BAR

Opened in 1927, this seaside bar in the Rosarito Beach Hotel had built a broad and loyal fan base long before the brash and boisterous clubs arrived in town. It's still a hit with those who want to watch the sun go down and salute the day's end while talking in a normal level of voice. Make time for a post-drink stroll down the only public pier on Baja's Pacific shoreline. *At the south end of town, overlooking the Pacific in the Rosarito Beach Hotel. 01152 (6) 612-11-11. Full bar; full lunch and dinner served in adjacent restaurant; karaoke Fri-Sun.*

CALAFIA

Two nightspots with beautiful coastal views and distinct atmospheres beckon at this venerable seaside resort south of town. The gringo set favors the outdoor Club 1773, where you can dance beneath the stars year round to English and Spanish rock. The local crowd is partial to Salón Mexicano, an indoor dance club with a live band on weekends that plays salsa, *cumbia* and other Mexican tunes. *5 miles south of town along the Hwy 1 free road. 01152 (6) 612-15-81. Full bar; restaurants adjacent; live music schedule varies by club.*

Another nightspot nearby Club Tequilas with a similar theme (and noise level) is the aptly named Boom Boom.

CLUB TEQUILAS

It's places like this that forged Rosarito's modern reputation as a bastion of wild, no-holds-barred hedonism. As the name suggests, distilled spirits flow freely inside this spacious club, where a mostly under-25 crowd gets down to ear-blasting hip-hop and modern rock. It's no less subtle outside, with a Flintstone-like facade reminiscent of the Baby Rock in Tijuana. *Between Blvd Juárez and the beach, 1 blk west of the Festival Plaza. No phone. Full bar.*

FESTIVAL PLAZA

If there's such a thing as an a la carte party experience in Baja, it would have to be this gaudy eight-story hotel in the south part of town. It has no fewer than 10 restaurants, clubs and cantinas, with names like **Rock & Roll Taco, Jazz Grotto, Sol Café** and **Cha Cha Cha Barefoot Bar**. Another, **El Museo**, claims to have the world's largest selection of tequilas, 299 in all. There's also a Ferris wheel and an amphitheater for concerts under the stars. It's mostly a younger scene, and during spring break the college crowd takes over completely, but the rest of the year the 30-plus crowd should find something worthwhile. *Corner of Blvd Juárez and Calle Nogal in the south part of town. (888) 337-8486, 01152 (6) 612-29-50. Live music schedules vary by establishment.*

PAPAS & BEER

Fans of the original Papas & Beer in Ensenada should feel right at home at this sprawling seaside club. There's the usual assortment of beer, well drinks and finger food, but the setting is quasi-tropical with banana trees, palms, wooden decks and a waterfall. There's also a volleyball court on the sand and fire rings for those cool seaside nights. It's mostly a young crowd, but with a good number of 30- and 40-somethings along for the ride. *On the beach in the south*

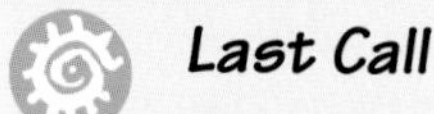

Last Call

The 3 a.m. last call common at nightspots across northern Baja may not seem unusual by North American standards, but for Mexicans (or other Latin Americans), it's early. In most of Mexico the carousing doesn't shift into high gear until well after midnight, and the new day will often have dawned before the last stragglers gather their things and head off into the sunrise.

part of town, 2 blks west of the Festival Plaza. 01152 (6) 612-02-44. Full bar; light menu; live music schedule varies.

RENE'S SPORTS BAR

As the name implies, it's a great place to catch the big game, but "something for everyone" would be a worthy tagline for this gringo-friendly restaurant/bar. Short on gimmicks or pretensions, Rene's is also a place to dance (salsa, *cumbia*, rock), sing along to mariachis, shoot a round of billiards or try your aim at darts—all till long after midnight. It's an "older" crowd mainly, which in Rosarito these days means anything from late-20s on up. *Along the Hwy 1 free road at the southern edge of town. 01152 (6) 612-10-61. Full bar; full menu to 10:30 pm; live music schedule varies.*

"I always wake up at the crack of ice."
—Sign inside a Rosarito nightclub

SALÓN MEXICANO

Friday and Saturday nights are busy times at this hotel lounge. It starts with the Fiesta Mexicana, a buffet dinner and floorshow featuring mariachis and folkloric dancers. Afterward the night-fever crowd takes over, with dancing to a live band playing disco, reggae and rock until 2 a.m. *At the south end of town in the Rosarito Beach Hotel. 01152 (6) 612-11-11. Full bar; full lunch and dinner served in adjacent restaurant.*

SEÑOR FROG'S

Once Rosarito earned its party town credentials, it was just a matter of time until Grupo Anderson's set up shop, and this is the local offering. Opened in 1999, Señor Frog's has the usual Anderson's recipe of high-octane drinks, dance music, tasty food and TV sports. And of course, there's the roving tequila server, ready to pour a long one down your hatch. *On Blvd Juárez in the south part of town, just north of Festival Plaza. 01152 (6) 612-43-75. Full bar; lunch and dinner served daily; live music schedule varies.*

Dining

Rosarito's ship may have come in big-time with *Titanic*, but the seaside town had made a name for itself well before that, thanks in no small part to the many excellent eating places. Dozens of restaurants crowd Boulevard Juárez in town, while many more line the Highway 1 free road some 20 miles south to La Misión. Seafood and Mexican fare are universal and American food abounds, but in this part of Baja, lobster reigns supreme.

Restaurant at Puerto Nuevo

Scores of restaurants serve the red crustacean, but for many people, lobster is synonymous with Puerto Nuevo, 11 miles south of town, where more than 30 restaurants cram a few square blocks known as Lobster Village. They range from simple diners with little atmosphere to romantic seaside lounges where a bill for two can push $100. A few restaurants date to the 1950s and have stayed in the same family for generations, while others have opened within the last 10 years. They all serve various kinds of seafood and a few other dishes, but the common thread is lobster served family style with rice, beans, flour tortillas and the inevitable chips and salsa.

Apart from lobster, this locale has enough other restaurants to bring you back for many weekends without ever trying the same place twice. They run the gamut, including down-home taco shops, seafood joints galore, Mexican restaurants with lavish murals, and a couple of very upscale spots that lend proper meaning to the word *elegante.*

Favorites

CALAFIA — **Varied Menu**

Fancy or casual, Calafia offers a most agreeable eating experience. Choose from an upscale menu served at one of five indoor or outdoor dining areas; or munch on tacos, quesadillas and other light fare served on an outdoor terrace. Either way, you'll enjoy choice surroundings, surveying miles of coastline and the Los Coronados Islands. *5 miles south of Rosarito. 01152 (6) 612-15-81. Restaurant open daily 8 am-11 pm. Taco bar open Fri-Sun 10 am-2 am,*

TITANIC UNLIMITED

There's no official restaurant of the movie *Titanic*, but if there were, it would probably be Calafia. The top floor of this expansive restaurant/club has become a de-facto shrine to the 1997 blockbuster, complete with models, paintings and photos of the ship, plus numerous *objets d'art* from the movie's making.

Sun 10 am-10 pm; closed Mon-Thu. Restaurant $10-26, taco bar $3.50-5.

CHABERT'S — Continental

After "seafood," "casual" has to be the most oft-spoken word to describe the Rosarito dining experience, but there are exceptions, none better known than Chabert's. Step inside, gaze up at the huge chandelier in the foyer and you'll know there's nothing ordinary about this restaurant, housed in a fully restored mansion. Entrees include rack of lamb, chicken Kiev, roast duck, steak and lobster. *Rosarito Beach Hotel, Blvd Juárez near south end of town. 01152 (6) 612-11-11, ext 356. Open Wed-Mon 5 pm-midnight, closed Tue; open Fri-Sat only during winter. $10.50-21.*

LA CASA DE LA LANGOSTA — Seafood

If you're looking for lobster without driving clear to Lobster Village, one compelling reason to stay put is this popular restaurant in the heart of Rosarito. Nor need you wait till the evening to dig into a spiny crustacean, with lobster omelets and burritos gracing the menu as well. (Remember, the name is Spanish for "the Lobster House.") The all-you-can-eat (and sensibly priced) Sunday brunch buffet is another worthy excuse for starting the day here. *On Blvd Juárez in Quinta Plaza. 01152 (6) 612-09-24. Open Thu-Tue 8 am-10 pm, later hours in summer; closed Wed. $7.70-22; Sunday brunch $7.*

LA CAZUELA DEL MOLE — Mexican

In a town where menu and pricing are geared toward the U.S. crowd, this spot flouts convention, to the benefit of all who seek honest Mexican cuisine at down-to-earth prices. As you might guess, this spot is known for its *mole,* the chocolate/chile-based sauce usually poured over chicken. The breakfasts are good, too, as are the *sopes* and *tacos dorados. Blvd Juárez between Calle Rene Ortiz and Calle Acacia, roughly opposite the police station. 01152 (6) 612-2910. Open daily 8 am-8 pm. $1.30-5.50.*

LA FLOR DE MICHOACÁN — *Taquería*

In a town where so much has changed, La Flor de Michoacán remains a reliable constant—for which we should all be grateful. The world needs more *taquerías* like this, a local institution since 1950. The homemade flavor is hard to top at any price in the *carnitas*, tacos, burritos or tortas. Well yes, they have changed one thing: opening a second location to serve the folks who know good, back-to-basics Mexican food when they taste it. ***Original location:*** *In a large, 2-story building on Blvd Juárez near north end of town, at corner of Calle Mexicali. 01152 (6) 612-18-58. Open Thu-Tue 9 am-10 pm.* ***Second location:*** *2 blks north of Festival Plaza Hotel on Blvd Juárez between Calle*

Eucalipto and Calle del Roble. 01152 (6) 613-02-78. Open daily 9 am, closing hours vary. 65¢-$2.80 per item.

LA FONDA **Varied Menu**

Not all seaside settings were created equal—something you may wish to dwell on as you linger over dessert, high above Playa La Misión. La Fonda's splendid views and romantic ambiance have few rivals on Baja's Pacific coast. The menu will suit any whim, with the obligatory fish and lobster entrees, plus offerings like prime rib, grilled quail and baked rack of lamb. *20 miles south of town, just north of Km 60 on the Hwy 1 free road. No phone. $8-26.*

Others

AZTECA RESTAURANT/BAR **Varied Menu**

$7-20. *Rosarito Beach Hotel, Blvd Juárez near south end of town. 01152 (6) 612-11-11, ext 365.*

EL NIDO **Steakhouse**

$5.50-21. *Corner of Blvd Juárez and Calle Eucalipto. 01152 (6) 612-14-30.*

LA LEÑA **Steak/Seafood**

$10-31. *On Blvd Juárez in Quinta Plaza. 01152 (6) 612-08-26.*

SENOR FROG'S **Mexican**

$3.70-16. *Corner of Blvd Juárez and Calle Nogal, next to Festival Plaza Hotel. 01152 (6) 612-43-75, 612-43-63.*

Puerto Nuevo

The focal point of Puerto Nuevo is Lobster Village, a few square blocks of restaurants and curio shops tucked between the Highway 1 free road and the beach. The village entrance is along the free road 10.7 miles south of the Rosarito Beach Hotel. The following are some of the more established restaurants that have proved reliable in terms of quality and service:

Lobster with all the fixings

EL GALEÓN

Near the center of the village, 1 blk east of the beach.

THE LOBSTER HOUSE

1 blk east of the beach, near the southwest corner of the village.

MIRAMAR

1 blk east of the beach at north end of the village.

ORTEGA'S

2 locations: At the extreme southeast corner of the village, and the extreme northwest corner of the village.

PUERTO NUEVO #1

On the left as you drive into the north entrance of the village.

PUERTO NUEVO #2
Near the north entrance of the village, next door to Puerto Nuevo #1.

SANDRA'S
Near the center of the village, 2 blks east of the beach.

Lodging

For more than 50 years, if you wanted to spend the night in Rosarito, the Rosarito Beach Hotel & Spa was the only game in town. For many folks it's still the *only* place, but Rosarito has come a long way in the last 20 or so years, as you'll discover driving down Boulevard Juárez. Several good-sized hotels line the main drag or can be found between it and the nearby ocean. There's even the makings of a skyline since the town's first high-rise hotels went up in the 1990s. Several more hotels and campgrounds dot the free road to Ensenada for the next 20 miles south before the route turns inland.

YOU KNOW YOU'RE IN ROSARITO WHEN ...

The hotel rules card in your room at the Festival Plaza advises guests that jumping on beds is not allowed.

While there is plenty of lodging these days, don't be surprised if you still find the town booked up for spring break, summer weekends and U.S. holidays. Not only will you want to make reservations, but you'll pay more during these peak periods. Room rates seem to fluctuate more than most Baja towns, depending on the time of year and day of the week. Conversely, though, you'll find some real bargains if you're here, say, on a weeknight in November. AAA-rated hotels are generally more expensive, ranging anywhere from about $50 to more than $200 a night. Non-rated hotels cover a wide range too, starting at $35 or less per night during off-peak times, to well over $100 a night during peak periods.

See Lodging & Campgrounds, Chapter 15.

TRAVELOGUE

Rosarito to Ensenada via Old Highway 1
(50 mi., 82 km.; 1.15 hrs.)

South of Rosarito, the free and toll roads to Ensenada run parallel for some 24 miles along the rocky Pacific shore. The two-lane old road is slower, but if sightseeing and shopping are your objectives,

Highway 1 pottery shop

this is the route of choice. Pulling over is possible all along the road and there's quicker access to such attractions as Lobster Village and a seemingly endless string of arts and crafts shops.

The free road turns inland at La Misión and scales a steep grade to a high plateau before winding down to meet the coast again at San Miguel. The free and toll roads merge at this point, on the northern outskirts of Ensenada, and follow the coast to the town entrance at Boulevard Costero.

00.0 **Rosarito, at the entrance to the Rosarito Beach Hotel.**

03.6 **Entrance to Fox Studios Baja.**

04.3 **Popotla, a scattered seaside settlement with a large trailer park for permanent residents.**

05.0 **Calafia Resort, built on terraces overlooking the sea, has dining, a disco, a museum and a mobile home park with overnight accommodations.**

08.7 **Las Gaviotas, a residential subdivision overlooking the ocean.**

10.7 **Puerto Nuevo, home of Lobster Village, the famed seaside community with more than 30 restaurants specializing in lobster.**

23.0 **La Misión, a quiet village located in a steeply walled valley. On the south side of the valley are the ruins of Mission San Miguel, founded in 1787. The highway climbs out of the valley past abrupt volcanic bluffs via a series of narrow switchback curves.**

35.3 **Junction with a graded dirt road leading 15 miles west to Valle Guadalupe.**

42.3 **San Miguel Village, a beach camp at the junction of highways 1 and 1-D. The rocky beach here is popular with surfers.**

43.7 **Junction with Highway 3, which leads northward to Guadalupe and Tecate (see *Highway 3 Travelogue*, page 159). Just past the interchange is El Sauzal, a sprawling community with a large fish cannery.**

47.2 Junction. Although Highway 1 swings inland here, the preferred route into downtown Ensenada (signed Centro) follows the coastline to the right.

49.7 Ensenada, at the intersection of boulevards Teniente Azueta and Lázaro Cárdenas (better known locally as Costero).

TRAVELOGUE

Tijuana to Ensenada via Toll Highway 1-D

(68 mi., 109 km.; 1:30 hrs.)

This divided, controlled-access highway resembles a U.S.-style freeway more than any other road in Baja California, except for the new toll road between Tijuana and Mexicali. Tollbooths await your fare at three stops along this route, which provides the fastest, safest link between the border and Ensenada. Stopping along the highway is prohibited; call boxes dot the way for travelers in distress. Numerous ramps provide access to seaside resorts and points of interest along this fast-growing corridor.

El Mirador, off Highway 1 toll road

From the border, follow the prominent "Ensenada Toll Road" (Ensenada Cuota) signs along Calle Internacional to Mexico Highway 1-D. Be alert and pick the proper exit lane, since the wrong choice could land you in downtown or in the midst of the Zona Río. Highway 1-D skips the downtown morass as it runs due west along the border fence, turning south to meet the first tollbooth at Playas de Tijuana. From there your route follows the scenic shoreline most of the way to Ensenada, passing miles of rolling hills, housing tracts, condo towers and some outstanding views of the Pacific. Two more booths charge tolls en route, one at the south edge of Rosarito, the other at San Miguel near the northern edge of Ensenada. In 2001, the total fee for passenger cars and light trucks was $6.60.

00.0 Tijuana (U.S. border crossing).

05.9 Exit for Playas de Tijuana and Bullring-by-the-Sea. No toll is charged to this point.

06.5 Toll station, Playas de Tijuana.

12.6 Real del Mar, a resort complex with a hotel, tennis courts and a golf course.

14.2 Exit for San Antonio and Tijuana/Rosarito KOA.

18.7 Rosarito Norte interchange; junction with Highway 1 to Rosarito. (Although most tourists take this highway to Rosarito, the town is described previously in the log for Old Highway 1, which passes directly through town.)

22.1 Rosarito Sur interchange; junction with Highway 1. To the east rises the impressive Mesa de Rosarito.

22.4 Toll station, Rosarito.

33.4 Exit for Cantamar and Puerto Nuevo; junction with Highway 1. Puerto Nuevo (Newport) is a fast-growing community with a hotel and Lobster Village, described above in Rosarito Beach under Dining, page 123.

41.3 Exit for La Fonda, site of a popular restaurant, and the village of La Misión, which is 2.9 miles beyond.

45.6 Exit for La Salina (see *Lodging & Campgrounds*, Chapter 15).

48.6 Exit for Bajamar, a resort development with houses, condominiums, a hotel, tennis and a golf course, the Bajamar Country Club.

52.4 El Mirador, a rest stop with a gift shop and restaurant. An overlook high above the water provides a sweeping coastal panorama. At this point, Highway 1-D makes a sharp turn, which requires a reduction in driving speed. The next several miles are subject to slides.

58.9 Exit for Playa Saldamando campground.

61.6 Toll station, San Miguel.

61.9 Exit for San Miguel Village; junction with Highway 1. The last eight miles to Ensenada are on a toll-free divided highway.

63.5 Junction with Highway 3, which leads northward to Guadalupe and Tecate *(see Highway 3*, page 159). Just past the interchange is El

Sauzal, a sprawling community with a large fish cannery. Many hotels, motels and trailer parks are located along the beach between here and Ensenada.

69.5 Ensenada, at the junction of boulevards Teniente Azueta and Lázaro Cárdenas.

Ensenada as seen from Lomas de Chapultepec

In retrospect, it's easy to see how Ensenada became the leading resort in northern Baja California. An hour's drive south of Tijuana, the city lies within weekend range for millions of Southern Californians, and has a natural setting that's hard to beat on either side of the border. Spread along the shores of the magnificent Bahía de Todos Santos, the city enjoys beautiful surroundings, sheltered from Pacific storm swells, and with mild year-round weather like that of nearby San Diego.

The attractions are many, including excellent fishing, first-rate shopping, nightclubs, and an ambiance that makes it hard not to relax. Nearby draws include beaches, the vineyards of the Valle de Guadalupe, and the famed geyser La Bufadora at the tip of Punta Banda.

Even so, the city has taken time to reach its potential as a resort, and for many years suffered the image of a somewhat seedy port town. That's changing, though, with several recent improvements, like the bayside *malecón* walkway, a new marina and a gentrified tourist district. A new cruise ship dock along Boulevard Costero marks

New cruise ship docks bring passengers closer to downtown Ensenada.

another step forward, bringing passengers within a short walk of downtown.

But Ensenada is much more than a tourist town, having grown far inland across foothills and canyons to reach a present-day population of 260,000. Manufacturing is growing in importance, and you needn't venture more than a few blocks inland to find neighborhoods with few, if any foreigners. Still, the sea and bay will surely remain the key to the city's livelihood. With its modern docking facilities, Ensenada is the busiest seaport in Baja California, home to a major fishing fleet and an important shipping point for farm goods from the Mexicali Valley.

It's come a long way from what Juán Rodríguez Cabrillo saw when he dropped anchor in 1542 and became the first European to make landfall in northern Baja. Little had changed in 1602 when Sebastián Vizcaíno sailed into the bay and was so enthralled by its grandeur that he named it for all the saints—"Ensenada de Todos Santos." However, a lack of fresh water would preclude development here for another 200 years, although Spanish galleons would sometimes call (as would the pirates who preyed on them). Whalers and fur traders put in here as well, but it was not till the early 1800s that ranchers arrived and put down the first meaningful roots.

In the ensuing decades, the locale served as a supply point for pioneers and missionaries probing Mexico's north, but the town did not really take hold until 1870, when gold was discovered at nearby Real de Castillo. Ensenada soon emerged as an important supply depot for miners, and in 1882 it became capital of the territory of Baja California Norte. Two years later the town became headquarters for a company formed to develop a huge land grant covering much of northern Baja, and Ensenada continued to prosper. The good times lasted until the early 1900s, when the gold played out, the land company folded, and the capital moved to Mexicali.

With those setbacks, Ensenada dwindled to a sleepy fishing village, although U.S. Prohibition drew some Americans south during the 1920s. Then in the 1930s two important events spurred a more lasting revival. One was agricultural development in the Mexicali Valley, which created the need for a seaport to export farm products. The other was the arrival of the paved highway from

Tijuana, which put the town within easier reach of American tourists.

Ensenada has been growing ever since, and today forms the southern edge of a long coastal metropolis that extends nearly uninterrupted clear to Tijuana and beyond. Yet for many Americans, the town's appeal is stronger than ever. Even now, it maintains a low-key ambiance with open space, beautiful vistas and a pace of life that has largely disappeared in Alta California.

DID YOU KNOW ...

that Ensenada is the largest *municipio* in all of Mexico? Of course, the *zona urbana* (urban area) reaches south only to Maneadero, but the city's jurisdiction extends clear to the Baja California Sur state line, nearly 400 miles to the south. Nearly a half-million people live in the total *municipio*.

Getting Around

In a city of 260,000, you may conclude that you'd be stuck without an automobile, but in Ensenada that's not necessarily so. It's true that most visitors drive here, but if you're staying in town, you'll discover the main tourist zone is a fairly compact area that's easily covered on foot.

Specifically, we're referring to Avenida López Mateos and Boulevard Costero, which have the largest concentration of restaurants, clubs and gift shops in the city. From anywhere in this zone, you're never more than a few minutes' walk from the *malecón*, Riviera del Pacífico, Plaza Cívica and other attractions. As it turns out, this is also the most congested part of town, and walking is often the fastest way to get about. On Saturday nights—"cruise night" in Ensenada—it may take a half-hour to drive a half-dozen blocks along López Mateos through the middle of downtown.

López Mateos is an excellent place to hire a cab for an out-of-town excursion. La Bufadora at the tip of Punta Banda and the wineries northeast of town along Highway 3 are the most popular destinations. Either one will cost about $30 round trip, or up to $40 for a full load of five or six passengers. For a ride back to your cruise ship, the going rate is $4 for up to four passengers, and $1 extra for each additional person. Like most of Baja, your typical Ensenada cab is a full-size, Detroit-built sedan at least 10 years old, with enough room to pack all but the largest of families.

If you're doing the driving, you'll find that Ensenada maintains a fairly uniform grid pattern once you get inland from López Mateos. Wherever you go, you'll encounter the usual Baja bugaboos such as missing street signs, smallish stop signs and inconspicuous traffic lights.

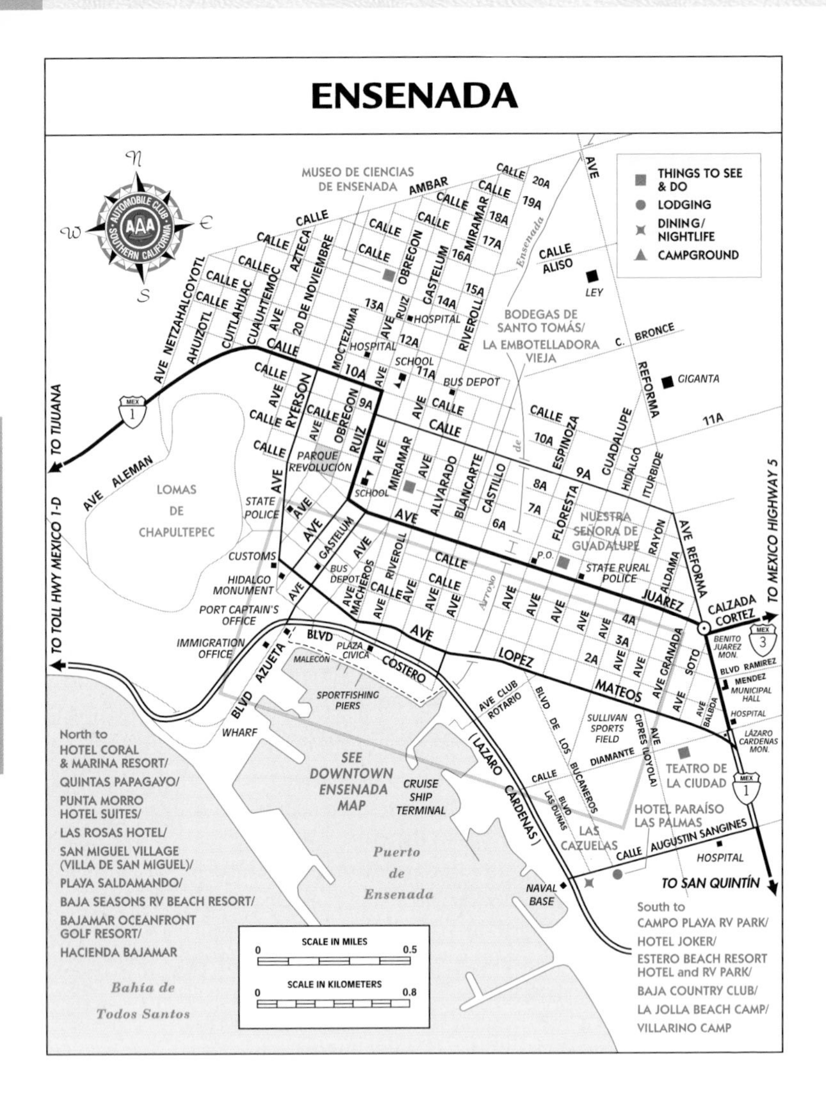

When it's time to leave town, if you have any doubts about which way to go, Boulevard Costero is a good starting point. Heading north, it turns into Highway 1 at the north edge of town. Heading south, Costero follows the shoreline to the naval base entrance, where a left turn on Calle Agustín Sangines leads a few blocks east to southbound Highway 1.

Things To See & Do

When it comes to sheer variety, Ensenada has few if any rivals for activities and attractions in Baja California. Outdoor recreation abounds, the shopping is first rate, and several excellent points of interest await discovery. What's more, return visitors will find the downtown and waterfront have

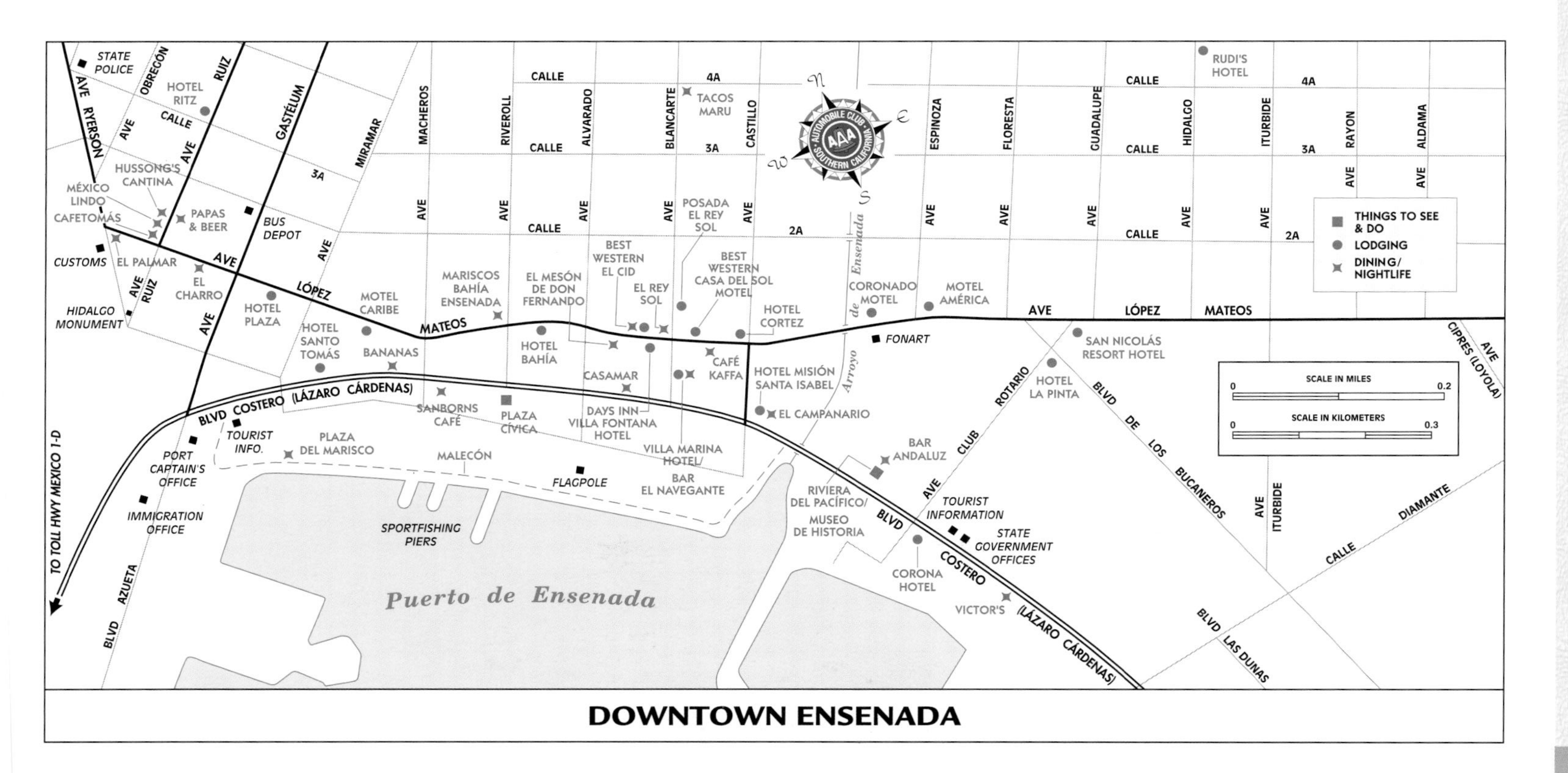
STATE POLICE
AVE RYERSON
OBREGÓN
HOTEL RITZ
RUIZ
CALLE
AVE
GASTÉLUM
MIRAMAR
3A
HUSSONG'S CANTINA
MÉXICO LINDO
CAFETOMÁS
PAPAS & BEER
BUS DEPOT
CUSTOMS
EL PALMAR
EL CHARRO
HIDALGO MONUMENT
HOTEL PLAZA
LÓPEZ
MATEOS
MOTEL CARIBE
HOTEL SANTO TOMÁS
BANANAS
MACHEROS
RIVEROLL
ALVARADO
BLANCARTE
CASTILLO
ESPINOZA
FLORESTA
GUADALUPE
HIDALGO
ITURBIDE
RAYON
ALDAMA
4A
2A
TACOS MARU
POSADA EL REY SOL
BEST WESTERN EL CID
EL REY SOL
BEST WESTERN CASA DEL SOL MOTEL
MARISCOS BAHÍA ENSENADA
EL MESÓN DE DON FERNANDO
HOTEL BAHÍA
CASAMAR
CAFÉ KAFFA
HOTEL CORTEZ
CORONADO MOTEL
MOTEL AMÉRICA
FONART
Arroyo de Ensenada
HOTEL MISIÓN SANTA ISABEL
EL CAMPANARIO
SAN NICOLÁS RESORT HOTEL
HOTEL LA PINTA
CIPRES (LOYOLA)
THINGS TO SEE & DO
LODGING
DINING/ NIGHTLIFE
SCALE IN MILES
0
0.2
SCALE IN KILOMETERS
0
0.3
BLVD COSTERO (LÁZARO CÁRDENAS)
SANBORNS CAFÉ
PLAZA CÍVICA
DAYS INN VILLA FONTANA HOTEL
VILLA MARINA HOTEL/
BAR EL NAVEGANTE
TOURIST INFO.
PLAZA DEL MARISCO
MALECÓN
FLAGPOLE
PORT CAPTAIN'S OFFICE
IMMIGRATION OFFICE
SPORTFISHING PIERS
TO TOLL HWY MEXICO 1-D
BLVD AZUETA
Puerto de Ensenada
BAR ANDALUZ
RIVIERA DEL PACÍFICO/ MUSEO DE HISTORIA
AVE CLUB ROTARIO
BLVD DE LOS BUCANEROS
TOURIST INFORMATION
STATE GOVERNMENT OFFICES
CORONA HOTEL
VICTOR'S
CALLE DIAMANTE
BLVD LAS DUNAS
AUTOMOBILE CLUB · SOUTHERN CALIFORNIA · AAA
DOWNTOWN ENSENADA

Nuestra Señora de Guadalupe, Ensenada's largest church

undergone a major renaissance, spurred by an ongoing urban renewal program.

An example of the renewal is the *malecón*, the bayside walkway that opened in 1997 and has become one of the city's most popular destinations. Stroll its length and you'll pass an enormous flagpole (more than 300 feet tall) and the largest fish market in Baja. Nearby is Plaza Cívica, with its enormous head figures of Mexican heroes. You'll head this way too if you plan on fishing, whale watching or any other sort of boat-based activity, since the local sportfishing and pleasure boat fleets are along the *malecón*.

Another requisite stroll is along Avenida López Mateos, where dozens of gift shops and craft stalls make it the town's top shopping destination. Numerous nightclubs, coffee bars and cafes also line the avenue, which has undergone its own transformation with new street signs, wider sidewalks, tile inlays, new landscaping and other improvements.

Farther south, one of the great jewels of northern Baja sits across the street from the bay: Riviera del Pacífico, a one-time casino and resort that during its early years played host to high-rolling gringos. Built in 1930, it is a masterpiece of Mediterranean architecture and one of the most attractive buildings in Ensenada, its stately white facade and red tile roof surrounded by lush, subtropical gardens. Inside, there's an art gallery, historical museum and beautiful handiwork throughout.

1000 REDUX

Most years the Baja 1000 is actually a 750- to 850-mile race, with the starting and finish lines in Ensenada. Only every third year is it a true 1000-mile event, with the finish line in La Paz.

Not all the major attractions lie near the water, such as Bodegas de Santo Tomás, one of the biggest wineries in the country, which occupies an entire city block. Along with tours and tasting, it's also a good place to buy an unusual keepsake or enjoy a gourmet meal. Other inland highlights include Nuestra Señora de Guadalupe, the city's main parish and, with its soaring twin bell towers, a major landmark. Museo de Ciencias de Ensenada, a tidy science museum, focuses on local marine life and oceanography. And there's the 460-seat Teatro de la Ciudad, Ensenada's leading performing arts venue.

Many travelers happily bypass the in-town attractions, however, to enjoy recreating in the nearby bay and Pacific. Fishing has perhaps the biggest fan base, and many boats stay busy year round hauling mostly Americans offshore to cast their lines in the bay and offshore waters. Surfing has plenty of adherents as well, mostly Southern Californians who head this way for quality waves without the hometown crowds. Some of the world's top riders come here every winter, however, to challenge the huge waves that break a few miles offshore at Islas Todos Santos.

For more information on Punta Banda, see *GreatestHits*, Chapter 3, and Side Route Maneadero to Punta Banda and La Bufadora, page 162.

Surfers and anglers aren't the only ones who migrate this way. California gray whales pass a few miles offshore between December and March on their way to the calving lagoons of southern Baja. Party boats head seaward daily to provide a close-up look at the mammals as they near the end of their annual migration. Divers, meanwhile, enjoy the ultimate close-up with sea life, exploring the ocean's depths off Punta Banda and Islas Todos Santos.

Niños Héroes monument, Plaza Cívica

Back on land you'll get a good sense of all that Ensenada has to offer by taking a short drive north of downtown to the prestigious hillside neighborhood of Lomas de Chapultepec. Pick from several lookout points along Avenida Alemán, from which you'll enjoy unsurpassed views of the city, bay and territory surrounding this booming seaside metropolis.

Top Attractions

BODEGAS DE SANTO TOMÁS

One of Mexico's largest wineries has a major aging and storage facility in Ensenada, complete with a gift shop, bookstore, concert hall, restaurants and a market. English-speaking guides conduct tours lasting about an hour, followed by tasting. A full-fledged cultural center is in the development stages. *Ave Miramar between calles 6 and 7. 01152 (6) 178-33-33, 174-08-29, 174-08-36. Tours daily at 10 and 11 am, noon, 1 and 3 pm. Tours with tasting, $2.*

Tours of the Santo Tomás Winery and vineyards in the Santo Tomás Valley, about 30 miles south of Ensenada, are available by appointment to groups of 10 or larger.

LOMAS DE CHAPULTEPEC

Outstanding views of Ensenada, the port and Pacific waters merit a visit to this attractive residential neighborhood near the north end of town. Avenida Alemán, which wraps around the hilltop, has several parking areas that offer different perspectives. Turning right from Calle 2, the view is of the city, port and foothills rising east of the city. Turning left provides a view that extends south to Punta Banda and seaward to the Todos Santos Islands. *At the north end of Calle 2.*

MALECÓN

Opened in 1997, this attractive bayside walkway has emerged as one of Ensenada's most popular strolling and gathering places. The centerpiece is an enormous 340-foot flagpole bearing a massive Mexican flag that is visible for miles. Along the *malecón's* half-mile length you'll stroll past Plaza Cívica, sportfishing piers and the state's largest fish market. *Along the harbor's edge, between Blvd Azueta and Ave Castillo.*

MUSEO DE CIENCIAS DE ENSENADA

Exhibits on astronomy, oceanography, marine life and endangered species highlight this small but informative museum. During the winter months the museum organizes offshore trips to see the California gray whale. *Ave Obregón between calles 14 and 15. 01152 (6) 178-71-92. Open Tue-Fri 8:30 am-5:30 pm, Sat 10 am-5 pm; closed Sun.*

MUSEO HISTORICO REGIONAL

A fine collection of photos, artifacts and exhibits on local history makes this museum a worthwhile stop on your downtown tour, but the building's past is a story in its own right. Built in 1886, it was an army barracks in its early years. Then, for more than 40 years this was the town prison, and cellblocks, guard towers and a solitary confinement cell still remain in place. *Ave Gastelum just west of Ave López Mateos. 01152 (6) 178-25-31. Open Tue-Sun 10 am-5 pm. Donation.*

Museo Historico Regional was for many years a prison

NUESTRA SEÑORA DE GUADALUPE

Opened in 1951, this Spanish Colonial-style church with its soaring twin towers is one of the most prominent structures in the city. The church appears more impressive on the inside, where marble columns dominate the main sanctuary. *Corner of Calle 6 and Ave Floresta.*

PLAZA CÍVICA

This landscaped court is a familiar landmark with its 12-foot bronze heads of national heroes Benito Juárez, Miguel Hidalgo and Venustiano Carranza. Another monument salutes the Niños Héroes (Children Heroes) of Mexican-American War fame. The plaza is a main staging area as well for horse-drawn carriage tours. *Blvd Costero at the foot of Ave Riveroll.*

RIVIERA DEL PACÍFICO

Riviera del Pacífico is sometimes referred to as Centro Cívico Social y Cultural.

Renowned for its splendid Mediterranean architecture, this building opened in 1930 as a glamorous resort and casino, and it remains one of the most attractive buildings in Baja. Its attractions include a history museum (see sublisting), an art gallery, and hallways full of lovely murals and fancy wood paneling. The centerpiece is the one-time casino, where a massive ornate chandelier hangs from the high ceiling. Beautifully landscaped grounds full of all sorts of subtropical plants surround the building and are another attraction. *Blvd Costero between Arroyo de Ensenada and Ave Club Rotario. Grounds open daily 8 am-7 pm, to 9 pm in summer.*

Riviera del Pacífico

Museo de Historia This small museum has a good collection of artifacts, and several excellent dioramas and murals depicting life in Baja California's early days. Guided tours are available in English and Spanish. Adjacent to the museum is an art gallery that features rotating exhibits. *In the northwest corner of the Riviera del Pacífico. 01152 (6) 177-05-94. Open daily 9 am-2 and 3-5 pm. Admission $1, ages 7-12 and students 50¢. Gallery hours vary; free admission.*

SHOPPING

In a locale full of attractions and diversions, shopping is almost surely the most popular pastime. With the abundance of shops, open-air stalls and marauding vendors, it would take one tightfisted tourist to head home without some sort of keepsake. There's virtually every manner of clothing, artwork or handcraft sold in Baja—jewelry, blankets, baskets, ceramics, leather goods, wrought iron, embroidered clothing and much more. And there are as many bargain-priced liquor stores and *farmacias* as you'd expect in any self-respecting border town.

The best-known shopping strip is **Avenida López Mateos,** where dozens of shops and stalls crowd the blocks between Avenida Castillo and Avenida Ruíz. Many more beckon a block away on **Boulevard Costero**. The prime shopping there is in the teeming network of art and craft stalls known as the **Centro Artesenal/Mexican Hand Crafts Center,** at the corner of Avenida Castillo.

A Perspective on Pricing

Before you dicker over the last two pesos on the Indian blanket you've already haggled down by 30 percent, just remember the shopkeeper has to feed a family, too, and he probably takes home a lot less at the end of the day than you. And unless you're tossing burgers for a living, the person who actually wove that blanket probably earns less in a day than you make in an hour.

If you're stocking up for a trip or otherwise need more mundane supplies, Ensenada has plenty of these sources as well. Around downtown, avenidas Ruíz, Juárez and Reforma all have a good number of shops selling food, auto parts, camping supplies and other consumer goods. Also, the city's numerous supermarkets, such as Gigante and Calimax, are excellent spots to pick up everyday goods at often attractive prices.

TEATRO DE LA CIUDAD

Musicals, dancing and theatrical productions reflecting Mexico's rich cultural heritage take place throughout the year in this 460-seat auditorium. *Calle Diamante between aves Reforma and Loyola.*

Outdoor Fun

DIVING

Northern Baja's best diving areas are within easy reach of Ensenada, with thick kelp forests that harbor a broad range of sea life like that off Southern California. Conditions vary by season but are generally best during the summer, when visibility can reach 60 feet or more. From Ensenada you'll either head southwest to Punta Banda or offshore to Islas de Todos Santos. Punta Banda, with several good diving coves along its north and south flanks, is within a 45-minute drive of downtown Ensenada. You'll need a boat to reach the Islas de Todos Santos, about eight miles from the harbor entrance.

Punta Banda is a popular diving area.

For more information on Punta Banda, see Side Route, page 162.

Almar *Ave Macheros between Ave López Mateos and Calle 1. 01152 (6) 178-30-13.* **Dale's La Bufadora Dive** *Just east of La Bufadora on Punta Banda. 01152 (6) 154-20-92.* **Juanito's Boats** Panga *rentals on the* malecón. *01152 (6) 174-09-53.*

FISHING

Fishing may be the single most popular outdoor activity in Ensenada, and local party boats stay busy year round with half- and full-day trips. With conditions much like those of Southern California, anglers catch a healthy assortment of cool-water dwellers such as bonito, bass, barracuda, lingcod and the inevitable bottom-dwelling rock cod.

Summer generally provides the best fishing, as yellowtail visit the inshore waters while albacore beckon farther offshore. When albacore are running, some boats may stay out 15 hours and travel up to 35 miles offshore to the so-called Outer Banks in their quest for the feisty game fish. Otherwise, the typical party boat trip lasts about eight hours and costs around $35. A Mexican fishing license costs another $9 or so per day (depending on the exchange rate), while tackle rents for about $5 per day.

Gordo's Sport Fishing Fleet *On the* malecón. *01152 (6) 178-35-15, 178-23-77. Website at www.gordos.8m.com.* **Javier's** *On the* malecón. *01152 (6) 176-32-34.* **Sergio's Sportfishing** *On the* malecón. *(800) 336-5454, (858) 454-7166, 01152 (6) 178-21-85. Website at www.sergios-sportfishing.com.*

GOLF

This is not a city known for its broad fairways or close-cropped greens, but a pair of fine golf courses do lie within a half-hour's drive of downtown. The more upscale is Bajamar, a sprawling 27-hole resort north of town between the ocean and the Highway 1 toll road. South of town there's the Baja Country Club, its 18 holes nestled in the rocky foothills east of Highway 1. Both have scenic settings and have earned loyal followings among American golfers.

Golfing at Bajamar

Baja Country Club (Semi-private) 18 holes; 6103 yards; par 72; 119 slope; 69.5 rating. Rates: $35-45. *9 miles south of downtown via Hwy 1, then 3 miles east. 01152 (6) 177-55-23.*

Bajamar Oceanfront Golf Resort (Semi-private) 27 total holes; the Lagos-Vista course is 18 holes, 5712 yards, 118 slope, 67.2 rating. The Vista-Oceano course is 18 holes, par 72, 122 slope, 69.1 rating. The Oceano-Lagos course is 18 holes, par 71, 117 slope, 67.4 rating. Rates: $45-80. *21 miles north of downtown, off Hwy 1-D at Jatay exit. (888) 311-60-76.*

SURFING

Surfing and northern Baja California have gone hand in hand for decades now, and Ensenada is the biggest center for the sport. While some Mexicans ride the local waves, most of the surfers are Southern Californians, lured south by consistent waves and relatively uncrowded conditions. It's no surprise that Baja's oldest surf shop is here: San Miguel surfboards.

Water temperatures off Ensenada are similar to those of Southern California, ranging from the mid-50s in the winter to the high 60s or low 70s in the summer.

The shop bears the name of one of the region's best-known surfing spots, Punta San Miguel, a lusty right-handed point break that works on most winter swells. The point is next to the village of San Miguel, about five miles north of the Ensenada city entrance off Highway 1. Other nearby spots include Salsipuedes, located north of the Highway 1 tollbooth; Tres M's and California, near the north entrance of town; and Estero Beach, along the shoreline south of downtown.

All those spots pale, though, next to Islas Todos Santos, home of the most vaunted wave in Baja California, if not North America. Located at the mouth of Bahía de Todos Santos, the twin islands catch the full brunt of winter swells from the North Pacific and deliver waves of monumental dimensions. The islands are synonymous with Killer's, a reef break off the northwest tip of Isla Norte that serves up winter waves of 30 feet or higher. Top surfers from around the world have ridden here, and boat service is available between the port and islands. A 20-foot *panga,* large enough to hold four surfers and their boards, costs about $150 for an eight-hour rental.

Juanito's Boats Panga *rentals on the* malecón. *01152 (6) 174-09-53.* **San Miguel Surfboards** *In Plaza Hussong, corner of Ave López Mateos and Calle Ruíz. 01152 (6) 178-10-07.*

WHALE WATCHING

The waters off Ensenada are on the home stretch for the California gray whales during their annual migration from the Arctic to the calving grounds of Baja California Sur. Between December and March, most whales pass between the shoreline and Todos Santos Islands, within sight of land and easy reach of whale-watching boats.

The rugged coastline north and south of town has some excellent vantage points for viewing the mammals. Punta Banda is one of the best viewing points in northern Baja, as some whales pass within a few hundred yards of the towering headland. Offshore trips offer a close-up look at the finned beasts as local sportfishing boats do double duty, providing whale-watching trips during the peak viewing months. Tours typically last three to four hours and cost about $20 for adults, with sizable discounts for children. Reservations are recommended. Most cruises have bilingual narrators who have an in-depth knowledge of the whales.

Gordo's Sport Fishing Fleet *On the* malecón. *01152 (6) 178-35-15, 8-23-77. Website at www.gordos.8m.com.*
Sergio's Sportfishing *On the* malecón. *(800) 336-5454, (858) 454-7166, 01152 (6) 178-21-85. Website at www.sergios-sportfishing.com.*

Nightlife

You would expect a seaside resort like this to have a zesty, carefree night scene, and Ensenada has just that. Weekends and holidays year round bring a festive atmosphere to the downtown of this, the largest seaport/resort on Baja's Pacific coast. Yet Ensenada is generally less rowdy than its northern neighbors Tijuana and Rosarito, where many young Americans seem to go with the express goal of drinking to a stupor.

Instead, this town draws a more diverse party crowd, including surfers, yachties, sun-bronzed seniors, off-road warriors and lots of curious folk who just want a peek inside Hussong's. All told, they far outnumber the under-21 set, and it's not unusual to see tourists and locals in equal numbers sharing the bar stools or dance floor.

If you want to avoid the crowds, weekday evenings are generally the best time to enjoy Ensenada's bar and club scene.

The bar and club scene is mainly downtown, amid the restaurants and shops along López Mateos and Boulevard Costero. "Bar and club scene" is a more apt phrase than "night scene," since this town parties on down when the sun is high in the sky too. Even in broad daylight, the crowds are liable to spill into the streets in front of some drink and dance spots on U.S. holidays, weekends, or when a cruise ship is in port.

We've made no attempt to list every bar or club in town. Some will appeal to solely a local crowd, others are just comfortable but undistinguished lounges, while still others are centers for decidedly illicit behavior.

BANANAS

A textbook high-tech disco with a fancy light show and high-volume DJ music, this venerable dance club is a steady favorite with the young and restless out for a good time. Plenty of Americans crowd the floor alongside the locals during busy tourist periods. *Blvd Costero between aves Miramar and Macheros. 01152 (6) 178-20-04. Full bar.*

BAR ANDALUZ

Housed in the Riviera del Pacífico, this stylish, low-key lounge is the perfect foil to the rowdy downtown bar and dance scene. Classy without being stuffy, it's a good place to slump back in your chair, nurse a drink and converse without having to shout over the music. Fancy woodwork and tiling all about befit this drinking spot inside one of Ensenada's most lovely and historic buildings. *Inside Riviera del Pacífico (use rear entrance). No phone. Full bar; light menu. Piano and saxophone music Fri-Sat; closed Mon.*

> **OLD BAR, NEW NAME**
>
> 
>
> Bar Andaluz's present-day name dates to 1979, when it reopened after an extensive restoration of Riviera del Pacífico. The bar first opened in 1930, under the name Bar del Emperador.

BAR EL NAVEGANTE

The decor and atmosphere are nondescript, but oh what a view from atop the Villa Marina Hotel, Ensenada's tallest building. A 360-degree panorama of city and bay are yours for the cost of one reasonably priced drink. Happy hour (5-7 p.m.) sweetens the deal and is a great way to salute the day's end. *Villa Marina Hotel, Ave Blancarte just west of Ave López Mateos. 01152 (6) 178-33-21, ext 2015. Full bar. DJ dance music Thu-Sun.*

HUSSONG'S CANTINA

Both Hussong's and Papas & Beer have their own gift shops on Avenida López Mateos.

In the same location since 1892, Baja's oldest and most famous watering hole is a peninsular classic. It's a cozy, well-worn haunt where sawdust covers the hardwood floor, early town photos adorn the walls and a bluish tobacco haze hangs in the air. Mariachi and string trio troupes provide the music and round out an atmosphere that money can't buy. A magnet for tourists and locals alike, Hussong's is best experienced on a weekday when the cruise ships aren't in port. *On Ave Ruíz just east of Ave López Mateos. 01152 (6) 178-32-10. Full bar.*

LA CAPILLA

All right, it's not a household name like its neighbors down the street, but for grownups with a taste for the more civilized diversions in life, this may be the most agreeable nightspot in Ensenada. The atmosphere leans baroque, with stained glass and ornate woodwork throughout the lounge. A gallery of famous visitors from yore fills the back wall, with glossy old black-and-whites of John Wayne, Anthony Quinn, Vickie Carr, Cheech & Chong, etc. Cuban jazz provides the live soundtrack, starting at 9 nightly. *At the El Cid Motor Hotel, Ave López Mateos between aves Blancarte and Alvarado. 01152 (6) 178-24-01.*

LA EMBOTELLADORA VIEJA

More than 80 varieties of wine from Baja and the rest of the world fill the racks inside this converted warehouse, earning it kudos from *Wine Spectator* magazine. Prices start at about $2 per glass; per-bottle prices range from less than $10 to more than $130. *Inside Bodegas de Santo Tomás, corner of Calle 7 and Ave Miramar. 01152 (6) 174-08-07. Live salsa, Latin jazz and string trio music; schedule varies.*

PAPAS & BEER

Tequila shots, jumbo-sized margaritas and a free flow of *cerveza* combine with an ear-blasting disco/rock soundtrack to make this the busiest nightspot in town. Built on three floors with a bar on each level, this place strives to please all comers, with live and recorded music, finger food, karaoke and many special events. The formula seems to work, drawing a healthy mix of gringos and locals across the age spectrum. *On Ave Ruíz just east of Ave López Mateos (across from Hussong's). 01152 (6) 174-01-45.*

Dining

If it's indeed possible to have too much of a good thing, then you could build a strong case that Ensenada has too many restaurants for its own good. This city has so many eating places that you may despair at settling on one when mealtime comes around.

Seafood is the undisputed king, as you'd expect from the largest port on Baja's Pacific coast, but it's just one of countless options.

A colorful restaurant at Plaza del Marisco

Chinese, steak, pizza and American-style coffee shops are a few of the viable choices, and that's just downtown along Boulevard Costero and Avenida López Mateos. These two main drags are at the heart of the tourists' dining scene. There isn't much those blocks don't offer up in terms of food or ambiance, be it stand-up taco stands, quasi-Mexican eateries aimed at gringos, or the oldest French restaurant in Mexico.

While downtown has the best range of options within a small area, they represent just a small fraction of what's out there. Citywide, Ensenada boasts hundreds of restaurants, some steps from your hotel, others on the outskirts of town or in neighborhoods seldom visited by foreigners. Savvy diners will do well to seek them out in their unending quest for new eating adventures.

Favorites

EL CHARRO **Specialty**

Chicken broilers twirl relentlessly on a rotisserie in the window of this homey downtown restaurant, where they've seduced passersby since the 1940s. Care to join the tradition? All right, but there's no telling what you'll order once you realize you can also have a charbroiled steak, charbroiled lobster, charbroiled fish filet or .... *Ave López Mateos between aves Gastelum and Ruíz. 01152 (6) 178-38-81. Open daily 11 am-2 pm. $6-20.*

EL MESÓN DE DON FERNANDO **Mexican/American**

It's impressive anytime you meet a person who's fully bilingual *and* bicultural, moving gracefully across international boundaries. The same goes for restaurants, and this fine cafe pulls it off with more aplomb than most. Burgers, Hawaiian shrimp, lobster thermidor and apple pie (!) grace the menu alongside a healthy list of Mexican favorites. *Ave López Mateos, one door south of Ave Alvarado. 01152 (6) 174-0155. Open daily at 7 am; Sun-Thu to 11 pm, Fri-Sat to midnight. $3.70-22.*

EL REY SOL **♦♦♦ French/Mexican**

Opened in 1947, El Rey Sol bills itself as "Mexico's most recommended restaurant," and upon further review, you may decide this isn't mere hype. Service, ingredients and preparation—amid elegant surroundings—have few rivals in Baja. That goes for breakfast, lunch or dinner, from the *enchiladas suizas* to the crab crepes. *Corner of aves López Mateos and Blancarte. 01152 (6) 178-17-33, 8-23-51. Open daily 7:30 am-11 pm. $8.75-21.*

PUTTIN' ON THE RITZ, SORT OF

You need not don a coat and tie or buy an evening gown, but El Rey Sol's refined atmosphere does suggest attire a tad nicer than your average beach bum. At a minimum, forego the shorts and sandals, and guys, wear a shirt with a collar.

LA EMBOTELLADORA VIEJA **Mediterranean**

A cavernous warehouse with huge oak wine barrels and intricate brickwork provide for Ensenada's most unusual restaurant setting. The cuisine is likewise unique, being best described as Mediterranean with Mexican influences. We'd be more specific, but the menu gets a full revamping three or four times every year. You'll *always* find a terrific selection of domestic and imported wines at this ritzy haunt, part of the Santo Tomás Winery. *Inside Bodegas de Santo Tomás, corner of Calle 7 and Ave Miramar. 01152 (6) 174-08-07. Open Wed-Mon at noon, closing times vary; closed Tue. $8-25 (exact prices may vary).*

LAS CAZUELAS **Mexican/American**

A low-key but not stuffy atmosphere with fancy woodwork and stained glass reflect this restaurant's distance from the hubbub of the main tourist strip. The extensive menu makes this a sure-fire bet for divergent tastes and budgets. Prime rib and *Camarones Las Cazuelas* (lobster-stuffed shrimp) top the roster of house specialties. *Just east of Blvd Costero on Blvd Sangines. 01152 (6) 176-10-44. Open daily 7 am-11 pm. $4-18.*

MARISCOS BAHÍA ENSENADA **Seafood**

With sensible prices, snappy service and more than 40 tasty seafood entrees, no wonder this place always seems busy. A downtown fixture for more than 30 years, it holds equal sway with locals and out-of-towners. The lively atmosphere is no place for a heavy date or a power lunch, and you may get cut off midsentence by a marauding string trio. By the way, the abalone and lobster are the only entrees over $10. *Corner of aves López Mateos and Riveroll. 01152 (6) 178-10-15, 8-31-51. Open daily 10 am-10 pm. $4.80-34.*

PLAZA DEL MARISCO **Seafood**

Whether you're watching every last *centavo,* seeking an honest-to-God Mexican experience or just like your seafood by the water's edge, this outdoor food court merits a visit. Fish tacos, seafood cocktails, tangy *caldos* (soups) and combination platters—all with low, low prices—are standard fare at any of the open-air booths. Half the fun is strolling past the gauntlet of fervid barkers, all convinced that *their* stand has the best seafood in Baja. *Near the north end of the* malecón, *between Blvd Costero and the waterfront. No phone. Open daily 7 am-6:30 pm (exact hours vary by stand). Tacos 50¢-$1.10, full-course meals $4.80-7.60.*

Others

CAFÉ KAFFA **Bakery**

Beverages 90¢-$3.20, baked goods 60¢-$2.70. *Ave López Mateos between aves Castillo and Blancarte. 01152 (6) 174-02-59.*

CAFETOMÁS **Bakery**

Beverages $1.10-2.40, baked goods 60¢-$2.50. *Plaza Hussong, corner of aves López Mateos and Ruíz. No phone.*

CASAMAR **Steak/Seafood**

$8-31.50. *Blvd Costero across from the* malecón *flagpole. 01152 (6) 174-04-17.*

EL CAMPANARIO **Mexican**

$3-9. *At the Hotel Misión Santa Isabel, corner of Blvd Costero and Ave Castillo. 01152 (6) 178-36-16.*

EL CID **Mexican**
$5-19. *At the El Cid Motor Hotel, Ave López Mateos between aves Blancarte and Alvarado. 01152 (6) 178-24-01.*

EL PALMAR **Seafood**
$5.30-10.50. *Corner of aves López Mateos and Ryerson. 01152 (6) 178-87-88.*

MÉXICO LINDO ***Taquería***
$1-2.75. *Ave Ruíz between Ave López Mateos and Hussong's Cantina. 01152 (6) 178-86-28.*

SANBORNS CAFÉ **Mexican/American**
$4.50-8. *Plaza Marina, on Blvd Costero between aves Macheros and Riveroll. 01152 (6) 174-09-71.*

TACOS MARU **Mexican**
$2-6. *Corner of Ave Blancarte and Calle 4. 01152 (6) 178-27-20.*

VICTOR'S **Mexican/American**
$3.50-10. *Blvd Costero, ½ blk south of Calle Las Rocas and state tourism office. 01152 (6) 173-13-13.*

Lodging

For information on special events in Ensenada, see *Special Events & Holidays*, Chapter 13.

When it's time to put your feet up for the night, few Baja towns can approach Ensenada in terms of variety or number of lodging choices. It's all here, including seaside resorts, standard-issue motor lodges, high-rise hotels, and crusty hovels off the tourist path.

What you won't find is a vacant room on summer weekends, U.S. holidays, or during special events—which this city has more of than any other in Baja. Call at least a week ahead of time to ensure a room during those peak periods. During other times, though, you'll have the run of the town, and you may be able to negotiate a discount off the posted rate.

THE "SKYLINE" OF ENSENADA

Based on decor and appointments alone, the Villa Marina Hotel would be about average among major Ensenada hotels, but step onto the balcony and think again. The 10-story hotel is Ensenada's tallest building, and from its upper floors you'll have breathtaking views of the city, bay and surrounding territory.

If it's important to be at the center of action, Avenida López Mateos and Boulevard Costero are loaded with midpriced hotels within a short walk of countless restaurants, nightclubs and curio shops. For something quieter or with a beachfront view, several fine properties dot the coastline north and south of town.

Mexico Highway 2

Tijuana to Tecate via Highway 2

(34 mi., 54 km.; 1 hr.)

Beyond the Tijuana downtown tourist scene is the border region that most locals see and know: that of big-block shopping malls, modern assembly plants and orderly rows of concrete apartments, and a rural landscape of rolling hills, orchards and ranchland. All of this is showcased along the free road between Tijuana and Tecate.

Highway 2 starts in Tijuana as Boulevard Díaz Ordaz and makes its way through the bustling commercial and industrial district of La Mesa. From here the road crosses a dam near the city's eastern flank before emerging into rolling open countryside that is slowly being absorbed by Tijuana's eastward sprawl. The road then climbs through rocky hills, dairy farms and olive groves for the balance of the drive to Tecate.

Being the free road, this route has its drawbacks, including heavy traffic, blind curves, potholes and missing guardrails, among other adventures. The route is four lanes undivided to La Presa ("the Dam"), where it narrows to two lanes for the rest of the way. Traffic is often heavy in the La Mesa district, and Boulevard Insurgentes often proves to be a faster-moving alternative. A divided route that starts in La Mesa, Insurgentes parallels Highway 2 for seven miles before the two routes merge.

00.0 Tijuana (San Ysidro border crossing). Proceed straight ahead and follow the signs to Paseo de los Héroes. Do not follow signs pointing to Rosarito and Tecate. Following this route eventually leads you to the Tecate toll road.

01.6 Corner of Paseo de los Héroes and Antonio Caso, where a large sign points south to Ensenada. Turn right here.

01.9 Junction with Boulevard Agua Caliente. Turn left and head east on Boulevard Agua

Caliente, which eventually becomes Boulevard Díaz Ordaz.

03.7 Caliente Racetrack. On the hills to the south is one of the city's most attractive residential neighborhoods.

05.7 Boulevard Lázaro Cárdenas, which goes northeast to Boulevard Insurgentes, the central bus station and Tijuana Airport.

09.8 Boulevard Díaz Ordaz reaches a fork. Bear left to continue to Tecate.

10.7 La Presa, Tijuana's easternmost suburb.

11.0 Rodríguez Dam and lake, once the sole source of Tijuana's water supply. The road follows the top of the dam and is quite narrow.

16.5 El Florido, a large housing development.

26.5 Junction with the toll road to Tecate. Passenger vehicles entering the toll road here must pay a $1.50 fare.

30.5 Rancho La Puerta, the famed health and fitness spa and resort catering to an exclusive clientele.

33.0 Tecate, at the tree-shaded plaza known as Parque Hidalgo. At the intersection here is Mexico Highway 3, which leads south toward and Ensenada (see Travelogue for Mexico Highway 3, page 159).

TRAVELOGUE

Tijuana to Tecate via Toll Highway 2-D

(21 mi., 35 km.; 0.30 hr.)

A modern four-lane highway with controlled access provides a fast alternative to Highway 2, albeit for a price. Highway 2-D starts in eastern Tijuana, where tollbooths collect fees from vehicles headed to and from Tecate. The tolls aren't cheap—about $4.50 for cars and light trucks, although this makes for a lightly traveled road, where congestion and slow vehicles are almost never a problem.

After crossing the border at Otay Mesa, drive 1.2 miles straight south to the first main boulevard and turn east. Follow this thoroughfare, Boulevard Industrial, through the *maquiladora* district, where many multinational firms have built huge assembly plants in recent years. After about two miles the toll road officially begins. Beyond the sprawling factories and housing developments, your route emerges into open countryside. First it follows a narrow canyon (watch out for falling rocks) before ambling over rolling hills, with occasional farms and ranches along the way. After 18 miles, the highway dips into the Tecate Basin, where exits lead into town.

AN EXPENSIVE "OOPS"

Unless you intend to drive clear to Tijuana, stay off the westbound toll road in Tecate. The westbound lanes offer no exits before you reach the eastern edge of Tijuana, where you'll have to pay *twice*—once for the westbound trip and again eastbound if you're returning to Tecate.

00.0 **Corner of Boulevard de los Aztecas with Boulevard Industrial. Heading south from the Otay Mesa border crossing (on Boulevard de los Aztecas), a sign points eastward toward Boulevard Industrial and the toll road.**

01.8 **Last chance to exit before the start of the toll road.**

05.3 **Toll station.**

16.0 **Exit for Mexico Highway 2 and west entrance to Tecate.**

20.8 **Exit for Mexico Highway 3, which heads south to El Sauzal and Ensenada.**

20.9 **Last exit for Tecate.**

Tecate

Parque Hidalgo, Tecate's main town square

Save the wandering signal of a San Diego radio station or the occasional colors of a California license tag, this could well be someplace in the *Bajio* region, far to the south on the Mexican mainland. The main square has a quaint colonial feel, while storefronts have that weathered, timeworn look that's oh-so Mexican, and barnyard animals wander on dusty side streets.

Hard to believe that the U.S. border is just a few blocks north of downtown. But then, Tecate has always been the great exception among Baja border towns, and may be the least Americanized city along Mexico's northern frontier. Set in a small valley surrounded by rolling, rocky hills, this town of 50,000 lies some 30 miles east of Tijuana and eons removed from its teeming crowds, acres of shops and boisterous night scene. Instead, Tecate attracts a more relaxed, thoughtful breed of tourist, some on day larks, others headed south for extended Baja treks.

At the same time, Tecate has several worthwhile attractions. Best known is the Cuauhtémoc Brewery, home of Tecate beer and by far the largest structure in town. It does tours and has a sunny beer garden, where a cold one is on the house. Nearby is the town's main square at Parque Hidalgo, where stately trees shade fountains, tile walkways and a Spanish-style gazebo. Near the west edge of town is another local institution—Rancho La Puerta, a renowned health resort that since 1940 has drawn rich and famous clients from around the world seeking physical and spiritual renewal.

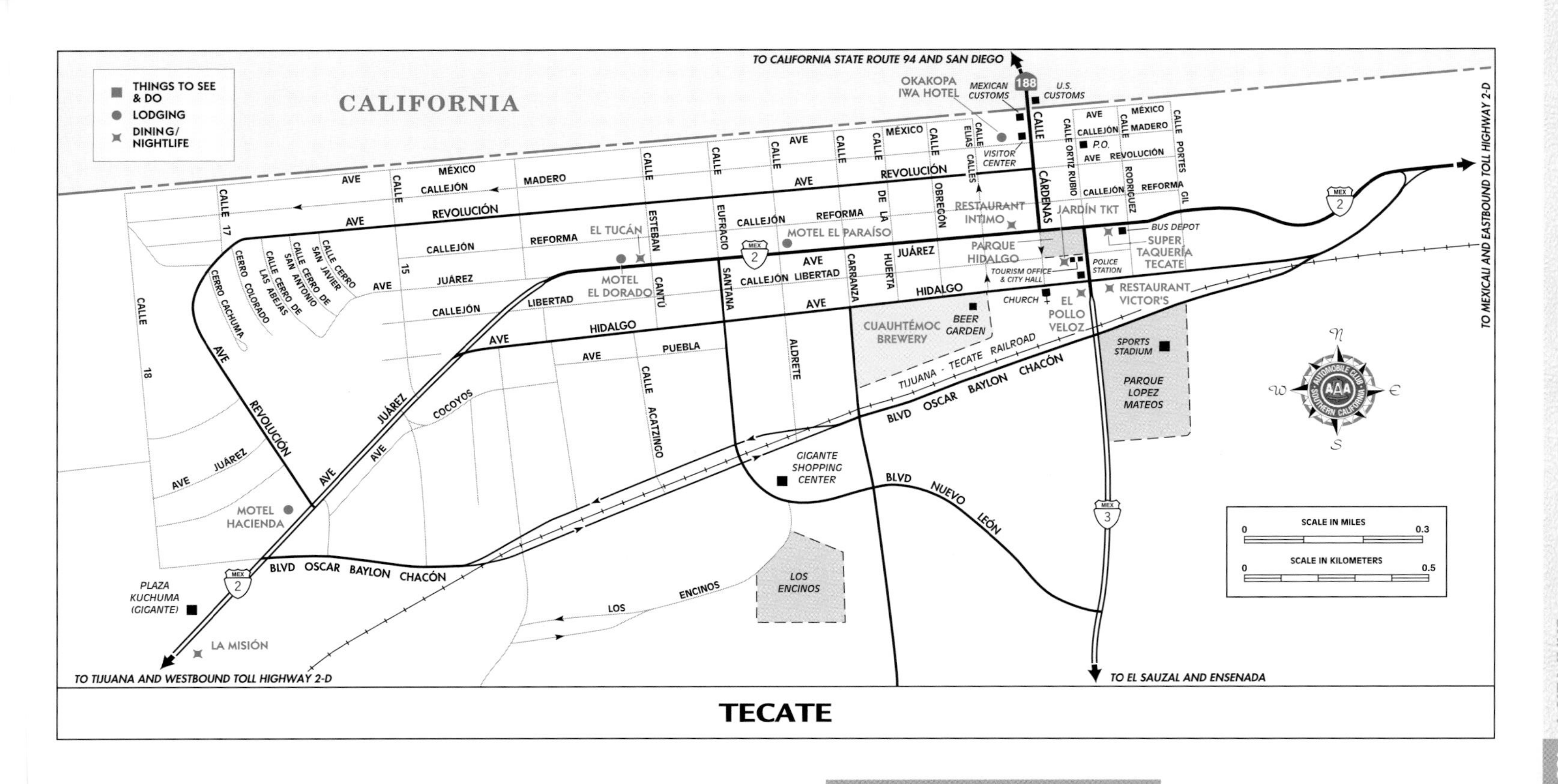
TECATE
CALIFORNIA
TO CALIFORNIA STATE ROUTE 94 AND SAN DIEGO
TO MEXICALI AND EASTBOUND TOLL HIGHWAY 2-D
TO EL SAUZAL AND ENSENADA
TO TIJUANA AND WESTBOUND TOLL HIGHWAY 2-D
THINGS TO SEE & DO
LODGING
DINING/ NIGHTLIFE
SCALE IN MILES
SCALE IN KILOMETERS
0
0.3
0.5
U.S. CUSTOMS
MEXICAN CUSTOMS
VISITOR CENTER
OKAKOPA IWA HOTEL
P.O.
BUS DEPOT
SUPER TAQUERÍA TECATE
RESTAURANT VICTOR'S
POLICE STATION
JARDÍN TKT
TOURISM OFFICE & CITY HALL
CHURCH
EL POLLO VELOZ
RESTAURANT INTIMO
PARQUE HIDALGO
BEER GARDEN
CUAUHTÉMOC BREWERY
SPORTS STADIUM
PARQUE LOPEZ MATEOS
GIGANTE SHOPPING CENTER
LOS ENCINOS
MOTEL EL PARAÍSO
EL TUCÁN
MOTEL EL DORADO
MOTEL HACIENDA
LA MISIÓN
PLAZA KUCHUMA (GIGANTE)
CALLE CÁRDENAS
CALLE ORTIZ RUBIO
CALLE PORTES GIL
RODRIGUEZ
CALLE ELIAS CALLES
CALLE OBREGÓN
CALLE DE LA HUERTA
CALLE CARRANZA
CALLE ALDRETE
CALLE EUFRACIO SANTANA
CALLE ESTEBAN CANTÚ
CALLE ACATZINGO
CALLE 15
CALLE 17
CALLE 18
AVE MÉXICO
AVE MADERO
AVE REVOLUCIÓN
AVE REFORMA
AVE JUÁREZ
AVE LIBERTAD
AVE HIDALGO
AVE PUEBLA
CALLEJÓN
CALLEJÓN LIBERTAD
TIJUANA - TECATE RAILROAD
BLVD OSCAR BAYLON CHACÓN
BLVD NUEVO LEÓN
LOS ENCINOS
COCOYOS
CALLE CERRO SAN JAVIER
CALLE CERRO DE SAN ANTONIO
CALLE CERRO DE LAS ABEJAS
CERRO COLORADO
CERRO CACHUMA
MEX 2
MEX 3
188

It's no surprise that an expensive spa would open in Tecate, given its scenic surroundings and a climate that may be the best of any town in northern Baja. Some 35 miles inland, the town lies beyond reach of nearly all the late-spring and early-summer fog that shrouds the Pacific coast. And at 1700 feet high, it escapes summer's worst heat while making for pleasantly brisk winter days.

The climate lends itself to growing grapes, olives and wheat, which thrive in the surrounding countryside, as they have for more than 100 years. First settled in 1831, Tecate is the oldest border town in Baja, the result of a land grant to a wealthy Peruvian rancher who later became the mayor of San Diego. (The present-day border was not drawn until 1848.) The town didn't really take off until the 1880s, when farming became an important industry here and in the nearby Guadalupe Valley. Further development came after the 1915 completion of a railroad between Tijuana and Mexicali, which spurred the export of farm products to the United States.

Tecate was known for exports of another kind, when a large distilling plant opened and the town became a staging point for smuggling whiskey and other spirits across the border during U.S. Prohibition. After Prohibition ended, beer replaced whiskey as the town's main income source when Cuauhtémoc Brewery opened in 1944.

These days, manufacturing drives economic growth as Tecate joins the boom in population and commerce along

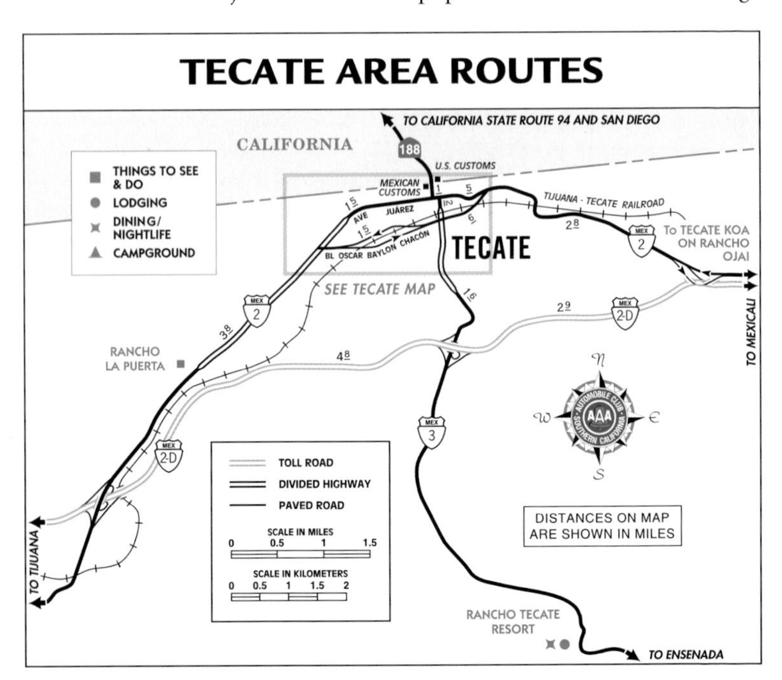

Crossing the Border in Tecate

Twenty years ago the average border-crossing wait in Tecate was about as long as a red light on Avenida Juárez, as this peaceful inland burg basked in quiet seclusion. The town remains a fairly subdued place, but the days of no crossing lines are but a memory as Tecate's population and industrial boom continue unabated. Still, the average waiting time for cars at the two-lane crossing gate is just a small fraction of that in most border towns. Even on weekend afternoons, the longest wait is seldom more than 15 minutes, and pedestrians have almost no wait at all.

Tecate's crossing gate lies at the north end of Calle Cárdenas, but when traffic backs up, the line of cars bends around the corner onto Avenida Revolución, two blocks below the border. Open from 6 a.m. to midnight, the border crossing lies about two miles south of California State Route 94, a bucolic two-lane highway that winds east-west across the rugged hills and ranchland east of San Diego. From the border crossing, it's about a 45-minute drive to the eastern suburbs of San Diego.

Tecate also sits at one of northern Baja's major crossroads. It is the largest town on Mexico Highway 2 between Tijuana and Mexicali, and the northern terminus of Mexico Highway 3, which meets the coast near Ensenada. From Tecate it is about 90 miles east to Mexicali, 30 miles west to Tijuana and 66 miles southwest to El Sauzal, near Ensenada.

Baja's northern frontier. The brewery remains the biggest employer, but several assembly plants have opened, shipping a variety of finished goods to the United States. At the same time, housing developments have spread across hillsides farther and farther from the old downtown. So far, however, Tecate has maintained its bona fide Mexican flavor and at least some of its small-town atmosphere—something fast disappearing along much of the border.

Top Attractions

CUAUHTÉMOC BREWERY

Opened in 1944, this brewery is the home of Tecate beer; it produces several other brands as well, including Dos Equis, Sol and Carta Blanca. It is by far the largest building in town, spanning three city blocks and employing 450 workers, who labor around the clock in three shifts six days a week. Free tours of the plant last about an hour and take place Monday through Friday, subject to an eight-person minimum. An attractive beer garden is on the premises as well, serving a cold one on tap to all visi-

In case you wondered, Tecate Beer was named for the town, not vice-versa.

Brewery and beer garden

tors. (Limit one per visit.) *Ave Hidalgo and Calle Carranza. Beer garden open Mon-Fri 10 am-6 pm, Sat 10 am-4 pm; closed Sun. Free tours Mon-Fri at 9, 10 and 11 am, and 3 and 4 pm. Sat tours by appointment only. For tour information, call 01152 (6) 654-20-11, ext 3470.*

PARQUE HIDALGO

Tecate's main plaza, or *zócalo,* is an attractive retreat and popular gathering spot for locals and tourists alike. A gazebo marks the center of the park and an impressive statue of Benito Juárez stands at its northeast corner. City hall, a small museum and the local tourism office all line the south edge of the park. *On Ave Juárez, 4 blks south of the border crossing.*

SAN DIEGO RAIL MUSEUM

Riding the rails becomes a cross-border experience as trains depart the Campo, California, museum and travel to Tecate, offering tours of the Cuauhtémoc Brewery, along with sightseeing and shopping around town. Tours take place two or three Saturdays a month, with occasional weekday excursions. *Tickets $40, ages 2-12 $20. (619) 595-3030.*

SHOPPING

Tecate lacks the huge network of gift shops and craft stalls of other border towns, but there are several good spots to pick up a keepsake. One is along **Calle Cárdenas** just below the border crossing, where pottery is the main specialty. Another good spot is the artisans market located on the south side of the Río Tecate, next to Parque López Mateos and just east of Highway 3. In addition, weekend vendors at Parque Hidalgo roll out a nice display of lacquer ware, blown glass, leather goods and other crafts.

Dining

It's a far cry from Tijuana or Ensenada, where the selection of restaurants is truly overwhelming, but Tecate is still a hard town to leave with an empty stomach. If there were one word to describe the local dining scene, it would have to be "authentic," as in a lack of singing waiters, trendy food or dollarized menus. Nearly all the restaurants count on locals as their main clientele, which makes this a great town for most back-to-basics dishes.

Taquerías and casual diners are a great place for the basic entrees, and the town is full of these. Downtown has the largest concentration, and virtually every block around Parque Hidalgo has at least one walk-up stand where you can fill up for less than $5. Stroll those same blocks and you'll note several fruit and juice stands, where a tall glass of fresh-squeezed orange juice costs about a dollar and a huge *licuado* (smoothie) runs less than $2. If you're looking for something more upscale, the best options are away from downtown. Even then, it's hard to exhaust your dining budget anywhere in this town.

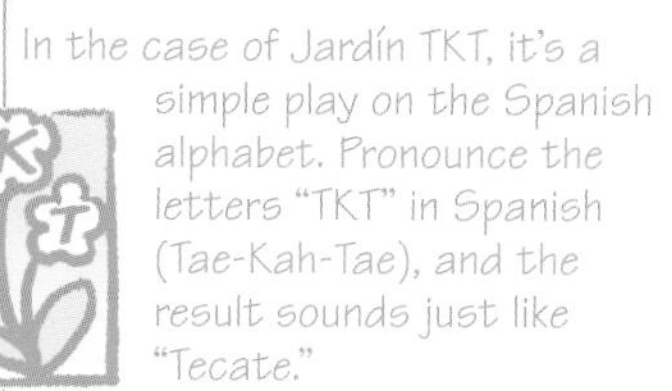

Favorites

JARDÍN TKT — **Mexican**

A town square like Parque Hidalgo would not be complete without a sidewalk cafe, and this is it. Cool your heels alongside the shaded plaza, watch the weekend crowd go by and order from a good selection of well-prepared Mexican standbys. *South side of Parque Hidalgo, near the State Tourism Office. 01152 (6) 654-34-53. Open daily 6 am-9 pm. $2.70-6.*

LA MISIÓN — **Steak/Seafood**

Ask the locals where they like to dine out, and this name comes up time and time again. On weekdays you're likely to hear the top brass from nearby foreign-owned assembly plants talking cross-border trade over their grilled steak or Tecate-style fish. On weekends, gringos and locals alike queue up for dinner or the Sunday breakfast buffet in this dignified but not overly formal restaurant. *Ave Juárez 1110, west of downtown and across from the Gigante shopping center. 01152 (6) 654-21-05. Open daily; Mon-Sat 11 am-10 pm, Sun 8 am-10 pm. $5.25-10.*

RANCHO TECATE — **Mexican/American**

Tecate's most upscale restaurant also has the most spectacular setting—off the road to Ensenada with panoramic views of rolling, stony mountains in every direction. "Upscale" is a relative term of course, and there's little on the menu that's outlandishly priced. Sunday brunch ($13) is a great way to enjoy country surroundings and try one of the nearly three dozen Baja California wines. *5 miles south of town off Hwy 3. 01152 (6) 654-02-66, 654-00-11. Open daily; Sun-Fri 7 am-10 pm, Sat 7 am-11 pm. $4.40-16.*

RESTAURANT INTIMO **Mexican**

If you're visiting Tecate to find the real Mexico, it doesn't get much better than this. From the velvet paintings on the walls to the tangy *albóndigas* (meatballs), a neighborhood diner like this is an essential part of the Mexican experience. Try a *comida corrida*, served daily in the afternoon, in which the server brings your meal to the table one course at a time—the way it's done in cities all over Mexico. *On Ave Juárez, half a blk west of Parque Hidalgo, between calles Cárdenas and Elias. 01152 (6) 654-48-19. Open Mon-Sat 7 am-9 pm; closed Sun. $2.70-5.50.*

Other Choices

EL POLLO VELOZ **Mexican**

$3-6. *Ave Hidalgo between Calle Cárdenas and Hwy 3. 01152 (6) 654-40-28.*

EL TUCÁN **Mexican**

$7.50-20. *Adjacent to Motel El Dorado, corner of Ave Juárez and Calle Cantu. 01152 (6) 654-13-33.*

RESTAURANT VICTOR'S **Mexican/Seafood**

$4.80-13.50. *Ave Hidalgo, just east of Hwy 3. 01152 (6) 654-18-01.*

SUPER TAQUERÍA TECATE ***Taquería***

$1.25-4.50. *Ave Juárez between calles Rubio and Rodríguez. No phone.*

Lodging

Unless you have an odd fondness for dairy farms or *maquiladora* plants, you can hit Tecate's highlights in a half a day or less, which means the town may not figure in your overnight plans. But if you elect to stay here, Tecate has a fair number of hotels and motor inns, though little that's overly fancy or expensive.

Highway 2 (Avenida Juárez in town) is the place to look for motor inn-style lodging, while the neighborhood around Parque Hidalgo has a few bare-bones, budget-priced inns priced under $15 a night. Then there's Rancho Tecate Resort, south of town on Highway 3, which has one of the most secluded and natural settings for an accommodation along Baja's northern frontier. The nearest camping is 13 miles east of town at KOA Kampground & RV Park, on the Highway 2 free road (see *Lodging &*

The Borderland's Playground of the Rich

You can't discuss Tecate without mentioning Rancho La Puerta, the famed health and fitness spa on a secluded hillside near the west end of town. Since its opening in 1940, the clientele has included movie stars, business execs, royalty and other moneyed types seeking relaxation and renewal. Care to join them? You can, for rates ranging from $1400 to more than $2000 a week. Or, take a peek on a Saturday morning, when free public tours are offered. For information, call (800) 443-7565.

Campgrounds, Chapter 15). Tecate has no AAA-rated lodgings, but several properties priced from around $20 to $100 are comfortable and should meet the needs of most travelers.

Mexico Highway 3

TRAVELOGUE

Tecate to El Sauzal

(66 mi., 107 km.; 1:30 hrs.)

There was a time when much of Southern California looked like this—rolling countryside where vineyards, orchards and pastures filled the valleys, separated by virgin hills that changed colors with the passing seasons. Those images have largely disappeared north of the border, as have roads like Mexico Highway 3—a meandering, two-lane byway that remains a major link in Baja.

Museum entrance, off Highway 3 in Valle de Guadalupe

Tecate sets the tone for this drive, set amid a picturesque inland valley with a semi-rural atmosphere and refreshing lack of U.S. influence. You quickly leave the town and its namesake valley behind as the highway scales a series of boulder-strewn hillsides and small upland valleys on its way south. Numerous curves and steep inclines demand your full attention on this first stretch, after which the road drops into a broad valley where scattered field crops and olive orchards thrive amid the ranchland.

Farther south, miles of vineyards take over as the main land use, signaling your arrival in the Guadalupe Valley, the leading wine district in Mexico. The main wineries in this region are Domecq and L.A. Cetto, whose front gates face each other on opposite sides of the highway. Two miles beyond is the turnoff to the village of Guadalupe, the valley's main settlement, founded by Russian immigrants in the early 20th century (see below). Tracking southwest, the rolling countryside continues to the seaside at El Sauzal, at the northern edge of Ensenada.

00.0 Tecate, at the junction of Mexico highways 2 and 3.

01.8 Junction with Mexico Highway 2-D, the Tijuana-Mexicali Expressway.

05.2 Rancho Tecate, a resort with tennis, swimming and a golf course under development.

17.5 Valle de las Palmas, an agricultural community with gasoline, stores and restaurants.

30.5 El Testerazo, a village with a cafe. To the west are prominent rocky peaks, 3000 to 4200 feet in elevation.

45.8 Entrance gates to Domecq and L.A. Cetto wineries. To the left is L.A. Cetto; tours daily 10 a.m.-4 p.m. Across the road is Domecq; tours Mon.-Fri. 10 a.m.-4 p.m., Sat. 10 a.m.-1:30 p.m. At this point, the highway enters a region containing extensive, well-maintained vineyards.

48.0 Valle de Guadalupe. Next to the elementary school are the ruins of Mission Nuestra Señora de Guadalupe (1834), last of the Baja California missions. Russian immigrants founded an agricultural community here early in the 20th century. Museo Comunitario del Valle de Guadalupe has a collection of pictures and artifacts about these Russian-Mexican settlers. This museum is located 1½ miles west of the junction of Highway 3 and the main road into town. Hours are Wed.-Sun. 9 a.m.-4 p.m.; dona-

tion. Guadalupe has two cafes, groceries, an inn and a clinic.

59.1 San Antonio de las Minas, a village with a restaurant and a pair of small markets.

65.6 El Sauzal, at the junction with Mexico Highway 1. Ensenada is six miles southeast.

Bienvenido to California's Other Wine Country

For gringos who think of Corona with lime or Cuervo Gold as Mexico's national libations, the thought of uncorking a Domecq '95 Cabernet Sauvignon or any Mexican wine might sound a bit strange. It shouldn't for those who have driven past the miles of vineyards along Highway 3 north of Ensenada.

Welcome to the Guadalupe Valley, the leading wine district in Mexico. Its miles of vineyards along Highway 3 north of Ensenada have warm summer days and evenings cooled by Pacific breezes, a climate perfect for wine grapes. The region lies near the southern edge of the Northern Hemisphere's primary wine-producing belt, between the 30th and 50th parallels.

Vineyards under summer's sun at L.A. Cetto

The wide range in temperatures is ideal for growing many different wine grapes, with cabernet, zinfandel, Chenin Blanc and Riesling ranking among the major varieties. Guadalupe accounts for the lion's share of northern Baja's wine production; along with the Santo Tomás Valley south of Maneadero, the two valleys produce 90 percent of Mexican table wines. Some growers send grapes to distilleries in mainland Mexico, where they're transformed into brandies.

Winemaking in northern Baja is nothing new, dating back to the founding of Misión Santo Tomás in 1791, yet outside of Mexico the region's wines have remained little known. By most accounts, their quality sagged until the late 1980s, when the government slashed tariffs on a wide range of goods. Facing the rigors of foreign competition, Mexican producers rose to the challenge; by the early 1990s Baja wines were beginning to earn international acclaim.

Production-wise, Domecq is king of Baja wineries, turning out more than 1.5 million cases per annum, followed by L.A. Cetto, whose annual sales top 400,000 cases. Santo Tomás ships more than 100,000 cases a year from its namesake valley farther south.

Still, Baja's wineries face an ongoing struggle to drum up business. Most of their production stays in Mexico, where the average consumer drinks less than 0.4 liters of wine (roughly a half bottle) per annum. Nor does it help that visiting Americans can return home with only a single liter of any alcoholic beverage.

The wineries have found one good means to promote themselves and have a grand time in the bargain. Each summer they stage the Fiestas de la Vendimia (Harvest Festivals)—10 days of street fairs, eating, concerts, tasting tours and more. Ensenada is the hub for the celebration, though many festivities take place at wineries and other venues across northern Baja.

The wineries welcome visitors for tasting and tours during the rest of the year, too. L.A. Cetto and Domecq, flanking opposite sides of Highway 3, are within easy driving distance of Ensenada and Tecate. Driving is the easiest way to reach the valley from nearby California, though some groups hail from cruise ships in port at Ensenada.

L.A. Cetto is open daily from 10 a.m. to 4 p.m.; Domecq is open Monday through Friday from 10 a.m. to 4 p.m. and Saturday from 10 a.m. to 1:30 p.m. In Ensenada, Santo Tomás offers tours and tasting at its headquarters on Avenida Miramar. Several smaller wineries in the area offer tours by prior arrangement.

Maneadero to Punta Banda and La Bufadora

(See map page 163.)

(14 mi., 23 km.; 0:30 hr.)

(See also *Lodging & Campgrounds*, Chapter 15.)

This short side trip makes an ideal excursion for visitors to Ensenada, and is also a popular family outing for locals. The route offers spectacular views of the Pacific and Bahía de Todos Santos en route to the main attraction, La Bufadora ("the Snorter")—a natural sea spout that sends columns of spray soaring into the air.

See *GreatestHits*, Chapter 3, for more on La Bufadora.

From its junction with Highway 1, BCN 23 winds through olive orchards and cultivated fields for a few miles, then leads onto Punta Banda, the mountainous peninsula forming the southern end of Bahía de Todos Santos. The area is growing rapidly, with shops, restaurants and vacation homes lining much of the route, although good-sized chunks of

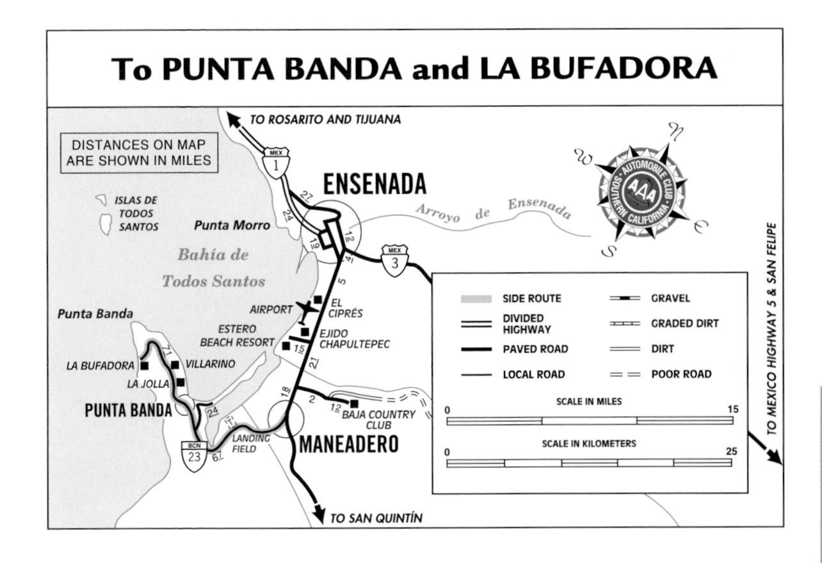

open space remain. Seven miles west of Maneadero is the turnoff to Baja Beach and Tennis Club, a private resort. Another mile west is a group of trailer parks and campgrounds on the shore of the bay; La Jolla Beach Camp and Villarino Camp offer extensive camping facilities.

The peak of Punta Banda measures 984 feet above sea level.

Beyond the trailer parks and campgrounds, the road twists and climbs toward the summit of the peninsula before dropping to the edge of a small rocky cove favored by skin divers and scuba divers. Near the western tip of Punta Banda, the road ends at a paved parking lot (nominal fee), with steps leading to La Bufadora. A long row of food stands and curio shops line the walkway leading to the viewing area and do a booming business on sunny weekends. Several dirt lots handle overflow parking during those periods.

Blankets galore for sale at La Bufadora

Besides La Bufadora, Punta Banda has excellent conditions for scuba diving, snorkeling and kayaking. Dale's La Bufadora Dive, located near the end of the road, rents complete diving equipment, wet suits and kayaks; phone 01152 (6) 154-20-92.

Chapter 5

Highway 3 South

Unless you have a weird fondness for towns with names like Ojos Negros, Héroes de la Independencia and Valle de la Trinidad, we could excuse you for making a non-stop dash across the southern leg of Mexico Highway 3. Those are the only towns of any consequence along this two-lane, 122-mile strip of pavement, which you might well dismiss as just a connecting route from the Pacific coast to the Colorado Desert. But then, this is Baja California, a land full of intrigue and surprises for those who care to venture past the pavement's edge and forego the normal comforts of life on the road.

Highway 3 charts a wandering southeast course from Ensenada to a desert junction with Mexico Highway 5, near the north edge of the Gulf of California and 32 miles north of San Felipe. Depending on your state of mind, this route is a key link to San Felipe, an approach

Parque Nacional Constitución de 1857

road for assorted outdoor adventures, or part of an interesting loop trip through the backcountry of northern Baja. Whatever your take, if you've come here from someplace the least bit urban, you may feel like you've entered a bucolic time warp as you drive across rolling foothills, verdant farming valleys and empty plateaus before making a climatic descent to the barren desert floor.

En route, Highway 3 provides a good hint of what potential diversions lie out there, skirting the base of mountains that harbor some of northern Baja's most secluded destinations. One is Laguna Hanson, east of Ojos Negros amid the rocky uplands of the Sierra de Juárez, with a feel that Southern California's mountains may have possessed 100 years ago. Fair to say that the cattle far outnumber the humans in the forest around this 4000-foot-high mountain lake, even during the peak tourist periods. Farther southeast, Mike's Sky Rancho enjoys a different sort of wilderness setting, perched atop a knoll on the north slope of the Sierra de San Pedro Mártir. A favorite haunt for the dirt bike crowd, Mike's comes off as a bastion of cushy living in a land where family-style meals and a roof over your head pass for creature comforts.

HIGHWAY 3 SOUTH

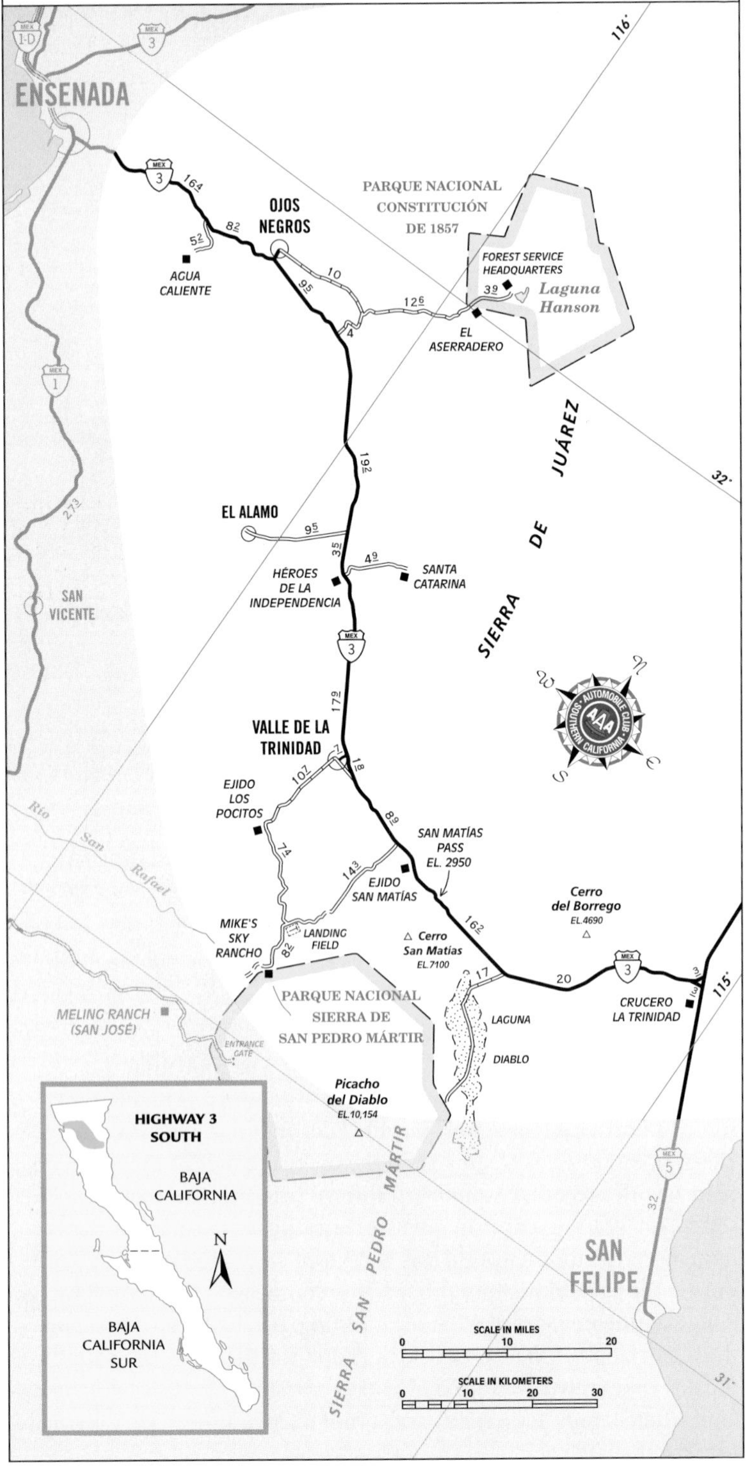

ENSENADA
OJOS NEGROS
AGUA CALIENTE
PARQUE NACIONAL CONSTITUCIÓN DE 1857
FOREST SERVICE HEADQUARTERS
Laguna Hanson
EL ASERRADERO
SIERRA DE JUÁREZ
EL ALAMO
HÉROES DE LA INDEPENDENCIA
SANTA CATARINA
SAN VICENTE
VALLE DE LA TRINIDAD
EJIDO LOS POCITOS
Río San Rafael
SAN MATÍAS PASS EL. 2950
EJIDO SAN MATÍAS
Cerro del Borrego EL.4690
MIKE'S SKY RANCHO
LANDING FIELD
Cerro San Matías EL.7100
CRUCERO LA TRINIDAD
MELING RANCH (SAN JOSÉ)
ENTRANCE GATE
PARQUE NACIONAL SIERRA DE SAN PEDRO MÁRTIR
LAGUNA DIABLO
Picacho del Diablo EL.10,154
SIERRA SAN PEDRO MÁRTIR
SAN FELIPE
AUTOMOBILE CLUB · SOUTHERN CALIFORNIA · AAA

HIGHWAY 3 SOUTH
BAJA CALIFORNIA
BAJA CALIFORNIA SUR

SCALE IN MILES 0 10 20
SCALE IN KILOMETERS 0 10 20 30

Highway 3 also provides the best paved approach for climbing Picacho del Diablo, at 10,154 feet the highest peak on the Baja peninsula. Height is not the main challenge of this arduous trek, where steep canyon walls, inclement weather and sheer remoteness have foiled the best-laid plans of many an experienced climber. A challenge of a far different sort takes place each June when the highway and surrounding wilderness double as a giant speed course for the Baja 500 off-road race. Thousands line the winding course to catch a fleeting glimpse of their favorite drivers as they put their machines—and bodies—through one of motor sports' most grueling tests.

Fields near Valle de la Trinidad

See *GreatestHits,* Chapter 3, for more on the Sierra de San Pedro Mártir.

The upshot is, this feral inland quarter offers far more than meets the eye—whether it's a scenic country drive you want, or the takeoff point for some of Baja California's premier adventures.

Experience...

- The unexpected joy of having a whole lake to yourself, camping midweek along the tree-lined shore of Laguna Hanson.
- Hauling a rainbow trout from the chilled waters of an alpine stream—a most un-Baja-like experience.
- Catching the first glimpse of the shimmering Sea of Cortez, driving down the east slope of San Matías Pass.
- A complete sense of detachment from the soulless malls, mega-freeways and red-tile sameness of suburbia while walking down the dusty streets of Valle de la Trinidad.

TRAVELOGUE

Ensenada to El Chinero, Junction with Highway 5

(122 mi., 195 km.; 3 hrs.)

This route may share the same number as Mexico Highway 3 between Tecate and El Sauzal, but the similarities begin and end there. The northern leg runs southwest to the Pacific coast, while this one tacks southeast toward the Gulf of California. If San Felipe is your destination, it makes for an interesting alternative to the drive down Highway 5 from the border at Mexicali. Otherwise, it stands as a worthwhile byway in its own right, crossing a large swath of northern Baja's most scenic inland countryside.

A bend in the road near Ojos Negros

Eastbound from Ensenada, the road twists and climbs through a range of chaparral-covered coastal hills before descending to the broad, green Valle de Ojos Negros, a good-sized farming and ranching center. Past the town of Ojos Negros, the road grows somewhat wider before you scale another set of hills onto a plateau known as the Llano Colorado. Still more hills follow before the road winds downward to reach the edge of the Valle de Trinidad, another farming and ranching center.

Beyond the fields and pastures of this peaceful valley the rugged peaks of the Sierra de Juárez and Sierra San Pedro Mártir mountains rise ahead. The highway cuts a path between them as it scales a canyon known as San Matías Pass. Beyond it lies the desert and the shimmering waters of the Gulf of California as the road quickly drops toward the junction with Highway 5. The mountains appear far more impressive from this side, their sheer granite peaks jutting upward much like the east face of California's Sierra Nevada. The eastern escarpment of Picacho del

REMEMBER EL ALAMO

Fame and fortune seemed destined for this corner of Baja in 1888 when gold was discovered at the village of El Alamo. Miners poured in by the thousands almost overnight, but the shiny metal soon played out and just as quickly the settlement was all but abandoned. Only a few people live in the vicinity of El Alamo today, 9.5 miles west of Highway 3 near Héroes de la Independencia.

Diablo looms mightily to the southeast as the highway descends to the desert floor.

00.0 **Ensenada, at the intersection of Avenida Benito Juárez (Mexico Highway 1), Avenida Reforma and Calzada Cortez. Follow Calzada Cortez eastward from the traffic circle.**

01.4 **Calzada Cortez reaches the junction with a boulevard marking the start of Highway 3. Turn left here.**

08.2 **El Gran 13, an amusement park with rides and playground equipment, a picnic ground, swimming pool and spa.**

16.4 **Junction with a 5.2-mile dirt road to Agua Caliente, a rustic tourist resort. This road should not be attempted in wet weather.**

24.6 **Junction with the paved road leading 1.2 miles to Ojos Negros, a farming and cattle-raising community with several markets, cafes and a nice park. A graded road leads eastward from Ojos Negros to the Sierra de Juárez and Laguna Hanson (see Side Route to Laguna Hanson, page 171).**

Side Routes

34.5 **Junction with a signed road to Parque Nacional Constitución de 1857; the road from Ojos Negros is the better choice.**

54.0 **Junction with a 9.5-mile dirt road leading to El Alamo, site of a short-lived gold rush in 1888. A few people remain living in the area today, along with scattered old buildings and other evidence of the brief mining era.**

57.5 **Héroes de la Independencia, a scattered settlement on Llano Colorado. The town has groceries, pottery stores, cafes and auto parts. Gasoline is sold in front of a small grocery store; a sign points the way from the highway. A dirt road branches north to the ruins of Misión Santa Catarina, founded in 1797.**

75.5 **Junction with the short, paved road to Valle de la Trinidad. This rapidly growing community is a farm market center of around 5000, with stores, cafes, a bank, an ice house, schools, an unusual conical church, a mechanic, tire repair and gasoline.**

Side Routes

San Felipe is 32 miles south of the junction of highways 3 and 5.

86.2 Junction with a good dirt road to Mike's Sky Rancho, which is 22.5 miles to the south (see Side Route to Mike's Sky Rancho, page 171).

88.2 Ejido San Matías, a roadside hamlet with two cafes, a small store and a tire shop.

91.0 San Matías Pass, elevation 2950 feet.

102.4 Junction with a dirt road leading first to Rancho Villa del Sol and Colonia San Pedro Mártir, then southeast to San Felipe. This rugged route passes close to the base of the Sierra de San Pedro Mártir; Cañón El Diablo, 20 miles south of the junction, is where many climbers begin the difficult ascent of Picacho del Diablo. (Another road, 1/10 mile to the east, leads to the same destinations, merging with the first road less than a quarter-mile south of Highway 3.)

121.5 El Chinero (also called Crucero la Trinidad), junction with Mexico Highway 5 (see Travelogue for Mexico Highway 5, the *Desert Northeast*, Chapter 12). About 0.7 mile south of the junction is a Pemex station and a cafe.

Side Routes

Ojos Negros to Laguna Hanson

(27 mi., 43 km.; 1:45 hrs.)

This unpaved side route offers a look at the high plateau country of the Sierra de Juárez—a land of cool mountain air, rocky peaks and thick forests of ponderosa pine. At its heart is Laguna Hanson, a shallow, intermittent lake at about 4000 feet in elevation, surrounded by tall pines, odd rock formations and excellent primitive campsites. Laguna Hanson (also known as Laguna Juárez) is the centerpiece of a small national park known as Parque Nacional Constitución de 1857.

HANSON'S EASTER MADNESS

If you're going to Laguna Hanson in search of solitude, avoid Semana Santa, or Easter Week. This is the busiest week of the year, drawing hundreds of campers, mainly from northern Baja. Things are generally quiet the rest of the year.

SIDE ROUTES from HIGHWAY 3 to LAGUNA HANSON and MIKE'S SKY RANCHO

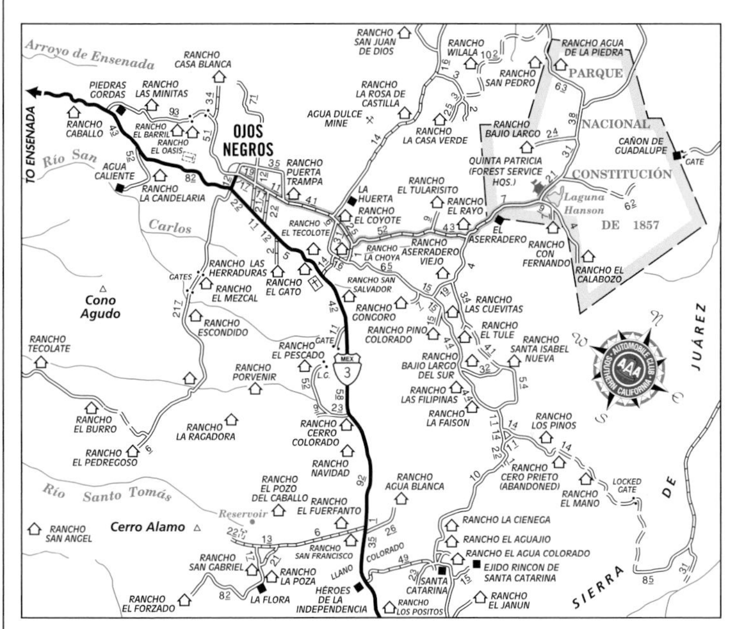

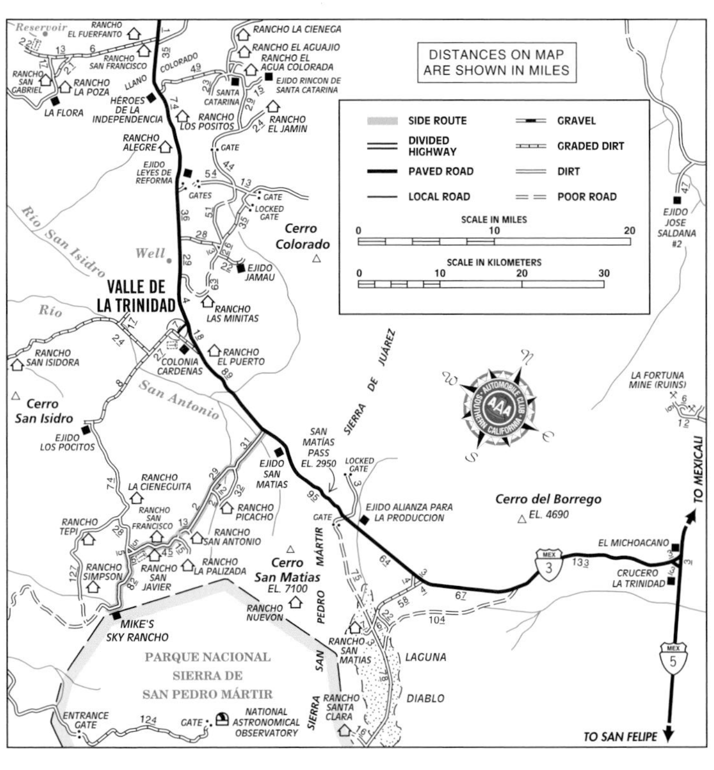

Laguna Hanson

Aside from standout scenery, solitude is one of the main attractions of this side route; the park gets very few tourists during most of the year, despite its proximity to major cities on both sides of the border. A passenger car can make the drive from Ojos Negros in dry weather, but may run into trouble on the rougher route that continues north to Mexico Highway 2.

From the pavement's end in Ojos Negros (1.2 miles north of Highway 3), turn right onto a wide graded road running eastward toward the mountains. The road passes several farms and ranches before ascending into brush-covered foothills. At mile 7.9 is a major junction; bear right here. Beyond the junction the road climbs steadily into the mountains. There are no steep grades, however, as the road winds upward, leaving the chaparral belt behind for a ponderosa pine forest. At mileage 20.4 is another important junction; bear left. The route swings north from here and enters Aserradero, a village of wooden buildings; the road leaves Aserradero ahead to the left. Just beyond the village is the southern entrance to Parque Nacional Constitución de 1857. A $3 per-person fee is sometimes collected here. Four miles beyond Aserradero is Laguna Hanson. A wide, hard-packed dirt road leads clear around the lake, providing access to various campsites set beneath the pines. Beyond Laguna Hanson, the route continues north for another 37 miles to meet Mexico Highway 2 at El Cóndor, about nine miles west of La Rumorosa.

Park regulations prohibit hunting at Laguna Hanson.

Highway 3 to Mike's Sky Rancho

(23 mi., 37 km.; 1:30 hrs.)

Perched atop a 3800-foot-high knoll in the Sierra San Pedro Mártir, Mike's Sky Rancho has been a favorite getaway for off-road motorcyclists and other outdoor enthusiasts since the late 1960s. Mike's offers motel-type accommodations, family-style meals, a pool, sycamore-shaded campsites and information about trips into the rugged country to the

PEDAL TO THE METTLE

Mountain bikers seeking new challenges can try the 43-mile trail from Mike's to the National Astronomical Observatory, at an elevation of 9200 feet in Sierra San Pedro Mártir National Park.

east. Hikers and mountain bikers put to good use an extensive network of trails crisscrossing the surrounding mountains. Anglers catch rainbow trout in a small stream that runs through Arroyo San Rafael, a wooded valley overlooked by the ranch.

Fording a stream near Mike's Sky Rancho

The road to Mike's leaves Highway 3 at a signed junction 10.7 miles southeast of Valle de Trinidad. The first half of the trip is over a dirt road rising gradually through semiarid landscape, with Cerro San Matías (elevation 7100 feet) visible to the east. The road becomes rougher and more winding as it approaches a junction at mileage 13.8. A 6000-foot graded airstrip belonging to Mike's is located here. A rough road to the right goes to Ejido Los Pocitos. Bear left to continue 8.2 miles farther over rough surface to the ranch. With slow and careful driving, a passenger car can make this trip during dry weather, although a high-clearance truck or jeep is still a better choice.

Mike's Sky Rancho offers the only indoor lodging of any kind in this region.

SUMMER IS MAS TRANQUILO

If you'd rather not share the great outdoors with marauding dirt-bikers, consider staying at Mike's Sky Rancho during the summer. The off-road crowd favors Mike's during the cooler months of the year, using the ranch as a base for excursions to the desert flatlands east of here.

Lodging at Mike's costs $45 a night per person, including two meals a day. Reservations are necessary. For more information, call 01152 (6) 681-55-14 (English is spoken); write P.O. Box 1948, Imperial Beach, CA 92032; or e-mail mikes@telnor.net.

Chapter 6

South of Ensenada

Time, progress, and the average tourist have all but ignored the huge expanse of countryside and miles of untamed coastline that stretch far to the south of Ensenada. Beyond the reach of most weekend travelers from the U.S. yet bypassed by nearly all long-distance trekkers, this vast quarter gets short shrift from the vast majority of outsiders. That's fine and well with those who'd gladly keep Baja California the way it is, but it sells short a region full of diverse attractions and scenic surprises.

Between the southern sprawl of Ensenada and the northern fringe of the Central Desert, Highway 1 threads its way through 200 miles of thinly populated territory, where the climate and geography mimic that of nearby Southern California. Cooling sea breezes and coastal fog provide mild weather year round along a picturesque shoreline that is

Pacific shoreline near La Bocana

equal parts rocky headlands and wide sandy beaches. Soaring mountains with fragrant pine forests and heavy winter snows guard the eastern flank and effectively seal this region off from the Colorado Desert. Baja's loftiest peak is located here—Picacho del Diablo, 10,154 feet in elevation and one of the most challenging climbs in all of Mexico. Between mountain and sea are miles of rolling hills and pocket valleys where cattle graze and vineyards flourish beneath the warm summer sun, while fertile coastal plains produce a bounty of fruit and truck crops. Small towns and ranchos dot the inland valleys and foothills, while remote fish camps and gringo vacation homes hug the water's edge.

The closest thing to an urban center here is San Quintín, the bustling hub of an ever-expanding agricultural empire that, in all of Baja California, is surpassed only by the Mexicali Valley. With 22,000 people, San Quintín is in no way a major metropolis or leading tourist venue, though it does bring in many vacationers for excellent hunting around its bay and wetlands, and for superlative deep-sea fishing.

By and large, however, the most inviting venues are well-removed from civilization, which winnows out all but the most dedicated of vaga-

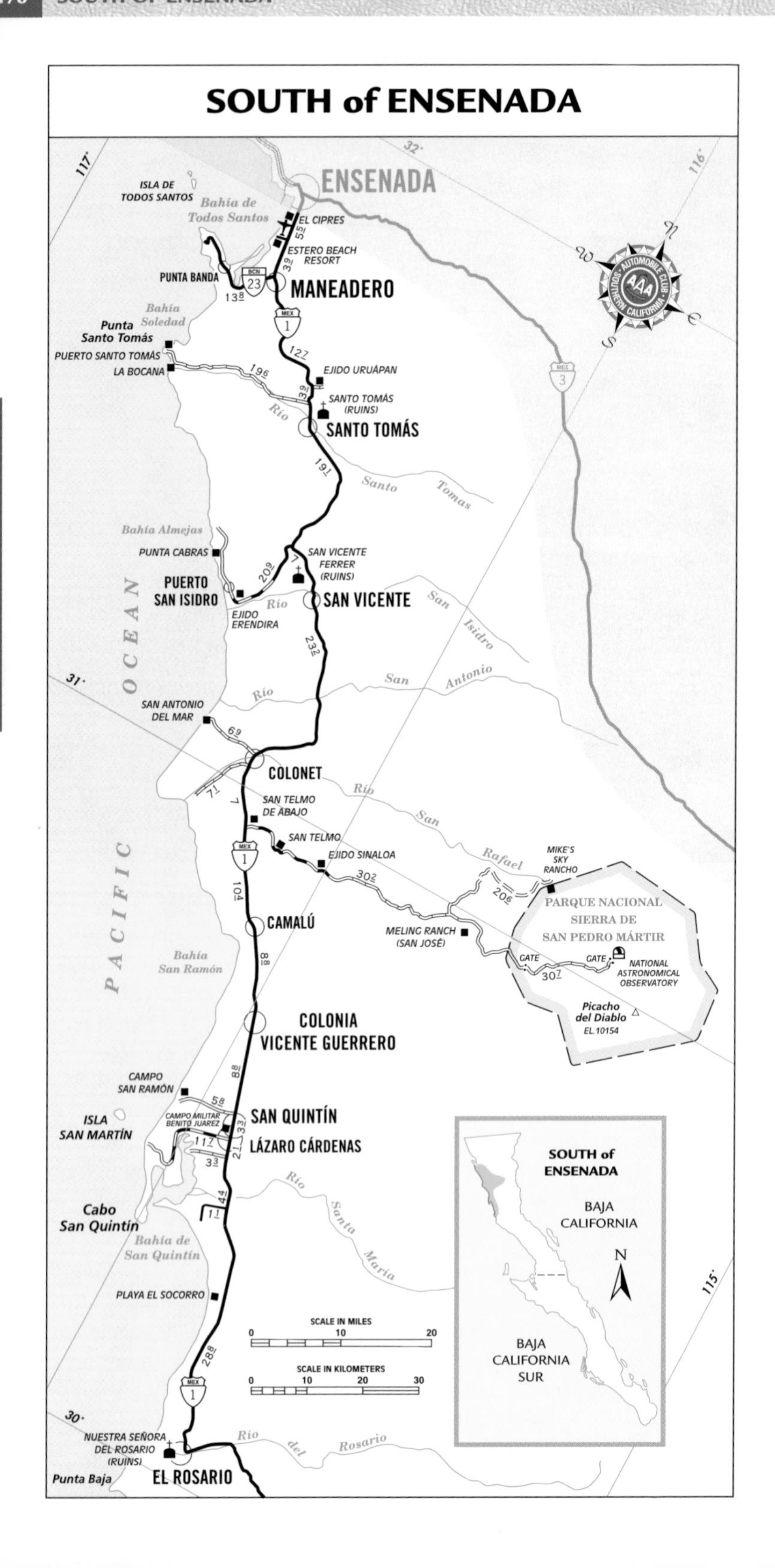

SOUTH of ENSENADA
ENSENADA
ISLA DE TODOS SANTOS
Bahía de Todos Santos
EL CIPRES
ESTERO BEACH RESORT
PUNTA BANDA
MANEADERO
Bahía Soledad
Punta Santo Tomás
PUERTO SANTO TOMÁS
LA BOCANA
EJIDO URUÁPAN
SANTO TOMÁS (RUINS)
SANTO TOMÁS
Río Santo Tomás
Bahía Almejas
PUNTA CABRAS
SAN VICENTE FERRER (RUINS)
PUERTO SAN ISIDRO
EJIDO ERENDIRA
SAN VICENTE
Río San Isidro
Río San Antonio
SAN ANTONIO DEL MAR
COLONET
SAN TELMO DE ABAJO
SAN TELMO
EJIDO SINALOA
Río San Rafael
MIKE'S SKY RANCHO
PARQUE NACIONAL SIERRA DE SAN PEDRO MÁRTIR
MELING RANCH (SAN JOSÉ)
GATE
NATIONAL ASTRONOMICAL OBSERVATORY
Picacho del Diablo
EL.10154
CAMALÚ
Bahía San Ramón
PACIFIC OCEAN
COLONIA VICENTE GUERRERO
CAMPO SAN RAMÓN
ISLA SAN MARTÍN
CAMPO MILITAR BENITO JUAREZ
SAN QUINTÍN
LÁZARO CÁRDENAS
Río Santa María
Cabo San Quintín
Bahía de San Quintín
PLAYA EL SOCORRO
SCALE IN MILES
0 10 20
SCALE IN KILOMETERS
0 10 20 30
NUESTRA SEÑORA DEL ROSARIO (RUINS)
Río del Rosario
Punta Baja
EL ROSARIO
SOUTH of ENSENADA
BAJA CALIFORNIA
BAJA CALIFORNIA SUR
N
AUTOMOBILE CLUB SOUTHERN CALIFORNIA AAA

bonds. Many side roads branch off of Highway 1, but just a few lend themselves to the low-slung family sedan. Solar panels and propane tanks are the power sources of choice at many outposts, where your late-night reading may well be done by flashlight. Of course the lack of people and creature comforts are the main draws for many who do venture here—anglers who cast their lines along desolate beaches, motor bikers raising clouds of dust along the endless web of backcountry trails, surfers in search of the perfect (read empty) wave.

Highway 1 near Santo Tomás

While this region has the feel of a bygone Southern California, things grow increasingly dry the farther south you go. By the time Highway 1 swings inland near El Rosario, the coastal headlands are all but devoid of vegetation. Not far beyond, the terrain transforms to chalk-colored mountains, cacti and jumbled rocks—icons of the textbook Baja, but no reason to miss the wonders that come before.

Experience . . .

- Shades of California's Big Sur as the afternoon's sun sinks toward a boding fog bank off the rocky shoreline of La Bocana.
- The heady aromas of eucalyptus trees and sizzling *carne asada* mingling in a shaded picnic ground in Santo Tomás.
- Treading the day's first—and last—footsteps along a deserted stretch of beach, somewhere west of Highway 1.
- The honky-tonk ruckus of a fisherman's cantina, where tales of the day's exploits improve with every round of cold *cerveza*.
- October's chill breeze sweeping through a grove of fiery yellow aspens, 9000 feet high in the Sierra de San Pedro Mártir.

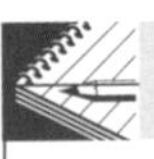

TRAVELOGUE

Ensenada to Colonet

(76 mi., 123 km.; 1:45 hrs.)

Ensenada's growth from a sleepy seaside town into a bustling metropolis is apparent as you head southward from the city's center. Highway 1 continues as a broad four-lane route as far as Maneadero, with sprawling shopping malls, apartment blocks, factories and other buildings lining the route. Eventually, those urban fixtures cede to a rich farming belt, where olives, chili peppers and assorted vegetables are the main crops. Countless produce stands crowd the roadside, tempting motorists with their pickled olives, honey, coconuts and bulging bags of assorted nuts.

NOTEWORTHY DINING

El Palomar restaurant, on Highway 1 in Santo Tomás, is a good, moderately priced dining alternative if you've opted to pass up Ensenada on your way south. The most unusual thing here: vintage currency notes from around the world adorn the walls. Open daily, 7 am-10 pm.

Beyond Maneadero, the coastal plain gives way to chaparral-clad hills, much like those of nearby Southern California, while the road grows narrower. Careful driving is essential as you cross a range of hills and drop into the broad and beautiful Santo Tomás Valley. Vineyards spread across the land in this, the second-largest wine district in Mexico. (The Guadalupe Valley near Ensenada is the biggest.) Beyond Santo Tomás, the road winds through more hills and narrow valleys en route to San Vicente, where beef and dairy cattle graze amid the pastures. Heading on to Colonet, the landscape grows drier and less rugged.

00.0 **Ensenada, at the intersection of boulevards Teniente Azueta and Costero (Lázaro Cárdenas). Follow Costero south to its end at the new naval base entrance, then turn left.**

01.9 **Junction with Highway 1, turn right.**

04.9 **El Ciprés, site of Ensenada Airport and a large military camp.**

06.5 **Turnoff to Estero Beach. The paved side road leads past several curio shops to a**

popular beach resort area. The sandy beaches and quiet waters of Bahía de Todos Santos are ideal for water sports.

08.6 Junction with road to Baja Country Club.

10.4 Maneadero, a community of about 55,000, at the junction with the paved road to Punta Banda (see Side Route to Punta Banda, page 162). This fast-growing agricultural market center has two Pemex stations, several small restaurants and many markets and other stores, including auto parts shops. Drivers should watch for unmarked speed bumps.

Side Routes

23.1 Ejido Uruápan, which offers camping, hunting and hot springs.

27.0 Junction with the graded dirt road to La Bocana and Puerto Santo Tomás (see Side Route to Puerto Santo Tomás, page 191).

29.0 Santo Tomás (see *Lodging & Campgrounds*, Chapter 15), a village that has become well known because of the domestic wine of the same name. A Pemex station and general store are located here. The ruins of Misión Santo Tomás lie just west of the trailer park.

45.9 Junction with the paved road to Ejido Eréndira (see Side Route to Ejido Eréndira, page 193).

52.2 A rough dirt road leads to the ruins of Misión San Vicente Ferrer, 0.5 mile to the west.

52.9 San Vicente, a busy farming center with a population of 6000. Facilities include two Pemex stations, several stores, cafes, motels and an auto parts store.

75.8 Colonet, at the junction to San Antonio del Mar (see Side Route to San Antonio del Mar, page 194). Colonet, a center for farmers and ranchers in the area, offers a selection of goods and services.

TRAVELOGUE

Colonet to Valle de San Quintín

(41.5 mi., 72.8 km.; 1 hr.)

A broad, flat plateau dotted with cultivated fields marks the terrain south of Colonet, while the highway widens slightly along this stretch. After descending a steep hill into the village of Camalú, the highway heads onto an expansive coastal plain, where more cropland spreads forth in all directions. Moving south toward Colonia Guerrero, the soaring Sierra San Pedro Mártir—Baja's highest mountain range—comes into view on the eastern flank, while the thin blue line of the Pacific lies off to the west.

Ripe tomatoes near San Quintín

Beyond Colonia Vicente Guerrero, the volcanic cones of Bahía de San Quintín gradually emerge to the south as the road makes a straight shot across miles more of level farmland. Tomatoes, strawberries and chili peppers rank among the primary crops across this fertile plain as you near the outskirts of San Quintín.

00.0 **Colonet, at the junction to San Antonio del Mar.**

01.7 **Junction with a good dirt road that leads to Cabo Colonet, site of a small fishing cooperative eight miles away.**

07.8 **San Telmo de Abajo, at the junction with an improved dirt road to San Telmo, Meling Ranch, the National Observatory and Mike's Sky Rancho (see Side Route to Meling Ranch, page 195).**

18.4 **Camalú, which has a Pemex station, clinic and a variety of supplies and services.**

27.1 **Colonia Vicente Guerrero (see *Lodging & Campgrounds*, Chapter 15) is a busy, fast-growing agricultural center. Facilities**

	include a motel, a hospital, Pemex station, telegraph and post office, stores and cafes. Vicente Guerrero also has the first traffic signal south of Maneadero.
27.5	**Turnoff to Posada Don Diego and Mesón de Don Pepe trailer parks.**
38.5	**Entrance to San Quintín (see *Lodging & Campgrounds*, Chapter 15).**
41.5	**Lázaro Cárdenas, at the military camp.**

Valle de San Quintín

Daybreak at Bahía San Quintín

We've made it clear already that San Quintín is not a major urban center, but with 22,000 souls it is the largest town for more than 700 miles along Highway 1—from Ensenada clear to Ciudad Constitución. It also has the only full-fledged bay between Ensenada and the Vizcaíno Peninsula, but even so, most travelers skip the town on their way up and down the peninsula.

There are two distinct faces to this town, one being the San Quintín Valley, a chain of homes and businesses strung haphazardly for several miles along Highway 1, with services of all types available for residents and travelers. Technically, there are two distinct settlements here—San Quintín and Lázaro Cárdenas—although they have grown into one large community with little to distinguish one from the

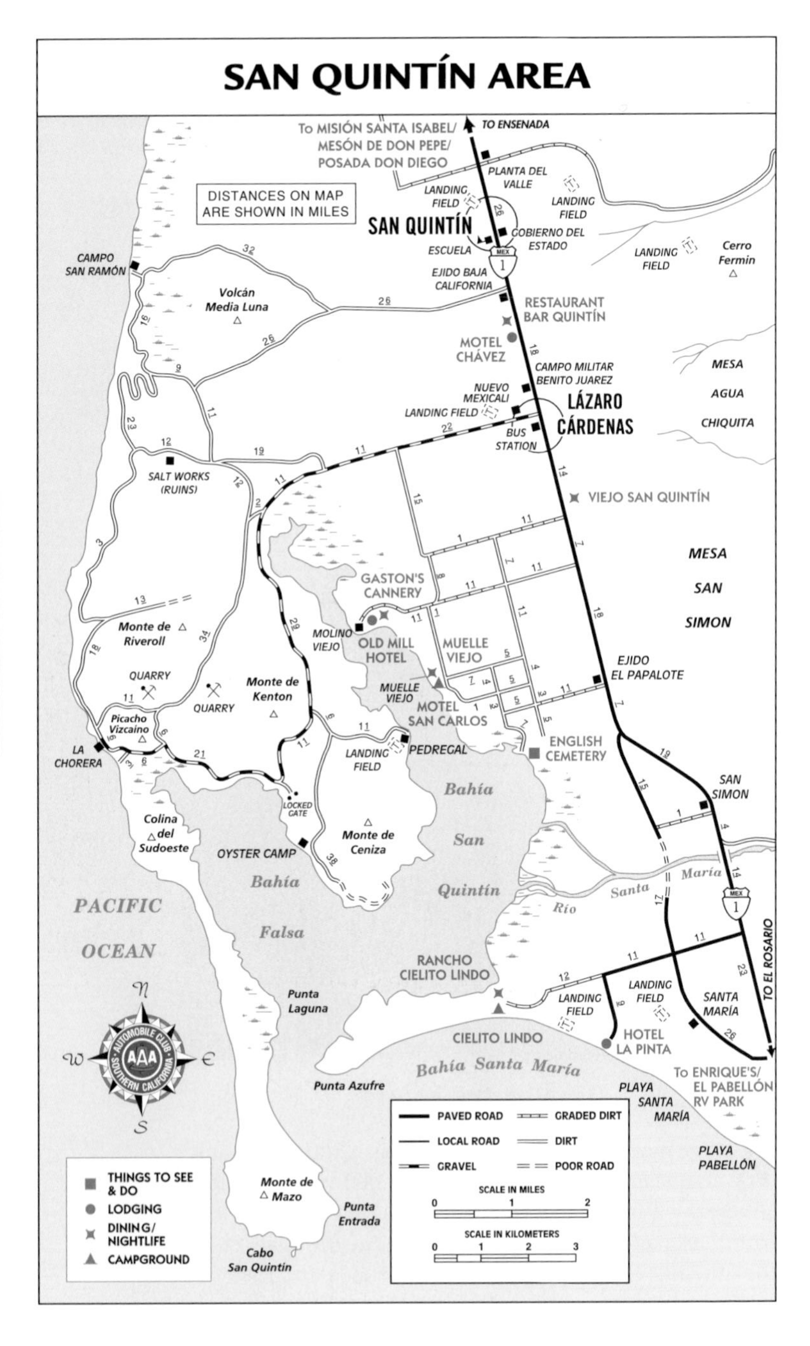

other. Together with Colonia Vicente Guerrero (about 10 miles farther north) they comprise the service center for a booming farming region that extends for many miles north and south along the coast, with strawberries, tomatoes, peppers, potatoes and barley being the main crops.

The other face is the nearby Bahía San Quintín, which ranks among the biggest tourist venues between Ensenada and Mulegé. Several hotels line the bay and serve as prime staging points for anglers and hunters, most from Southern California. The sheltered waters of this U-shaped bay separate the rich farmland of Valle de San Quintín from an impressive chain of six extinct volcanic peaks that rise to the west. Beyond them lies the open sea, reachable only by a series of remote dirt roads. Surfers sometimes ply these and other roads in search of empty waves.

WRONG-WAY WHALES

California gray whales are not unknown inside Bahía San Quintín. They sometimes make an errant turn during their southward migration to the lagoons of Baja California Sur and may remain in the bay for days before making their way back out to sea.

Top Attractions

ENGLISH CEMETERY

Time and the elements have taken their toll on the aged gravesites of this bayside graveyard, where the names have faded from the old wooden crosses. Only a single English tomb remains legible, on the left side of the main road leading into the cemetery. The cemetery does remain in use, though, as local families continue to bury their deceased here. The simple crosses of the English graves provide a poignant contrast from the elaborate marble and statuary work marking so many of the Mexican tombs. *About 2 miles west of Hwy 1, on the eastern shore of Bahía San Quintín.*

English and Mexican gravesites share space at San Quintín's English Cemetery

Outdoor Fun

FISHING

If you're at all familiar with ocean fishing off Southern California, then the San Quintín catch will hold few surprises for you. Water temperatures run about the same as farther north, ranging from 55 to 60 degrees in winter and 65 to 70 degrees during the summer months. Yellowfin, albacore and yellowtail are the prime game fish, although such warm-water gamesters as marlin and dorado are known to show up here during the summer. Other species that you'll likely hook include such Southern California standbys as sea bass, barracuda, bonito, rock cod, white fish and halibut.

"You Know Your're In Mexico When . . ."

A pack of local teens can plunk down a string of orange cones along a major highway to flag down motorists and offer cups of cola in exchange for donations for the big back-to-school dance—with the full blessing of the local constable. We saw it (and contributed) on Highway 1 in San Quintín.

Several outfits offer trips out of Bahía San Quintín, working the banks and secret hot spots up to 20 miles off the coast or around Isla San Martín, about five miles offshore. While most anglers come here for deep-sea fishing, you needn't leave terra firma for a rewarding experience. Playa Santa María, near the Hotel La Pinta along San Quintín's outer bay, is an excellent place for surf-fishing, or clam-digging when the tide goes out. Another good surf-fishing spot is Playa Socorro, about nine miles south on Highway 1 from the Hotel La Pinta turnoff.

If you're heading offshore, you'll find fishing boats available ranging from 22- or 23-foot skiffs *(pangas)* to full-fledged cruisers close to 30 feet long. Daily rates per boat range from $160 for a panga to more than $300 for a fully outfitted cruiser. All-expense packages including two days of fishing on a cruiser, food and lodging cost from $250 to $500 per person. License, bait and tackle may cost extra.

See Recreation in the *Appendix*, Chapter 16, for information on fishing licenses.

El Capitan Sportfishing *Near the Old Mill Hotel, 01152 (6) 162-17-16.* **Mike's Sportfishing and Lodge** *Near Pedregal colony and oyster farm on San Quintín's inner bay, (888) 862-6001.* **Old Mill Sportfishing** *At the Old Mill Hotel, (619) 691-7864.* **Pedro's Pangas** *Near the Old Mill Hotel, (888) 568-2252.* **San Quintín Sportfishing** *At Rancho Cielito Lindo Hotel, near Playa Santa María, (760) 951-5774. Website at www.sanquintin.com.* **Tiburón Pangas** *On San Quintín's inner bay next to Old Mill Hotel, 01152 (6) 170-08-21.*

HORSEBACK RIDING

Rental horses are available for riding along the beach at El Pabellón, just south of Playa Santa María along San Quintín's outer bay. For more information, visit any of the hotels along the inner or outer bay.

HUNTING

The wetlands around Bahía San Quintín are one of Baja's top hunting grounds, thanks largely to black brant, a type of goose that settles here between December and February. Hunters also bag their share of quail, doves and migrating ducks during the rest of the year.

See Recreation in the *Appendix*, Chapter 16, for information on hunting regulations.

Mexican law requires that you be accompanied by a guide while you are hunting, and several guide services are available. A typical full-day excursion on board a skiff *(panga)* in the inner bay costs about $120 to $130 per boat, which can hold up to three hunters. The fee includes transportation, decoys and cleaning.

El Capitan Sportfishing *Near the Old Mill Hotel, 01152 (6) 162-17-16.* **Tiburón Pangas** *On San Quintín's inner bay next to Old Mill Hotel, 01152 (6) 170-08-21.*

SURFING

Hard-core surfers yearning for empty waves should have their wishes fulfilled along the remote coastline near San Quintín. Of course they should be empty, given their great distance from town and the narrow, bumpy roads one must traverse to reach the top breaks. A few of these spots include Playa Santa María and Cielito Lindo, both beach breaks along the outer bay near the Hotel La Pinta; and Playa San Ramón, a beach break due west of San Quintín. Farther north, Rincón de Baja is a right point break on the coast west of Camalú that works on winter swells. Bear in mind that water temperatures in this area are similar to Southern California's, which means wet suits are desirable through most of the year.

Dining

Please tell us that you were not looking for valet parking, cloth napkins or some chichi type of ambiance. We didn't think so, 'cause if you were, you've come to the wrong neck of the peninsula. What San Quintín does offer is a decent variety of solid, no-nonsense eateries, mainly geared toward locals of modest means or long-distance trekkers. Countless *taquerias*, seafood stands and more upscale establishments are strung along the Highway 1 business strip. Off the highway, each of the bayside and beachside hotels have their own adjacent restaurant. In case you

WHAT WOULD THE HEALTH BOARD SAY?

On the menu at one local restaurant is an entrée listed as *cucarachas*—that's right, cockroaches! Turns out that's the local name, at least at this establishment, for *sincronizadas*, the popular ham, cheese and tortilla dish known and loved by millions of Mexicans.

couldn't guess, casual attire is the norm virtually anywhere you go. By no means, though, is San Quintín the final word on where to eat in this region. Beyond the town's confines, you're never too far from a place to eat along Highway 1 anywhere in this part of Baja.

Favorites

GASTON'S CANNERY **American**

A tad pricey for these parts, but the steak and seafood servings are generous at this popular fishermen's haunt. Best deal is to bring your own fresh-caught fish to the chef and have him fix it to your liking for $10—hot bread, soup or salad, and cheesecake included. With its woodsy interior, deer antlers on the walls and stone fireplace, this place feels more like some north woods hunting lodge than a Mexican bayside resort. *Next to the Old Mill Hotel on San Quintín Bay. No phone. Open daily 5:30 am-9:30 pm. $3.50-23.*

> **WATCH YOUR TRACKS**
>
> Planning on dinner at Muelle Viejo or Gaston's Cannery? Pay heed to the route you take to either of these bayside restaurants. It's easy to make the wrong turn and get lost after dark amid the daunting maze of unlit, dusty roads.

RESTAURANT BAR QUINTÍN **Mexican**

Peso pinching? Take a load off your feet and fill up on the spicy, decidedly authentic enchiladas or tacos with the usual fixings for around $4. Or after a hard day's drive, indulge in the steak and lobster for a tad less than $20 while choosing from a lengthy list of Baja wines. You'll be fine in your usual Baja duds, though, amid the typical, informal San Quintín ambiance. *On the west side of Hwy 1, next to the Motel Chávez, near kilometer 193. 01152 (6) 165-23-76. Open daily 7:30 am-10:30 pm; bar till 1 am. $3.25-18.50.*

VIEJO SAN QUINTÍN **Mexican**

Walk through the front doors, inspect the menu and admire the splashy paintings on the walls, and you'll know you're not in gringolandia anymore. Good food, hearty portions and sensible prices make this place a favorite with locals and savvy travelers alike. Breakfasts are outstanding, especially the *machaca*. We've found the service to be snappy here every time we've stopped in. *On east side of Hwy 1, near kilometer 197 and directly across from the post office. No phone. Open daily 8 am-9 pm. $2.80-8.*

Others

MISIÓN SANTA ISABEL **Mexican**

$3.25-9. On the east side of Hwy 1 at the north end of town, near kilometer 188. (6) 165-23-09. Open daily 7 am-11 pm.

MUELLE VIEJO **Steak/Seafood**

$7.50-20. Next to the Hotel San Carlos on San Quintín Bay. 01152 (6) 163-42-06. Open daily 7 am-10:30 pm.

RANCHO CIELITO LINDO **Steak/Seafood**

$5-20. Adjacent to hotel of the same name. Same turnoff as Hotel La Pinta, 3½ mi west of Hwy 1, near outer San Quintín Bay. 3-11 pm.

Lodging

Once more we're guessing that the finer things in life are not essential to your everyday existence, because if they are, you'll be in trouble here—or anywhere else between Ensenada and Loreto for that matter. By "finer things" we mean satellite TV, Jacuzzis, 24-hour room service and other trappings that we would take for granted in other locales. Don't bother looking for swimming pools, either—a concession to San Quintín's mild sea-side climate.

English milling equipment at the Old Mill Hotel

What you will find are plenty of basic, clean and inexpensive places to rest your head for the night, many priced well under $50. All told, San Quintín has the best lodging selection of any town in this region, with numerous hotels along Highway 1 and the nearby bay. The bayside inns attract a mostly non-Mexican crowd, many of them anglers from Southern California who head south to fish the bay and offshore waters. With that in mind, it's a good idea to call ahead if you'll need a room on a weekend night. Highway 1, for its part, draws a healthy cross section of Mexicans, gringos and other trekkers from around the world. If you'd rather stay somewhere else, Santo Tomás, San Vicente, Colonet and El Rosario all have basic, low-priced accommodations of one sort or another.

See *Lodging & Campgrounds,* Chapter 15.

LOCATION, LOCATION, LOCATION

If price and value were the only criteria, then the Hotel La Pinta south of San Quintín wouldn't be a great deal. Its setting along Playa Santa María, however, is unrivaled in northern Baja. Most rooms overlook this lovely beach, where "sleep by the surf" isn't a mere cliché.

If you're driving an RV or towing a trailer, you'll find that San Quintín has this region's best selection of developed campgrounds. "Developed" is the operative word here, because the rural reaches beyond San Quintín have plenty of other places to camp, from remote beaches to the high country of the Sierra San Pedro Mártir, many miles from the nearest paved road.

Valle de San Quintín to El Rosario

(37 mi., 53.2 km.; 1 hr.)

These are miles of transition—and anticipation—as the last vestiges of Southern California-style landscape fade in the rearview mirror while the great Central Desert looms just ahead. The road narrows on this stretch as the sprawling farmland and chaparral-covered slopes disappear and the terrain turns ever more barren. You'll cross a series of bridges—narrow by U.S. standards—fording the riverbed of the Río Santa María and several arroyos that are usually dry, as you near the south end of the San Quintín Valley.

Climbing high above the ocean, Highway 1 swings inland some 30 miles south of San Quintín as you prepare to leave the Pacific behind for the next 200 miles. From here you will enjoy commanding views of the ocean and endless miles of virgin coastline, while folds of barren, eroded badlands march away toward the northeast. Turning south once more, a broad inland valley spreads forth as the highway dips into El Rosario, near the northern fringe of the Central Desert.

00.0 **Lázaro Cárdenas, at the military camp.**

00.3 **First turnoff to Bahía San Quintín. This gravel road leads four miles to the shore. A better road follows and provides access to bayside hotels.**

02.4 **Junction with the dirt road to Muelle Viejo, the ruins of a pier constructed by an unsuccessful English colony, and to the Old Mill Hotel.**

08.6 **Junction with the paved road to the Hotel La Pinta and the Cielito Lindo Hotel. Each of these hotels is about three miles off the pavement.**

11.8 **Turnoff on a dirt road to El Pabellón RV Park.**

17.3	**Junction with the unmarked short dirt road to Playa del Socorro, a seaside village that offers sportfishing and scuba diving.**
37.3	**Rosario de Arriba, the primary settlement of El Rosario.**

El Rosario

For many years El Rosario marked the end of the pavement, which made it the final outpost of civilization in northern Baja California. Only the best-equipped and most determined explorers ventured south beyond here toward the Central Desert. That changed with the completion of the Transpeninsular Highway in 1973, and then by Baja's microwave telephone system.

Mama Espinosa's, Highway 1 in El Rosario

Even now, this quiet farming town of about 4000 maintains a certain frontier-like atmosphere, being the largest settlement between San Quintín and Guerrero Negro, more than 220 miles to the south. El Rosario also has the last reliable gas available to southbound travelers for 200 miles. Other services like lodging, restaurants and auto parts shops make this an important highway stop for travelers headed in both directions. (Mama Espinosa's restaurant is a traditional stop-off for many Highway 1 nomads.)

El Rosario actually consists of two communities, located near the west end of a valley formed by the Río del Rosario. The main settlement is El Rosario de Arriba, which lies along Highway 1 in the upper part of the valley. The much smaller Rosario de Abajo lies about a mile southwest via a dirt road on the south bank of the Río del Rosario. The latter settlement is home to ruins of Misión Nuestra Señora del Rosario. Also here is **Museo de El Rosario**, a small museum with a modest collection of photos and local artifacts. A good place to get more information on

FILL 'ER UP ... OR ELSE

If you have any doubts about your fuel supply, top off your tank before heading south from El Rosario. The next reliable gas is in Villa Jesús María, 200 miles away.

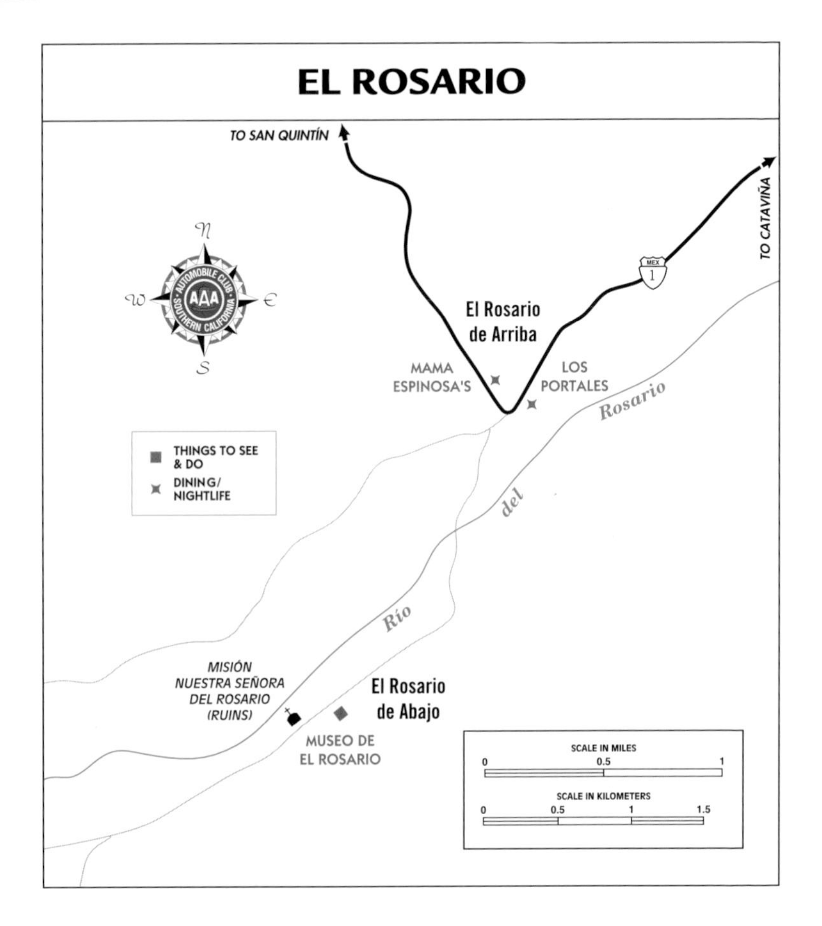

the museum and mission ruins is at Mama Espinosa's, near the bend of Highway 1 in El Rosario de Arriba.

MAMA ESPINOSA'S ♦ **Mexican/Seafood**

More than four decades before the Transpeninsular Highway went through, Doña Anita Grosso de Espinosa was making homemade Mexican dishes for early Baja trekkers. Her family is still at it, serving lobster omelets, tacos and burritos that rank among the best we've had in Baja. The beans, rice and other fare are also first-rate at this famed roadside establishment, which has gained enduring affection among legions of diehard Baja rats. *At the bend of Hwy 1. 01152 (6) 165-87-70. Open daily 6 am-10 pm. $4-14.*

LOS PORTALES **Seafood**

$3.20-13. On the south side of Hwy 1, just east of the bend, in El Rosario. 01152 (6) 165-88-80. Open daily 6 am-10 pm.

Side Routes

Highway 1 to La Bocana and Puerto Santo Tomás

(See map page 192.)

(20 mi., 32 km.; 1 hr.)

Superb scenery, camping and a host of other outdoor activities along a rugged stretch of Pacific shoreline draw adventurers to this, the first coastal access south of Punta Banda. Sturdy passenger cars can make the drive along the graded dirt road, which makes for a scenic highlight in its own right as it traverses the fertile Santo Tomás Valley to meet the ocean at La Bocana.

From Highway 1 the road branches off at Ejido Ajusco, just north of Santo Tomás. After passing vineyards, pasture land and grain fields, it narrows and hugs the north wall of the valley, where you may get a glimpse of the original road following the sandy streambed below. At 13.9 miles the road comes to a fork, heading left to a campground and cement plant, while the right fork leads to La Bocana and Puerto Santo Tomás. Bearing right, your first view of the ocean comes at 17 miles as the route swings northwest toward Puerto Santo Tomás. Scattered vacation homes, from simple trailers up to good-sized permanent dwellings, dot the coastline here. Pocket beaches, thick offshore kelp beds and rocky seaside cliffs conspire to lend a Central California feel as the final destination draws near. Careful driving is important here, as the road is rough in spots over these last few miles.

Situated on a sheltered cove beneath a rocky headland, Puerto Santo Tomás earns its living from the sea, both from commercial fishing and the visiting Americans who venture here to enjoy the coastal ambiance and related activities. Sportfishing is a big draw, with sheepshead, lingcod and rock cod lurking in the kelp beds, while yellowtail, calico bass and bonito all abound farther offshore. Hiking, kayaking, sailboarding and beachcombing enjoy a fan base as well. Trails suitable for motorcycles and

Autumn hues along the road to Puerto Santo Tomás

SIDE ROUTES from HIGHWAY 1 between SANTO TOMÁS and COLONET

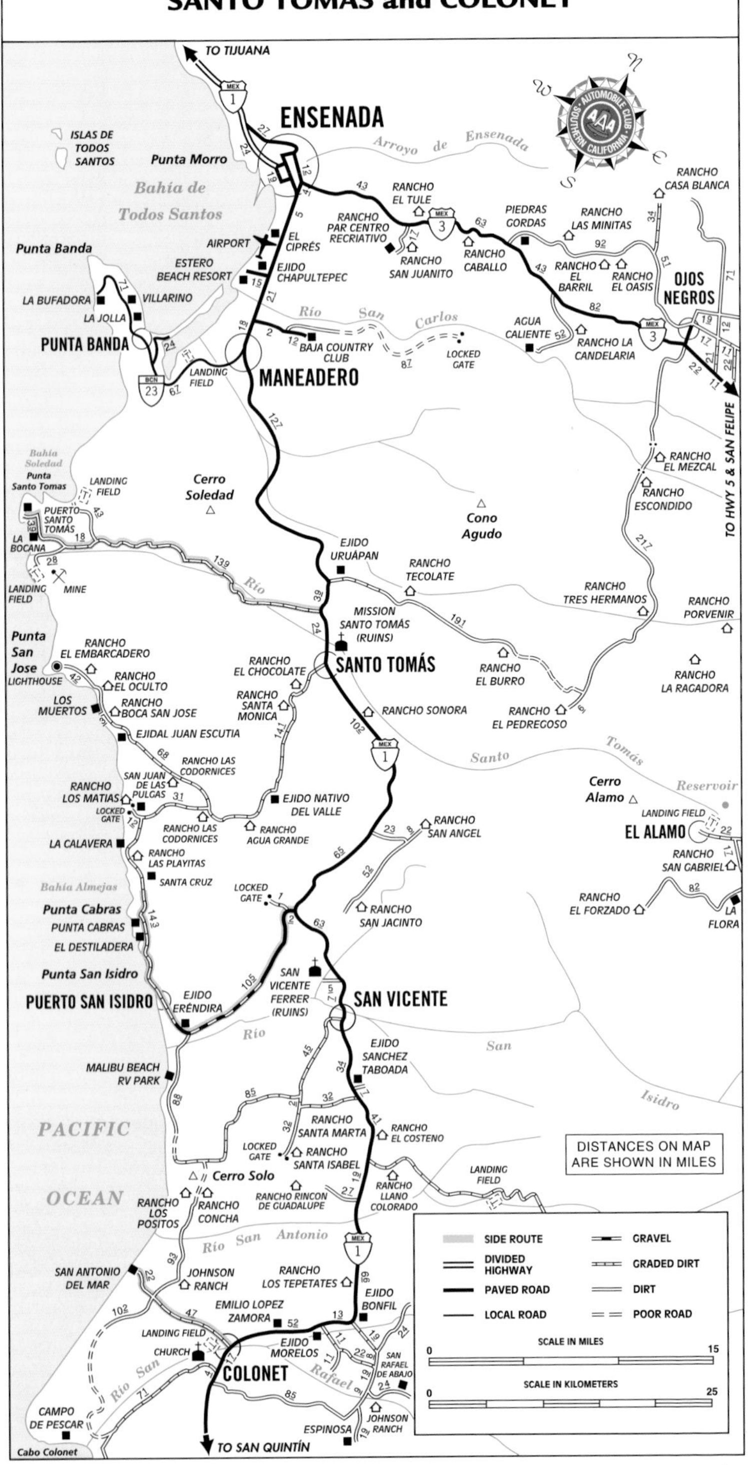

four-wheel-drive vehicles also crisscross the area.

Real Santo Tomás, a self-described tourist/fishing resort, is the main destination for most visitors, offering rustic cabins with gas stoves and electricity, campsites, a small store and boats for rent. A restaurant operates when the owners know that guests are coming, and a small hotel is under construction. For more information, call (714) 256-2577 or a number in Ensenada, 01152 (6) 174-56-83.

SLOW AND EASY

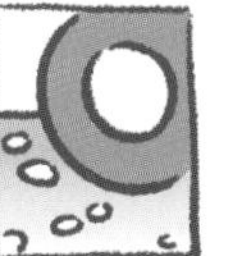

Loose gravel is one more reason to take it easy on unpaved roads like the one to La Bocana. Taking a bend too fast could send you skidding off the roadway and down a steep embankment.

Highway 1 to Ejido Eréndira, Puerto San Isidro and Points North

(See map page 192.)

(13 mi., 21 km.; 0:45 hr.)

A scenic swath of coastline with rugged cliffs, rocky shoals and spouting blowholes beckons travelers at the end of a side road winding through miles of picturesque landscape that is a page out of Southern California's rural past.

A signed junction, located seven miles north of San Vicente, marks the start of a paved road that follows the east wall of a shaded, sycamore-lined canyon and past chaparral-covered hillsides. About 6.4 miles from the main highway, the road crosses a bridge as the canyon empties into a large, wider arroyo, which the route then follows for 4.3 miles to a junction. Potholes mar this road in spots, but it's generally in good condition till it nears the ocean, where the pavement ends and is replaced by a largely rough dirt surface. To the right is the farming community of Ejido Eréndira, located just inland from the ocean.

Typical northern Baja scenery, en route to Ejido Eréndira

For a community of its modest size, Ejido Eréndira comes well equipped with markets, cafes, a hotel and Pemex station. Cabins, RV slots and fishing boats are all available for rent. One mile beyond Ejido Eréndira the road reaches the beach and swings north as the pavement ends. It follows the coast to Puerto San Isidro, site of a government-operated oyster and abalone hatchery and a tiny settlement of seaside homes. The road continues northward along the rocky coastline for five miles to Punta Cabras, a collection of rustic beach homes and an electric plant under construction.

There is little in the way of sandy beach, but the rugged headlands, lush kelp beds and rocky shelves jutting from the water make this ride another scenic treat. Perhaps the biggest surprise are the several blowholes—miniature versions of La Bufadora near Ensenada—that send their salty plumes spraying along the offshore reefs. North of Punta Cabras is a long sandy beach, the crescent-shaped Bahía Almejas.

Colonet to San Antonio del Mar

(See map page 192.)

(8 mi., 12 km.; 0:30 hr.)

If it's your first time at San Antonio del Mar, try to avoid returning to Highway 1 after dark. It's very easy to lose your way amid the criss-crossing dirt roads.

Camping, surf-fishing and clam-digging are the main activities that draw visitors to this remote stretch of coastline west of Colonet. A long, extremely wide beach meets the Pacific here, backed by good-sized sand dunes and sprawling wetlands that attract a wide variety of marine birds.

The partly graded dirt road leading here leaves Highway 1 at a signed junction at the north edge of Colonet, and is in fairly good condition all the way to the coast; passenger cars should have no problems in dry weather. The route follows sparsely vegetated, gently rolling terrain for the first 4.3 miles, when a sweeping view of the ocean comes into view and the road makes a short but steep descent to the coastal lowland. At 4.7 miles is a junction, where a turn to the right leads about a half-mile to a string of beach homes, with access to the beach available.

Heading farther north, on a road leading through the coastal wetlands, brings you to Rancho Los Positos, a small settlement atop a seaside bluff with commanding views of the coastline in both directions. Camping is available for a small nightly fee and the landowners have lots available for lease.

Highway 1 to Meling Ranch

(See map page 196.)

(31 mi., 50 km.; 1:45 hrs.)

For decades, Meling Ranch has maintained a Baja California tradition for rustic but comfortable lodging, hearty meals and solitude amid the foothills of the Sierra San Pedro Mártir. That tradition appeared threatened following the 1998 death of family matriarch Aida Meling, who was born and raised at the ranch, and had managed the 2500-acre spread for more than 40 years. The ranch remained in family hands after the elder Meling's death, but closed for more than two years while surviving kin sought someone new to put in charge.

Finally, in the fall of 2000, the ranch reopened and once more hosts guests who make the long drive up from Highway 1 or fly in to the adjacent dirt airstrip. The ranch offers hiking, fishing, hunting and mule trips deep into the mountain wilderness, and also serves as a milestone on the long off-pavement drive from Highway 1 to the alpine wilds of Parque Nacional Sierra de San Pedro Mártir.

Wide and graded most of the way, the road to the ranch is suitable for passenger cars with good tires during dry weather. Beyond the ranch, however, only sturdy, high-clearance vehicles should take on the drive upward to the national park. From the village of San Telmo de Abajo on Highway 1, about eight miles south of Colonet, the road winds between low, scrub-covered hills for 5.8 miles to the small village of San Telmo, which is picturesquely nestled in a small bowl-shaped valley. Beyond San Telmo the road passes Ejido Sinaloa and enters hilly country. At mileage 17.3 is the junction with a road on the left leading to Rancho Buenavista. The route to Meling Ranch now ascends a rocky arroyo, emerges onto a high ridge and winds through low hills to a junction at mileage 31.1. The turnoff for Meling Ranch is 0.4 mile ahead; the main road continues to the National Observatory.

Meling Ranch, also known as San José, came into being through a marriage uniting two pioneering families—the Melings and the Johnsons. Both families settled in northern Baja California in the early 1900s. The ranch house, rebuilt after the ranch itself was destroyed in 1911 during the Mexican Revolution, is a fine example of structures from that era.

The ranch accommodates guests at $75 per night for room and board, and reservations are necessary at least seven

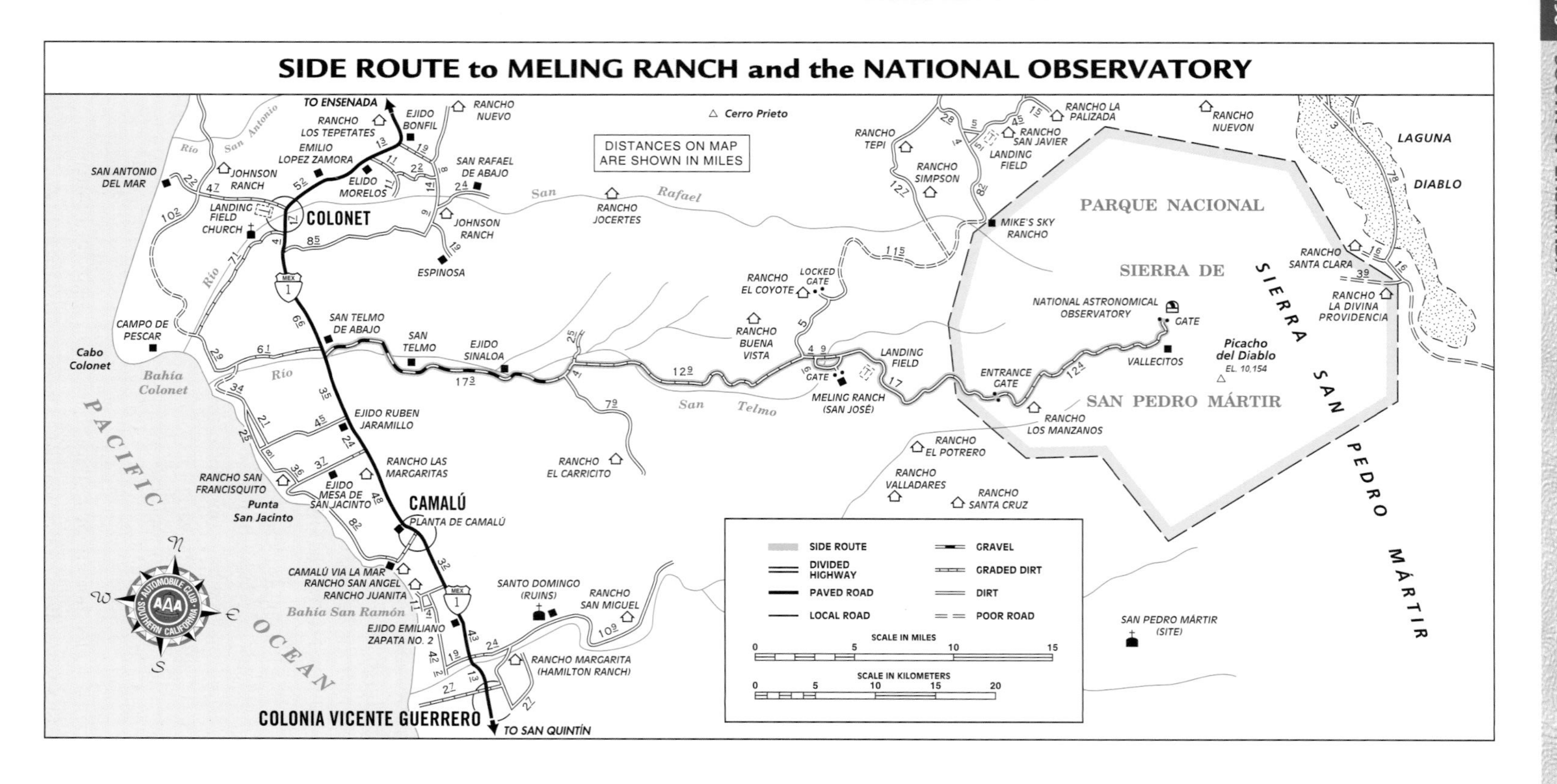
SIDE ROUTE to MELING RANCH and the NATIONAL OBSERVATORY
DISTANCES ON MAP ARE SHOWN IN MILES
PARQUE NACIONAL SIERRA DE SAN PEDRO MÁRTIR
SIERRA SAN PEDRO MÁRTIR
LAGUNA DIABLO
Picacho del Diablo
EL. 10,154
NATIONAL ASTRONOMICAL OBSERVATORY
GATE
VALLECITOS
ENTRANCE GATE
RANCHO LOS MANZANOS
MIKE'S SKY RANCHO
RANCHO LA PALIZADA
RANCHO SAN JAVIER
LANDING FIELD
RANCHO NUEVON
RANCHO SANTA CLARA
RANCHO LA DIVINA PROVIDENCIA
RANCHO SIMPSON
RANCHO TEPI
LOCKED GATE
RANCHO EL COYOTE
RANCHO BUENA VISTA
MELING RANCH (SAN JOSÉ)
RANCHO EL POTRERO
RANCHO SANTA CRUZ
RANCHO VALLADARES
SAN PEDRO MÁRTIR (SITE)
Cerro Prieto
San Rafael
San Telmo
RANCHO JOCERTES
RANCHO EL CARRICITO
EJIDO SINALOA
SAN TELMO
SAN TELMO DE ABAJO
RANCHO NUEVO
SAN RAFAEL DE ABAJO
JOHNSON RANCH
ESPINOSA
EJIDO BONFIL
RANCHO LOS TEPETATES
EMILIO LOPEZ ZAMORA
EJIDO MORELOS
COLONET
TO ENSENADA
LANDING FIELD
CHURCH
SAN ANTONIO DEL MAR
San Antonio
Río
CAMPO DE PESCAR
Bahía Colonet
Cabo Colonet
RANCHO SAN FRANCISQUITO
Punta San Jacinto
EJIDO MESA DE SAN JACINTO
EJIDO RUBEN JARAMILLO
RANCHO LAS MARGARITAS
CAMALÚ
PLANTA DE CAMALÚ
CAMALÚ VIA LA MAR
RANCHO SAN ANGEL
RANCHO JUANITA
Bahía San Ramón
EJIDO EMILIANO ZAPATA NO. 2
SANTO DOMINGO (RUINS)
RANCHO SAN MIGUEL
RANCHO MARGARITA (HAMILTON RANCH)
TO SAN QUINTÍN
COLONIA VICENTE GUERRERO
PACIFIC OCEAN
SIDE ROUTE
DIVIDED HIGHWAY
PAVED ROAD
LOCAL ROAD
GRAVEL
GRADED DIRT
DIRT
POOR ROAD
SCALE IN MILES
SCALE IN KILOMETERS
AUTOMOBILE CLUB SOUTHERN CALIFORNIA
AAA

days in advance. For more information or to reserve a space, call Baja Reservations at (888) 411-2252.

Meling Ranch to the National Observatory

(See map page 196.)

(30 mi., 48 km.; 1:15 hrs.)

The remarkably clear air atop the high Sierra San Pedro Mártir prompted the Mexican government to build a modern astronomical observatory on a rounded summit 9000 feet in elevation, across from Picacho del Diablo, highest point on the peninsula. Thanks to the graded road built to aid construction of the observatory, visitors now have a chance to explore Parque Nacional Sierra de San Pedro Mártir —a magnificent region of rocky peaks, pine forests, streams and meadows. The road to the observatory is rough and steep, requiring high-clearance vehicles. Snowfalls are common in winter, and are often measured in feet at higher elevations.

National Observatory

From the Meling Ranch turnoff, the route meanders through open fields and foothills before climbing into the mountains. This road demands extra caution in several areas, with its steep drop-offs, and rocky, deeply rutted spots that can take their toll on any vehicle. The road enters the forest rather abruptly at Corona de Abajo Meadow (elevation 6825), which also marks the park entrance. No entry fee is charged, but the park does accept donations.

Beyond the entrance station, the road continues for another 12 miles to a highway work station, where a gated road leads to the observatory. Tours of the observatory take place on selected Saturdays during the warmer months; the road is closed at other times. Gazing at the nighttime sky, it's no surprise the National Autonomous University of Mexico chose this location to place the nation's largest telescope; viewing conditions are considered among the best on Earth. The earthbound views are likewise impressive; from the observatory and nearby viewpoints they take in Picacho del Diablo, the Colorado Desert and the Gulf of California. To the west is an inspiring vista of hills all the way to the Pacific Coast.

See *GreatestHits*, Chapter 3, for more on Parque Nacional Sierra de San Pedro Mártir.

Chapter 7

Central Desert

Somewhere south of El Rosario, as Mexico Highway 1 twists its way through miles of barren hills and mesas, the sharp eye will catch sight of the first gaunt cirio tree, clinging precariously to some rocky slope. Dozens and then hundreds more soon follow, and with them vast boulder fields teeming with sagebrush, yucca, elephant trees and towering cardón cacti, all this backed by ruddy mountains, chalk-colored buttes and a bright blue sky that seems to go on forever.

By most accounts the mythical place known as the "real Baja" begins somewhere far south of the border fence at San Ysidro, and longtime Baja fans will forever disagree on just where it begins. All agree, though, the Central Desert—with its immense open spaces, magnificent flora and dusty back roads leading to far-off haunts—captures the essence of Baja California.

But while that's so, it's hard to paint this region with even the broadest of strokes, given its tremendous size, and diversity in climate and geog-

Fishing boats at dawn, San Francisquito

raphy. From a geographer's standpoint, the Central Desert runs from El Rosario almost to La Paz, comprising more than half the peninsula's total territory. Our scaled-down version is considerably smaller but is still huge, spanning coast to coast and more than 300 miles along Highway 1, with untold wonders looming far from the pavement.

Leaving El Rosario, the desert tips its hand slowly as the bleak landscape gradually transforms to a prolific wonderland of strange rock formations, cacti of all manner, and a bounty of other desert flora. So it goes for the next 150 miles as Highway 1 bobs and weaves through the heart of the desert with arid hills, palm oases, desolate lakebeds and the famed rock garden near Cataviña.

In time, the rugged topography gives way to a flat—some would say boring—expanse of coastal plain known as the Vizcaíno Desert. Gray and tan are the primary colors of this lonesome expanse, where coastal winds send clouds and fog scudding low across the sandy terrain. Still, this forlorn place enjoys a stark beauty in its own right, and harbors one of Baja's greatest attractions of all. Each winter in the sheltered waters of Scammon's Lagoon and Estero de San José, the cycle of life begins for thousands of California gray whales as mothers bear their calves and

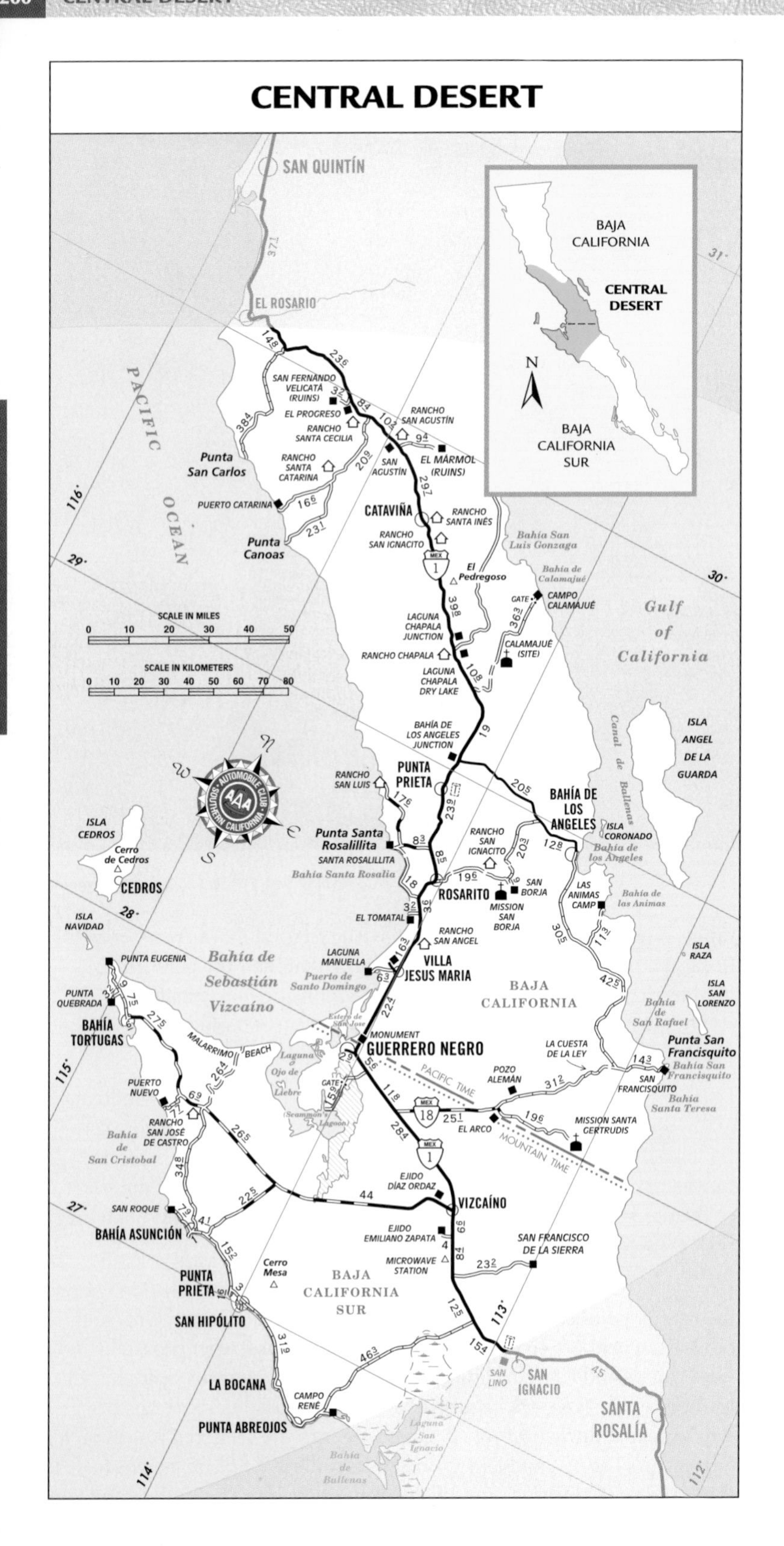
CENTRAL DESERT
SAN QUINTÍN
EL ROSARIO
BAJA CALIFORNIA
CENTRAL DESERT
BAJA CALIFORNIA SUR
N
PACIFIC OCEAN
SAN FERNANDO VELICATÁ (RUINS)
EL PROGRESO
RANCHO SANTA CECILIA
RANCHO SANTA CATARINA
RANCHO SAN AGUSTÍN
SAN AGUSTÍN
EL MÁRMOL (RUINS)
Punta San Carlos
PUERTO CATARINA
Punta Canoas
CATAVIÑA
RANCHO SANTA INÉS
RANCHO SAN IGNACITO
Bahía San Luis Gonzaga
Bahía de Calamajué
El Pedregoso
GATE
CAMPO CALAMAJUÉ
Gulf of California
LAGUNA CHAPALA JUNCTION
RANCHO CHAPALA
CALAMAJUÉ (SITE)
LAGUNA CHAPALA DRY LAKE
SCALE IN MILES
0 10 20 30 40 50
SCALE IN KILOMETERS
0 10 20 30 40 50 60 70 80
BAHÍA DE LOS ANGELES JUNCTION
ISLA ANGEL DE LA GUARDA
Canal de Ballenas
AUTOMOBILE CLUB SOUTHERN CALIFORNIA
AAA
RANCHO SAN LUIS
PUNTA PRIETA
BAHÍA DE LOS ANGELES
ISLA CORONADO
Bahía de los Angeles
ISLA CEDROS
Cerro de Cedros
CEDROS
Punta Santa Rosalillita
SANTA ROSALILLITA
Bahía Santa Rosalia
RANCHO SAN IGNACITO
ROSARITO
SAN BORJA
MISSION SAN BORJA
LAS ANIMAS CAMP
Bahía de las Animas
ISLA NAVIDAD
EL TOMATAL
RANCHO SAN ANGEL
ISLA RAZA
PUNTA EUGENIA
Bahía de Sebastián Vizcaíno
LAGUNA MANUELLA
VILLA JESUS MARIA
Puerto de Santo Domingo
BAJA CALIFORNIA
ISLA SAN LORENZO
PUNTA QUEBRADA
Bahía de San Rafael
BAHÍA TORTUGAS
Estero de San José
MONUMENT
GUERRERO NEGRO
MALARRIMO BEACH
Laguna Ojo de Liebre
LA CUESTA DE LA LEY
Punta San Francisquito
Bahía San Francisquito
PACIFIC TIME
POZO ALEMÁN
SAN FRANCISQUITO
PUERTO NUEVO
GATE
Bahía Santa Teresa
RANCHO SAN JOSÉ DE CASTRO
(Scammon's Lagoon)
MEX 18
EL ARCO
MISSION SANTA GERTRUDIS
MOUNTAIN TIME
Bahía de San Cristobal
MEX 1
EJIDO DÍAZ ORDAZ
VIZCAÍNO
SAN ROQUE
BAHÍA ASUNCIÓN
EJIDO EMILIANO ZAPATA
SAN FRANCISCO DE LA SIERRA
MICROWAVE STATION
Cerro Mesa
PUNTA PRIETA
BAJA CALIFORNIA SUR
SAN HIPÓLITO
SAN LINO
SAN IGNACIO
LA BOCANA
CAMPO RENÉ
SANTA ROSALÍA
PUNTA ABREOJOS
Laguna San Ignacio
Bahía de Ballenas
116° 29° 30° 31° 28° 115° 27° 113° 114° 112°

prepare for the long voyage north to their Arctic feeding grounds. Nearby these two lagoons is the "urban center" of the Central Desert in the town of Guerrero Negro, whose 12,000 souls make this the largest settlement for hundreds of miles. Aside from the whales, Guerrero Negro is not much of a tourist town, but does make a good springboard to the many adventures that await within a few hours' drive.

Eighteen side routes lead into Baja's Central Desert, by far the most of any region on the peninsula.

In desert canyons to the east, missions San Borja and Santa Gertrudis stand frozen in time, surrounded by granite walls and ranchland that hasn't changed since the Spaniards laid their cornerstones more than 200 years ago. Yet the missions are comparatively new in a region where Indians had long before left their mark with magnificent rock paintings. Hidden in remote mountain gorges, some of those works are considered among the most impressive on earth. Farther east still lies the gulf coast and remote outposts like San Francisquito and Bahía de los Angeles, which offer outstanding sportfishing, water sports of all types, and scenic grandeur that can only be seen to be believed. Somewhere in the midst of it all is the soul of Baja California.

Experience...

- The amusing discovery that bovine skulls half-buried in the sand, buzzards glaring down from crooked-armed cactus plants and other age-old desert clichés actually exist in real life.
- Little block houses in garish tones of chartreuse, purple and pink clashing comedically with the barren brown hills of Bahía Tortugas.
- The sense of dog-tired, body-trembling accomplishment known only to those who have just driven 120 miles of gravel-strewn, washboard-surface road.
- That eerie, edge-of-the-earth feeling you get as you step from your vehicle at the tip of the Vizcaíno Peninsula, 90 miles from the pavement's end.
- Walking beneath a rocky ledge, staring up in silent wonderment at an enormous fresco of Indian pictographs, painted hundreds of years before the first European explorers set foot in the Americas.
- Tears of primal joy rolling down the face of a fellow traveler after stroking the head of a 45-foot gray whale in Scammon's Lagoon.

TRAVELOGUE

El Rosario to Cataviña

(76 mi., 122 km.; 2 hrs.)

Averaging only about 6 inches of rainfall a year, El Rosario qualifies as a desert, though it's not a particularly picturesque one, surrounded by barren hills and canyons in muted shades of beige and brown. That changes soon enough, however, as Highway 1 turns eastward, traversing the irrigated croplands of the wide Arroyo del Rosario for a few miles before climbing out through a range of low, deeply eroded hills. In short time, the flora of the Central Desert begins sprouting amid the crooked terrain and the landscape takes on the classic imagery of Baja.

With its blue skies, expansive views and plethora of unique vegetation, the Central Desert of Baja California easily ranks as one of North America's most fascinating desert regions. Range after range of hills separated by broad valleys follow before Highway 1 enters the so-called "Rock Garden," a breathtaking region of huge boulder formations interspersed with cirio trees, giant cardón cacti and other plants for which Baja is famous. With a few changes in vegetation, the landscape closely resembles California's Joshua Tree National Park.

Rock garden near Cataviña

In return, this stretch of road requires careful driving, with countless bends, sharp drop-offs and several deep arroyos that are subject to flash flooding. In times past the road has been rough and marred with countless potholes, although a recent repaving project has largely cured that problem—at least for now. In the heart of the Rock Garden are the tiny outposts of Cataviña and Rancho Santa Inés. Again, bear in mind that El Rosario has the last reliable gas for the next 200 miles.

00.0 El Rosario.

04.4 A bridge carries Highway 1 across Arroyo del Rosario.

09.0 Cirio trees begin to appear, their weird forms reaching skyward in a profusion of

shapes. Aside from a small stand in Sonora on the Mexican mainland, these plants grow nowhere else in the world.

14.2 Junction with a good dirt road leading 39 miles to Punta San Carlos and a network of roads which provide access to several fishing camps.

37.9 Signed junction with an unpaved road to the adobe ruins of Misión San Fernando Velicatá, founded in 1769 by Father Junípero Serra, who went on to establish Alta California's chain of missions. Passenger cars can make this trip in dry weather.

39.6 El Progreso, which has a cafe. Once a busy construction camp, El Progreso is now all but abandoned.

46.4 Junction with the road to Puerto Catarina and Punta Canoas (see Side Route to Puerto Catarina, page 215).

54.3 San Agustín, which consists of an abandoned government-built trailer park and a highway maintenance camp. From behind the camp a sandy road leads to Rancho San Agustín.

56.6 Junction with a good dirt road leading to El Mármol (see Side Route to El Mármol, 216). Near the junction are two cafes.

Side Routes

64.0 Highway 1 now enters a region of impressive, boulder-strewn countryside. The Mexican government has created a park here, and the natural environment is protected by federal law.

73.9 Arroyo de Cataviñacito, a deep arroyo with tall blue fan palms and occasional pools of water. The first elephant trees appear here, their short, fat trunks seemingly squatting among the boulders.

76.0 Cataviña (see *Lodging & Campgrounds*, Chapter 15), set in the midst of "rock garden" scenery. A market, two cafes and a mechanic's shop are on the left; on the right is a government-built trailer park and the Hotel La Pinta, which sometimes sells gasoline. Hiking across the beautiful desert landscape is possible in any direction from the village.

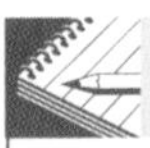

TRAVELOGUE

Cataviña to Bahía de los Angeles Junction

(65 mi., 105 km.; 1:30 hrs.)

The jumbled boulders of the "rock garden" stretch some ways past Cataviña, giving way eventually to mesas and buttes as Highway 1 heads southeast across the Central Desert. The last word on the grandeur of this geological wonderland comes some way south of the garden in the form of El Pedregoso. Comprised entirely of jumbled boulders, this massive heap of granite stands solitary alongside the roadway. Before the completion of Highway 1, it was a major landmark for Baja travelers—impossible to miss and unmistakable in form.

El Pedregoso, south of Cataviña

The rocky terrain begins to cede after the road crosses a narrow arroyo, then climbs to a 2700-foot summit before dropping quickly to the edge of a dry lake. The surroundings grow more and more barren as the route meanders through a range of low hills, rising to a 2200-foot saddle before descending once more to the basin of Laguna Chapala. This vast, desolate lakebed is dry most of the time, filling with shallow water or turning to mud only after the heaviest of rains.

Another range of low, barren hills looms next, beyond which the route crosses a sandy plain to the junction with the road to Bahía de los Angeles. Along these miles is an outstanding showcase of central Baja's magnificent flora; cirio, cardón, cholla, ocotillo, elephant trees and yucca válida all abound for much of the way.

00.0 Cataviña.

00.7 Junction with the 0.8-mile paved road to Rancho Santa Inés, which offers a clinic, motel, campground, cafe, a gravel airstrip and information for off-road explorers.

07.4 Rancho San Ignacito. In late 1973, road crews working north and south met here as they completed the paving of Highway 1. A small monument on the west side of the highway marks the spot.

18.6 El Pedregoso, a mountain composed entirely of jumbled boulders. Before the completion of the paved highway, this was an important landmark for peninsula travelers.

33.4 Laguna Chapala Junction. Here a dirt road, signed Calamajué, provides access to Bahía San Luis Gonzaga and other points along the northeastern shore of the peninsula. At the junction is a cafe.

34.2 Rancho Chapala. Stretching away to the east is the broad expanse of Laguna Chapala, with its bed of cracked clay.

50.9 Junction with a rough road to Campo Calamajué, a fish camp.

64.2 Junction with the paved road to Bahía de los Angeles (see Side Route to Bahía de Los Angeles, page 217). A highway patrol station is located here. The junction is sometimes called Punta Prieta, although the original settlement bearing this name is eight miles to the south.

TRAVELOGUE

Bahía de los Angeles Junction to Guerrero Negro

(80 mi., 129 km.; 1:45 hrs.)

Yet another transition zone looms as Highway 1 leaves one distinct desert behind for another. The extensive foliage and rugged topography of the Central Desert disappears—for a while—as the route heads due south toward the Pacific coast and the flat, lonely expanse of the Vizcaíno Desert.

Some 15 miles of sandy flatlands mark the outset of this drive, beyond which the road worms its way into another set of hills. Elephant trees and cirios predominate here as the vegetation gradually thins out, a harbinger of things to come. Use the utmost caution here as the sharp curves, steep drop-offs and a narrow roadway require constant vigilance. The road straightens out as you approach the village of Rosarito, where a range of wide, flat buttes hugs the eastern horizon.

> **TIME OUT**
>
> Remember to set your watch one hour ahead when you head south across the 28th parallel, the dividing point between the Pacific and Mountain time zones.

Beyond Rosarito, the highway gradually descends toward the Vizcaíno Desert and Guerrero Negro. The air turns cool and a steady breeze almost always blows in from the nearby ocean, bringing frequent fog and low clouds with it. Scattered clumps of saltbrush are the primary vegetation as you make your way across this, one of the most desolate stretches anywhere along Highway 1.

00.0 Junction to Bahía de los Angeles.

08.4 Junction with the short paved road to the village of Punta Prieta. A bustling construction camp during the paving of Highway 1, Punta Prieta is now a sleepy little hamlet. Facilities include a store, a cafe, a small military camp and a highway maintenance station. On the east side of the highway is a paved airstrip.

18.3 Brief view of the Pacific Ocean from a low summit.

Side Routes

23.9 Junction with a rough gravel road to Santa Rosalillita (see Side Route to Santa Rosalillita, page 221).

Side Routes

32.1 Rosarito, a village with a store, a cafe and a shrine. Rosarito also marks the junction with the dirt road to Mission San Borja (see Side Route to Mission San Borja, page 223).

39.0 Junction with a dirt road leading north along isolated beaches for 18 miles to Santa Rosalillita. This area is popular with surfers.

42.5 Junction with a rough dirt road to El Tomatal.

49.2 Turnoff to Rancho San Angel.

58.7 Villa Jesús María, a farming village with a Pemex station, two cafes and a small store. A paved road leads west to Ejido Morelos, a government-sponsored cattle-raising project, and Laguna Manuela, a lagoon with a fish camp and a sandy beach.

78.1	The 28th parallel separates the states of Baja California and Baja California Sur. Erected on the latitude line is a 140-foot-high steel monument in the form of a stylized eagle. On the west side of the monument are Hotel La Pinta, a trailer park and a new army base. Military personnel are almost always on duty here, checking vehicles for guns, drugs and other contraband. On a 2000 research trip, southbound drivers also had to pay a 10-peso fee to have their vehicles sprayed with an insecticide designed to prevent the spread of pests threatening agriculture.
80.0	Junction with the paved road to the town of Guerrero Negro, two miles to the west.

Guerrero Negro

Salt fields near Guerrero Negro

Spread along the edge of a desolate coastal plain where a chill wind relentlessly blows in from the sea, Guerrero Negro may at first glance seem like the least likely of tourist towns in all of Baja. But with its massive salt works and the annual arrival of thousands of gray whales, this friendly town of 12,000 has two claims to fame that have earned it prominence far beyond the Baja peninsula.

WHAT'S IN A NAME?

The name "Guerrero Negro" is the Spanish translation of *Black Warrior*, a Hawaii-based whaling ship that was wrecked at the entrance of Scammon's Lagoon in 1858.

If you drive around town at all, it soon becomes apparent that Guerrero

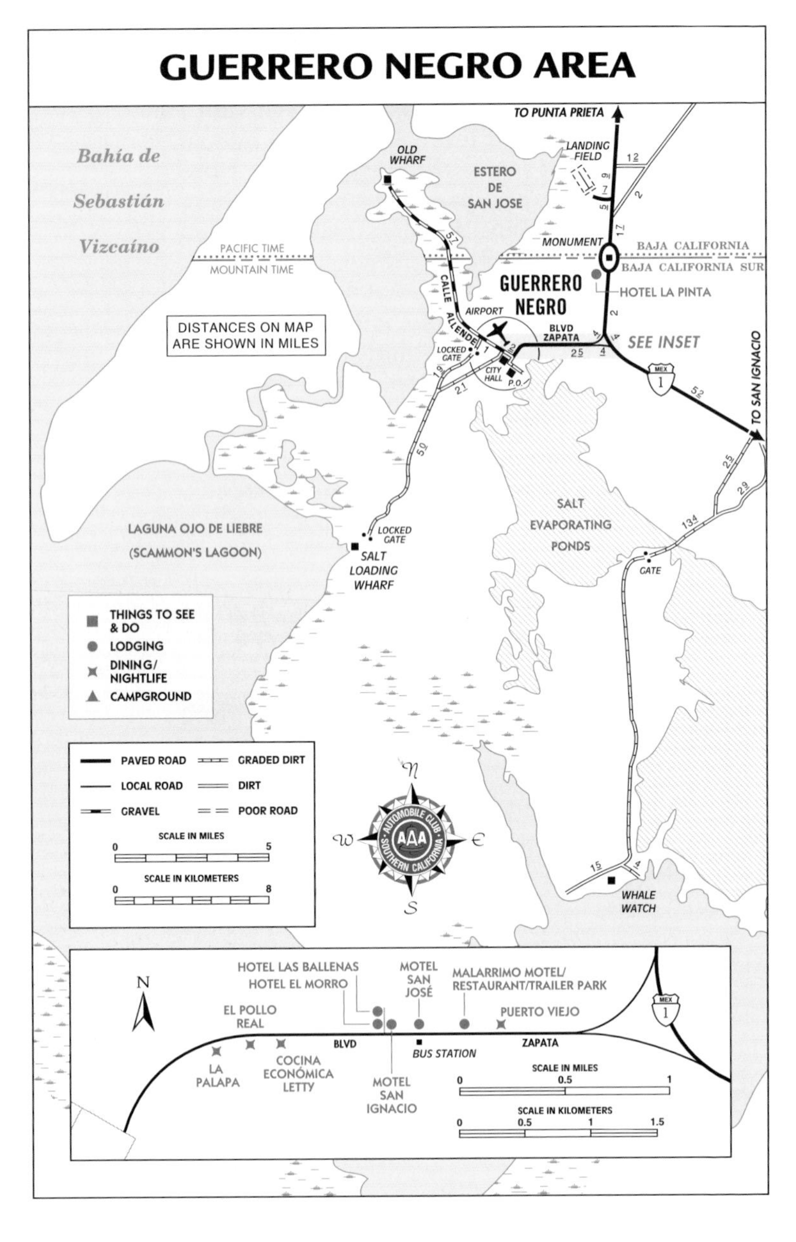

Negro is really two towns in one. To the east is Boulevard Zapata, the only part many visitors see, with its numerous hotels, restaurants, markets and other tourist services. Farther west there's the company town operated by Exportadora de Sal, the Mexican government/Mitsubishi Corp. consortium that purports to be the world's largest producer of salt. With its spotless streets, manicured lawns, and orderly rows of well-kept homes, the company town stands in striking contrast to the rather disheveled appearance of the surrounding neighborhoods.

Keeping Your Cool in Guerrero Negro

If it's your first time here, the mild climate may prove to be a surprise in its own right. Although it's more than 400 miles below the border, Guerrero Negro remains cool and foggy throughout the year, tempered by the chilly waters of the nearby Pacific. High temperatures during summer run in the low- to mid-70s, while winter days average about 10 degrees cooler—about the same as coastal Southern California. Rainfall, meanwhile, is extremely light and the few plants that do live in this desert region rely on fog as their main source of moisture.

The company's stamp extends well beyond the town limits, with its thousands of evaporating ponds to the south and west, where it harvests salt for shipment to ports all along the Pacific Rim. When flooded with seawater, the ponds quickly dry beneath the desert sun, leaving the salt behind, ready to be scooped up and shipped offshore. Backed by a few low-slung sand dunes and wind-blown shrubs, the vast white fields provide an eerie feel akin to some far-off polar wasteland.

Of course the salt works are just a footnote for most of the tourists who flock here each winter to visit Scammon's Lagoon (Laguna Ojo de Liebre), the largest calving ground for the gray whales. Scammon's and nearby Estero San José are the northernmost destinations for the famed mammals on their annual migration from the seas off Alaska. Hunted to near extinction in the late 19th and early 20th centuries, the whales have put on a dramatic recovery in recent decades, and today form the backbone for a thriving seasonal tourist industry. When the whales depart, the vast wetlands around the lagoons remain a birdwatcher's paradise.

Monument at the 28th Parallel

Guerrero Negro also marks a major milestone for Highway 1 travelers, poised at the 28th parallel, which divides the states of Baja California and Baja California Sur. The huge stylized eagle just north of town marks the state line and serves as a landmark for miles in all directions. For both travelers and Central Desert dwellers, Guerrero Negro is also the biggest service center for all of central Baja. Along with restaurants, Pemex stations and lodging, the town has campgrounds, auto parts stores and repair shops, a hospital, and the closest thing to a supermarket for hundreds of miles.

Top Attractions

SALT EVAPORATING PONDS

One of the most unusual industrial tours you may ever take is a guided excursion through Exportadora de Sal's huge salt-evaporating operation. Tours last about two hours and provide a close-up look at the evaporation ponds, the huge salt-dredging equipment and the docks where salt is loaded on barges for transfer offshore to larger ocean-going vessels. Tours are free if you contact the company directly, or $12.50 per person if arranged through one of the local tour companies. With advance notice, the tour operators can usually provide an English-speaking guide. For tour information, call Malarrimo Eco-Tours or Laguna Tours (see listings under Whale-Watching below) or call Exportadora de Sal, 01152 (1) 157-05-05, ext 223.

Outdoor Fun

BIRD WATCHING

When the gray whales head north from the nearby lagoons each spring, the prolific bird life of the surrounding wetlands becomes the main attraction for visiting wildlife enthusiasts. More than 110 bird species live part- or full-time along the shores of Estero de San José and Scammon's Lagoon. Best known of them are the giant ospreys (sea eagles), which you might observe nesting atop utility poles near the wetlands. One of the best ways to observe bird life is along the road to the old salt-loading wharf, which passes through miles of virgin wetlands in Estero de San José. The local eco-tour outfitters offer bird-watching tours as well; these typically last four hours and cost $25, box lunch included.

For tour information, call Malarrimo Eco-Tours or Laguna Tours. (See listings under Whale Watching, below.)

WHALE WATCHING

Perhaps the greatest attraction in all of central Baja plies the nearby waters of Estero de San José and Scammon's Lagoon, where thousands of California gray whales bear their young between December and March. Scammon's, the larger and better known of the two, alone accounts for more than half of all gray whale calves born in all Baja lagoons.

While you can view the finned beasts from the shore of either lagoon, a boat tour will provide a much closer look—perhaps close enough to reach out and pat one on the head. Most boat tours focus on Scammon's Lagoon. It's possible to join a boat trip, or make advance reservations through one of the local eco-tour operators. Pre-arranged tours last about four hours, including transportation to and from the lagoons, and cost about $45 per person. Tours departing directly from the lagoon cost slightly less. The following companies offer tours departing from Guerrero Negro:

See *GreatestHits*, Chapter 3, for more on whale watching.

Malarrimo Eco-Tours *Near the east edge of town on the north side of Blvd Zapata. 01152 (1) 157-01-00. Website at www.malarrimo.com.* **Laguna Tours** *In the center of town on the north side of Blvd Zapata. 01152 (1) 157-00-50. Website at www.bajalaguna.com.*

Dining

Guerrero Negro is long on low-priced, straightforward restaurants, where Mexican and seafood are the cuisine of choice. A plethora of taco stands and unpretentious diners line Boulevard Zapata, the busy, dust-blown main drag. Two of the top picks with the tourist crowd are the Malarrimo and Puerto Viejo, both near the east end of Zapata. Several others line Zapata near the center of town.

If you're camping and need to re-supply, La Ballena (Spanish for "the Whale") is a small supermarket with the best selection of groceries between Ensenada and Ciudad Constitución. It's on the north side of Zapata in the center of town.

Favorites

MALARRIMO ◆ **Mexican/Seafood**

One of the best restaurants on Baja's Pacific coast, Malarrimo has long been a must-stop for legions of Highway 1 trekkers. Everything on the menu is good, and the seafood is superb, fresh-caught from the nearby Pacific. The All Seafood Bowl—a hearty stew brimming with chunks of fresh fish, clams, shrimp and more—is a personal favorite. The service is reliably friendly and prompt as well. *Near the east edge of town on the north side of Blvd Zapata. 01152 (1) 157-02-50. Open daily 7 am-11 pm. $3.50-12.*

A Restaurant and Museum In One

Even if you aren't hungry, you need to pay at least one visit to the Malarrimo Restaurant and the adjacent, aptly named, Scavenger's Bar. Buoys, lanterns, oars, life vests and ship parts of all description adorn the ceiling and walls—all relics that have washed ashore at Malarrimo Beach. It's worth the stop (and price of a soft drink) to see these remarkable pieces of flotsam and jetsam. For more information on this remote beach, see Side Route Rancho San José de Castro to Malarrimo Beach on page 235—part of the loop trip round the Vizcaíno Peninsula.

Others

COCINA ECONÓMICA LETTY **Mexican**
$2.50-5. *In the center of town, south side of Blvd Zapata. No phone.*

EL POLLO REAL **Mexican**
$2.50-7. *In the center of town, south side of Blvd Zapata. No phone.*

LA PALAPA **Seafood**
$2.25-10. I*n the center of town, south side of Blvd Zapata across from the Pemex station. 01152 (1) 157-16-48.*

PUERTO VIEJO **Mexican/Seafood**
$3-17. *At the east edge of town, north side of Blvd Zapata. 01152 (1) 157-14-72.*

Lodging

Traveler's destination though it is, Guerrero Negro has nothing that remotely resembles a resort hotel. Perhaps that reflects the nature of the local tourist scene or the kind of travelers who put in here—mostly gray-whale lovers and Highway 1 vagabonds. Either way, Guerrero Negro has several low-priced inns, where style and fancy appointments take a back seat to economy and function. All but one of the town's hotels are scattered on or near Boulevard Zapata, the main drag coming off Highway 1.

Otherwise, there's the Hotel La Pinta, part of the venerable Baja California chain, located next to the 28th parallel monu-

¿HAY UNA RECAMARA?

During the whale-watching season from late December through late March, you'll need reservations to ensure having a room in Guerrero Negro. Many hotel clerks speak only Spanish, so whoever's calling should have at least a passing knowledge of the language.

ment just north of town. It's the most upscale hotel in town (comparatively speaking), with rooms priced around $73 a night. There is an adjacent campground as well. Boulevard Zapata presents a better value, however, with a going rate of $18 to $30 for one or two persons in a clean, no-frills room. Cable TV is almost non-existent, as are air conditioning and swimming pools—seldom sought out in this mild seaside climate.

Don't forget — more information is found in *Lodging & Camgrounds,* Chapter 15.

TRAVELOGUE

Guerrero Negro to San Ignacio

(89 mi., 142 km.; 1:45 hrs.)

The 28th parallel marks the gateway to Baja California Sur, but the barren vastness of the Vizcaíno Desert offers few hints to the wonders that lie ahead—rugged desert peaks, lush palm oases and some of the most spectacular coastline on the continent. The desert does enjoy a stark beauty in its own right, and as the miles go by, the landscape slowly hints at the glories for which Baja's southern state is famous. This stretch of highway also serves as the takeoff point for some the most interesting side trips in all of Baja.

Leaving Guerrero Negro, Highway 1 swings inland and begins its west-to-east traverse to the Gulf of California. While its course is straight and flat, the road is narrow in places, which calls once more for careful, heads-up driving. Halfway to San Ignacio is the town of Vizcaíno, the only settlement along this lonely route and the service center for nearby Ejido Díaz Ordaz, the largest farming cooperative in central Baja. Beyond Vizcaíno, the first signs of the Central Desert begin to reappear along Highway 1, in the form of cardón cacti, yucca válida and dense thickets of low-lying brush. To the east, the jagged outline of Sierra de San Francisco comes into view.

Some 25 miles beyond Vizcaíno, a group of flat-topped volcanic cones appears, and the ruddy complexion of the surrounding countryside lends further evidence to the area's past volcanic activity. By now the road bears almost due east as it leaves the flat terrain of the Vizcaíno Desert for a series of roller-coaster hills on the outskirts of San Ignacio. While Highway 1 bypasses the town itself, the vast palm groves just off the road leave no doubt that the turnoff is near.

00.0 Junction to Guerrero Negro.

05.6 Junction with the graded road to the shore of Scammon's Lagoon, signed Laguna Ojo de Liebre (see Side Route to Scammon's Lagoon, page 224).

Side Routes

17.1 Junction with the gravel highway to El Arco (see Side Route to El Arco, page 226).

Side Routes

45.4 Vizcaíno (sometimes called Fundolegal), with about 2400 inhabitants, has a Pemex station, three motels, an RV park, cafes, a market, a pharmacy and auto parts. A paved side road leads five miles to Ejido Díaz Ordaz (sometimes called Vizcaíno). Pavement on the side road ends after 16 more miles, beyond which a graded dirt road leads onto the remote Vizcaíno Peninsula. (See Side Route Loop Trip From Highway 1 Around the Vizcaíno Peninsula, page 230).

Side Routes

52.4 A paved road leads to Ejido Emiliano Zapata, a large dairy-farming *ejido*, or collective agricultural settlement.

57.4 Estación Microóndas Los Angeles, the first of 23 microwave relay stations along Highway 1 in Baja California Sur. The stations are closed to the public.

61.3 Junction with graded dirt road to San Francisco de la Sierra (see Side Route to San Francisco de la Sierra, page 240).

Side Routes

73.6 Junction with a graded dirt road to Punta Abreojos (see Side Route to Punta Abreojos, page 238). A cafe is located at the junction.

Side Routes

85.8 Junction with a 0.6-mile paved road to a good paved airstrip.

88.6 Junction with the 0.9-mile paved road to San Lino and Paredones, two villages on the outskirts of San Ignacio.

88.9 Junction with the 1.1-mile-long paved road to San Ignacio. Opposite the junction is a Pemex station.

Highway 1 to Punta Canoas and Puerto Catarina

(See map below.)

(46 mi., 74 km.; 2:30 hrs.)

Descending through scenic desert toward unspoiled shores along the Pacific, this trek actually has two destinations. The branch to Punta Canoas is used to measure the mileage and time provided here. Whichever destination you choose, the trip is for seasoned, well-prepared adventurers in high-clearance, heavy-duty vehicles, with four-wheel drive highly desirable. There are no facilities at all, which means you'll need plenty of food, water and gasoline, and be prepared to camp out. In return, the drive provides rich displays of ocotillos, cardón cacti and elephant trees en route to remote Pacific

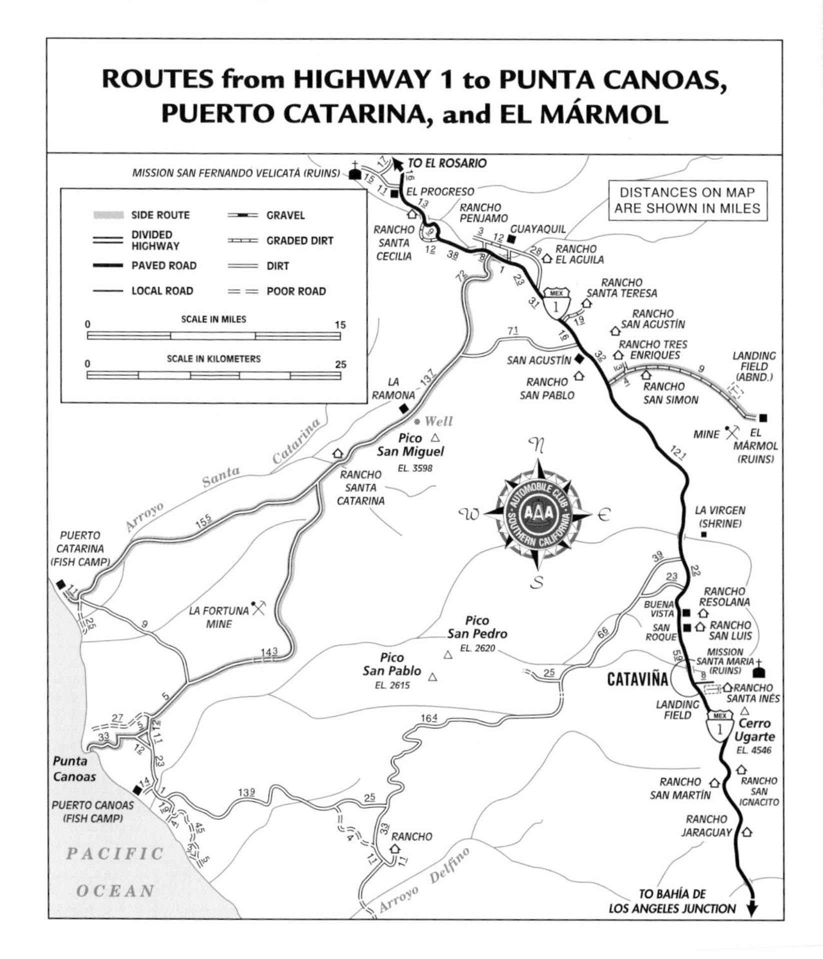

beaches that offer clam-digging, shell-collecting, tidepool-exploring and unmatched solitude. Surfers occasionally visit, lured more by lack of other surfers than by quality waves.

From its junction with the highway 5.6 miles southeast of Rancho Santa Cecilia (or 29 miles northwest of Cataviña), the road quality gradually deteriorates, although a few sandy stretches present the only substantial obstacles to passenger vehicles as far as Rancho Santa Catarina. This friendly settlement is home to families who raise cattle and a few crops. Fresh water is available here for washing and for radiators. Beyond the ranch, the road climbs to a plateau, reaching a junction at mileage 20.9. To the right, via 16.6 miles of rough road, is Puerto Catarina, the one-time shipping port for onyx from El Mármol. Bearing left takes you toward Punta Canoas, down a road that becomes narrow and rough as it crosses the coastal hills. At mileage 40.2 is another junction; bear left. At mileage 41.9 is a fork. To the right the road leads 3.3 miles to Punta Canoas, site of a seasonally occupied fish camp. Numerous campsites await explorers here, along a shelf high above the rocky coastline.

Highway 1 to El Mármol

(See map page 215.)

(9 mi., 16 km.; 0:30 hr.)

Spanish for "The Marble," El Mármol was once an active onyx-mining center, prospering from the early 1900s until a drop in demand for the mineral forced the camp's closure in 1958. In 1993 limited mining resumed, but there is little evidence of sustained recent activity. Signposts of the past abound at this remote site, though, with blocks and chips of onyx strewn across the barren landscape alongside the quarry. A walk through the remains of the camp reveals the ruins of adobe buildings, a schoolhouse made of unpolished onyx, the carcasses of long-abandoned trucks, and an interesting cemetery. Use caution walking about here; several deep, uncovered wells present hazards.

Otherworldly rocks at El Mármol

The signed junction with the road to El Mármol is 2.2 miles southeast of San

Agustín on Highway 1. The smooth, graded road is suitable for any type of vehicle during dry weather. After leaving the main highway, the road runs 0.4 mile to a junction with a remnant of the old peninsular road; on the right is a wooden corral and small gravel quarry. At mileage 0.9 the road passes a windmill and another corral before veering to the right. From there, the road takes a straight course across open countryside that is sparsely covered with cacti and brush. The road also flanks an abandoned airstrip before reaching El Mármol, 9.4 miles from Highway 1.

Highway 1 to Bahía de los Angeles

(See map page 219.)

(42 mi., 68 km.; 1 hr.)

(See also *Lodging & Campgrounds*, Chapter 15.)

With high, barren mountains as a dramatic backdrop to the west and numerous islands jutting up from the deep blue waters of the Gulf of California, Bahía de los Angeles rates among the most scenic outposts in all of Baja. Better known to most gringos as "L.A. Bay," Bahía de los Angeles is flanked by steep headlands to the north and south, and protected by 45-mile-long Isla Angel de la Guarda, which offers a fine sheltered anchorage for boats.

Launch ramp at Bahía de los Angeles

Besides its natural protection and grandeur, other factors come into play here to make this a premier venue for a myriad of outdoor pursuits. The town and bay are Baja's gateway to the so-called Midriff Region of the gulf, where it narrows to less than 60 miles across in spots. Surging tidal currents race up and down the gulf along this stretch, pulling up nutrients from deeper waters to form the foundation for a prolific food chain. As a result, the waters off Bahía de los Angeles enjoy some of the best sportfishing conditions in all of Baja.

> ***DON'T COUNT ON IT***
>
> While gas pumped from barrels is usually available in Bahía de los Angeles, the supplies are nothing to take for granted. Frequent long lines and steep mark-ups should be a further deterrent against counting on gasoline in this remote village.

The nutrient-rich waters are also a favored haunt by whales, and nearly

Morning at Bahía de los Angeles

a dozen species may show up during the year in the nearby Canal de Ballenas (Channel of Whales). Orcas, blues, sperm whales and even a few grays are among those to be found in this narrow strait between the shoreline and Isla Angel de la Guarda. South of the bay is Isla Raza, a reserve for migrating waterfowl and an outstanding spot for bird-watching. The bay and offshore islands also provide some excellent kayaking opportunities, while during the winter, the prevailing northeast winds are good for windsurfing. Fishing and diving trips, and other boat excursions can be arranged in town and at the nearby camps. For those who brought their own boat, several ramps dot the shoreline.

Students in Bahía de los Angeles who wish to study beyond eighth grade have a long way to go. The closest high school is in Guerrero Negro, more than 120 miles away.

The town itself is home to about 800 people, with a tiny "downtown" that touts a plaza park, town hall, and a museum devoted to the region's natural history and culture. Facilities include stores, restaurants, a bakery, trailer parks and several small motels. Other campgrounds dot the bay's shoreline outside of town. There is no Pemex station, but gasoline pumped from 55-gallon drums is usually available.

CALLING COSTA DEL SOL

Lodging reservations are usually not necessary in Bahía de los Angeles, but if you do want to call ahead, only one hotel has a telephone. It's the Hotel Costa del Sol, linked via satellite to Mexico City. The phone number is 01152 (5) 151-41-95.

The drive to Bahía de los Angeles is a scenic experience in its own right, though one that requires your full attention at the wheel, thanks to the many potholes and rough spots in the pavement. Leaving Highway 1 at a well-marked junction 8.4 miles north of Punta Prieta, the route heads east across a sandy plain where the typical vegetation of Baja's Central Desert is particularly abundant. Cardón, cholla and garambullo cacti, along with cirio, ocotillo and yucca válida are among the many types of flora on display. Brightly colored wildflowers carpet the desert floor during the early spring as well, while barren desert peaks rise in all directions.

Side Routes

About 10 miles from Highway 1, the road passes through a gap in the mountains before it descends to the edge of a large dry lake. At mileage 28 you pass the signed junction with a rough dirt road south to Misión San Borja. (The road to the mission from Rosarito on Highway 1 is better.)

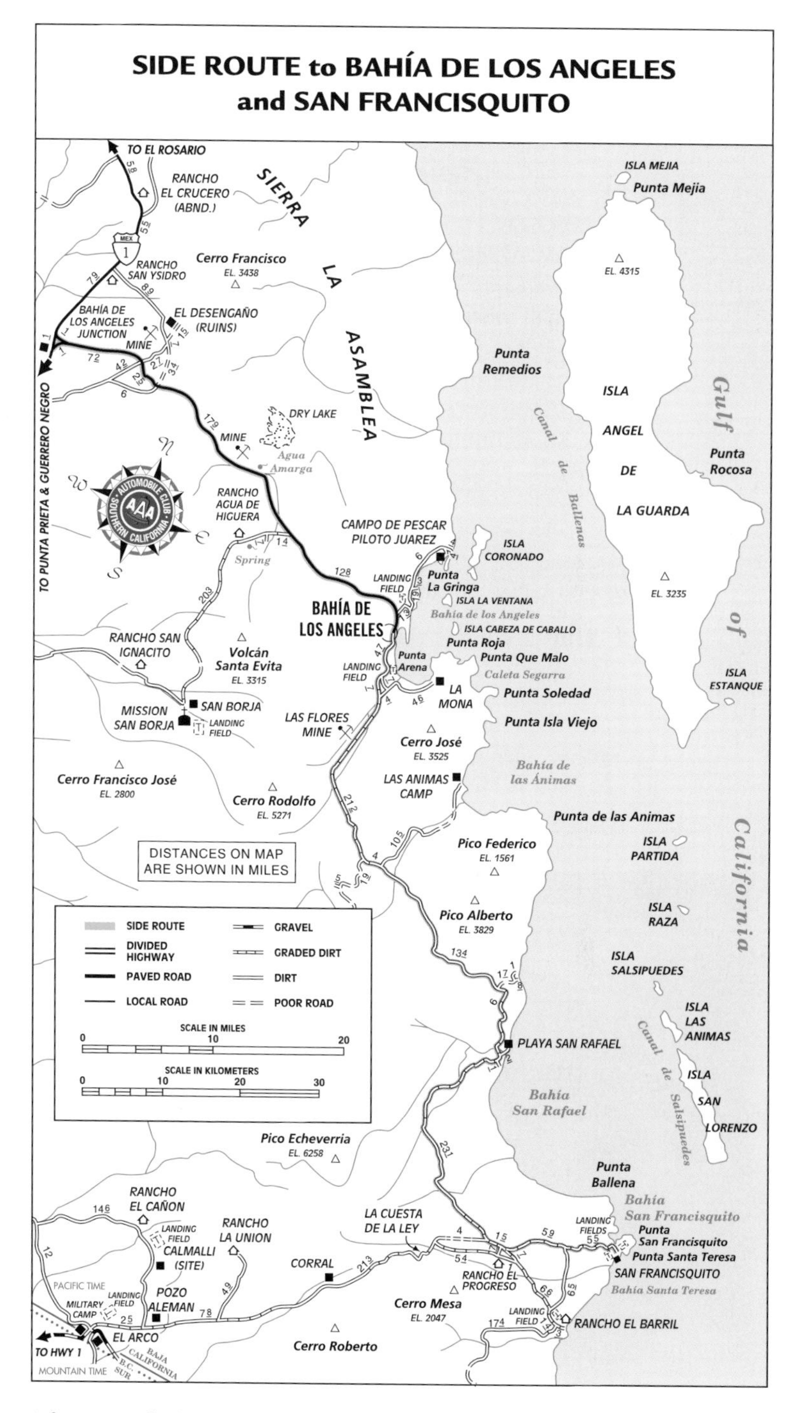

After a gentle downhill run through a canyon, the gulf suddenly looms ahead, providing one of the most dramatic views in all of Baja as the road drops quickly to the shoreline. Dirt roads run both north and south from the town, past vacation homes to remote beaches where good campsites can be found. In addition, a graded road winds southeastward to remote San Francisquito, 81 miles away. (See Side Route to San Francisquito, below.)

Points of Interest

MUSEO DE HISTORIA NATURAL Y CULTURA

West side of plaza park. No phone. Open daily 9 am-noon year round, and 2-4 pm except summer. Donations accepted. This small museum features excellent displays on sea life in the Gulf of California and Baja California fauna. Indian artifacts are also on display, as is a vintage Auto Club map of Baja California from the pre-Transpeninsular Highway days. Books on the region in English and Spanish are sold as well.

Bahía de los Angeles to San Francisquito

(See map page 219.)

(81 mi., 130 km.; 3:45 hrs.)

This journey through scenic desert hills and valleys to a secluded bay on the Gulf of California is graded all the way and presents a great opportunity to enjoy Baja's beauty at its unspoiled best. Given the extreme isolation along this route, you can drive for many miles without seeing another vehicle, which means traveling with a fully equipped, sturdy, high-clearance truck is a must. The route follows an inland course for most of its length, due to the rugged nature of the coastline. The scenery can be spectacular, however, with colorful mesas, desert peaks and some impressive stands of Central Desert foliage.

The desert sun has faded this sign south of Bahía de los Angeles.

The destination is a rustic fishing resort known as Punta San Francisquito, located on Bahía Santa Teresa, a small, attractive bay with a long sandy beach. The camp has cabañas for rent, along with a restaurant and bar, electricity during the evening hours, fishing boats and an airstrip. Fishing and snorkeling trips are available, as are outings to cave paintings in the nearby desert. Camping is allowed for a small fee. Many guests arrive by airplane, often flying in and leaving the same day. Overland visitors often arrive in convoys of dirt bikes, dune buggies or other off-road vehicles. About a mile north of the resort is Bahía San Francisquito, with a beautiful cove sheltered by rugged headlands. A small fish camp with a mechanic's shop is located here.

Occasional arrows painted on rocks along this side route point the way toward San Francisquito.

The road to San Francisquito begins near the southern edge of Bahía de los Angeles, turning right, then bearing left to head south across the desert, a short way inland from the bay. A fork appears at mileage 4.7, the left branch leading toward homes along the shoreline; bear right. Continuing south, the road heads through a huge stand of cardón cacti, then passes between two mountain ranges and climbs through a range of hills. At mileage 27 a side route goes north to Las Animas Camp, a remote fishing camp on a scenic lagoon. A large sign directs you southeast toward Punta San Francisquito.

Farther south, the road climbs through more hills before dropping almost to the shoreline of the lovely Bahía San Rafael. Several small islands rise from the gulf waters here, while farther offshore lies the form of Isla Tiburón—the largest island in the Gulf of California. The road once more heads inland, climbs a steep grade, then gradually descends in an easterly direction toward the coast. At 68 miles is a junction; a right turn heads toward El Arco, while a left turn leads the final 13 miles to San Francisquito. Along the way two roads branch southeast to El Barril, a large cattle ranch and site of a number of American vacation homes. Keep left at each junction as you continue northeast toward San Francisquito. As the seaside camp comes into view, the road swings around the airstrip and appears to bypass the resort before turning southeast to reach the final destination.

Highway 1 to Santa Rosalillita

(See map page 222.)

(10 mi., 16 km.; 0:45 hr.)

A tiny village spread along a sandy stretch of Pacific shoreline, Santa Rosalillita lends itself to a variety of ocean-related activities. Fishing is the main source of income for most of the 150 residents, and a small packing house sends most of the catch to Ensenada. Sea bass, hal-

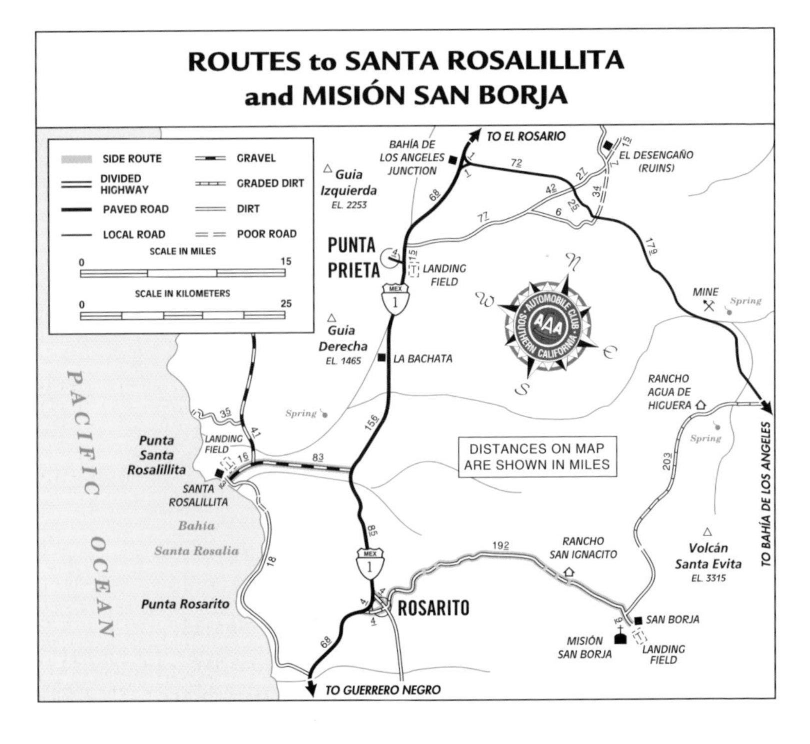

ibut, corvina, white fish and shark are the main take from the offshore waters, while lobster and abalone thrive in kelp beds closer to land. Also, Pismo clams are abundant along the broad beach that fronts the tiny hamlet.

For many visitors, fishing both from the beach and offshore is the primary draw to Santa Rosalillita. Local commercial fishermen charge reasonable rates for excursions of a few hours using their boats. Scuba divers are also drawn this way, mainly to work the kelp beds off Punta Rosalillita, just north of the village. Windsurfing is popular too during the winter and early spring, when the prevailing northwest winds blow almost every afternoon. Several surf spots beckon as well both north and south of the village, with the best waves during the winter. Beyond a market and small café, however, there is nothing in the way of tourist services. Camping is permitted, though, at no charge along the beach.

ONE ROCKY ROAD

The road to Santa Rosalillita is not particularly rough by Baja standards, but fist-sized pieces of gravel in the roadbed provide a strong hint that it's not a good idea to go too fast on this route.

From Highway 1, a wide gravel road leads to Santa Rosalillita and is suitable for a carefully driven passenger car. Leaving the highway 15.6 miles south of Punta Prieta, the road follows the shoulder of a wide arroyo, tracing the path of an older road in the sandy wash below. At mileage 8.3 it reaches a junction with a gravel road that leads north to Rancho San Luis, with access to some remote stretches of coastline. The road crosses a dirt airstrip at mileage 8.4 before looping down to the beach and into Santa Rosalillita, 9.9 miles from Highway 1.

An alternate return route, not suitable for standard automobiles, leads south from Santa Rosalillita past a chain of lovely, remote beaches. The road meanders along the shoreline for 15 miles, passing beaches covered with small, smooth stones, volcanic rocks and pearly white turban shells. Several good spots for wintertime surfing break off the rocky points. At Playa Altamira, a good camping spot, the road turns inland and runs about three miles to meet Highway 1 at a junction 6.8 miles south of Rosarito.

A young local cruises Santa Rosalillita's beach.

Rosarito to Misión San Borja

(See map page 222.)

(21 mi., 35 km.; 2 hrs.)

Set in a broad valley at the foot of the Sierra San Borja lies the site of the final mission established by Jesuit priests on the Baja California peninsula. Misión San Francisco de Borja was founded in 1759, shortly before the Jesuits' expulsion from the Americas, though it wasn't till 1801 that the Dominicans completed the present-day stone church. San Borja today is one of only two Spanish missions still standing in the state of Baja California (the other is Santa Gertrudis) and the destination for a rough but scenic drive through the Central Desert.

At its peak the mission served more than 3000 Indians, but diseases of the white man decimated the native population and the mission was abandoned in 1818. Local ranchers helped preserve the church, however, and the Mexican government later restored the structure to near-original condition. It

FROM THE ENDS OF THE EARTH

Several days, even weeks, sometimes pass between visits by outsiders to San Borja. However, the mission guest book reveals that visitors do come from all over the world—Asia, Europe, even as far as South Africa.

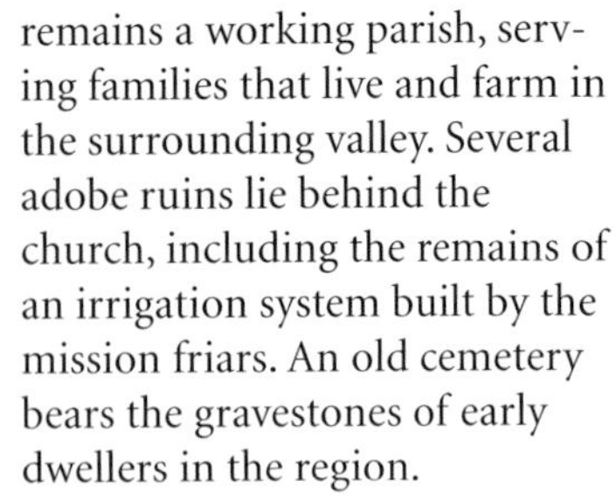

remains a working parish, serving families that live and farm in the surrounding valley. Several adobe ruins lie behind the church, including the remains of an irrigation system built by the mission friars. An old cemetery bears the gravestones of early dwellers in the region.

Misión San Borja, above and below, is a worthy destination for the properly equipped explorer.

The best road to San Borja, which starts in the tiny hamlet of Rosarito (not to be confused with the booming coastal town near Tijuana), is nonetheless totally unsuited for passenger cars. There are no steep grades, but the single-track road has a high crown and numerous rough and rocky spots that demand a sturdy high-clearance vehicle. For those with the right vehicle and equipment, though, the trip to this mission is well worth the time and effort.

From Rosarito, the route bears right just past a small weather station and leads northeast across a scenic swath of desert, passing a series of colorful mesas and buttes. At mileage 13.4 is a junction; bear left. About two miles beyond the junction is Rancho San Ignacito, a large cattle ranch with a stone-walled corral and a deep well. Beyond the ranch the road makes a rough climb out of a small arroyo and then descends gradually to the peaceful valley that harbors the mission.

Another road leads north from the mission for 20 miles to meet the paved route between Highway 1 and Bahía de los Angeles. Though long on scenery, this road is even rougher than the one from Rosarito; it is steep and narrow, with numerous rocky arroyo crossings.

Highway 1 to Laguna Ojo de Liebre (Scammon's Lagoon)

(See map page 227.)

(15 mi., 24 km.; 0:45 hr.)

As Baja California's biggest wintertime destination for the California gray whales, Scammon's Lagoon also attracts plenty of human visitors during the whales' annual migration to its shallow waters. While many visitors join organized whale-watching tours out of Guerrero Negro, many drive straight to the lagoon to join boat trips or just view the whales from the shore.

An access road from Highway 1 leads to the southeast shoreline, where tour boats embark and whales can usually be seen from shore. The drive itself is an experience, its last 10 miles running through salt-drying flats owned by Exportadora de Sal. The stark white landscape in spots seems more befitting of a polar icecap than a Baja California lagoon. You can often see huge dredging machines harvesting salt here. The salt company road is only open during the whale-watching season, which runs from late December through the end of March. (Exact dates vary from year to year.) While the whales are the chief attraction, the route also reveals a wealth of bird life, with large numbers of herons, cormorants and pelicans thriving in the vast wetlands surrounding the lagoon.

See *GreatestHits*, Chapter 3, for more on whale watching.

From Highway 1, a hard-pack dirt road branches southwest at a point 5.6 miles south of the Guerrero Negro turnoff. The well-marked junction bears the signs "Laguna Ojo de Liebre" and "Parque Natural de la Ballena Gris/Gray Whale Natural Park." While wide and graded its entire length, the road has some sandy spots over the first couple of miles, but during dry weather (which is nearly all the time) a passenger car can make the trip with slow and cautious driving.

Scammon's Lagoon shoreline

After leaving Highway 1 the road passes several junctions; some have signs with a picture of a whale and an arrow pointing the way. Side roads here belong to the salt company and are closed to public use. After passing a salt company checkpoint at mileage 3.9, the road crosses a levee between two huge sets of evaporating ponds. After another 10 miles the road comes to a small shack bearing the sign "Parque Natural de la Ballena Gris/Gray Whale Natural Park." A $3 admission is sometimes collected here. Just beyond the shack is a fork, with the left branch leading to the best beach to observe the whales. Binoculars help, since the mammals are usually some distance offshore. Small boats depart on whale-watching tours from the same shoreline. Bird-watching tours are also available during the months the road is open. Overnight camping is allowed, although no facilities exist.

Highway 1 to El Arco

(See map page 227.)

(25 mi., 41 km.; 1 hr.)

A one-time mining town and way stop along the old Highway 1, El Arco exists today as a peaceful if worn-looking community that serves as a center for the surrounding ranches. Located just north of the state line between Baja California and Baja California Sur, this scattered village offers little to attract most visitors, but serves as a jump-off point for numerous points of interest. Gasoline is pumped from drums, but drivers should not take this supply for granted. Within the village itself, an army camp and a fair-sized church are the main landmarks, and a landing field is located just to the south.

Horsing around at a rancho near El Arco

The road to El Arco, designated Mexico Highway 18, leaves Highway 1 at a well-signed junction located 17.1 miles southeast of Guerrero Negro. Leading northeast from this junction, the road runs through flat, barren terrain until mileage 6.6, when dense desert vegetation suddenly springs from the landscape. Cardón, yucca válida, elephant trees, cholla cacti and a variety of shrubs all grow in this "living desert." The road charts a gradual uphill course before rounding a small range of steep, barren hills and dropping into El Arco. The roadway is elevated with a gravel surface, but many drivers choose to use the smoother dirt paths that parallel the main road for much of its length. There are no meals or lodging of any type along this route or those that follow out of El Arco.

El Arco to Misión Santa Gertrudis

(See map page 227.)

(21 mi., 32 km.; 1:10 hrs.)

Nestled in a narrow canyon beneath the red-rock sierra of central Baja, Misión Santa Gertrudis presents a

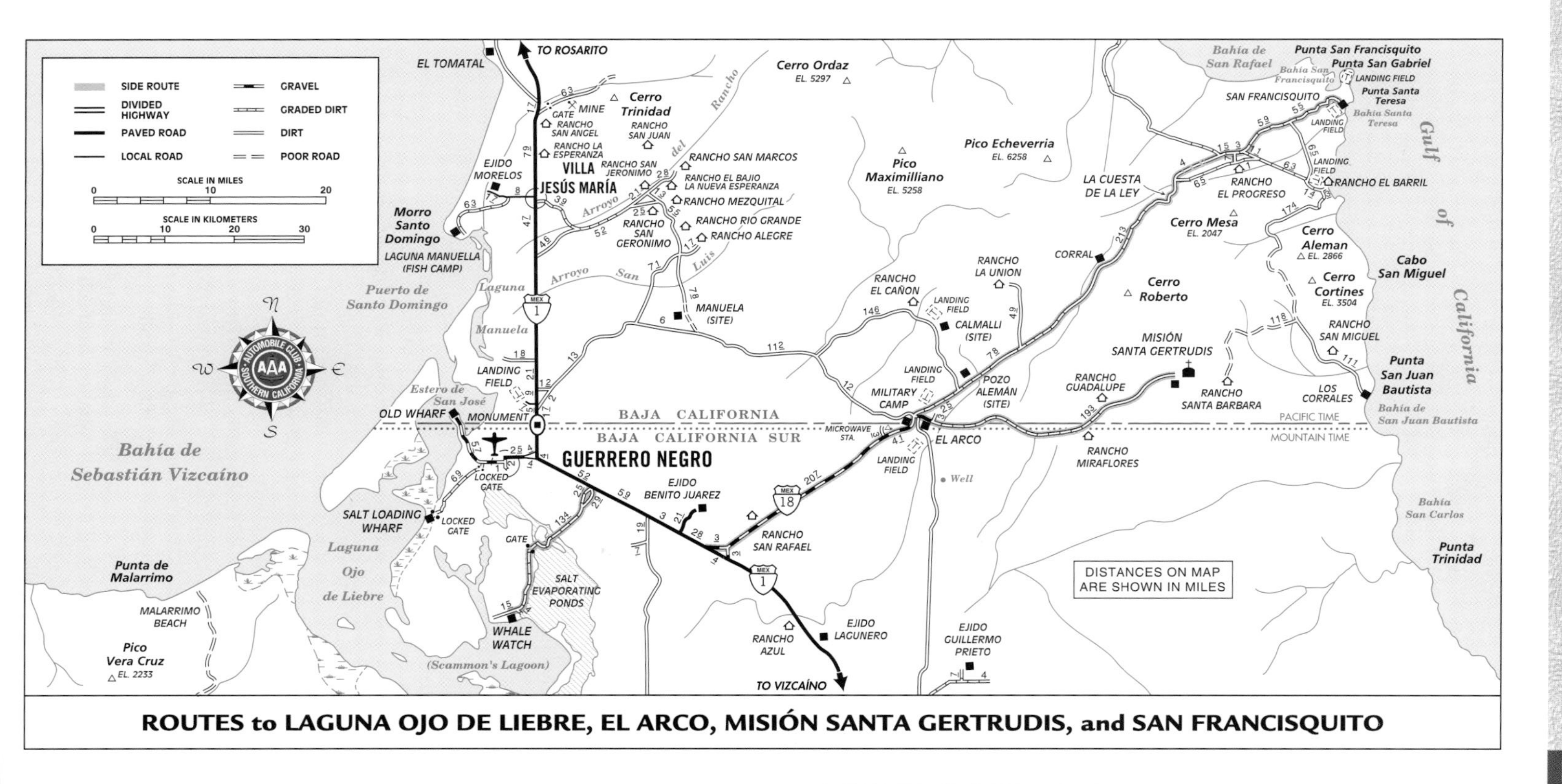

ROUTES to LAGUNA OJO DE LIEBRE, EL ARCO, MISIÓN SANTA GERTRUDIS, and SAN FRANCISQUITO

Be careful to get on the proper road to your destination when leaving El Arco. It's easy to make a wrong turn, which could send you driving miles in the wrong direction.

lovely if remote target—one worthy of the time and effort involved for the properly equipped explorer. This is among the least-visited of all the intact missions in Baja California (not surprising given its distance from Highway 1) though it does attract a year-round trickle of visitors from all over the world. The biggest turnout takes place each year on November 16, when pilgrims from throughout Baja arrive for the Fiesta de Santa Gertrudis de la Magna.

Founded by the Jesuits in 1752, Misión Santa Gertrudis was an important supply center during the mission era, being about midway between missions San Ignacio and San Borja on the dusty old road known as El Camino Real. After the Jesuits were expelled from Baja California in 1768, the Dominicans arrived and built the small stone church in 1796. Almost from the start, Santa Gertrudis suffered from a shortage of fresh water, and many Indians succumbed to diseases, helping lead to its abandonment in 1822.

While the mission was never fully completed, the chapel remains in use, serving the handful of ranch families that still live in the area. The chapel was deteriorating until the late 1980s, when a restoration project commenced. (Work on the chapel continues on an intermittent basis.) Several other ruins occupy the grounds, including the remains of an irrigation system dating from the 18th century and a restored adobe belfry. A small museum features some interesting artifacts from the mission's heyday, including the original confessional booth and robes the early padres wore. In addition, several cave-painting sites can be found in the surrounding mountains. Information is available at the mission.

ALMS FOR THE CHURCH

Donations are not required, but Misión Santa Gertrudis will accept any contributions to aid the ongoing restoration of its chapel.

The route to Misión Santa Gertrudis heads east from El Arco across typical central Baja mesa and butte country, with the standard assortment of Central Desert foliage. The road is wide and graded nearly all the way, but washboard sections do exist, making this another trip best left to trucks with sturdy tires. The route begins where the main road through El Arco makes a hard right turn and heads south from the army camp, crossing an arroyo. A worn sign in front of a schoolhouse points the way east toward the mission. En route, the road passes two forks that lead to local ranchos; bear left at both of them. At 21 miles from the center of El Arco, the road pulls into the small oasis that is home to the mission.

El Arco to San Francisquito
(See map page 227.)

(47 mi., 75 km.; 2:30 hrs.)

The road from El Arco to Bahía San Francisquito is reasonable by Baja off-road standards and suitable for most high-clearance vehicles, but it wasn't always that way. Before the late 1970s, the route featured one of Baja's most formidable driving challenges in the form of La Cuesta de la Ley, a harrowing plunge that dropped 400 vertical feet in less than half a mile. Only trekkers with four-wheel-drive could make the trip in those days, before a major regrading eased the precipitous incline (or "ruined" it, some old-timers say) to accommodate a wider range of vehicles. Today it remains a lonely, lightly traveled road with no services of any type before reaching San Francisquito, located along a remote stretch of Gulf of California shoreline.

Buggy and beachside lodging, San Francisquito

From the junction by the town hall in El Arco, the route commences in a northeasterly direction, climbing through a steep and narrow arroyo at the outset. At mileage 2.5 is a short access road leading 0.2 mile to the deserted town of Pozo Alemán. A busy gold- and copper-mining center in the early 1900s, Pozo Alemán lies abandoned and decaying today—a real-life ghost town worthy of a Hollywood western set. Beyond Pozo Alemán, the road emerges onto a flat plain, then enters a region of rocky arroyos dotted with huge cardón cacti. At mileage 9.9 a road leads left to Rancho La Unión; bear right. The road to the gulf now climbs through a series of steep-sided valleys toward an open plateau that continues rising gradually toward La Cuesta de la Ley. At mileage 30 La Cuesta de la Ley begins its descent, along with the long downward journey to the coast. A major fork is located at mileage 37.0; to the right is a cattle ranch known as Rancho El Barril, while the left branch leads another 10.4 miles to San Francisquito.

Side Routes

Located on Bahía Santa Teresa, San Francisquito is a rustic fishing resort, most of whose visitors fly in, using a nearby landing strip. For details about this settlement, see Side Route, Bahía de los Angeles to San Francisquito, page 220.

Loop Trip From Highway 1 Around the Vizcaíno Peninsula

(See map page 231.)

Sticking westward like a dagger into the Pacific Ocean, the Vizcaíno Peninsula is one of the most remote regions not only in Baja California, but the entire Mexican Republic. Only a few thousand people reside in this huge hook of land, where the barren landscape and poor roads only increase the sense of desolation. But for those with the time, inclination and the right vehicle, a journey around the Vizcaíno Peninsula makes for one of the best high adventures in Baja. This is a land of vast coastal plains, virgin beaches, beautiful bays and coves, and strange desert badlands befitting some distant world.

However, those same qualities help make this a trip only for seasoned off-road explorers equipped to handle the worst that Baja has to offer—extreme isolation, poor roads, a lack of fresh water, limited facilities, frequent dust storms, desert heat and thick coastal fog. Services (such as they are) are limited to the cannery towns, which include Punta Abreojos, La Bocana, Bahía Asunción and Bahía Tortugas. Gasoline is available, in some places pumped from drums, but it is often expensive and supplies can be erratic. Lodging, where it exists, is extremely modest in nature, although fine primitive campsites can be found throughout the peninsula. Wood, however, is scarce. Beyond the cannery towns, a handful of ranchos and tiny fishing villages are the only outposts of civilization, scattered far apart along the roads and remote shoreline.

The lonely road to the Vizcaíno Peninsula

For the most part, the main route between Vizcaíno and Bahía Tortugas is well signed, periodically maintained, and receives a small but steady flow of traffic. A passenger car or small RV can handle this road, but a sturdy high-clearance truck is by far the best option. Off this main route, several roads have bad spots that can trap or damage a low-slung car. For driving anywhere on the peninsula, take along extra water, food and gasoline, and check your equipment against the Suggested Supply Lists in the *Appendix*, Chapter 16.

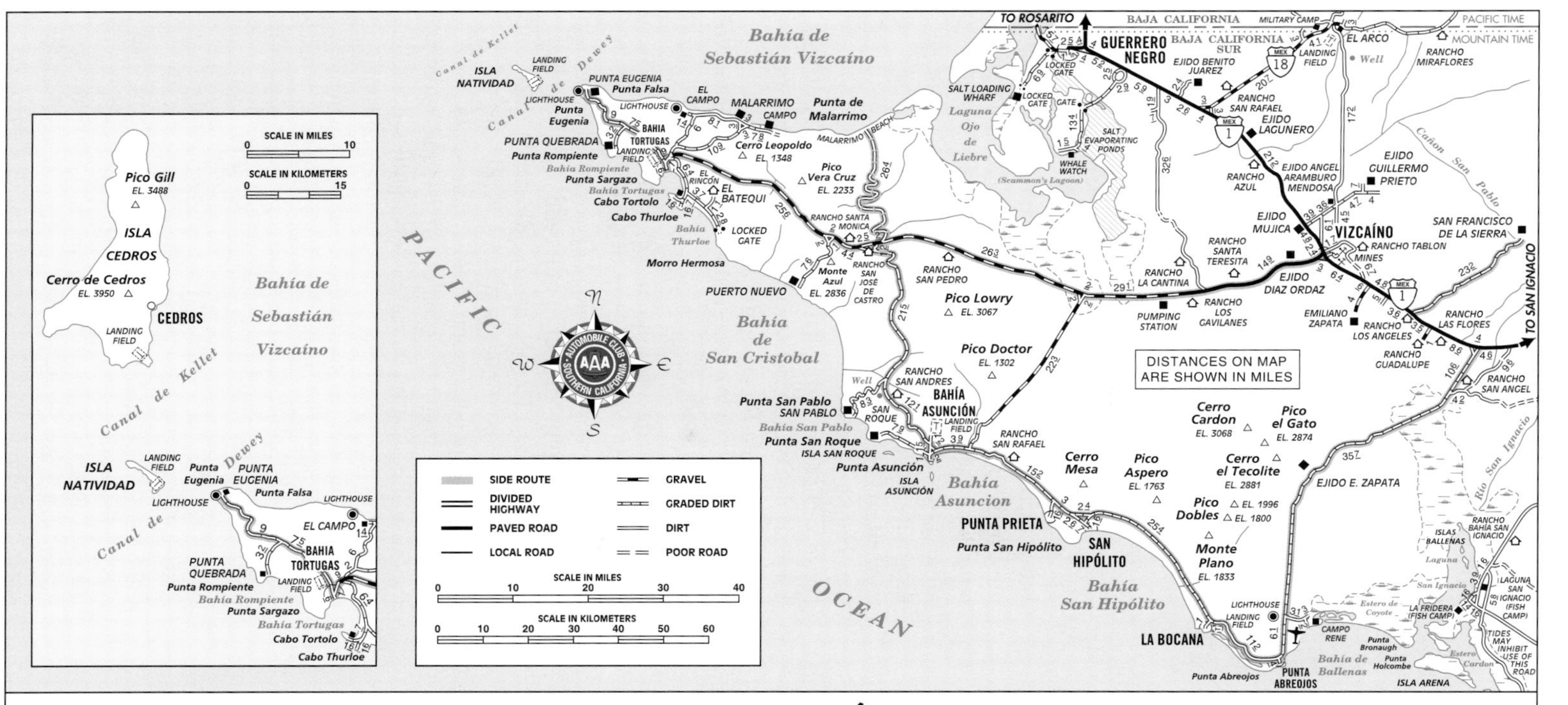
SIDE ROUTES of the VIZCAÍNO PENINSULA
DISTANCES ON MAP ARE SHOWN IN MILES
SIDE ROUTE
DIVIDED HIGHWAY
PAVED ROAD
LOCAL ROAD
GRAVEL
GRADED DIRT
DIRT
POOR ROAD
SCALE IN MILES
SCALE IN KILOMETERS
AUTOMOBILE CLUB · SOUTHERN CALIFORNIA
AAA
PACIFIC
OCEAN
BAJA CALIFORNIA
BAJA CALIFORNIA SUR
PACIFIC TIME
MOUNTAIN TIME
TO ROSARITO
TO SAN IGNACIO
GUERRERO NEGRO
EL ARCO
RANCHO MIRAFLORES
EJIDO BENITO JUAREZ
RANCHO SAN RAFAEL
EJIDO LAGUNERO
RANCHO AZUL
EJIDO ANGEL ARAMBURO MENDOSA
EJIDO GUILLERMO PRIETO
EJIDO MUJICA
VIZCAÍNO
RANCHO TABLON
MINES
SAN FRANCISCO DE LA SIERRA
RANCHO SANTA TERESITA
RANCHO LA CANTINA
EJIDO DIAZ ORDAZ
PUMPING STATION
RANCHO LOS GAVILANES
EMILIANO ZAPATA
RANCHO LOS ANGELES
RANCHO LAS FLORES
RANCHO GUADALUPE
RANCHO SAN ANGEL
EJIDO E. ZAPATA
SALT LOADING WHARF
LOCKED GATE
SALT EVAPORATING PONDS
WHALE WATCH
Laguna Ojo de Liebre
(Scammon's Lagoon)
Bahía de Sebastián Vizcaíno
PUNTA EUGENIA
Punta Falsa
EL CAMPO
MALARRIMO
CAMPO
Punta de Malarrimo
MALARRIMO BEACH
Cerro Leopoldo
Pico Vera Cruz
RANCHO SANTA MONICA
BAHIA TORTUGAS
LANDING FIELD
LIGHTHOUSE
PUNTA QUEBRADA
Punta Rompiente
Bahía Rompiente
Punta Sargazo
Bahía Tortugas
Cabo Tortolo
Cabo Thurloe
Bahía Thurloe
EL RINCÓN
EL BATEQUI
Morro Hermosa
PUERTO NUEVO
Monte Azul
RANCHO SAN JOSÉ DE CASTRO
RANCHO SAN PEDRO
Pico Lowry
Pico Doctor
Bahía de San Cristobal
RANCHO SAN ANDRES
BAHÍA ASUNCIÓN
Punta San Pablo
SAN PABLO
Bahía San Pablo
SAN ROQUE
Punta San Roque
ISLA SAN ROQUE
Punta Asunción
ISLA ASUNCIÓN
Bahía Asuncion
RANCHO SAN RAFAEL
PUNTA PRIETA
Punta San Hipólito
SAN HIPÓLITO
Bahía San Hipólito
Cerro Mesa
Pico Aspero
Cerro Cardon
Pico el Gato
Cerro el Tecolite
Pico Dobles
Monte Plano
LA BOCANA
Punta Abreojos
PUNTA ABREOJOS
CAMPO RENE
Bahía de Ballenas
ISLA ARENA
ISLAS BALLENAS
RANCHO BAHÍA SAN IGNACIO
LAGUNA SAN IGNACIO (FISH CAMP)
LA FRIDERA (FISH CAMP)
TIDES MAY INHIBIT USE OF THIS ROAD
Río San Ignacio
Cañon San Pablo
ISLA NATIVIDAD
Punta Eugenia
Canal de Kellet
Canal de Dewey
Pico Gill
ISLA CEDROS
CEDROS
Cerro de Cedros

Gasoline supplies have been known to run out in the peninsula's cannery towns. Be sure to have a full tank before leaving Vizcaíno.

Two routes lead from Highway 1 to the peninsula, one starting at Vizcaíno Junction, 45 miles southeast of Guerrero Negro, the other at an unsigned junction 15 miles west of San Ignacio. The following route descriptions are organized as a semi-loop trip starting at Vizcaíno Junction, with each segment outlined as a separate side route. Unless you are staying on the Vizcaíno-Bahía Tortugas road, consider traveling in a caravan with at least one other vehicle. Conditions can change, hours may lapse between passing vehicles, and help is a long way off.

Vizcaíno Peninsula:
Vizcaíno to Rancho San José de Castro

(See map page 231.)

(74 mi., 119 km.; 4 hrs.)

The road leading onto the Vizcaíno Peninsula is durable and graded but its gravelly surface is still rough for the most part, with many long washboard sections. Drifting sand is another problem in spots. The surface is raised most of the way, and signs appear at the most important junctions. Rancho San José de Castro is used here as a convenient route-dividing point. The highway continues west from here to Bahía Tortugas and is the lifeline between Highway 1 and that little port town. (The Bahía Tortugas description follows.) Vizcaíno has the last gasoline before Bahía Tortugas, 103 miles away. Ejido Díaz Ordaz, just west of Vizcaíno, is the last chance for food or supplies of any kind.

Begin by taking the Vizcaíno turnoff from Highway 1 and following the paved road past the irrigated fields, orchards and vineyards of Ejido Díaz Ordaz. The farmland ends abruptly after a few miles and is replaced by flat, barren desert. The pavement ends after 21 miles, and the graded road continues west across scrub-covered desert. After passing a group of small ranches, the road heads through a remote region of salt flats and lagoons, as the sense of desolation increases. Beyond the salt flats the road begins its gradual ascent into the mountains that dominate most of the peninsula, sometimes slicing abruptly through ridges, at other times following natural gaps in the hills. Elephant trees and cacti begin to appear, and the bay is occasionally visible to the right.

At mileage 48.0 is a signed junction with a graded dirt road that heads southwest to join the coastal road 3.9 miles south of Bahía Asunción. At mileage 70.6, the road reaches the hard-to-find Malarrimo Beach turnoff; it is on the right-hand side about .5 mile east of the San José de Castro sign. After another .5 mile, a dirt road on the left leads 1.3 miles south to Rancho San José de Castro and connects to the older dirt road leading south to Bahía Asunción. Rancho San José de Castro, a cattle ranch with a large spring, is also a residence for magnesite miners. There are no tourist facilities, but ranchers sell cold drinks and can provide information and directions.

Vizcaíno Peninsula:
Rancho San José de Castro to Bahía Tortugas

(See map page 231.)

(31 mi., 50 km.; 2 hrs.)

Beyond the junction with the road to San José de Castro, the road to Bahía Tortugas continues westward, gradually climbing its way farther into the arid mountains. The only turnoff along this long, lonely stretch comes at mileage 6.8, where a dirt road veers off to the left and winds eight miles south to the fishing village of Puerto Nuevo. Beyond this turnoff the road heads through a narrow valley between the mountains, following the ridge contours and at times cutting a path right through the mountains themselves.

Spanish for "Turtles Bay," Bahía Tortugas did not earn its name for being a home to the shelled reptiles, but rather because the bay's shape resembles that of a turtle.

The surroundings are utterly desolate along this stretch, although sculpted cliffs, eroded badlands and other weird landforms make for some of the most interesting scenery along Baja's Pacific coast. The barren mountains on either side belie the fact that the ocean is just a few miles away, even as the road approaches Bahía Tortugas. Finally, at mileage 31.3 the road drops out of the mountains and the bay suddenly appears at the entrance to town.

Bahía Tortugas, the "metropolis" of the Vizcaíno Peninsula

With a population of around 3000, Bahía Tortugas qualifies as the "metropolis" of the Vizcaíno Peninsula and is the main destination for outsiders visiting the peninsula. The town's status is not surprising, given its setting along a large round bay that is one of the finest natural harbors on Baja California's Pacific Coast. Tucked beneath barren hills on the north side of the bay, Bahía Tortugas earns its keep from the sea. A fishing fleet works the offshore waters, while lobster and abalone are harvested closer to land. A good-sized cannery packs various types of seafood, much of which is flown or trucked to Ensenada.

Let There Be (Late) Light

At the western extreme of the Mountain Time Zone, Bahía Tortugas sees the last daylight of any town in Baja California Sur. It's almost a full degree in longitude west of Guerrero Negro and five degrees west of Cabo San Lucas. Accordingly, there's enough ambient light for a few rounds of stickball until after 9 p.m. on summer evenings. Of course, early birds are sure to squawk about the late sunrises.

Though almost devoid of vegetation, Bahía Tortugas enjoys a scenic beauty all its own, its barren brown hills rising in sharp relief against the dark blue waters and kelp beds of central Baja's Pacific coast. Neat rows of buildings in vibrant shades of purple, pink, yellow, etc. provide a further contrast amid the desolate surroundings. Despite its remote location, Bahía Tortugas receives plenty of outside influence. Along with a small but steady flow of overland visitors, the town is a frequent port of call for pleasure boaters traveling up and down the Pacific coast of Mexico. (The bay is a good place if you're trying to hitch a ride by boat.) The town has an orderly feel to it, with a generally welcome attitude toward outsiders. One thing Bahía Tortugas does lack is fresh water, which means its supply must be brought in by ship or truck, or distilled from seawater in the town's small desalinization plant.

REDEFINING THE WORD "REMOTE"

Just how isolated is the Vizcaíno Peninsula? From Punta Eugenia, at the westernmost tip, the nearest paved road is 100 miles away, the nearest bank is 165 road miles away in Guerrero Negro, and the nearest theater is 420 miles distant in San Quintín. The closest McDonald's? In Ensenada, 540 miles away.

For the traveler there are three rustic motels, numerous stores and cafes, telephone and radio communications, laundry service, a medical center, auto repairs and a Pemex station. Lodging is quite cheap, with clean but very basic rooms costing $15 or less per night. Expect plenty of fresh fish on the restaurant menus here, although service can be rather slow at times. From Bahía Tortugas a dirt road runs 16.5 miles to Punta Eugenia at the western tip of the Vizcaíno Peninsula.

Vizcaíno Peninsula: Bahía Tortugas to Punta Eugenia

(See map page 231.)

(16 mi., 25 km., 0:30 hr.)

At the extreme western tip of the Vizcaíno Peninsula, Punta Eugenia marks the end of the road, more than 120 miles west of Highway 1. A tiny, windswept hamlet with just a few dozen buildings, Punta Eugenia relies on fishing for its livelihood, with lobster being the primary catch, as evidenced by the hundreds of lobster traps stacked along the dusty streets. Like so much of this peninsula, the setting is scenic and stark at once, as the taupe hills of the desert meet up with a rocky, wave-lashed coastline befitting New England or Big Sur. Isla Natividad, a popular surfing destination, cuts a low profile about five miles offshore and is easily visible most of the time. The much-larger Isla Cedros, site of a fish-packing plant and salt-loading wharf, lies 13 miles to the northwest and is visible on clear days.

Lobster traps and boat at Punta Eugenia

Punta Eugenia has no conventional services of any type for travelers, but boat trips can be arranged through local fishermen to both Isla Natividad and Isla Cedros. The boat ride to Isla Natividad takes about 20 minutes, while Isla Cedros takes about 1½ hours to reach by boat. (See Side Route to Isla Cedros, page 239.) Information on pricing and pickups is available from fishermen.

Side Routes

The road to Punta Eugenia is much like the one from Rancho San José de Castro to Bahía Tortugas—a dusty, two-lane route with some washboard sections, taking a roller coaster-like path through the mountains before winding down to the water's edge. The lone turnoff is 7.5 miles west of Bahía Tortugas and heads south to the fishing village of Punta Quebrada, an even smaller version of Punta Eugenia.

Vizcaíno Peninsula:
Rancho San José de Castro to Malarrimo Beach

(See map page 231.)

(26 mi., 43 km.; 2:30 hrs.)

An arduous journey leads from the main road to Malarrimo Beach, one of the remotest—and most fascinating—beaches in all of Baja California. Located on the north shore of the Vizcaíno Peninsula, the beach not only gets the brunt of wintertime swells, but lies at the receiving end of the prevailing ocean currents that circulate clockwise around the North Pacific. As a result, the beach acts as a huge catch basin for flotsam and jetsam from far corners of the ocean.

Huge redwood logs, World War II food tins, Japanese fishing floats, timbers from sunken vessels and trash thrown overboard from ships have all turned up on this remote strand. Stories of cases of Scotch and other valuable items washing ashore are probably true, but the beach has been pretty well picked over since the treasure-trove came to light in the early 1960s. Even now, though, the determined beachcomber will likely turn up some items of interest, manmade or otherwise. During a 1999 expedition, an Auto Club research team found the remains of a gray whale.

The remains of a gray whale, washed ashore at Malarrimo Beach

The drive to Malarrimo Beach presents a worthy adventure in its own right, following a road that is one of the roughest on the peninsula and subject to periodic closures due to rockslides, washouts and other hazards. Four-wheel-drive is necessary to negotiate some of the worst patches of this narrow, twisting route.

The turnoff from the Vizcaíno-Bahía Tortugas road is about .2 mile east of the road leading to Rancho San José de Castro. From there the route winds north through a series of narrow, steep-walled arroyos for several miles before emerging onto a barren mesa, providing some excellent views of some colorful eroded canyons. The road then makes a steep rugged descent into one of the gaping canyons and follows a streambed toward the Pacific Ocean. The road becomes sandy over the final few miles, and driving on the beach itself is not advisable, due to patches of quicksand that have trapped more than one vehicle over the years. The beach itself is very windy, and the best campsites are just inland near the mouth of the canyon. Driftwood for fires is in abundant supply.

Vizcaíno Peninsula:
Rancho San José de Castro to Bahía Asunción

(See map page 231.)

(35 mi., 56 km.; 1:45 hrs.)

This long and lonely drive is among the scenic highlights of the Vizcaíno Peninsula, showcasing its desolate beauty as it winds through canyons and across mesas, hills and stark coastal plains to Bahía Asunción. Even by Baja standards, the feeling of isolation is extreme along the dusty byway that leads to this remote coastal town, and it is easy to cover the 35 miles without seeing another vehicle. Bahía Asunción, a windblown village of 1650 sitting on a low peninsula across from rocky Isla Asunción, typifies the small cannery towns of the Vizcaíno Peninsula. Like Bahía Tortugas, Bahía Asunción lives off the fishing, abalone and lobster trades, its packing plant sending goods by truck to Ensenada and other towns.

TASTY TACOS

Made with fillets freshly hauled from the nearby Pacific, the fish tacos at Restaurant El Mayico, on the main drag in Bahía Asunción, rank among the best in Baja.

For a settlement of this size, the range of facilities is decent, including basic accommodations, cafes, small markets, a pharmacy and a health center, laundry service, telephone service and gasoline. There's also an army base and a dirt airstrip—seemingly standard equipment for remote Baja settlements. A graded road leaves town from behind the health center and runs 7.9 miles northwest along the coast to the fishing village of San Roque.

The graded road to Bahía Asunción branches south from the Vizcaíno Junction-Bahía Tortugas route .5 mile west of the Malarrimo Beach turnoff. Follow the signed road to the left 1.3 miles to San José de Castro, bear left, go 4.3 miles, then turn right (south) onto the dirt road to Bahía Asunción. From this junction the road climbs into a range of dark brown mountains covered with an impressive assortment of Baja flora. After crossing a saddle, the road descends onto a wide, sloping plain, with the ocean visible far to the west. The road enters a shallow arroyo and follows the sandy bottom for 1.5 miles, then winds upward to a gap between a flat-topped volcanic butte and a range of barren hills. Later the road runs through a range of low, chalk-colored hills before heading southeast along the base of a volcanic mesa. Rounding the south end of the mesa, the road angles gradually toward the ocean as it emerges onto a lonely coastal plain. After dropping into another sandy arroyo, the road turns south and reaches Bahía Asunción at mileage 37.5.

On the beach at Bahía Asunción

An alternate route returns from Bahía Asunción to the Vizcaíno-Bahía Tortugas road, following the road to Punta Abreojos (see following side route) for the first 3.9 miles to a junction where you turn left. This graded dirt and gravel road runs 22.5 miles northeast to the Vizcaíno-Bahía Tortugas road and is the shortest route back to Highway 1. The road is short on scenic value, though, crossing miles of flat, sparsely vegetated desert.

Vizcaíno Peninsula:
Bahía Asunción to Punta Abreojos
(See map page 231.)

(59 mi., 93 km.; 2 hrs.)

Another far-flung cannery town lies at the journey's end of this, one of the easier legs of the loop trip around the Vizcaíno Peninsula. A handful of sandy stretches present the only hazard of note along the regularly graded road, which hugs the contour of the Pacific shoreline to Punta Abreojos. En route the road passes another canning town, La Bocana, along with fishing villages and miles of virgin beaches.

A village of 1200, Punta Abreojos lies on a sandy spit between the ocean and a salt marsh at the western edge of Bahía de Ballenas (Whales Bay). About 20 miles west across the bay is the entrance to Laguna San Ignacio, one of the winter calving grounds for the California gray whale. A series of wetlands lie between the village and lagoon, as do large expanses of barren mud flats that were once earmarked for development as a huge salt-evaporating operation. Punta Abreojos is another village with a fishing cooperative and a cannery that sends its products to the markets of the north. Facilities for the traveler include a store, a cafe, gasoline drums, a telegraph office and radio communications. An airstrip is located just north of town.

The road to Punta Abreojos follows the curve of the shoreline along the edge of an arid coastal lowland, running about a half-mile inland from the beach most of the way. Several dirt roads provide access to the flat, sandy shore, which is littered with a variety of shells. A large number of primitive campsites line the beach, but relentless winds and a lack of wood limit their appeal. Fishing from shore can be excellent, however.

Leaving Bahía Asunción, 3.9 miles from town is a junction with a graded road that leads northeast to the Vizcaíno-Bahía Tortugas road. The road continues southeast along the coast, passing a small shrine 18 miles from Bahía Asunción, just before the junction with a dirt road to the fishing village of Punta Prieta. At mileage 21.7, a road branches right to San Hipólito, another fishing village.

North of the junction is the unusual form of Cerro Mesa, with its vivid layers of magenta and green rock. The road continues to follow the coastline to La Bocana, reached by a turnoff at mileage 47.7. This cannery town of 900 has stores, cafes, a clinic, gasoline and mechanical assistance. Beyond La Bocana the road veers inland and skirts a shallow inlet to the entrance of Punta Abreojos, a 10.9-mile drive. The surface along this final stretch is smooth, hard-packed dirt, which allows for speeds of up to 50 mph and serves as a natural airstrip.

Vizcaíno Peninsula: Punta Abreojos to Highway 1

(See map page 231.)

(53 mi., 85 km.; 2 hrs.)

A long drive across empty, barren desert leads back to Highway 1 on the southeastern-most leg of the loop around the Vizcaíno Peninsula. A carefully driven passenger car can make the trip on this wide, graded road, although the jarring washboard surface can make the trip uncomfortable in any vehicle. Leaving Punta Abreojos, the route passes an airstrip before swinging north across the featureless desert. At mileage 6.1 is a signed junction with a road that leads 3.1 miles east to Campo René, a popular fishing spot where rustic cabañas and windy campsites can be found on the beach.

After skirting the southern flank of flat-topped Cabo Santa Clara Mesa, the road bears northeast across rolling, cactus-covered terrain. A group of volcanic peaks rise from the desert on the western skyline. Approaching Highway 1 the road enters a "forest" of cardón cacti. Visible in the distance to the south is Laguna San Ignacio. The road meets Highway 1 at a junction 15 miles west of San Ignacio and 28 miles southeast of Vizcaíno.

SPANISH, BAJA STYLE

Cardonal is the Spanish word for a huge, forest-like stand of cardón cacti.

Isla Cedros

(See map page 231.)

Rising high and rugged above the Pacific, Isla Cedros is far removed from the normal Baja tourist circuit, lying some 60 miles west of Guerrero Negro and 13 miles off the tip of the Vizcaíno Peninsula. The island's sole town, Cedros (also called El Pueblo), is a busy place, though, with fishing and salt being the twin pillars of the economy. Near the southwest corner of the island, the town has a fish-packing plant and a deep-water port that serves as transshipment point for salt harvested at Guerrero Negro. Salt arrives by barge from the mainland to be loaded on ocean-going ships, which in turn ship it around the world. About 3000 residents live full-time in the town.

HITCHIN' A (BOAT) RIDE

Boat transportation can be arranged with local fishers from Punta Eugenia to Isla Natividad and Isla Cedros. Natividad is about 20 minutes away by skiff, while Cedros is $1\frac{1}{2}$ hours away. At Isla Cedros you can arrange a boat trip to Islas San Benito.

Isla Cedros has several attractions for the outdoor-minded. A few of the rugged island's peaks reach heights of more than 3000 feet, and hiking trails lead to the tallest one, 3950-foot Monte Cedros. Diving is good off the north and south ends of the island, while fishing is good for barracuda, bass and yellowtail. For the visitor, the town of Cedros offers a few cafes, a couple of low-priced inns and taxi service. A local airline, Aero Cedros, serves the town with twice-weekly flights from Guerrero Negro and Ensenada. Boat transit can be arranged as well, through fishermen in Punta Eugenia, at the westernmost tip of the Vizcaíno Peninsula.

Isla Cedros falls in the Pacific time zone, one hour earlier than Guerrero Negro.

South of Isla Cedros, off the western tip of the Vizcaíno Peninsula, is the small, low-lying Isla Natividad. The main draw to this island is surfing, especially the south shore, which ranks with Baja's top spots to catch summer swells rumbling out of the South Pacific. Huge northwest swells, suited for experts only, break off the island's northern tip during the winter months. West of Isla Cedros are Islas San Benito, a clump of three islands known for their excellent diving, and fishing for bass and yellowtail in their extensive kelp beds.

See *GreatestHits*, Chapter 3, for more on San Francisco de la Sierra.

Highway 1 to San Francisco de la Sierra

(See map page 231.)

(22 mi., 35 km.; 1:30 hrs.)

The flatlands of the desert give way to red-rock mesas, yawning canyons and cooler temperatures along the rocky road to San Francisco de la Sierra, high in the Sierra San Francisco. This tiny settlement, at an elevation of 4500 feet, is the jump-off point for intrepid explorers who come from around the world to see the famed cave paintings of central Baja.

Those drawings, considered the most spectacular in all of Baja, enjoy the full protection of the federal government and require permission (available in San Ignacio) to view them. Visitors are also required to be accompanied by local ranchers, who serve as authorized guides. Known as Californios, those ranchers make their homes in San Francisco de la Sierra and the surrounding mountains, and are descendants of Spanish ranchers who settled the highlands in the 1700s. Raising mules, horses and goats, they have remained much removed from the mainstream of Mexican life. The settlement here has a school, church and small store. There is no restaurant, but meals are available upon request.

Cañon Santa Teresa, in the heart of Sierra San Francisco

The road to San Francisco de la Sierra is graded in some areas, but has some very rough and narrow sections as it winds into these rugged mountains. Only sturdy trucks with plenty of clearance and good tires should attempt this drive. Leaving Highway 1 at a signed junction 27.6 miles northwest of San Ignacio, the road heads across level desert for the first six miles before beginning a sharp, winding ascent onto a mesa. Southeast of the mesa, a vast, lonesome canyon comes into view as the road continues upward. Climbing ever higher, the meager vegetation of the flatlands gives way to barrel cactus, agave, occasional cirios, and closely spaced brush. At about 18 miles from the start, your destination comes into view as the road skirts the side of a deep, gaping chasm on the final approach to San Francisco de la Sierra.

NICE AND EASY

Steep drop-offs, blind curves and a rough roadbed narrowing to one lane in spots demand more caution than normal as you climb into the Sierra San Francisco. If you're going to see the cave paintings, you'll probably be driving east across the desert in the early morning—directly into the sunlight. Slow down and take your time.

Chapter 8

San Ignacio & Down the Gulf

The 28th parallel marks the border between Baja California and Baja California Sur, but if the lay of the land and ambiance count for anything, then Baja's southern state truly begins on the outskirts of San Ignacio. Some 80 miles beyond the state line, the flat and barren landscape of the Vizcaíno Desert gradually cedes to rolling terrain with rugged peaks on the horizon as Highway 1 nears the northernmost of Baja Sur's oasis towns.

San Ignacio is a fitting introduction to Baja Sur, plunked amid a vast grove of date and fan palms that far outnumber the town's 2000 souls. Balmy days and blue skies are the norm year round, which you would expect in Baja Sur, and they come in sharp contrast to the cool overcast that prevails along the Pacific Coast. Beyond San Ignacio the terrain

Palm oasis and Misión San Ignacio

grows still more dramatic as Highway 1 passes three enormous extinct volcanic cones known as Las Tres Vírgenes and approaches the Gulf of California.

The gulf's splendor unfolds slowly as the highway meets the water's edge in Santa Rosalía. A busy town of 11,000, Santa Rosalía retains many trappings from its days as a copper-mining center, developed by the French in the late 1800s. The town has a distinct look from all others in Baja, with its Gallic past manifest in its buildings, which include an iron church designed by the architect of the Eiffel Tower.

Farther south is the sleepy village of Mulegé, just inland from the gulf and poised alongside a river of the same name. With its vast palm oasis and slow pace of life, Mulegé enjoys a near idyllic atmosphere that may best capture the outsider's romanticized notion of what a small Baja town should be. Mulegé lies near the mouth of Bahía Concepción, an awe-inspiring, 30-mile-long bay that ranks among the greatest scenic treasures not only of Baja, but the whole of Mexico. Even with the completion of Highway 1 in 1973, the bay has remained largely undeveloped, but word is out about its unmatched beauty. Retirement and vacation homes have sprung up along its western shore, and during the

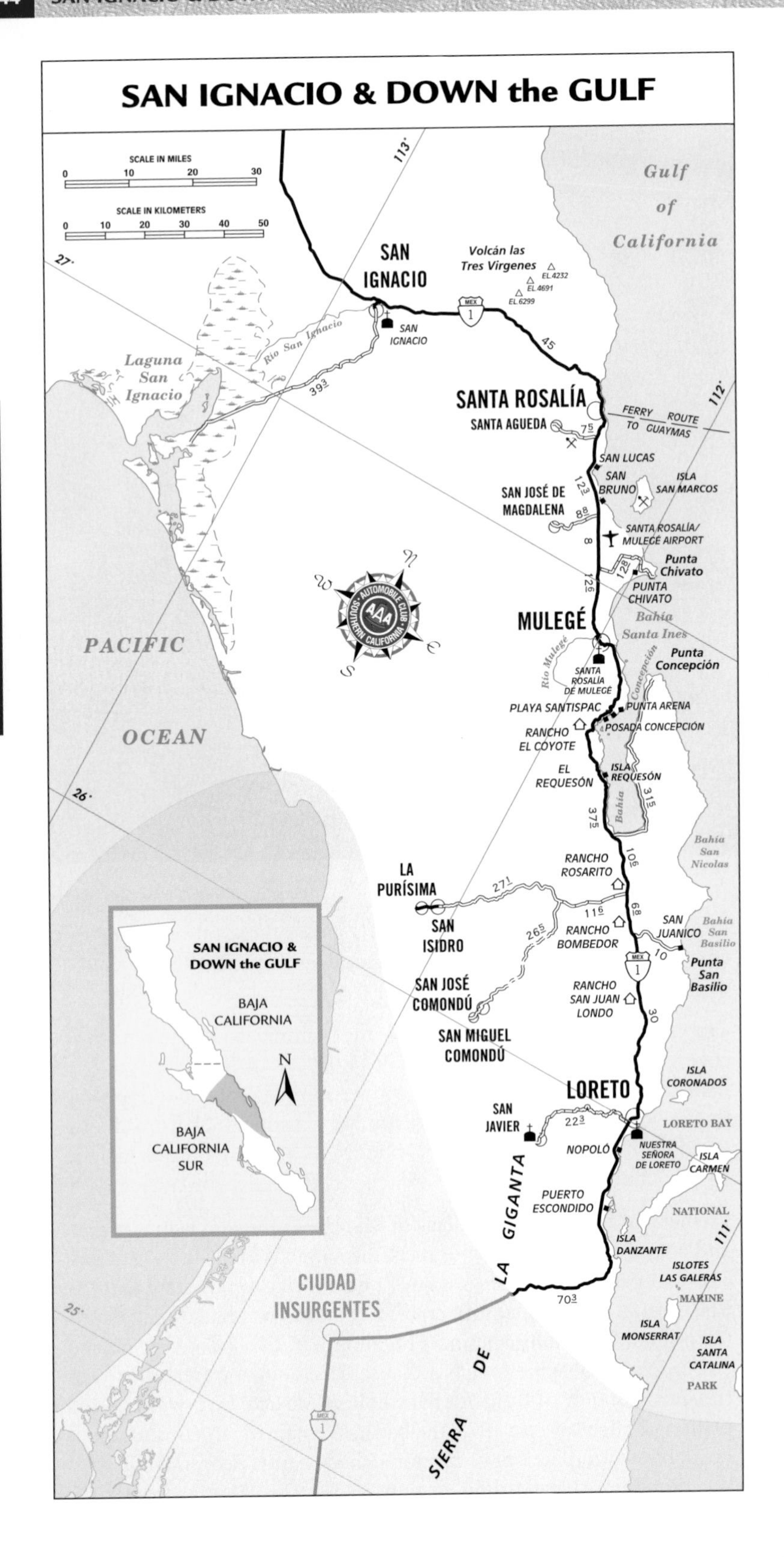

SAN IGNACIO & DOWN the GULF
SCALE IN MILES
0 10 20 30
SCALE IN KILOMETERS
0 10 20 30 40 50
Gulf of California
SAN IGNACIO
Volcán las Tres Virgenes
EL.4232
EL.4691
EL.6299
SAN IGNACIO
Río San Ignacio
Laguna San Ignacio
SANTA ROSALÍA
SANTA AGUEDA
FERRY ROUTE TO GUAYMAS
SAN LUCAS
SAN BRUNO
ISLA SAN MARCOS
SAN JOSÉ DE MAGDALENA
SANTA ROSALÍA/ MULEGÉ AIRPORT
Punta Chivato
PUNTA CHIVATO
MULEGÉ
Bahía Santa Ines
Punta Concepción
Río Mulegé
SANTA ROSALÍA DE MULEGÉ
PLAYA SANTISPAC
PUNTA ARENA
RANCHO EL COYOTE
POSADA CONCEPCIÓN
EL REQUESÓN
ISLA REQUESÓN
Bahía Concepción
PACIFIC OCEAN
Bahía San Nicolas
RANCHO ROSARITO
LA PURÍSIMA
SAN ISIDRO
RANCHO BOMBEDOR
SAN JUANICO
Bahía San Basilio
Punta San Basilio
SAN JOSÉ COMONDÚ
RANCHO SAN JUAN LONDO
SAN MIGUEL COMONDÚ
ISLA CORONADOS
LORETO
SAN JAVIER
LORETO BAY
NOPOLÓ
NUESTRA SEÑORA DE LORETO
ISLA CARMEN
PUERTO ESCONDIDO
ISLA DANZANTE
ISLOTES LAS GALERAS
LORETO BAY NATIONAL MARINE PARK
ISLA MONSERRAT
ISLA SANTA CATALINA
CIUDAD INSURGENTES
SIERRA DE LA GIGANTA
SAN IGNACIO & DOWN the GULF
BAJA CALIFORNIA
BAJA CALIFORNIA SUR
AUTOMOBILE CLUB SOUTHERN CALIFORNIA AAA

winter RVs by the hundreds stake their claims to plots of beachfront along a chain of picturesque coves.

Still farther south is Loreto, cradle of European civilization in the Californias and the last town before Highway 1 swings inland from the gulf. Founded in 1697, Loreto is the oldest permanent settlement in Baja California. Unchanged with the passing centuries is the spectacular setting of this town, between the ruddy peaks of the Sierra de la Giganta and the azure waters of the gulf, with desert islands floating offshore.

Until completion of the Transpeninsular Highway in 1973, many residents and travelers got about in this region using centuries-old dirt roads built by the Jesuits.

This being Baja, some of your finest moments will come far from the pavement's edge. There's the tiny mission town of San Javier, nestled high in the Sierra de la Giganta amid surroundings that have few equals in either of the Californias. Other remote villages with names like La Purísima, San Isidro and Comondú lurk high in the sierra, reachable from Highway 1 by only the sturdiest of off-road vehicles. On the Pacific Coast there's Laguna San Ignacio, the last of the California gray whales' winter calving grounds to remain totally undeveloped. The gulf, for its part, boasts one of Mexico's newest biosphere preserves, Loreto Bay National Marine Park. A mecca for diving, sportfishing and kayaking, this offshore preserve derives most of its grandeur beneath the waves. That's saying a lot in a region with arguably the most magnificent scenery on the Baja California peninsula.

Experience ...

- A spell of quiet reflection, soothing for the pious and unchurched alike, sitting before the gilded altar of Misión Nuestra Señora de Loreto.
- Pulling off the road along Highway 1 and staring in silent reverence across the turquoise waters of Bahía Concepción.
- Discovering shades of brown and red you didn't know existed as the new day's sun's rays angle across the Sierra de la Giganta, somewhere along the road to San Javier.
- Friendly locals who greet you for no good reason as they pass you on the street in San Ignacio.
- The aromas of salt air, sage and fresh-baked *pan dulce* all vying for your attention during your early-morning stroll along the banks of the Río Mulegé.

San Ignacio

Río San Ignacio, just north of its namesake town

Reaching San Ignacio is without a doubt one of the great joys for Highway 1 travelers, welcome relief after crossing miles of spare, flat scrubland. Northernmost of Baja's oasis towns, San Ignacio personifies nearly all the attributes associated with such—thousands of palms crowding a languid river, pastel storefronts alongside a shaded main plaza, and a lovely mission surrounded by narrow streets with simple thatched-roof homes.

Stony hills and taupe mesas surround this peaceful hamlet, which lies at the floor of a broad arroyo about a mile off Highway 1 via a winding access road. That road is a scenic treat in its own right, crossing an earthen dam across the broad Río San Ignacio and passing through a forest of date palms, which form the backbone of the farm-based economy. Oranges, figs and grapes are other important crops, nourished by the town's namesake river, which flows underground before surfacing on the outskirts of the community.

WHAT'S IN A NAME?

Before the Jesuits renamed it San Ignacio, the Indians knew it as "Kada-kaaman," or "Creek of Weeds."

The river supported a large Indian settlement before Jesuit missionaries arrived in the early 1700s, founding the mission in 1728. It was the Jesuits who planted the date palms that crowd the riverbanks, and in 1733 they began work on the mission church. They were expelled, though, before they could complete the building, which the Dominicans accomplished in 1786. They abandoned the mission in 1840, but the church remains a working parish today.

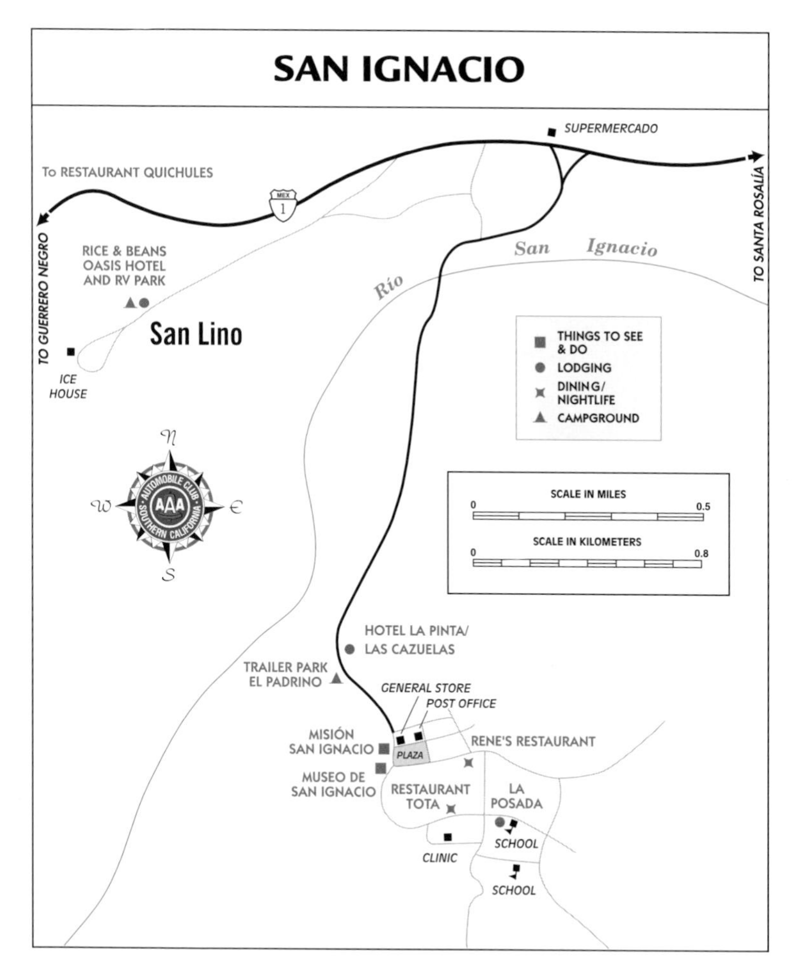

The mission is also the largest and most impressive building in much of central Baja, but these days it's a gray whale skeleton at the Highway 1 turnoff that lets you know the town is nigh. The skeleton befits a town that serves as jump-off point to Laguna San Ignacio, one of the grays' three main calving lagoons. The whales have helped make a name for San Ignacio, as tourists from around the world converge here during the winter before traveling down 40 miles of dirt road to the sheltered waters of the lagoon.

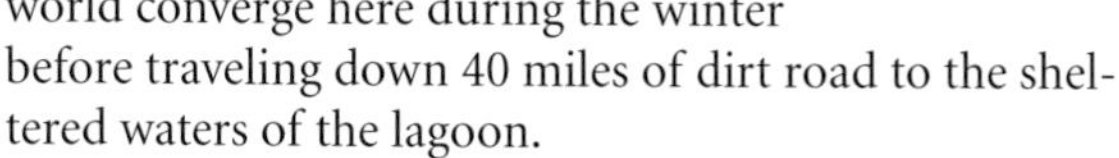

FYI ...

T.J. Cabo

The midway point on Highway 1 between the U.S. border and Cabo San Lucas is about 2½ miles west of San Ignacio.

The rugged mountains northeast of town harbor the area's other great attraction—the cave paintings of Sierra San Francisco. The famed murals bring many travelers through San Ignacio, since this is one of only two towns (the other is La Paz) where permission is granted to gain access to the painting sites.

For more information on the murals, see *GreatestHits*, Chapter 3.

Misión San Ignacio

San Ignacio pulls in its share of other travelers heading up or down Highway 1, being the only settlement for many miles with markets, restaurants, gasoline or mechanical assistance. By themselves, though, the mission, palm groves and simple, small-town charms are enough to bring many back this way time and time again.

Top Attractions

MISIÓN SAN IGNACIO Completed in 1786, this imposing stone mission remains a working parish, and by itself merits a stop in San Ignacio. With its ornate façade, towering belfry and soaring entryway, the church ranks with the grandest of missions in all of Baja. The lava-block walls measure four feet thick and have helped keep the building in excellent condition. Inside, the frescoes are beginning to show their age but remain viewable, while the altars and statuary remain impressive works of art. *On the west side of the main square. No phone.*

GET ABOVE IT ALL

A rocky mesa east of the main square affords an excellent overlook of San Ignacio, the surrounding countryside and the mission church rising from the vast palm groves. A rough trail leads to the summit.

MUSEO DE SAN IGNACIO This small but informative museum is a good place to learn about the history and geography of central Baja. The greatest emphasis is on the cave paintings of San Francisco de la Sierra, including life-sized replicas of the vaunted murals. One drawback is that all the descriptive text is in Spanish only. Next to the museum is a local office of the National Institute of Anthropology and History (INAH), the place to obtain the required permission to visit the paintings. *Next door to mission. No phone. Open Tue-Sat, 8 am-6 pm, May through Oct till 3 pm. Free.*

Government permission is required to visit the cave paintings of Sierra de San Francisco. Permission is granted upon completing a short application at Museo de San Ignacio.

Outdoor Fun

WHALE WATCHING

San Ignacio is the starting point for nearly all tourists bound for Laguna San Ignacio to see the California gray whales. This pristine, shallow inlet lies along the Pacific coastline southwest of town, the middle of the three main calving grounds for Baja's most famous mammals.

Laguna San Ignacio has a reputation for having the friendliest whales of any Baja lagoon, with many of the gentle giants eagerly approaching boats. Perhaps that's because San Ignacio is the only lagoon to remain entirely undeveloped, save for a few tiny fish camps. It seems sure to stay that way for the foreseeable future, as the Mexican government in 2000 scrapped plans to build a huge salt-evaporating operation along the lagoon's shoreline.

See *GreatestHits*, Chapter 3, for more on whale watching.

Day outings last about seven hours, including the 80-mile round-trip drive on the dirt road between San Ignacio and the lagoon, plus a guided boat trip and lunch. Overnight trips are available as well, with lodging at seasonal camps along the shoreline. Boat tours in the lagoon last around 2½ hours and cost $30 per person. Vans providing transport from town to the lagoon charge around $130 for up to 10 passengers. While various hotels, markets and campgrounds provide information about tours, the main operator is Ecoturismo Kuyima, located on the main plaza across from the mission, phone 01152 (1) 154-00-70.

In addition, two San Diego-based outfitters operate campsites at the lagoon and organize tours departing from the San Diego area. They are:

Baja Discovery *(800) 829-2252 or (619) 262-0700. Website at www.bajadiscovery.com.* **Baja Expeditions** *2625 Garnet Ave, San Diego, CA 92109. (800) 843-6967. Website at www.bajaexpeditions.com.*

Dining

With all of 2000 residents, San Ignacio is not a place for exquisite dining, but the town's attractions and strategic location along Highway 1 ensure a steady stream of visitors who keep several decent restaurants in business. You'll find the usual assortment of Mexican and seafood platters, served amid casual surroundings with the inevitable *norteña* music playing in the background.

LAS CAZUELAS — **Mexican**
$4.50-11. *In the Hotel La Pinta, on entrance road leading to town plaza. 01152 (1) 154-03-00.*

RENE'S RESTAURANT — **Mexican/Seafood**
$4.50-14.50. *One block east of the main plaza. 01152 (1) 154-01-53.*

RESTAURANT QUICHULES — **Mexican/Seafood**
$3-11. *2 miles northwest of town on Hwy 1. No phone.*

RESTAURANT TOTA — **Mexican**
$4-13. *3 blocks east of the main plaza. No phone.*

Lodging

Unless you're camping, you have your choice of just two places to stay in San Ignacio. There's Hotel La Pinta, a typical, comfortable branch of the small Baja California chain, and La Posada, a small, no-frills inn that attracts the peso-pinching set. Finding a vacant room is not a problem during most of the year, but it's another matter during the whale-watching season, when La Pinta may sell out for several weeks in advance. La Posada doesn't have quite the demand, but may still fill up early in the day, so reservations are advisable. La Pinta rooms cost about $75 per night, while La Posada rooms fetch about $25.

For campers, San Ignacio has several small trailer parks with tent and RV sites. Best known is El Padrino, on the road leading into town from Highway 1 (across from Hotel La Pinta) and the only one with any hookups or other creature comforts.

See *Lodging & Campgrounds*, Chapter 15, for listings.

TRAVELOGUE

San Ignacio to Santa Rosalía
(45 mi., 72 km.; 1:15 hrs.)

More than 500 miles from the border, Highway 1 reaches the shores of the Gulf of California at last, with the first sighting about 34 miles east of San Ignacio. Following that is a rapid, winding drop from the desert plateau to the water's edge, just north of Santa Rosalía.

While it is one of the great climaxes of Highway 1, reaching the gulf is by no means the sole highlight of this drive. Leaving the palm groves of San Ignacio behind, the route soon returns to arid surroundings, winding through more miles of low hills as it approaches Las Tres Vírgenes, which rank among the great scenic highlights anywhere along Highway 1. A string of three massive volcanic cones, Las Tres Vírgenes (The Three Virgins) rise majestically above the surrounding desert, the tallest of which stands 6547 feet above sea level. Highway 1 skirts their base before it drops onto a cacti-covered plateau.

At the plateau's edge comes that first view of the gulf, along with the steepest grade on all of Highway

1, as you embark on seven miles of weaving switchbacks and hairpin turns. Drive these miles with extreme caution and be extra alert for trucks rounding the curves; passing without the greatest care is an invitation for disaster. Rockslides are also a hazard here. Dozens of shrines line the shoulders, bearing witness to those who failed to negotiate this roadway. At the bottom of the grade the road turns south and hugs the coast to the junction with the main street of Santa Rosalía.

Highway 1's precipitous grade near Santa Rosalía

00.0 **Junction with the paved road into San Ignacio.**

08.7 **Junction with a rough dirt road to Rancho Santa Marta, a departure point for mule trips to ancient Indian cave paintings in the rugged mountains north of San Ignacio.**

23.9 **Excellent viewpoint for Las Tres Vírgenes.**

34.1 **First view of the Gulf of California.**

35.0 **Beginning of a series of steep grades and tight curves, as the highway plunges 1000 feet to the shore of the gulf.**

41.0 **The shore of the Gulf of California.**

45.4 **Junction with the main street of Santa Rosalía.**

Santa Rosalía

Each of Baja's gulf coast towns has its unique personality, but none to quite the degree of Santa Rosalía. In both appearance and atmosphere, this bustling port settlement of 11,000 stands out not just from other gulf towns, but the rest of Baja California. Credit that to the French, who founded Santa Rosalía in the 1880s as a company town for copper mining and smelting. The heydays of the copper industry are long gone, but the town's Gallic roots

Santa Rosalía, with its distinctive French architecture

remain apparent in the colorful bungalow-style homes, local French bakery and one-of-a-kind church designed by A. Gustave Eiffel, he of Eiffel Tower fame.

For the first seven decades, copper and Santa Rosalía were inseparable, and the town prospered under the auspices of El Boleo Copper Company, which turned this into one of the leading mining centers in Mexico. The French-owned firm imported Indian labor from Sonora, built a pipeline to bring in water and constructed a port to handle shipments of processed ore. Eventually the best deposits played out, which combined with a world drop in copper prices to force the mine's closure in 1954.

Santa Rosalía is the seat of government for the *municipio* of Mulegé, which also includes the towns of Guerrero Negro, San Ignacio and Mulegé.

While the few efforts to revive the industry have seen limited results, mining remains important to the local economy. These days, however, the main quarry is gypsum, shipped mostly to the United States for use as additives in plaster and cement. Some gypsum is mined on the mainland, but the largest source is four miles off the coast at Isla San Marcos.

Truth be told, Santa Rosalía will not win many beauty contests as seaside towns go. Evidence of the mining past is all too apparent in the decaying remains of the smelter and mining equipment, and the town has not done a very good job of cleaning up after itself. The beaches, to use the term loosely, are gray and rocky, seeing few visitors besides the local populace. As such, Santa Rosalía offers few hints of the scenic splendor that lies farther south, and the town hosts fewer tourists than any other along Baja's gulf coast.

¡QUÉ RICO!

Panadería El Boleo, on Avenida Obregón between calles 3 and 4, just may be the best bakery in Baja California Sur, with its mouth-watering baguettes and other French-style pastries and breads. In a country not known for its exquisite baked goods, many Highway 1 travelers consider El Boleo a must-stop.

Be all that as it may, the town still merits a visit, certainly for Iglesia Santa Bárbara de Santa Rosalía, the all-metal church that was shipped here in sections from France and assembled in 1897. Elsewhere, the northern plateau (Mesa Norte) provides a panoramic view of the old copper smelter and some fine examples of

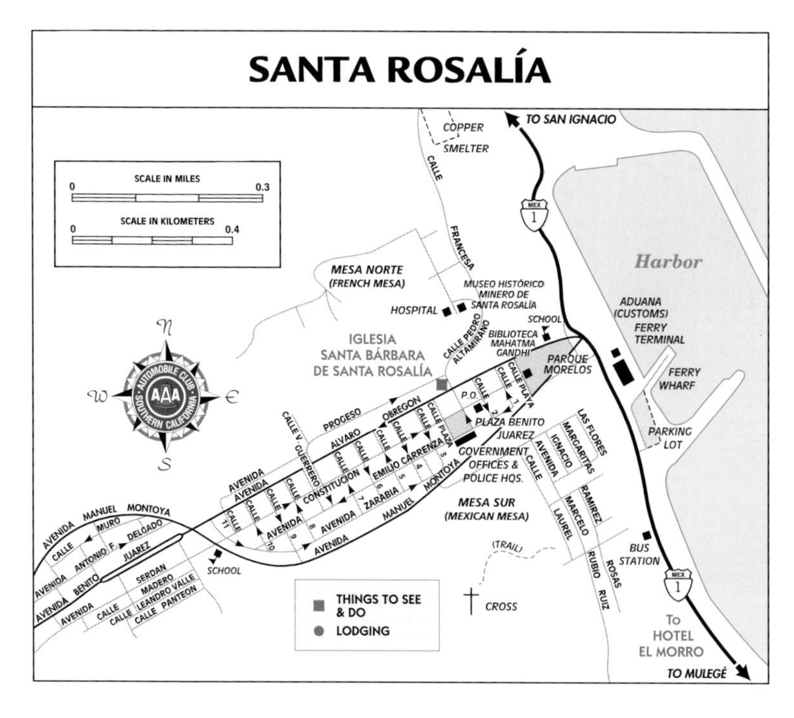

French colonial architecture. Also, rolling stock from El Boleo's short-line railroad can be seen around town, most notably a locomotive at the corner of Highway 1 and Avenida Obregón. More icons of the past grace the walls of the public library, Biblioteca Mahatma Gandhi, which boasts a fine collection of early photographs of the town.

Attractions aside, Santa Rosalía is an obligatory stop for all those coming or going across the gulf on the Baja California Ferry, which links central Baja with the mainland port of Guaymas. The ferry runs twice a week from the fair-sized harbor, which shelters the local fishing fleet plus assorted commercial and pleasure craft. For the traveler, Santa Rosalía also has several small hotels, cafes and markets, not to mention Pemex stations, auto parts stores and repair shops.

See *Appendix*, Chapter 16, for more on the Baja California Ferry.

Top Attractions

IGLESIA SANTA BÁRBARA DE SANTA ROSALÍA

This prefabricated iron church is more than 100 years old but has withstood the test of time superbly, remaining in excellent condition as well as a working parish for the local population. Designed by A. Gustave Eiffel, the church had earned considerable recognition several years before it arrived in Santa Rosalía. It first stood alongside the Eiffel Tower during the 1889 World Exposition in Paris, an example of a church built to withstand the fierce

Iglesia Santa Bárbara

heat of equatorial climates. Following the fair, the church was disassembled and sat in storage for several years before El Boleo company officials discovered the pieces and had them shipped to Santa Rosalía. The interior of the church is more traditional in appearance, highlighted by some lovely stained glass work. *On Ave Obregón, 4 blocks west of Hwy 1.*

TRAVELOGUE

See map on page 285.

Santa Rosalía to Mulegé

(38 mi., 61 km.; 1 hr.)

If Santa Rosalía falls short of scenic expectations, the highway farther south soon makes up for it as the beauty of the gulf begins to unfold in deep blue waters juxtaposed against rugged coastal headlands and desert islands.

Heading south from Santa Rosalía, the highway follows the shoreline for about four miles, providing some excellent views of Isla San Marcos, best known for its large gypsum mine. The route turns briefly inland before returning to the gulf, only to lose the coast once more as the shoreline swings east toward Punta Chivato. There is little of scenic interest as the route passes through several miles of barren countryside before dropping rapidly into Mulegé.

00.0 **Junction with the main street of Santa Rosalía.**

05.2 **Junction with the 7.5-mile dirt road to Santa Agueda, a quaint farming village that produces papayas, mangos and dates, and has a spring that is the source of Santa Rosalía's water. Although graded its entire length, the road has a rough, washboard surface and a couple of bad spots that could damage a passenger car.**

09.4 **San Lucas, a fishing village situated on an attractive, palm-lined cove. Good camping beaches can be found both north and**

south of the village. A signed turnoff leads to San Lucas RV Park.

14.7	San Bruno, a village with an airstrip that has grown up around a fishing cooperative on the gulf shore, 0.8 mile from Highway 1.
17.4	Junction with the dirt road to San José de Magdalena (see Side Route to San José de Magdalena, page 278).
21.8	Entrance to the Santa Rosalía Airport.
25.2	A gravel road leading to Punta Chivato, site of a seafront hotel (see *Lodging & Campgrounds*, Chapter 15). The hotel is currently closed for remodeling. Nearby are a good dirt airstrip and a cluster of vacation homes.
37.9	Mulegé. Turn left to enter the main part of town.

Río Mulegé

Nestled amid a teeming palm oasis between rolling desert hills and its namesake river, Mulegé basks in a setting that is sublime, even by Baja California Sur standards. This peaceful village of 5000 straddles the palm-shrouded Río Mulegé, about two miles upstream from the Gulf of California. Between its blissful surroundings and proximity to the gulf, this town has predictably become a popular haunt for North Americans vacationing or staying on as seasonal residents.

The name Mulegé (pronounced "Moo-le-HEY") is a contraction of the Yuman Indian words for "large creek of the white mouth," and reflects the town's attraction to its earliest residents. The river and its substantial Indian population helped make this one of the earliest towns in southern Baja, settled by Jesuit priests, who in 1705 founded Misión Santa Rosalía de Palermo. (It was later changed to Santa Rosalía de Mulegé.) The first mission church was destroyed in 1770 by a *chubasco* and flood that leveled much of the town, but it was soon rebuilt at its current site above the south bank of the river. It remained open until declining Indian populations forced its abandonment in 1828. A small settlement remained, but the outside world did not return in force till 1847, when U.S. troops tried unsuccessfully to seize the town during the Mexican-American War.

These days the Americans have returned, along with Canadians and visitors from many other lands who have discovered this town since the completion of Highway 1 in 1973. Some stay for weeks or months, while others put in briefly on their way down Highway 1 or flying in at the local airstrip. Consequently, south of Ensenada on Highway 1 Mulegé is the first tourist town of consequence, with hotels, restaurants, a pair of Pemex stations, and the usual

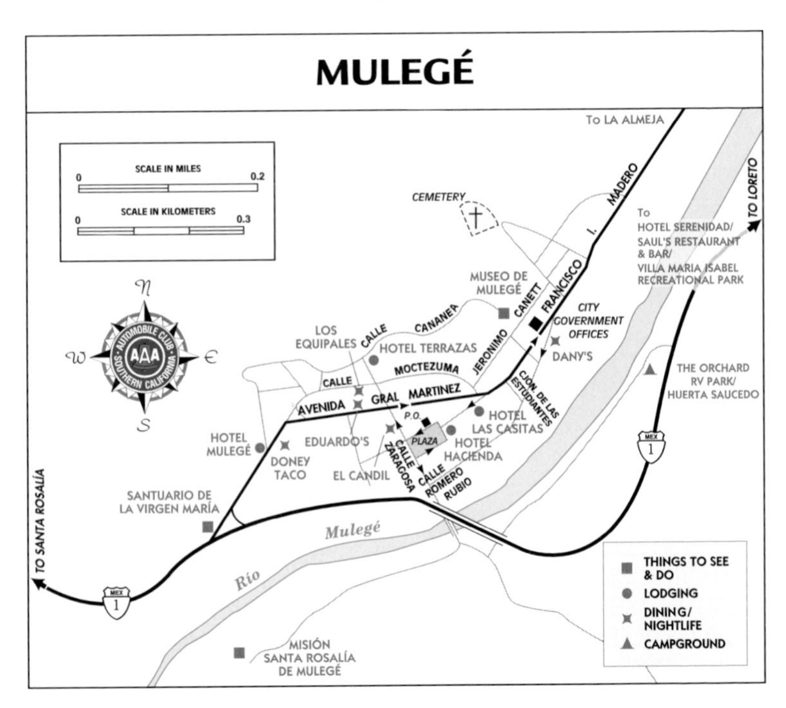

Park It and Walk

Mulegé is another Baja town where the best way to get around is on your own two feet. Not only is walking the only way to really explore the town, but Mulegé is decidedly not auto-friendly. Although the downtown streets are paved and in good condition, they're also very narrow and restricted to one-way traffic. For cars and pickups it's a tight fit, and for RVs it's a potential nightmare.

assortment of markets, auto parts stores and repair shops. So far, the town has absorbed the tourist inflow while retaining the serene atmosphere that brought so many here in the first place.

The Río Mulegé, for its part, remains the main source of the town's prosperity as it has since pre-Hispanic days. Its waters nourish huge groves of date palms, along with crops of oranges, figs, bananas and olives. The river also harbors several RV parks and a growing number of vacation homes along its shady banks. High above the river, the mission has been restored and returned to use as the local parish. The church is modest both in size and design, and it's almost always locked except for Mass. Instead, it's the location that makes this mission special. A lookout just behind the church affords outstanding views of the river and the vast grove of palms that line its banks from the distant foothills to the shoreline of the gulf.

While the mission and lovely river are Mulegé's main attractions, a small museum and shrine to the Virgin Mary are also worth a visit. But far more beckons beyond the town's confines. Mulegé marks the northern gateway of the Bahía Concepción, a 30-mile-long bay with awe-inspiring scenery that's equal to any in Baja California. The bay is a recreator's paradise where diving, fishing and kayaking are the primary activities. Outside the bay, the open gulf beckons with more places for diving and some of the best sportfishing to be found in the Sea of Cortez. Back on terra firma, the Indian paintings of San Borjitas and La Trinidad are the destination for an excellent day trip in the mountains outside of town.

With all those activities and the town's idyllic atmosphere, it's easy to see why some people move to Mulegé and resolve never to leave. Many pull up stakes within a few years and head back north, though, when they find the pace of life a tad too slow. Summer's brutal heat doesn't help either, and many locals leave town during the steamy days of August, September and early October. But every year a few more homes spring up around town, built by those who visit, fall in love and vow to put down roots in this tranquil oasis village.

Top Attractions

CAVE PAINTINGS

Dozens of cave painting zones dot the rugged Sierra de Guadalupe west of Mulegé, including two of the finest in Baja California. One is about 18 miles west of Mulegé at Cañon La Trinidad, home to three major murals that can only be reached with a four-mile round-trip hike and, depending on the season, a short swim through a stream considered to be the headwaters of the Río Mulegé. The other area is San Borjitas, 35 miles northwest of town, which was considered the most impressive site in Baja until the discovery of the Sierra de San Francisco murals in the early 1960s. An easy hike of less than a mile each way leads to a single mural site, inside a large granite cave.

Cave paintings in Cañon de Trinidad

The Mexican government requires a camera permit for either La Trinidad or San Borjitas. A per-day permit costs the peso-equivalent of about $3 for still photos and $30 for a video camera. Licensed guides can assist you in obtaining a permit.

A licensed guide is required to visit either of these zones. Most hotels and campgrounds in Mulegé can provide more information about the painting sites and help in arranging a guided tour. Another good source is El Candil restaurant on Calle Zaragoza in the center of town. These tours should be considered an all-day affair, due in part to the lengthy off-road drive required on the approach to either zone. The going rate for a tour to La Trinidad is about $40, while the tour of San Borjitas runs about $55. Prices usually include the guide, transportation, food and beverages.

MISIÓN SANTA ROSALÍA DE MULEGÉ

This L-shaped, stone-hewn church has been through several restorations since the missionaries departed in 1828, and it remains in active use today as the town parish. The main attraction is not the mission itself but the commanding view of the oasis from a nearby lookout. It is one of the most photographed views in Baja. A nearby hilltop provides a still

Misión Santa Rosalía de Mulegé

more panoramic vista, not only of the oasis, but of the town, the church and surrounding desert. *Above the south bank of the Río Mulegé, just upstream from the bridge that carries Hwy 1 across the river.*

MUSEO DE MULEGÉ

Built in 1907, this former penitentiary has become the local storehouse for displays and artifacts recalling the history of Mulegé and its environs. Along with Indian and early settler artifacts, the museum showcases the works of local artists. *On a hilltop overlooking the town. Open Mon-Sat 9 am-1 pm. Admission $1.20.*

RÍO MULEGÉ

Though not a "point of interest" in the traditional sense, this sleepy, palm-shrouded river lies at the core of the town's identity. A stroll along the river's south bank, via a footpath from the Hotel Serenidad to the Highway 1 bridge, is part of the Mulegé experience.

SANTUARIO DE LA VÍRGEN MARÍA

This attractive shrine to the Virgin Mary includes a panoramic painting of Mulegé. A flight of steps leads to the shrine, overlooking Highway 1 and the Río Mulegé. *At the west end of town.*

SHOPPING

It can't compete with the likes of Tijuana or Cabo San Lucas, but Mulegé has several arts and crafts shops with a nice selection of clothing and handicrafts. The place to look is in the heart of downtown, mostly along Calle Zaragoza and Avenida General Anaya.

Outdoor Fun

DIVING

The only dive shop in Mulegé is Cortez Explorers (formerly Mulegé Divers), which has scuba and snorkeling gear for sale and rent, along with air, guidebooks and other outdoor equipment. The shop organizes guided trips to Isla Santa Inés, and Punta Concepción, on the eastern flank of Bahía Concepción. Snorkeling trips start at $30 per person, while scuba excursions (equipment included) can cost $70 or more. The shop does not offer a full-fledged scuba certification course, but does have an introductory class for about $80.

ONE-STOP OUTFITTER

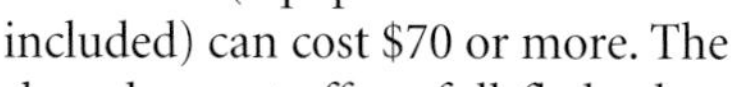

Along with scuba and snorkeling gear, Cortez Explorers also rents mountain bikes and ATVs—useful not only for exploring the surrounding hills and coastline, but also for puttering about town.

Sea temperatures around Mulegé range from the mid-80s in late summer to around 60 degrees during the winter.

See map on page 285.

Then there's EcoMundo, a self-described outdoor education recreation center on Bahía Concepción, which offers tours that combine snorkeling and kayaking. EcoMundo may also have the best deal on rental snorkeling gear in Baja, starting at $5 per day, with even lower rates for multi-day rentals.

Cortez Explorers *On Calle Moctezuma near the west entrance to town. 01152 (1) 153-05-00. Website at www.cortez-explorer.com.* **EcoMundo** *On the sand at Playa Concepción on Bahía Concepción, 15 miles south of town. Information available at office next to Hotel Las Casitas, in center of Mulegé at Calle Madero 50. 01152 (1) 153-04-09. E-mail at ecomundo@aol.com.*

FISHING

Mulegé is sometimes overlooked as a sportfishing destination, overshadowed by the likes La Paz, Cabo San Lucas, the Midriff region and other hot spots. But the nearby waters hold their own against any in Baja, with most of the major game species passing through at some point during the year. Marlin and sailfish are late-summer visitors to these seas, which lie near the northern limit of their range, but it is the middleweight game fish that are Mulegé's claim to fame.

Mulegé provides some of the best mid-weight fishing in the entire gulf, sending plenty of happy anglers home with ice chests packed full of dorado, yellowtail, tuna and sierra. While the mid-weights are seasonal in nature, smaller species like cabrilla, pargo and grouper swim these waters throughout most of the year. Now and then, the fishing heats up within a mile or two of shore, but the best action is normally farther offshore, typically near Isla San Marcos, Isla San Inés and Punta Concepción.

Nearly all fishing is done from *panga* motor launches, which usually launch from Playa El Faro or the Río Mulegé near the Hotel Serenidad. Other boats launch from Punta Chivato, 12 miles north of Mulegé. *Panga* rates are among the lowest in Baja, averaging $110 to $120 per day for a 22-foot boat, including bait and tackle. The best way to arrange a trip is through one of the major tourist hotels in town, which usually have some English-speaking staff on hand. Cortez Explorers (see listing above, under Diving) also arranges fishing trips.

KAYAKING

Mulegé makes the list of truly outstanding kayaking areas along the coast of Baja California, even by the elevated standards of the Sea of Cortez. The town itself is not much of a kayaking destination, but just a few miles to the south lies Bahía Concepción. With its sheltered waters, superlative scenery and abundance of marine life, this pristine bay has few equals along the peninsula and attracts adventure-seeking paddlers from the world over. The shallow waters along the shoreline and islands also lend themselves to snorkeling as part of any kayaking trip. For more ambitious paddlers, Mulegé is the starting point for the long-distance voyage to Loreto. The 84-mile trek can be done in as little as five days, but most people take seven or eight days, which makes for a more leisurely and rewarding experience. Guided expeditions along this coast are available through Baja Seafaris, a San Diego-based tour company.

Kayaks along Bahía Concepción

See *GreatestHits*, Chapter 3, for more on Bahía Concepción.

Along Bahía Concepción, the main outfitter is EcoMundo, which has earned a reputation for its affordable rentals and emphasis on environmental awareness. Single-seat kayaks rent for $25, while two-seaters rent for $35, with discounts on either model for multi-day rentals. Guided kayak trips start at $45 for a half-day outing, and information on longer treks is available. Besides EcoMundo, some freelance outfitters may rent kayaks for use on the bay during the winter tourist season.

See map on page 285.

Baja Seafaris *(619) 462-3761. E-mail at seafaris@juno.com.*
EcoMundo *On the sand at Playa Concepción on Bahía Concepción, 15 miles south of town. Information available at office next to Hotel Las Casitas, in center of Mulegé at Calle Madero 50. 01152 (1) 153-04-09. E-mail at ecomundo@aol.com.*

Dining

Small town though it is, Mulegé is well stocked with good restaurants—no surprise really, given the influx of travelers here during most of the year. And so it's not hard to find American-style food around town, plus the usual seafood/Mexican conventions. If there were one word to describe the dining scene across the board, it would be "casual," as in no rigid dress codes, no reservations and no stuffy atmospheres. It also means your dining budget will stretch farther there than in most larger tourist towns.

When mealtime comes around, you'll find that downtown has the biggest concentration of restaurants, but by no means is that the only place to look. Some of the locale's best eateries lie farther south along Highway 1 or along the sandy shores of the gulf.

Favorites

DANY'S **Taquería**

The simple menu and lack of pretensions can't disguise the fact that this is perhaps the best taco stand in central Baja. Service is prompt, ingredients are fresh, and the chicken, fish and *carne asada* tacos just taste a mite better here on the banks of the Río Mulegé. *On Calle Rubio near the intersection with Ave Madero. No phone. $1-4.*

EDUARDO'S **Varied Menu**

Honors for Mulegé's most diverse menu go to this popular gringo haunt. Sunday is Chinese day, and on Wednesday night the kitchen trots out a different buffet each week, replete with a well-stocked salad and soup bar. Burgers and hot dogs are standard fare throughout the week, along with seafood and the usual Mexican dishes. *Ave General Martínez across from the Pemex station. 01152 (1) 153-02-58. Open daily 4-10 pm, except Sun 1:30-8:30 pm and Wed 4:30-10 pm. Closed late May through Oct 20. $3-10.*

EL CANDIL **Mexican/Seafood**

On the one hand, the service can be leisurely and the entrée lineup is fairly standard for this part of Baja. On the other hand, the portions are huge and everything is made fresh daily from scratch, which helps explain this restaurant's enduring appeal (four decades and counting). The restaurant and adjacent bar are another big hangout for ex-pats, and a great place to get the lowdown on local attractions. *In the center of town on Calle Zaragoza. No phone. Open daily 8 am-10 pm. $3-10.*

HOTEL SERENIDAD **Varied Menu**

Saturday night pig roasts with their massive buffet, mariachis and jumbo margaritas have reached near-legendary status at this hotel's restaurant. Some folks plan their Baja trips around a weekend stay in Mulegé just to catch the feeding frenzy and party. Italian night on Thursday is a more low-key highlight, and the Mexican/American menu is reliable throughout the week. *At the Hotel Serenidad, 2½ miles east of town center. 01152 (1) 153-05-30. Open daily 6 am-10 pm. Closed in Sep. $4-18, pig roast $14.*

RAY'S PLACE **Mexican/Seafood**

Tacos, burgers, the day's fresh catch and ice-cold *cerveza* are served steps from the water's edge on Bahía Concepción and come mighty close to producing a casual diner's nirvana. With his perennial smile and easy call of your name, owner Ray Lima just may be the friendliest restaurateur in Baja. *On the sand at Playa Santispac, 13 miles south of town. No phone. Open Mon-Sat 2-11 pm, Oct-Jun; till 8 pm, Jul-Sep. Closed Sun. $4.50-9.50.*

See map on page 285.

Others

DONEY TACO **Taquería**

$1-4.50. *Near the west entrance of town on the road leading in from Hwy 1. No phone.*

LA ALMEJA **Mexican/Seafood**

$3-13. *Palapa-roof restaurant on the sand, at Playa El Sombrerito, 3 miles northeast of town via Ave Madero. No phone.*

LAS CASITAS **♦ Mexican**

$3-13. *In the hotel of the same name on Calle Madero in the center of town. 01152 (1) 153-00-19.*

LOS EQUIPALES **Varied Menu**

$6.50-13. *Calle Moctezuma, just west of Calle Zaragoza. 01152 (1) 153-03-30.*

SAUL'S RESTAURANT & BAR **Mexican/Seafood**

$3.80-14. *¼ mile south of Hotel Serenidad entrance on Hwy 1. No phone.*

Lodging

Tourist towns in Baja come in many different stripes, many of which have done fine without a single ritzy, big-bucks resort. Case in point is Mulegé, a town of more back-to-basics accommodations—that is if you opt for a room at all. For many visitors, "lodging" Mulegé-style means an RV, parked along the river bank or on a lovely beach along Bahía Concepción. Pitch a tent or just roll out a bedroll beneath the stars, and you'll pay just a few bucks a night to sleep in a setting with few equals.

"UPSCALE" IN MULEGÉ

Honors for Mulegé's best all-around hotel go to the Hotel Serenidad, east of town at the mouth of the river. It's higher priced than the digs in town, but still a good value with its attractive grounds, comfortable rooms, secure parking, nice-sized pool and tennis court.

Of course camping out can have its downside, including mosquitoes along the river and a dearth of shade (except beneath *palapas*) along the shoreline. If it's a hotel room you need and you don't need to be completely pampered, Mulegé is sure to fill your needs. While most hotels are not AAA-approved, you will find several clean but unpretentious properties around town, priced mostly in the $30 to $35 range.

See *Lodging & Campgrounds*, Chapter 15, for listings for campgrounds in Mulegé and along Bahía Concepción.

During the peak tourist season, from mid-November through early spring, you'll do well to call ahead for reservations. Campgrounds can be even more problematic, and the "No Vacancy" sign may go up for weeks at a time.

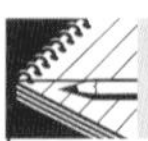

TRAVELOGUE

Mulegé to Loreto

(84 mi., 136 km.; 2 hrs.)

The shady palm groves, sleepy river and placid atmosphere of Mulegé are an alluring combination, yet belie the scenic beauty that awaits farther south along one of the most spectacular stretches of Highway 1.

Just east of town, the road picks up the gulf shore for a dozen miles and heads south through barren coastal hills before reaching the northern edge of the Bahía Concepción. From here Highway 1 climbs a low saddle before emerging onto a long, sandy plain. For the next 25 miles the road follows the shoreline and provides breathtaking panoramas of aquamarine waters, volcanic islands, placid coves, and Punta Concepción across the bay in the distance.

Bahía Concepción

Beyond the south edge of the bay, the route heads inland and winds through scrub-covered hills before dropping to a coastal plain as it nears the junction to Loreto. All along this drive, the rugged backbone of the Sierra de la Giganta rises boldly to the west, its arid peaks reaching heights of nearly 6000 feet. Check your fuel gauge before leaving Mulegé; there are no gas stations between here and Loreto.

See map on page 285.

00.0 Junction to Mulegé.

00.7	Junction with a road leading to Misión Santa Rosalía de Mulegé.
01.7	Junction with the entrance road to the Villa María Isabel RV/Trailer Park.
02.4	Junction with the entrance road to Hotel Serenidad.
10.4	Playa Punta Arena, a popular windsurfing spot.
13.1	Playa Santispac, a developed public beach on one of the bay's loveliest coves.
14.5	Posada Concepción, a campground on the shore of Bahía Tordillo.
14.8	Entrance road to EcoMundo, a diving and kayaking outfitter specializing in ecological tours of Bahía Concepción.
16.8	Rancho El Coyote, opposite a pair of lovely coves with enticing public beaches.
26.6	El Requesón, a small island connected to the shore by a sandspit. The narrow spit is a public beach.
36.6	Unmarked junction with a lonesome dirt road that loops around the southern end of Bahía Concepción, then goes north along the eastern side of the bay for 36 miles to Punta Concepción. The road passes a few fish camps, a huge stand of cardón cacti and expanses of pristine desert. The last few miles are very rough.
45.3	Rancho Rosarito, a ranch in a small oasis.
46.9	Junction with a road across the Sierra de la Giganta to San Isidro, La Purísima, San José de Comondú and San Miguel de Comondú (see Side Route to La Purísima, page 279).
51.0	Rancho Bombedor, site of a small roadside cafe.
55.1	Junction with a scenic dirt road to San Juanico and Bahía San Basilio.
58.8	Junction with another road leading to Punta San Basilio, site of a bayside camp with development under way.
64.8	Unmarked junction with a dirt road to Rancho San Juán Londo, 0.2 miles from the highway in a palm grove. This is the site of a Jesuit *visita*, or visiting station, dating from 1705.
83.7	Junction with the paved road to Loreto.

Loreto

Misión Nuestra Señora de Loreto

Shoehorned between the arid peaks of the Sierra de la Giganta and the shores of the deep-blue gulf, Loreto can sweep visitors off their feet with its beautiful surroundings, but that is only the beginning of this town's appeal. There is a hospitable spirit, an unusually long list of outdoor diversions and an alluring, slightly worn-at-the-edges feel. Moreover, this town boasts a historical tradition unrivaled in Baja, being the oldest permanent settlement in the Californias, dating to 1697 when Spanish padres founded Misión Nuestra Señora de Loreto.

The local mission (completed in 1752) remains in use to this day and is without a doubt the most recognizable building in town. Close by is the Plaza Cívica, an inviting cobblestone beauty surrounded by lush tropical vegetation, with the obligatory gazebo at its heart. The grandeur of Loreto's physical setting is manifest along the *malecón*, a lovely brick promenade fronting the gulf. A bounty of recreational pursuits—fishing, kayaking and diving—are available amid those waters and scattered islands, 800 square miles of which comprise Loreto Bay National Marine Park. Pick the right time of year and you may even see a pod of blue whales cruising this, the newest aquatic national park in the country.

"OLDEST" DEFINED

The first Spanish settlement in Baja California dates to 1535, when Hernán Cortés founded a small outpost at the site of the modern-day La Paz. It was abandoned after two years, though, leaving Loreto as the oldest permanent settlement in Baja.

With all that in mind, it is no surprise that Loreto has emerged as the most important tourist town between

Ensenada and La Paz, or that Fonatur—the government's tourist development agency—has targeted this town for seemingly bigger and better things. Yet Loreto so far has never lived up to the billing of those who would see it become one of Baja's premier resorts, even with government-backed developments and a modern international jetport.

An example of that lies about 15 miles down the coast at Puerto Escondido, a would-be resort for the well-heeled that was to have fashionable hotels, time-shares, restaurants and RV parks built around a sparkling marina. It may yet happen, but so far it's little more than the concrete shells of half-finished buildings, abandoned cul-de-sacs covered with broken glass, and a few yachts bobbing around in the harbor. More successful has been Nopoló, five miles south of town, scene of an all-inclusive resort complete with a manmade harbor, tennis courts and the only golf course between Ensenada and Los Cabos.

But if major developments remain a dream, then Loreto's modest size surely remains one of its greatest cachets. With just 9000 souls today, it isn't hard to imagine how the site of the present-day town must have appeared when the Spaniards arrived. It was October 15, 1697, that Padre Juan María Salvatierra made landfall and established the town's namesake mission, 72 years before San Diego would become the first town in *Alta California*.

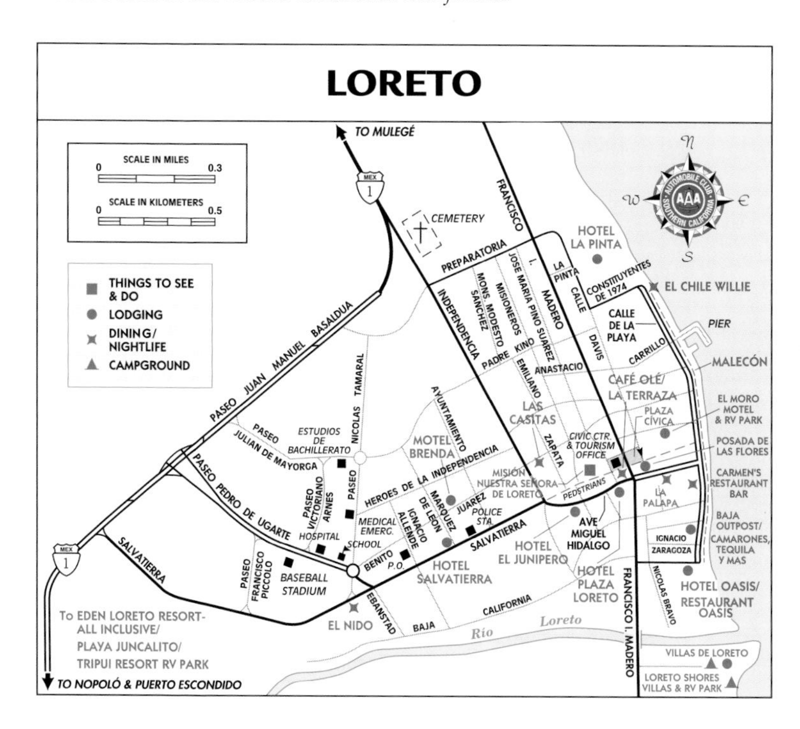

For the next 132 years, Loreto would serve as capital of Baja California and hold sway as the peninsula's commercial and military hub. That ended abruptly in 1829 when a hurricane devastated the city and the capital was moved to La Paz. Loreto all but disappeared until the early 1900s, when Mexican fishermen began returning to work offshore waters that were prolific even by Baja standards. American sport anglers began flying in as well, but the flow of outsiders did not really pick up until the completion of Highway 1 in 1973. Tourism and fishing are by no means the only modern-day industries. Neighboring orchards turn out rich harvests of citrus fruits, mangoes and dates, and the town is government seat for the *municipio* of Loreto.

Hotel façade, Loreto

If Loreto has not taken off as many had thought, the uncomfortably hot summers may share part of the blame. Late summer and early fall also bring the lion's share of the annual rain as the famous *chubascos* douse the town with short but violent downpours, flooding the streets and sending diehard tourists scurrying beneath the nearest palm-frond roof. Winter and spring are near perfect, however, with warm days, comfortable evenings and weeks of uninterrupted sunshine. Even at those times, Loreto seldom feels overwhelmed by the influx of outsiders, and many Highway 1 warriors keep their stays fairly short—lending credence to the tag line chosen for the town's 1697-1997 anniversary: "300 years old and still undiscovered."

Getting Around

Nearly all of the highlights in Loreto lie fairly close together, so here goes with our standard small-town-Baja advice: Park it and walk. The mission, Plaza Cívica, shopping district and *malecón* are all within a few minutes of each other on foot, and you may even make a discovery or two that you'd miss from behind the wheel.

If you need to leave town and don't have your own set of wheels, Loreto's taxi fleet makes its informal headquarters just south of the Plaza Cívica on Calle Madero. Plan to pay about $10 for a lift to either the airport or Nopoló. You shouldn't pay more than $5 for a ride anywhere within town.

Top Attractions

MALECÓN

Looking seaward along the **malecón** *in Loreto*

Loreto's front door to the sea is a nearly mile-long brick walkway with an unforgettable, amphitheater-like view of the gulf. With a late-afternoon sea breeze blowing and the sun's rays front-lighting the brownish-red peaks of Isla del Carmen, it is entirely possible—for fleeting moments at least—that there is no more idyllic a location on the Baja peninsula. *Where Calle de la Playa parallels the sea.*

MISIÓN NUESTRA SEÑORA DE LORETO

Completed in 1752, the mission that stands today is the descendent of the Jesuit padres' first religious outpost in the Californias, dating to 1697. It withstood numerous earthquakes, floods and the ruinous 1829 hurricane before undergoing an extensive renovation, completed in 1976. The building is of fairly simple design and probably more impressive on the inside, with its high arched ceiling and a beautiful gilded altar. *On Calle Salvatierra in the center of town.*

Museum As much an attraction as the mission itself, this small historical/religious museum has an excellent collection of artifacts dating back to the region's early colonial days. A few of these include a crucifix and paintings of Christ from the 18th century, and a hand-painted chest from the Philippines that dates to the 17th century. There's also a good display of 19th-century cowboy gear. English-speaking docents are usually available to provide tours and information. *Next to the mission. Open Wed-Mon 9 am-6 pm. Admission $2. 01152 (1) 135-04-41.*

PLAZA CÍVICA

Plaza Cívica

Loreto's version of the traditional Mexican *zócalo*, this peaceful town square is the center of civic and social activities. It's a thoroughly pleasant spot to relax and take in the local scene (assuming one tires of the *malecón*). Across from the plaza is the municipal hall, an attractive colonial-style building that contains, among other things, the local tourism office. *In the center of town, 2 blocks west of the mission on Calle Salvatierra.*

SHOPPING

Tourist town that it is, Loreto has a good number of shops and open-air stalls brimming with handicrafts, paintings, pottery, clothing and other souvenirs. The heaviest concentration is in the middle of town along calles Hidalgo and Salvatierra. Fortuitously perhaps, the local bank is to be found in the heart of this zone, at the corner of Salvatierra and Calle Madero.

Outdoor Fun

BOATING

With five neighboring islands, numerous sheltered beaches and coves, and excellent fishing and diving nearby, Loreto is a natural location from which to embark on a boat trip, whether for a few hours or a weeklong voyage. It's a long way down Highway 1 to tow a boat, and even farther for those sailing from the west coast of the U.S. or Canada, although that doesn't deter some intrepid salts.

BEEN THERE, DONE THAT?

If the opportunities listed here aren't enough, Loreto's tour and recreation outfitters offer many more kinds of guided tours. Possibilities include Bahía Concepción, Mission San Javier, Mulegé-area cave paintings, hiking trips and walking tours about town.

Fortunately, if you don't have your own boat, it's still possible to arrange a tour out of Loreto. Las Parras Tours offers two- and four-hour sailing trips during the windy winter months, with prices ranging from $15 to $39 per person (subject to a minimum number of persons). Longer adventures of up to a week are also available, exploring the Sea of Cortez on single- and double-hull craft in the 22- to 27-foot range. Baja Sailing, based in Calistoga, California, is the best-known purveyor of such trips, charging about $1000 for a weeklong voyage. Some local hotels may also offer sailing trips of a few hours exploring the local waters.

Baja Sailing *(800) 398-6200 or (707) 942-4550. Website at www.paddlingsouth.com/sailadd.* **Las Parras Tours** *Calle Francisco I. Madero 16, ½ block south of Plaza Cívica. 01152 (1) 135-10-10. Website at www.tourbaja.com.lasparras.html.*

DIVING

Loreto is a place where nature's grandeur extends beyond the shoreline and beneath the waves without missing a beat, which ensures its status as one of the finest diving locales in

Baja California. It's no accident that in 1996 President Ernesto Zedillo signed a law designating the offshore waters to be Loreto Bay National Marine Park, only the second such preserve in Mexico. Covering 800 square miles and a chain of five islands, the park is designed to protect one of the country's great undersea ecosystems, with commercial trawling and netting prohibited within its boundaries.

Given the superlative conditions, it's no surprise that Loreto has several dive shops and outfitters catering to varying interests and experience levels. Guided trips are available to all five of the marine preserve's islands, which include, from north to south, Isla Coronado, Isla del Carmen, Isla Danzante, Isla Monserrat and Isla Santa Catalina. While the variety of experiences is enormous, Isla Coronado receives the most visitors (especially first-timers), since it is the nearest island to Loreto. Isla del Carmen receives many visitors too, having several good dive spots off its northern and eastern shores. A few spots along the local shoreline afford good snorkeling, including Punta Nopo, Punta Escondido and Juncalito; outfitters in Loreto can provide details.

Water temperatures off Loreto range from the mid-60s in winter (cool enough for wet suits) to the upper 80s by late summer. Visibility ranges from 20 to 50 feet during the winter and improves to 120 feet in the late summer and early fall.

Pricing for trips varies almost as much as the range of experiences available. At the low end, snorkeling trips to Isla Coronado's popular sea lion colony run between $35 and $45. Scuba excursions to some of the closer-in sites average $70 to $80 for a two-tank drive, while outings to more distant locations can cost substantially more. Outing prices usually include snorkeling gear, while complete scuba gear is available at extra cost. For aspiring scuba divers, several shops offer open-water certification, priced at about $350 for a comprehensive course. Major outfitters and agencies include these:

Arturo's Sportfishing *Calle Hidalgo, ½ block west of the* malecón. *01152 (1) 135-07-66.* **Baja Outpost** *Near the south end of the* malecón. *01152 (1) 135-11-34, (888) 649-5951. Website at www.bajaoutpost.com.* **Las Parras Tours** *Calle Francisco I. Madero 16, ½ block south of Plaza Cívica. 01152 (1) 135-10-10. Website at www.tourbaja.com.lasparras.html.* **The Loreto Center** *Corner of Ave Hidalgo and Pino Suárez. 01152 (1) 135-07-98 or (800) 848-4333. Website at www.loreto-center.com.*

FISHING

Half a century ago the cobalt seas off Loreto rated as one of the finest of Baja fishing holes, teeming with all the middle- and heavyweights known to the Sea of Cortez. That was before a flotilla of commercial boats, both domestic and foreign, began working these seas along with the local *panga* fleet. As a result, the local stocks have

PACKAGE DEALS

Several local hotels book inclusive fishing/lodging packages, typically four days, three nights, with two days of fishing. Prices vary by hotel, but packages are usually good deals compared to booking your lodging and fishing boat separately. Some hotels with packages are La Pinta, Oasis, Plaza Loreto, Posada de las Flores and Eden Loreto Resort.

taken a substantial hit, which means fewer and smaller fish than in decades past.

Even now, though, Loreto fishing can be darn good, provided you come at the right time of year. One of those times is November through March, when yellowtail pass through in substantial numbers. Another is June through August, when dorado show up in force. Marlin and sailfish provide some summer and early fall action as well, but for most anglers, dorados are the stars of the local lineup. Whatever you're casting for, odds are you'll be a good distance from the mainland, usually off the northeast tip of Isla del Carmen or north of Isla Coronado. The hot spots may vary from week to week, but the larger fish seldom venture close to the local shoreline.

Wherever the fishing is, you'll almost certainly be doing it from a *panga*, king of the seas off Loreto. The popular motorized skiffs rent for between $125 and $180 per boat, per day, or about $30 more for the slightly larger, better-equipped *super pangas*. Some outfits rent small cruisers in the 24- to 26-foot range, with daily rentals running $240 to $280 a day. The following are some of the larger fishing services and tour outfitters that book fishing trips:

BUYER BEWARE

An inexpensive fishing boat rental may prove to be a false savings if the price doesn't include bait, tackle and license, and the boat may not have a radio or other emergency gear.

Alfredo's Sport Fishing *Across from the* malecón *at the marina. 01152 (1) 135-04-09.* **Arturo's Sportfishing** *Calle Hidalgo ½ block west of the* malecón. *01152 (1) 135-07-66.* **Baja Big Fish Company** *Paseo Hidalgo 19, between Calle Madero and the* malecón. *01152 (1) 135-04-48, voice mail at (888) 533-2252. Website at www.bajabigfish.com.* **The Loreto Center** *Corner of Ave Hidalgo and Pino Suárez. 01152 (1) 135-07-98 or (800) 848-4333. Website at www.loretocenter.com.* **Ricardo's Sport Fishing** *Francisco Madero 118. 01152 (1) 135-01-26.*

GOLF

If you want to chase a golf ball and you're somewhere between Ensenada and Los Cabos, you can play wherever you like, as long as it is Campo de Golf Loreto, located near the Fonatur-run Eden Loreto Resort.

Campo de Golf Loreto (Public) 18 holes; 6542 yards; par 72; N/A slope; N/A rating. Rate: $40, golf cart $35 extra. *In Nopoló near Eden Loreto Resort, 5 miles south of town. 01152 (1) 133-05-54.*

On the links, Campo de Golf Loreto

HORSEBACK RIDING

Picturesque beachfronts and remote foothill oases are the kinds of venues that lend themselves wonderfully to horseback outings, and you'll find both in Loreto. El Chile Willie restaurant offers guided equestrian trips to a small oasis known as Primer Agua, and through the desert to an old lighthouse at El Bajo outside of town. Either outing costs $45 including lunch, with snorkeling gear provided on the El Bajo trip. Or if you prefer, rent a horse and ride on your own along the beach for $9 an hour. This is a cool-weather activity, with horses available only from October into the early spring. **El Chile Willie restaurant.** *Near the north end of the* malecón. *01152 (1) 135-06-77.*

KAYAKING

If variety is the spice of life, then the kayaking scene in Loreto is as good as you'll find anywhere in Baja California. Whether it's a quick paddle along the local shoreline, a tour of nearby islands or a two-week expedition to La Paz, Loreto outfitters cater to every interest, budget and experience level.

There are three basic approaches to kayaking here. The most economical is renting a kayak without the benefit of a guide, which, unless you're a novice, is a good way to explore the local inshore waters. Some adventurous types travel offshore to one of the neighboring islands, but such a journey is only for the most experienced of paddlers. Either way, plan on paying about $5 an hour or $25 per day for a single-seat model, while a two-seater should cost about $7.50 per hour or $30 per day.

A step up in price are the popular guided tours to either Isla Coronado or Isla del Carmen, in which you'll travel to one of the islands on a larger boat and then set off to explore by kayak. The typical cost is $50 to $60, which normally includes your guide, rental snorkeling gear and lunch.

Then there are the long-range guided tours, which are the most expensive but offer the ultimate paddling adventures. Taking a week or longer, paddlers and their guides explore the remote coastline south of Loreto or the islands of Loreto Bay National Marine Park, camping at secluded beaches along the way. The final word in long-range tours from Loreto is the 200-plus mile trek to La Paz, taking from 10 days to two weeks. Tour prices start around $800 and climb to well over $1000.

Below are some of the major outfitters operating out of Loreto:

Blue Waters Kayaking and Paddling South offer multi-day expeditions only.

Baja Outpost *Near the south end of the* malecón. *01152 (1) 135-11-34, (888) 649-5951. Website at www.bajaoutpost.com.* **Blue Waters Kayaking** *Call in U.S. at (415) 669-2600. Website at www.ehot.com/share/cgi-bin.* **Las Parras Tours** *Calle Francisco I. Madero 16, ½ block south of Plaza Cívica. 01152 (1) 135-10-10. Website at www.tourbaja.com/lasparras.html.* **The Loreto Center** *Corner of Ave Hidalgo and Pino Suárez. 01152 (1) 135-07-98 or (800) 848-4333. Website at www.loretocenter.com.* **Paddling South** *See Las Parras Tours in Loreto, or in U.S. call (800) 398-6200 or (707) 942-4550. Website at www.tourbaja.com/paddlsth.html.*

TENNIS

"Tennis anyone?" is not exactly the most common phrase that you'll hear in Baja, but if you're in Loreto when the urge to play hits, you're in luck. One of the biggest tennis complexes on the peninsula is at Nopoló, the Fonatur resort complex.

See *GreatestHits*, Chapter 3, and Side Route to Puerto López Mateos, *South of Loreto*, Chapter 9, for more on whale watching at Puerto López Mateos.

Centro Tenístico de Loreto 8 lighted courts for public play. *In Nopoló near Eden Loreto Resort, 5 miles south of town. Call the Eden Loreto Resort, 01152 (1) 133-07-00 or directly to the tennis complex, 133-01-29. $7 per court, per hour during daylight; $10 per court, per hour after dark. Free for Eden Loreto Resort guests. Reservations recommended Oct-Apr.*

WHALE WATCHING

No, the California gray whales do not frequent the seas off Loreto, but the town does lie within a reasonable drive of the southernmost of the grays' Pacific coast calving lagoons, namely Bahía Magdalena. The nearest point on that bay is Puerto López Mateos, about a two-hours' drive southwest across the peninsula and an excellent day trip. This small port settlement near the north end of the bay is one of the best places in Baja to view the whales from land, and it has a sizable fleet of boats for guided tours.

Organized tours from Loreto visit the bay on an almost daily basis during the peak whale-watching months from late-December through the end of March. Tours cost about $100, including round-trip transportation, lunch and time on the water. Any hotel or travel agency in

Loreto can provide more information or make reservations.

> **DO THE MATH**
>
> At 90 feet, the average blue whale is nearly 3½ times as long as the super pangas that transport tourists into the gulf to see them.

As for the gulf, an occasional pod of grays does make it this far north, but a much bigger attraction—literally—comes around in February-March when blue whales make their annual local appearance. These behemoths of the deep, which average 90 feet in length, appear in the waters between Isla del Carmen and Isla Monserrat. Baja Outpost, a locally based ecotourism agency, specializes in outings to see the blues, using long-range, 27-foot *super pangas.* Tours last about seven hours and cost $135 per person. Along with most local hotels, the following outfitters offer whale-watching tours:

Baja Outpost *Near the south end of the* malecón. *01152 (1) 135-11-34, (888) 649-5951. Website at www.bajaoutpost.com.* **Las Parras Tours** *Calle Francisco I. Madero 16, ½ block south of Plaza Cívica. 01152 (1) 135-10-10. Website at www.tourbaja.com.lasparras.html.* **The Loreto Center** *Corner of Ave Hidalgo and Pino Suárez. 01152 (1) 135-07-98 or (800) 848-4333. Website at www.loretocenter.com.*

Dining

Loreto is one of those classic *palapa*-roof-eatery-next-to-the-sand towns where seafood is on the menu virtually everywhere, replete with a bed of rice, bowl of salsa and greasy tortilla chips on the table, and plenty of cold *cerveza* to chug it all down. You come to expect that from Sea of Cortez towns, but you also come to expect some variety in the fare (at least in the larger towns), and Loreto has that. Quiz the local snowbirds or year-round ex-pats, and they surely will have a favorite spot for getting a burger or club sandwich once they've seen one too many fish tacos. Most eateries are moderately priced, although we have enjoyed some excellent meals at the lower end of the price range.

> **SEE YOU IN OCTOBER**
>
> You may find some Loreto restaurants closed during the late summer and early fall, generally reopening sometime in October.

Our favorite restaurants are so widely dispersed as to defy geographical categorization, but if it's around mealtime and you're not sure what you're hungry for, try taking a walk down the *malecón* or the blocks surrounding the Plaza Cívica. Not only will it help work up your appetite but you'll have the chance to stick your head inside a number of worthy establishments.

Oh yeah, one more thing—if you're looking for *los arcos dorados* (golden arches), the nearest set is in Ensenada, more than 600 miles north.

Favorites

CAFÉ OLÉ **Mexican/Seafood**

The menu, ambiance and prices are what you'd expect from a down-to-earth, true-to-itself diner that brings in the *yanquis* and locals alike without selling its Mexican soul. Nothing is more than $5, but the *machaca* burritos, *flautas* and inevitable fish tacos rank with the best eats in town at any price. Not so hungry? Try a *licuado* (fruit smoothie) or a tall glass of fresh-squeezed orange juice. *On Calle Madero, just south of Plaza Cívica. 01152 (1) 135-04-96. Open daily; Mon-Sat 7 am-10 pm, Sun 7 am-2 pm. $1.70-4.50.*

EL CHILE WILLIE **Mexican/Seafood**

Creativity and atmosphere are strong suits at this spacious, popular restaurant, next to the crashing waves of the gulf. The staff works hard to put its unique stamp on the day's catch, serving the likes of fish filet in pineapple/curry sauce, fish filet Sicilian-style, and chile relleno with lobster or crab. *Near the north end of the* malecón. *01152 (1) 135-06-77. Open daily 7 am-11 pm. $5.50-17.50.*

EL NIDO **♦♦ Steakhouse**

Mesquite-grilled steaks along with chicken and seafood are reliably good at this ever-popular restaurant, perhaps the best of the small El Nido chain. The food and ambiance are surely the most gringofied in town, and the Eden Resort staff frequently recommends it to guests when they head into town. A great place to head after a couple of weeks on the road and you yearn for familiar surroundings. *At the entrance of town, 1 mile east of Hwy 1 at Salvatierra 154. 01152 (1) 135-02-84. Open daily 1-10:30 pm. $4-18.*

RESTAURANT OASIS **Mexican/Seafood**

To be honest, this hotel restaurant can be a bit erratic, ranging from just ordinary to superlative. But when it's in top form (usually during peak tourist season), superlative is not an exaggeration to describe the quality or presentation of the food; the seafood is particularly outstanding. One thing you can always rely on is the casual yet romantic atmosphere—alongside the beach and a stand of coco palms that rustle in the evening sea breeze. *At the Hotel Oasis, south end of the* malecón. *01152 (1) 135-01-12. Open daily, 5:30-11 am, noon-3 and 6:30-8:45 pm. $4.50-20.*

Others

CAMARONES, TEQUILA Y MÁS **Mexican/Seafood**
$8-15. *At Baja Outpost, near the south end of the* malecón. *01152 (1) 135-11-34.*

CARMEN'S RESTAURANT BAR **Mexican/Seafood**
$3-12. *Across from the* malecón *between Calle Jordan and Paseo Hidalgo. 01152 (1) 135-05-77.*

LA PALAPA **Mexican/Seafood**
$4.50-17. *On Paseo Hidalgo, ½ block west of the* malecón. *01152 (1) 135-11-01.*

LAS CASITAS **Varied Menu**
$4.50-16. *Calle Juárez between calles Independencia and Zapata. 01152 (1) 135-11-04.*

LA TERRAZA **Mexican/Seafood**
$6-16. *On Calle Madero, just south of Plaza Cívica (upstairs from Café Olé). 01152 (1) 135-04-96.*

Lodging

With its beautiful setting, many diversions and strategic location a half-day's drive from La Paz, you would expect Loreto to have many places to stay, and it does. The town has yet to become a full-fledged resort, but there is a good selection of inexpensive to moderately priced hotels, along with campgrounds, B&Bs and a few one-of-a-kind establishments. What is hard to find in Loreto is cushy Cabo-style resorts with multiple pools, in-room bars, satellite TV and other first-world niceties. (About the only exceptions, noted below, are Eden Loreto Resort and the recently opened Posada de las Flores.)

If money's an issue, you'll generally pay less by setting your sites away from the shore. Even a block or two inland can mean considerable savings, with several no-nonsense hotels priced at $25 to $50 per night. To sleep next to the water's edge, plan on paying $70 to $100 for comfortable but uninspiring digs. Uninspiring, that is, except for the gentle breeze blowing in from the gulf, with an unforgettable view of Isla del Carmen in the distance.

LOVE IT OR LOATHE IT

In a locale short on luxury accommodations, the great exception is the Eden Loreto Resort, five miles south of town. With its tasteful guestrooms, meticulously manicured grounds, clothing-optional hot tub and country club-like atmosphere, this is a place you're destined either to hate or love. No one under 18 allowed.

See *Lodging & Campgrounds*, Chapter 15.

Highway 1 to San José de Magdalena

(See map below.)

(9 mi., 15 km.; 0:30 hr.)

A winding road with some excellent canyon vistas leads to this lovely oasis village in the rocky foothills above Highway 1. Groves of stately palms, colorful flower gardens and thatched-palm dwellings interspersed with concrete-block houses make San José de Magdalena an inviting destination, within easy reach of the main highway. Farming supports the local economy, as it did during Baja's colonial days, when the village was a visiting station of Misión Santa Rosalía de Mulegé. Garlic, dates, citrus fruit, and vegetables are the main crops today. Evidence of the past can be seen in the old stone walls running along the valley floor and in the ruins of a chapel built by the Dominicans in 1774. Higher up in the mountains are the ruins of Misión Guadalupe, reachable by horseback from Rancho San Isidro, 10 miles southeast of San José de Magdalena.

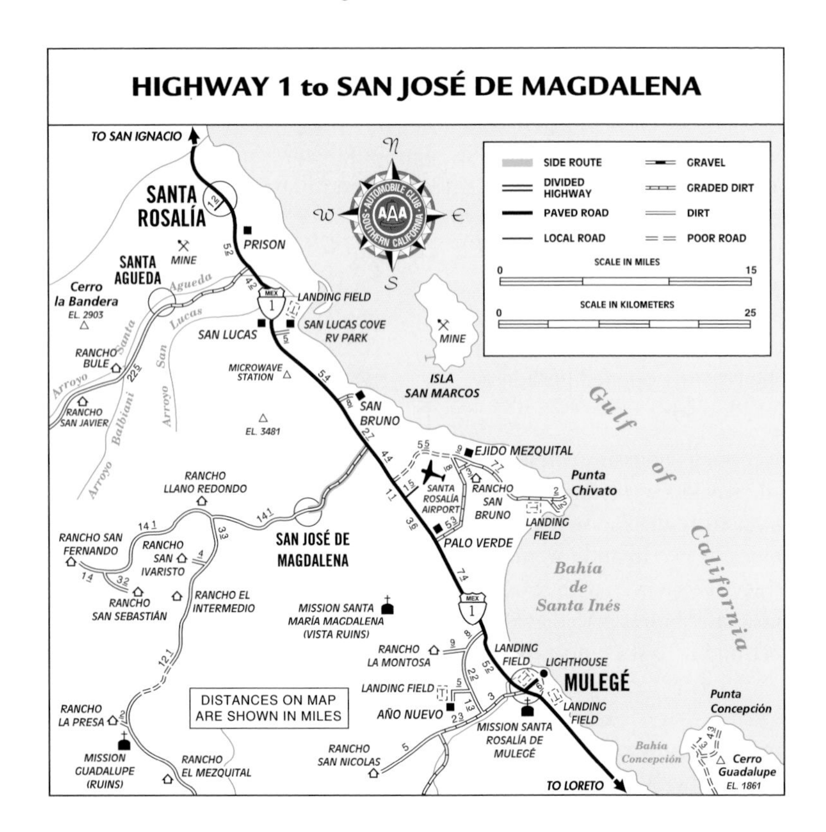

A passenger car can take the graded dirt road to the village with few difficulties, but beyond it the road turns rough and is only suitable for high-clearance vehicles. From a well-marked junction 17.5 miles south of Santa Rosalía on Highway 1, the road branches west and traverses a sparsely vegetated plain for 3.5 miles. It then enters a range of barren foothills and negotiates a series of short, steep grades before dropping into a palm-lined canyon. After following the edge of the canyon past several ranches and an interesting cemetery, the road crosses a streambed and arrives in San José de Magdalena, 8.8 miles from Highway 1.

Highway 1 to Ciudad Insurgentes via La Purísima

(See map page 282.)

(118 mi., 190 km.; 5 hrs.)

With its teeming tracts of palms, fruit trees and irrigated cropland, the Valle de la Purísima is a welcome site for trekkers heading across the rugged Sierra de la Giganta. Guarded by barren mountains, soaring cliffs and the landmark butte known as Cerro El Pilón, this valley sits amid dramatic surroundings, and is a worthy destination for adventure-minded explorers with the right vehicle. Two small towns occupy the valley floor—La Purísima and San Isidro, whose residents work the land and make this one of the most productive oases in Baja Sur. An extensive irrigation system taps spring waters to nourish abundant crops of mangoes, dates, grapes, citrus fruit and assorted vegetables.

Better known of the two towns is La Purísima, which dates to 1730, when a Jesuit mission relocated here from a site several miles away. Stone ruins are all that remain of the mission today, however, as diseases took their toll on the native Indians and led to its abandonment in 1822. The town was revived in the late 19th century, when Mexican farmers returned to till the valley's fertile land. Their descendants remain today, heirs to a quiet village with a well-worn appearance and the feel of a bygone era. About 1200 people call La Purísima home, with civic life centered around a prim main square with an attractive municipal hall. For tourists the town offers modest lodging, a restaurant, gasoline from barrels, auto parts and a post office.

A wide, well-graded road leads across the sierra to La Purísima, and is suitable for most high-clearance vehicles with sturdy tires. The road starts at a junction 47 miles south of Mulegé (or 37 miles north of Loreto) on Highway 1. After cutting across five miles of open desert, the road winds through a series of narrow, heavily vegetated canyons walled by steep volcanic bluffs, reaching a junction at mileage 11.3. To the left is the road to San José de Comondú and San Miguel de Comondú; to the right is a seldom-used portion of the old La Purísima/San Isidro road. Proceed straight ahead. Scaling a rocky grade, the road tops a low ridge a mile beyond the junction, then descends into a long, winding valley. The route meanders in and out of the valley, at times crossing the bleak, boulder-strewn hillsides.

Though not as scenic, the drive from Ciudad Insurgentes to La Purísima can be made by most passenger cars. For more information, see Side Route Ciudad Insurgentes to La Purísima in *South of Loreto*, Chapter 9.

Finally, at mileage 30.7 Valle de La Purísima pulls into view, and a 700-foot drop to the valley floor commences. The road descends via a series of steep switchbacks before straightening out to become a palm-lined avenue. A stone aqueduct parallels the avenue as it passes orchards and field crops before reaching San Isidro, 35.2 miles from the start. This hamlet has a cafe, limited supplies, a telegraph, a clinic and a rustic motel. Three miles farther down the valley is La Purísima.

Beyond La Purísima, the road continues down the valley for another 3.5 miles to a junction. The right fork is a graded road running northward for 30 miles to San Juanico with a hard-to-follow, unimproved route that continues to San Ignacio. The route to Ciudad Insurgentes bears left here and climbs out of the valley onto a high mesa. Paved most of the way, it then heads southward, winding among barren rounded hills. Thirteen miles from the junction is a signed road to the fishing village of Las Barrancas, site of a joint German/Mexican solar energy project. At mileage 76.8 from Highway 1 (or 34.8 miles from La Purísima), the road arrives at Ejido Francisco Villa—a dusty, windblown farming cooperative. The Comondú road angles in from the left here, while another road veers right to the small farming town of Poza Grande; proceed straight ahead for Ciudad Insurgentes.

Valle de la Purísima

The road continues south across the open desert and irrigated fields of the Santo Domingo (Magdalena) Plain. About 22 miles past Ejido Francisco Villa is the junction with a 1.5-mile side road to Santo Domingo, a farming community with a store, a cafe and gasoline. Two miles farther is the junction with the road coming in from Loreto and Misión San Javier. Fifteen miles farther south is Ciudad Insurgentes.

Highway 1 to Ciudad Insurgentes via Comondú

(See map page 282.)

(103 mi., 165 km.; 5 hrs.)

Ringed by rocky peaks and barren volcanic mesas, the twin villages of Comondú provide a sharp contrast from their arid, sparse surroundings, tucked amid a teeming green oasis at the floor of a seven-mile-long valley. San José de Comondú and its companion village San Miguel de Comondú have a combined population of about 600, most of whom earn their living from working the land. Nearby springs provide the water to grow citrus fruit, dates, figs, grapes, sugarcane and other crops.

San José de Comondú is the larger of the two villages and the site of a Jesuit mission that moved here in 1737. Evidence of those early days remains around town in the form of a school and many homes built from the carved stone used to construct the original mission sanctuary. (The sanctuary was torn down in the 1930s.) The sacristy is the only mission building that remains standing, serving today as the parish for the valley's residents. The original bells, which date from 1708, remain as well, hanging from a standard alongside the church. Nearby the mission is a handsome colonial-style main square that further lends an ambiance of a place frozen in time. Services in town are limited to a small grocery store and a clinic. Two miles to the west, San Miguel presents a worn look with many deserted buildings but still has an aura of historic charm. It has a post office, telegraph service and a general store that also sells gasoline.

The route to Comondú crosses the Sierra de la Giganta and for the first 11.3 miles shares the same road as the one leading to San Isidro and La Purísima. Beyond that first stretch, which is wide and graded, the road is narrow and winding with several steep, rocky grades. As such, this trip is only suitable for sturdy, high-clearance vehicles. The route begins at an unmarked junction with Highway 1, 47 miles south of Mulegé and 37 miles north of Loreto. Heading west, the road cuts a straight path across open

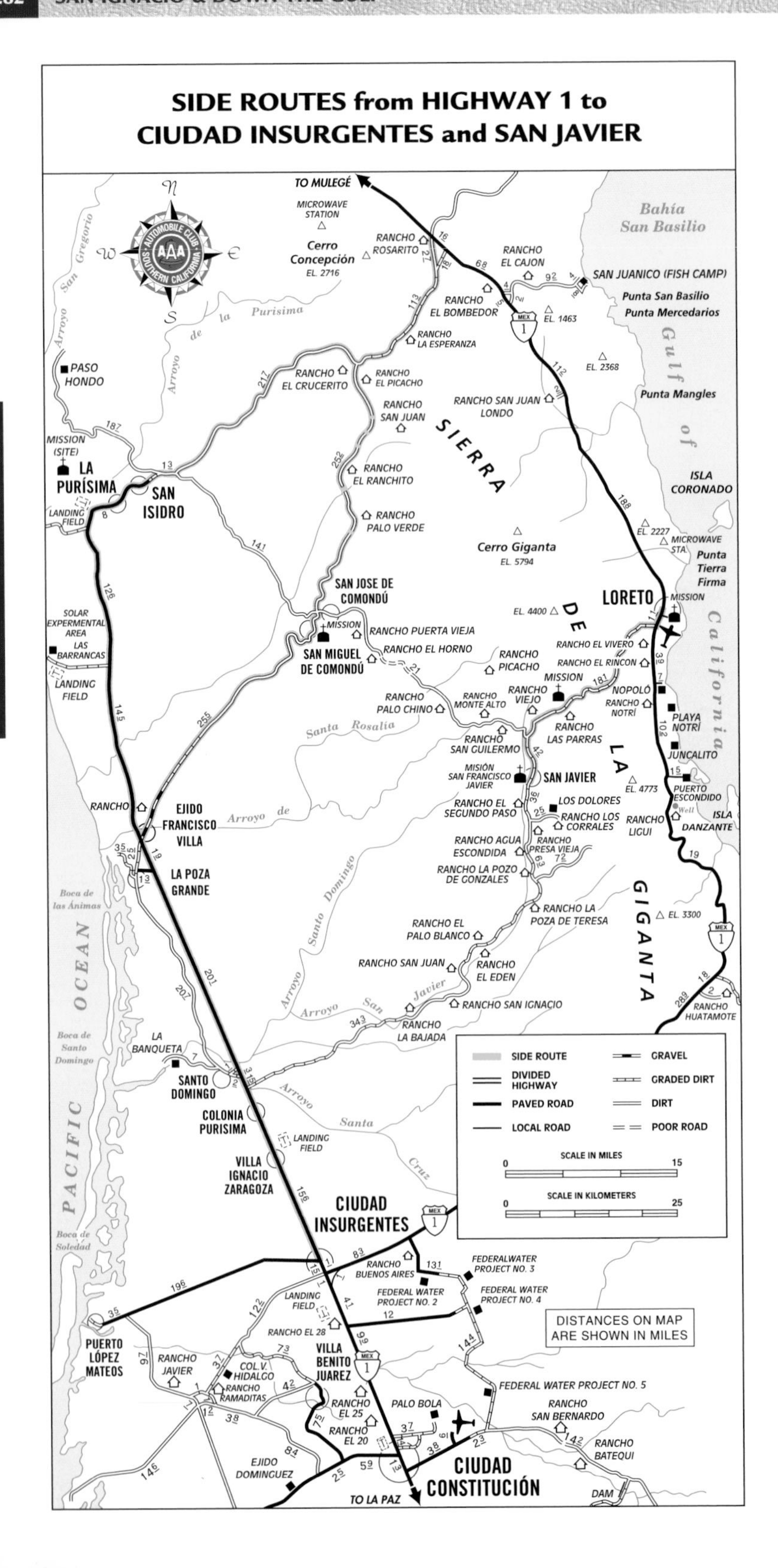

SIDE ROUTES from HIGHWAY 1 to
CIUDAD INSURGENTES and SAN JAVIER
TO MULEGÉ
MICROWAVE STATION
Cerro Concepción
EL. 2716
RANCHO ROSARITO
RANCHO EL CAJON
SAN JUANICO (FISH CAMP)
Bahía San Basilio
Punta San Basilio
Punta Mercedarios
RANCHO EL BOMBEDOR
RANCHO LA ESPERANZA
EL. 1463
EL. 2368
Arroyo de la Purisima
Arroyo San Gregorio
PASO HONDO
RANCHO EL CRUCERITO
RANCHO EL PICACHO
RANCHO SAN JUAN
RANCHO SAN JUAN LONDO
Punta Mangles
Gulf of California
SIERRA DE LA GIGANTA
MISSION (SITE)
LA PURÍSIMA
SAN ISIDRO
LANDING FIELD
RANCHO EL RANCHITO
RANCHO PALO VERDE
ISLA CORONADO
Cerro Giganta
EL. 5794
EL. 2227
MICROWAVE STA.
Punta Tierra Firma
SAN JOSE DE COMONDÚ
LORETO
MISSION
EL. 4400
SOLAR EXPERMENTAL AREA
LAS BARRANCAS
LANDING FIELD
SAN MIGUEL DE COMONDÚ
RANCHO PUERTA VIEJA
RANCHO EL HORNO
RANCHO EL VIVERO
RANCHO EL RINCON
RANCHO PICACHO
MISSION
NOPOLÓ
RANCHO NOTRÍ
PLAYA NOTRÍ
JUNCALITO
RANCHO PALO CHINO
RANCHO MONTE ALTO
RANCHO VIEJO
RANCHO LAS PARRAS
Santa Rosalía
RANCHO SAN GUILERMO
MISIÓN SAN FRANCISCO JAVIER
SAN JAVIER
EL. 4773
PUERTO ESCONDIDO
Well
ISLA DANZANTE
RANCHO
EJIDO FRANCISCO VILLA
Arroyo de Santo Domingo
RANCHO EL SEGUNDO PASO
LOS DOLORES
RANCHO LOS CORRALES
RANCHO LIGUI
RANCHO AGUA ESCONDIDA
RANCHO PRESA VIEJA
LA POZA GRANDE
RANCHO LA POZO DE GONZALES
Boca de las Ánimas
RANCHO LA POZA DE TERESA
EL. 3300
PACIFIC OCEAN
RANCHO EL PALO BLANCO
RANCHO SAN JUAN
RANCHO EL EDEN
Arroyo San Javier
RANCHO SAN IGNACIO
RANCHO HUATAMOTE
Boca de Santo Domingo
LA BANQUETA
RANCHO LA BAJADA
SANTO DOMINGO
Arroyo Santa Cruz
COLONIA PURISIMA
LANDING FIELD
VILLA IGNACIO ZARAGOZA
CIUDAD INSURGENTES
Boca de Soledad
SIDE ROUTE
DIVIDED HIGHWAY
PAVED ROAD
LOCAL ROAD
GRAVEL
GRADED DIRT
DIRT
POOR ROAD
SCALE IN MILES
0 15
SCALE IN KILOMETERS
0 25
RANCHO BUENOS AIRES
FEDERALWATER PROJECT NO. 3
LANDING FIELD
FEDERAL WATER PROJECT NO. 2
FEDERAL WATER PROJECT NO. 4
DISTANCES ON MAP ARE SHOWN IN MILES
PUERTO LÓPEZ MATEOS
RANCHO EL 28
RANCHO JAVIER
COL. V. HIDALGO
RANCHO RAMADITAS
VILLA BENITO JUAREZ
FEDERAL WATER PROJECT NO. 5
RANCHO EL 25
PALO BOLA
RANCHO SAN BERNARDO
RANCHO EL 20
RANCHO BATEQUI
EJIDO DOMINGUEZ
CIUDAD CONSTITUCIÓN
TO LA PAZ
DAM
AUTOMOBILE CLUB SOUTHERN CALIFORNIA
AAA

Other Routes to Comondú

Two other routes leading to Comondú are longer journeys, but don't require four-wheel drive. One route starts near Loreto and follows the road to San Javier for the first 16.6 miles before reaching a fork at Rancho Viejo. (See Side Route to San Javier.) From Rancho Viejo the route heads 27 miles northeast across the Sierra de la Giganta on a partly graded dirt road with only a couple of rough spots. Driven carefully, a high-clearance vehicle with two-wheel-drive should have few difficulties on this route. Total driving distance is about 44 miles from Loreto.

The other route is longer still, leading 65 miles north from Ciudad Insurgentes. The road is paved for the first 41 miles and a carefully driven passenger car can make it the entire way. This approach is less scenic, however, as it does not cross the Sierra de la Giganta. For more details, see Side Route Ciudad Insurgentes to Comondú and La Purísima in *South of Loreto*, Chapter 9.

desert for five miles, then begins a gradual ascent through a steep-walled canyon. At mileage 11.3 is an unsigned, four-way intersection. Straight ahead is the road to San Isidro and La Purísima, while to the right is an abandoned road. Turn left for Comondú. The road now winds upward over grades of up to 15 percent to reach the summit of the Sierra de la Giganta. Only experienced drivers with the sturdiest of four-wheel-drive vehicles can safely take this steep grade.

Beyond this section, the road crosses a plateau, climbs another summit and drops through a rocky arroyo. After traversing low hills for several miles, the road comes to the edge of a deep canyon. There, nestled far below amid a forest of date palms are the twin hamlets of Comondú. Just ahead, near a roadside cemetery, is a junction.Straight ahead is a graded road to San Isidro and La Purísima. Turning left, the road drops sharply via a series of steep switchbacks to the valley floor, reaching San José de Comondú at mileage 36. Just beyond is San Miguel de Comondú.

The road between San Javier and the La Purísima-Ciudad Insurgentes route can be difficult if not impossible to negotiate following heavy rainfall.

Continuing west from Comondú, a graded road winds down the canyon, which gradually opens up onto a wide, sparsely vegetated coastal plain. The road is wide, well-graded and easy to follow. About 25 miles beyond Comondú (or 61 miles from Highway 1) the road arrives at Ejido Francisco Villa, where it joins the La Purísima/Ciudad Insurgentes route. From here it's 40 miles south to Ciudad Insurgentes. (For more information on this road, see Side Route to Ciudad Insurgentes via La Purísima.)

Loreto to Misión San Javier

(See map page 282.)

(23 mi., 37 km.; 1:30 hrs.)

Misión San Javier is the destination for one of the most rewarding side routes in Baja. Not only is it one of North America's most beautiful Spanish missions, but the drive offers superlative views of mountains, canyons and the gulf. The mission is the centerpiece of the village of San Javier, which has a small store, cafe, telephone and a divided parkway instead of the usual plaza. The village sits at the bottom of a deep valley beneath towering walls of dark gray stone, and serves a minor farming and ranching district.

On the road to San Javier

Sturdy, high-clearance vehicles are best for the winding dirt road to the town, although passenger cars can make it with cautious driving. The mission can also be reached from the Pacific side of the peninsula, but this approach is considerably longer and involves many rocky arroyo crossings.

From a signed junction 1.1 mile south of the Loreto turnoff, the road to San Javier leads westward from Highway 1 through rolling foothills for about six miles. It then begins a gradual, winding climb into the rugged Sierra de la Giganta, following the steep wall of a deep arroyo. At mileage 10.5 the road swings to the left and provides a sweeping view of the gaping canyon below and the Gulf of California in the distance. Rancho Las Parras, 12.2 miles from Highway 1, has a small stone chapel and groves of citrus and olive trees. Six miles beyond the rancho is a junction with a rough road to Comondú, 25.8 miles to the north. From this junction the road gently winds 4.4 miles through a narrow canyon to reach San Javier.

Beyond the mission, the road continues southwest down the canyon, fording several arroyos and passing several small ranches. The canyon gradually widens into a broad valley, where irrigated farms line the road. Some 44 miles beyond San Javier, a drive of almost three hours, the road finally reaches the junction with the paved route between La Purísima and Ciudad Insurgentes. From here it's 15.5 miles south to the junction with Highway 1 in Ciudad Insurgentes.

See *GreatestHits*, Chapter 3, for more on Misión San Javier.

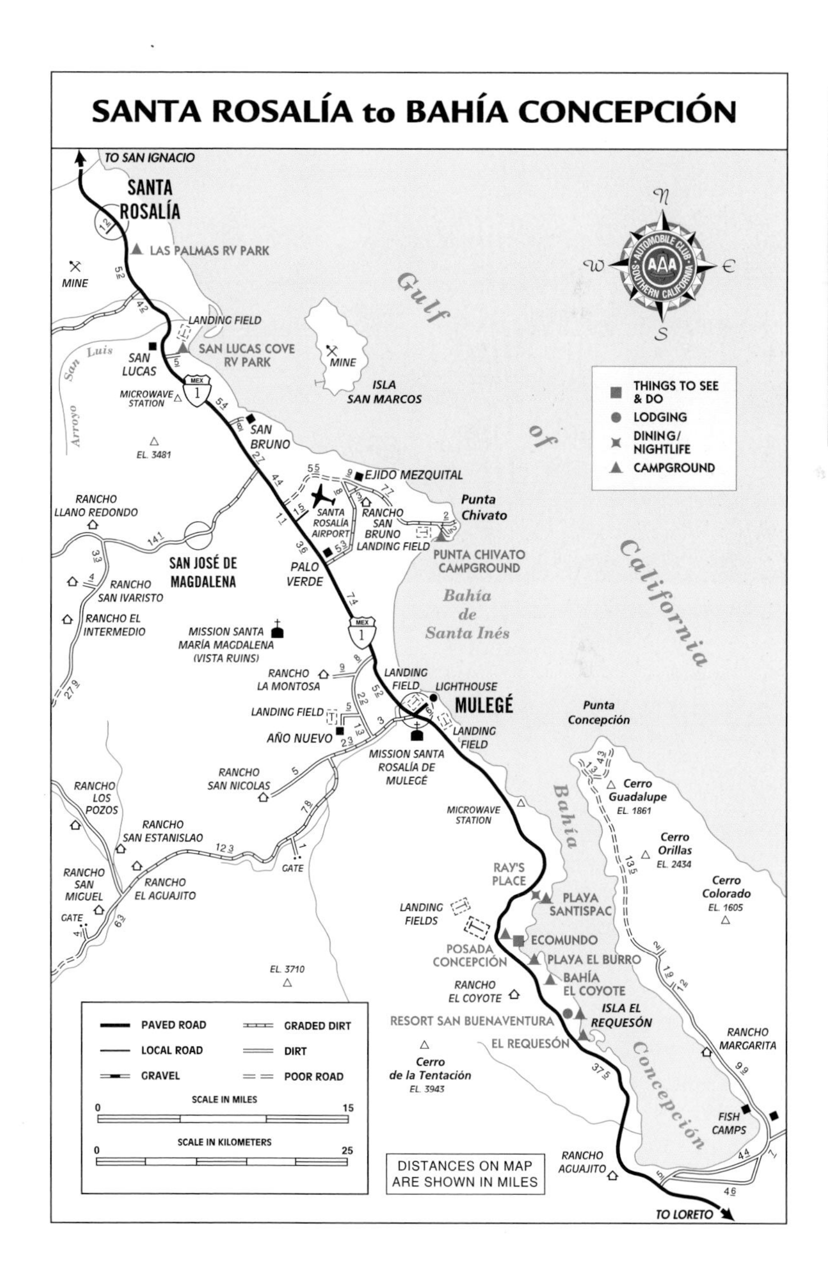

Chapter 9

South of Loreto

Baja California Sur is the least populous of all the 31 states in Mexico—a fact you may well surmise while on the long drive between Loreto and La Paz. Only two towns have more than 10,000 people along this 220-mile stretch of Highway 1, which most people travel over in all due haste. Truth be told, the drive can be mundane in spots once the road heads inland on a course that is well removed from mountains, sea and other scenic highlights of Baja. But Highway 1 belies the wonders that are out there—many miles from the main route but beckoning anyone with a sense of purpose or adventure. What's more, you needn't have knobby tires, four-wheel-drive or a month's worth of provisions to leave the main road and enjoy the best of what this region has to offer.

Of course, much of the terrain lies beyond reach of any vehicle, thanks in large part to the Sierra de la Giganta, the jagged barrier down the

On the road to Puerta Agua Verde, somewhere east of Highway 1

eastern flank of the peninsula from Loreto to the outskirts of La Paz. Highway 1 crosses the range south of Loreto and serves up a few last breathtaking views as it leaves the Sea of Cortez's grandeur behind. Beyond the sierra is a coastal plain that spreads toward the Pacific Ocean. At its heart is the Santo Domingo Valley (or Magdalena Plain), a major farming district that looks more like California's Central Valley than something you'd expect to find in Baja. Ciudad Constitución and Ciudad Insurgentes lie at the hub of this bustling region and are the only real towns along Highway 1 between Loreto and La Paz. Neither one is a tourist destination by any stretch, but they do serve as the gateways to some of the greatest attractions of the unknown Baja.

To the north of these towns is the easiest route to the La Purísima and Comondú valleys, each home to a postcard-perfect oasis and nestled along the west slope of the Sierra de la Giganta. To the southeast lie the mission and village of San Luis Gonzaga, miles from the nearest pavement and plunked amid another beautiful palm oasis.

The biggest attraction of all is to the west with Bahía Magdalena. "Mag Bay," as most North Americans call it, is the centerpiece of a 130-mile network of protected waterways along the Pacific Coast, and a place

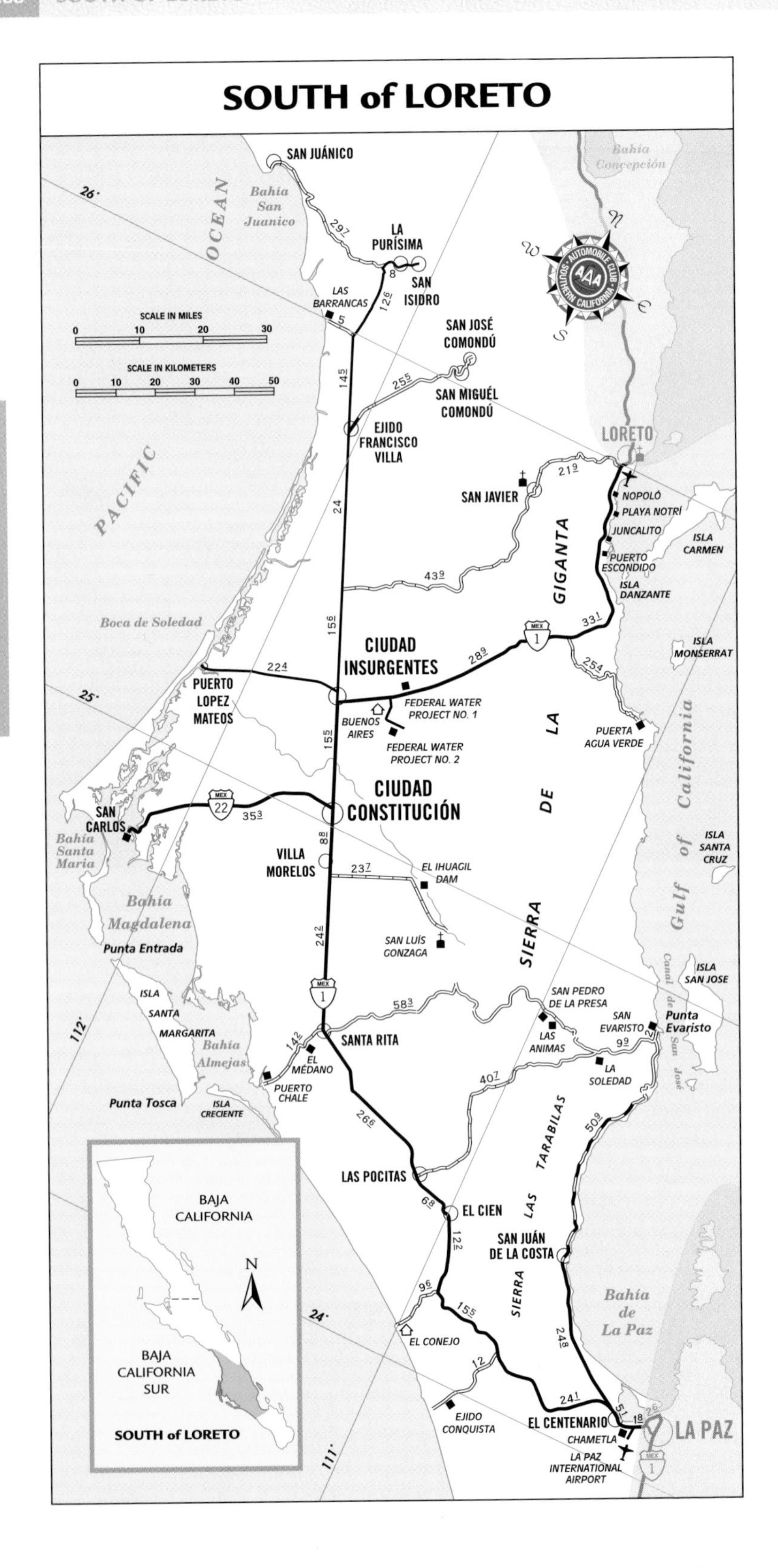
SOUTH of LORETO
SAN JUÁNICO
Bahía San Juanico
OCEAN
PACIFIC
LA PURÍSIMA
SAN ISIDRO
LAS BARRANCAS
SCALE IN MILES
0 10 20 30
SCALE IN KILOMETERS
0 10 20 30 40 50
SAN JOSÉ COMONDÚ
SAN MIGUÉL COMONDÚ
EJIDO FRANCISCO VILLA
Bahía Concepción
LORETO
SAN JAVIER
NOPOLÓ
PLAYA NOTRÍ
JUNCALITO
PUERTO ESCONDIDO
ISLA CARMEN
ISLA DANZANTE
GIGANTA
Boca de Soledad
CIUDAD INSURGENTES
ISLA MONSERRAT
PUERTO LOPEZ MATEOS
FEDERAL WATER PROJECT NO. 1
BUENOS AIRES
FEDERAL WATER PROJECT NO. 2
PUERTA AGUA VERDE
LA
CIUDAD CONSTITUCIÓN
DE
SAN CARLOS
Bahía Santa Maria
VILLA MORELOS
EL IHUAGIL DAM
Gulf of California
ISLA SANTA CRUZ
Bahía Magdalena
SIERRA
Punta Entrada
SAN LUÍS GONZAGA
ISLA SAN JOSE
Canal de San José
ISLA SANTA MARGARITA
SAN PEDRO DE LA PRESA
SAN EVARISTO
Punta Evaristo
SANTA RITA
LAS ANIMAS
Bahía Almejas
EL MÉDANO
LA SOLEDAD
PUERTO CHALE
Punta Tosca
ISLA CRECIENTE
TARABILAS
LAS
BAJA CALIFORNIA
LAS POCITAS
EL CIEN
SAN JUÁN DE LA COSTA
SIERRA
Bahía de La Paz
BAJA CALIFORNIA SUR
SOUTH of LORETO
EL CONEJO
EJIDO CONQUISTA
EL CENTENARIO
CHAMETLA
LA PAZ
LA PAZ INTERNATIONAL AIRPORT
AUTOMOBILE CLUB · SOUTHERN CALIFORNIA · AAA

that lends itself to superlatives. It is the largest bay in Baja California, home to the only deepwater port on the Pacific coast of Baja Sur (San Carlos), and is widely considered the top natural harbor on the Pacific Coast between San Diego and Acapulco.

Puerta Agua Verde, along the remote gulf coast

For most overland travelers, however, Bahía Magdalena remains off the beaten path. Geographical isolation helps, given the bay's distance from major population centers and transit hubs. (The nearest commercial airport is 100 miles away in Loreto.) Tourist facilities, such as they are, are limited to San Carlos and Puerto López Mateos, the only towns of consequence along the bay. Otherwise, the bay and its sprawling wetlands are almost entirely undeveloped, instead supporting a huge ecosystem that harbors marine and bird life of all description. The stars of that cast are the California gray whales, which make the bay the southernmost of their winter calving grounds.

Perhaps the bay's greatest appeal lies in its sheer remoteness, something it shares with the rest of this region. It's that same mystique that so much of Baja provides—going someplace of great beauty and significance, yet unknown to all but the most seasoned of explorers.

Experience ...

- Peek-a-boo views of the Sea of Cortez and offshore islands from Highway 1 as it winds high into the Sierra de la Giganta.
- Pods of gray whales unseen but clearly heard in the dark—diving, cavorting and spouting within earshot of the shoreline at Puerto López Mateos.
- Catching first glimpse of the verdant oasis and mission towers of San Luis Gonzaga ... and suddenly, the last 20-plus miles of bone-jarring road are worth the effort.
- Fresh-baked *pan dulce*, roasted corn and a slab of rotisserie-broiled pork fusing as one oh-so-Mexican aroma along a busy sidewalk in Ciudad Constitución.

Loreto to Ciudad Constitución

(90 mi., 144 km.; 2 hrs.)

The blue waters, desert isles and rugged sierra of the gulf coast are at their most beautiful driving south on Highway 1 from Loreto, but not for too long as the route soon swings inland once more. Two hundred miles will pass before the road meets the sea again near La Paz, as Highway 1 scales the Sierra de la Giganta and heads toward the farm belt of the Magdalena Plain.

Corn field near Ciudad Constitución

Leaving Loreto, the highway skirts the base of the Sierra de la Giganta, whose brownish-red slopes rise sharply from the gulf. Offshore, Isla del Carmen basks in the azure waters as the road passes miles of picturesque coves and fine beaches. Some 15 miles south is the turnoff to Puerto Escondido, beyond which the route turns west, climbing ever higher to cross the sierra. Nearing the summit, a series of odd, hat-shaped peaks come into view before the road gradually descends along the edge of a deep canyon.

Continuing southwest, the road soon levels out as you reach the broad, gently sloped Santo Domingo Valley. Though extremely arid, this sandy lowland has developed into a major farm center, thanks to wells tapping a vast underground aquifer. Miles of cropland stretch forth as the route heads west toward Ciudad Insurgentes, where it turns south toward Ciudad Constitución. Be alert for slow-moving farm vehicles and pass with care.

00.0 Junction with the paved road to Loreto.

01.1 Junction with a rough dirt road to Misión San Javier (see Side Route to Misión San Javier, *San Ignacio & Down the Gulf*, Chapter 8). This road is best suited for sturdy, high-clearance vehicles.

Side Routes

01.6 Junction with the paved road to Loreto's airport. Aeromexico and Aero California

both offer flights here. (See *Appendix*, Chapter 16, Transportation section.)

05.1 Nopoló, site of a government-sponsored Fonatur resort complex, which includes the Eden Loreto Resort.

09.9 A dirt road to Playa Notrí, a sandy beach.

13.7 Junction with the short dirt road to Juncalito, a fishing village, where boats for sportfishing are available. The road continues beyond the village to a public beach.

15.6 Junction with the 1.5-mile paved road to Puerto Escondido (Puerto Loreto), a deep-water port that once served commercial vessels. This bay has been earmarked for development by Fonatur, but so far with few results. Current facilities include an RV Park (see *Lodging & Campgrounds*, Chapter 15) and a marina with a boat ramp.

34.5 A steep, scenic dirt road leads southeast to Puerta Agua Verde, a fishing village on the gulf. Campsites are available on nearby beaches.

45.0 Turnout overlooking a rugged canyon.

63.5 Entrance to Ley Federal de Aguas #1, a government-sponsored water project that provides fresh water for nearby farms. It has a large Pemex station.

65.6 Rancho Buenos Aires and Ley Federal de Aguas #2, a major farming development.

74.0 A red, white and green monument marks the junction with Ciudad Insurgentes, a town of about 12,000 with stores, cafes, two Pemex stations, banks, an auto parts store and mechanical assistance. The center of town is to the right. The main street continues north as a paved road for 66 miles, then as a graded dirt road along the coast. Branches lead to San Javier, Comondú, La Purísima (see Side Route to La Purísima and Comondú), and San Juánico (Scorpion Bay), a popular surfing area. Another road heads west from town 20 miles to Puerto López Mateos. (See Side Route to Puerto López Mateos.)

Side Routes

Side Routes

90.0 Ciudad Constitución, at the junction with the paved road (Mexico Highway 22) to San Carlos (see Side Route to San Carlos).

Cuidad Constitución

In a land where English is the widely spoken second language, tourism employs thousands and foreign influence is everywhere, Ciudad Constitución is an island of comparative isolation, perhaps the least Americanized of major cities in Baja California. The word "major" may seem a stretch, but with 55,000 people, Ciudad Constitución is the third-largest city in Baja California Sur. And while it's not a tourist town in any normal sense, this is an important stopping point for Highway 1 vagabonds. The city's sheer size sees to that, being the only place with full services between Loreto and La Paz.

Ciudad Constitución is the largest town on Highway 1 between Ensenada and La Paz.

Ciudad Constitución owes nearly all its size and livelihood to the fields and orchards of the surrounding Santo Domingo Valley (sometimes called the Magdalena Plain), the largest farming district in Baja California Sur. This was a small roadside village till the 1960s, when wells tapped a vast underground aquifer and transformed the arid valley into a huge patchwork of productive farms. A bounty of crops now thrive beneath the year-round sun, including wheat, garbanzo, cotton, corn, alfalfa, sorghum and citrus fruit. Some farms also turn out large numbers of livestock. Ciudad Constitución holds sway too as the government seat for the *municipio* of Comondú, which also includes Ciudad Insurgentes.

Looking north along Bulevard Olachea in Ciudad Constitución

While it is no tourist town, Ciudad Constitución has a good variety of services, including lodging, a trailer park, restaurants, markets, a hospital, banks and coin laundries. If auto repairs are a pressing need, you'll find parts stores, repair shops and dealerships, along with several Pemex stations. What's more, Ciudad Constitución is an ideal jump-off point for day trips to the surrounding territory. There is nothing that remotely resembles a resort, but if clean, no-nonsense lodging and restaurants are all you need, you'll have few problems here.

For those who choose (or are forced) to stop here, Ciudad Constitución enjoys another advantage, being far lower-priced than Baja's resort towns. A week's lodging at one of the town's business-class hotels would cost you about the same as a single night's say at some Los Cabos hotels.

Dining

In case you hadn't guessed, Ciudad Constitución is not a town known for its gourmet dining, but it's still the largest town in this part of Baja and center of a thriving farm belt—factors that alone ensure a ready supply of restaurants. Highway 1 (locally called Boulevard Agustín Olachea) is the best place to look come mealtime, and has several clean, reasonably priced eateries. In addition to these choices, there are several low-priced *taquerias.*

ESTRELLA DEL MAR **Seafood**
$5-22. *West side of Hwy 1, .1 mile north of turnoff to San Carlos (next to Super Pollo) 01152 (1) 132-09-55.*

NUEVO DRAGÓN **Chinese**
$4.80-5.50. *East side of Hwy 1, Blvd Agustín Olachea 1134. 01152 (1) 135-01-84.*

RINCÓN JAROCHO **Seafood**
$5-20. *East side of Hwy 1, 1 block south of turnoff to San Carlos. 01152 (1) 132-25-25.*

SUPER POLLO **Chicken/Mexican**
$2.75-7. *West side of Hwy 1, just north of turnoff to San Carlos. 01152 (1) 132-28-88.*

Lodging

"Economical" is the operative word for lodging in Ciudad Constitución, a town that has no AAA-approved inns, but

See *Lodging & Campgrounds*, Chapter 15, for listings.

does have several clean, no-frills hotels. The majority of these are on or near Boulevard Olachea, the in-town name for Highway 1. Air-conditioned rooms with one or two beds typically run $12 to $37 per night.

Ciudad Constitución to La Paz

(130.0 mi., 208 km.; 2:45 hrs.)

The scenic coastline of Baja Sur seems worlds removed as Highway 1 strikes south through miles more of fertile cropland, which spreads well beyond Ciudad Constitución. Eventually the farm belt gives way to seemingly endless empty badlands as one yearns for the first glimpse of La Paz.

Leaving Ciudad Constitución, Highway 1 takes a straight shot for more than 30 miles across perfectly flat terrain, angling southeast at the tiny village of Santa Rita. From here, miles of chalk-colored hills, mesas and eroded gullies follow. Here and there you'll catch a glimpse of the distant Pacific or Gulf waters as the highway crosses the narrowest stretch of the entire peninsula, less than 30 miles between coasts. A steady procession of dips and curves on this often-narrow road demands your full attention behind the wheel.

Typical Highway 1 view, somewhere north of La Paz

Finally, more than 100 miles from Ciudad Constitución, the journey's destination comes into view. A teepee-shaped shrine marks the spot atop a high bluff, where the Gulf of California and Bahía de La Paz spread forth. A string of pink and white buildings crowd the far side of the bay, while a pair of brown desert peaks rise behind them at this first sighting of La Paz.

Dropping rapidly, the road soon reaches a broad coastal plain, thick with cirios, cholla, cardón cacti and other Baja flora. Beyond the hamlet of El Centenario, the route follows the contour of the bay, with La Paz's low-slung skyline shimmering in the distance. On the outskirts of town, you'll reach the famed Dove of Peace Monument, gateway to this scenic bayside capital.

00.0 **Ciudad Constitución, at the junction with the highway to San Carlos.**

01.3 **Junction with the paved road leading 3.8 miles east and .6 mile north to the Ciudad Constitución airport.**

08.1 **Villa Morelos, a tiny farming community with a cafe.**

10.3 **Junction with the dirt road to El Higuajil Dam and Misión San Luís Gonzaga (see Side Route to Misión San Luís Gonzaga).**

Side Routes

33.7 **Santa Rita, a village with a store, cafe and a church. At the north end of the village a dirt road branches west to Puerto Chale (see Side Route to Puerto Chale).**

Side Routes

52.0 **Junction with a mostly graded dirt road to a ranching region that includes the villages of San Pedro de la Presa and Las Animas. Winding along streams through the scenic Sierra de la Giganta, the road descends to San Evaristo on the gulf coast, 68 miles to the northeast.**

61.3 **Las Pocitas, a village with a picturesque church, a clinic and a cafe. A graded road leads northeast to La Soledad and San Evaristo.**

69.0 **El Cien, a settlement with a Pemex station, highway department camp and a cafe.**

81.2 **Junction with the 12-mile dirt road to El Conejo, a wind-blown Pacific beach that is popular with surfers. Any high-clearance vehicle can make the trip.**

96.6 **A good graded dirt road to Ejido Conquista and the Pacific coast.**

109.7 **A summit with a sweeping panorama of Bahía de La Paz; a turnout leads to a tepee-shaped shrine. Highway 1 now begins a sharp descent.**

117.6 **Site of an agricultural inspection station. All vehicles are required to stop.**

120.4 **Junction with a scenic paved road leading 25 miles north along the shore of Bahía de La Paz to the mining settlement of San Juán de la Costa. Phosphorus mined here is shipped by freighter to processing plants elsewhere in Mexico for use in the production of fertilizer. The town has gasoline and groceries. A dirt road follows the coast 45 miles farther north to the village of San Evaristo; its economy is based on fishing and salt evaporation and it has a protected cove. From there a road winds southwest through the Sierra de la Giganta and connects with Highway 1.**

121.9 **El Centenario, a small town of about 2000 inhabitants on the shore of the bay, has a Pemex station. The skyline of La Paz is visible across the water.**

125.6 **Chametla, a settlement at the junction with the 2.1-mile paved road to La Paz International Airport.**

127.1 **At the "Dove of Peace" monument, Camino a las Garzas veers to the right, providing a convenient bypass of central La Paz for Los Cabos-bound motorists.**

130.0 **La Paz, at the intersection of calzadas Abasolo and 5 de Febrero. Turn right here for Highway 1 south to Cabo San Lucas; straight ahead, the road along the bay shore leads to downtown La Paz and to Pichilingue, the Baja California Ferry port (see Transportation in the *Appendix*, Chapter 16).**

Side Routes

Ciudad Insurgentes to Comondú and La Purísima

(See map page 298.)

This is the longer but easier approach to these twin pairs of oasis towns, located on the west slope of the Sierra de la Giganta, heading north from Highway 1 in Ciudad Insurgentes. (The more northerly route, described in *San Ignacio & Down the Gulf,* Chapter 8, is more direct as it crosses the sierra from the east, but only sturdy off-road vehicles with four-wheel-drive can safely make this approach.) The route is paved clear to La Purísima and the neighboring town of San Isidro, located 72 miles north of Ciudad Insurgentes. San Miguel de Comondú and San José Comondú are slightly closer at 64 miles from the same starting point, but a slightly longer drive as a dirt road covers the final leg to these communities. The road is wide and graded, however, and passenger cars driven with care should be able to make the drive.

From Ciudad Insurgentes, the same route heads north toward both destinations for the first 41 miles, passing through miles of fertile cropland that eventually give way to barren desert. In Ejido Francisco Villa, a dusty, windblown farm cooperative near the Pacific Coast, the routes diverge as a gravel road forks to the right toward Comondú, while the paved road continues straight ahead toward La Purísima.

Town square and municipal hall, La Purísima

The Comondú route turns from gravel to dirt a few miles beyond Francisco Villa as it heads north-east across the coastal plain. Eventually the road winds into the steep, narrow canyon that shelters the two communities and a large oasis, about 25 miles off the paved road. A shallow arroyo crossing near the town's entrance may pose a problem for some low-slung cars.

The route to La Purísima runs almost due north from Francisco Villa, passing a side road to the fishing village of Las Barrancas (site of a joint German/Mexican solar energy project) and winding among barren coastal hills. Twenty-seven miles from Francisco Villa, it reaches the junction of a dirt road leading north another 30 miles to the seaside village of San Juánico (better known to North Americans as Scorpion Bay), home to one of Baja Sur's best-known surfing spots. From this junction, the paved road continues another four miles into the heart of La Purísima, with some outstanding views of the oasis and neighboring mesas.

For complete details on both destinations, see Side Route to Ciudad Insurgentes via Comondú and Side Route to Ciudad Insurgentes via La Purísima, in *San Ignacio & Down the Gulf,* Chapter 8.

Side Routes

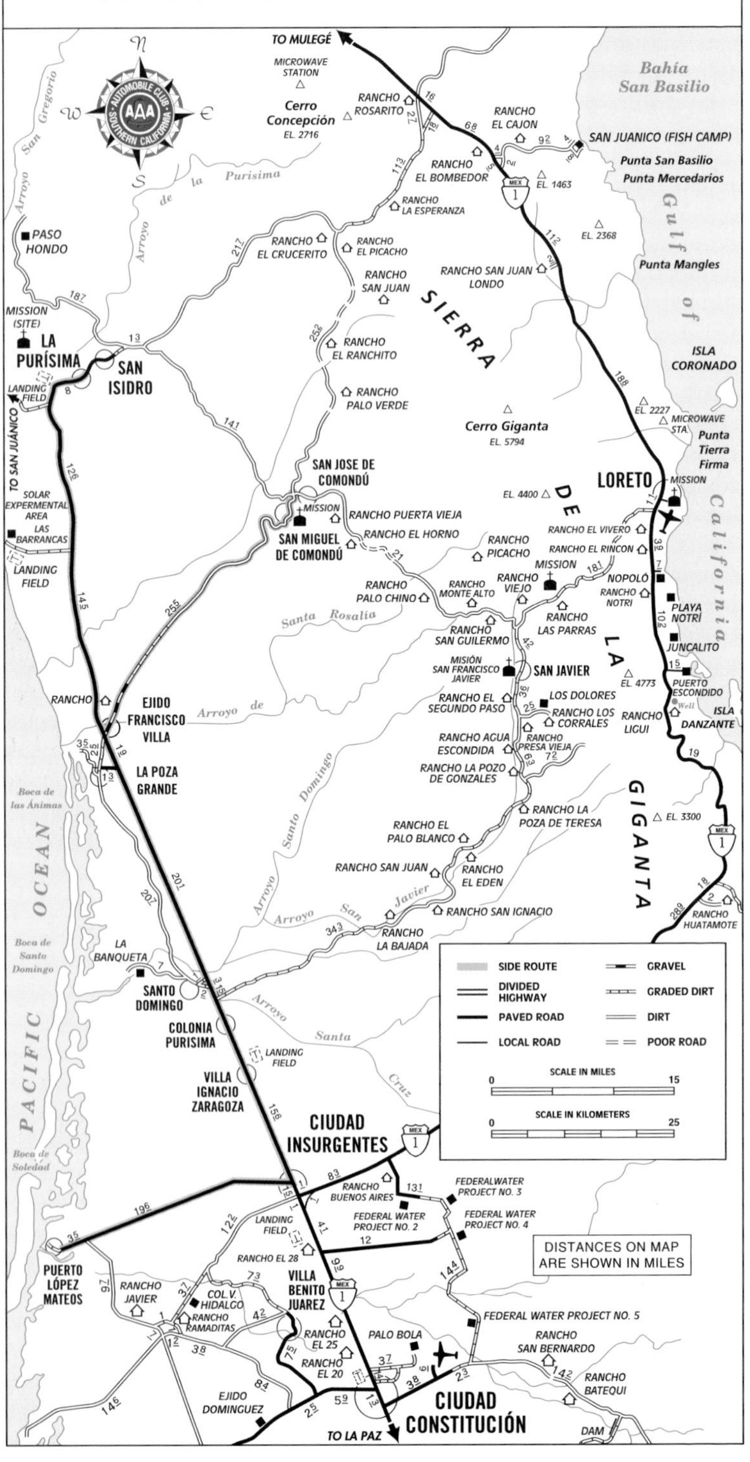
CIUDAD INSURGENTES to LA PURÍSIMA, COMONDÚ and PUERTO LOPEZ MATEOS
TO MULEGÉ
MICROWAVE STATION
Cerro Concepción
EL. 2716
RANCHO ROSARITO
RANCHO EL CAJON
SAN JUANICO (FISH CAMP)
Punta San Basilio
Punta Mercedarios
Bahía San Basilio
RANCHO EL BOMBEDOR
EL. 1463
RANCHO LA ESPERANZA
EL. 2368
Gulf of California
PASO HONDO
RANCHO EL CRUCERITO
RANCHO EL PICACHO
RANCHO SAN JUAN
RANCHO SAN JUAN LONDO
Punta Mangles
SIERRA DE LA GIGANTA
MISSION (SITE)
LA PURÍSIMA
SAN ISIDRO
LANDING FIELD
TO SAN JUANICO
RANCHO EL RANCHITO
RANCHO PALO VERDE
ISLA CORONADO
Cerro Giganta
EL. 5794
EL. 2227
MICROWAVE STA.
Punta Tierra Firma
SAN JOSE DE COMONDÚ
LORETO
MISSION
SOLAR EXPERIMENTAL AREA
LAS BARRANCAS
SAN MIGUEL DE COMONDÚ
RANCHO PUERTA VIEJA
RANCHO EL HORNO
EL. 4400
RANCHO EL VIVERO
RANCHO EL RINCON
RANCHO PICACHO
RANCHO PALO CHINO
RANCHO MONTE ALTO
RANCHO VIEJO
NOPOLÓ
RANCHO NOTRI
PLAYA NOTRÍ
Santa Rosalía
RANCHO SAN GUILLERMO
RANCHO LAS PARRAS
JUNCALITO
MISIÓN SAN FRANCISCO JAVIER
SAN JAVIER
EL. 4773
PUERTO ESCONDIDO
Well
ISLA DANZANTE
RANCHO
EJIDO FRANCISCO VILLA
Arroyo de
RANCHO EL SEGUNDO PASO
LOS DOLORES
RANCHO LOS CORRALES
RANCHO LIGUI
RANCHO AGUA ESCONDIDA
RANCHO PRESA VIEJA
LA POZA GRANDE
RANCHO LA POZO DE GONZALES
Boca de las Ánimas
RANCHO LA POZA DE TERESA
EL. 3300
RANCHO EL PALO BLANCO
Arroyo Santo Domingo
RANCHO SAN JUAN
RANCHO EL EDEN
Arroyo San Javier
RANCHO SAN IGNACIO
RANCHO HUATAMOTE
RANCHO LA BAJADA
PACIFIC OCEAN
Boca de Santo Domingo
LA BANQUETA
SANTO DOMINGO
Arroyo Santa Cruz
COLONIA PURISIMA
LANDING FIELD
VILLA IGNACIO ZARAGOZA
CIUDAD INSURGENTES
Boca de Soledad
SIDE ROUTE
DIVIDED HIGHWAY
PAVED ROAD
LOCAL ROAD
GRAVEL
GRADED DIRT
DIRT
POOR ROAD
SCALE IN MILES
SCALE IN KILOMETERS
RANCHO BUENOS AIRES
FEDERALWATER PROJECT NO. 3
FEDERAL WATER PROJECT NO. 2
FEDERAL WATER PROJECT NO. 4
LANDING FIELD
DISTANCES ON MAP ARE SHOWN IN MILES
PUERTO LÓPEZ MATEOS
RANCHO EL 28
RANCHO JAVIER
COL.V. HIDALGO
RANCHO RAMADITAS
VILLA BENITO JUAREZ
FEDERAL WATER PROJECT NO. 5
RANCHO EL 25
PALO BOLA
RANCHO SAN BERNARDO
RANCHO EL 20
RANCHO BATEQUI
EJIDO DOMINGUEZ
CIUDAD CONSTITUCIÓN
TO LA PAZ
DAM

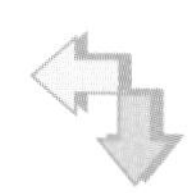

Ciudad Insurgentes to Puerto López Mateos
(See map page 298.)

(20 mi., 32 km.; 0:30 hr.)

Located near the northern edge of Bahía Magdalena, Puerto López Mateos makes its living from the sea and bay, although on a more modest scale than the bay's other port town, Puerto San Carlos. There is no deepwater port, only limited lodging, and the nearest gasoline is in Ciudad Insurgentes. But this town of 2400 does have ready access to the open sea and some of the Pacific Coast's best whale-watching opportunities.

Like San Carlos, López Mateos' busiest tourist season corresponds with the arrival of the gray whales in the winter, when the town throws an annual festival celebrating their return. A fleet of *pangas* and other small fishing boats double as whale-watching boats for visitors during these months. The port is ideally situated for whale watching, as the north entrance of the bay, Boca de Soledad, is a short boat ride away and a major gathering point for the giant mammals. The town is also an excellent place for viewing the whales from the shoreline, since the bay narrows to barely a mile in breadth.

Fishing boats at rest, Puerto López Mateos

López Mateos is a center for other outdoor activities throughout the year, including fishing, sailboarding, bird watching and kayaking. Fishing *pangas* are available for rent but are not allowed in the bay south of Boca de Soledad during the whale-watching months. Sailboards and kayaks are also barred from the same area during this period. For overnight visitors, there is a single small hotel, and a primitive campground on the bay at Playa Soledad. Rooms may also be available for rent in local homes.

See *GreatestHits*, Chapter 3, for more information on whale watching at López Mateos and San Carlos.

The route to López Mateos begins in Ciudad Insurgentes at a junction 1.5 miles north of Highway 1, crossing flat expanses of farmland and typical Baja desert on its way to the port. The road is paved for all but the last mile, turning to graded dirt on the outskirts of town.

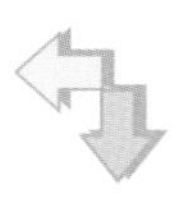

Ciudad Constitución to Puerto San Carlos

(See map page 301.)

(36 mi., 58 km.; 0:45 hr.)

With a population of about 4500, San Carlos is the largest settlement along Bahía Magdalena and serves a deepwater port that was originally built to ship farm products from the Santo Domingo Valley. Not many farm goods pass through today, but the port remains a busy place, with its commercial fishing fleet and packing plant for tuna and sardines. The seasonal whale-watching trade has helped create a limited tourist infrastructure, including several hotels, restaurants and markets. There's also a rustic campground, a public beach, auto repair shops and a Pemex station.

Dockside at Puerto San Carlos

Though not the most scenic of routes, Mexico Highway 22 provides speedy access to San Carlos and the bay from its junction with Highway 1 in Ciudad Constitución. The route is flat nearly all the way, passing through several miles of irrigated farmland before emerging into open desert covered with such typical Baja vegetation as cardón, cholla, pitahaya and assorted brush. Reaching the edge of the bay, the road crosses a bridge and enters San Carlos, situated on an irregular peninsula.

Diesel fuel is not sold at the Pemex station in San Carlos, but is available at the nearby deepwater port.

San Carlos gets some visitors throughout the year, but by far the busiest time is the winter, when the gray whales arrive at the end of their long southward trek. Hotel reservations are often necessary during this season, which peaks between mid-January and late March. (Many whale-watchers come and go in a single day.) The town pays homage to its finned visitors with a series of signs along the main street (Puerto La Paz) providing information about the whales and their migration. A small tourism office operates near the town's entrance during the whale-watching season as well. Whale-watching boats from the port find the best viewing near Punta Entrada at the main entrance of the bay.

EARLY BIRD GETS THE WHALE

Morning is usually the best time for whale watching in Bahía Magdalena. Like other calving lagoons, there is generally less wind and the bay is calmer than during the afternoon.

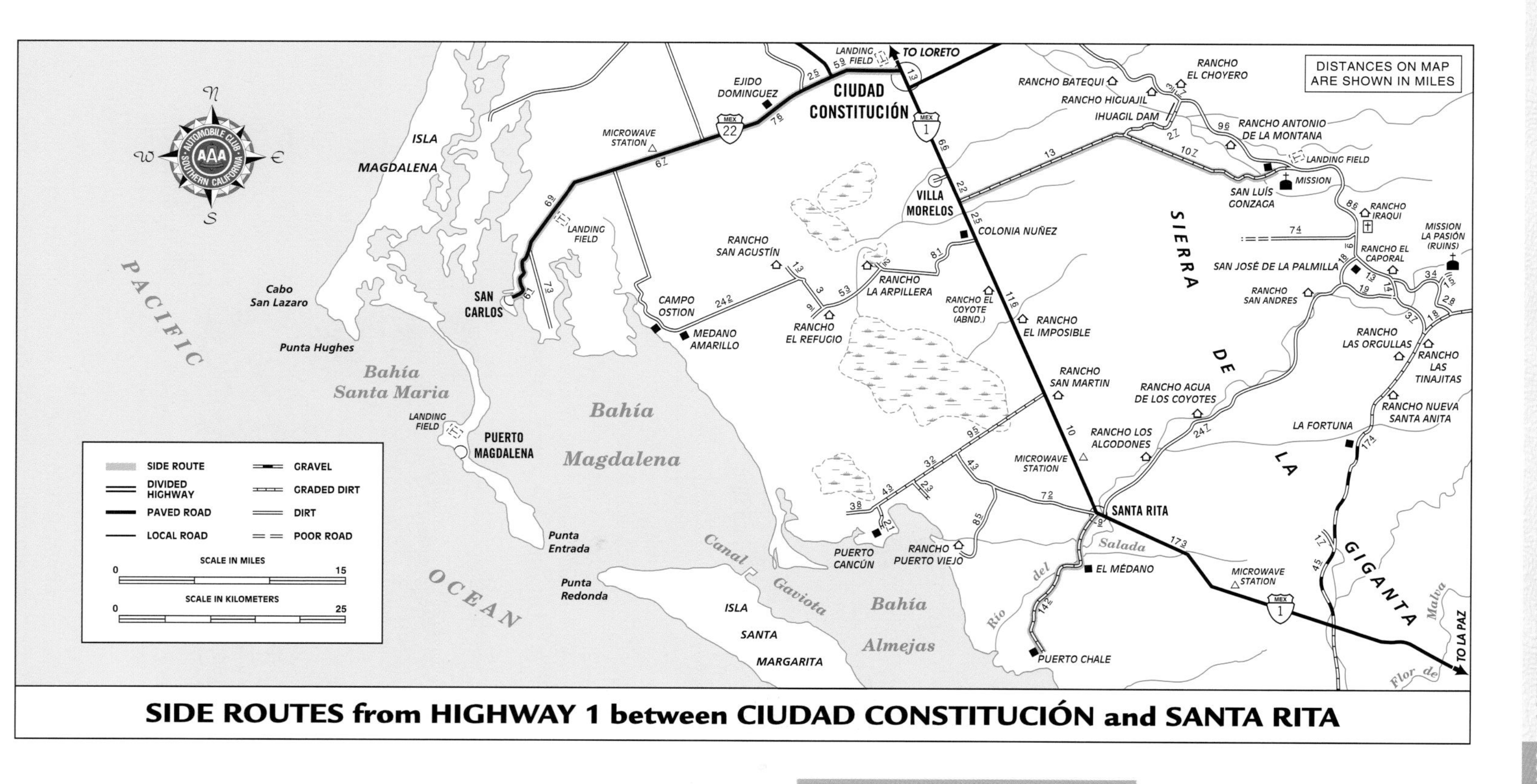

SIDE ROUTES from HIGHWAY 1 between CIUDAD CONSTITUCIÓN and SANTA RITA

HIDE AND SEEK

Migratory birds and marine life are not the only ones to have found refuge in Bahía Magdalena. Japanese submarines used the bay as a hideout during World War II.

Aside from the whales, other pursuits include kayaking along the mangrove-lined shore, sailboarding and bird watching. Migratory birds frequent the bay year round, but winter brings the largest numbers, with ducks, black brant and osprey the most prevalent species.

See *Lodging & Camgrounds*, Chapter 15, under San Carlos, for listings.

San Carlos has no AAA-approved lodging, but does have several inns ranging from austere to fairly comfortable. Rates range from about $13 to $65 per night.

Arrangements for whale-watching and fishing trips are available at most hotels.

Highway 1 to Misión San Luís Gonzaga

(See map page 301.)

(24 mi., 39 km.; 1 hr.)

Take away its modern school building, and the village of San Luis Gonzaga could easily stand as a museum piece from a long-past era. The stone mission, founded in 1737, is still in use and has a colorful, well-kept interior. The mission and a companion building formerly used for living quarters face a large open area that qualifies as the town's center. Two other stone buildings face this square—an abandoned store, and a former public building that now serves as a kind of dormitory. Several farmhouses are adjacent as well. Cattle ranching and date palms support the inhabitants of this small, remote hamlet.

Ready to cross a shallow stream following late summer's rains, near San Luís Gonzaga

The route to this village is well graded and is suitable for a passenger car with good tires and a sturdy suspension. From Highway 1, at a point 2.2 miles south of Villa Morelos (10 miles south of Ciudad Constitución), turn east on the road marked Presa Higuajil. After a mile, cultivated fields give way to native desert covered with cardón and a variety of other desert foliage. Thirteen miles from the pavement brings you to a junction with the road leading to Presa Ihuagil. Continuing straight ahead here, it's a 2.5-mile drive to Presa Higuajil, a dam with a modest-sized reservoir that is a major waterfowl sanctuary and excellent bird-watching location.

Bearing right at the junction, the graded dirt road continues southeast for another 10.7 miles to San Luis Gonzaga, crossing a wide plain and scaling a low ridge before dropping into the broad valley that is home to the mission and surrounding settlement.

Santa Rita to Puerto Chale

(See map page 301.)

(15 mi., 24 km.; 0:30 hr.)

A tiny, remote village along the windswept shore of Bahía Almejas, Puerto Chale has no tourist facilities, but attracts outsiders nonetheless for the recreational opportunities that beckon offshore. Bahía Almejas (Clams Bay) is the southernmost adjunct of the huge Bahía Magdalena complex. Nearly all the families who live here earn their living from fishing or taking visitors on guided outings. Diving, fishing and whale watching are all excellent, depending on the season.

Diving trips can be arranged to Isla Santa Margarita, some 20 miles distant, which separates the bay from the open sea. (The prime target is a sunken boat in about 30 feet of water off Punta Tosca, at the southern end of the island.) Boat trips are also available to view California gray whales between January and early April. On the fishing front, snapper, snook and corbina lurk amid the mangroves along the shoreline, although most anglers head for the open sea, where tuna, dorado, rooster fish and other big-game species abound. The town itself has a market and a small church, but no dining or auto repair facilities whatsoever.

From Highway 1, the route is wide and graded for the most part and negotiable by sturdy passenger cars. Sharp, fist-sized rocks can be a menace, however, and demand careful driving at moderate speeds. The road leaves the main highway just north of the village of Santa Rita and descends gently through barren countryside, passing the tiny hamlet of El Médano before crossing an arroyo en route to Puerto Chale.

Chapter 10

La Paz & Environs

Nine hundred two miles from the U.S. border, Mexico Highway 1 ascends to the crest of a rounded desert hill, and far ahead to the southeast spreads one of the most awaited—and cherished—sites in all of Baja California. A string of pastel buildings hugs the curving shoreline as you cast your eyes for the first time on the magnificent city and bay of La Paz.

Government seat for the state of Baja California Sur, La Paz is arguably the most picturesque of Mexico's 31 state capitals and by any measure one of the most beautiful cities in the country. La Paz emanates all that is right with the Baja peninsula: clean desert air, world-class fishing, uncrowded beaches, friendly locals, and the warm, clear waters of the gulf that attract divers from around the globe.

With its balmy year-round climate, La Paz is a natural magnet for snowbirds fleeing frigid winter climes far to the north. Drive the main

Isla Espíritu Santo, Bahía de La Paz

drag, Paseo Alvaro Obregón, in February and the license tag in front of you will as likely be from Oregon or British Columbia as Baja California Sur. Visiting yachts from around the world put in at the town's marinas, hailing from lands as far removed as Ireland and South Africa. Odds are your waiter at La Terraza speaks at least passable English, and the many nearby gift shops are clearly aimed at tourists from *el norte*.

Yet somehow this town of 180,000 absorbs that influx without losing its essential Mexican character. You will *not* be accosted by fast-talking time-share vendors; the old man selling hammocks will *not* chase you for three blocks; and there's a refreshing lack of sterile, pre-fab restaurants with the same menu as the ones in L.A. or Phoenix. La Paz draws an eclectic crowd, as you'll quickly note from the Nikes, Birkenstocks, Topsiders and *huarache* sandals treading the seaside *malecón*—*the* place to see and be seen in town.

For our purposes, La Paz is more than just the bayside town, but a region stretching roughly 80 road miles in a southeasterly arc along the Sea of Cortez. To the north of downtown is Pichilingue, the deepwater port where ferries come and go between the mainland. Beyond it lies a

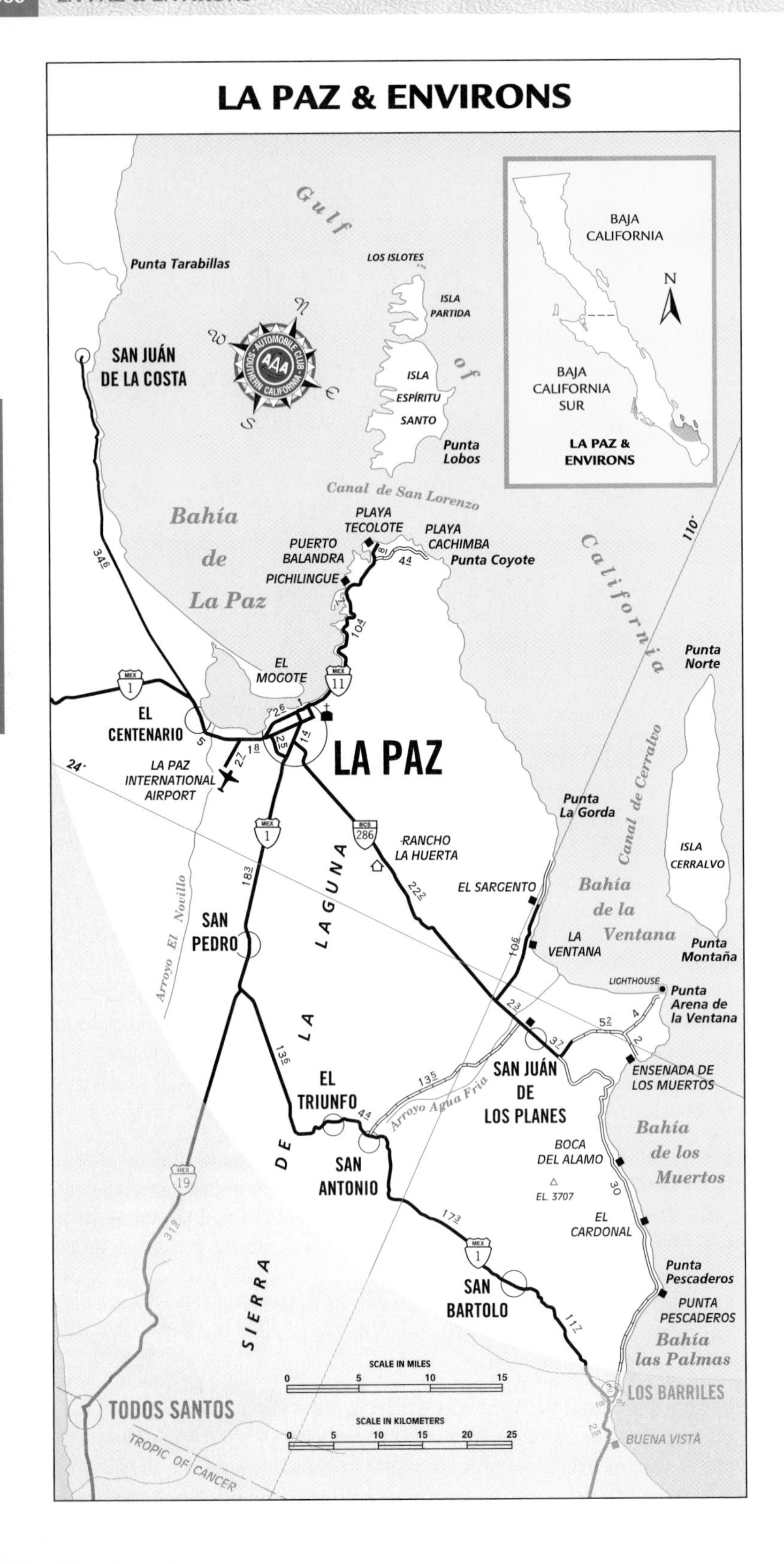

LA PAZ & ENVIRONS
Gulf of California
Punta Tarabillas
SAN JUÁN DE LA COSTA
LOS ISLOTES
ISLA PARTIDA
ISLA ESPÍRITU SANTO
Punta Lobos
Canal de San Lorenzo
BAJA CALIFORNIA
N
BAJA CALIFORNIA SUR
LA PAZ & ENVIRONS
Bahía de La Paz
PLAYA TECOLOTE
PUERTO BALANDRA
PLAYA CACHIMBA
Punta Coyote
PICHILINGUE
EL MOGOTE
EL CENTENARIO
LA PAZ
LA PAZ INTERNATIONAL AIRPORT
24°
110°
Punta Norte
Punta La Gorda
Canal de Cerralvo
ISLA CERRALVO
RANCHO LA HUERTA
EL SARGENTO
Bahía de la Ventana
LA VENTANA
Punta Montaña
LIGHTHOUSE
Punta Arena de la Ventana
Arroyo El Novillo
SAN PEDRO
LAGUNA
DE LA
SIERRA
EL TRIUNFO
SAN JUÁN DE LOS PLANES
ENSENADA DE LOS MUERTOS
Arroyo Agua Fría
Bahía de los Muertos
SAN ANTONIO
BOCA DEL ALAMO
EL. 3707
EL CARDONAL
Punta Pescaderos
PUNTA PESCADEROS
SAN BARTOLO
Bahía las Palmas
SCALE IN MILES
0 5 10 15
SCALE IN KILOMETERS
0 5 10 15 20 25
LOS BARRILES
BUENA VISTA
TODOS SANTOS
TROPIC OF CANCER

series of attractive beaches—gently sloped, seldom crowded, each with its own open-air, *palapa*-roofed diner.

Southeast of town, a two-lane road dubbed Baja California Sur 286 forks off toward another string of far-flung beaches with names like La Ventana, Punta Arena and Ensenada de los Muertos. Highway 1, meanwhile, charts an inland course as it heads south from town through desert and the rugged canyons of the Sierra de la Laguna before reaching the coast once more at Los Barriles. Beyond the water's edge, the bay, gulf and several islands are essential parts of this region. Isla Cerralvo is surrounded by some of the best fishing waters in all of Mexico, while Isla Espíritu Santo and Isla Partida are renowned as diving and kayaking venues.

John Steinbeck helped put all this in the public eye when he extolled La Paz's virtues in his 1941 tome "The Log From the Sea of Cortez." John Wayne and a host of other Hollywood stars did so in the 1950s when they would venture south between movie or TV shoots to fish the Gulf of California, long before Highway 1 linked the town with the U.S. mainland.

Fishing is still a marquee attraction, although other outdoor pursuits have gained an ever-widening fan base. And there remain the visual beauty, relaxed pace of life and enduring spirit of friendship—befitting a town whose name is Spanish for "The Peace." As the plaque reads on the Dove of Peace Monument near the city's northern entrance, "And if you want peace, I offer it to you in the sunny peace of my bay."

Experience ...

- Beads of sweat dripping from the glass of an oh-so-cold piña colada beneath a *palapa*-roofed restaurant on Playa El Tecolote.
- Getting up close and personal to tickle the whiskers of a sea lion while diving off Isla Espíritu Santo.
- Your first sight of a blue marlin, vaulting skyward at the end of a 40-pound test line, in the final throes of a 90-minute struggle between man and fish.
- Ten thousand lights twinkling along the water's edge and across the hills as crimson fades to black across the bay at day's end.
- Guys and girls trading coy glances, couples locked arm in arm, and families strolling as one during the Sunday evening promenade along the *malecón.*

Getting Around

Unlike most Mexican cities, La Paz is a sprawling, low-density community, which means you'll need some kind of wheels to get around at great length. Luckily, though, the main tourist scene is confined to a fairly small area along the water's edge, namely Paseo Obregón. Strap on a sturdy pair of sandals or walking shoes and you'll do fine in ambling along this busy venue, scene of cafes, hotels, gift shops and the *malecón* bayside walk. Major points of interest like the main square *(zócalo)*, cathedral

FOLLOW THE SUN

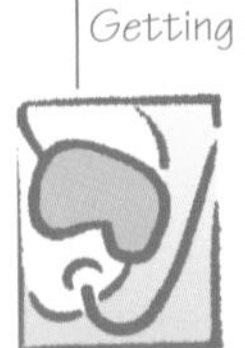

Getting your bearings in La Paz can be confusing at first, seeing as how the shoreline faces northwest instead of eastward like other towns along the gulf. You'll note this when the evening sun sinks across the bay instead of inland.

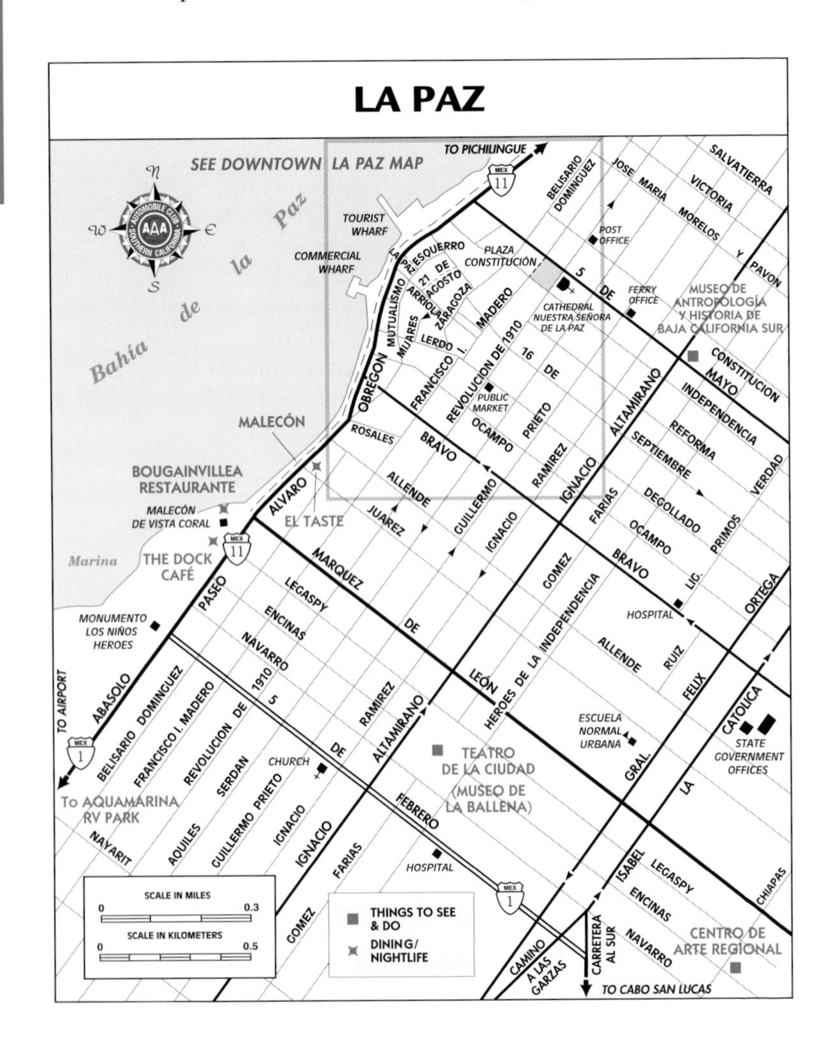

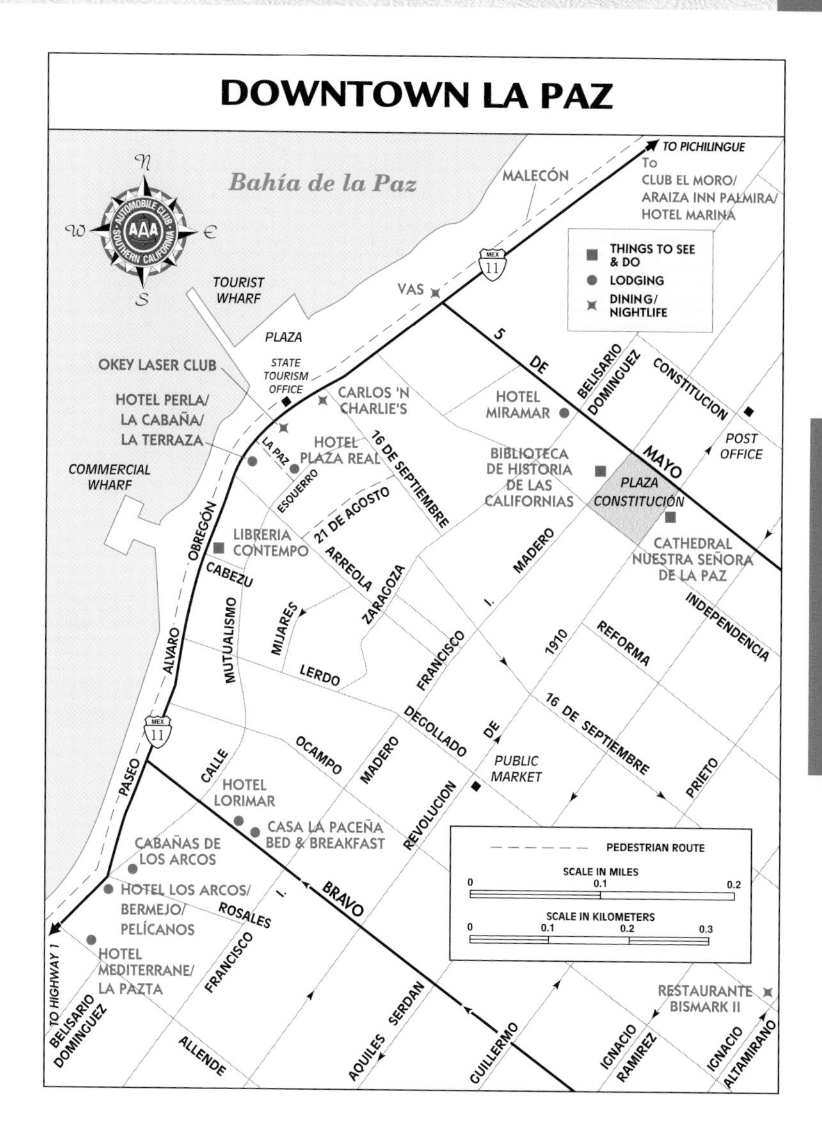

and Museum of Anthropology are a few short blocks inland and within a short hoof of the waterfront.

Stroll Obregón for any length of time and you'll hear the refrain of "*¿Taxi? ¿Taxi?*" from a brigade of cabbies hustling for a fare. They can be annoying until you hire one, but once you have, they are a great and not-too-expensive way to get about. Hourly fares run around $10, about the same rate you'll pay for a lift to the airport (eight miles southwest of downtown.)

La Paz just may be the only city its size or larger in Mexico where the motorists generally yield to pedestrians at crosswalks.

If you're intent on serious backcountry exploring, we'll assume that you've brought your own wheels or plan to rent a vehicle here. If you plan to stray beyond town or the port at Pichilingue, it's the only realistic means of getting around.

Things to See & Do

Why read an essay about things to see and do in La Paz when what you really need to do is take a walk down Paseo Obregón? This single seaside avenue provides a wonderful look at the many diversions this city and environs offer.

On the bay side of the avenue there's the famed *malecón* walkway, a narrow beach, two tourist piers and a tidy plaza fronting the picturesque harbor. Cross the street and there's nearly a mile's worth of gift shops, travel agencies and recreation outfitters worked in amid hotels, clubs and open-air restaurants. Not only is this La Paz's prime shopping district, but a great place to find out more about the region's many outdoor activities.

The *malecón,* for its part, is an essential part of the La Paz experience, and one that nearly all tourists enjoy, no matter how many times they've been here. Tread this walkway on a Sunday evening and you'll join legions of tourists and locals in the time-honored ritual of a weekly promenade up and down the palm-lined bayside. For *paceños,* it's a practice that dates back decades as friends and strangers mingle, and perhaps marvel at their good fortune of calling this seaside town their home.

If your main goal in travel is to expand your shopping horizons, the other side of Obregón will surely catch your interest first. Dozens of gift shops and open-air stalls await your perusal along several blocks of street front, so take your time and inspect all the wares before you open your wallet. These same blocks are a great place to learn more about the attractions that await offshore, with several agencies that offer fishing, diving and kayak trips, among other sorts of outings.

Plaza Constitución

For gringos coming south, it was the waters of the bay and gulf that made a name for La Paz, and for many years the town reigned supreme as both the sportfishing and diving capital of Baja. By most scores the fishing crown has moved south to Cabo and the East Cape, but La Paz

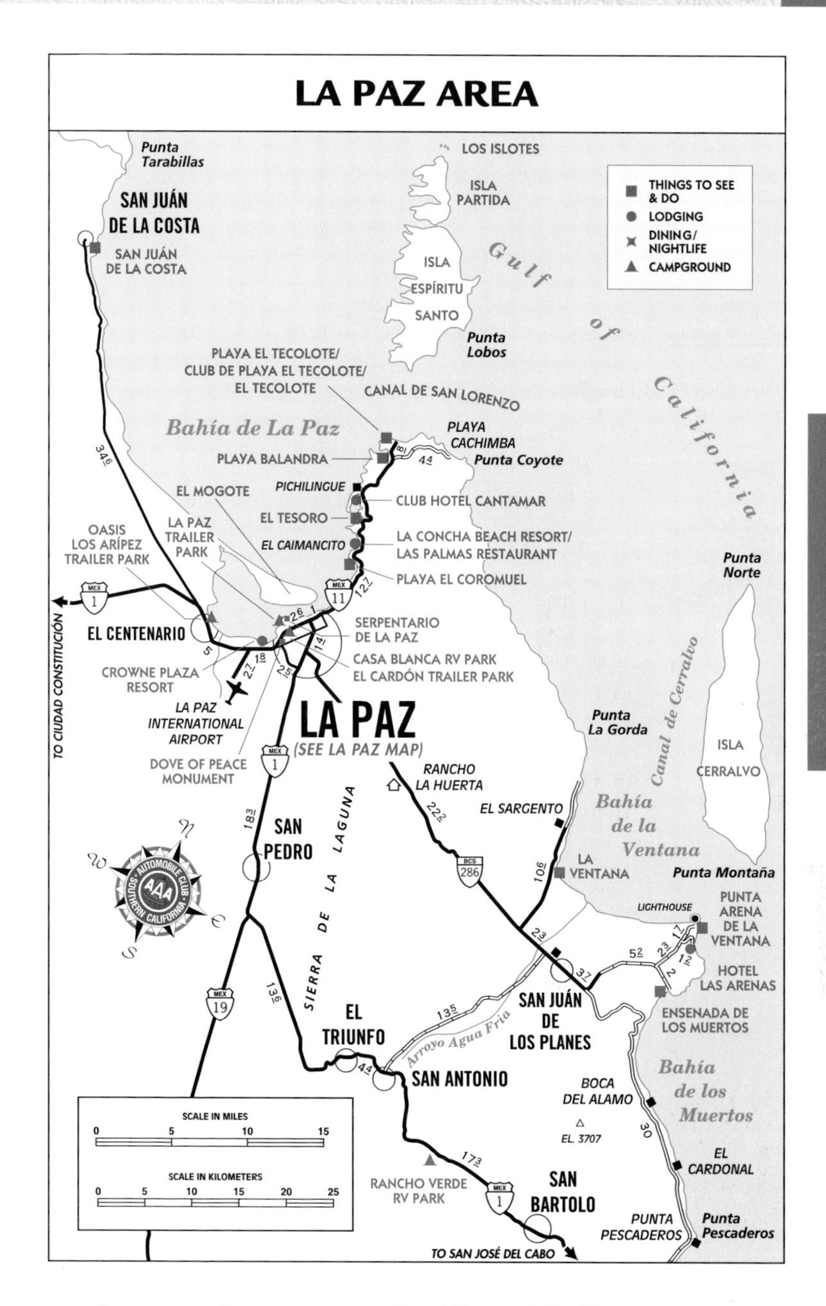

remains a great place to cast your line. The catch inside the bay is not what it once was, but the open waters of the gulf remain a bastion for game fish and hunting grounds for those who pursue them with bait and hook.

For undersea explorers, the waters off La Paz are among the premier diving areas in Baja, with seamounts, shipwrecks, rugged islands and other venues lending themselves to every skill level. Another nice thing is the warm seawater, with surface temperatures reaching the high 80s by late summer. About the only downside is the long boat ride you'll likely take, since the best dive spots are well off the mainland shore.

Kayaking is another great way to explore the local waters, from the inner harbor to islands well removed from the city. By far the most popular destination is Isla Espíritu Santo (Holy Spirit Island), near the upper edge of La Paz Bay and by some scores one of the top kayaking spots in the country. Paddling trips around this island and elsewhere can range from a couple of hours to several days, and provide the most intimate look at the sea and shoreline.

OUTFITTERS UNLIMITED

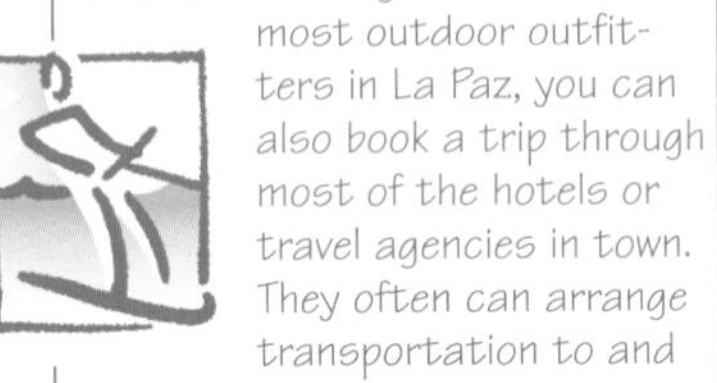

While Paseo Obregón has the most outdoor outfitters in La Paz, you can also book a trip through most of the hotels or travel agencies in town. They often can arrange transportation to and from your hotel as well.

Water recreators soon become familiar with the gulf's amazing variety of sea life—everything from tropical fish to sea lions, giant manta rays and huge (but harmless) whale sharks. A fair number of California gray whales show up in these waters during the winter, as do a smattering of other species, including massive blue whales—the largest animals on earth. Your best bet for viewing a whale, however, is by joining a daylong guided tour to Bahía Magdalena on the Pacific coast, southernmost of the gray whales' winter calving grounds.

Back on land, meanwhile, Paseo Obregón is not the only place in town worth spending time. A few blocks inland is Plaza Constitución, a small, inviting park that is the town's *zócalo*. Two of La Paz's best known old buildings flank the plaza, including the town's main cathedral, Nuestra Señora de La Paz, and the Biblioteca de Historia de las Californias, which was the government center for most of Baja Sur's pre-statehood days. A few blocks farther up the street is the Museo de Antropología y Historia (Museum of Anthropology and History), a must-stop for those who aspire to learn more about the early days of Baja Sur.

Elsewhere, there's the Teatro de la Ciudad (Theater of the City), a good-sized performing arts complex that also touts an art gallery and the Museo de la Ballena (Whale Museum), a tribute to gray whales and other finned giants of the sea. Then there's the Dove of Peace Monument, which at first glance looks more like a whale's tail. Near the town's north entrance, the huge white sculpture of a dove merits a closer inspection by all who pass this way, at least on your first visit to this peaceful bayside town.

Top Attractions

BIBLIOTECA DE HISTORIA DE LAS CALIFORNIAS

Housed in the old state capitol building, this small library boasts a display of vivid paintings depicting the early days of Baja California Sur. There's a good collection of books in Spanish and English about the early history of the Californias. The building dates to 1881 and served as Baja California Sur's government center until 1963. It was rededicated as a library in 1981. *North side of Plaza Constitución. No Phone. Open Mon-Fri 8 am-8 pm. Free.*

DOVE OF PEACE MONUMENT

At first glance, this huge, sculpted gateway to La Paz may appear to be a giant whale's tail. A second look confirms this is a dove with wings spread in full flight, which suits the town's Spanish name. A plaque in front greets visitors with an inscription that reads: "And if you want peace *(paz)*, I offer it to you in the sunny peace of my bay." *At the north entrance of town at the junction of Hwy 1 and Camino a las Garzas.*

MALECÓN

The *malecón* is a major gathering spot for any Mexican port town, but even more so in La Paz. Hugging the east flank of the inner bay, La Paz's *malecón* lies across the street from the tourist shopping district. Along the way are a pair of wharves that serve visiting tour boats and are perfect for an evening stroll. Perhaps the epicenter of the *malecón* is the park next to the State Tourism Office. There's a large gazebo here, plus a plaque that marks a red-letter day in local history—Queen Elizabeth's arrival by sea during her 1983 cruise up the west coast of North America. *Along the water's edge on Paseo Obregón, between Calle Marquez de León and north edge of town.*

***Enjoying a stroll along the* malecón**

MUSEO DE ANTROPOLOGÍA Y HISTORIA DE BAJA CALIFORNIA SUR

One of Baja Sur's top museums, this modern, attractive facility merits a stop if you care the least bit about the history or early peoples of Baja's southern state. Lavish murals, dioramas and elaborate exhibits combine to provide a tour de force of the state and city's geography and early days. Beyond the local state, Mexico's War of Independence, the Mexican-American War and the Mexican Revolution all receive good coverage. Still more displays cover the geology, flora and fauna of Baja Sur. *Corner of Ignacio Altamirano and 5 de Mayo. 01152 (1) 122-01-62 or 25-65-24. Open Mon-Fri 8 am-6 pm, Sat 9 am-2 pm.*

NUESTRA SEÑORA DE LA PAZ

A handsome twin-towered church, La Paz's main parish anchors the southeast side of Plaza Constitución. While this one lacks the size or baroque grandeur of many of Baja's missions, it still merits a walk inside, if just for the lovely stained glass. The present building dates to 1861, when it replaced the city's original mission church. Large bilingual plaques recall the church's history and some of the early settlement of La Paz. *South side of Plaza Constitución.*

Cathedral Nuestra Señora de La Paz

SERPENTARIO DE LA PAZ

Opened in late 2000, this attractive new facility purportedly has the second-largest collection of snakes in Mexico. It has a wide variety of reptiles and other ground-hugging creatures native to Baja and elsewhere in Latin America, including various rattlesnakes, gopher snakes, a boa constrictor, tarantulas and scorpions. *On Calle Brecha California, 1 blk east of Playa Sur and 1 blk south of Ave Nueva Reforma (near La Posada de Engelbert). 01152 (1) 122-56-11. Open Tue-Sun 10 am-6 pm, closed Mon. Admission $10 for non-La Paz residents.*

During its first 40 years, Nuestra Señora de La Paz had only one tower. The church's second tower wasn't added until the early 1900s.

SHOPPING

Paseo Obregón has the highest concentration of outdoor clothing, arts and crafts in the entire city, spread along a seven-block stretch between Calle Bravo and Calle 5 de Mayo. Your best bet here is to buy nothing on your first walk up the street—just check the wares and note the prices as you go. On your way back you'll be set to buy—with a working knowledge of selection, quality and what's a fair price to pay. Elsewhere about town, blankets, ser-

TIME TO RE-SUPPLY?

La Paz has the biggest, best-supplied supermarkets in Baja California Sur, with a good selection of groceries and sundries of all description. Major chains include CCC (Centro Comercial Californio), with two locations, and Supermercados Aramburo, with three locations around town.

apes, rugs and other woven goods are the specialty at Artesanía Cuauhtémoc (The Weaver), on Abasolo (Highway 1) between calles Jalisco and Nayarít. Another shopper's highlight is Centro de Arte Regional, a good-sized pottery workshop that makes and sells ceramic works at reasonable prices, at the corner of calles Chiapas and Encinas.

TEATRO DE LA CIUDAD

A 1500-seat theater presents a variety of music, stage and dance productions, but that's just one of the attractions at this modern complex. Adjacent to the theater is a gallery showcasing the works of artists from Baja Sur and the rest of Mexico. Nearby is the Museo de la Ballena (Whale Museum), a place to learn about whales of all species, with a strong focus on the California gray whale. *Corner of Miguel Legaspy and Héroes de la Independencia. 01152 (1) 125-02-07 or 122-91-96. Art gallery open Mon-Fri 8 am-8 pm. Whale Museum open Tue-Sun, 9 am-2 pm. Theater ticket prices vary according to performance. Donation only for gallery and Whale Museum.*

Teatro de la Ciudad

Outdoor Fun

BEACHES

Balandra A distinctive, mushroom-shaped rock punctuates this sheltered strand along a narrow inlet, off the highway north of Pichilingue. Swimming and wading are both excellent in these waters, and a small coral reef provides one of few good snorkeling spots along the mainland near La Paz. Also, a nearby trail leads up a hill to an excellent viewpoint above the inlet. *12 miles north of town and 3 miles north of Pichilingue, off the road to El Tecolote.*

El Coromuel This smallish, sandy strand is a good place to swim, wade or sunbathe, and conveniently close to town. An open-air seafood restaurant makes this a good one-stop beach if you're not up for a long drive. *2½ miles north of town on the road to Pichilingue.*

El Tecolote A long, sandy strand with open-air restaurants, *palapa* huts and access to various water sports, El Tecolote takes honors as the most popular beach among *paceños* and visitors alike. Wading and swimming are quite good along this gently sloped beach, although it gets some waves, being partly exposed to the open gulf. Kayak and snorkeling trips embark from here across the Canal de San Lorenzo to Isla Espíritu Santo, four miles away across the Canal de San Lorenzo. *14 miles north of town and 5 miles north of Pichilingue.*

El Tesoro This small, crescent-shaped strand is a good destination for swimming, wading and sunning in a reasonably quiet environment without driving clear north to El Tecolote. A restaurant on the sand has seafood and cold drinks. *8 miles north of town on the road to Pichilingue.*

San Juán de la Costa It's a long drive to this remote beach with few services and many gravelly spots, best known for its phosphorus mine and loading pier. On the other hand, it's never crowded and it's a lovely drive to get here, between the blue bay and the ruddy slopes of the Sierra de la Giganta. *29 miles northwest of town along the western shore of Bahía de La Paz.*

DIVING

Diving the seas off La Paz can mean anything you want it to: Exploring a shipwreck 100 feet beneath the surface, snorkeling with hundreds of vibrant tropical fish along a shallow inshore reef, stroking a sea lion on the head, or gazing up at a circling school of hammerhead sharks. The possibilities are endless, although most visiting divers will be heading for one of a dozen or so locations.

The most popular dive spot is **Los Islotes,** at the extreme northern edge of La Paz Bay, where scores of friendly sea lions await the daily boatloads of snorkelers and scuba divers. A clump of small, rocky islands, Los Islotes lie north of **Isla Espíritu Santo,** which offers several more outstanding diving spots. Inshore, the island has several good shallow reefs with tropical fish and colorful coral heads that make for excellent snorkeling. Deeper zones nearby are home to sunken ships, rocky reefs and undersea caves. El Bajo, a group of undersea pinnacles east of Espíritu Santo, is famous for attracting schools of hammerhead sharks and other open-water fish throughout the year. Farther southeast, **Isla Cerralvo** affords excellent diving at varying depths off its north and south ends.

Snorkeling off Los Islotes, Bahía de La Paz

Outing prices vary considerably, depending on your destination and whether you're snorkeling or scuba diving. Snorkeling trips start at less than $50, while extended scuba trips can cost several hundred dollars. A typical day outing to Los Islotes and Isla Espíritu Santo runs about $90 per person, equipment not included. Equipment rentals are available through any outfitter in town, with snorkeling gear running $10 to $15 per day, while scuba gear can fetch $60 to $90, depending on what equipment you need. Scuba instruction is available for all experience levels; beginners can expect to pay around $350 for open-water certification.

See *GreatestHits,* Chapter 3 for more on Isla Espíritu Santo.

Major diving outfitters include the following:

Baja Diving & Service *Paseo Obregón between 16 de Septiembre and Callejón La Paz. 01152 (1) 122-18-26 or 122-70-10. Website at www.bajadivingservice.com.* **Cortez Club** *At La Concha Beach Resort, 3 miles north of town on the road to Pichilingue. 01152 (1) 121-61-20. Website at www.cortezclub.com.* **Scuba Baja Joe** *Paseo Obregón between calles Ocampo and Degollado. 01152 (1) 122-40-06. Website at www.scubabajoe.com.* **Scubaja** *Corner of Paseo Obregón and Calle Nicolás Bravo. 01152 (1) 122-74-23. Website at www.scubaja.com.* **Sea & Scuba** *Corner of Paseo Obregón and Calle Ocampo. 01152 (1) 123-52-3.*

FISHING

Heading seaward in the predawn light to fish the Gulf of California remains the most classic of La Paz adventures. While the Cape Region has superseded La Paz as the fishing capital of Baja, the local seas remain a bastion for the game fish that made Baja famous. All those species ply the depths at one time or another during the year, though odds are slim you'll catch them all on the same day.

La Paz Bay itself is not the best of fishing grounds, although things pick up as you reach the bay's northern limits. Beyond the bay, though, the waters of the gulf can provide some of the most outstanding fishing in all of Baja California. For most visiting anglers, that means heading southeast of town to the waters near **Isla Cerralvo**. All of Baja's game fish pass this way during the year as they migrate up and down the gulf, and dozens of boats may work this zone when the action's hot. When the game fish aren't biting, smaller but good-eating species like cabrilla, grouper and sierra can provide some action along the inshore waters. Farther north, **Canal de San Lorenzo,** off the south end of Isla Espíritu Santo, and **San Juán de la Costa** are often excellent spots.

See *GreatestHits,* Chapter 3, for more on fishing in La Paz.

Guess who's coming to dinner?

Some anglers choose to fish from a full-fledged cruiser, but most opt for a *panga,* the venerable outboard-motor skiff that is the backbone of the local fleet. Most *pangas* embark from beaches well-removed from the city, including **El Tecolote** to the north, and **Punta Arena, La Ventana** and **Ensenada de los Muertos** to the southeast. *Pangas* usually cost $180 per boat for a full day's fishing and normally hold two or three anglers. Cruisers fall mainly in the 28- to 30-foot range and cost around $350 per day, holding up to four anglers.

Major fishing outfitters in La Paz include the following:

Baja Diving & Service *Paseo Obregón between 16 de Septiembre and Callejón La Paz. 01152 (1) 122-18-26 or 122-70-10. Website at www.bajadivingservice.com.* **Fishermen's Fleet** *Office at Hotel Los Arcos, corner of Paseo Obregón and Calle Rosales. 01152 (1) 122-13-13.* **Jack Velez Fleet** *Office at Hotel Los Arcos, corner of Paseo Obregón and Calle Rosales. 01152 (1) 122-27-44.* **Viajes Coromuel** *Corner of Paseo Obregón and Calle Rosales, next to Hotel Los Arcos. 01152 (1) 122-80-06.* **Viajes Lybsa** *Corner of Paseo Obregón and Calle Degollado. 01152 (1) 122-60-01 or 122-60-02.*

KAYAKING

Prolific sea life and sparkling clear waters, along with beautiful islands and coast combine to make greater La Paz one of the top kayaking areas not only in Baja California, but in all of Mexico. A La Paz kayaking trip can mean whatever you want—from a quick jaunt around the inner bay to a multi-day excursion exploring many miles of shoreline. Odds are you'll want to combine your outing with snorkeling, fishing or camping, or maybe all of the above.

Baja Expeditions and Mar y Aventuras are the principal providers of long-range kayak tours that include overnight camping.

While there are many good paddling destinations, the one that stands out from the rest is **Isla Espíritu Santo,** near the northwest edge of the bay and by many accounts the finest kayaking destination in Baja. Along with its great scenic beauty, the island has numerous sheltered coves, excellent diving conditions, and several suitable spots for putting ashore. **Isla Partida,** its smaller, next-door neighbor, shares those same attributes. Farther north, several islands attract long-range paddlers, including **Isla San Francisco, Isla San José** and **Isla Santa Cruz.** Closer at hand, **El Mogote,** the sand spit across the bay from La Paz's main shoreline, and **Playa Balandra,** a few miles north of Pichilingue, make for good short-range trips.

Pricing varies immensely and there is something to match any budget. A few hotels offer kayaks either free or at a nominal charge to guests for paddling around the nearby bay. Other firms offer kayaks for rent by the half-day or day, while a few outfitters specialize in guided, inter-island outings lasting a week or more. Daily rentals typically cost $40 to $60, depending whether you use a one-seat or two-seat model. Daylong trips to the ever-popular Isla Espíritu Santo run $90 to $120, including boat transportation, lunch and snorkeling gear. Excursions lasting a week or longer start around $900 and can cost well over $1000.

Major kayaking outfitters in La Paz include the following:

Baja Diving & Service *Paseo Obregón between 16 de Septiembre and Callejón La Paz. 01152 (1) 122-18-26 or 122-70-10. Website at www.bajadivingservice.com.* **Baja Expeditions** *2625 Garnet Ave, San Diego, CA 92109. (800) 843-6967. Website at www.bajaexpeditions.com.* **Cortez Club** *At La Concha Beach Resort, 3 miles north of town on the road to Pichilingue. 01152 (1) 121-61-20. Website at www.cortezclub.com.* **El Tecolote** *At Playa El Tecolote.* **Mary Aventuras** *Calle Topete between calles 5 de Febrero and Navarro, near Marina de La Paz. (800) 355-7140 (toll-free in U.S.); 01152 (1) 122-70-39 (La Paz office). Website at www.bajakayak.com.*

ONE-STOP WATER SPORTS

Club de Playa El Tecolote is the main purveyor for water-sports equipment rentals and trips at La Paz area beaches. Among other things, this beach club offers wave-runners and kayaks for rent, along with trips to Isla Espíritu Santo, water-skiing and "parasail" rides.

WHALE WATCHING

With a stroke of luck, you may just spot a pod of whales during your boating escapades out of La Paz. Gray whales, sperm whales, humpbacks, orcas and majestic blue whales are all known to the local waters, with your best chance of seeing them between January and April. Even then, however, it's not a sure thing, and thus La Paz is normally not thought of as a major whale-watching destination.

By far your best chance of seeing a whale is heading north to Bahía Magdalena, where California gray whales bear their calves from January to early April. It's a 160-mile drive to this huge Pacific coast bay, which makes for a full-day trip from La Paz. It's worth the effort, though, if you want a close-up look at the mammals and maybe a chance to pat one on the head. Daylong tours cost $100-$130, meals included, departing early in the morning and returning that same evening. Overnight trips are available as well, with lodging at Puerto San Carlos. Some of the companies offering these tours include the following:

Baja Diving & Service *Paseo Obregón between 16 de Septiembre and Callejón La Paz. 01152 (1) 122-18-26 or 122-70-10. Website at www.bajadivingservice.com.* **Baja Quest** *Calle Sonora between calles Topete and Rangel, near Marina de La Paz. 01152 (1) 123-53-20.* **Cortez Club** *At La Concha Beach Resort, 3 miles north of town on the road to Pichilingue. 01152 (1) 121-61-20. Website at www.cortez club.com.* **Viajes Coromuel** *Corner of Paseo Obregón and Calle Rosales, next to Hotel Los Arcos. 01152 (1) 122-80-06.* **Viajes Lybsa** *Corner of Paseo Obregón and Calle Degollado. 01152 (1) 122-60-01 or 122-60-02.*

Nightlife

When it comes to late-night merrymaking, La Paz lives up to its name for the most part. "The Peace" generally prevails along the streets of downtown and the waterfront, although it's not entirely quiet when darkness falls upon the bay. A fair number of clubs and drinking spots draw good-sized weekend crowds, but with a more subdued tone that never approaches the drunken frenzy of Tijuana or Cabo San Lucas. That's right in keeping with a town that tacitly asks outsiders to conform to the local standards of behavior, not the other way around.

Many of La Paz's nightspots gear themselves toward the local crowd, which is not to say that outsiders are unwelcome, just that you may feel out of place if you're the only non-Mexican in the place. For the out-of-town crowd, Paseo Obregón has the most action, with several spots where tourists and locals mix comfortably, especially during the peak tourist season. Luckily as well, most are within walking distance of several major hotels. All that assumes, of course, that you're not content with a stroll down the *malecón* or to linger over a late-night dinner at some bayside bistro. You may well decide that such a subdued approach fits the bill just fine, thank you.

> **CUTTING SLACK FOR SMOKERS**
>
> 
>
> Depending on your point of view, Mexico is behind the times or refreshingly sensible when it comes to smoking in public. Only a few restaurants ban lighting up entirely, while most of the rest have smoking and non-smoking sections.

CARLOS 'N CHARLIE'S

Drinking, dancing and food are all abundant at this Paseo Obregón fixture, the self-billed "Home of the Mother

Mardi Gras, Family Style

"Fun," "festive" and "genteel" are a few words that spring to mind for describing La Paz's version of *Carnaval*, the Spanish word for the Mardi Gras. Paceños and visitors show how to live it up for the pre-Lenten celebration without the bawdy, hell-raising antics of New Orleans, Río and other less restrained spots. Singles, oldsters, small fry and everyone in-between flock to Paseo Obregón as the waterfront thoroughfare closes to through traffic at dusk for six nights leading up to Ash Wednesday.

Margarita." It's a standard setup of the Grupo Anderson's chain—a restaurant/bar that doubles as a dance club when the hour grows late. Sip your drinks and munch your finger food at the sidewalk cantina, then dance all night beneath the stars to the English/Spanish party tunes. *Corner of Paseo Obregón and Calle 16 de Septiembre, across from the tourism office. 01152 (1) 122-92-90. Full bar; full menu till midnight; dancing Tue, Thu-Sat.*

LA CABAÑA

If you like to dance and your tastes run the least bit Latin, then head on over to this venerable club at the Hotel Perla. It's a mainly local crowd, leavened with enough *turistas* to keep things interesting, with a healthy mix of singles and couples, young and old. Check the schedule for the night's theme—disco, salsa, *cumbia,* English-language oldies and more. *01152 (1) 122-07-07. Paseo Obregón between calles Arreola and La Paz. Full bar; live music Wed-Sun.*

LA CONCHA BEACH RESORT

Stop by on a weeknight and the Palapa Bar is a fine place to watch the sun sink across the bay. Weekends are another story, with live music, including folkloric dancers for Friday night's Mexican Fiestas. Next door, the Palmita Sports Bar is a thoroughly gringo experience, with a spacious game room and satellite TV. *3 miles northeast of town on the road to Pichilingue. 01152 (1) 121-61-61. Full bar.*

OKEY LASER CLUB

A perennial favorite with the young single crowd, this boisterous club whoops it up with the best of them along Obregón. It's all about dancing here, with a soundtrack of bilingual party tunes. *No phone. On Paseo Obregón between calles Muelle and Degollado. Full bar.*

PELÍCANOS

This low-key bar is a long-time favorite for gringos and locals alike to toast another day's end as the sun slides beneath the western skyline. The fishing crowd has always gravitated to this spot, nursing beers and spinning yarns of the morning's action off Cerralvo. It's worth a stop just to see the nice display of old black and white photos, including vintage shots of Pancho Villa, Ike, and Clark Gable. *In the Hotel Los Arcos, corner of Paseo Obregón and Calle Rosales. 01152 (1) 122 27-44. Full bar.*

Dining

Eating out in La Paz is a reflection of the town itself—very Baja-like, but with a healthy dose of international influence. The bayside town is at its best when serving up the Baja basics, as in fresh seafood, steaks and the usual assortment of traditional Mexican dishes. Pasta, burgers, deli sandwiches and other foreign favorites get their just dues as well, but so far the town has steered clear of any U.S.-style chain restaurants.

If you've read the chapter from the beginning, you may be thinking that the dining scene is centered along the bayfront, in which case you'd be correct. Stroll the length of Paseo Obregón and you'll never be more than a half-block from one or more eateries, with many more a short ways inland. By no means is the waterfront the only place to look, but if you want to check out a large number of restaurants without driving all over town, let the search begin here.

For the most part, dressing up for dinner in La Paz means a pair of long pants and a shirt with a collar on it. Otherwise it's Baja-casual, as in a pair of shorts, a shirt or blouse and footwear of some kind. That suits the price scale here, which runs about average for Baja but at the low end as Mexican resorts go. Unless you're running up a long bar tab, there are plenty of good restaurants where a twosome can enjoy the day's fresh catch for $20 or less, tax and tip included.

Favorites

BOUGAINVILLEA RESTAURANTE **International**
Aside from the dress code, this place strikes a decidedly upscale note in an otherwise casual town. Presentation, preparation and service are all first-rate at this classy bay-side restaurant at the south end of the *malecón*. What's to like? Elaborate salads, superb wood-baked pizza, surf and turf, ribs, and the inevitable variety of fresh-caught seafood. Dress-wise, you might opt for a collared shirt

over the basic crew neck or tank top. *Along La Paz Bay in Malecón de Vista Coral development. 01152 (1) 122-77-44. Open daily 1 pm-midnight. $5-23.*

THE DOCK CAFÉ **Mexican/American**

La Paz has (so far) staved off the southward advance of U.S.-style franchise eateries, but resident gringos need *somewhere* to go when the urge strikes for a taste of home. Enter The Dock Café, where the menu features fried chicken, cheeseburgers, corn beef hash and *homemade apple pie.* For the Mexican crowd, flautas, enchiladas and chimichangas are there as well. Being on the marina, this place pulls in a steady flow of boaters, especially in the winter months. *At Marina de La Paz, at the end of Calle Legaspy. 01152 (1) 125-66-26. Open daily, 8 am-11 pm. $5-24.*

LA PAZTA ♦♦ **Italian**

Half a block from the waterfront, this cozy cafe lends a continental flare to its subtropical surroundings. Settle in amid the international crowd and savor the mingling aromas of rosemary, garlic and fresh-ground coffee. Service can be a bit leisurely at times, but it's worth the wait once you order from the eclectic lineup of seafood, pasta, meat and fowl entrees. *On Calle Allende, ½ block southeast of Paseo Obregón. 01152 (1) 125-11-95. Open daily 7 am-11 pm. $6.50-10.*

LAS PALMAS RESTAURANT **Mexican/International**

Food and ambiance share top billing at this beachside restaurant amid a sunny, palm-laden resort on the road to Pichilingue. Culinary adventures abound during the week, including Sunday brunch, Thursday night Italian buffets and Saturday night barbecue feasts. Friday nights are always fun with their Mexican Fiesta, replete with live music, folkloric dancing, piñatas and a free splash of tequila with your buffet dinner. *At La Concha Beach Resort, 3 miles northeast of town on the road to Pichilingue. 01152 (1) 121-61-61. Buffet meals $15; a la carte, $12-25.*

LA TERRAZA **Mexican/Seafood**

Downstairs from the famed Hotel Perla, this breezy, open-air restaurant exudes the spirit of La Paz, situated along the heart of the *malecón* and holding equal sway with visitors and the local crowd. There's no better place to watch the world go by, and the food is invariably fresh and well prepared. We especially like the soups, most notably the *caldo tlalpeño,* oozing with garbanzo beans, cilantro and other fresh garden pickings. *On Paseo Obregón, between calles Arreola and La Paz. 01152 (1) 122-07-77. Open daily 7 am-10:30 pm. $4-13.*

Other Choices

BERMEJO **Mexican/Seafood**
$5.25-23.50. *Inside Hotel Los Arcos, corner of Paseo Obregón and Calle Rosales. 01152 (1) 122-27-44 ext 638.*

CARLOS 'N CHARLIE'S **♦ Mexican**
$5-15. *Corner of Paseo Obregón and 16 de Septiembre. 01152 (1) 122-92-90.*

EL TASTE **♦ Mexican/Seafood**
$5-18. *Corner of Paseo Obregón and Calle Juárez. 01152 (1) 122-81-21.*

EL TECOLOTE **Seafood**
$3-10. *On the sand at Playa El Tecolote, 17 miles north of La Paz. No phone.*

RESTAURANTE BISMARK II **Seafood**
$4-20. *Corner of calles Degollado and Altamirano. 01152 (1) 122-48-54.*

VAS **Mexican/Seafood**
$3.50-16. *On the* malecón, *corner of Paseo Obregón and Calle 5 de Mayo. 01152 (1) 122-75-10.*

Lodging

It's a long cry from the sprawling luxury hotels that crowd the beachfronts in Los Cabos, but La Paz is a great place in its own right to put up for the night. In truth, a large part of the town's cachet lies in its very lack of huge resorts that seem overbuilt for their surroundings. Instead, value almost always trumps pretense in La Paz, possibly the most affordable of resort destinations in all of Mexico.

The town is full of fair- to midsize hotels, comfortable but not extravagant, most priced well under $100 per night. Some are only a few years old, like the mid-rise properties that have sprung up along the bayside marinas. Others have long, distinguished histories, such as La Perla, a bayfront landmark along Paseo Obregón since 1940, the same year that Steinbeck sailed into town.

Nearly all visitors here gravitate toward the bay, so it's no surprise that most of the larger, better-equipped hotels are at or very close to the water's edge. Several fine hotels line Obregón in the heart of the tourist zone, but you'll have to cross the avenue to be on the beach itself. If a room right on the shoreline is imperative, be prepared to pay more and stay somewhere besides downtown. Elsewhere, La Paz is full of inexpensive rooms, priced well under $50 a night for those who don't mind walking a few blocks to the bay. Some draw mostly Mexicans, while others draw a healthy mix of younger travelers from points around the world—backpack and outdoor-loving types who want to stretch their budgets.

La Paz is one place, too, where many visitors never see the inside of a hotel room, since the town and environs are a prime destination for the RV crowd. Several campgrounds are scattered about the town, most equipped with hookups, showers, food stores and other perks of the good life. Beyond the town, several campgrounds are little more than a flat spot to park a trailer or RV along some remote but lovely stretch of beachfront.

See *Lodging & Campgrounds*, Chapter 15.

As far as hotels go, those with AAA approval are generally more expensive, while the best bargains are among the non-approved properties.

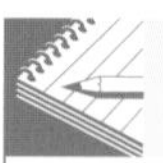

TRAVELOGUE

La Paz to Los Barriles
(65 mi., 105 km.; 1:45 hrs.)

If Cabo San Lucas is your primary destination, then there's a choice of routes driving south from La Paz. Mexico Highway 19 makes for the faster drive as it heads directly south toward the Pacific coast, passing through the seaside town of Todos Santos and saving about an hour's travel time. Highway 1, meanwhile, tacks southeast as it heads across hills and canyons toward another rendezvous with the Gulf of California, passing through several small towns along the way. It returns to the gulf shoreline at Los Barriles, a small but fast-growing tourist enclave and a hub of recreation on the East Cape.

As the outskirts of La Paz fade behind, Highway 1 returns to the open desert as you pass

Highway 1, south of La Paz

through more miles of typical dry land vegetation. Just past the hamlet of San Pedro is the junction with Highway 19. Bearing left keeps you on Highway 1, which proceeds to climb into the rugged foothills of the Sierra de la Laguna. Beyond the village of El Triunfo, the route descends to the bottom of a narrow, steep-sided valley, where you'll pass through the town of San Antonio. Emerging from the valley, the highway winds across another arm of the sierra and follows the course of another canyon to San Bartolo. Leaving the mountains behind, the road reaches the gulf once more at Los Barriles, on the shore of Bahía las Palmas.

00.0 **La Paz, at the intersection of Calzadas Abasolo and 5 de Febrero. To proceed south on Highway 1, take 5 de Febrero southeast for 1.1 mile to Boulevard Forjadores, then bear right.**

Side Routes

02.3 **Junction with the paved road (BCS 286) to San Juan de los Planes (see Side Route to San Juan de los Planes, page 328). A Pemex station is at the corner of this junction.**

16.5 **San Pedro, a small community serving the surrounding farms and ranches.**

19.6 **Junction with Mexico Highway 19 to Todos Santos and Cabo San Lucas (see Travelogue for Mexico Highway 19, *The Cape Region*, Chapter 11, page 332).**

33.0 **El Triunfo, a picturesque mountain village with a cafe and a church. El Triunfo was once a rich gold and silver mining camp, and at one time was the largest settlement in the south of Baja California. The mines closed in 1926, but with the increase in precious metal values, mining has resumed at some locations. Numerous old buildings line the highway, and on a hill just south of the village are the remains of the old smelter. Handwoven baskets are for sale on the north side of the highway.**

37.7 **San Antonio, an attractive farming center located in the bottom of a deep arroyo. San Antonio's history also includes a mining boom. Facilities include groceries, eating**

establishments and gasoline. Past the junction with the village's main street, Highway 1 climbs sharply out of the canyon.

55.0 San Bartolo, a sleepy town strung out along a palm-lined canyon, produces guavas, oranges, avocados and other fruits. Groceries, local fruits and meals are available.

66.2 Junction with the paved road leading into Los Barriles. This road leads 0.3 mile to another junction in the center of this small town. Turning left, the road continues paved for another 0.7 mile, followed by eight miles of dirt road leading north along the scenic coast to the resort community of Punta Pescadero. The road goes on to the village and resort of El Cardonal (see *Lodging & Campgrounds,* Chapter 15), to Boca del Alamo and farther northwest to San Juan de los Planes.

La Paz to Pichilingue and Beaches to the North

(See map page 329.)

(17 mi., 29 km.; 0:40 hr.)

The easy drive to Pichilingue and the beaches to the north makes an enjoyable half-day excursion from La Paz—a full day if you want to recline on the sand, stay for dinner and watch the sun go down over Bahía de La Paz. Also known as Mexico Highway 11, this paved route is a northward continuation of Paseo Alvaro Obregón—La Paz's bay-front thoroughfare. The road hugs the shore of Bahía de La Paz and provides some excellent views of cactus-covered hills, mangrove thickets and the clear blue waters of the bay. Playa El Coromuel, an attractive beach that is popular with locals, is 2.6 miles from Calle 5 de Mayo, the last major street of the city. About a mile farther north are La Concha Beach Resort and El Caimancito, which has a public beach, a restaurant and the state governor's mansion.

For schedules and more information on ferry service to Mazatlán and Topolobampo, see the Transportation section in the *Appendix*, Chapter 16.

Nine miles north of town the road reaches Pichilingue, La Paz's deepwater port and home to the terminal used by the ferries traveling between La Paz and the mainland ports of Mazatlán and Topolobampo. In addition, Pichilingue is also home to a commercial fishing fleet, warehouses, a hotel and several restaurants. Just after the ferry terminal is Playa Pichilingue, another popular beach. A short distance beyond, the road cuts inland, passing a paved spur that runs northwest to the shore of Puerto Balandra, a lovely inlet that makes a good spot for a picnic. A trail here leads up a hill to an excellent viewpoint above the inlet. Past Puerto Balandra, the road runs another mile north to Playa El Tecolote, where the pavement ends.

A ferryboat at La Paz's deepwater port, Pichilingue

A sandy, broad strand with gentle waves, thatched-roof restaurants and *palapas* for rent, Playa El Tecolote is one of La Paz's most popular seaside retreats for locals and visitors alike. The view north looks across Canal de San Lorenzo to Isla Espíritu Santo, the region's top destination for divers, kayakers and wildlife observers. From here a good dirt road lined with scenic desert plants runs eastward along the shore for another three miles to a gravel mine and Playa Cachimba, a popular surf-fishing spot.

La Paz to San Juán de los Planes

(See map page 329.)

(29 mi., 45 km; 1 hr.)

An excellent day-long excursion from La Paz, the side trip to Los Planes provides the chance to visit a fast-growing agricultural region and to explore some of the beautiful, isolated beaches southeast of the city. Leaving Highway 1 at a well-marked junction on the southern outskirts of La Paz, a paved road signed "BCS 286" runs between rolling hills for nine miles before climbing onto the northern shoulder of the Sierra de la Laguna. At

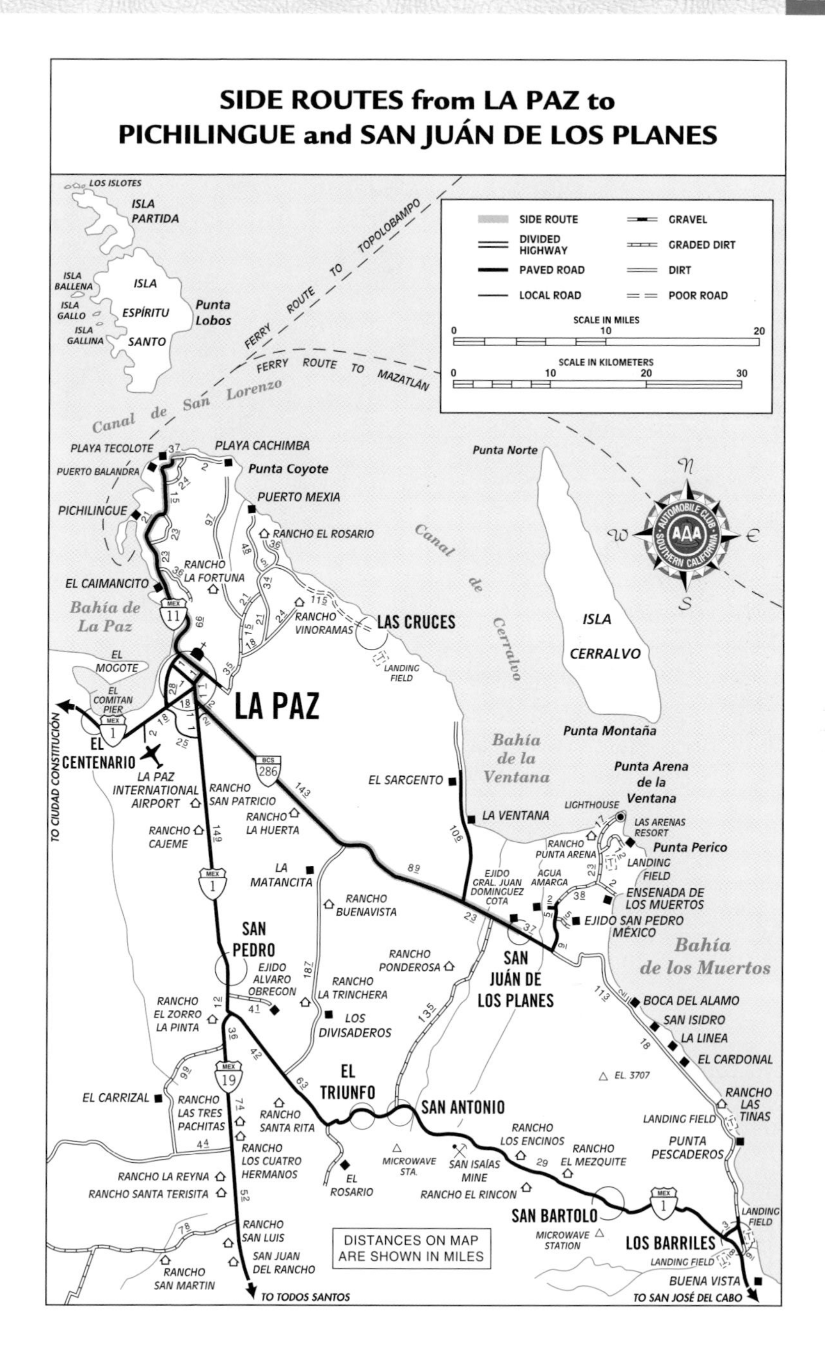

mileage 11.9 you'll reach Rancho La Huerta, a long-established cattle ranch with a brick chapel, small cemetery and cafe.

Beyond La Huerta the road passes turnoffs to several more ranches as it winds through countryside covered with cardón, cholla, pitahaya, copalquin (a small deciduous tree) and heavy underbrush. At mileage 15.9 the road

Fishing boat and pelicans, Ensenada de los Muertos

crests, providing a fine view ahead to the cultivated fields of Los Planes, the blue expanse of Bahía de la Ventana, and barren, mountainous Isla Cerralvo. From the summit the road makes a long, steady descent onto a level coastal plain, where it reaches a junction at mileage 23.7. To the left, a good paved road leads seven miles to El Sargento and La Ventana, fishing and ranching villages on the western shore of lovely Bahía de la Ventana. Continue straight ahead for Los Planes. At mileage 25.8 is an intersection with a new road on the right that leads 13.5 miles to the village of San Antonio on Highway 1.

From here the route continues 3.2 miles farther to San Juán de Los Planes (or Los Planes, in local parlance), the center of a developing farming region. An underground aquifer here provides water for cotton, corn, chiles, tomatoes, beans and other crops. Los Planes is a friendly town of about 1000 with a cafe, markets, phone service and a health center.

LIVESTOCK ALERT!

San Juán de los Planes makes an excellent side trip, but beware of wandering livestock. A hazard throughout Baja, cattle, burros and other farm animals are especially common on the pavement here. Use extra caution along these roads, on which we strongly advise against driving at night.

The pavement continues past the center of town for a few miles en route to Ensenada de los Muertos (Deadman Bay), 9.5 miles to the northeast. This beautiful, curving bay has a small fish camp, and is a major staging point for sport fishermen out of La Paz. Primitive but scenic campsites are abundant here, and the swimming and fishing from shore are excellent. The bay is also a popular anchorage for pleasure craft from North American ports.

Two miles shy of Ensenada de los Muertos is a signed dirt road that leads north toward Punta Arena de la Ventana, directly opposite Isla Cerralvo on the eastern shore of Bahía de la Ventana. This road leads past a cattle ranch, an airstrip and a group of salt-evaporating ponds to reach the isolated Las Arenas Resort along the northeast shore of the bay. North of the hotel is a lighthouse. This bay is another popular starting point for sport anglers.

Chapter 11

The Cape Region

Welcome to the Mexico of a thousand travel brochures, glossy posters and gringo daydreams—a land of tropical beaches, fish tacos, towering cacti, roving mariachis, and a climate that gives proper meaning to the phrase "endless summer." All those icons and many more exist in Baja's Cape Region—from the go-go glitz of Cabo San Lucas to the smallest towns with their tranquil charm of Old Mexico. All that's left is to find the boundaries of this region, and for that there's no one answer.

Ask a geographer and you'll be told the Cape Region extends clear to La Paz, a full 140 miles up Highway 1 from Cabo San Lucas. Ask a travel agent and you'll surely hear about Los Cabos—the sliver of coastline from San José del Cabo to Cabo San Lucas with the so-called "Corridor" of developments in between. Either answer has its merits, but for

Land's End, Cabo San Lucas

highway-bound nomads, neither one quite fills the bill. With fully half the population of Baja California Sur, La Paz can be deemed a region in its own right, and at the same time, it's hard to focus just on the narrow strip of Los Cabos.

From our standpoint, the boundary lines fall somewhere in the middle, reaching north along both the Pacific and Gulf of California coasts, but giving a wide berth to greater La Paz. On the Gulf side, the Cape Region extends past the white beaches and azure waters of the East Cape to the palm-cloaked village of Los Barriles, where Highway 1 emerges from the mountains. On the Pacific side it runs north past more than 40 miles of untamed coastline to reach Todos Santos, a one-time sugar-mill town turned artists colony, smack dab on the Tropic of Cancer.

Between the coastlines rise the cragged peaks of the Sierra de la Laguna, southernmost in the 1000-mile long chain of peninsular ranges that tumble seaward at the famed arch rock of Land's End. Reaching heights of more than 7000 feet, these are the tallest mountains in Baja California Sur and receive the most rain of any spot in Baja—up to 35 inches per year.

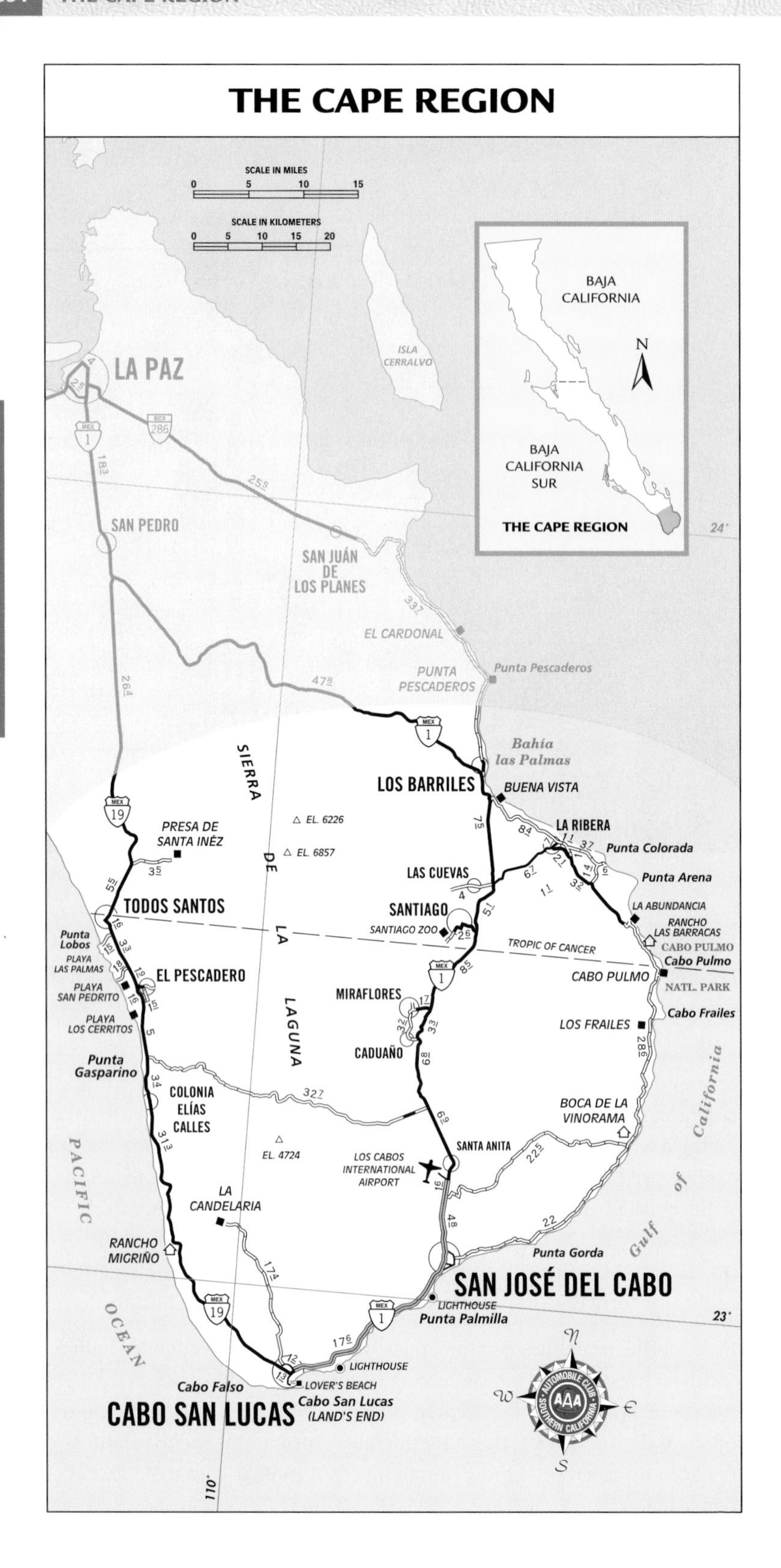
THE CAPE REGION
SCALE IN MILES
0 5 10 15
SCALE IN KILOMETERS
0 5 10 15 20
BAJA CALIFORNIA
N
BAJA CALIFORNIA SUR
THE CAPE REGION
24°
LA PAZ
ISLA CERRALVO
SAN PEDRO
SAN JUÁN DE LOS PLANES
EL CARDONAL
PUNTA PESCADEROS
Punta Pescaderos
Bahía las Palmas
SIERRA DE LA LAGUNA
LOS BARRILES
BUENA VISTA
LA RIBERA
Punta Colorada
Punta Arena
PRESA DE SANTA INÉZ
EL. 6226
EL. 6857
LAS CUEVAS
TODOS SANTOS
SANTIAGO
SANTIAGO ZOO
LA ABUNDANCIA
RANCHO LAS BARRACAS
CABO PULMO
Cabo Pulmo
NATL. PARK
TROPIC OF CANCER
Punta Lobos
PLAYA LAS PALMAS
PLAYA SAN PEDRITO
PLAYA LOS CERRITOS
EL PESCADERO
MIRAFLORES
CADUAÑO
LOS FRAILES
Cabo Frailes
Punta Gasparino
COLONIA ELÍAS CALLES
BOCA DE LA VINORAMA
Gulf of California
PACIFIC OCEAN
EL. 4724
SANTA ANITA
LOS CABOS INTERNATIONAL AIRPORT
LA CANDELARIA
RANCHO MIGRIÑO
Punta Gorda
SAN JOSÉ DEL CABO
LIGHTHOUSE
Punta Palmilla
23°
LIGHTHOUSE
LOVER'S BEACH
Cabo Falso
CABO SAN LUCAS
Cabo San Lucas (LAND'S END)
AUTOMOBILE CLUB SOUTHERN CALIFORNIA
AAA
N
W
E
S
110°

Without exception, the major towns are along the seashore and each has a distinct personality, though all share a strong degree of outside (read North American) influence. While generalities can be a tricky thing, a few will help you get a better handle on both these towns and the region as a whole. Think of Cabo San Lucas as a rowdy nightclub, San José del Cabo as a trendy boutique, and the Corridor (with four 18-hole golf courses) as a huge fairway. Farther north, Todos Santos is a sawdust art gallery, while Los Barriles lies at the hub of a huge aquatic park.

Sprinkled here and there are a handful of lesser-known burgs with their own claims to fame—Miraflores and its leatherwork shops, Santiago with the only zoo in Baja Sur, and La Ribera as the gateway to the renowned diving of Cabo Pulmo. These and other towns with names like Las Cuevas, El Pescadero, Santa Anita, etc., have retained their down-home feel and sense of laid-back timelessness—immune so far to the forces that have transformed so much of Baja's southernmost region.

Experience ...

- Losing yourself while diving amid a huge school of sergeant majors and other tropical fish, within a stone's throw of the sand at Lover's Beach.
- Cascades of red and purple bougainvillea sagging untrimmed across a pastel storefront in San José del Cabo.
- A kaleidoscope of strange neon and pastel colors spread beneath your eyes as you snorkel through an undersea world of coral off Cabo Pulmo.
- Melodic echoes reverberating up and down the Cabo San Lucas' Marina District as a bevy of clubs rattle and hum toward dawn's early light.
- Walking through the crumbled remains of an abandoned sugar mill in Todos Santos, which somehow seems to fit right in with the surrounding palm oasis.

Los Barriles

Looking north along the coast toward Los Barriles

Spread along the shore of Bahía las Palmas (Palms Bay) at the north edge of a coastal plain, Los Barriles is yet another Baja Sur town with a serene atmosphere and resplendent setting. Small town though it is, it reflects the changing face of the Cape Region, as outside forces make their presence felt on the landscape and the lives of those who live there.

Given its placement on Highway 1 and its natural attributes, it's no wonder that the outside world has discovered Los Barriles. Hotels, RV parks and restaurants aimed at gringo taste buds line the palm-shrouded streets of this town, which seems to be in transition between its traditional fishing village roots and the promise of a more prosperous future. Currents of change are visible in other ways too, with English signage everywhere, a modern minimall on the edge of town, and the spread of California-style beachfront homes.

AIRPORT AND TAXI TIPS

Unless La Paz figures prominently in your vacation plans, Los Cabos International Airport is your best bet for flying to Los Barriles. Los Cabos is about 44 miles south of town, about 25 miles closer than La Paz. Arranging transport between the airport and town is best done through one of the local hotels.

If tourism is the town's main business, then fishing and windsurfing are its twin pillars, and have made Los Barriles a known name in circles far beyond Baja Sur. From late November to early March, northeasterly winds blow with force almost every day, making this Baja's top windsurfing locale. During the peak months of December and

January, winds of 15 mph or more blow almost daily, drawing adherents from around the world.

Sportfishing ebbs during those windblown months, but from May through October the offshore waters come alive as big game species migrate up and down the gulf. Fishing trips can be arranged through the local hotels, with craft ranging from *pangas* to full-fledged cruisers. While the fishing is usually good all summer, the stream of visitors slows to a crawl during August and September, when the heat and humidity are their worst, and tropical storms are possible. Some hotels and restaurants close their doors during much of this period.

All year long, however, Highway 1 travelers find Los Barriles to be a reliable stopover for more mundane services, including a Pemex station, auto parts stores, markets and a clinic. There's also an airstrip for fly-in visitors.

Outdoor Fun

DIVING

Los Barriles itself is not thought of as a first-class diving destination, but within a few miles north or south are several outstanding dive spots for which Baja's East Cape is so well known. Heading north along the coast, Punta Pescadero and El Cardonal each have reefs with excellent diving, the latter having a small growth of coral. A dirt road leads to either venue, but *pangas* are the preferred way to access either spot. Still farther north, the southern end of Isla Cerralvo sees its share of divers boating up from Los Barriles. Heading south, there's Cabo Pulmo, which affords some of the best diving in the entire Cape Region and is the most popular destination for outings out of Los Barriles. Boating trips to Cabo Pulmo run about $60 for snorkeling and $110 for scuba diving. If you'd prefer to stay put, the shoreline has a few small reefs that can be reached directly from the beach.

Most hotels have at least snorkeling gear for rent along with information on nearby diving destinations. Snorkeling gear typically rents for $10 a day, while scuba gear runs $20 or more, varying widely according to your equipment needs. Boating tours and complete equipment rentals are available through Vista Sea Sport, a full-service dive shop on the beach at Buena Vista.

Vista Sea Sport *South of Los Barriles, off Hwy 1 near Km 107. 01152 (1) 141-00-31.*

FISHING

Virtually all of the major Baja game fish ply the waters off Los Barriles at some point during the year and have

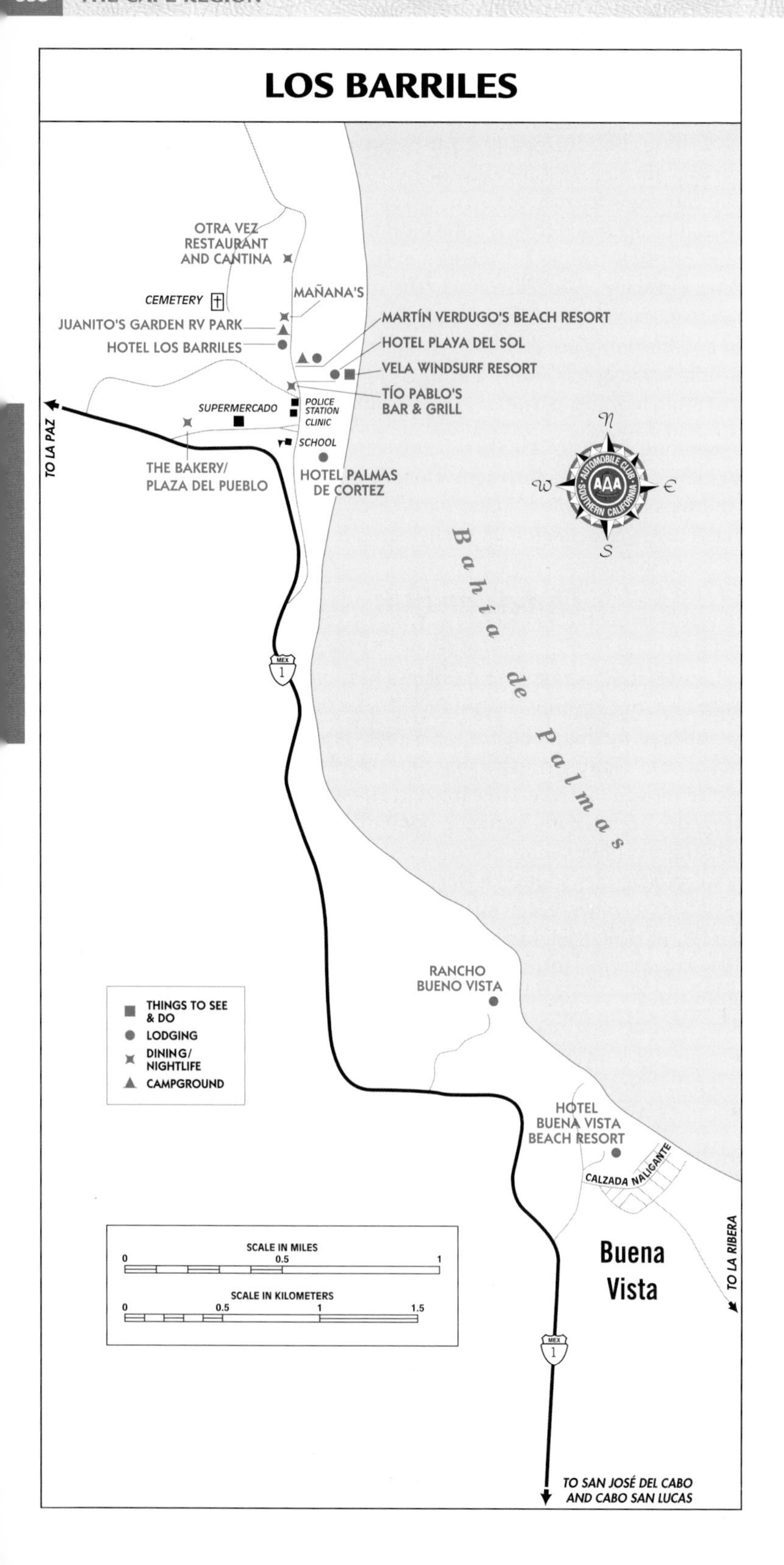
LOS BARRILES
OTRA VEZ RESTAURANT AND CANTINA
CEMETERY
MAÑANA'S
JUANITO'S GARDEN RV PARK
HOTEL LOS BARRILES
MARTÍN VERDUGO'S BEACH RESORT
HOTEL PLAYA DEL SOL
VELA WINDSURF RESORT
TÍO PABLO'S BAR & GRILL
SUPERMERCADO
POLICE STATION
CLINIC
SCHOOL
THE BAKERY/ PLAZA DEL PUEBLO
HOTEL PALMAS DE CORTEZ
TO LA PAZ
Bahía de Palmas
AUTOMOBILE CLUB SOUTHERN CALIFORNIA
AAA
N
S
E
W
MEX 1
RANCHO BUENO VISTA
HOTEL BUENA VISTA BEACH RESORT
CALZADA NALIGANTE
Buena Vista
TO LA RIBERA
TO SAN JOSÉ DEL CABO AND CABO SAN LUCAS
THINGS TO SEE & DO
LODGING
DINING/ NIGHTLIFE
CAMPGROUND
SCALE IN MILES
0
0.5
1
SCALE IN KILOMETERS
0
0.5
1
1.5

helped earn the town a loyal following of anglers. Marlin and sailfish lead the cast of heavyweights and are the hot ticket when they reach their peak run from late spring through the summer. Tuna, wahoo, dorado and roosterfish lead the middleweight lineup, with the best fishing during the summer. During the slower winter months, yellowtail provide the most action.

Smoking and vacuum-packing services for your fish are available in Los Barriles.

While package trips through local hotels are very popular, it's also possible to rent boats by the day or half-day. Day-long *panga* outings start around $130 per vessel, while a full day on board a fully equipped 30-foot cruiser can cost $300 or more per boat. Reservations are often necessary from late spring through midsummer.

Baja Fishing and Resorts *For information and reservations call (800) 368-4334.* **Pacific West Sportfishing** *For information and reservations call (800) 700-7022 or (805) 493-5444.*

WINDSURFING

Steady northeasterly breezes are an almost daily occurrence along the southern Sea of Cortez between November and March, and in few places are they stronger or more reliable than the waters off Los Barriles. As a result, the town has earned international acclaim for winter windsurfing, as aficionados flock here from around the world.

Catching an early-season northeast breeze off Los Barriles

Given the strong winds that regularly blow here, these waters are best left to experts. The season's highlight comes in early January with the Vela Neil Pryde Baja Championships, a week of sailboard racing sponsored in part by the local Vela Windsurf Resort. The prime windsurfing outfitter for the entire East Cape, Vela offers all-inclusive vacations, complete with modern equipment, lodging, food, and instruction for all skill levels except beginner.

Vela Windsurf Resort *On the beach in front of the Hotel Playa del Sol. For information and reservations call (800) 223-5433.*

Dining

Truth be told, the most popular meal in Los Barriles might be the box lunch—standard fare for anglers on their all-day fishing trips. Other than that, seafood is the inevitable king of cuisine in Los Barriles, which means the menu will vary during the year according to what's biting that week. If you've been fishing yourself, nearly all of the hotel restaurants will prepare your fresh catch to your liking, with your choice of side dishes. Otherwise, Los Barriles has plenty of eateries serving good Mexican food, and a few gringo-owned spots serving home-style cooking for their visitors from *El Norte.*

Favorites

OTRA VEZ RESTAURANT AND CANTINA — **Varied Menu**

Steak and seafood beneath a *palapa* roof is not exactly a unique concept for Baja, but it *is* when you throw in Thai food, home-grown herbs, family-made dressings, and vegetables organically grown in nearby Santiago. So it goes at this American-owned restaurant in the heart of town. Anglers flock this way for the Fishermen's Special—their fresh-caught fish prepared to order with all the fixings for $6. Stop by on Thursday evenings during the winter, when musically inclined gringos get down with their weekly jam sessions. *In the center of town, ¼ mile north of Hotel Los Barriles. 01152 (1) 141-02-49. Open Wed-Sun 8 am-10 pm, closed Tue; also closed Aug 15-Sep 30. $6-13.*

Others

THE BAKERY — **Baked Goods/American**

$2-6.50 (Breakfast and lunch only). *In the strip mall (Plaza del Pueblo) at the entrance to town. No phone.*

MAÑANA'S — **Mexican/American**

$6.50-14. *Near center of town, between Tío Pablo's and Otra Vez. 01152 (1) 141-03-44.*

TÍO PABLO'S BAR & GRILL — **♦ American**

$4-14. *South part of town, near the entrance road from Hwy 1. 01152 (1) 142-12-14.*

Lodging

For AAA-approved hotels, see *Lodging & Campgrounds,* Chapter 15.

Water sports center that it is, Los Barriles has no shortage of lodging oriented toward the outdoor enthusiast. Several hotels specialize in package vacations for windsurfing, fishing or both, and several also rent kayaks, mountain bikes and other equipment. Diving, hunting and ATV trips can also be arranged. While Los Barriles has little in terms of AAA-approved accommodations, there are several hotels and resorts to choose from both here and in the nearby village of Buena Vista. As usual, the best lodging bargains are at the local campgrounds, where rates run less than $15 a night. Nightly room rates start around $45 and climb to more than $200. Package deals can vary widely in cost.

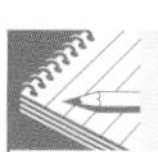

TRAVELOGUE

Los Barriles to San José del Cabo

(50 mi., 81 km.; 1:15 hrs.)

Highway 1's encounter with the gulf proves very brief as you depart Los Barriles and cross another desert plain toward the growing resort region of Los Cabos. Even without the coastline, this is still a scenic journey as you pass beneath the eastern face of the Sierra de la Laguna.

Leatherworker in Miraflores

Leaving Los Barriles, the road skirts the gulf shoreline for a few miles before striking across the long, cactus-covered plain. En route you'll pass the turnoff to the East Cape road, along with roads leading to little towns such as Santiago, Miraflores and Caduaño. Just south of Santiago the road officially enters the Tropics, passing a large spherical monument that marks the Tropic of Cancer.

The first hint of what lies ahead comes just past the village of Santa Anita, at the turnoff to the Los Cabos Airport. Suddenly the highway widens to four lanes, accompanied by a gauntlet of English-language billboards touting hotels, restaurants, timeshares, nightclubs and other tourist-geared ventures. Before long, auto shops, mini-malls, condo complexes and other buildings spring up roadside as you reach the northern fringe of San José del Cabo.

0.0 **Junction with the paved road leading into Los Barriles.**

2.6 **Junction with the entrance road of the Hotel Rancho Buena Vista. Across the road is a ¾-mile road leading to a lookout with outstanding views up and down the coastline along the East Cape.**

3.3 **Junction with a dirt road to the Hotel Buena Vista Beach Resort.**

Side Routes

10.7 Junction with a paved road to La Ribera, then graded roads to Punta Colorada, Cabo Pulmo and Los Frailes (see Side Route to Cabo Pulmo, page 395). To the right is Las Cuevas, a quiet farming village with no tourist facilities.

15.8 Junction with the paved road to Santiago. This attractive agricultural community of about 4000 people sits on a pair of hills separated by a shallow, palm-forested canyon. On the northern hill, 1.6 miles from Highway 1, is the town plaza, along with a Pemex station, an inn with a restaurant, and several cafes and stores. Just beyond the southern hill is the Santiago Zoo, the only one in Baja California Sur.

17.8 The Tropic of Cancer, marked by a spherical concrete monument representing the 23.27 North Latitude parallel.

24.3 A Pemex station at the junction with the 1.7-mile paved road to Miraflores, a farming town known for its vegetables and cheeses. By the end of the paved road at the town entrance is a leather shop that does retail sales. Facilities in Miraflores include stores and cafes.

27.6 Junction with the graded dirt road to Caduaño, another small farming community. The town center is about a mile from the main highway.

34.6 Junction with a winding scenic road signed "Los Naranjos," which goes across the tree-covered landscape of the Sierra de la Laguna to El Pescadero and Todos Santos on Mexico Highway 19. Sturdy, high-clearance vehicles are necessary.

39.9 Santa Anita, a sleepy little town with a bus depot, along with several cafes and small stores.

41.5 Junction with the 0.9-mile paved road to Los Cabos International Airport (see Transportation in the *Appendix,* Chapter 16).

48.1 Junction with Calle Zaragoza, which leads to the center of San José del Cabo.

San José del Cabo

Los Cabos Municipal Hall

Highway 1 rejoins the coastline for the final time on its long trek south at San José del Cabo, and a splendid encounter it is when desert foothills tumble toward the water's edge alongside a sprawling, lush lagoon. Orchards, palm groves and arid scrubland share a narrow coastal shelf with this scenic town, centered on a quaint downtown square and lovely twin-towered church.

That San José del Cabo rose to resort status is no great wonder. Just don't confuse it with its brassy neighbor down the road in Cabo San Lucas. Whereas Cabo San Lucas is modern, loud and raucous (and proudly so), San José del Cabo imparts a tone of gentrified elegance that all but begs you to unwind. Still, this town defies such descriptions as "staid" or "sleepy," but might best be captured in the phrase "something old, something new."

Something old lingers in the narrow streets and alleyways of downtown, with their pastel storefronts, arched building ways, *palapa*-roofed restaurants and shaded main plaza. With its tony restaurants, highbrow gift shops and lovely mission church, this is the part of town best-known to tourists, who seem to outnumber the locals on the sidewalks most of the time. Calle Zaragoza and Boulevard Mijares are the main thoroughfares of this aged quarter, where many structures date to the 1800s.

Beyond its downtown core, San José del Cabo presents a decidedly modern tone as time-shares, condos and mini shopping malls spread across the desert and coastal hills. On the shoreline south of town a chain of resort hotels has sprung up between the beachfront and a wide boulevard with a distinct California feel to it. Those upscale hotels are the most visible products of the tourist zone funded in part by Fonatur, Mexico's tourist development agency.

BOOKWORM ALERT!

Libros Books, located at Mijares 41, has one of the best selections of English magazines and paperbacks in southern Baja. You can't miss it, with the big "USA Today" sign out in front.

Such modern trappings are a far cry from 1730, when hordes of flies and other pests forced Jesuit priests to move their newest mission site from the coastline to a hilltop location six miles inland. Misión San José del Cabo had a short and tumultuous history, rocked by rebellion in 1734 and abandoned in 1767 after diseases had killed off most of the native population. The settlement remained as a military outpost, however, and took further root during the 1800s. Ranching and farming fueled the village's growth through most of the 20th century, as cane fields, orchards and grazing cattle became fixtures in the region. By the 1970s, the village had grown into a full-fledged town as the Transpeninsular Highway and the Los Cabos International Airport opened, and Fonatur targeted the locale as a future resort destination.

San José del Cabo's growth continued with the dawn of a new century, as its modern face looms ever larger in size and interest to outsiders. The town has spread northward toward the airport, seven miles distant, and westward down the Highway 1 corridor, where fairways, condos and world-class resorts are snapping up the best remaining sea-view plots. Still more growth looms in the years ahead if plans proceed to pave the East Cape road, which runs 60 miles up the gulf shoreline toward the village of La Ribera.

Palms at Estero San José

Such developments will clear the way for more people to enjoy the quaint spirit of San José del Cabo and the splendors of Baja's Cape Region. How well the town manages that growth without destroying the virtues that created it will be the supreme challenge as the 21st century unfolds.

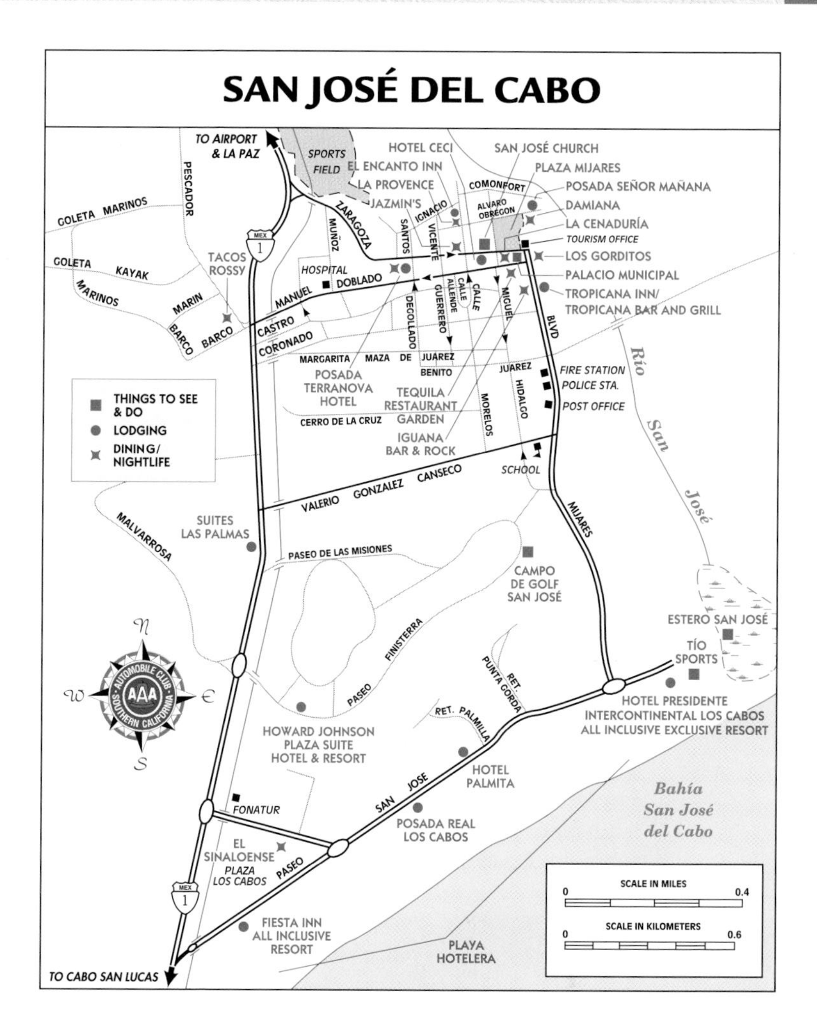

Getting Around

Simply put, if you're perusing the downtown, you need to get out of your car and let your feet do the work. The streets are narrow, parking is tight and traffic laws are strictly enforced. And besides, it's a fairly compact area in which it's easy to miss the details if you're busy angling for a parking place.

It's only a mile from the Fonatur zone to the heart of downtown, but if you're going much farther, you will probably need some sort of wheels. If you don't rent a car, rest assured that taxis abound, although the rates do run on the steep side.

TWO-TIMING TAXI FARES

Down in Los Cabos the cabbies have two sets of rates—one for the locals and another for tourists, the latter being about 20 percent higher. How do they know who's who? Oh, they have their ways ....

From the Fonatur zone to the center of town, the posted rate is about $3.50 per carload. To the airport it's about $14, while a jaunt to downtown Cabo San Lucas (20 miles away) runs a bit less than $30. Whether you rent a car or hire a cab is something your own needs will dictate—assuming, of course, that you didn't drive here yourself down Highway 1.

Things To See & Do

Sans the wacky nightlife, massive yacht basin and fancy shopping plazas of Cabo San Lucas, San José del Cabo comes off as one low-key town. But with its splendid surroundings, recreational opportunities and lovely, gentrified downtown, this end of the Corridor packs considerable cachet.

San José's attractions center around two main venues—the downtown and the nearby seashore. Downtown is the more inclusive of the two—a place where tourists and locals alike come to mingle, shop or just watch the world go by. From the corner of Mijares and Zaragoza, walk just a couple of blocks and you'll catch the essence of the old San José del Cabo. The town hall, mission church and main plaza all lie within a few steps of each other, as does a myriad of galleries and gift shops that beg closer inspection. If you're a seasoned Baja shopper, you'll probably note that local wares rank a notch or two higher in terms of taste and workmanship.

San José's beaches are an outdoor mecca.

Down at seaside, people tend to head their own way for their recreation of choice, but one place you need to see is Estero de San José. The magnificent, palm-shrouded lagoon is almost never crowded and is the perfect setting for an evening stroll, or perhaps a kayaking tour across its placid waters.

Just east of here is La Playita, a broad, soft-sand beach with good summer surf and panoramic vistas both east and west along the coastline. This beach is home to the local *panga* fleet, which means you'll be headed this way for deep-sea fishing, launching during lulls in the surf. Beyond the *estero* to the west there's Playa Hotelera, so named for its location in front of the Fonatur hotels. With a rather steep drop-off, it's not the greatest place for swimming or surfing, but it's just fine for sunning or a seaside walk, and thus gets its share of use from hotel guests. Farther west there's Playa Costa Azul ("Blue Coast Beach"), a lovely, popular strand that's home to restaurants, shops and Zippers—a sizzling reef break that rates with the top surfing spots in southern Baja.

Costa Azul marks the eastern end of the fabled Corridor, where an abundance of opportunities await outdoor enthusiasts. Swimming, beachcombing and diving are superb at different venues along these 20 miles of shoreline, with more than a dozen named beaches and coves. Of course, for many folks the Corridor is all about golf, with six courses spread along this stretch, including four within a 10-minute drive of San José. Two more are on the way, which will further cement this region's reputation as the top golfing destination in Mexico. Still more pursuits include horseback riding (Playa Costa Brava is a popular site), hiking, and ATV-riding through the arid foothills above the Corridor coastline.

In many ways the Corridor is a tamer version of the East Cape road, a 60-mile, dirt and washboard route that hugs the shoreline northeast of San José. Diving, fishing and camping are major draws for those who make this trek, many miles from the nearest fairway or luxury hotel. The focal point, if there is one, would be Cabo Pulmo, an outstanding destination for undersea explorers, with the only substantial coral reef on the west coast of North America.

Top Attractions

ESTERO SAN JOSÉ

One of the Cape Region's most inviting destinations is only a few blocks from the center of San José del Cabo, and literally next door to the luxury hotels of the Fonatur zone. As such, this idyllic 125-acre estuary is also the region's most accessible outdoor attraction. Even so, it feels removed from the town or tourist scene, due to the immense thicket of palms and other plant life. A footpath winds through the palms between the Hotel Presidente Intercontinental and Boulevard Mijares near the post office, just south of downtown. *Main entrance next to Hotel Presidente Intercontinental, east end of Paseo San José.*

PALACIO MUNICIPAL

Built in 1927, this traditional structure with a prominent clock tower is a more modern reflection of the town's colonial roots. The offices face an inner patio typical of

Mexican municipal halls. *On Blvd Mijares, 1 block south of Plaza Mijares.*

PLAZA MIJARES

The epicenter of San José's social and business scene, this lovely cobbled plaza is a happening place around the clock. A handsome gazebo, shade trees and benches attract tourists and locals of all ages, from strolling young couples and preschool-aged tykes on up to seniors watching the town go by. The local tourism office is located here, while the town's cultural center is located at the north edge of the plaza. *Corner of Blvd Mijares and Calle Zaragoza.*

SAN JOSÉ CHURCH

Built in 1940, this twin-towered church is the town's best-known landmark, built at the site of the original Misión San José del Cabo in 1730. Above the front entrance is a tile mosaic that depicts the slaying of the parish priest during the 1734 Indian rebellion. *On Calle Zaragoza along west side of Plaza Mijares.*

Shopping along Boulevard Mijares

SHOPPING

As Baja towns go, this one has nowhere near the most shopping, but what San José del Cabo lacks in sheer volume, it makes up for in style and quality. The tasteful boutiques and galleries of Zaragoza and Mijares are a cut above those of other tourist strips. Fine arts, hand-made crafts, silver, gold and chic fashions are all in abundant supply. There's something for everyone, though, including the tacky and mundane, and several stalls on Mijares have the age-old favorites. In the end, however, you may spend a bit more here, but you probably won't go home with some slipshod piece of pottery or overgrown sombrero destined to gather dust on some forsaken closet shelf.

Outdoor Fun

ATV TOURS

For more ATV tour companies, see listings under Cabo San Lucas.

The lovely beaches, desert landscape and rugged hills surrounding San José del Cabo cry out for exploration, and an ATV is a good way to see them in a limited amount of time. First time or not to the Cape, you may find a guided tour to be an excellent and cost-effective way to explore the grandeur beyond the town limits.

Tour options are as varied as the surrounding territory, whether a three-hour trip to nearby Punta Gorda, a half-day jaunt through the canyon lands above the Corridor, or a full-day trek to Cabo Pulmo, including a snorkeling plunge in the Sea of Cortez. If your destination is along the coast, you'll probably follow the shoreline on your way there, and take an inland route through the desert on the way back.

Tours can run anywhere from 90 minutes to all day, priced from less than $30 to around $130. There is no minimum number of persons required for most outings. Should you prefer to explore on your own or just want a means of getting about, ATV rentals run $20 per hour and $80 per day.

Desert Park *At the Meliá Cabo Real Beach & Golf Resort, 7.5 miles southwest of town. 01152 (1) 144-00-00 ext 3500 or (1) 144-01-27.* **Tío Sports** *Next to Estero San José in front of the Hotel Presidente Intercontinental. 01152 (1) 142-45-99.*

BEACHES

La Playita Wider and more gently sloped than Playa Hotelera, this strand is a popular surfing spot and serves as home base for the town's fishing *panga* fleet. It's a good place for wading into the surf, as long as you avoid the surfers or fishing boats. Easiest access is off the road heading up the East Cape. *½ mile east of town in front of Estero San José.*

Pangas ***on the sand, La Playita***

Playa Hotelera Lovely and seldom crowded, this beach in front of the Fonatur hotels is a fine venue for sunning or strolling, but not for swimming, due to its steep incline and pounding shore break. *South of downtown in front of the Fonatur hotels.*

DIVING

The waters directly off San José del Cabo don't offer much for divers, but the town is centrally located for outings up the East Cape to Cabo Pulmo or down the Corridor to Bahía Chileno and Bahía Santa María. You can rent snorkeling gear in town before setting out to explore the nearby undersea wonders.

Bahía Chileno and Bahía Santa María are each within a 20-minute drive of town, with signs pointing their way off of Highway 1. Cabo Pulmo is most easily reached by driving north up Highway 1 to the La Ribera turnoff and then heading southeast along the coast. It's about 60 miles from town by this route, all but the last six miles on paved roads. (See Side Route to Cabo Pulmo.) Scuba and snorkeling gear are available for rent at Cabo Pulmo, which has three operating dive shops. Guided tours can be arranged both at Cabo Pulmo and at Tío Sports in San José del Cabo, with prices ranging from around $40 to more than $100 depending on duration and venue. Snorkeling gear in town rents for around $12 a day.

Costa Azul Surf Shop *On the Corridor just west of town on inland side of Hwy 1. 01152 (1) 147-0071.* **Tío Sports** *Next to Estero San José in front of the Hotel Presidente Intercontinental. 01152 (1) 142-45-99.*

FISHING

If you have visions of hooking a marlin, sailfish or other hulking game fish from the deck of a fully equipped cruiser, then head on down to Cabo San Lucas, which rightly claims to be billfish capital of the world. Stay in San José and you'll have a different experience, in which you'll launch through the waves in one of the venerable skiffs known as *pangas.*

Without a marina, San José relies on its *panga* fleet, based at La Playita, the beach just east of town. Scores of the small craft head seaward from here, bound primarily for the Gorda Banks, a pair of submerged shoals about 10 miles off the coast. (Your own skipper may head elsewhere, depending where the action is.) While you just might catch a trophy-sized marlin, more likely you'll bring back a tuna, dorado, roosterfish, or other mid-sized specimen.

Panga trips from La Playita are typically priced for southern Baja, running about $150 for six hours on board a 22-foot skiff or $180 on one of the slightly larger, better equipped *super pangas.* Either boat can handle up to three anglers, although two are a better fit. Add a few dollars more for box lunch, bait and a tip for good service. Nearly all of the local hotels or travel agencies can arrange a trip, but you can save a few dollars by going to the beach and dealing directly with the boat owner.

GOLF

Palm Springs meets Carmel along the southern shore of the Cape Region, where half a dozen courses grace the desert shoreline between San José del Cabo and Cabo San Lucas. Either town could claim bragging rights as the golfing capital of Baja California, although four of the six dot the Corridor between the two towns. San José has just a single course itself, but three more lie within eight miles, toward this end of the Corridor. All these courses can claim magnificent desert and sea vistas, which helps them charge greens fees topping $200 per round.

Cabo Real Golf Course (Semi-private) 18 holes; 5920 yards; par 72; 115 slope; 68.7 rating. Rates: $85-180. *On the Corridor, 7½ miles southwest of town. 01152 (1) 144-00-40.*

Campo de Golf San José (Public) 9 holes; 2879 yards; par 35; N/A slope; N/A rating. Rates: 9 holes, $45; 18 holes, $75. *Situated among the condominiums and hotels in the resort area south of downtown. 01152 (1) 142-09-05.*

PUTTING AROUND IN SAN JOSÉ

If you're not a full-fledged golfer or just want a fun time for the whole family, check out the Caddy Shack Golf Course with its nine holes of miniature golf, in Plaza Los Cabos shopping center. It's $5.50 per round for adults, $3.25 for ages 13 and under.

El Dorado Golf Club (Public) 18 holes; 5771 yards; par 72; 125 slope; 68.1 rating. Rates: $94-214, 10- to 25-percent discount for guests of selected hotels. *On the Corridor, 6 miles southwest of town. (800) 393-0400, 01152 (1) 144-54-51.*

For more area golf courses, see listings under Cabo San Lucas.

Palmilla Golf Club (Public) 18 holes; 6130 yards; par 72; 110 slope; 66.5 rating. Rates: hotel guests $93.50-192.50, non-hotel guests $115.50-214.50. *On the Corridor, 4 miles southwest of town. (800) 637-2226, 01152 (1) 144-52-50.*

HORSEBACK RIDING

Should you grow weary of the surf and sea, or simply seek a new way to enjoy the splendor around San José del Cabo, a horseback ride might be your ticket. Take your choice between the beach (Playa Costa Brava) and the arid foothills high above the Corridor—or combine them on a single longer outing. Rates are rather high here, ranging from $35 for a one-hour ride to $60-65 for two hours. Riding lessons in Spanish and English are available.

Cuadra San Francisco Equestrian Center *On the Corridor, 7½ miles west of town in front of Meliá Cabo Real Beach & Golf Resort, 01152 (1) 144-01-60.*

KAYAKING

You needn't leave town to embark on a rewarding kayaking trip in San José del Cabo. Estero San José, with its still waters, scenic shoreline and abundant bird life, is an ideal destination for paddlers of all skill levels. Single-seat units, available next to the *estero*, rent for $10 an hour while two-seaters cost $15 per hour. Along the East Cape, Los Frailes and Cabo Pulmo are excellent venues to combine kayaking with snorkeling. Hotels and travel agencies can provide you with information on organized trips.

Let's Be Clear About This

Summertime brings the warmest water of the year, but diving conditions may be less than optimum along the southern shoreline of the Cape. South swells during these months stir up the bottom and reduce the visibility, although you can still see a fair amount of sea life. Winter has the best visibility, but water temperatures can drop to the low 60s, cool enough to merit at least a partial wet suit.

Tío Sports *Next to Estero San José in front of the Hotel Presidente Intercontinental. 01152 (1) 142-45-99.*

SURFING

A thousand miles below the border, San José del Cabo may seem like a long way to go in search of the perfect wave, but warm seas, year-round sunshine and some choice surf have drawn many gringos south for just that. By California standards at least, the local waves are still uncrowded, but there's little chance you'll have them to yourself as more and more outsiders take note of Baja's southernmost coast.

Killer Hook Surf Shop, on Hidalgo between Zaragoza and Doblado in downtown, has surfing gear for sale and information on local breaks, but does not rent equipment.

By most accounts, the Cape's premier surfing spot is just west of town at Zippers, a reef break off Playa Costa Azul that churns out head-high or larger waves during the south swells of summer. Bahía Chileno, Punta Palmilla and several unnamed spots break farther down the Corridor, though access isn't as convenient.

At the south edge of town, in front of Estero San José, is La Playita, a reliable beach break during the summer. Farther east, a string of spots produce good surf along the East Cape, starting at Punta Gorda and reaching north to Punta Colorada. These spots only work on south swells, however—the only ones that reach into the otherwise sheltered waters of the Gulf of California.

SEASIDE SPANISH

In case you didn't know them already, here are a few Spanish words translated to help you around Los Cabos: *Playa* is "beach," *mar* is "sea," *cabo* is "cape," *bahía* is "bay," and *estero* is "estuary" or "tideland."

If San José seems like a long way to bring your own gear, you will find surfboards and related equipment for rent. Surfboards rent for $15 per day or $63 per week, including wax, a leash and roof racks for your vehicle. Body boards rent for $10 per day or $6 for a half-day, including swim fins. Partial wet suits ("spring suits" in surfer parlance) fetch $3 per day and are a good investment during the cool winter months. And if you're a beginner, lessons are available at $25 per hour.

Costa Azul Surf Shop *On the Corridor just west of town on inland side of Hwy 1. 01152 (1) 147-00-71.*

Nightlife

If we've conveyed the impression that San José del Cabo rolls up its proverbial sidewalks as soon as the sun goes down, don't jump to conclusions just yet. Granted, the night moves of this town do tend toward the mild side, at least compared to Cabo San Lucas. And yes, the crowd here is, by and large, more low-key than in that rowdy town down at the other end of the Corridor.

Westin Regina offers one of the many places for after-dark entertainment

But if San José del Cabo doesn't rock on until the dawn's early light, there is plenty to do once the crimson fades from the western sky. That goes for folks of all ages and a broad range of tastes, which means the town again flouts any generalities. If it's a six-string strummed on a garden patio, you've got it. If it's zesty rock beneath a thatched roof on the beach, you've got it. And if it's a rockin' dance club in the heart of downtown, once more San José del Cabo has got you covered.

ARRECIFES RESTAURANT

With rooms starting around $250 a night, the Westin Regina Resort is clearly a place aimed at the well-heeled among us. Care to join them? You can for an evening without cashing in your retirement plan, as you nurse a nightcap in the bar of this subdued, elegant dining establishment. We could all get used to this, surveying the panoramic view of the arch-shaped hotel, its dramatic water-themed landscape and the Sea of Cortez. *On the Corridor 6 miles west of town. 01152 (1) 142-90-00. Full bar; live jazz nightly, 7-10 pm except Tue.*

DAMIANA

If your ideal of San José del Cabo nightlife is a guitar-strumming duo crooning soft romantic numbers on a bougainvillea-shrouded patio, here's your spot. Ease back and order your favorite mixed drink or imported wine, unless you want to try a menu that's had a write-up in the pages of *Bon Appetit* magazine. *East side of Plaza Mijares. 01152 (1) 142-04-99. Full bar; live music 7-9 pm Wed-Sat.*

IGUANA BAR & ROCK

Downtown rattles till the tiny hours of the morning at this high-spirited club, where locals and *turistas* mix things up seven nights a week. Still, it's a more grown-up scene than your average Cabo San Lucas club, which should suit a lot of folks just fine. It's a healthy cross-section all around—singles and pairs from early 20s up to 40-something, dancing to English and Spanish rock. *Blvd Mijares 24. 01152 (1) 142-02-66. Full bar; full menu until 10 pm; live music Thu-Sat.*

TEQUILA RESTAURANTE GARDEN

All right, this place is known for its namesake spirit, with some 80 types of tequila awaiting for sale. But it's also known for its cuisine *and* Latin jazz nights, with a four-piece combo that takes to the secluded patio's stage twice a week. *Calle Doblado just west of Blvd Mijares. 01152 (1) 142-11-55. Full bar; full menu till 10 pm; live music Thu-Fri.*

TROPICANA BAR AND GRILL

If the salsa is just too hot for your blood, get a more traditional Latin music fix at the Tropicana between 7 and 9 p.m., when a six-piece mariachi band plays.

This venerable downtown spot has gone through several nighttime incarnations, though few as lively as the current one, with live Cuban salsa vibes rattling the thatched roof six nights a week. They'll even teach you a few dance steps to help shake the night away. *Blvd Mijares between Calle Juárez and Calle Doblado. 01152 (1) 142-15-80 or 142-09-07. Full bar; full menu till 10:30 pm; live music Tue-Sun. Schedule may vary by season.*

ZIPPER'S BAR & GRILLE

For the rat race-fleeing, Corona-swilling, cheeseburger-in-paradise set, weekend nights at Zipper's surely rate with the most classic of Baja experiences. The beer is cold and the music is hot as the tropical evenings rock to live bands in English beneath the jumbo-sized *palapa* roof. For those seeking the perfect wave, it's all part of a one-stop vacation, a few steps across the sand from one of the top reef breaks in Baja Sur. *South of town on Playa Costa Azul. No phone. Full bar; lunch and dinner served daily; live music Fri-Sat.*

Dining

If Double Whoppers, Domino's Pizza or Dairy Queen sundaes served in squeaky-clean, air-conditioned surroundings are your notion of ideal vacation fare, here's a hot tip: Grab your car keys and head for Cabo San Lucas, where you'll find all those and more. San José del Cabo is refreshingly (or distressingly, depending on your point of view) free of the *yanqui*-style fast-food chains that have made inroads at the other end of the Corridor.

On the other hand, the average visitor to San José seems to be looking for something different, and if that includes you, then you'll have few problems finding something to suit your palate and pocketbook alike. Seafood and Mexican are the main fare, naturally, but you'll also find prime rib, pasta, and cheeseburgers served with a heap of fries. In terms of setting, you may have lunch at a funky taco stand known best to locals, while dinner could be at a critically acclaimed dining house known far beyond southern Baja. As a rule, expect to pay higher prices the closer you get to Plaza Mijares.

Favorites

DAMIANA ♦ **Mexican/Continental**

In a town that's long on intimate, romantic places to eat, the atmosphere at Damiana has few peers. Take your choice from a pair of dining salons or a lovely outdoor patio (candlelit by night) dominated by a magnificent, huge old bougainvillea. Then choose among a long list of tempting ways to fix your favorite selection of seafood or steak. *East side of Plaza Mijares. 01152 (1) 142-04-99. Open daily 11 am-10:30 pm. $12-36.*

EL SINALOENSE **Seafood/Mexican**

It may lack the quaint charm or colorful facade of restaurants down on Zaragoza and Mijares, but this place *does* have a terrific ocean view from its outdoor deck above Paseo San José. And the menu reflects its distance from town (and the big-buck resorts) with its down-to-earth pricing. The daily specials run $9 or less, and you can't spend more than $4 for a complete breakfast. Toss in first-rate food and service, and you have one of the Cape Region's outstanding values. *Plaza Los Cabos shopping center. 01152 (1) 142-29-50. Open daily 8 am-10 pm. $4.80-16.50.*

LA CENADURÍA **Varied Menu**

In a town that plays heavily off its Old Mexico feel, this restaurant has a leg up, housed in a fully restored, 1860's-era adobe in the heart of downtown. Somehow your barbecued chicken or *Pescado Siete Puertos* (Seven Ports Fish) just taste a tad better beneath the stars on the rooftop deck as you gaze across at Plaza Mijares. Lavish murals and Luis Miguel's latest CD playing in the background enhance an atmosphere that is *muy romantico. Calle Zaragoza across from Plaza Mijares. No phone. Open daily noon-11 pm. $7.50-13.*

LOS GORDITOS **Mexican/Seafood**

In the heart of downtown and a flight of stairs up from

the sidewalk, there's no better place to sit back and enjoy the local scene. You pay for the setting with a menu that's a bit on the high side, but the daily specials (a beer included) are a good deal at around $9, and there's a great selection of vegetarian entrees for less than $10. *Corner of Blvd Mijares and Calle Zaragoza. 01152 (1) 142-37-33. Open daily 8 am-midnight. $8-38.*

TACOS ROSSY ***Taquería***

All right, this is a taco stand, with a simple menu at that, and it *is* a bit out of the way. But the dozen or so plastic tables are usually full, not only with locals but resident gringos who love to turn their friends on to a tasty, very Mexican eating experience. This is the only place in Baja we know of with scallop tacos, and they also have fish, shrimp and *carne asada* tacos. Oh yeah, the coleslaw is on the house and the beers run only about a buck. *On Calle Doblado, just west of Hwy 1, next to La Fabula Pizza. No phone. Open daily 7 am-mid-afternoon. Tacos 90¢-$1.30 each.*

ZIPPER'S BAR & GRILLE **Varied Menu**

A profound cross-cultural experience this is not—just a carefree surfside eatery with tasty food and ice-cold *cerveza*, capturing the idealized notion of the tropical beach holiday. It's right on the sand with surfboards hanging from the *palapa* ceiling, while burgers, prime rib, and fish and chips share top billing with traditional Mexican platters. *South of town on Playa Costa Azul. No phone. Open daily 11 am-10 pm. $7-20.*

Others

IGUANA BAR & ROCK **Mexican/Seafood**

$4-15. *Calle Zaragoza between calles Coronado and Doblado. 01152 (1) 142-02-66.*

JAZMIN'S **Mexican/Seafood**

$7.50-22. *Corner of calles Zaragoza and Morelos. 01152 (1) 142-17-60.*

LA PROVENCE **♦♦♦ Continental**

$8-20. *Corner of calles Morelos and Obregón. 01152 (1) 142-33-73.*

POSADA TERRANOVA **Mexican**

$5-10. *Calle Degollado just south of Calle Zaragoza. 01152 (1) 142-05-34.*

TEQUILA RESTAURANTE GARDEN **Mexican/Seafood**

$12-25. *Calle Doblado just west of Blvd Mijares. 01152 (1) 214-11-55.*

TROPICANA INN ♦ **Varied Menu**
$5.50-26. *Blvd Mijares between calles Juárez and Doblado. 01152 (1) 142-15-80 or 42-09-07.*

Lodging

For AAA-approved hotels, see *Lodging & Campgrounds,* Chapter 15.

Drive along Paseo San José, that broad parkway south of downtown, and you'd be forgiven for thinking that San José del Cabo had little more than newish, high-priced hotels on the beach, where swim-up bars, saunas and full-fledged gyms were standard equipment. The same could be said after examining the even more expensive resorts sprouting off Highway 1 on your way west toward Cabo San Lucas. But that's only half the story in a town that defies generalizations.

Pool at Tropicana Inn

Beyond the big-bucks resorts of the Fonatur zone and the Corridor are several modest to middle-class establishments. For those who take the effort to look, there are many quarters within reach of the most frugal travelers. It may mean giving up your fancy digs and sea-view rooms, but downtown you'll find several inns priced under $50 a night on Calle Zaragoza, Calle Obregón and Calle Degollado. What's more, you'll be in the heart of the prime shopping and eating zone.

SAN JOSÉ ON A BUDGET

Hotel Ceci, across from the mission on Calle Zaragoza, is not only one of the lowest-priced inns, but quite likely the best deal in town. Its 20 rooms are simple and clean, with TV and AC. Sorry, no cable or room service, but hey, you can probably swing $14 a night.

The beachfront hotels are like those in most other resort towns, which means the rates will vary widely with the passing seasons. The same room that runs $150 in the winter may fetch less than $100 during late summer. Savvy (but polite) bargaining may also save you quite a few bucks off the posted rates.

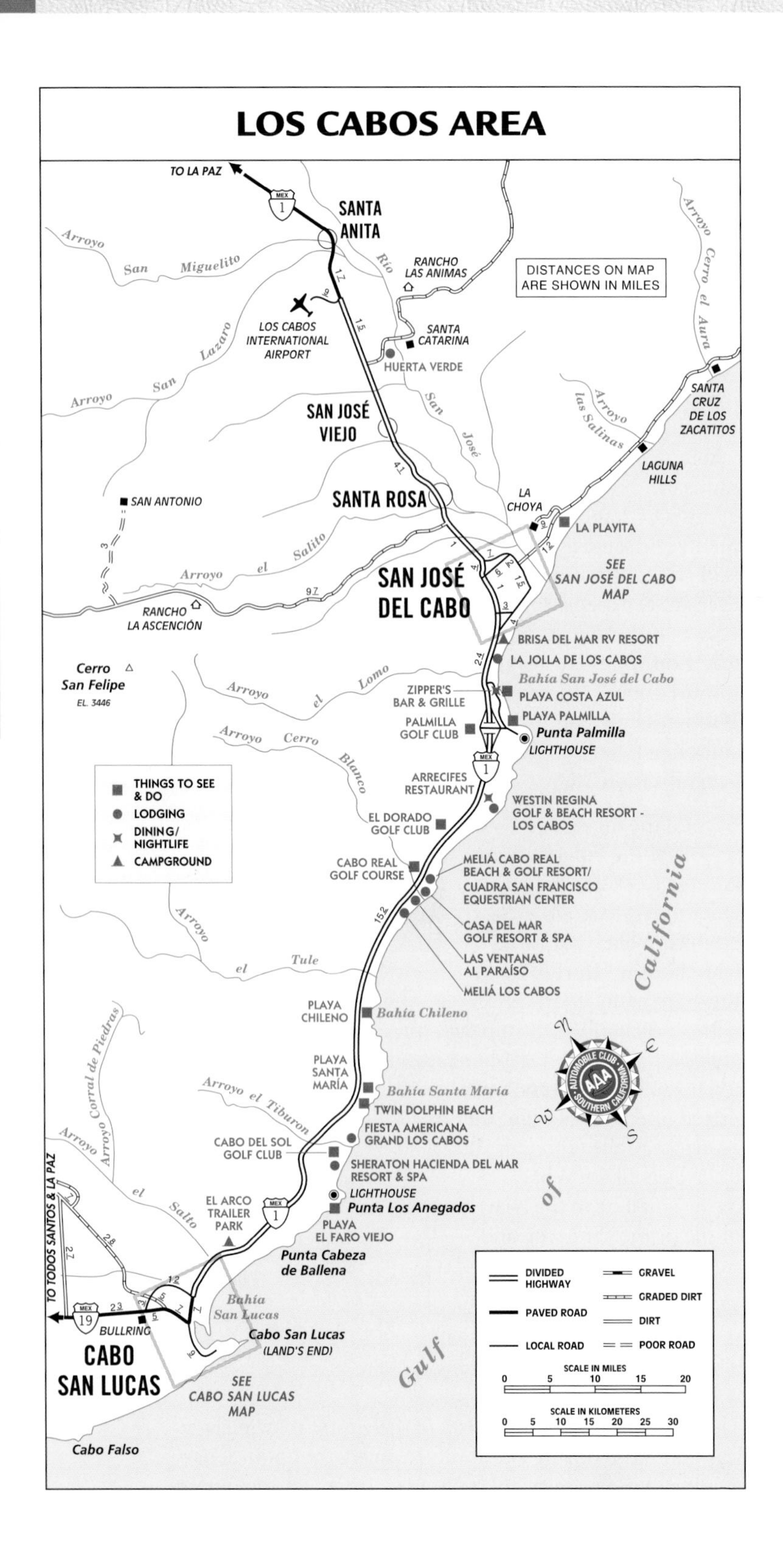
LOS CABOS AREA
TO LA PAZ
SANTA ANITA
RANCHO LAS ANIMAS
DISTANCES ON MAP ARE SHOWN IN MILES
Arroyo San Miguelito
Río San José
LOS CABOS INTERNATIONAL AIRPORT
SANTA CATARINA
HUERTA VERDE
Arroyo San Lazaro
Arroyo Cerro el Aura
SANTA CRUZ DE LOS ZACATITOS
SAN JOSÉ VIEJO
Arroyo las Salinas
LAGUNA HILLS
SANTA ROSA
SAN ANTONIO
LA CHOYA
LA PLAYITA
Arroyo el Salito
SAN JOSÉ DEL CABO
SEE SAN JOSÉ DEL CABO MAP
RANCHO LA ASCENCIÓN
BRISA DEL MAR RV RESORT
LA JOLLA DE LOS CABOS
Cerro San Felipe
EL. 3446
Bahía San José del Cabo
Arroyo el Lomo
ZIPPER'S BAR & GRILLE
PLAYA COSTA AZUL
PALMILLA GOLF CLUB
PLAYA PALMILLA
Punta Palmilla
LIGHTHOUSE
Arroyo Cerro Blanco
THINGS TO SEE & DO
LODGING
DINING/ NIGHTLIFE
CAMPGROUND
ARRECIFES RESTAURANT
WESTIN REGINA GOLF & BEACH RESORT - LOS CABOS
EL DORADO GOLF CLUB
CABO REAL GOLF COURSE
MELIÁ CABO REAL BEACH & GOLF RESORT/ CUADRA SAN FRANCISCO EQUESTRIAN CENTER
CASA DEL MAR GOLF RESORT & SPA
LAS VENTANAS AL PARAÍSO
MELIÁ LOS CABOS
Arroyo el Tule
PLAYA CHILENO
Bahía Chileno
Gulf of California
Arroyo Corral de Piedras
PLAYA SANTA MARÍA
Bahía Santa María
Arroyo el Tiburon
TWIN DOLPHIN BEACH
AUTOMOBILE CLUB AAA SOUTHERN CALIFORNIA
FIESTA AMERICANA GRAND LOS CABOS
CABO DEL SOL GOLF CLUB
SHERATON HACIENDA DEL MAR RESORT & SPA
Arroyo el Salto
LIGHTHOUSE
Punta Los Anegados
EL ARCO TRAILER PARK
PLAYA EL FARO VIEJO
TO TODOS SANTOS & LA PAZ
Punta Cabeza de Ballena
Bahía San Lucas
BULLRING
Cabo San Lucas (LAND'S END)
CABO SAN LUCAS
SEE CABO SAN LUCAS MAP
Cabo Falso
DIVIDED HIGHWAY
GRAVEL
GRADED DIRT
PAVED ROAD
DIRT
LOCAL ROAD
POOR ROAD
SCALE IN MILES
0 5 10 15 20
SCALE IN KILOMETERS
0 5 10 15 20 25 30

Best of the Corridor Beaches

More than a dozen beaches, each with its own attributes and adherents, dot the shoreline of the Corridor between San José del Cabo and Cabo San Lucas. Some are just a few steps from Highway 1 while others require a substantial walk to circumvent resort hotels and other private property. As such, you'll find everything from a rollicking fiesta atmosphere to secluded tranquillity that just may be worth the hike. We haven't listed them all here, but a few of the more popular and sublime stretches of sand follow.

Playa Chileno

Playa Chileno Convenient access, good facilities, and excellent swimming and snorkeling conditions make this attractive strand one of the top all-around beaches for families along the Corridor. Among other things, there's a dive shop with equipment for rent. *8 miles northeast of Cabo San Lucas at Km 14.*

Playa Costa Azul Swimming is fair here, but this beautiful, kilometer-long strand is best known as home of the Zippers surfing spot. Snacks and refreshments are available here, and Zippers restaurant is a popular lunch and dinner spot. Surfboard and body board rentals are available across Highway 1 at Costa Azul surf shop. *At the east end of the Corridor, between Kms 28 and 29.*

Playa Palmilla This beautiful, crescent-shaped beach provides the best swimming along the Corridor, with nearly a mile of protected shoreline. Snorkeling is possible as well, and local youths are known to dive for golf balls from the nearby Palmilla Golf Club. Pepe's Restaurant, along the access road to the beach, is a popular seafood joint. *Entrance at Km 27.*

Playa Santa María Swimming and snorkeling are excellent at this attractive beach, fronting a lovely horseshoe-shaped bay. But bring your own shade, food and liquid refreshments—things not available here. *7 miles northeast of Cabo San Lucas, just east of the Hotel Twin Dolphin.*

Twin Dolphin Beach "Seclusion" is the key word at this picturesque strand, actually a series of beaches broken by rocky outcrops. Access requires a lengthy walk down the hill from a lot next to the Hotel Twin Dolphin. Swimming and sunbathing are excellent at this beach, also known as Playa Las Viudas (Widows Beach). *Below the Twin Dolphin Hotel, between Kms 11 and 12.*

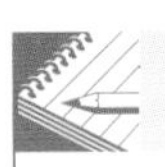

TRAVELOGUE

San José del Cabo to Cabo San Lucas
(21 mi., 34 km.; 0:30 hr.)

Twenty miles (and radically different mindsets) separate San José del Cabo and Cabo San Lucas, but a nonstop building boom is rapidly filling the space between these towns as they become the pillars of a single, larger resort area. This is the Corridor, the upstart coastal strip through which Highway 1 cuts a path on this final leg of the 1059-mile journey from the border to the Cape.

Highway 1 heads southwest out of San José del Cabo as a four-lane expressway and quickly picks up the shoreline, where new developments abound. Amid them are signs of things to come: concrete shells of fast-rising hotels and condos, yellow earthmovers clearing hilltops for new projects and billboards (all in English) pointing the way to new openings.

So far, the Corridor's inherent beauty has come through fairly intact, with many fine views of the sea and still-pristine beaches. Some beaches belong to private hotels, but several are open to the public, with dusty side roads leading their way from the highway. Near the west end of this drive, just shy of Cabo San Lucas, is the first view of the arch rock of Land's End, at the southernmost tip of the peninsula.

00.0 **Junction with Calle Zaragoza into San José del Cabo.**

01.3 **Junction with a palm-lined boulevard leading to the beach resort development marked "Zona de Hoteles."**

03.8 **Entrance road to the Hotel Palmilla resort.**

05.7 **Entrance road to the Westin Regina Resort.**

06.2 **Entrance road to the El Dorado Golf Club.**

07.5 **Entrance road to the Meliá Cabo Real Beach & Golf Resort.**

10.8 **Entrance road to the Hotel Cabo San Lucas.**

12.9 **Entrance road to the Hotel Twin Dolphin.**

14.1 **Entrance road to Sheraton Hacienda del Mar, Cabo del Sol Golf Club, Hotel Ritz**

	Carlton, Hotel Fiesta Americana and Puerto del Sol condominiums.
16.3	**Junction with the paved road leading to the Cabo Bello development, which includes the Hotel Calinda Beach Cabo San Lucas. At this point, Land's End comes into view.**
18.2	**Entrance road to the Cabo San Lucas Country Club.**
19.0	**Junction with Mexico Highway 19 leading north to Todos Santos, San Pedro and La Paz.**
19.8	**Cabo San Lucas, at the junction with Boulevard Marina, which leads to the waterfront.**

Cabo San Lucas

Cabo San Lucas marina

When day breaks across the southern tip of the Baja California peninsula, it does so over a town that never sleeps, where fun and carousing prevail under the sun and stars without reprieve. Cabo San Lucas can be a place to relax, but that's to miss the point of a resort that plays hard all day and parties just as hard till dawn's first light. "Cabo," as it is known for short, has come a long way from its days as a remote haunt for yachters and hard-core sportfishers, which a 1976 Auto Club guidebook described as "a quiet, unassuming town." Today's Cabo is anything

"Chicks Dig Me, Fish Fear Me"
—T-shirt for sale in Cabo.

but that, having transformed itself into a raucous, commercial resort aiming to please all sorts of visitors.

Though 1000 miles from the U.S. border, Cabo may be the most Americanized of towns not just in Baja, but all of Mexico. You may agree, walking amid the downtown marina district with its big-block condos, air-conditioned shopping plazas and American-style burger stands. In the marina, million-dollar yachts from ports around the world rest at their moorings, while a steady stream of tour boats shuttle visitors seaward on all manner of pleasure trips. All this in a setting where English is the predominant tongue for tourists and many locals.

CITY SLICKERS TILL THE END

How to spot the Mexico City visitors in Los Cabos: The men arrive in dark polyester slacks with patent leather shoes while the women wear their spike heels and black nylons—even in the relentless heat of late summer.

That Cabo became an international resort was perhaps inevitable, given its placement at the tip of Baja and many natural attributes. With its fine natural harbor, Cabo was a natural spot to construct a marina, and it was never a hard sell to attract boaters here. Known as "Marlin Alley," the offshore waters provide some of the most prolific sportfishing in the world, with anglers hooking more than 50,000 billfish each year. For divers, Cabo serves as the gateway to a string of lovely coves along the cape's southern edge, while several seamounts lurk offshore, as does a huge underwater canyon just a few meters off Land's End.

Cabo's allure dates far back, and nomadic Pericú Indians were already living in the area when Juán Rodríguez Cabrillo became the first European explorer to make landfall here in 1542. Pirates were soon using Cabo as a hideout, lying in wait to ambush Spanish galleons sailing in from across the Pacific, a practice that continued well into the 1700s.

Pelicans off Land's End

The fishing and yachting crowds from the United States discovered Cabo following World War II, but the town remained a quiet place into the 1970s, and by the time Highway 1 opened in 1973, it still had only 1500 people. Cabo has been growing steadily ever since, to a present-day total of about 30,000 full-time residents. Transformed though it has been, Cabo has managed to retain much of its intrinsic beauty. It's easy to see it in a

Extra! Extra!

It's hard not to keep up with local events and the tourist scene—not with four English-language newspapers, all free, circulated throughout the Cape Region. There's the monthly *Baja Sun* with its pullout section on Baja California Sur, the twice-monthly *Gringo Gazette,* the monthly *Cabo Life* and the bilingual monthly *Los Cabos News.* If you want to keep up with world affairs, you'll find *USA Today, The Wall Street Journal* and the *Los Angeles Times*, plus the international editions of *Time* and *Newsweek*. Other than the freebies, which are omnipresent, the best place to find reading material is at Libros Books in Plaza Bonita.

place where the desert meets the sea one last time before the arch rock of Land's End dips beneath the waves.

Getting Around

Whether to drive or not to drive is the foremost question for transit in most Baja towns, and Cabo is no exception. In the end there is no pat answer, as it depends on where you are staying and where your interests lie. As a general rule, you're better off walking if circumstances allow. The marina district, with its myriad of restaurants, clubs, shops, etc., is far more easily seen and experienced on foot. If you're staying in the center of town, the marina and its satellite attractions will probably be within reasonable walking distance. But if your lodging is elsewhere, it still makes sense to catch a cab to town, or drive and park someplace before getting about on foot.

If you're headed down the Corridor, you can still leave the car parked and catch the bus. There's service between here and San José del Cabo every half-hour until 8 at night, and with fair warning, drivers will stop along the way to let you out. Of course a set of wheels can often be your best bet, whether for golfing, dining, beach hopping or just exploring the territory.

Things To See & Do

For all its growth and new attractions, Cabo San Lucas remains all about the sea and the multitude of water-based experiences, taking full advantage of its modern harbor, year-round outdoor climate and convergence of two major bodies of water.

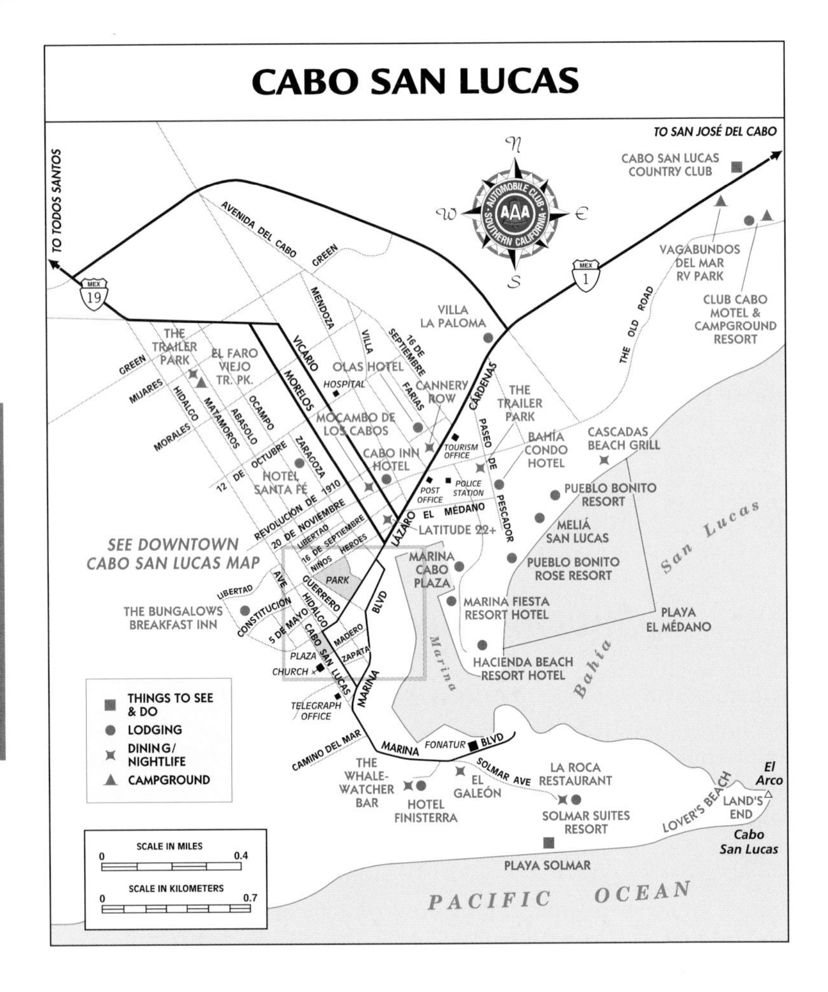

Cabo has always been an angler's haunt, and its reputation for deep-sea fishing has only increased with the town's rise to major resort status. The offshore waters aren't known as "Marlin Alley" for nothing, with more billfish (marlin, sailfish, etc.) caught annually than any comparable venue in the world. The highlight of the sportfishing scene is the Bisbee's Black and Blue tournament (named for black marlin and blue marlin), held each October since 1981. Many anglers still take their fish home, but with growing pressure from commercial and sportfishing interests, "catch and release" has become the mantra of the day.

Given the focus on billfish, the local fishing fleet is comprised primarily of full-fledged cruisers designed to go after such species. It's possible to hook one of those big fish from an open-deck *panga*, and some anglers do enjoy that challenge. In general though, *pangas* are the vessel of choice for small to mid-size game fish.

Divers are another group who will find Cabo to be one of Baja's premier destinations. The southern edge of the cape lends itself to all types of underwater adventures and skill levels. For a quick snorkeling trip, nothing beats Lover's Beach at Land's End, one of Cabo's essential experiences and a short boat ride from either Playa El Médano or the marina. Farther south along Land's End is Pelican Rock (Roca Pelícanos), a slightly more challenging spot about 20 feet in depth, reachable by boat or swimming from Lover's Beach. Along the Corridor, Bahía Chileno and neighboring Bahía Santa María are

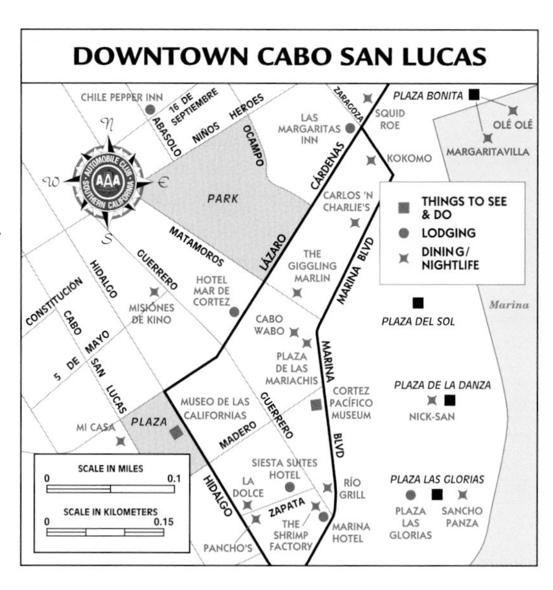

"Coffee, Tea or a Time-share?"

We would be remiss not to address a certain downside to the fast times and fun beneath Cabo's eternal sun. The lust for the greenback is endemic at times, as seen in the brigades of smooth-talking shills who ply the downtown streets, hawking restaurants, strip joints, "booze cruises," etc. By far the worst, though, are those hustling time-shares, who have turned their sneaky tactics into an art form.

A typical ruse starts with a well-chiseled man or buxom young lass who wants to know where this good-looking tourist has been all his/her life. Take the bait and you may spend half a day at a high-pressure spiel tailored to get you to sign the dotted line *now*. Another popular come-on lurks in the pop-up stands that promise fun times at suspiciously low prices—e.g. two sunset cruise tickets for $10 (the regular price is $70). The deeply discounted price is for real, complete with its own fast-talking pitch. ("This offer is good till ... uh ... noon today.")

This is not to dissuade you from visiting Cabo or strolling the downtown, just a word to the wise that many locals (as opposed to natives—a rarity in Cabo) make it their goal in life to separate you from your hard-earned *dinero*. In Baja, like anywhere else, if it sounds too good to be true, it almost certainly is.

both excellent for viewing marine life in sheltered, shallow waters.

For experienced scuba divers, some of Baja's greatest adventures lurk offshore. One is just off Land's End, where a huge submarine canyon plunges to depths of nearly 3000 feet. The focal point here is a remarkable "sand-fall" in which a cascade of sand tumbles from 20 feet beneath the surface to the canyon's floor. Farther offshore lie the Gorda Banks, a pair of shoals 8½ and 11 miles off the coast, each more than 100 feet below the surface. The banks are a prime gathering spot for some of Baja's biggest sea life, attracting whale sharks—the largest fish in the world—along with manta rays and super-sized game fish.

Surfers also choose among several locations, including Bahía Chileno, Punta Palmilla and a number of other breaks along the Corridor. Heading north along the Pacific coast, Migriño is the best spot close to town. Surfers from California will find the Cape's tepid seas far more inviting than the chilly surf back home, with water temperatures topping 80 degrees during summer and early fall. Winter is another story, as temperatures can drop to the low 60s—warmer than up north but still cool enough to merit some sort of wet suit.

See sidebar, page 359, for more on Corridor beaches.

If a quick dip in the brine is all that you want, the Corridor has several good swimming beaches, several in front of luxury hotels. The best of the Corridor strands may be Bahía Chileno, where scenic beauty, easy access and inviting inshore waters are a hard-to-beat combination. It's a very popular beach with locals on weekends. Within the town itself, Playa El Médano is the primary swimming beach, just east of the marina in front of a long string of resort hotels. However, the commercialization can be disturbing, with an endless parade of souvenir vendors and inflated prices on some rather ordinary food and drinks.

Golfing, Cabo San Lucas style

Whale watching is another water-based diversion, at least from late December to early April, when some California gray whales venture this far south during their annual migration from the Arctic. Pilot whales, humpbacks, orcas and even a few blue whales—the world's largest living creatures—are also known to these waters. Still other aquatic activities include "para-sailing" around the bay (a standard at Mexican beach resorts), kayaking (Land's End is a popular destination), sailing and windsurfing. Playa El Médano is a good place to get information or rent equipment for any of these.

> **SOMETHING FOR EVERYONE**
>
> Cabo Mil 96 FM, the Cape's only FM radio offering, has got to be the only radio station in Mexico—or anywhere else—where you can hear Air Supply, AC-DC and Mexican *ranchera* legend Vicente Fernandez, all in the same block of music.

Back on *terra firma*, Cabo has become one of Mexico's leading destinations for golfers from all over North America. Five 18-hole courses beckon within a dozen miles, with more under construction or in the planning stages. Cabo's emergence as a golfing mecca makes perfect sense, given the scant rainfall, balmy year-round weather, and lovely desert and sea vistas. But it is not for the faint of wallet, as greens fees can top $200 for an 18-hole round. Elsewhere on land, horseback riding and ATV tours present a good way to reach backcountry and undeveloped coastline that would be otherwise inaccessible.

In town, meanwhile, Cabo is a nirvana for that most civilized of tourist pastimes, namely shopping. For clothing, jewelry, art and keepsakes of all description, Cabo has the best choice of items in all of Baja Sur. There's no one dominant shopping district unless you count all of downtown, where block after block is full of goods for every taste and budget.

While footloose downtown, you'll find a couple of stops that are completely free. One is the Cortes Pacífico Museum, where the game fish of the local waters are showcased with attractive full-scale models. Another is the Museo de las Californias, a salute to the Cape region's history, dating back into pre-Columbian times. Finally, if you're coming off a tough night hopping among those downtown clubs, you'll have plenty of company if you just relax at poolside, nursing your way back to health before heading back out to do it again.

Top Attractions

CORTÉS PACÍFICO MUSEUM

If it's big and finned and swims in the waters of Baja California, then you'll find a likeness of it in this small museum in the heart of the tourist zone. Every major game fish known to the gulf and Pacific waters has its own full-scale model adorning the walls. Bilingual pictures and charts of other Baja fish make this a worthwhile stop. *On*

Blvd Marina just south of Madero. No phone. Open daily 11 am-10 pm. Free.

LAND'S END

Baja's signature landmark, this wind-worn chain of granite headlands tumbles seaward at the southern tip of the peninsula, officially separating the Pacific from the Gulf of California. At the very tip is the famed arch rock El Arco, whose image has graced countless postcards, posters and travel brochures. A close-up visit to El Arco is easily done through a flotilla of water taxis, many with glass bottoms, that depart the marina through most of the day. *At the southwest tip of Cabo San Lucas. Boats depart daily from marina in front of Plaza las Glorias and Playa Médano, 9 am-4 pm. Last pickup from Lover's Beach at 4:45 pm. $8.*

... AND I HAVE AN ARCH ROCK TO SELL YOU

We've heard tales from those who claimed they jawboned the price of a $30 serape down to less than $6, putting the screws on some hopelessly outwitted vendor. Do we believe them? Uh-huh, just like yarns of the 400-pound sailfish that snapped the 30-pound test line, inches shy of the gaffe.

See *GreatestHits,* Chapter 3 for more on Land's End.

MUSEO DE LAS CALIFORNIAS

In a town with no real sense of history, the past lives on in this modest-sized museum in the core of downtown. Historic photos, fossils and historical artifacts are heady reminders that there really was life in Los Cabos before Burger King, Cabo Wabo and the mega-resorts. *On downtown plaza south of Madero. No phone. Open daily 9 am-4 pm. Free.*

Headgear for sale, somewhere along Calle Hidalgo

SHOPPING

Cabo San Lucas has more of almost everything for the *turista* than anyplace else in Baja California Sur, and shopping is no exception. Cabo's got all bases covered—from those neon-bright Indian blankets and R-rated T-shirts on up to the most elegant of fine arts and jewelry.

Calle Hidalgo comes off as a beach-oriented version of Tijuana's Avenida Revolución, with its seemingly endless blocks of open-air shops full of clothing, crafts and souvenirs of all kinds. Nearby streets of the same vein include **Madero, Lázaro Cárdenas** and **Guerrero**. The **Marina District** presents still more ways to spend your money, with scores of shops ranging from the mundane to the most upscale sellers of jewelry, artwork and designer-label clothing. **Plaza Nautica, Plaza Bonita, Plaza del Sol, Plaza del Mar** and **Plaza Real Mall** are the main centers of activity along Boulevard Marina, the main thoroughfare of this district. Yet another good shopping zone is on the north side of the marina near the sport fishing dock, where dozens of vendors sell keepsakes of all types from a complex of open-air stalls.

Outdoor Fun

ATV TOURS

From the hubbub of downtown Cabo it's just a few minutes' riding time by ATV to the untamed shore and sand dunes of the Pacific coast. Odds are you'll be headed that direction if you join a guided ATV tour from one of several companies in Cabo San Lucas. The standard route heads up the coast to expansive sand dunes and El Faro Viejo (Old Lighthouse), about three miles north of town. It's a three-hour trek, taking it slow and with time for viewing the coast and hot-dogging about the dunes. A longer trip takes in the tiny village of La Candelaria, some 18 miles north of town in the foothills above the Pacific Coast. While these are the most popular tours, you can arrange custom outings that explore the nearby desert or that depart from San José del Cabo or Los Barriles.

For more ATV tour companies, see listings under San José del Cabo.

Price-wise, three-hour tours cost about $45 for a single-seat cycle and $60 for a double-seater. Six-hour trips run about $100. Hourly and daily rentals are available, too, should you wish to travel on your own. Rates range from $20 per hour to $75 per day for a single- or double-seat model. You can arrange a trip by contacting a company directly, although most of the major hotels also book tours. Several freelance outfits rent ATVs along Boulevard Marina, but you are likely to have a more rewarding experience with one of the established operators.

Baja's Moto Rent *In front of Hotel Presidente. 01152 (1) 142-20-11.* **Baja's Water Sports & ATV's** *3 locations on Playa El Médano, and at Plaza las Glorias hotel, Pueblo Bonito Resort, Villa Del Palmar Hotel and Bahía Hotel. 01152 (1) 143-20-50.* **Cabo Moto Rent** *On Blvd Marina between Blvd Lázaro Cárdenas and Morelos. 01152 (1) 143-08-08.* **Rancho Tours** *On east side of marina, across from Marina Sol Resort. 01152 (1) 143-54-64.* **Tío Sports** *In front of Hotel Meliá San Lucas, behind Playa El Médano. 01152 (1) 143-29-86.*

BEACHES

See *GreatestHits*, Chapter 3 for more on Lover's Beach.

Lover's Beach (Playa del Amor) Baja's southernmost beach allows the unique experience of walking "coast to

Lover's Beach

coast" from the Gulf of California to the Pacific Ocean in just a couple of minutes. This lovely, hourglass-shaped strand is flanked on either side by the towering granite crags of Land's End. Diving is excellent on the gulf side of the beach, but any swimming is usually dangerous off the Pacific side. *Near the southern tip of Land's End. Accessible by boat from the marina and Playa El Médano.*

Playa El Faro Viejo The first Pacific coast beach north of town, this secluded strand is named for an old but still-standing lighthouse that was replaced years ago by an automated one. Most visitors get here on horseback or with guided ATV tours. *About 2 miles north of Land's End.*

Playa El Médano The most popular beach in all of Baja, this sun-washed, two-mile-long strand is the center of Cabo's outdoor scene. Swimming and wading are excellent in the warm, sheltered waters of the bay, and the beach is definitely *the* place for socializing with your fellow vacationers. El Médano has become a full-service beach of sorts, with several restaurants and bars bringing food and drinks to your location on the sand. Also, there's information or rentals for nearly all of Cabo's outdoor activities—sailing, diving, kayaking, boat tours, para-sail rides and more. The beach does have its downside, which includes an endless stream of vendors, expensive food and beverages, and seasonal crowds during the winter and U.S. holiday periods. *East of the marina along Bahía San Lucas.*

Playa Solmar The only in-town beach on the Pacific, Playa Solmar is an attractive place for sunbathing or strolling, but strong currents and undertow make swimming dangerous

Water Sports, Etc.

Looking for still more outdoor fun? A kayak to paddle about, a wave-runner to speed around the bay in, or a thrilling "para-sail" ride 600 feet above the water? All these and more are available at Playa El Médano, where several outfitters offer a full range of activities. There's information and/or rentals for virtually every activity that Cabo San Lucas has to offer. Among these are the Activity Center, phone 01152 (1) 143-30-93, Cabo Acuadeportes, phone 143-01-17, and JT Water Sports, phone 147-53-28.

here. Several resort hotels front this strand and their bars are the best spots in town for watching the sun set. *Just north of Land's End on the Pacific side of the peninsula.*

BOAT CRUISES

Board a boat in most Baja ports and you're probably going diving, fishing or out to see a whale. Not so in Cabo San Lucas, where boating takes on a host of possibilities known nowhere else on the peninsula. It could mean riding the breeze on an ocean racing yacht, a glass-bottom boat ride to Land's End, a romantic dinner cruise along the shoreline, or a proverbial "booze cruise"—those frolicking, open-bar excursions for which Cabo is famous. Other tours combine food and recreation, like the sailing trips down the Corridor coastline, where you'll go swimming or snorkeling in a sheltered bay before enjoying a buffet lunch on the way back.

A cruise combining diving and lunch typically costs $40 per person, snorkel gear included, although the cost may vary by vessel and length of trip. Dinner cruises also run about $40, while drinking-only excursions run slightly less. The best deal going is a short hop to Land's End with an optional stop at Lover's Beach, which usually costs less than $10.

A schooner heads seaward for a sightseeing cruise.

A walk around the marina is the best way to learn about these cruises and other trips available. Reservations are advised for eating or drinking cruises. Land's End outings, on the other hand, require no reservations, and boats depart on a regular basis until about 4:30 p.m. Just be sure to arrange for a pickup if you have a boat drop you off at Lover's Beach.

Some of the boat companies offering eating or drinking cruises or private charter cruises include the following, all based at the marina:

Tour boats visiting Land's End are based along the southwest side of the marina, between the Plaza Las Glorias hotel and the sportfishing pier.

Kaleidoscope *01152 (1) 148-73-18.* **La Princesa Cruises** *01152 (1) 143-76-76.* **Pez Gato** *01152 (1) 143-37-97.* **Pirate Ship Cruises of Cabo** *01152 (1) 147-54-53.* **Sun Rider** *01152 (1) 143-22-52.* **Vancouver Star** *01152 (1) 143-21-88.*

DIVING

Next to sportfishing, exploring the ocean's depths has got to be Cabo San Lucas' most vaunted outdoor pursuit, and with good reason. Within a short boat ride of the marina, the variety of diving experiences available is staggering.

There are sheltered coves full of colorful fish, offshore banks inhabited by whale sharks, huge rays and other behemoths, and a yawning submarine canyon that plunges close to 3000 vertical feet.

Along with its many destinations, Cabo has an abundance of outfitters providing transportation, equipment and diving instruction. Prices range tremendously, depending on destination and time involved. A snorkeling trip to Lover's Beach via water taxi can cost as little as $7, while a four-day scuba package exploring the best local dive sites can cost $400 or more. Or you can spend nothing more than the gas for your car by driving to Bahía Chileno or Bahía Santa María. These two bays also rank with the most popular venues for party boats, which typically charge $35 to $50 for a three- to four-hour snorkeling cruise. The most popular trip, though, is the jaunt to Lover's Beach, with departures from the marina and Playa El Médano. Reservations are not required.

Rentals of all types are readily available, too, with snorkeling gear costing $10 to $12 per day, while a complete scuba gear package (tanks, wet suit, regulator, etc.) runs $65 to $85 for 24 hours. Scuba instruction is available for divers of all skill and experience levels. Beginners seeking full certification for open-water diving can expect to pay $350 to $400 for a four- or five-day course.

Among the companies offering snorkeling and scuba trips are the following:

Aero Calafia *01152 (1) 143-43-02.* **Amigos Del Mar** *On the marina, across from the sportfishing dock. (800) 344-3349 or 01152 (1) 143-05-05.* **Cabo Acuadeportes** *On Playa El Médano in front of Hotel Hacienda and at Bahía Chileno. 01152 (1) 143-01-17.* **Fleet Solmar** *On the marina, across from the sportfishing dock. (800) 344-3349, 01152 (1) 143-06-46 or 143-35-35.* **Land's End Divers** *On the marina, Plaza las Glorias Local A-5. (800) 675-3483 or 01152 (1) 143-22-00.* **Neptune Divers** *On the marina, Plaza las Glorias Local A-18. 01152 (1) 170-09-19.* **Pacific Coast Adventures** *(scuba only) On the marina in the Baja Cantina, Plaza las Glorias 01152 (1) 143-10-70.* **Tío Sports** *On Playa El Médano in front of Hotel Meliá San Lucas. 01152 (1) 143-29-86.* **Underwater Diversions De Cabo** *Plaza Marina Local F-5. (949) 728-1026 or 01152 (1) 143-40-04.*

Companies offering trips designed primarily for snorkeling include the following:

Cabo Expeditions *On the marina at Plaza las Glorias Local C-7. 01152 (1) 143-27-00.* **Pez Gato** *At the marina, Plaza las Glorias dock. 01152 (1) 143-37-97.* **Sun Rider** *Plaza las Glo-*

rias dock. 01152 (1) 143-22-52. **Vancouver Star** *Tickets at Baja Cactus Jewelry in Plaza Nautica. 01152 (1) 143-21-88.*

FISHING

Before golf, the wacky night scene and a slew of seaside resorts came along, fishing was Cabo's original drawing card. In the post-World War II years before Highway 1 went through, anglers with the time and means made a steady pilgrimage to these waters, which early on gained the nickname "Marlin Alley." Fishing no longer hogs the spotlight but remains a marquee attraction, with more billfish hooked from local waters than anywhere else in the world.

Billfish—marlin, sailfish and swordfish—have always been the primary prey for Cabo anglers, who keep several scores of boats and their crews busy through most of the year. This is sportfishing as the layman would imagine it—fighting a tenacious foe from a swivel chair on a full-fledged cruiser, several miles from land. Cabo does have its share of open skiffs (*pangas*), the craft of choice for catching smaller gamefish such as yellowtail and dorado, and they cost less to rent. In the waters of Marlin Alley, though, they're upstaged by their larger brethren.

CATCH IT NOW, EAT IT LATER

Want to take some of your catch home? Have your fish vacuum-packed or smoked in Cabo for long-term storage. Smoking costs about $4.50 a pound, including storage and packaging. Vacuum-packing runs $1.50 a pound, which covers freezing, storage and sealing your filets in one-pound packages.

How much you'll spend depends on the size and type of boat you rent. The classic Cabo fishing cruiser is a 28- or 31-footer, carrying four or six anglers respectively, and costing $350 to $500 for eight hours of fishing. *Pangas*, carrying two or three anglers, start as low as $140 or a half day, while a 50-foot cruiser carrying up to eight anglers can fetch $1500 or more a day. Most of the major operators have their offices along the marina, including those listed below, unless otherwise noted. You can also arrange a fishing trip through any of the larger hotels in town.

If you don't catch and release, local taxidermists charge $680 and up to mount a billfish.

Dream Maker Sportfishing *01152 (1) 143-72-66.* **Fiesta Sportfishing Los Dorados** *(888) 757-2226, 01152 (1) 143-16-30.* **Fleet Solmar** *(800) 344-3349, 01152 (1) 143-06-46 or 3-35-35.* **Gaviota Sportfishing Fleet** *Bahía Condo Hotel, Playa El Médano. (800) 932-5599, 01152 (1) 143-04-30.* **Gricelda's Sport Fishing** *01152 (1) 143-49-35.* **Minerva's Baja Tackle** *Corner of Blvd Marina and Madero. 01152 (1) 143-12-82.* **Picante Sportfishing** *(714) 572-6693, 01152 (1) 143-24-74.* **Pisces Fleet** *01152 (1) 143-12-88.* **Ursula's Sportfishing** *Blvd Marina across from Plaza Las Glorias hotel. 01152 (1) 143-69-64.*

GOLF

Cabo San Lucas anchors the west end of Baja's golfing cornucopia, touting half a dozen courses within a half hour's drive, although just two of those lie at this end of the Corridor. Cabo has made no bones about promoting itself as Mexico's top golfing destination, though, and with its many luxury resorts the town has actively wooed those who can afford the steep green fees. Besides those listed here, a new course designed by Tom Weiskopf is under construction on the shoreline just west of the Jack Nicklaus-designed Cabo del Sol Golf Club.

For more area golf courses, see listings under San José del Cabo.

Cabo del Sol Golf Club (Public) 18 holes; 5843 yards; par 72; 116 slope; 66.8 rating. Rates: hotel guests $130-220; non-hotel guests $143-220. *On the Corridor, 5 miles northeast of town. Phone 01152 (1) 143-31-49; (800) 386-2465.*

Cabo San Lucas Country Club (Semi-private) 18 holes; 6135 yards; par 72; 126 slope; 69.9 rating. Rates: $100-154, 25 percent discount for hotel guests. *On east edge of town, just north of Hwy 1. Phone 01152 (1) 143-46-53, (888) 328-8501.*

HORSEBACK RIDING

If you want to "get away from it all" in Cabo without driving for miles or boarding a boat, your best bet may be the back of a horse. Both the hillsides and beaches are attractive options in this land where the desert meets the sea. Sunset rides along the beach are an especially popular—and romantic—choice. Prices range from $20 for a one-hour trot into the nearby hills or along the beach, and up to $65 for a 3½-hour ride to El Faro Viejo (Old Lighthouse). Guided outings will normally take up to 15 persons without special arrangements. Reservations are recommended.

Due to the intense midday heat, local stables do not offer rides between noon and 2 or 3 p.m.

Sanluqueña *Junction of Hwy 1 and Hwy 19 in front of La Sanluqueña Bullring. No phone.* **Red Rose Riding Stables** *At northeast edge of town, near the entrance to the Cabo San Lucas Country Club. 01152 (1) 143-48-26.* **Reyes Collins** *Hotel Meliá San Lucas. 01152 (1) 143-36-52.*

SURFING

Cabo San Lucas may be a water sports nirvana, but you'll have to head at least a few miles out of town on Highway 1 or Highway 19 in your quest for good waves. Several spots dot the Corridor, the best ones being the reef breaks at Bahía Chileno and Punta Palmilla. Up the Pacific coast, the first really good spot is about 19 miles north at Migriño Bay, a right point break that works on winter swells.

"It Depends On How You Define 'Ocean' "

In geographical terms, the official dividing point between the Pacific Ocean and Gulf of California is at Land's End in Cabo San Lucas. The reasoning makes sense, this being the southernmost point on the Baja California peninsula, but it's not the only place to draw the line. The Corridor presents a transition zone of sorts as the warmer waters of the gulf mix with the cooler Pacific waters—one reason anglers catch so many species of fish here.

Land's End: Where the Pacific meets the Gulf?

From the surfer's standpoint, the limits of the Pacific extend well up the East Cape, as ocean swells continue to make their presence known. Of course the action is limited to the southerly swells of April through October, since north and west swells fail to wrap around the cape. By this measure, the Pacific extends clear north to Punta Colorada, near the village of La Ribera and 70 miles from Land's End.

WHALE WATCHING

While Cabo San Lucas lies well south of the California gray whales' calving lagoons, a fair number of the mammals do show up in the local waters during the winter months. Mother whales and their newborn calves often head south to the cape or into the Sea of Cortez for "trial runs" before embarking on their long migration to the Arctic. It's not unusual to spot whales from the rocky headlands above the Pacific, and tour boats schedule daily whale-watching cruises between January and March.

Cruises from the marina typically last two hours and cost $40. Just don't expect a close encounter or to pat any whales on the head, as you might in the calving lagoons. However, you might have the good fortune of spotting some other species; humpbacks and killer whales ply these waters during December and January, while pilot whales and even a few huge blue whales appear during January and February.

If you want an up-close look at the grays and money is not a problem, Aero Calafia offers full-day outings to Bahía Magdalena. Flying north along the Pacific shoreline, you may spot pods of the mammals from the air before landing and boarding a motor launch for a whale-watching tour in the bay. All-inclusive tours cost $330 per person.

Aero Calafia *Office at Plaza las Glorias hotel. 01152 (1) 143-43-02.* **Cabo Acuadeportes** *On Playa El Médano in front of Hotel Hacienda. 01152 (1) 143-01-17.* **Cabo Expeditions** *Plaza las Glorias Local C-7. 01152 (1) 143-27-00.* **Land's End Divers** *On the marina, Plaza las Glorias, Local A-5. (800) 675-3483, 01152 (1) 143-22-00.*

Nightlife

If this town were to have a civic anthem, it would have to be *Livin' La Vida Loca*. When darkness falls across the cape, the living truly is *loca* up and down boulevards Marina and Lázaro Cárdenas, where knots of marauding gringos hop from one club to the next long past the witching hour. The profile weighs heavily toward college-age California kids who head south for tequila, suds, Jell-O shots and all-night carousing, all legal here at 18. Of course, the young-at-heart are welcome too, and you'll see plenty of revelers middle-aged and older whooping it up in splashy sundresses or garish Hawaiian shirts.

In the streets, bad-boy locals peel rubber between speed bumps in their mini-pickups and ancient Toyota sedans, in a comedic attempt to win the eyes if not the eternal affection of some sun-bronzed California beach babe. Nor do the fast times stop at the water's edge, as party boats weigh anchor at sunset for open-bar "booze cruises" along the inshore waters.

Where the living is loca *when the sun goes down*

Cabo San Lucas has been a town of consequence for barely two decades, but in short order has won a reputation as the rowdiest night spot in Baja if not all of Mexico. Cabo has worked hard to cultivate this image, and it's perfectly normal to see the DJs encourage club-goers, in perfect English, to knock back another stiff one and "dance sexy" as they shake their booty in a raucous disco frenzy.

In fairness, there is more to Cabo than booze-swilling, hell-raising antics. Just a few blocks away, you can toast an idyllic day's end on a subdued, romantic note at an open-air lounge on a cliff high above the Pacific, where a sharp eye will observe whales spouting offshore during the winter months. Or if you prefer, you can also relax while nursing a glass of imported wine and tapping your foot to the sounds of a live jazz quartet.

In short, Cabo has something to suit the most wild or genteel of mindsets, and in a town renowned for its nightlife, we've only listed a comparative handful of spots that reflect the overall scene. *Our inclusion of certain establishments should not be construed as an endorsement of the conduct promoted there.*

Night Spots

CABO WABO

If you're a devout rock 'n' roller with racks full of hard-edged rock CDs and a drawer brimming with concert T's dating back to the late '70s, you probably already know about this raucous establishment, owned by former Van Halen vocalist Sammy Haggar. The Haggar stamp emanates throughout this place, where autographed posters and gold record plaques fill the walls, while Aerosmith, Guns 'N Roses, Kiss and other greats of their genre scream over the deafening sound system. The music turns live on the weekends, sometimes featuring Haggar himself. *In Plaza de las Mariachis on Blvd Marina. 01152 (1) 143-11-88. Full bar; full menu till midnight; live music Thu-Sun.*

CARLOS 'N CHARLIE'S

By Cabo standards at least, this is a fairly tame establishment, one more pillar of Grupo Anderson's nationwide restaurant/watering hole chain. There is plenty of drinking with dancing to English and Spanish rock till 2 in the morning, but things seldom get too out of hand—comparatively speaking. *Blvd Marina between Ocampo and Zaragoza 01152 (1) 143-21-80. Full bar; full menu until midnight.*

THE GIGGLING MARLIN

Were Cabo to designate an "official nightclub," it might be this landmark spot downtown, which seems bent on having just a little more unbridled hedonism and over-the-top attitude than anywhere else. Age-wise it's a diverse crowd, with everyone from college students to sun-bronzed seniors encouraged to drink up and boogie to the disco/rock soundtrack as if there were no *mañana*. The tagline hints at the devil-may-care Cabo mindset: "If our food and drinks are not up to your standards, please lower your standards." *Corner of Blvd Marina and Matamoros, across from Plaza Mariachi. 01152 (1) 143-11-82. Full bar; full menu until 1 am.*

> **THE MARLIN'S REVENGE**
>
> Cabo's signature photo op still has to be—no, not Land's End—but the booth inside The Giggling Marlin, where the crested fish exacts his revenge as you are suspended upside down next to a caricature of a chortling marlin, fishing rod clutched in fin.

KOKOMO

Eating and drinking (or vice versa) outweigh atmosphere at this tropically themed downtown establishment. Still, there is a good party spirit by day or night at this restaurant/bar/dance club, known for its superduper-sized margaritas. Another bonus: Ladies drink free after 10 p.m. *On Blvd Marina across from Plaza Bonita. 01152 (1) 143-52-52. Full bar; full menu until 11 pm.*

LATITUDE 22+

In a town full of fast talk and pretensions, this homey restaurant/bar takes the counter tack, proudly bragging of its nonendorsement by major cruise ship lines. Yachties, anglers and locals stake out the bar stools amid an atmosphere best described as tropical/maritime, complete with the din of clacking billiards and Jimmy Buffet (who else?) crooning from the stereo. It's also hard to knock a place where a prime rib dinner can be had for less than $7.50. *Blvd Lázaro Cárdenas between Morelos and Vicario. 01152 (1) 143-15-16. Full bar; full menu until 11 pm. Closed Tue.*

PLAZA DE LAS MARIACHIS

Anyplace in Cabo that sells dollar *cervezas* or tequila shots for just over a buck and margaritas for around $2 is going to attract a legion of fans. So it goes at this outdoor square in the heart of downtown, not a restaurant or club per se, but a place to see, be seen and consume liquid refreshments—not necessarily in that order. Along with the booze, there's a taco stand (open till 1 a.m.) to take care of your late-night munchies, several curio stalls and Cuban cigars sold from a walk-in humidor. *Corner of Blvd Marina and Matamoros. No phone. Full bar.*

RÍO GRILL

Dancing, drinking and dining hold equal sway at this venerable downtown favorite that packs 'em in by night and day. "Happy hour" takes on new meaning here, spanning from 4 to 9 p.m., winding down just as the band strikes up on weekend nights. With classic rock, blues and reggae played live, and a DJ play list that runs the gamut, it's hard not to find something you'll want to dance to. *Corner of Blvd Marina and Vicente Guerrero, across from Plaza las Glorias hotel. 01152 (1) 143-13-35. Full bar; full menu until 11 pm. Live music Thu-Sat.*

YOU KNOW YOU'RE IN CABO WHEN ...

... happy hour starts at 8 o'clock in the morning, as it does at one watering hole in the Marina District.

SANCHO PANZA

If the notion of relaxing to Latin jazz or B.B. King while sipping a glass of domestic or imported wine appeals to you, then this is your spot in Cabo. Choose from more than 100 wines from around the world at this self-proclaimed "wine bar café," and admire the cubist paintings adorning the walls between sets. The libations, music and art share billing with a menu that is described as "Mediterranean with a touch of Latin America." *Next to the marina in Plaza las Glorias. 01152 (1) 143-32-12. Full bar; full menu until 11 pm; live music schedule varies. Closed Sun.*

SQUID ROE

A fixture amid the Marina District party scene, this open-air drinking-and-dancing spot provides another irreverent take on the insanity of it all. There's sawdust on the floor, waiters dancing on tabletops, and sardonic maxims painted on the walls. (e.g. "If drunks could fly, this place would be an airport," or "Beauty is in the eye of the beer-holder.") The beer is cold and the margaritas are potent, but like so many Cabo spots the main attraction isn't so much the booze but the music (disco and classic rock), the unusual theme, and crazy antics put on by patrons and employees alike. *Blvd Lázaro Cárdenas just east of Zaragoza. 01152 (1) 143-06-56. Full bar.*

THE WHALE-WATCHER BAR

The wacky shenanigans of the Marina District are but a few blocks away, although you'd never know it, sipping a nightcap at this aptly named open-air bar overlooking the Pacific. A roving string trio provides a gentle reminder that Cabo is indeed still part of Mexico. The views are best enjoyed with a clear head, but if you so desire, there are more than two dozen kinds of tequila, and champagne priced up to $240 per bottle. *At the Hotel Finisterra, above the marina. 01152 (1) 143-33-33, ext. 19. Full bar; full menu until 8 pm; live music nights vary by season.*

> **WHALE OF A VIEW**
>
> The Whale-Watcher Bar lives up to its name, at least during the winter months, when a good number of California gray whales wander this far south during their annual migration from the Arctic. January through March are the best viewing months.

Dining

We never cease to be amazed by the long lines of sunburned tourists waiting to place their orders at the franchised burger stands down on Boulevard Marina. Served in familiar surroundings with the AC stuck at full blast, the burgers are just as juicy and the fries no less crispy than the ones we're used to in Phoenix or Fresno. That's fine and well, although it begs the question, Just what is travel for, anyhow?

Since those icons of foreign investment are hard to miss (and those so inclined will seek them out anyhow), don't bother looking here for their listings. Luckily too, Cabo San Lucas is awash with good restaurants that will remind you that yes, you really are in a foreign land. Surroundings alone should see to that—toes dug in the sand while gazing at Land's End, or admiring the vivid mural in some al fresco restaurant downtown. In all candor, sometimes "atmosphere" is really just "Mex Lite," such as the string trio that serenades you with *La Cucaracha*, or the waiter who rocks your head back to deliver a long shot of Cuervo Gold. (There are those who seem to view this as a profound cross-cultural experience.)

Typical restaurant sign art, downtown Cabo San Lucas

Now that we've gotten in our two *centavos'* worth, be assured that Cabo has an amazing assortment of restaurants, and you'll be hard-pressed to come away dissatisfied. It's all here, from hole-in-the-wall taco stands and walk-up smoothie bars to gourmet establishments where dinner for two can rival the cost of a night in some fancy hotel suite. The nightspots mentioned in the section above serve food day and night, generally a credible range of burgers, seafood and quasi-Mexican entrees.

If numbers provide some perspective, a recent visitor's guide listed 115 restaurants in this town of 25,000—not including the nearby Corridor (20 more listed there) or the many back-street haunts favored by locals. We haven't listed them all here, but encourage an adventurous spirit come mealtime.

Favorites

CASCADAS BEACH GRILL **Mexican/International**

It's hard to beat the setting at this outdoor restaurant beneath a *palapa* roof on the sand at the more tranquil east end of Playa Médano. Depending on the night, you'll partake in your pasta, fresh lobster or Mexican platter to the sound of live jazz, a string duo or mariachi troupe. By day, there's always that great view of Land's End across the bay. *On the sand in front of the Club Cascadas de Baja hotel. 01152 (1) 143-03-07. Open daily 7 am-10:30 pm. Live music 7-10 pm. $8-28.*

LA ROCA RESTAURANT **Mexican**

Call it touristy if you want, but Saturday night's Mexican buffet with mariachis and the folkloric dance show affirm that it's possible to find Mexican culture in Cabo. The highlight here isn't so much the food or mariachis (predictable enough) but the dance show, in the same vein as the one that has entertained generations at Mexico City's Palace of Fine Arts. *At the Hotel Solmar Suites, on the Pacific side of Land's End. 01152 (1) 143-35-35. Sat night buffet starts at 6:30 pm, $23.50. Restaurant open daily 6 am-10 pm. Mariachi music Wed-Mon, 6-9 pm. $10.50-20.*

MI CASA **Mexican/Seafood**

A pleasant all-around dining experience, Mi Casa does a superlative job in turning out both the catch of the day and traditional mainland Mexican platters. The super-thick, homemade tortillas may be the best in all of Los Cabos. Of course it helps when you're enjoying your meal amid surroundings that are festive and romantic at once, with vivid murals jazzing up a terraced outdoor courtyard with the inevitable *palapa* roof. *On Calle Cabo San Lucas across from the main square. 01152 (1) 143-19-33. Open daily noon-4 and 5-10 pm. $7.50-21.*

> **EVERYWHERE YOU WANT TO BE?**
>
> American Express and many Cape area businesses seem to be in cahoots, which means your VISA or MasterCard will not be welcome at many restaurants. Inquire before you order, lest you end up washing dishes.

MISIÓNES DE KINO **Mexican/Seafood**

You'd never guess that this peaceful neighborhood diner was just two short blocks north of Cabo Wabo and the rest of the downtown club scene—at least not while enjoying one of their creative seafood platters, next to the trickling fountain on the cozy patio, with salsa and reggae tunes in the background. A personal favorite is the seafood burrito, laden with fish, octopus, scallops and shrimp. *Corner of Vicente Guerrero and 5 de Mayo. 01152 (1) 143-01-52. Open daily 1-10:30 pm. $8.80-16.50.*

MOCAMBO DE LOS CABOS **Seafood**

Substance trumps style beneath the enormous *palapa* roof at this slightly staid but always reliable restaurant with one of the longest seafood menus in town. A loyal following of *turistas* and locals seems to believe that the hearty portions and superb preparation are a good deal for the money. (Most entrees run in the $12-15 range.) Case in point is the *Camarones Mocambo*, a large helping of shrimp wrapped in bacon and stuffed with cheese for around $14. *Corner of 20 de Noviembre and Leona Vicario. 01152 (1) 143-21-22 or 3-60-70. Open daily 11 am-11 pm. $8-31.*

PANCHO'S **Mexican**

This is Cabo's self-described most authentic Mexican restaurant, and they could be on to something here, with a menu featuring a long list of traditional dishes from Oaxaca and the Yucatan Peninsula. (Banana leaf-wrapped tamales, anyone?) For less-adventurous types, steak and lobster sizzling on the mesquite grill are worthy offerings. And with dollar beers and 400-plus kinds of tequila (from 50 cents to $50 a shot), Panchos is a sure-fire crowd-pleaser for Cabo's party-hearty sect. *Corner of Hidalgo and Zapata. 01152 (1) 143-09-73. Open daily 7 am-11 pm. $4-35.*

THE TRAILER PARK **Steak/Seafood**

In a town where anything more than 10 years old is ready for the historical registry, the Trailer Park, which opened in 1979, is nearly a legend. Owned by a U.S.-Mexican couple, this popular restaurant blends the two cultures in a way that suits much of the bronzed-hide, fun-in-the-sun gringo set who flock to Cabo. Nothing is cheap on the long chalkboard menu, but the portions are colossal and the atmosphere is typical Cabo-casual. A second restaurant at La Golondrina has joined the original one at El Faro Viejo. **El Faro Viejo** *Corner of calles Mijares and Abasolo. 01152 (1) 143-19-27. Open Thu-Tue 5-10:30 pm; closed Wed.* **La Golondrina** *On Paseo de Pescador, 1 block south of Lázaro Cárdenas. 01152 (1) 143-05-42. Open Tue-Sun 5-10:30 pm; closed Mon. $15-43.*

DRINK THIS WITH TWO HANDS

There's an undeclared war under way to claim the biggest margarita in Cabo San Lucas, and some glasses do appear large enough to float a good-sized fishing panga. For now, the mother-of-all-margaritas award must go to the Trailer Park, where the enormous glasses resemble a goldfish bowl fused to a stem.

Others

CANNERY ROW **American**

$6-15. *Blvd Lázaro Cárdenas between Gómez Farias and Francisco Villa. 01152 (1) 148-60-70.*

EL GALEÓN **♦♦ Italian**

$8-26. *West side of Land's End on Blvd Marina, across from sportfishing dock. 01152 (1) 143-04-43.*

LA DOLCE **Pizza/Pasta**

$7-11.50. *Corner of Hidalgo and Zapata. 01152 (1) 143-41-22.*

LATITUDE 22+ **Sandwiches/Seafood**

$3.50-8. *Blvd Lázaro Cárdenas between Morelos and Vicario. 01152 (1) 143-15-16.*

MARGARITAVILLA **Mexican/American**

$10.50-31. *Blvd Marina in Plaza Bonita. 01152 (1) 143-00-10.*

NICK-SAN — **Japanese**

$8-25. *Blvd Marina in Plaza de la Danza. 01152 (1) 143-44-84.*

OLÉ OLÉ — **Spanish**

$5-31. *On the marina, next to the boat ramp in Plaza Bonita mall. 01152 (1) 143-06-33.*

RÍO GRILL — **Varied Menu**

$10-20. *Corner of Blvd Marina and Vicente Guerrero, across from Plaza las Glorias hotel. 01152 (1) 143-13-35.*

SANCHO PANZA — **International**

$14-26. *Blvd Marina in Plaza las Glorias. 01152 (1) 143-32-12.*

THE SHRIMP FACTORY — **Seafood**

$9-34. *On Blvd Marina across from Plaza las Glorias. 01152 (1) 143-50-66.*

Lodging

If your notion of Cabo-style lodging is that of world-class resorts overlooking tropical beaches, secluded coves or verdant fairways, well, there's something to that. Cabo bills itself as a high-end destination for golfers, anglers and other well-moneyed tourists, but that doesn't present the entire picture. There are plenty of moderately priced hotels for those who can't afford (or have too much sense) to spend hundreds of dollars per night. They won't all have sea views or fancy decor, but unless the hotel is where you plan to hang out, they should more than suit your needs.

For AAA-approved hotels, see *Lodging & Campgrounds*, Chapter 15.

Los Cabos magazine and *Los Cabos Visitor's Guide,* both available around town, are excellent sources for information on lower-priced accommodations and those not AAA approved.

Pick the right time of year and a location a few blocks from the water, and you can find rooms starting for less than $50 a night. Campers get the best deal of all, with even the most expensive of trailer parks charging around $20 a night for two people. More typically, major resorts along the water's edge charge $150 to $400 per night in

Ignorance Is Bliss ...

... until it's time to settle up at your stay's end, when you realize that your hotel rate also includes a 12 percent sales tax and a service charge of up to 15 percent. It's standard practice in Cabo that these are not included in the posted rate. In fairness, a 2- to 10-percent service charge is more typical, but combined with the sales tax you're still looking at an extra 14 to 22 percent tacked on to your bill. Check it out and count the cost before signing your name anywhere.

Going upscale in Cabo: Hotel Finisterra pool

season, although you could easily spend much more. You can plunk down more than $2000 a night for a suite the size of a small house, where last night's guest may have been some movie star unwinding after a three-month shoot. Wherever you stay, be mindful that during all but the peak season (December through Easter), some friendly but shrewd bargaining could result in a good-sized discount off the rack rate.

Mexico Highway 19

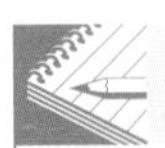

TRAVELOGUE

Cabo San Lucas to Todos Santos

(48 mi., 77 km.; 1:15 hrs.)

The only paved route along the Pacific in Baja California Sur, Highway 19 follows the shoreline all the way to Todos Santos as it sets out on the western leg of a loop trip around the Cape Region. The air is cooler here than on the gulf coast, and the views are magnificent as the highway threads its way between the ocean and the western slope of the Sierra de la Laguna.

Drifting sand is an occasional problem on Highway 19, at times flowing clear across one or both lanes of the highway.

Leaving Cabo San Lucas, the highway soon picks up the shoreline and heads north along a rolling coastal plain, keeping the Pacific within view clear to Todos Santos. Scattered farms line the road's eastern flank, while several lovely, unspoiled beaches lie just to the west. Some of these strands are public and have campgrounds ranging from primitive to highly developed. Word is out about these beaches, which host an ever-growing number of foreign visitors each year. Surfing is outstanding in several spots as well. While a rural atmosphere prevails all along this route, signs of growth are emerging, with large vacation homes sprouting in spots along the ocean and billboards promising more to come.

00.0	Cabo San Lucas, at the junction with Mexico Highway 1.
1.5	Junction with the main thoroughfare leading into Cabo San Lucas.
14.6	Rancho Migriño, a beachfront development.
33.5	Colonia Elías Calles, a small farming community surrounded by fields and orchards. Several nice beaches lie just to the west.
40.1	Junction with a good dirt road to Playa Los Cerritos, a beautiful, wide strand with a private trailer park and public beach camping. Rental surfboards and bodyboards are available.
41.6	Junction with a paved road leading to El Pescadero (see *Lodging & Campgrounds*, Chapter 15), a farming and fishing town of 1500 located just east of the highway. Several dirt roads lead from the pavement to the center of town, where stores and cafes ring a small plaza. El Pescadero is a junction with a road leading across the Sierra de la Laguna to Mexico Highway 1, five miles north of Santa Anita.
43.5	Turnoff for San Pedrito RV Park, a campground with numerous beachfront sites.
46.8	Junction with a dirt road to Playa Punta Lobos, where fishermen launch their boats, and also a popular picnic spot with local residents.
48.4	Todos Santos, town center.

Beach Walkers Beware

Heavy surf, steep drop-offs and powerful undertows add up to one lethal combination along the Pacific beaches south of Todos Santos. Drownings are fairly rare, but some beach walkers have been literally snatched off the shore by the occasional rogue waves that can sweep over a beach without warning. Playa Las Palmas and Playa Los Cerritos are the only beaches that are considered safe for swimming, the latter being a popular surfing spot. But regardless of which beach you visit or what time of year, be alert, and when you're anywhere near the surf line, never turn your back to the water.

Todos Santos

Civic Plaza, center of city and social life in Todos Santos

If Cabo San Lucas has an alter ego on the Cape, it must be 45 miles up the west coast in the relaxed pace, homey art galleries and well-worn feel of Todos Santos. Here's a town that's never played to the tourist crowd, but has still won loyal fans, wooing some to make this their full-time home. It's not hard to see why, in a town with as grand a setting as any on Baja's Pacific coast, plunked amid a teeming palm oasis between the ocean and the towering Sierra de la Laguna. Consequently, the town has grown steadily in recent years, especially since the completion in 1986 of Highway 19 as a paved route. While some say the influx of newcomers has destroyed the small-town atmosphere, this village of 6000 retains a rustic, lived-in charm, sans the brand-name hotels and restaurants of Los Cabos.

The timeless sense befits a town that dates to 1724, when the Jesuits founded Misión Santa Rosa de Todos Santos and planted fields of sugar cane in the surrounding oasis. The original mission is long gone, rocked by early Indian rebellions, and it closed in 1840 after diseases decimated the native population. Gone too are the cane fields, which withered in the 1950s when their water source ran dry, though their legacy lives on in the crumbled shells of the local sugar mills. Orchards, vegetables and other less-thirsty crops have replaced the cane, joining ranching,

FEET, DO YOUR THING!

Day-trippers from Cabo San Lucas often seem glued to the steering wheel as they drive about in their rental cars. That's a sure way to miss out on the town's essential character. Todos Santos was built to a human scale, and walking is the best way to get around.

fishing and, increasingly, tourism as mainstays of the economy.

MEXICO'S ART CAPITAL

While Todos Santos has the most galleries for its size of any town in Baja, the biggest art colony in Mexico is on the mainland. That would be San Miguel de Allende, a landlocked colonial town in the state of Guanajuato, 150 miles northwest of Mexico City.

You could hit the town's high points in a day, browsing the art galleries and artisan shops with time left to walk the civic plaza, visit the cultural center and enjoy a leisurely lunch. The Hotel California is a point of pilgrimage for some, but contrary to popular belief, it did not inspire the fabled song by the Eagles. Elsewhere, the remains of two sugar mills bear witness to an earlier era; the remnants of Molino de los Santana sit near the west end of Juárez, while Molino El Progreso sits decaying on Rangel next to the aptly named El Molino ("The Mill") Trailer Park.

Sugar mill ruins, west of downtown

Beyond the town's borders, a long chain of lovely, wave-lashed beaches runs southward nearly all the way to Cabo San Lucas. Dirt roads off Highway 19 lead to these remote strands that are the favored haunts of adventurous surfers, campers, and gringos fleeing colder climes. The ocean plays no small part in blessing Todos Santos with the best all-around climate on the Cape. Tempered by onshore breezes, winter days are slightly warmer than La Paz or Los Cabos, while summer days run up to 10 degrees cooler than neighboring towns. Even so, late summer and early fall brings weeks on end of sultry days, as the tourist trade grinds almost to a standstill. Come mid-August, many shopkeepers close their doors and hang out signs that read "Back on October 1."

Top Attractions

CENTRO CULTURAL

This restored brick building started out as the town's first schoolhouse before gaining a new lease on life as the center for the local arts and culture scene. Art exhibits, photos and a fair collection of local artifacts fill the exhibit rooms, and an impressive mural, painted in 1933, graces the front entryway. The center hosts numerous plays and other cultural events throughout the year, including Todos Santos' annual art festival in late January. *Avenida*

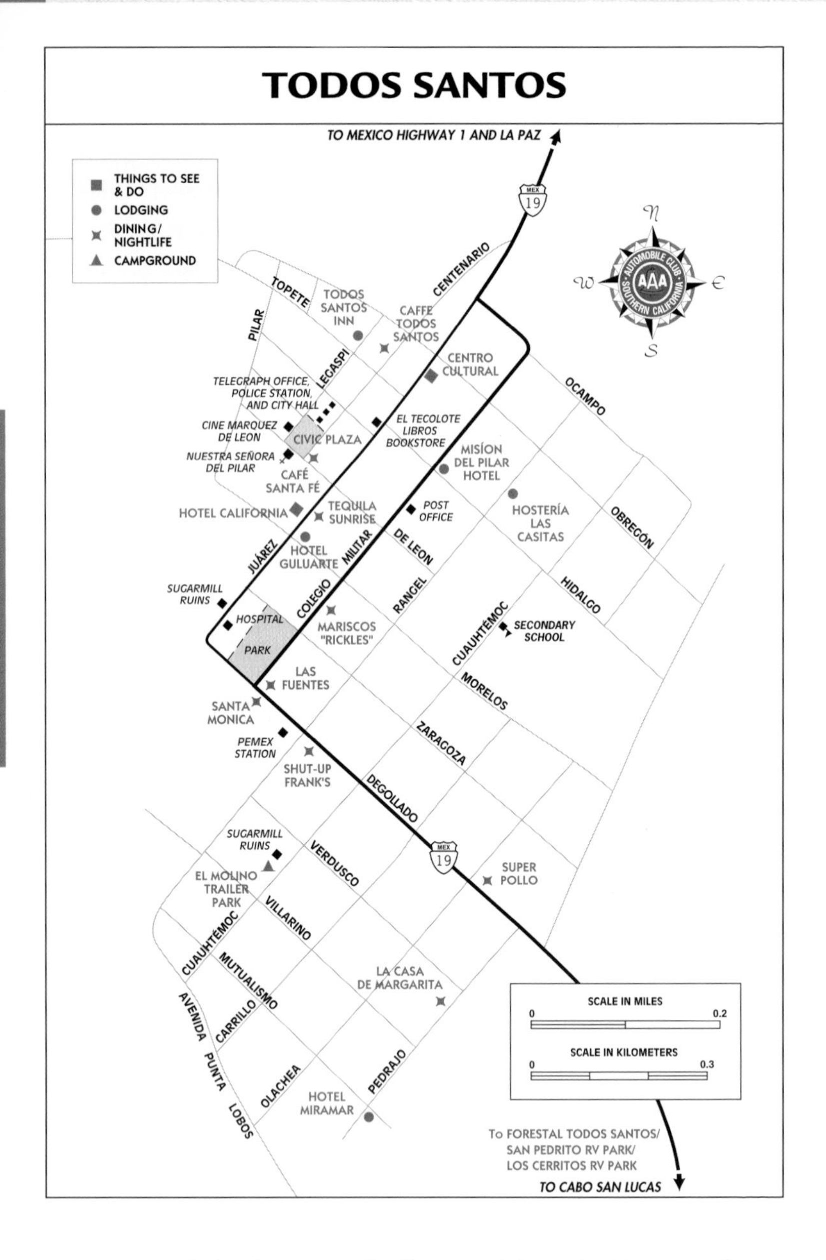

Juárez between calles Topete and Obregón. No phone. Open Mon-Fri 8 am-7 pm. Free.

WORDS TO LIVE BY?

A quote in Spanish above the outside entrance of the Centro Cultural translates to read, "The money spent on culture is not an expenditure, but an investment."

CIVIC PLAZA

Todos Santos' civic and social life centers around this main square, which is the best spot for viewing the townscape. From its hillside perch, the plaza provides a commanding view of both the town and nearby coastline, which brings many locals this way at day's end to watch the sun sink into the Pacific. Two of the town's most prominent buildings front the square, including the theater and the mission church. Cine Gral. Manuel Márquez de León flanks the north side of the plaza, where it has hosted live music, dance and dramatic performances since 1944. Nuestra Señora del Pilar dominates the west side and merits a walk-through for its impressive stained glass and statuary. *At the center of town, bordered by Legaspi, Centenario, Hidalgo and Márquez de León.*

Inside the sanctuary at Nuestra Señora del Pilar

FORESTAL TODOS SANTOS

Anyone who's ever wondered about the desert plant life while driving the roads of Baja should find the answers to their questions at this botanical garden. Foot paths wind through several spacious gardens, which feature virtually all the major plant species native to the Baja peninsula. Other sections showcase desert foliage from other parts of the world. *Off Hwy 19, 3 miles south of town near Km 56. No phone. Open Mon-Fri 8 am-2 pm, Sat-Sun 8 am-7 pm. Free.*

HOTEL CALIFORNIA

Built in 1928, this small, colonial-style inn made a name for itself by claiming to be the inspiration behind the famous Eagles' song. While those claims are of dubious origin, the hotel still brings many visitors to Todos Santos. In early 2001 the hotel was closed and on the selling block, but a gift shop across the street keeps the quasi-mystique alive by selling T-shirts, mugs and other goodies feting the rocking '70s tune. *On Juárez, just west of main plaza.*

Outdoor Fun

BEACHES

Playa Las Palmas One of the loveliest beaches off Highway 19, this strand is backed by lush wetlands and a burgeoning forest of palms. The brick and mortar shell of an abandoned home stands amid the palms, as do scattered remains of a one-time sugar plantation. *Off Hwy 19, 3 miles south of town near Km 56.*

Playa Los Cerritos Another scenic gem, this wide, unbroken strand stretches for several miles and has one of the

Playa Los Cerritos

few safe swimming areas south of Todos Santos. Surfing is also good, and there is a shop that rents surfboards and body boards. *Off Hwy 19, 8 miles south of town, near Km 64.*

Playa Punta Lobos A long, lovely beach with excellent mountain views, this is the closest accessible beach south of Todos Santos. This is also the primary beach for the area's commercial fishermen, who come and go in their skiffs during lulls in the surf. It is totally unsuited for swimming, however. *Off Hwy 19, 2 miles south of town, near Km 54.*

GET YOUR BEACH READING HERE

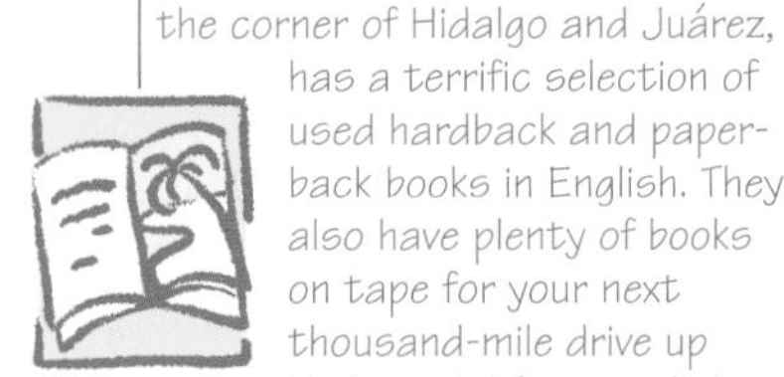

El Tecolote Libros Bookstore, at the corner of Hidalgo and Juárez, has a terrific selection of used hardback and paperback books in English. They also have plenty of books on tape for your next thousand-mile drive up Highway 1. It's open daily from 10 a.m. to 5 p.m.

Playa San Pedrito Home to a large, fully equipped campground, this popular beach attracts many surfers and seasonal residents. There are many primitive and full-service campsites, along with a restaurant, pool and laundry facilities. A day-use fee may be charged. *Off Hwy 19, 5 miles south of town, south of Km 59.*

SURFING

Surfers will forever debate the merits of different spots and where the best waves are in Baja. When it comes to access, though, Todos Santos is easily the best locale on the Pacific coast of Baja Sur. While many good breaks line the southern state's Pacific shoreline, most are well removed from major highways. From Todos Santos, however, numerous spots lie within a few minutes' drive and can be reached by a standard passenger car. One drawback, though, is safety, since most swells break with full force along the steep west-facing beaches.

Playa Cerritos is probably the best place for beginners, especially near the sheltered north end. More advanced wave riders head for Playa San Pedrito, with its grinding reef break in front of a popular campground. Several less tame breaks, suitable only for advanced surfers, lie off the pavement north of town. The best known of these is a right point-break known as La Pastora.

Surfboards for rent at Playa Los Cerritos

Like most of Baja's Pacific coast, winter generally brings bigger, more consistent surf to this locale. Water temperatures average in the upper 60s during these months, though even colder seas follow in late spring, when temperatures can drop to the lower 60s. By late summer, however, the ocean warms to around 80 degrees. If Todos Santos seems too far to bring your own gear, local shops rent surfboards for $10 a day and body boards with swim fins for $5 a day.

Todos Santos Surf Shop *3 locations: East side of Hwy 19 at the south edge of town; at the corner of Rangel and Zaragoza, 1 block east of Hwy 19; and at Playa Los Cerritos, off Hwy 19 near Km 64.*

Dining

Todos Santos belies its diminutive size with a fine selection of good restaurants—in keeping with its status as an up-and-coming tourist resort. Just don't come here looking for the name-brand franchises of *El Norte*, which never did mesh well with any artist's colony. Luckily, Todos Santos does a credible job of looking after both native and foreign palates.

SUMMER SIESTA

Odds are you won't be visiting Todos Santos during the steaming days of late summer or early fall, when tourism slows to a crawl across the Cape Region. But in case you do come, be aware that many merchants close up shop and head for cooler climes during this time.

It's possible to spend a tidy sum on eating here, although locals and budget travelers seem to get the long end of the bargain, with numerous taco stands and simple *loncheriás* where it's hard to spend more than $5. Colegio Militar (as Highway 19 is known in town) has several such establishments, especially near the bus stop. Mexican food and seafood otherwise lead the gastronomic lineup, and you could make a case for naming fish tacos as the town's official cuisine. Todos Santos has more to offer than that, however, whether pasta, burgers, U.S.-style baked goods or other decidedly non-Baja offerings.

Favorites

CAFÉ SANTA FÉ **♦♦ Italia**

There are plenty of good reasons to visit Todos Santos, and one of the best is the northern Italian cuisine of this widely acclaimed restaurant, which draws loyal patrons from all over the Cape. Homemade pasta, fresh seafood, a lengthy wine list, and organic herbs and vegetables provide the groundwork for a memorable dining experience. *South side of the civic plaza in the center of town. 01152 (1) 145-03-40. Open Wed-Mon noon-9 pm; closed Tue. $8-20.*

LAS FUENTES **Mexican**

With its plastic furnishings and *norteño* music playing in the kitchen, this is not the hippest spot in town, but who cares? When the friendly waitress brings your $7 shrimp dinner, you may decide this is one of the Cape's great sleepers. The service is prompt too, but you may just lose track of time while lounging on the outdoor patio, surrounded by tropical trees and three gurgling fountains. *Corner of Colegio Militar and Degollado (across from the Pemex station). 01152 (1) 145-02-57. Open daily 7 am-9 pm. $3-10.50.*

SHUT-UP FRANK'S **Mexican/American**

A self-described "sports bar and grill," this spot hits a home run with the wayward gringo crowd pining for a taste of home. All-you-can-eat spaghetti, rib eye steak, and stuffed pork shoulder are a few of the nightly specials aimed at the ex-pats. Frank's also touts the "best burger in Baja"—impossible to confirm but a good deal at around $4. Enjoy your meal, down a cold one and watch the big game on one of three satellite TVs. *On Degollado (Hwy 19), just south of the Pemex station. 01152 (1) 145-01-46. Open daily 7 am-10 pm. $4-22.*

Other Choices

CAFFE TODOS SANTOS **Mexican/Seafood**

$5.25-14.50. *Centenario 33, between Topete and Obregón. 01152 (1) 145-03-00.*

LA CASA DE MARGARITA **Mexican/Seafood**

$3.50-10.50. *On Pedrajo, between Verduzco and Villarino. 01152 (1) 145-01-84.*

MARISCOS "RICKLES" **Seafood**

$3.50-9. *Colegio Militar between Morelos and Zaragoza. No phone.*

SANTA MONICA **Mexican**
$3-10. *Corner of Colegio Militar and Degollado, next to the Pemex station. 01152 (1) 144-00-79.*

SUPER POLLO **Chicken/*Antojitos***
$2.80-6.80. *Corner of Degollado and Olachea. 01152 (1) 145-00-78.*

TEQUILA SUNRISE **Mexican**
$3-9. *On Juárez, across from the Hotel California. 01152 (1) 145-00-73.*

Lodging

The bad news is, there aren't any swim-up bars, opulent spas or $500-a-night honeymoon suites awaiting you here. The good news is, if you were looking for those, you probably weren't planning to spend much time here in the first place. Todos Santos has never aimed to please extravagant tastes, leaving that role to Los Cabos while jealously guarding its small-town atmosphere. Having said that, Todos Santos offers a fair supply of lodging, including simple hotels, quaint bed and breakfast inns, campgrounds and private homes for rent—all at some of the lowest prices in Baja Sur.

'TWAS A LOVELY PLACE

SE VENDE

The Hotel California was a past and possible future pick as one of Todos Santos' best lodging values. Before going on the block in 1999, its simple but clean rooms fetched $25 to $35 per night, and the overall atmosphere was full of Colonial charm.

Hotel-wise, Todos Santos has nothing rated by AAA, but there are some clean and perfectly comfortable places to stay. Priced from around $10 to $120 per night, you'll find inns of one sort or another scattered from downtown to the outer fringes of the community. Some of the pricier inns, while not AAA-approved, rival those in large towns, in terms of comforts and services. Be forewarned that some of these close during the sultry days of August

"Cottage Industry" Defined

What Todos Santos lacks in big-time resorts it makes up for, at least in part, with its variety of tiny but creative inns. Many residents have turned innkeepers by converting private homes into one- or two-unit guesthouses, charging nightly, weekly or monthly rates. Information on these is available at local businesses and in *El Calendario de Todos Santos,* the town's monthly English-language newsletter.

through early October, when the tourist trade reaches its annual ebb.

If you are looking for more choices, AAA-approved properties or simply more comforts of a first world-style hotel, you're just and hour's drive from La Paz or Cabo San Lucas.

Mexico Highway 19

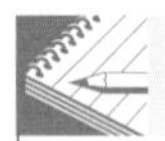

TRAVELOGUE

Todos Santos To Highway 1 Junction

(32 mi., 51 km.; 0.45 hr.)

First paved in 1986, Highway 19 is the fastest route between La Paz and Cabo San Lucas, saving about an hour's time compared to Highway 1. If scenery counts, though, it's still hard to sell short this route, which meets Highway 1 some 19 miles south of La Paz. Together with Highway 1, Highway 19 forms the western leg of a scenic loop trip around Baja's Cape Region.

Heading north from Todos Santos, Highway 19 leaves the palm oasis and the coast behind to cross miles of desert covered with brush and cacti. To the east, the peaks of the Sierra de la Laguna form a solid barrier almost to Highway 1. The mountains are the main scenic highlight on this leg, where few people live and there are no real points of interest. A few ranches line the route, which means that livestock on the road are a hazard.

00.0 **Todos Santos, town center.**

5.5 **Signed road to Presa de Santa Inéz, a dam tucked in the foothills of the Sierra de la Laguna.**

28.3 **Club Campestre El Carrizal, a country club with a pool and a restaurant.**

31.9 **Junction with Mexico Highway 1, just south of the village of San Pedro.**

Side Routes

The East Cape Drive

Highway 1 to La Ribera,
(7 mi., 11 km.; 0:15 hr.),
Cabo Pulmo, and
(23 mi., 37 km.; 0:45 hr.) and
San José del Cabo
(63 mi., 102 km.; 3:30 hrs.)

Virgin beaches, pocket coves and lovely turquoise waters backed by rugged desert headlands highlight this, the longest seacoast side route in Baja California. Deep-sea fishing, camping and diving along Baja's only coral reef are added attractions on this drive, which plies a long stretch of the East Cape, one of Baja's most picturesque and fastest-growing coastal regions. This road hugs the gulf most of the way from La Ribera to San José del Cabo, but remains unpaved south of La Abundancia, a stretch of 46 miles.

For some reason, most of the passenger cars that brave the East Cape road are rentals.

While this coast remains mostly undeveloped, change is afoot and each year a little more open space gives way to new tracts of vacation homes. The *municipio* of Los Cabos has announced plans to eventually pave the road's entire length, a move that will surely accelerate the pace of growth. Meanwhile, low-slung cars and small RVs can safely drive the dirt road, but all travelers should take it slow and easy, as the rusted hulks of abandoned vehicles alongside the road would suggest. Be prepared for a long, jarring drive over miles of washboard surface, and several rough and rocky patches—a trek that can take its toll on even sturdy vehicles and their occupants.

Beautiful coastline, south of Cabo Pulmo

The route leaves Highway 1 at a junction about 11 miles south of Los Barriles, heading eastward through seven miles of farm fields and desert to seaside La Ribera. A village of about 2000, La Ribera (also called La Rivera) has stores, a

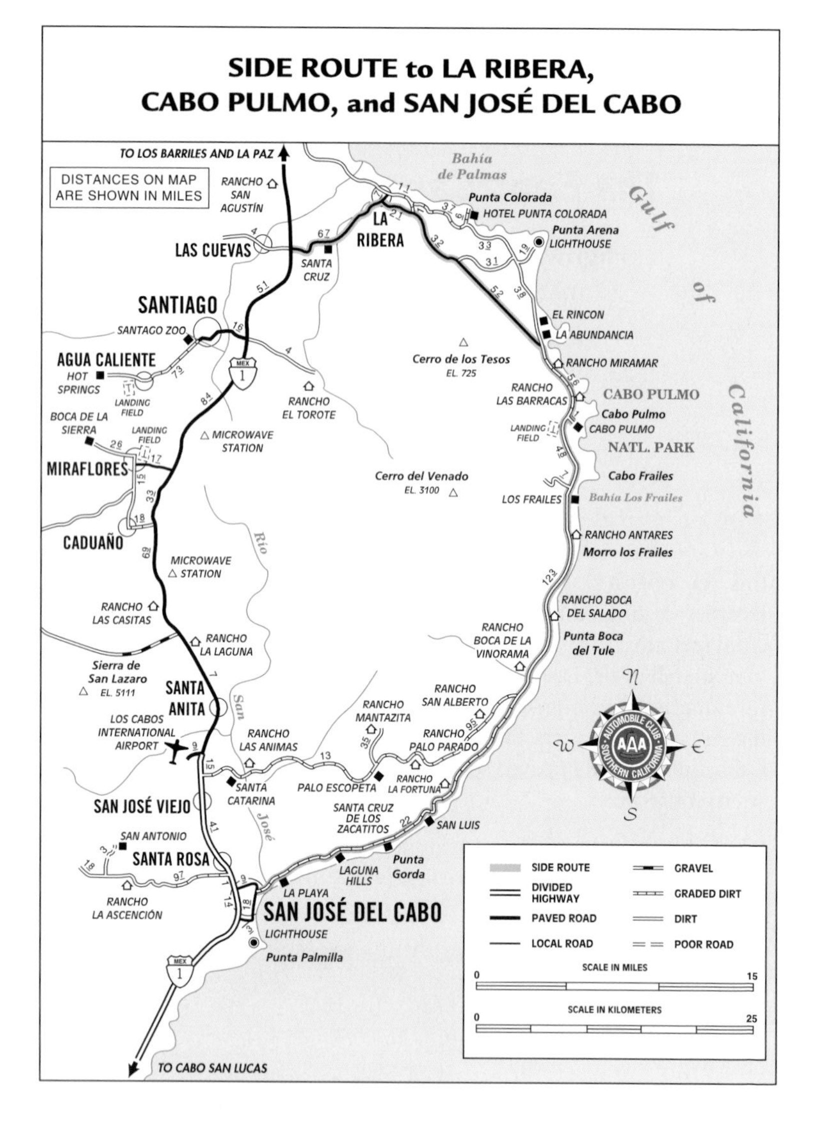

cafe, a trailer park and a Pemex station. From a junction 6.7 miles east of Highway 1, two roads head southeast from La Ribera. One is a graded dirt road that crosses rolling scrub-covered countryside for 5.5 miles to the Hotel Punta Colorada, situated atop a low bluff overlooking a lovely beach. The other route is paved and takes a more inland course across 11 miles of hilly terrain to reach the coast near La Abundancia, where it joins a dirt road.

From the pavement's end, the dirt road parallels the shoreline to the village of Cabo Pulmo, one of Baja's top diving destinations. A knot of thatched huts and small restaurants on a lovely tropical beach, this tiny hamlet is the center of activity for Cabo Pulmo National Park, a marine preserve established in 1997. Centerpiece for the park is the only coral reef on the Gulf of California, and one of only three in all of North America. There are eight major reef fingers, varying widely in depth and marine life, including some within easy reach of the shoreline. Cabo Pulmo has three dive shops renting scuba and snorkeling gear, with arrangements made for offshore trips. Sportfishing is excellent as well, outside the boundaries of the national park.

Church at La Ribera

Beyond Cabo Pulmo, the route runs slightly inland for five miles before reaching the village of Los Frailes, named for the nearby promontory that forms the easternmost point of the Baja peninsula. This hamlet has vacation homes, trailers and a hotel. Miles more of scenic coast and desert landscape follow, with numerous campsites tucked between the road and the water's edge. At mileage 40, beyond a wide sandy wash near Rancho Vinorama, is a junction with a graded road leading 24 miles across the coastal hills to Highway 1. Three miles past the junction, a massive wild fig tree sits next to the road. Six miles beyond, the rusting hulk of a large vessel lies just offshore—visible after a short walk down to the water's edge. The coastline here remains mostly undeveloped, but signs of rapid growth abound in new vacation housing tracts with names like "Laguna Hills," "EaSt-CAPE" and "Tortuga Beach." The influence is distinctly non-Mexican, with English-language signs everywhere, and U.S. and Canadian license plates on most vehicles.

Average diving visibility off Cabo Pulmo ranges from 30-45 feet in the winter to 50-80 feet in late spring and summer.

DIVE SHOP DATA

Diving shops at Cabo Pulmo include Pepe's Dive Center, Cabo Pulmo Divers and Pulmo Reef Dive Shop. Pepe's is the only one with a telephone, 01152 (1) 141-00-01. Snorkeling gear costs about $10 a day, while scuba gear runs $45 to $65 per day. Guided tours start at $25.

Several miles farther south, the road swings slightly inland, and heads through densely vegetated terrain before scaling a low ridge that provides your first glimpse of San José del Cabo. Farther west, after crossing a series of dirt roads, the road arrives at the junction of Calle Mijares, the main thoroughfare of San José del Cabo.

Chapter 12

The Desert Northeast

Red rock peaks, palm canyon hideaways, RVs lined up beneath the winter sun along the shimmering Sea of Cortez. Some drive south for days on Highway 1 to find such trappings for which Baja California is famous, yet they all exist within a weekend's drive of gringolandia. So it goes in Baja's northeast flank, a huge and mostly empty quarter with nearly all the scenic wonders and outdoor diversions that you'd look for hundreds of miles farther south.

It starts east of Tecate where the land tilts sharply upward to reach a high inland plateau and the rocky peaks of the Sierra de Juárez. Sealing the desert off from any coastal influence, those highlands create one of the driest regions in North America. The Colorado Desert, on the west shore of the Gulf of California, gets less than 3 inches of rain in an

Heading seaward at dawn, Bahía San Luis Gonzaga

average year. While the highlands are a temperate place, summers are extremely hot on the desert floor, with daytime highs climbing well above 100 degrees.

Yet in the heart of that low, flat desert is the second-largest city in all of Baja: Mexicali, population 800,000. Pressed hard against the U.S. border, Mexicali is overlooked by most gringos, who pass through quickly on their way elsewhere. But Mexicali has done just fine without them, being capital of Baja's northern state, a growing manufacturing center and the hub of a vast farm belt that thrives off the waters of the Colorado River.

While not a major tourist town, Mexicali is still the main gateway to this region, with two major highways bisecting it. Mexico Highway 2 charts an east-west course along the northern frontier, scaling the plateau east of Tecate and making for the Rumorosa Grade, which drops 4000 feet in a dozen spectacular miles to reach the desert floor. From there, Highway 2 continues east across the desert, skirting the north edge of the vast Laguna Salada and the southern flank of Mexicali before crossing the prolific farmland of the Mexicali Valley to the banks of the Colorado.

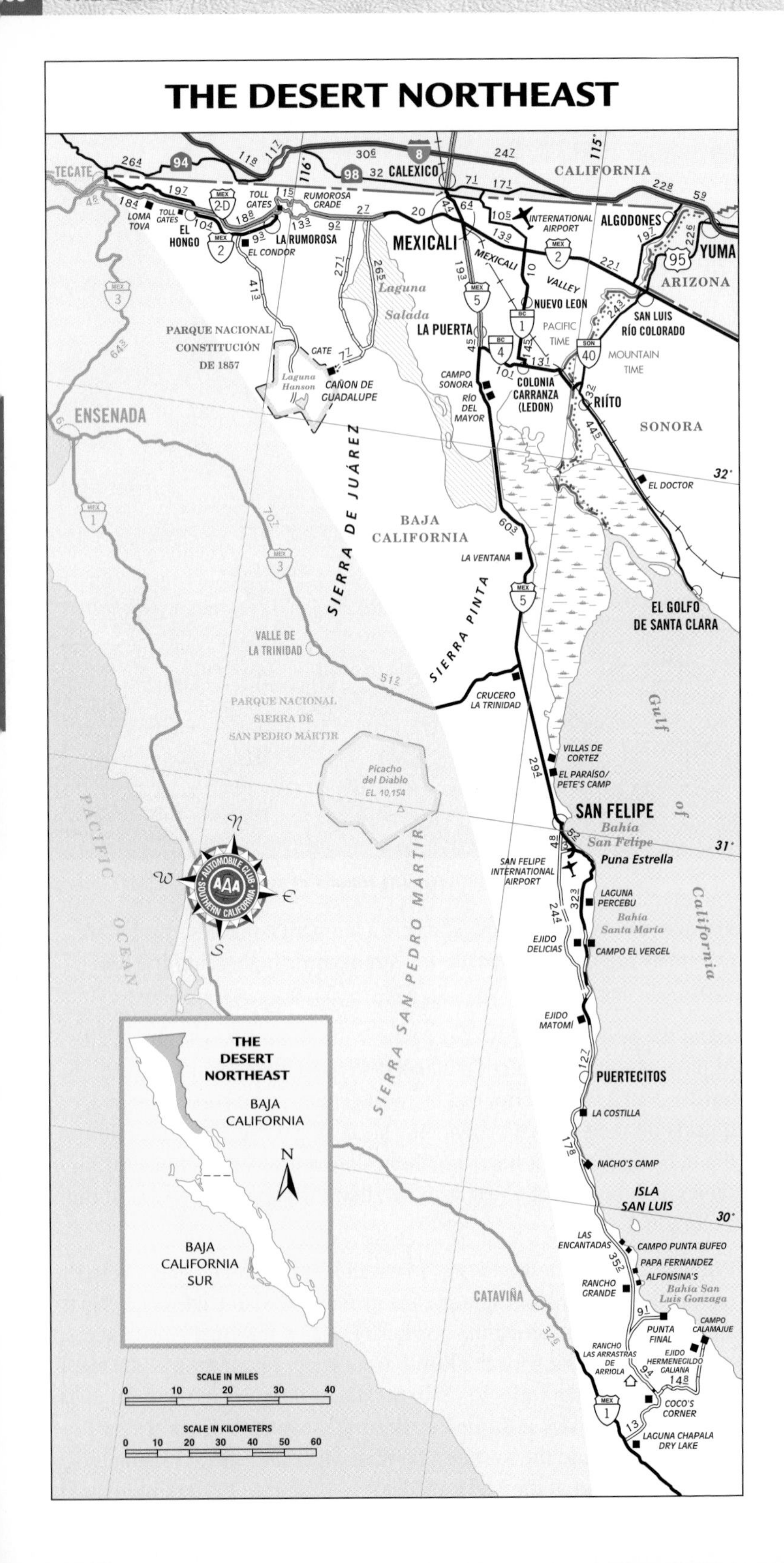
THE DESERT NORTHEAST
TECATE
CALEXICO
CALIFORNIA
ALGODONES
YUMA
ARIZONA
INTERNATIONAL AIRPORT
MEXICALI
MEXICALI VALLEY
NUEVO LEON
SAN LUIS RÍO COLORADO
PACIFIC TIME
MOUNTAIN TIME
LOMA TOVA
TOLL GATES
EL HONGO
RUMOROSA GRADE
LA RUMOROSA
EL CONDOR
Laguna Salada
LA PUERTA
CAMPO SONORA
RÍO DEL MAYOR
COLONIA CARRANZA (LEDON)
RIÍTO
SONORA
EL DOCTOR
PARQUE NACIONAL CONSTITUCIÓN DE 1857
GATE
Laguna Hanson
CAÑON DE GUADALUPE
ENSENADA
SIERRA DE JUÁREZ
BAJA CALIFORNIA
LA VENTANA
SIERRA PINTA
EL GOLFO DE SANTA CLARA
VALLE DE LA TRINIDAD
CRUCERO LA TRINIDAD
PARQUE NACIONAL SIERRA DE SAN PEDRO MÁRTIR
Picacho del Diablo
EL. 10,154
Gulf of California
VILLAS DE CORTEZ
EL PARAÍSO/ PETE'S CAMP
SAN FELIPE
Bahía San Felipe
Puna Estrella
SAN FELIPE INTERNATIONAL AIRPORT
LAGUNA PERCEBU
Bahía Santa María
EJIDO DELICIAS
CAMPO EL VERGEL
EJIDO MATOMÍ
PUERTECITOS
LA COSTILLA
NACHO'S CAMP
ISLA SAN LUIS
PACIFIC OCEAN
SIERRA SAN PEDRO MÁRTIR
AUTOMOBILE CLUB SOUTHERN CALIFORNIA AAA
THE DESERT NORTHEAST
BAJA CALIFORNIA
BAJA CALIFORNIA SUR
LAS ENCANTADAS
CAMPO PUNTA BUFEO
PAPA FERNANDEZ
ALFONSINA'S
Bahía San Luis Gonzaga
RANCHO GRANDE
CATAVIÑA
PUNTA FINAL
CAMPO CALAMAJUE
RANCHO LAS ARRASTRAS DE ARRIOLA
EJIDO HERMENEGILDO GALIANA
COCO'S CORNER
LAGUNA CHAPALA DRY LAKE
SCALE IN MILES
0 10 20 30 40
SCALE IN KILOMETERS
0 10 20 30 40 50 60
32°
31°
30°
115°
116°

Highway 5, meanwhile, heads straight south from the border, passing farmland, salt flats and countless miles of empty desert to reach the seaside town of San Felipe. Near the north edge of the Gulf of California, San Felipe has long been a haven for the snowbird set, and well it should be, with its balmy days and oh-so-blue skies that prevail even in the "dead" of winter. There's quite a fan base with the younger crowd too, evidenced by the throngs of college students and off-roaders who flock this way for spring break and major U.S. holidays.

Until completion of the Transpeninsular Highway in 1973, many residents and travelers got about in this region using centuries-old dirt roads built by the Jesuits.

Beyond San Felipe, Highway 5 heads southward along the gulf past scores of beach camps to the tiny village of Puertecitos. The paved road ends here, but a dirt track continues for another 120 miles across rocky hills, steep canyons, desert scrubland and some of Baja's loveliest shoreline before reaching Mexico Highway 1, deep in the Central Desert.

Taking it easy at Cañon de Guadalupe

Someday this road may be paved, a move that would swing Baja's back door wide open. For years state and federal officials have mulled plans to build an eastern expressway into the heart of the peninsula, saving hours of travel time for thousands of would-be tourists. For good or ill, such a highway would bring more development of all types, leaving an indelible mark on this desert region. For the time being, a short drive beyond the vibrant streets of Mexicali, northeastern Baja remains mostly untamed, with untold back roads, canyons, empty shorelines and other secrets awaiting discovery.

Experience ...

- Daybreak's soft, pink glow spreading gently across the granite crags of the Sierra de Juárez, 3000 feet above your tent flap.
- Easing back in a pool of hot mineral water at Cañón de Guadalupe and feeling a hundred muscles unknot after a six-mile desert hike.
- Craning your neck to look up at a cardón cactus taller than a five-story building in Valle de los Gigantes.
- Munching fish tacos along a sun-splashed sidewalk in San Felipe, across the street from the boat that hauled the fish from the sea that morning.
- Stepping out of your car along some remote desert road to celebrate in the endless blue sky, solitude and vast tracts of empty space.

Mexicali

Universidad de Baja California

Cheek by jowl with the United States but 100 miles from the nearest seacoast or major U.S. city, Mexicali may seem like the least likely border metropolis in Mexico. On second look, it makes perfect sense that Mexicali sprang up on the Colorado Desert and within 100 years grew into a prospering city of 800,000.

The *municipio* of Mexicali extends south to San Felipe and east to the Colorado River.

The first thing to understand is that while Mexicali is on the border, it has never been a border town in the traditional sense. You'll search in vain for the painted burros, reams of craft stalls, raucous beer joints or other icons that pervade Tijuana and so many other towns on Mexico's northern flank. No, Mexicali earns its keep by other means, being capital of the state of Baja California, hub of a vast farming empire, and a major manufacturing center for Mexican and foreign-owned companies.

The result is a booming, vibrant city that ranks among the richest of major urban areas in Mexico. Mexicali exudes its wealth on many levels—from the prim residential neighborhoods near the border to the endless flow of automobiles along calzadas Juárez and López Mateos to the swarms of young people with their disposable pesos patrolling Plaza Cachanilla on weekend afternoons. The biggest single icon of that wealth would be the Centro Cívico-Comercial, a huge urban renewal project along Calzada Independencia that is home to the state capitol. Various city and federal government offices, hotels, hospitals, restaurants, a bullring and other buildings also comprise this sprawling district in the city's heart.

Early on, agriculture built this city, blessed by a year-round growing season and nourished by the nearby waters of the Colorado River. It's no accident that Mexicali was founded in 1903, the year after the completion of the Imperial Canal, which tapped the river waters and opened the region to mass-scale farming. The Colorado River Land Company owned most of the land, and brought in Chinese immigrants to work the new farming region. The Chinese comprised most of Mexicali's early population, and by 1920 they had established La Chinesca, the city's Chinatown, which remains an important part of the downtown border district.

Mexicali residents are nicknamed *cachanillas,* after a plant that thrives in the surrounding desert.

Meanwhile, Mexicali became the capital of the then-territory of Baja California Norte in 1915, an early sign that the city would diversify beyond a farming center. Tourism became a busy trade during U.S. Prohibition in the 1920s and early '30s, when many Americans came south not just to the city's cantinas, but its casinos and bordellos.

Today farming remains a major pillar of the valley's economy, evidenced by the endless patchwork of field crops, orchards and pastureland that thrive on this vast desert plain. Cotton, wheat, citrus fruit, ranching and countless vegetables are the mainstays of the valley, whose bounty reaches market shelves across much of North America. As the 21st century arrived, though, manufacturing had surpassed agriculture to become Mexicali's leading moneymaker. Some of Mexico's largest companies have set up shop here, producing plastics, glass, steel, auto parts, textiles and processed food, among many other things. *Maquiladoras,* those "in-bond" plants owned and operated by multinational firms, have become another dynamo, assembling components into finished consumer products for reshipment to the United States and other countries.

State capitol monument

Travelers know Mexicali as a major crossroads, where Highway 5 heads south toward San Felipe, while Highway 2 runs east-west across the northern edge of Baja. The city also marks the northwest terminus of the nation's railroad system, with service more than 1000 miles southeast to Guadalajara. The bus station provides direct links to mainland Mexico as well, with daily service to Guadalajara, Mexico City and countless cities along the way.

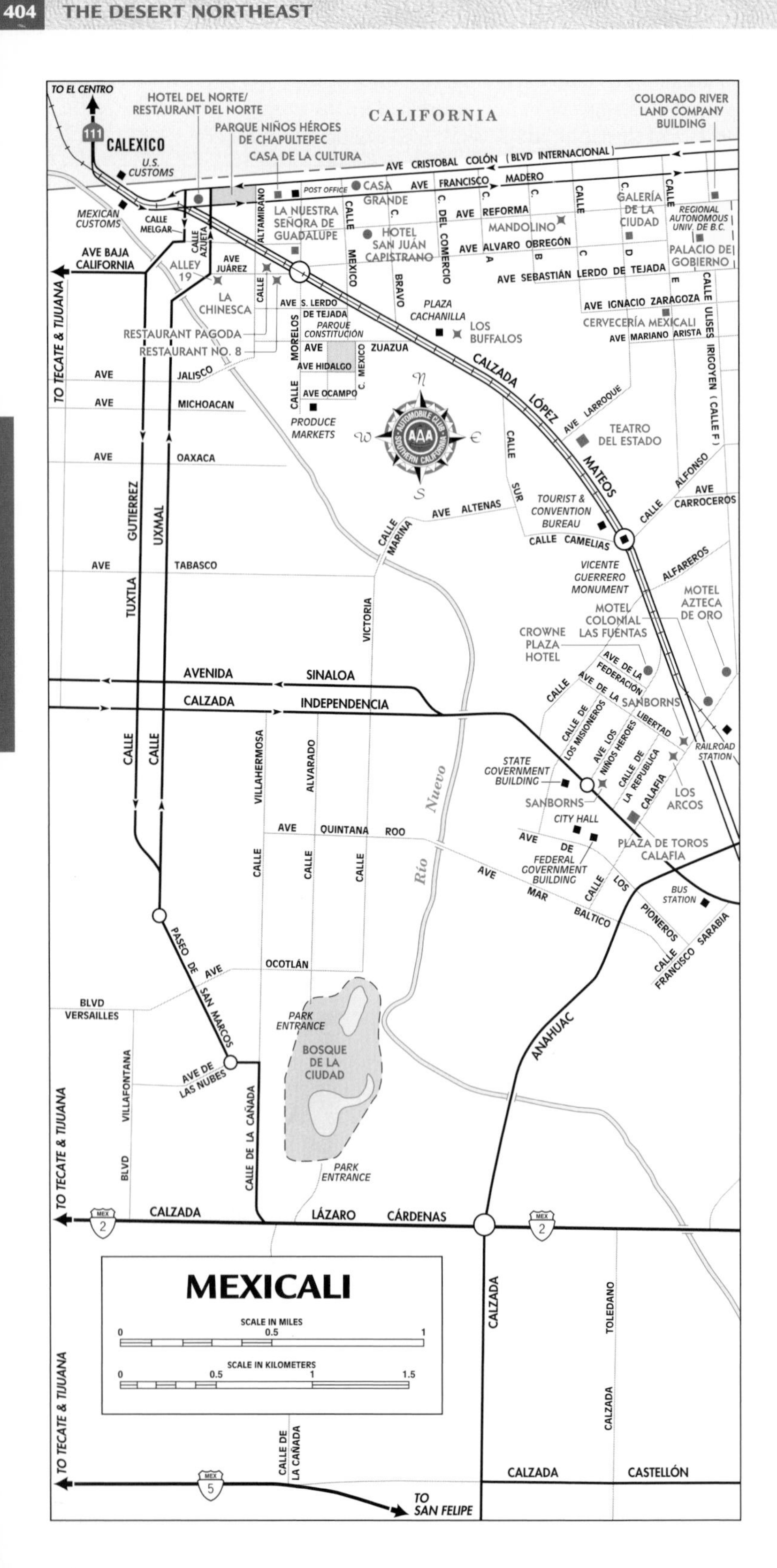
MEXICALI
SCALE IN MILES
0 0.5 1
SCALE IN KILOMETERS
0 0.5 1 1.5
TO EL CENTRO
111
CALEXICO
CALIFORNIA
HOTEL DEL NORTE/ RESTAURANT DEL NORTE
PARQUE NIÑOS HÉROES DE CHAPULTEPEC
CASA DE LA CULTURA
COLORADO RIVER LAND COMPANY BUILDING
U.S. CUSTOMS
MEXICAN CUSTOMS
AVE CRISTOBAL COLÓN (BLVD INTERNACIONAL)
AVE FRANCISCO MADERO
POST OFFICE
CASA GRANDE
LA NUESTRA SEÑORA DE GUADALUPE
HOTEL SAN JUÁN CAPISTRANO
GALERÍA DE LA CIUDAD
REGIONAL AUTONOMOUS UNIV. DE B.C.
PALACIO DE GOBIERNO
MANDOLINO
AVE REFORMA
AVE ALVARO OBREGÓN
AVE SEBASTIÁN LERDO DE TEJADA
AVE IGNACIO ZARAGOZA
CERVECERÍA MEXICALI
AVE MARIANO ARISTA
CALLE MELGAR
CALLE AZUETA
ALTAMIRANO
AVE BAJA CALIFORNIA
ALLEY 19
AVE JUÁREZ
LA CHINESCA
RESTAURANT PAGODA
RESTAURANT NO. 8
AVE S. LERDO DE TEJADA
PARQUE CONSTITUCIÓN
AVE ZUAZUA
AVE HIDALGO
AVE OCAMPO
PRODUCE MARKETS
MORELOS
C. MEXICO
CALLE MEXICO
BRAVO
C. DEL COMERCIO
PLAZA CACHANILLA
LOS BUFFALOS
CALZADA LÓPEZ MATEOS
AVE LARROQUE
TEATRO DEL ESTADO
CALLE ULISES IRIGOYEN (CALLE F)
AVE JALISCO
AVE MICHOACAN
AVE OAXACA
AVE TABASCO
TO TECATE & TIJUANA
TUXTLA GUTIERREZ
UXMAL
CALLE SUR
TOURIST & CONVENTION BUREAU
CALLE CAMELIAS
AVE ALTENAS
CALLE MARINA
CALLE ALFONSO
AVE CARROCEROS
ALFAREROS
VICENTE GUERRERO MONUMENT
MOTEL COLONIAL LAS FUENTAS
MOTEL AZTECA DE ORO
CROWNE PLAZA HOTEL
VICTORIA
AVENIDA SINALOA
CALZADA INDEPENDENCIA
AVE DE LA FEDERACIÓN
AVE DE LA LIBERTAD
SANBORNS
RAILROAD STATION
CALLE DE LOS MISIONEROS
AVE LOS NIÑOS HEROES
CALLE DE LA REPUBLICA
CALAFIA
LOS ARCOS
STATE GOVERNMENT BUILDING
CITY HALL
PLAZA DE TOROS CALAFIA
FEDERAL GOVERNMENT BUILDING
AVE DE LOS PIONEROS
BUS STATION
CALLE FRANCISCO SARABIA
AVE MAR BALTICO
AVE QUINTANA ROO
VILLAHERMOSA
ALVARADO
Río Nuevo
PASEO DE SAN MARCOS
AVE OCOTLÁN
BLVD VERSAILLES
BLVD VILLAFONTANA
AVE DE LAS NUBES
CALLE DE LA CAÑADA
PARK ENTRANCE
BOSQUE DE LA CIUDAD
ANAHUAC
CALZADA LÁZARO CÁRDENAS
MEX 2
CALZADA TOLEDANO
CALZADA CASTELLÓN
MEX 5
TO SAN FELIPE

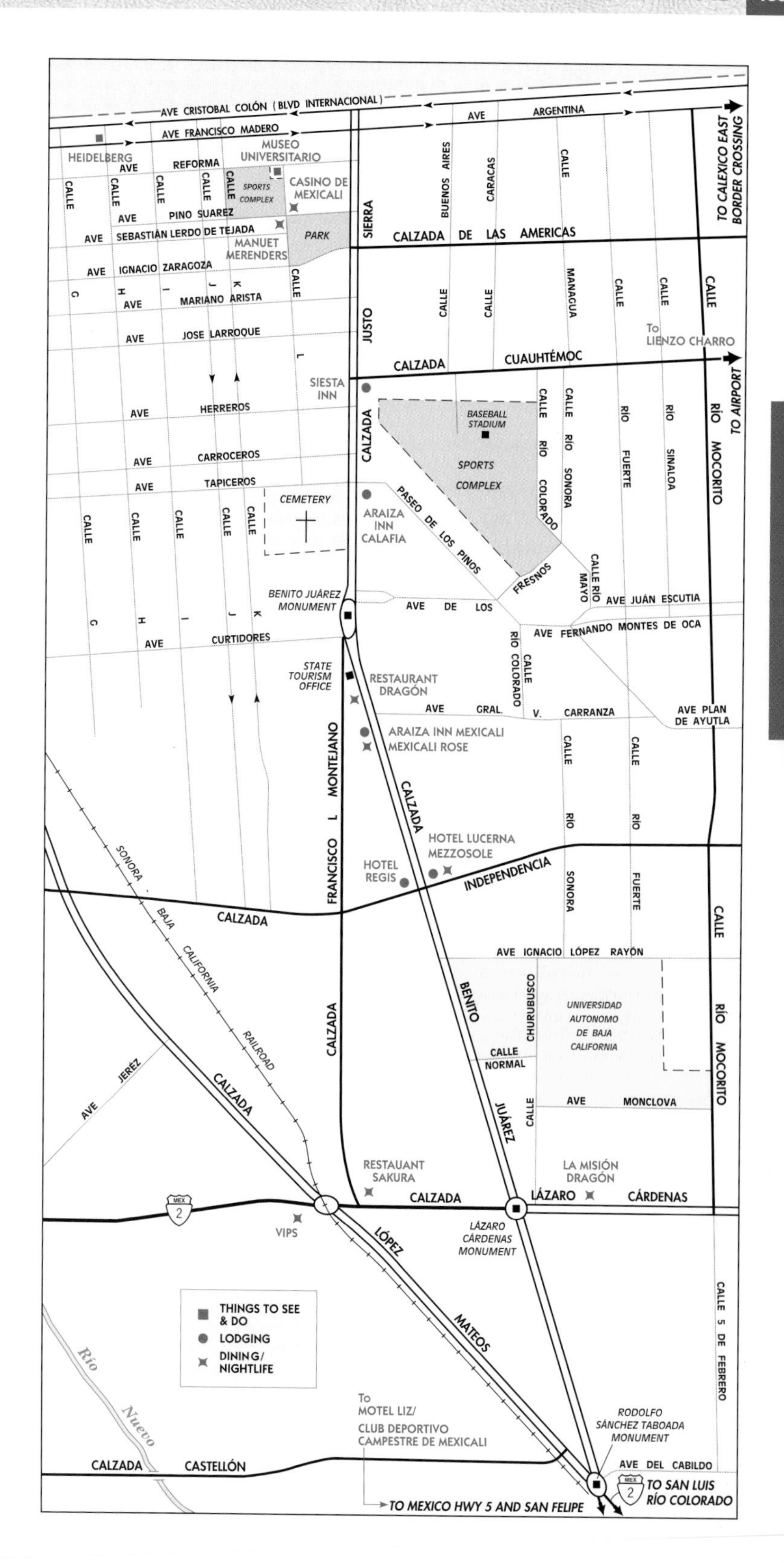
AVE CRISTOBAL COLÓN (BLVD INTERNACIONAL)
AVE FRANCISCO MADERO
AVE ARGENTINA
HEIDELBERG
MUSEO UNIVERSITARIO
AVE REFORMA
SPORTS COMPLEX
CASINO DE MEXICALI
AVE PINO SUAREZ
AVE SEBASTIÁN LERDO DE TEJADA
PARK
MANUET MERENDERS
AVE IGNACIO ZARAGOZA
AVE MARIANO ARISTA
AVE JOSE LARROQUE
CALZADA DE LAS AMERICAS
CALZADA CUAUHTÉMOC
SIERRA
JUSTO
CALZADA
To LIENZO CHARRO
TO CALEXICO EAST BORDER CROSSING
TO AIRPORT
SIESTA INN
BASEBALL STADIUM
SPORTS COMPLEX
AVE HERREROS
AVE CARROCEROS
AVE TAPICEROS
CEMETERY
ARAIZA INN CALAFIA
PASEO DE LOS PINOS
FRESNOS
CALLE RÍO MAYO
AVE JUÁN ESCUTIA
BENITO JUÁREZ MONUMENT
AVE DE LOS
AVE FERNANDO MONTES DE OCA
AVE CURTIDORES
STATE TOURISM OFFICE
RESTAURANT DRAGÓN
AVE GRAL. V. CARRANZA
AVE PLAN DE AYUTLA
ARAIZA INN MEXICALI
MEXICALI ROSE
FRANCISCO L MONTEJANO
HOTEL LUCERNA
MEZZOSOLE
HOTEL REGIS
CALZADA INDEPENDENCIA
SONORA BAJA CALIFORNIA RAILROAD
AVE IGNACIO LÓPEZ RAYÓN
UNIVERSIDAD AUTONOMO DE BAJA CALIFORNIA
CALLE NORMAL
CALLE CHURUBUSCO
AVE MONCLOVA
CALLE RÍO MOCORITO
CALZADA BENITO JUÁREZ
AVE JERÉZ
RESTAUANT SAKURA
LA MISIÓN DRAGÓN
CALZADA LÁZARO CÁRDENAS
MEX 2
VIPS
LÁZARO CÁRDENAS MONUMENT
CALZADA LÓPEZ MATEOS
CALLE 5 DE FEBRERO
THINGS TO SEE & DO
LODGING
DINING/ NIGHTLIFE
Río Nuevo
To MOTEL LIZ/ CLUB DEPORTIVO CAMPESTRE DE MEXICALI
RODOLFO SÁNCHEZ TABOADA MONUMENT
AVE DEL CABILDO
CALZADA CASTELLÓN
TO SAN LUIS RÍO COLORADO
TO MEXICO HWY 5 AND SAN FELIPE

Be all that as it may, most travelers pay little mind to Mexicali itself, passing through quickly on their way to other destinations. There is an image problem, since the city lacks compelling scenery and the weather gravitates to extremes. Summers are extremely hot, with high temperatures that top 100 degrees and sometimes 110 from mid-May into late September. Winters are very comfortable, however, with daytime readings that average in the 60s and nighttime lows that seldom dip to freezing. Rainfall is very light, averaging just 3 inches annually. Aside from

Crossing The Border

Far removed from Southern California's urban areas and not a major tourist town itself, you might think crossing the border in Mexicali would be a snap, but the reality can be far different. Queue up at the main crossing gate on Sunday afternoon, or during the early-morning or late-afternoon rush hours during the week, and you may wait an hour or more as traffic stacks up for many blocks along Avenida Cristobal Colón.

¡Bienvenido a México!

For many years, Mexicali's sole port of entry was in the heart of the downtown border district at the west end of Avenida Cristobal Colón. That changed in 1997 with the opening of Calexico East, a crossing designed primarily for commercial traffic, but open to all types of vehicles. Calexico East has helped relieve some of the wait, although population growth on both sides of the border and growing international trade ensure more cross-border traffic than ever in the future.

Coming from Calexico, the main border crossing lies at the southern end of California State Route 111, the primary north-south highway through California's Imperial Valley. Crossing into downtown Mexicali, you can either turn east onto Avenida Francisco Madero or proceed straight ahead on Calzada López Mateos, which runs southeast and eventually becomes Mexico Highway 5. Heading north, traffic lines up along Avenida Cristobal Colón, which approaches the crossing gate from the east.

Calexico East lies six miles east of downtown, near the eastern end of Avenida Cristobal Colón and just south of California State Route 98. Similar to the Otay Mesa crossing in Tijuana, the average wait is usually somewhat shorter than downtown. Calexico East is open from 6 a.m. to 10 p.m., while the main crossing stays open 24 hours a day.

summer, then, you're apt to find Mexicali an agreeable place. And on closer look you'll discover a city full of surprises and contradictions, with enough attractions to bring the thinking traveler back time and time again.

Getting Around

Assuming you are not traveling beyond Mexicali, there are two basic options for getting about this town. If you're here mainly to shop, visit the old downtown and perhaps get some Chinese food, then park your car in Calexico, pay the lot fee and cross the border on foot. The main shopping district is adjacent to the crossing gate, and La Chinesca (the equivalent to Chinatown) is only a couple of blocks away. If you're venturing farther south, say, to a bullfight, a major shopping mall or one of the "nicer" Chinese restaurants, you can always hire a taxi. Squads of cabbies queue up next to the crossing gate, with fairly fixed rates to major destinations. From the border to Plaza Cachanilla, plan on paying about $4; to the Toreo (bullring) or the major hotels along Calzada Benito Juárez, expect to pay $5 or $6. Pack a full load (four or five people) in a cab and you may pay a dollar or two more.

Public transportation in Mexicali is about as affordable as it gets. You can ride the entire length of a bus route for less than 30 cents.

Now, if you're out to explore the city at length, you're probably better off driving across the border. Beyond a few busy boulevards, driving in Mexicali is not especially daunting. Except for Mexico Highway 2, which skirts the city's southern boundary, Mexicali has nothing resembling a freeway or expressway. For the most part, the city conforms to a conventional grid, interrupted by the Río Nuevo (New River) and a few diagonal boulevards. If you were to name a main drag, it would be Calzada López Mateos, one of those thoroughfares that defies the conventional grid. Angling southeast from the border crossing, López Mateos is the route you will pick up on your way to Mexico Highway 5 and San Felipe. Along the way it passes the huge Plaza Cachanilla shopping center, Teatro del Estado (State Theater), several hotels, and within a block of the bus and railroad stations.

BIG, BAD WEDNESDAY

Wednesday is usually the worst day to cross the border, when Mexicali residents head north by the thousands to Calexico's weekly Las Palmas swap meet. The backups start well before dawn at both crossings and last until midafternoon.

Drive on López Mateos or a few other *calzadas* (Independencia, Benito Juárez, Francisco L. Montejano, Justo Sierra) and you'll have to deal with traffic circles. Known as *glorietas* in Spanish, traffic circles are known to strike fear in the

¡Viva La Musica!

Two of our favorite radio stations in all of Baja California are in Mexicali, spreading good cheer and Latin vibes across both sides of the border. One is 106.7 FM, the self-billed "Fiesta Mexicana," which serves up a zesty mix of Spanish tunes old and new—salsa, rock, *banda*s and more. The other is the oldies-oriented Estereo 89.9 FM, where *ranchera* tunes, *boleros* and other romantic songs of decades past keep tugging at cross-border heartstrings.

hearts of North Americans, but with careful driving and a little practice, you should soon be at ease with them. Like many Mexican cities, traffic lights here are frequently small and stop signs can be easy to miss. With that in mind, "alert" is the key word for driving safely in Mexicali.

Things to See & Do

Truth be told, for most Americans headed this way, Mexicali is little more than a giant speed bump on the long drive south to San Felipe. You might agree at first, seeing how it isn't long on scenic grandeur and lacks the shopping/nightlife scene of most border towns. But in a city full of surprises and contradictions, there are plenty of compelling reasons to stop and take a look around.

You'll realize that within a few steps of the downtown border gate, beginning with the pagoda that fetes the role Chinese immigrants played in this city's development. Not far beyond it lies a well-worn neighborhood known as La Chinesca, the largest Chinatown in Mexico, where Chinese shops and restaurants line the streets with their distinctive green and gold signage. La Chinesca is a stand-in of sorts for any large tourist district. There's nothing here that approaches Tijuana's Avenida Revolución, but there are enough gift shops to send nearly all shoppers back with something to declare to customs.

After you've walked the downtown, a good place to relax and take in the local color is at Parque Niños Héroes de Chapultepec, a tidy park full of large trees, statues and broad walkways that was the city's original main square. If the sun demands an indoor break, take a seat in La Nuestra Señora de Guadalupe, downtown's main church and hard to miss with its graceful bell tower and salmon-hued exterior.

Beyond downtown, there's plenty more to be explored, including stately monuments, museums, historic buildings and other trappings that you would expect to find in a modern state capital. Unless you're a world-class walker, you'll need a taxi or your own wheels to see it all in fairly short order. A good way to start is with a drive east down Avenida Obregón, a pleasant thoroughfare that dead-ends at the Regional Autonomous University of Baja California. The highlight of this attractive campus is the university rectory, a 1920s-era gem that once served as the state capitol building.

The governor could keep a sharp eye on state affairs in those days, since he lived less than two blocks away in a residence that today holds the city's main art museum, Galeria de la Ciudad. An airy, modern complex, Galeria de la Ciudad showcases the works of artists from both sides of the border, and is one of the city's chief cultural centers. Nearby you'll find two more 1920s buildings that have retained their grandeur. One is a Cervecería Mexicali, a one-time brewery that sits vacant but well-maintained two blocks south of the rectory on Avenida Zaragoza. The other is the former Colorado River Land Company headquarters, a Spanish-Colonial masterpiece that sits across the street from the university on Avenida Reforma.

The former state capitol building, now part of the Autonomous University of Baja California

Like Obregón, Reforma runs east-west and has a pleasing air about it as it bisects one of the city's most attractive residential sections. Near its east end is another of the city's standout attractions, the autonomous university-run museum (Museo Universitario). Compact yet comprehensive, the museum lends proper attention to the land and early peoples of northeastern Baja. Rotating exhibits are an added bonus that merit more than one visit to this modern, well-run facility.

Beyond these quiet neighborhoods are the ever-busy boulevards and *calzadas*, where Mexicali's imposing traffic circle monuments pay tribute to the likes of Benito Juárez, Lázaro Cárdenas and other national heroes. You'll find these stately monuments around the university too, but the biggest and best examples are on Calzada López Mateos, Calzada Benito Juárez and other main thoroughfares.

Elsewhere, there's Bosque de la Ciudad, a welcome greenbelt on the city's southern flank and the largest urban park in all of Baja. A zoo, narrow-gauge train and a natural history museum combine to ensure this park's popularity with local families, which means your best bet is to visit on a weekday. Then there's Teatro del Estado, a 1050-seat theater on Calzada López Mateos that hosts plays, dance and music productions from throughout the country.

As for sports and recreation, landlocked Mexicali can't compete with most coastal resorts, but the city has attractions with which few others can compete. One is bullfights at Plaza de Toros Calafia, the 10,000-seat bullring in the Centro Cívico-Comercial. Another is *charreadas* (Mexican rodeos), held at Lienzo Charro de Mexicali. Golfers, meanwhile, enjoy some of the lowest green fees in Baja at the Mexicali Country Club (Club Deportivo Campestre de Mexicali).

Top Attractions

BOSQUE DE LA CIUDAD

The name in Spanish means "Forest of the City," and while it may be a stretch to call this a "forest," Bosque de la Ciudad is the largest city park not only in Mexicali, but in all of Baja California. With a small zoo, natural history museum and picnic area, the park is a magnet for local families, especially on weekends. There's also a miniature train that gives rides around the park's perimeter. *In the southwest part of town; entrances on Blvd Lázaro Cárdenas, and at the corner of Ave Ocotlán (del Fuego) and Calle Alvarado. Open daily 9 am-5 pm. Admission $1; ages 11-16, 75¢; ages 3-10, 50¢; parking $1.10.*

CASA DE LA CULTURA

Built in 1916, this former schoolhouse is today one of the city's main centers of art, hosting exhibits that change on a monthly basis. *01152 (6) 552-96-30. On Ave Madero between calles Altamirano and Morelos. Open Mon-Fri 8 am-8 pm, Sat 9 am-1 pm. Closed Sun and from mid-June till late Aug.*

GALERÍA DE LA CIUDAD

Mexican artists and some of their U.S. counterparts showcase their works inside this small art gallery, operated by the Cultural Institute of Baja California. The gallery moved to its present location, the one-time state governor's residence, following a major remodeling project in 1998. *1209 Ave Alvaro Obregón between calles D and E. 01152 (6) 553-58-74. Open Mon-Fri 9 am-8 pm, Sat 9 am-1 pm, closed Sun. Free.*

HISTORIC BUILDINGS

Colonial Mexico this is not, where baroque cathedrals, stately municipal buildings and sweeping archways surround centuries-old plazas, but Mexicali does have several well-preserved old buildings. The most notable ones are within a few blocks of the border, including the following:

Cervecería Mexicali This one-time brewery opened in 1923 and for decades slaked the thirst of local residents. It's empty now but remains attractive, despite a major fire in 1986. *Corner of Calle E and Ave Zaragoza.*

Colorado River Land Company Building The former headquarters of this company, which played a key role in the development of the Mexicali Valley's vast farm irrigation system, were housed in this attractive Spanish Colonial-style building, completed in 1924. *Ave Reforma at Calle Ulises Irigoyen (Calle F), across from the Autonomous University of Baja California.*

La Nuestra Señora de Guadalupe Built in the 1920s and remodeled in 1957, this single-tower, Colonial-style church is one of the most prominent buildings in the old downtown border district. *Corner of Ave Reforma and Calle Morelos.*

Palacio de Gobierno Completed in 1922, this building was the original state capitol for Baja California before its conversion into the rectory for the Autonomous University of Baja California. *Ave Reforma at Calle Ulises Irigoyen (Calle F).*

Avenida Juárez, near the border in La Chinesca, is not to be confused with the much-larger Calzada Benito Juárez, which runs south toward Mexico Highway 5.

LA CHINESCA

"Chinatown," would be the English translation to describe this section of downtown, the largest Chinese neighborhood in Mexico. La Chinesca is centered around the intersection of Calle Altamirano and Avenida Juárez, a block south of Calzada López Mateos and a short walk from the main border crossing. Gateway to the neighborhood is a handsome pagoda at Plaza de Amistad, just a few steps from the border gate. La Chinesca is well past its prime, achieved in the 1920s and '30s, due in part to the declining number of Mexicali residents who claim pure Chinese ancestry. (Only about 2000 remain.) It still has a good number of interesting shops, Chinese restaurants and buildings that house more than two dozen Chinese family associations.

Chinese pagoda near the entrance to La Chinesca

MUSEO UNIVERSITARIO

One of the finest museums in Baja, this modern, attractive facility fits a great deal of information inside a fairly compact structure. The museum, operated by the Regional Autonomous University of Baja California, features some excellent permanent exhibits on the history, geography, geology and peoples of Baja California. Other display rooms host temporary exhibits that change every three to four months. *Ave Reforma at Calle L. 01152 (6) 552-57-15. Open Mon-Fri 9 am-6 pm, Sat-Sun 10 am-4 pm. Admission 80¢.*

PARQUE NIÑOS HÉROES DE CHAPULTEPEC

The closest thing to a main plaza, or *zócalo*, in Mexicali is this attractive, shaded park, literally across the street from the U.S. border fence. It's a welcome rest stop for those crossing the border on foot and a good place to take in the local scene. *3 blocks east of the border crossing between aves Cristobal Colón and Francisco Madero.*

We saw it at Dorian's department store in Plaza Cachanilla in late 1999—a brand-new Olivetti manual typewriter, on sale for about $105.

SHOPPING

Mexicali has only a fraction of the gift shops, craft stalls and specialty stores you'd find in Tijuana or Ensenada, but there's enough shopping to keep most visitors busy for the better part of an afternoon. The heaviest concentration is in the old downtown directly across from the main border gate, along streets such as Calle Azueta, Calle Melgar, Avenida Cristobal Colón and the northern end of Calzada López Mateos. Jewelry and leather goods are the chief wares, although most of the usual Mexican keepsakes are in evidence. What Mexicali lacks in artisan shops it makes up for with an abundance of *farmácias*, liquor stores, and doctor and dentist's offices—aimed mostly at visiting tourists.

CULTURE SHOCK CASE

A sure sign you've entered Mexico is when you see huarache sandals, fake Nikes and retro-style platform shoes with six-inch heels all sitting in the same footwear display case, a dozen paces from the downtown border crossing.

Valley Girls, Etc.

So where do Mexicans go to shop, take a walk or simply hang out on a blazing hot Saturday afternoon? In Mexicali the place to go is Plaza Cachanilla—far and away the largest North American-style shopping mall in Baja California, with somewhere close to 300 retail outlets. You may not buy anything but you'll still enjoy a walk through this vast, single-floor mall—a testament to the growing middle class along Mexico's prosperous northern frontier. It's hard to miss on your way down Calzada López Mateos, 1.3 miles from the international border.

If by chance you'd like a look at the Mexican version of a sprawling, U.S.-style shopping mall, Mexicali has a couple of whoppers. One is Plaza Cachanilla, on Calzada López Mateos a little more than a mile south of the border. Another is Plaza Fiesta, across from the Centro Cívico on Calzada Independencia.

Teatro del Estado

TEATRO DEL ESTADO

Musicals, plays and dance productions featuring performers from Mexico and abroad pass through this modern, 1050-seat auditorium. There's also a 100-seat hall that hosts local dancers and musicians in a coffee house-style setting. *Calzada López Mateos, 1½ miles south of the U.S. border, just south of Plaza Cachanilla. 01152 (6) 554-64-18.*

TRAFFIC CIRCLE MONUMENTS

Mexican cities have long been known for their imposing traffic circle *(glorieta)* monuments saluting national heroes, and Mexicali is no exception. Some of the local examples are especially impressive, located where some of the city's main thoroughfares intersect. A few of the biggest are **Benito Juárez** (intersection of Calzada Benito Juárez, Calzada Francisco L. Montejano and Calzada Justo Sierra), **Lázaro Cárdenas** (Blvd. Lázaro Cárdenas at Calzada Benito Juárez), **Rodolfo Sánchez Taboada** (Calzada López Mateos at Calzada Benito Juárez) and **Vicente Guerrero** (Calzada López Mateos at Calle de la Compresora). Several smaller but still handsome monuments are to be found in the neighborhood near the Autonomous University of Baja California, along Avenida Alvaro Obregón, Avenida Reforma and Avenida Tejada.

Outdoor Fun

GOLF

Northeastern Baja's only golf course is at the Mexicali Country Club (Club Deportivo Campestre de Mexicali), which welcomes golfers from across the border and is one of the most affordable courses in Baja. If you don't mind the summer heat, greens fees from June through September are just $20.

Club Deportivo Campestre de Mexicali (Semi-private) 18 holes; 6516 yards; par 72; 133 slope, 71.0 rating. Rates: $20-40. *On Hwy 5 at kilometer 2.5, 5 miles south of downtown. 01152 (6) 563-61-70.*

Spectator Sports

BULLFIGHTING

Toros face their human foes beneath the desert sun all but two months of the year in Mexicali, where the season runs from March through December at the 10,000-seat Plaza de Toros Calafia. Bullfights are strictly a Sunday afternoon event, and take place every second or third weekend throughout the season. Tickets cost between $12.50 and $25, with seats on the shaded side of the ring fetching the highest prices.

For more information on bullfighting or *charreadas* in Mexicali, or a schedule of upcoming events, call the Mexicali Tourist and Convention Bureau at (877) 700-2092 or 01152 (6) 566-11-16.

Plaza de Toros Calafia *In the Centro Cívico-Comercial, corner of Calzada Independencia and Calle Calafia. 01152 (6) 557-14-17.*

CHARREADAS

Mexican *charros,* or rodeo performers, display their ranching and equestrian skills on an occasional basis in *charreadas,* at Lienzo Charro, located in the eastern part of the city. *Charreadas* take place about once a month between September and April, usually on Sundays or major Mexican holidays.

Lienzo Charro *4 miles east of Calzada Justo Sierra on Carretera a Compuertas (the highway to the airport). 01152 (6) 565-00-20.*

Dining

If you and your crew have arrived in Mexicali on empty stomachs, you have a problem—how on earth to choose from among the tremendous assortment of restaurants. You would expect a booming city of 800,000 to have many good restaurants, but even then, the selection in Mexicali is truly astounding. The variety goes far beyond all Baja conventions and has few rivals in the entire peninsula.

Chinese restaurant, Mexicali-style

For the uninitiated, the first surprise is sure to be the many Chinese restaurants. The city boasts more than 100 in all, ranging from weary back street diners to palatial dinner houses that seat hundreds and fill their parking lots with license tags from both sides of the border. They are a natural outgrowth of the city's earliest days, when Chinese laborers were recruited to farm the Valle de Mexicali, and brought their culinary traditions with them. Most of the restaurants are Cantonese style, which reflects the origin of the early immigrants, but the cuisine has evolved a bit to satisfy local palates. For instance, it's standard practice to see a bowl of sliced limes at your table, and just a few drops of their juice can transform the character of many entrees.

Mexican restaurants also run the gamut, from walk-up taco stands and plain-Jane diners on up to highbrow dining rooms where government and business leaders convene. Steaks are a staple at many of the better restaurants, which take extra pride in their broiler selections. (Northern Mexico has a well-earned reputation for serving the best steaks in the country.)

A drive around town will present many more possibilities, as you discover that Mexicali is a place for German, Japanese and Italian dining, or lingering over breakfast in one of several U.S.-style coffee shops. Finally, we'd be remiss not to point out that Mexicali has one of Baja's widest selections of *comida rapida*, or fast food. Burger King, McDonald's, KFC, Dunkin' Donuts and other U.S. icons have set up shop here, mainly on the major boulevards away from the border district, and do steady business around the clock, especially with the younger set.

Favorites

ALLEY 19 **Chinese**

Not the biggest or fanciest place in town, but this homey diner takes honors as the oldest Chinese restaurant in Mexicali, with the same family and location since 1928. In the heart of La Chinesca, this spot pulls in regulars both from Mexicali and the Imperial Valley for its generous, sensibly priced entrees. *On Ave Juárez, just east of Calle Azueta. 01152 (6) 552-95-20. Open daily 11 am-9 pm. $3.80-7.75.*

CASINO DE MEXICALI **International**

Pass through the doors in the brick-stone exterior, then gaze around at the white linen tablecloths, sprigs of greens and designer lighting, and it's hard to believe you aren't somewhere on Melrose. A local favorite for special occasions, this may be the most all-around, stylish restaurant in town, with a menu destined to please the hardest-to-please groups. Burgers, burritos, gourmet tacos, steaks and poultry are all available, and at fair-minded prices that belie the classy surroundings. *Corner of Calle L and Pino Suarez. (6) 552-58-93. Open daily; Mon-Sat 7 am-11 pm, Sun 7 am-7 pm. $6-12.*

HEIDELBERG **German**

German food in Baja? Just another reminder that you're in a multifaceted city where not everything is as we expect it. The Mexican staff works hard to please with its renditions of typical German cuisine, with a few local dishes thrown in. Steaks, poultry and lamb dishes highlight the lineup, served in a Bavarian village atmosphere. *Corner of Ave Madero and Calle H. 01152 (6) 554-20-22. Open Mon-Sat noon-11 pm; bar open till 1 am. $10-16.*

LA MISIÓN DRAGÓN — Chinese

Famous for its elaborate architecture and beautifully landscaped grounds, this is without a doubt the grandest of Chinese restaurants, inside and out, in Mexicali. You'll feel like you're entering the emperor's palace as you cross the grounds with their bridges and waterfalls, while wood-paneled walls and a huge dragon mural greet you inside. The cuisine measures up to the elaborate decor. Try the Dragon Plaza-style duck or hot peppers filled with shrimp, along with the superlative egg rolls. *Blvd Lázaro Cárdenas 555, 1 block east of Cárdenas monument and Calzada Benito Juárez. 01152 (6) 566-44-00. Open daily 11 am-midnight. $14-22.*

> **LOOK THE PART**
>
> Mexicali enjoys a more sophisticated atmosphere than almost anywhere else in Baja, so let your attire reflect that when dining in one of the nicer restaurants. Coat and tie aren't necessary, but it's amazing how service improves when you give the T-shirt, tennies and shorts the night off.

LOS ARCOS — ♦♦ Seafood

Mexicali is not a big seafood town, but if the craving strikes, it's hard to go wrong at this festive, colorfully decorated establishment. Never mind that you're a couple of hours from the nearest seashore, Los Arcos surely has one of the most exhaustive seafood menus in all of Baja. It's part of a small northern Baja chain with two more branches in Tijuana. *Calle Calafia at Ave de la Libertad, near Plaza de Toros. 01152 (6) 556-09-03. Open daily 11 am-10 pm (Thu-Sat to 11 pm). $6-20.*

MANDOLINO — Italian

Scaloppine beef, *flete* fish, and a big assortment of pizza and pastas highlight the choices at one of the most popular Italian restaurants in Baja. Service is friendly and the decor is typically Italian. The upstairs piano bar merits a visit as well, whether or not you're planning on dinner. *Ave Reforma between calles B and C. 01152 (6) 552-95-44. Open daily 11 am-11 pm. $6-12.*

MEZZOSOLE — ♦♦♦ Italian

Soft lighting and lavish murals on the ceiling and walls in an intimate dining room help lend a cosmopolitan atmosphere worthy of Baja's state capital. Favored by travelers and locals alike, this restaurant is located in one of Mexicali's most upscale hotels. The seafood linguini and Gorgonzola steak are two of our top picks from the extensive continental menu. *In the Hotel Lucerna, corner of Calzada*

Benito Juárez and Calzada Independencia. 01152 (6) 564-70-00 ext 620. Open daily noon-midnight. $7-14.

RESTAURANT DEL NORTE **Mexican**

It's a few steps to the U.S. Customs offices, but the feeling is closer to downtown Guadalajara in this popular diner, a local fixture since 1950. *Carne asada, tortas, chiles rellenos* and other Mexican favorites are served in a basic but friendly atmosphere, at very affordable prices. This is a hard place to miss, on the ground floor of the art-deco hotel by the same name. *In the Hotel del Norte, next to the downtown border crossing. 01152 (6) 552-81-01, ext 42. Open daily 7 am-10 pm. $1.90-7.50.*

Others

CAFETERÍA CALAFIA **Steak/Mexican**

$4.50-13. *In the Araiza Inn, Calzada Juárez, just south of Ave Curtidores and the Benito Juárez monument. 01152 (6) 564-11-00 ext 728.*

LOS BUFFALOS **Steak/Seafood**

$5.50-13. *In Plaza Cachanilla between the Ley supermarket and Cappel department store. 01152 (6) 552-22-85.*

MANUET MERENDERS **Mexican**

$2-8. *Calle L between Ave Tejada and Pino Suarez (across from Casino de Mexicali). 01152 (6) 552-56-94.*

RESTAURANT DRAGÓN **Chinese**

$4-10.20. *Calzada Benito Juárez, just south of the Benito Juárez monument. 01152 (6) 566-20-20 or 566-39-55.*

RESTAURANT NO. 8 **Chinese/Mexican**

$3.80-6. *In La Chinesca, Ave Juárez just west of Calzada López Mateos. 01152 (6) 552-54-35.*

RESTAURANT PAGODA **Chinese/Mexican**

$3-8. *In La Chinesca, Ave Juárez just west of Calzada López Mateos (across from Restaurant No 8). 01152 (6) 552-21-75.*

RESTAURANT SAKURA **Japanese**

$5-20. *Corner of Blvd Lázaro Cárdenas and Calzada Montejano. 01152 (6) 566-48-48.*

SANBORNS **Varied Menu**

$3-10. *Next to Centro Cívico: Corner of Calzada Independencia and Ave Niños Héroes. 01152 (6) 557-04-11. Near railroad station: Corner of Calzada López Mateos and Calafia. 01152 (6) 557-02-12.*

VIPS **Coffee Shop**

$4.50-8.50. *Corner of Blvd Lázaro Cárdenas and Mexico Hwy 5, next to Wal-Mart. No phone.*

Lodging

Because it is not a resort town and sits right across from California, you might never consider spending a night (or longer) in Mexicali. Then again, why not? For anyone with the initiative and interest to explore this city, Mexicali has a large number of hotels in all levels of price and comfort.

For information on lodging in nearby Calexico, see the *AAA Southern California-Las Vegas TourBook.*

The city's nicest properties lie some distance from the border, along calzadas Juárez, Justo Sierra and López Mateos. At the other end of the price scale are several worn hotels in and around La Chinesca, a few of which double as dens of questionable moral activity and are hard to recommend at any price. In between, Mexicali has a several comfortable hotels in the low- to mid-priced range. Because it's not a tourist destination, Mexicali generally has lower hotel rates than other northern Baja cities. A few AAA-approved hotels charge $100 or more a night, but most others run less than $50.

Mexico Highway 5

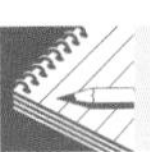

TRAVELOGUE

Mexicali to San Felipe

(124 mi., 198 km.; 2.30 hrs.)

This journey across Baja's northern desert serves up a kaleidoscope of contrasts—barren wasteland, rich farming districts, mountains, sea, dry lakebeds and more—all within a 2½-hour drive. Even so, most *nortemericanos* pass through quickly en route to San Felipe.

Heading north across the border you must approach the crossing along Avenida Cristóbal Colón, a one-way westbound street that follows the border fence.

The outset is a contrast in itself as you drive through Mexicali. From the border, the most direct way to reach Highway 5 is via Calzada López Mateos, one of the city's main north-south thoroughfares. Leaving the Mexican port of entry, turn right and follow this broad boulevard southeast to the traffic circle where it meets Highway 5.

Highway 5 takes some time to clear the urban sprawl of Mexicali, beyond which it leads south through some 30 miles of farmland as it skirts the western edge of one of Mexico's most productive agricultural regions. Looking east you can also see steam plumes rising from the Cerro Prieto geothermal electric plant, which exports some of its power to the United States.

Beyond the fields and pastureland, the route continues south through miles of barren desert, with the rugged peaks of the Sierra de Juárez rising to the west. Some 45 miles below the border, the highway sets out atop an 11-mile-long levee crossing the southernmost portion of the vast intermittent lake known as Laguna Salada. If you don't find the lake empty and cracked across the bottom, then it will be muddy or filled with shallow water, depending upon the season and the amount of rainfall that year.

The sun-baked lakebed of Laguna Salada

Leaving the levee behind, Highway 5 passes through the volcanic basalt hills of the Sierra Pinta, another unusual sight with their dark, otherworldly appearance that jumps out surreally from the surrounding desert. Nearing the junction with Mexico Highway 3, the view west is of the Sierra San Pedro Mártir, crowned by 10,154-foot Picacho del Diablo, Baja's highest peak. And as San Felipe draws near, the Gulf of California appears to the east as the road bends to follow the shoreline. A pair of white arches signal your arrival to this seaside town.

00.0 **Mexicali (U.S. border crossing).**

01.2 **Entrance to Plaza Cachanilla, Mexicali's largest shopping center.**

02.7 **Junction with Calzada Independencia.**

03.9 **Junction with Calzada Lázaro Cárdenas.**

05.0 **Traffic circle at Sánchez Taboada Monument. Bear right, then take the right fork, which heads south.**

05.7 **Junction with Mexico Highway 2 west to Tecate and Tijuana (see Travelogue for Mexico Highway 2, page 149).**

07.7 **A paved road branches west to Club Deportivo Campestre de Mexicali, which has a golf course and other sports facilities.**

25.0	La Puerta, a roadside farming center with a Pemex station, cafe and store. A paved road here leads east to the farming communities of Zakamoto and Ejido Nayarít.
29.5	Junction with highway BCN 4, a paved route that crosses the Mexicali Valley to Coahuila (Colonia Nuevas) and continues to El Golfo de Santa Clara on the Sonora side of the gulf (see Side Route to El Golfo de Santa Clara). Highway 5 narrows from four lanes to two lanes at this point.
37.7	Campo Sonora, the first of several rustic trailer camps along Río Hardy.
40.6	Río del Mayor, a village with an Indian museum. Located by the police station, it is called Museo Comunitario, Centro Cultural Cucapá.
48.8	At this point, the highway, elevated by a levee, sets out across the southern end of Laguna Salada.
70.9	La Ventana, which has a Pemex station and café.
92.9	El Chinero, also known as Crucero la Trinidad, the junction with Mexico Highway 3, which leads westward to Valle de Trinidad and Ensenada (see Travelogue for Mexico Highway 3 South, page 168). About 0.7 mile south of the junction is a Pemex station and a cafe.
111.8	A dirt road branches left to Villas de Cortez, the first of a string of trailer camps on the gulf shore north of San Felipe. Facilities in these camps range widely in terms of facilities.
115.7	A graded one-mile road to El Paraíso/ Pete's Camp, a long-established, popular camp with tent and RV spaces, showers, a disposal station and a restaurant-bar.
123.8	San Felipe, at the junction of Mexico Highway 5 and Avenida Mar de Cortez. Less than a mile north of here are the twin arches marking the entrance to the town.

Side Routes

San Felipe

Looking north from Virgin of Guadalupe Shrine, San Felipe

Call this Baja's backdoor to the Sea of Cortez, a sun-baked desert town that spreads along the shimmering waters of the gulf near their northernmost reach. It's a town where wildflowers bloom in January, the tide may rise or fall 20 feet within a few hours, and Baja's highest mountain peaks guard the western flank in rugged splendor. And it's a town where twin white arches rise above a wide traffic circle to greet weary travelers who just drove 2000 miles from someplace in the Frozen North.

It's not hard to see why San Felipe has been a resort town for so long, luring Americans south in large numbers since the early postwar years, and why the first paved road reached here from the U.S. in 1951. Year-round sun, a stunning backdrop and the waters of the gulf were and still are big attractions, and while the once-superb fishing has declined, the town has become a haven for the off-road vehicle set. As a result, San Felipe has grown from around 1000 souls in 1950 to 20,000 today.

ONLY IN SAN FELIPE ...

... can the sight of a little old lady rumbling down the street on an all-terrain cycle not evoke any second looks or smart-aleck remarks.

The town's population may swell by another 5000 during the second half of March, when U.S. college kids arrive for spring break, jamming hotels, trailer parks and even beach camps to capacity. The same thing happens during U.S. holiday weekends, when the off-road crowd arrives in force. Either group brings all the antics

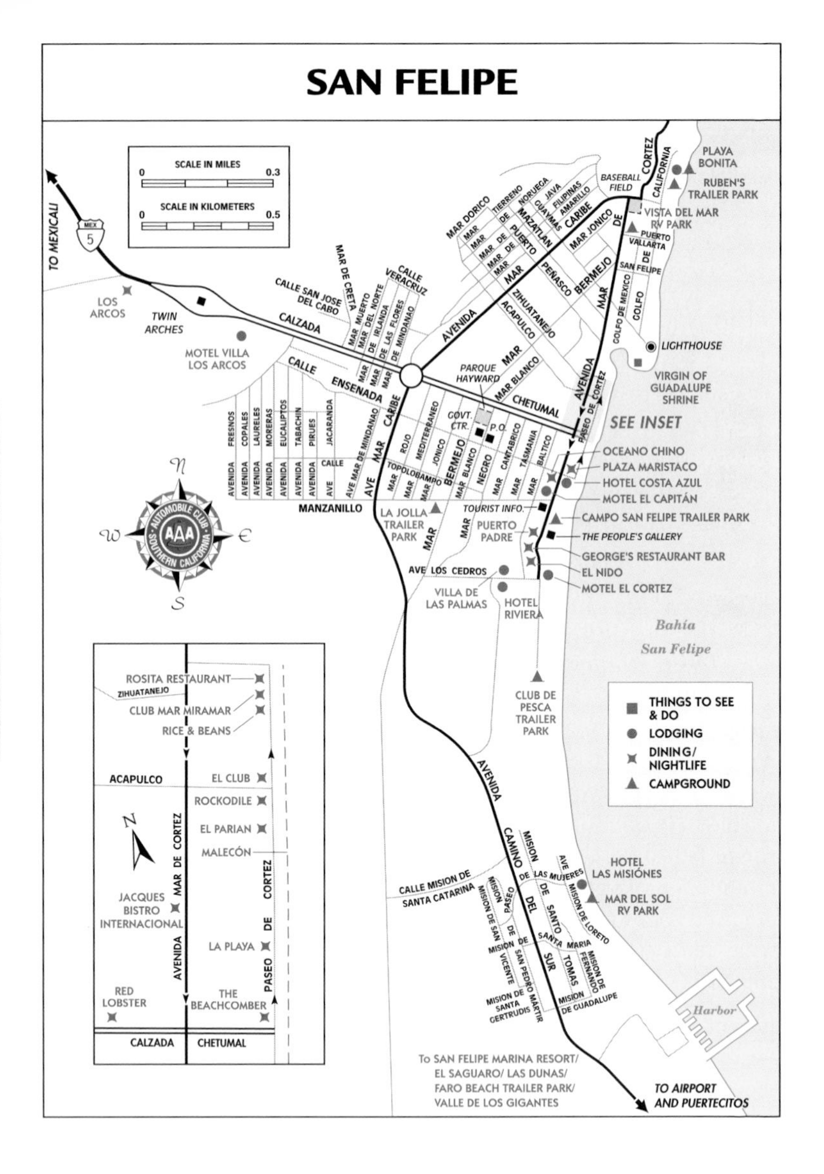

associated with dirt bikes, parties and a free flow of alcohol, while leaving a trail of litter in their wake. A few off-road races and other events also bring the crowds, but apart from those times, this town is a fairly quiet place.

Say what you will about their mindset, the young and rowdy produce a windfall for the local economy. They've created a booming rental business for ATVs, personal watercraft and other mechanized toys, while pouring greenbacks into local hotels, restaurants and clubs.

Then there are the snowbirds, a more subdued breed comprised mostly of U.S. and Canadian retirees who ride out part or all of the winter here. Many head south in campers, motor homes or trailers and settle in the locale's many RV parks, returning north when the days heat up. The snowbirds also mean quite a boon to local coffers, and the town salutes them with the Welcome Snowbirds Fiesta at the start of winter, with mariachis, folkloric dancers, gifts from local shops and more.

Winter's appeal is obvious to anyone who has been here during those months, when San Felipe basks in near-perfect weather, with shirtsleeve days, cool nights and weeks on end of sunshine. (Averaging less than three inches of rainfall per year, San Felipe is one of the driest towns in Baja.) What rain does fall here comes mainly during late summer, when occasional *chubascos*, or tropical storms, sneak up the gulf and strike with short but violent downpours. Otherwise, summers aren't quite as hot as up the road in Mexicali, but the discomfort may be worse, thanks to the stifling humidity wrought by the gulf.

Even so, summer is a happening time in San Felipe, and the town invariably fills up over 4th of July and Labor Day weekend. So far, though, the town has drawn peso-wise tourists for the most part, and you'll find no fairways, yacht basins or luxury hotels. That may change before too long, as state tourism officials keep talking up San Felipe as the next big thing—the Los Cabos of the north, with all the trappings of a world-class resort. For now, the town remains within reach of the average tourist.

Getting Around

It's a long boat ride from San Diego around Cabo San Lucas to San Felipe, and the town no longer has scheduled air service from the U.S., which means you'll almost surely be driving here. Well yes, there is bus service from Tijuana, Mexicali and Ensenada, but in a town that's all about motorized marauding, the real question is how much you'll need to drive.

Twin arches mark your arrival in San Felipe

If you're sticking near the *malecón* and nearby shopping strip, your best bet is to park and walk. Otherwise you'll need some sort of wheels, since San Felipe is fairly spread out, with many hotels and campgrounds quite a ways from the city center. Some people do this in their off-road cycles, but unless you brought your

ATTITUDE IS EVERYTHING

If by chance you need a lift to the airport, how much you pay will depend greatly on your demeanor, as one cabby explained to us: "If it's an American with an attitude, $18, if it's a friendly American, $15."

own, prepare to pay $100 or more per day to rent one.

Aside from Highway 5, the only paved road out of town runs south along the shoreline, where rebuilding continues following a 1997 storm that left a trail of gaping potholes, washed-out dips and other damage south of Punta Estrella. Once complete, an all-new road will extend 52 miles to Puertecitos.

Things to See & Do

Well-worn or not, the phrase "fun in the sun" aptly describes the mindset of San Felipe and the droves who head here for holiday and vacation breaks. At least that goes for the thousands of spring-breakers and off-road fiends who look for good times in this, the closest town on the gulf to the U.S. border.

It was fishing that first made a name for San Felipe, back in the early post-World War II years, when the paved road arrived and the waters of the upper gulf ranked with the most productive in all of Baja. Those days are history, thanks to over-fishing and other factors, but a good-sized *panga* fleet still offers day outings to nearby waters. The better action, though, lies well to the south, where several larger boats head for multi-day excursions.

Shredding the dunes in San Felipe

The decline of fishing has been mirrored by the rise of off-road motor sports, which have come to symbolize the modern-day San Felipe. Every U.S. holiday weekend brings a long line of pickups, campers and SUVs parading down Highway 5, dirt bikes and all-terrain vehicles in tow. Those who don't have their own off-road toy need not fret, since San Felipe teems with rental ATVs, lined in neat rows and primed for boisterous days of sand-shredding and back-country marauding.

By and large, though, the proliferation of ATVs has not marred the intrinsic beauty of the desert. Perhaps the best place to appreciate that is at Valle de los Gigantes ("Valley of the Giants") an undeveloped park south of town where huge cardón cacti tower above the desert floor. Even four-wheel-drive trucks are known to have sunk in the soft sand of this valley—not such a bad thing if it keeps the crowds at bay.

KEEPING UP WITH THE GOMEZES

San Felipe has two monthly newsletters with the latest news about the town and local North American community. One is the *San Felipe Newsletter*; the other is the *Gringo Gazette*. A good source of general information is the *Baja Sun*.

You need not leave town, though, to enjoy a good look at the grandeur of this region. Climb the stairway to the Virgin of Guadalupe Shrine, where the city, bay and desert spread out beautifully beneath the eternal sun. The shrine is just a short walk north of the *malecón*, San Felipe's front doorstep to the sea. Like so many Baja towns, the *malecón* is the best place to take a seaside stroll or watch the world go by. It has a nice beach, too, although at high tide it shrinks to only a few yards in width, and seldom seems to get many visitors.

A block west of the *malecón* is Avenida Mar de Cortez, the town's main shopping drag and a place with the feel of a single huge bazaar. A plethora of vendors sell their wares along this multi-block strip, with all the gewgaws that make Baja tourist towns what they are. Truth be told, you may find an overabundance of goods that are lowbrow in taste and quality, including a truly astounding assortment of tawdry-messaged T-shirts. Still, even the most sophisticated travelers should have few problems finding an appropriate keepsake.

Top Attractions

MALECÓN By Baja standards at least, San Felipe's seafront promenade is not the most tranquil or romantic, but it is a good place to walk about, eat a fish taco or just relax and observe the endless parade of humanity. For first-timers here, the three-block walkway is a great place to observe first-hand the enormous tidal changes of the upper gulf. At high tide the waves lap within a few feet of the seawall; at low tide it's a quarter-mile's walk or more reach the water's edge. *Along Paseo de Cortéz.*

SHOPPING Baja tourist towns are defined by their endless assortment of curios, and San Felipe is no exception. In this case the center of it all is Avenida Mar de Cortez, with three blocks of air-conditioned shops, sidewalk stands and open-air stalls selling every manner of clothing, arts and handcrafts. Ceramics, blown glass, jewelry, beachwear, blankets and other Baja standards can be found along this stretch, with more on Calzada Chetumal and the nearby *malecón.*

A TOUCH OF CLASS

Some of San Felipe's classiest keepsakes are sold at The People's Gallery, owned by a U.S. couple, in Plaza Caliente on Avenida Mar de Cortez. A wonderfully eclectic assortment of arts and crafts produced by talented local artists defies nearly all Baja conventions.

VALLE DE LOS GIGANTES The name in English translates to "Valley of the Giants," and it's apparent why when you come upon this stand of towering cardón cacti. Some are up to 50 feet tall and more than 100 years old, thriving amid a sublime desert setting. A cardón plucked from this park was transported to Seville, Spain, for Mexico's national exhibit at the 1992 World's Fair. A roadway sign points to the valley, which is open during daylight hours. A resident attendant controls access. A sandy access road demands careful driving for all types of vehicles to avoid getting stuck. *13½ miles south of town center, then about 2 miles southwest on a sandy road. Donation.*

VIRGIN OF GUADALUPE SHRINE Your best in-town view of San Felipe, the gulf, and surrounding mountains and desert is afforded from this shrine to Mexico's most revered holy image. Just north of this hilltop lookout is a lighthouse and massive headland known as Punta San Felipe, elevation 940 feet. Together they make one of this town's most popular photo subjects. *Atop a concrete stairway, north of the* malecón *and just east of Ave Mar de Cortez.*

Outdoor Fun

FISHING

Fishing was San Felipe's original marquee attraction, and was perhaps the biggest factor in bringing the first paved road south from the U.S. border. In decades past, Bahía San Felipe teemed with prolific schools of fish, including the famed totoaba, a burly game fish that topped 200 pounds in size and helped put this town on the map. Those days are long gone now due to several factors, including shrimp boats that destroyed nearby spawning beds and gill-netting boats that over-fished the remaining

Pangas ***on the beach in front of the*** **malecón**

stocks. The damming of the Colorado River played a role too, all but choking off the flow of fresh-water nutrients into the gulf.

CASTING FROM SHORE

"Surf fishing" is a misnomer of sorts in these calm upper gulf waters, but the bass and corvina action is decent in places along the miles of sandy beaches stretching south of town.

Even so, the seas off San Felipe still provide some action, and a pair of artificial reefs built in 1992 have become magnets for more and larger fish. Seabass, corvina and croaker are the main catch, as they were in the town's early days, though today's fish are fewer and far smaller than their ancestors. After being reduced to near-extinction by the 1980s, the totoabas have staged a modest comeback, but it remains illegal to catch and keep them. The local fishing season extends year round, and a few larger game fish make it this far north during the summer.

Unless you bring your own boat, the way to fish the local bay is by renting a *panga*—the tried and true motor launch of Baja fishing fleets. Most stay within 10 miles of the coast, although some head for Consag Rock, 18 miles offshore and a good spot for croaker and seabass. *Panga* rates average $40 per person, with a minimum of two people for a daylong guided trip. The best place to hire a panga is at the north end of the *malecón*.

Beyond the local bay, a number of charter boats head farther south to the more productive waters around Bahía San Luis Gonzaga and the Midriff region off Bahía de los Angeles. Most charter outings last a minimum of three days, operating out of the marina south of town: **Enchanted Island Excursions** *Phone 01152 (6) 560-95-84 or 550-42-02.* **Tony Reyes Fishing Tours** *Phone (714) 538-9300 or (714) 538-8010.*

MOTOR SPORTS

WHEEL AND DEAL

Rental rates for ATCs are sometimes subject to negotiation, and you may get a price break if you come early or business is slow. Dress the wrong way or bring the wrong attitude and you may pay more ... if you get to rent at all.

For many people the essence of the San Felipe experience is hot-rodding through the desert on a four-wheel, all-terrain cycle with a trail of flying sand and smoke in their wake. In fact, a whole stable of assorted vehicles ply the desert around San Felipe—dirt bikes, dune buggies, assorted trucks and the venerable Baja Bugs. But if you don't have your own set of wheels, it's a good bet you'll be heading forth in one of those all-terrain cycles (ATCs).

Riding on the beach is strictly forbidden for all motorized vehicles.

The best way to rent an ATC is by contacting one of the many informal rental agencies that park their cycles on street corners all over town, charging rates by the hour or day. Specifics will vary from one stand to the next, but these days the cycle of choice is a two-seat Yamaha or Honda equipped with a 125- or 300-cc engine. Most come equipped with automatic transmissions.

Smaller cycles typically rent for $15 or $20 per hour, while larger models fetch $20 or $25 hourly. Expect to pay slightly more during busy holiday periods. Daily rates run $100 to $150 for smaller cycles and about $50 more for larger models, although those rates too can vary according to season. Nearly all stands have a minimum age requirement of 12 or 13 years old, and all riders under 18 will need parental permission.

A series of nearby sand dunes are a big draw for ATC riders, who find them the most appealing for airborne stunts and other hotdog maneuvers. Others prefer to explore the desert on an extensive network of dirt roads and trails.

OFF-ROAD TOURS

If you don't have an off-road vehicle or you'd prefer not to explore the backcountry on your own, guided tours are another way to discover the remote desert and coastline around San Felipe. Casey's Baja Tours offers guided expeditions in radio-equipped, four-wheel-drive Chevrolet Suburbans with trained, English-speaking guides. Tours start at $25 and 3½ hours in length, with longer, more expensive trips available, visiting destinations such as Valle de los Gigantes, Puertecitos, hidden waterfalls and more.

Casey's Baja Tours *On Calle Mar y Sol, next to El Cortez Hotel. 01152 (6) 577-14-31. Website at www.lovebaja.com.*

Nightlife

"The best day you'll never remember." *—Tagline at a San Felipe nightclub.*

Given its rowdy reputation, you'd be forgiven to imagine San Felipe as the desert's nocturnal answer to Cabo San Lucas or Rosarito Beach—in other words, block upon block of whimsically themed clubs with thundering sound systems, happy hours that begin around noon and an all-night flow of high-octane refreshments. That would be an exaggeration, though, for while San Felipe does have its share of rocking nightlife, it's not in the same league as the biggest party towns.

The *malecón* is the happening place after dark, with several drinking and dance clubs that simmer most of the time, busting loose during the periodic *yanqui* invasions. If you don't count yourself among the young and restless (or at least restless), San Felipe does have its kinder and gentler side. The *malecón* is a fairly subdued (if not terribly sophisticated) scene when America's youth go home and the locals return to their favorite barstools. Elsewhere around town, you won't have to look far to find not only some peace and quiet, but—dare say—even something romantic.

THE BEACHCOMBER

A sports bar and disco in one, this popular nightspot is a lot like San Felipe itself—low-key most of the time but party central whenever the boisterous gringos hit town. There's something for everyone here—billiards, darts, karaoke in English and Spanish, and all of the big U.S. sporting events broadcast live. *Where Calzada Chetumal meets the* malecón. *01152 (6) 577-21-22. Full bar; dancing Fri-Sat and U.S. holidays; live entertainment schedule varies.*

CLUB BAR MIRAMAR

In San Felipe since 1948 and at the same location since '63, this friendly, unpretentious watering hole takes a back-to-basics approach to indoor fun. Billiards and Ping-pong provide some extra percussion while Garth Brooks, the Stones and Selena croon on the jukebox. On weekends it's more a tourist scene while during the week the snowbirds and other ex-pats hang out at their favorite barstools till 3 a.m. *Near the north end of Paseo de Cortéz. 01152 (6) 577-11-92. Full bar, light menu.*

EL SAGUARO

The perfect antidote to the theatrics of excitable gringos is a short drive south of downtown at this subdued beach-side bar. Honors go here as well for the most romantic haunt on the upper gulf. For something livelier, try the Saturday night *parillada* (steak grill) during summer and early fall, when Hawaiian and folkloric dancers perform on the outdoor esplanade. *In the San Felipe Marina Resort, 3 miles south of downtown. 01152 (6) 577-14-55, ext 284. Full bar, light menu.*

ROCKODILE

No one works harder to win the affections, or greenbacks, of the college/dirt bike crowd than this massive bar/disco/pool hall/restaurant. At the heart of the *malecón* scene, Rockodile has no fewer than five bars, along with a restaurant, a large dance floor and a sand volleyball court plunked in the middle of it all. The house specialty drinks (dubbed "Rockodile" and "AMF") are colossal in size, and if they leave your mind in a daze, you can remember your night on the town with a keepsake from the official Rockodile gift shop. *Paseo de Cortez just north of Calle Acapulco. 01152 (6) 577-12-19.*

Rockodile entrance

Full bar; full menu until 11 pm; DJ entertainment nightly; live entertainment schedule varies.

Dining

The upper Sea of Cortez gives up a lot fewer fish than it did 50 years ago, but you'd never it know from a walk through San Felipe's restaurants, where platters of broiled filets, golden-fried shrimp, fish tacos and steaming clams get gobbled up by the thousands on busy weekends.

Yes, San Felipe remains a seafood-lover's town, even if the fishing fleet must cast its nets farther afield than it once did. A stroll up Paseo de Cortez (across from the *malecón*) will verify that, with a bevy of open-air stands and sit-down diners serving up the daily catch. This strip has some of the best deals in town, with fish taco plates for a dollar or two at the sidewalk stands, and wholesome dinners starting under $5 at most of the sit-down restaurants. Head a block or two inland or to one of the nicer hotels and the prices begin to rise.

TIMING MAY BE OFF

If it's 9 p.m. and the lights are out at your favorite restaurant when the book says it's open till 10, please try not to take it out on us. Some local restaurants may close early during low season, and may stay open late when things are really hopping about town.

By no means, though, is seafood the last word on dining in San Felipe. Thanks to all those damn *yanquis*, this has become a great town to order a steak, rack of barbecued ribs, pizza or Chinese takeout. You may even find a waitress who understands the concept of *eggs over easy*. Serving the gringo has become a big business in San Felipe, and with Mexicali just two hours away, many restaurants make regular runs north to stock up on U.S.-brand foods sold in the border town's sprawling *supermercados*.

What you won't find in San Felipe, though, are Ronald McDonald, The Colonel or some freckled-faced girl named Wendy. For good or ill, Corporate America has yet to bestow this town with the wonders of standardized menus, drive-up windows and servers who say, "Would you like fries with that?"

Favorites

EL NIDO ♦♦ **Steakhouse**

This local steakhouse with the familiar wagon wheels in front is first pick for many gringos when guests arrive, or they just want a nice meal on the town. Mesquite-broiled steaks, chicken and seafood lead the cast of U.S.-style entrees, served in a softly lit dining room. Think of a slightly fancier version of George's (see next listing) and you'll get the idea. *Ave Mar de Cortez 348 (south of Calle Manzanillo). 01152 (6) 577-10-28. Open Thu-Tue 2-10 pm. $3.50-20.*

GEORGE'S RESTAURANT BAR ♦ **Steakhouse**

If you're looking for a thoroughly American experience, from the name to the charbroiled steaks right down to the cushy vinyl booths, this restaurant turns the trick as well as any in San Felipe. In the same vein as El Nido, this place is big with the red meat-loving snowbird set, who also flock in for the American-style breakfasts. *Ave Mar de Cortez Sur 336 (south of Calle Manzanillo). 01152 (6) 577-10-57. Open daily 6:30 am-9:30 pm. $2.50-13.*

LAS DUNAS **Mexican/Seafood**

A sweeping view across the bay may bring you here the first time, but the award-winning seafood should ensure many happy returns. Shrimp leads the cast of fresh-caught entrees, and the versions prepared with *chipotle* sauce, tequila and cilantro have all earned top honors at the town's annual Shrimp Festival competition. This is San Felipe's closest brush with "fine dining," but casual attire will still get you through the front door. *In the San Felipe Marina Resort, 3 miles south of downtown. 01152 (6) 577-14-55 ext. 285. Open daily 7 am-10:30 pm. $5-16.50.*

LOS ARCOS **American/Italian**

Whether it's pizza, meatloaf, spaghetti and meatballs or a hot beef sandwich, stop by enough times and you'll probably find all your favorites here, just as long as they aren't seafood, rice or beans. Owned by a Canadian-Mexican couple, this is the most un-Mexican restaurant in town, but it fills a big niche for all the ex-pats looking for some home cooking. *At the north entrance to town, just beyond the arches. 01152 (6) 577-25-85. Open Fri-Wed 11 am-9 pm, closed Thu. $3.40-13.50, pizzas $4.75-10.25.*

PLAZA MARISTACO **Seafood**

Part of the Mexican experience is picking a place to eat from a mass of food stalls, where squads of over-zealous barkers try to convince you that their stall is the best in town. In San Felipe, this is the place. It's also the best place when you're counting every peso, with fish taco combo plates fetching as little as a buck. Mariscos Conchita and 7 Mares are two personal

IN CASE YOU DIDN'T KNOW...

The name "Maristaco" is a contraction of *marisco* (Spanish for "seafood") and taco, which pretty well sums up the choices at this assemblage of open-air food stalls. The barkers can be annoying (but also amusing) until you pick a stall, but once you do they are courteous and prompt with their service.

favorites among the 20 or so stands. *At the south end of Paseo de Cortez. No phone. Open daily, hours vary by season. $1-10, with individual tacos starting at less than $0.70.*

Others

EL CLUB — **Mexican**
$2.80-13.30. *Corner of Paseo de Cortez and Acapulco. 01152 (6) 577-11-75.*

EL PARIAN — **Mexican/Seafood**
$4.90-10. *Paseo de Cortez between Acapulco and Chetumal (next to Rockodile). No phone.*

JACQUES BISTRO INTERNACIONAL — **International**
$7.50-22. *Ave Mar de Cortez, north of Chetumal. 01152 (6) 577-14-66.*

LA PLAYA — **Mexican**
$3.25-9.50, tacos $0.85-1.30. *Paseo de Cortez, 2 doors north of Chetumal. 01152 (6) 577-19-73.*

OCEANO CHINO — **Chinese**
$5-11. *Ave Mar de Cortez, between calles Ensenada and Manzanillo. 01152 (6) 577-26-59.*

PUERTO PADRE — **Mexican/Seafood**
$2.75-7.50. *Ave Mar de Cortez south of Calle Manzanillo. 01152 (6) 577-13-35.*

RED LOBSTER — **Seafood**
$4.50-21. *Calzada Chetumal between Ave Mar de Cortez and Mar Baltico. 01152 (6) 577-15-71.*

RICE & BEANS — **Mexican/Seafood**
$4.50-10. *Paseo de Cortez between Zihuatanejo and Acapulco. 01152 (6) 577-17-70.*

ROCKODILE — **Burgers/Tacos**
$1.50-8. *Paseo de Cortéz, just north of Calle Acapulco. 01152 (6) 577-12-19.*

ROSITA RESTAURANT — **♦ Mexican/Seafood**
$4.50-10. *North end of Paseo de Cortez. 01152 (6) 577-17-70.*

Lodging

See *Lodging & Campgrounds*, Chapter 15.

For thousands of San Felipe visitors, their closest brush with a hotel room is a postage-stamp plot of desert dirt about the width and length of a motor home. San Felipe has always been like that, a camper-and-trailer kind of resort, with fewer hotels than you might expect—which reflects the lifestyles of the snowbirds and sand dune warriors who flock here in such large numbers. And it's the only town we know of in Baja where a fleet of old house trailers has been converted into hotel rooms.

Some might say that San Felipe feels like a poor man's Cabo, since there are no truly upscale properties. In fairness, however, this town has a good number of hotels to choose from, some quite nice if not world-class. The best digs are down along the water's edge, with A/C, satellite TV, nice-sized swimming pools and other things that gringos have come to expect. Move a block or two inland and the lodging is more basic, but still comfortable for the most part.

Most San Felipe hotels charge between $40 and $90 per night, with generally higher summer rates (unlike most desert resorts) than winter. Be advised, too, that rooms or campsites can be scarce at any price during spring break and U.S. three-day weekends. Unless you've come to raise some hell yourself, consider planning your visit around those select periods.

UPSCALE, SAN FELIPE-STYLE

The closest thing you'll find here to a luxury resort would be the San Felipe Marina Resort. The Ritz-Carlton it is not, but $100 or so gets you a night's stay in a well-appointed semi-suite with a vaulted ceiling and a fabulous view across the bay.

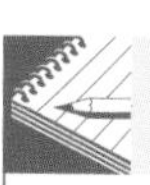

TRAVELOGUE

San Felipe to Puertecitos

(52 mi., 83 km.; 2:15 hrs.)

The twin white arches of San Felipe mark the end of Mexico Highway 5, but the paved road continues south for more than 50 miles to the tiny bayside town of Puertecitos. The word "paved" is subjective in spots along the southern portion of this road, however, due largely to the heavy toll that nature has exacted. Hurricane Nora in 1997 was the main culprit, leaving countless potholes and washed-out dips in its wake south of Punta Estrella. A major resurfacing project is under way, but in early 2001, the route remained in poor condition approaching Puertecitos. All that has not deterred the growing number of part- and full-time residents who have set up housekeeping at the many beach camps and residential communities that line the shore off this route.

Leaving town, the highway hugs the contour of Bahía San Felipe for the first eight miles as you head southeast past an ever-growing series of hotels, campgrounds and condominiums. The roadway is good here, although drifting sandbanks are known to cover the pavement in spots. Beyond this stretch, the road swings due south and stays a short way inland until it reaches Puertecitos. En route, you'll pass numerous side roads jogging east to beachside *campos*, where Americans and Canadians have their vacation homes or park their RVs for the winter. However, there remains nothing in the way of roadside facilities all along this long section.

High and dry during low tide at Puertecitos

Bad as the surface is in spots, the road itself is straight and level nearly all the way, and offers outstanding views of the Sierra San Pedro Mártir to the west. The flora is typical Baja, with mesquite, cholla, ocotillo, elephant trees, and the peninsula's northernmost stands of cardón cacti. You can make this trek in a passenger car ... if you have good tires, take it slow, and drive with vigilance at all times.

00.0 Traffic circle at the junction of Mexico Highway 5 and Avenida Mar Caribe (street name for the beginning of the route.)

01.0 Junction with a dirt road that also leads to Puertecitos. This road takes an inland route and sees only limited use, except during occasional off-road races.

01.9 Entrance to Hotel Las Misiónes and Mar del Sol RV Park.

02.6 Entrance to the commercial harbor.

03.0 Entrance to the San Felipe Marina Resort.

06.3 Junction with the paved road to San Felipe International Airport.

06.9 La Hacienda, a condominium development.

10.5 Turnoff to Faro Beach and Punta Estrella, at the southern end of Bahía San Felipe.

15.1 A sandy road leads southwest to Valle de los Gigantes, a group of very large cardón

cacti. In the opposite direction a sign points to Colonia Gutierrez Polanco.

19.1 A sandy spur road leads 2½ miles to Laguna (Rancho) Percebú, a growing community of American beach houses, a campground and a restaurant.

25.5 Turnoff to Campo Santa María, a large collection of trailers and vacation homes.

28.4 The village of Ejido Delicias, with a doctor, ambulance and a small store. On the beach opposite are a lighthouse and Campo El Vergel, a large settlement.

39.0 Junction with the inland road leading north toward San Felipe.

53.5 Puertecitos, overlooking a small bay. At the northern entrance is a municipal delegation and a small Mexican community called Ejido Matomí. Most of Puertecitos, however, is inhabited by Americans who lease their homes and trailer sites from the owners of the land. Facilities include a motel, a cafe and bar, a small general store, a Pemex station (not always open) and an airstrip. Arrangements are available here for camping, cabaña rentals, fishing boats, trailer rentals and boat launching. Fishing is good outside the shallow bay, which becomes dry during extreme low tides. The short road branching to the southeast point of the bay passes a rocky footpath leading to natural hot springs; depending on the tide, three separate pools are filled with water of varying temperatures.

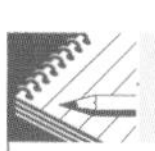

TRAVELOGUE

Puertecitos to Bahía San Luis Gonzaga

(45 mi., 72 km.; 4 hrs.)

For decades the road south of Puertecitos had a well-earned reputation as one of the most brutal routes in all of Baja California. That changed in 1987, with a major upgrade of this remote byway, but even now the surface remains a rough washboard, and sturdy, high-clearance vehicles are the

Bahía San Luis Gonzaga

best way to go. Carry adequate emergency equipment for this lonely stretch, where isolation is one of the main allures. While the route has been realigned, the tortuous, rocky route of yore is still in plain view alongside the new roadway. The new route does bypass Huerfanito Grade, which for many years earned the dubious distinction for being one of the most treacherous pieces of road in all of Baja.

Vegetation is sparse along the way, but interesting rocks in red, orange and brown make up for that in scenic value, as do the shimmering waters of the gulf. The best views come between miles 11 and 19, where the route crosses a range of hills just inland from the water's edge. Remote as this route may be, signs abound in the miles past Nacho's Camp, advertising campsites and lots for sale. The road here is level and runs close to shore. Another range of hills looms and the road crosses a series of sandy arroyos in the last six miles shy of Bahía San Luis Gonzaga.

By most accounts, Bahía San Luis Gonzaga (not to be confused with the mission of the same name in Baja California Sur) is one of the most beautiful bays along Baja's coast. The arid, barren landscape only adds to the sense of isolation that epitomizes Baja's gulf coast, with brilliant sunshine by day and billions of stars by night.

00.0 Puertecitos, in front of the Pemex station.

05.7 Campo La Costilla, a small private camp at the edge of an attractive cove, where the natural slope of the beach makes an excellent launch ramp. Refreshments can be purchased here.

11.3 The first of many good camping spots along the rocky gulf shore.

18.2 Nacho's Camp, a group of aging beach homes owned by Americans.

19.8 Another beach settlement with an adjacent airstrip.

35.0 Campo Los Delfínes, an abandoned private campground with several good primitive camping spots.

38.4 Junction with the road to Las Encantadas.

40.0 Junction with a 1.3-mile dirt road to Campo Punta Bufeo, a collection of homes owned by Americans and an airstrip. Refreshments and simple meals are available.

45.7 Bahía San Luis Gonzaga, at the junction with the 0.9-mile road to Papa Fernandez's camp. The resort offers meals, refreshments, boats and motors for rent, and occasionally gasoline and oil. Fishing is excellent and is one of the big draws to this remote camp.

48.4 Bahía San Luis Gonzaga, at the entrance to Rancho Grande, a water purification/ice plant and a campground. A 1.6-mile side road leads to Alfonsina's Camp, located on a narrow sandspit facing the bay. Facilities include a small hotel, a campground, a restaurant, an airstrip and gasoline. Vacation homes line the sandspit next to the camp.

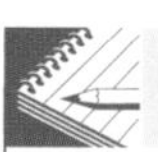

TRAVELOGUE

Bahía San Luis Gonzaga to Mexico Highway 1

(37 mi., 63 km.; 2 hrs.)

In theory, a low-slung passenger car or small RV can make this drive—at least northbound from Highway 1—but like so many Baja routes, this route is best left to high-clearance vehicles equipped for the rigors of off-road driving.

Passing beyond the shoreline of Bahía San Luis Gonzaga, the route meets the junction of the road leading to Punta Final, at the southern end of the bay. Beyond the bay, the road ascends several miles through gently sloping terrain where prolific blooms of wildflowers highlight the flora each spring. Beyond this stretch your route enters a range of hills with some fine stands of elephant trees. Amid these hills the road winds through a canyon, just beyond which lies Rancho las Arrastras. A short distance past the ranch is Coco's Corner, where the road forks left and then meets another road leading southwest to Mexico Highway 1.

00.0 Bahía San Luis Gonzaga, at the entrance to Rancho Grande.

10.1 Junction with the road to Punta Final, a private beach community. No services are available here.

24.2 Coco's Corner, located at the junction with the road leading southwest to Mexico Highway 1. Turn right at the junction for Highway 1. A left turn leads east, then north to Hermenegildo Galiana and to Campo Calamajué on the gulf.

37.3 Junction with Highway 1, just north of Laguna Chapala and 33.7 miles south of Cataviña.

Toll road fees between Tecate and La Rumorosa equal about $4.05 for standard automobiles and light-duty trucks, and $8.20 for campers and motorhomes. Vehicles towing trailers pay $1.80 per each additional axle.

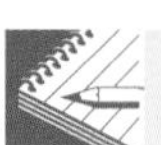

TRAVELOGUE

Tecate to La Rumorosa via Toll Highway 2

(38 mi., 61 km.; 0:45 hr.)

A modern four-lane highway now runs across the top of Baja California from the eastern suburbs of Tijuana to the western edge of Mexicali, following the 1999 completion of the final link, between Tecate and La Rumorosa. The new toll road makes for speedy transit between the two communities, and the only slowdown you're likely to encounter is at the tollbooth near Colonia El Hongo. So far, traffic has proved to be very light along this route, due no doubt to the tolls.

Leaving Tecate, Highway 2 climbs steeply for the first several miles as it scales the high plateau between the coastal plain and the Colorado Desert. The highway then climbs gradually, passing miles of empty countryside before peaking at La Rumorosa, where it converges with the free road and begins the long descent to the desert floor. At

4300 feet, La Rumorosa is high enough to get occasional snowfalls, although rarely heavy enough to shut the highway down.

00.0 **Tecate town center, at the junction of the Highway 2 free road and Highway 3. Head east on the Highway 2 free road (Avenida Juárez) to the toll road entrance.**

03.3 **Toll road entrance at the eastern edge of Tecate.**

18.0 **Exit for Colonia El Hongo. A tollbooth collects fees for vehicles leaving the toll road here. Just past the exit it is the tollbooth for traffic continuing to La Rumorosa.**

34.5 **Exit for La Rumorosa, located at the eastern edge of a boulder-strewn plateau. Facilities in the town include stores, cafes, a Pemex station and mechanical assistance.**

38.8 **La Rumorosa tollbooth. The free road and toll road from Tecate merge here.**

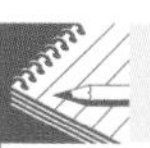

TRAVELOGUE

Tecate to La Rumorosa via Old Highway 2

(40 mi., 64 km., 1:00 hr.)

The new Highway 2 toll road is now the swiftest route between Tecate and La Rumorosa, but it has hardly replaced the old free road, which still handles most of the traffic between these two towns. What's more, the free road provides ready access to the small towns and numerous side roads that branch into the surrounding countryside, which the toll road bypasses.

Leaving Tecate, the free road begins a long, gradual climb onto the high plateau between the coast and desert. You pass orchards, scattered field crops and ranches pass along the way, as well as a number of rustic resorts and campgrounds that draw mainly Mexican guests. Climbing higher, the terrain becomes more desolate—mainly jumbled rocks and a few needle-leaf trees—as the highway climbs to the plateau's eastern edge at La Rumorosa.

00.0	Tecate, at the junction of Mexico highways 2 and 3.
3.0	Junction of Highway 2 (free road) and Highway 2D (toll road).
12.0	Entrance to Rancho Ojai RV Park.
13.8	Loma Tova, a village with a Pemex station and cafe.
20.8	Colonia El Hongo, a fast-growing farming community with cafes and stores. A partially paved road winds seven miles southwest to Hacienda Santa Verónica, a cattle ranch with a hotel and trailer park.
30.2	El Condor, a settlement with a Pemex station and restaurant, at the junction with a graded road to Laguna Hanson in the Sierra de Juárez.
38.4	La Rumorosa, located at the eastern edge of a boulder-strewn plateau. Facilities in the town include stores, cafes, a Pemex station and mechanical assistance.
40.2	La Rumorosa tollbooth. All eastbound vehicles, except for local traffic, must pay a fee here as the free and toll roads merge.

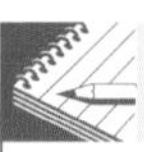

TRAVELOGUE

Highway 2-D
La Rumorosa to Mexicali

(42 mi., 68 km.; 1 hr.)

Highway tolls for travel between La Rumorosa and Mexicali equal about $1 for standard automobiles and light-duty trucks, and $4 for campers and motorhomes. Vehicles towing trailers pay $1 additional per axle.

Until recently, the drive between Tijuana and Mexicali included a crumbling, two-lane stretch of mountain road, fraught with dead-man's curves, missing guardrails and steep inclines that slowed large trucks to a crawl. That was the old Rumorosa Grade, one of the most perilous stretches of paved road in all of Baja California. Those days are gone for good, with the 1996 completion of a modern four-lane toll road that provides far smoother passage between La Rumorosa and the desert floor. Two lanes in each direction scale either side of a yawning canyon along the east face of the Sierra de Juárez.

While the old, free route is now a thing of the past, tolls on the modern highway are fairly low by Baja standards—about 85 cents for cars and light trucks, and about $3.60 for motor homes. Tollbooths at the top of Rumorosa Grade collect fees for traffic in both directions.

Between highlands and desert on Rumorosa Grade

One thing that has not changed is that this remains one of the most spectacular mountain roads on the continent, winding past strangely jumbled rock formations and jagged peaks with breathtaking vistas of the Colorado Desert. On clear days the view extends north to California's Salton Sea. And while the new highway represents a vast improvement over the old, steep drop-offs, heavy winds and numerous curves still demand careful driving.

From the base of the grade, Highway 2-D makes a straight shot east across the barren Colorado Desert, passing the north edge of Laguna Salada. From there it crosses a fold of low hills before dipping into the Mexicali Valley, one of Mexico's biggest farming areas. The route skirts the southern edge of Mexicali, but several boulevards branch off it and lead toward the city's center.

00.0 Tollbooth at La Rumorosa.

22.6 Junction with a graded dirt road along the edge of Laguna Salada to Cañon de Guadalupe. (See Side Route to Cañon de Guadalupe.)

Side Routes

28.6 End of the four-lane expressway, marked by a monument.

35.2 Colonia Progreso, a village with a large municipal building, a motel, restaurant and a Pemex station.

39.8 A well-marked turnoff heads toward downtown Mexicali and the U.S. border. Highway 2 bears right and continues east to the Highway 5 junction and San Luis Río Colorado.

44.6 Mexicali, at the traffic circle intersection of Mexico highways 2 and 5. (See Travelogue for Mexico Highway 5, page 418.)

Side Routes

Highway 2-D to Cañon de Guadalupe

(See map page 443.)

(35 mi., 57 km.; 1:15 hrs.)

Dozens of oases dot the deserts of Baja California, and one of the most picturesque is among the closest to the U.S. border. It is a long trek off the pavement to Cañon de Guadalupe, more than 30 miles by either of two available routes. The payoff is evident upon arriving at this shady, secluded palm forest nestled beneath the shadow of the jagged Sierra de Juárez. The massive, A-shaped spire of Picacho Rasco stands high above the canyon to the southwest, while toward the northeast your views stretch toward Laguna Salada and the desert ranges of southeastern California.

The route across Laguna Salada is about one mile shorter.

A cold creek runs year-round through this rugged canyon, while hot springs well up from underground, feeding their 107-degree water to bathing pools in the more developed campsites. In sum, it is the consummate setting for a deep-desert retreat. Three campgrounds line the canyon, offering sites that range from primitive to highly developed. A restaurant and cantina serve the campgrounds, as does a small store selling food, ice and firewood. Hiking trails lead to a small waterfall and Indian petroglyphs. Given its beautiful setting and available activities, Cañon de Guadalupe draws many visitors from both sides of the border, with Southern Californians coming to camp for a weekend or longer, and Mexicali residents taking day outings, primarily on Sundays.

A dune buggy pulls in to Cañon de Guadalupe

Two turnoffs from Highway 2 lead to the canyon. Coming from Tecate, the first road turns off the highway just east of kilometer 28 and threads a path between the western edge of Laguna Salada and the Sierra de Juárez. The surface is rough in spots with some sections of washboard. Follow the road 27 miles south before reaching a junction that leads another seven miles west to the canyon.

The second turnoff is 2.5 miles east, across from a Pemex station, and heads south across the dry lakebed of the

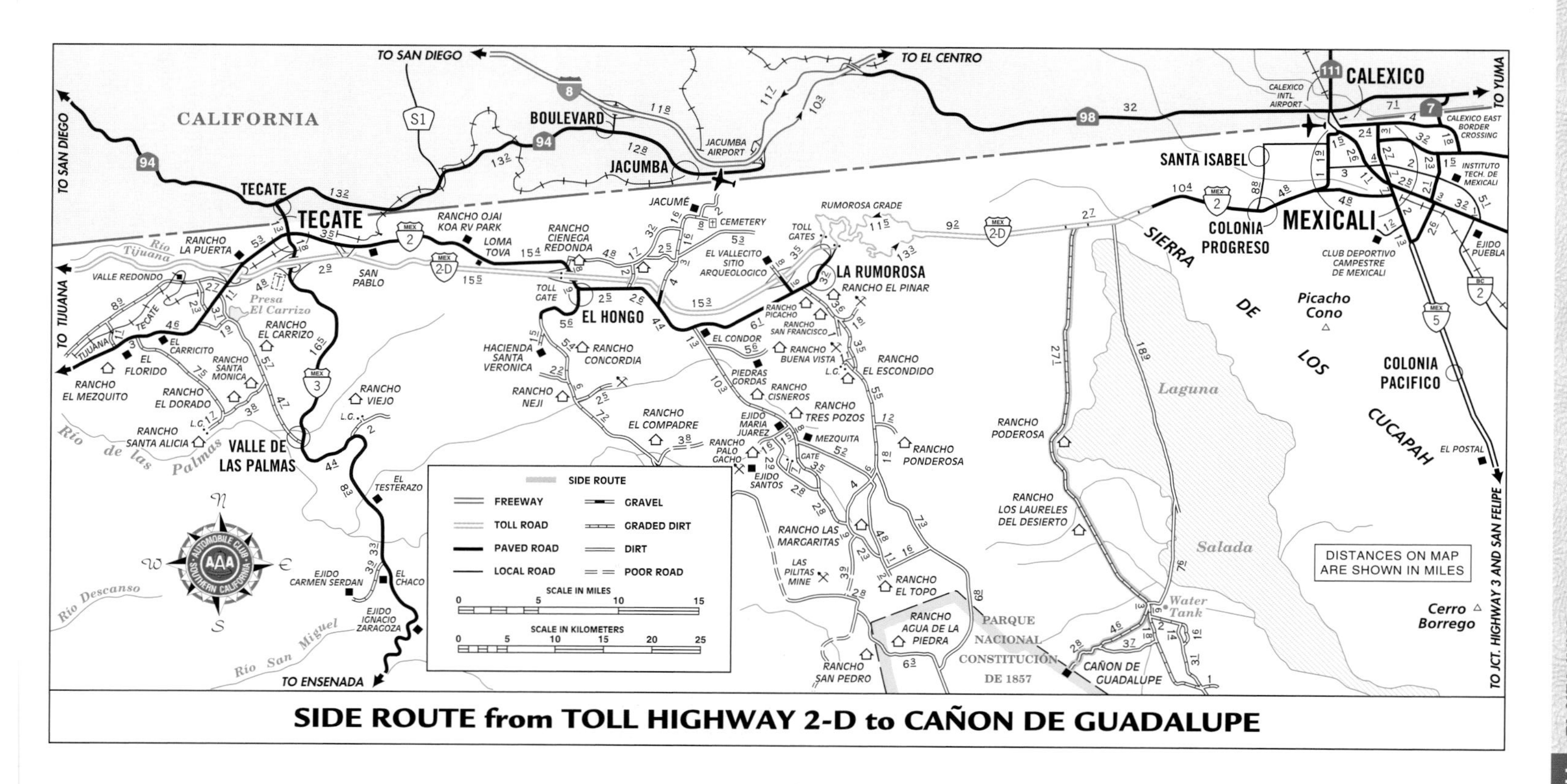

SIDE ROUTE from TOLL HIGHWAY 2-D to CAÑON DE GUADALUPE

laguna. (You must be heading eastbound on Highway 2 to make this turnoff.) Smooth and flat, it is only one lane wide but suitable for highway-speed driving. About 26.8 miles from Highway 2 is a junction with a graded dirt road that leads 7.7 miles west to the canyon and campgrounds. Turn right and follow the signs to the canyon entrance.

SUMMER SIZZLES

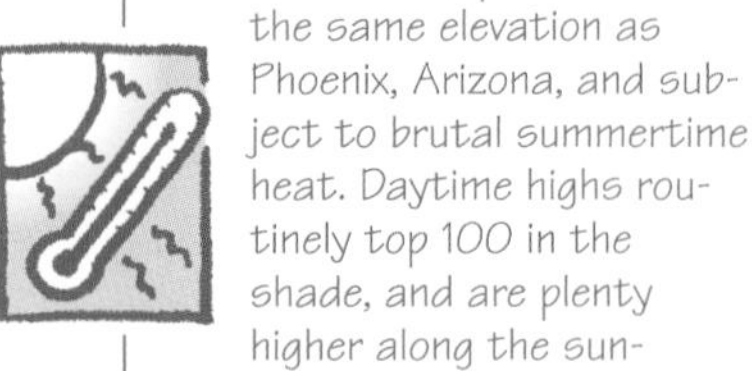

At 1100 feet above sea level, Cañon de Guadalupe is at about the same elevation as Phoenix, Arizona, and subject to brutal summertime heat. Daytime highs routinely top 100 in the shade, and are plenty higher along the sun-scorched roads approaching the canyon—no place to be on a summer afternoon.

By either route, most of the way is passable to vehicles of all types, but the last few miles lend themselves only to high-clearance trucks, jeeps and SUVs. Four-wheel-drive is not necessary, but the sharp dips, protruding rocks and broken roadbed are no place for RVs or passenger cars.

Several signs along both roads point toward the canyon entrance.

Under most conditions, you'll save time taking the road across the lakebed; it's smoother and has little washboard surface. After rainstorms, though, you may find the roadway under water or transformed to mud. If in doubt, use the road along the lake's edge or contact one of the campgrounds (see below) to verify conditions. Neither route is suitable for night driving; aside from safety concerns, it's easy to make a wrong turn and get lost in the desert.

Cañon de Guadalupe gets most of its visitors during the cooler months of the year and campsite reservations are often necessary. Weekends and holidays can be especially crowded. Nightly fees range from $10 to $50, depending on campsite, season and day of the week. For more information or to make a reservation, call (949) 673-2670, or call the Baja Safari travel club (toll-free) at (888) 411-2252.

Mexicali to San Luis Río Colorado, Sonora

(See map page 447.)

(41 mi., 66 km.; 1 hr.)

The only overland route linking Baja California to the Mexican mainland, Mexico Highway 2 strikes east across the farmlands of the Mexicali Valley before crossing the Colorado River into the state of Sonora. Stay on this road long enough and it intersects with Mexico Highway 15, which heads southeast along the mainland's west coast for nearly 1000 miles before turning inland toward Mexico

Baja's Smallest Border Town

The name is Spanish for "the Cotton Plants," but that's the last thing most visitors have on their mind when they come to Los Algodónes, a friendly town at the far northeast corner of Baja California. For many Americans, this burg of 14,000 is the place to go for affordable dental and medical care, as well as prescription drugs that sell for a fraction of their U.S. price.

Better known as simply "Algodónes," the town is a quiet place during the sweltering summer months, but in the winter it positively booms as snowbirds by the thousands head this way. (Yuma, Arizona, is 10 miles to the east and one of the largest snowbird havens in the United States.) U.S. retirees provide a lucrative business for the many doctors and dentists who hang their shingles in Algodónes' downtown tourist district. Dentists seem to draw the most customers, with more than a dozen offices located within two blocks of the border crossing. Most visitors park on the U.S. side and cross the border on foot, since the main tourist area is comprised of only a few square blocks. The crossing is open daily from 6 a.m. to 8 p.m.

Border fence near Algodónes

As for cotton, Algodónes is aptly named, since it's the service center for one of the leading cotton-growing areas in Mexico. Nearby as well is Morelos Dam, which straddles the international border and is the main irrigation source for the prolific farmlands of the Mexicali Valley.

City. This side route covers Highway 2 only as far as San Luis Río Colorado, on the east bank of the Colorado.

With a population of 135,000, San Luis Río Colorado is a busy border community that thrives from agriculture (cotton and wheat are the main crops), highway transportation and international trade. It has an attractive plaza park that's surrounded by businesses, a classic church and government buildings, including a state tourism office. Nearby is the main tourist district, which in turn is close to the border crossing, 23 miles south of Yuma, Arizona.

Vehicle permits are required for travel into mainland Mexico (except Golfo de Santa Clara), and are available at the border in San Luis Río Colorado. (See *Tourist Regulations* and *Travel Tips*, Chapter 2.)

Highway 2, for its part, sees comparatively few tourists despite its proximity to the U.S. border. Heading eastward across the flat Mexicali Valley, it traverses one of Mexico's

Stay alert for slow-moving farm vehicles entering and leaving this section of Highway 2.

most important farming areas, where cotton, wheat, dairy farming and vegetables are the mainstays. Side roads provide access to El Golfo de Santa Clara and Algodónes, Baja's easternmost border town.

From its junction with Mexico Highway 5, Highway 2 traverses a sprawling industrial district before striking out across miles of irrigated cropland broken by occasional small farming towns. At mileage 6.0 is a paved road leading to the village of Ejido Puebla and the Cerro Prieto Geothermal Zone, site of a large geothermal electrical generating facility. Mileage 14.0 brings the junction with BCN 1, a paved route that leads north to the Mexicali Airport (Gral. Rodolfo Sánchez Taboada International Airport) and south to BCN 4 en route to El Golfo de Santa Clara (see Side Route to El Golfo de Santa Clara, Sonora). Farther east, at mileage 36.8, is a junction with the paved highway that heads 17 miles north to the border town of Algodónes. Finally at mileage 38.3, Highway 2 reaches the toll bridge crossing the Colorado River. Paid in pesos, the toll is about 50 cents.

Side Routes

Highway 5 to El Golfo de Santa Clara, Sonora

(See map page 447.)

(69 mi., 112 km.; 2 hrs.)

A sun-washed fishing village at the far northern edge of the Gulf of California, El Golfo de Santa Clara is a favorite side route for many Baja trekkers, although it lies in the state of Sonora, far removed from any other settlement. The town also attracts good-sized crowds from Arizona to ride dirt bikes and ATVs down the beach, watch the sun set over the gulf and sleep beneath the stars. U.S. holiday periods bring the most visitors here. At other times, all is mostly quiet in this remote town of 3000. Though perched at the edge of one of North America's driest deserts, El Golfo is long on natural grandeur, with the peaks of northern Baja clearly visible across the shimmering waters of the gulf. The tidal range is tremendous here, and the

On the beach at Golfo de Santa Clara

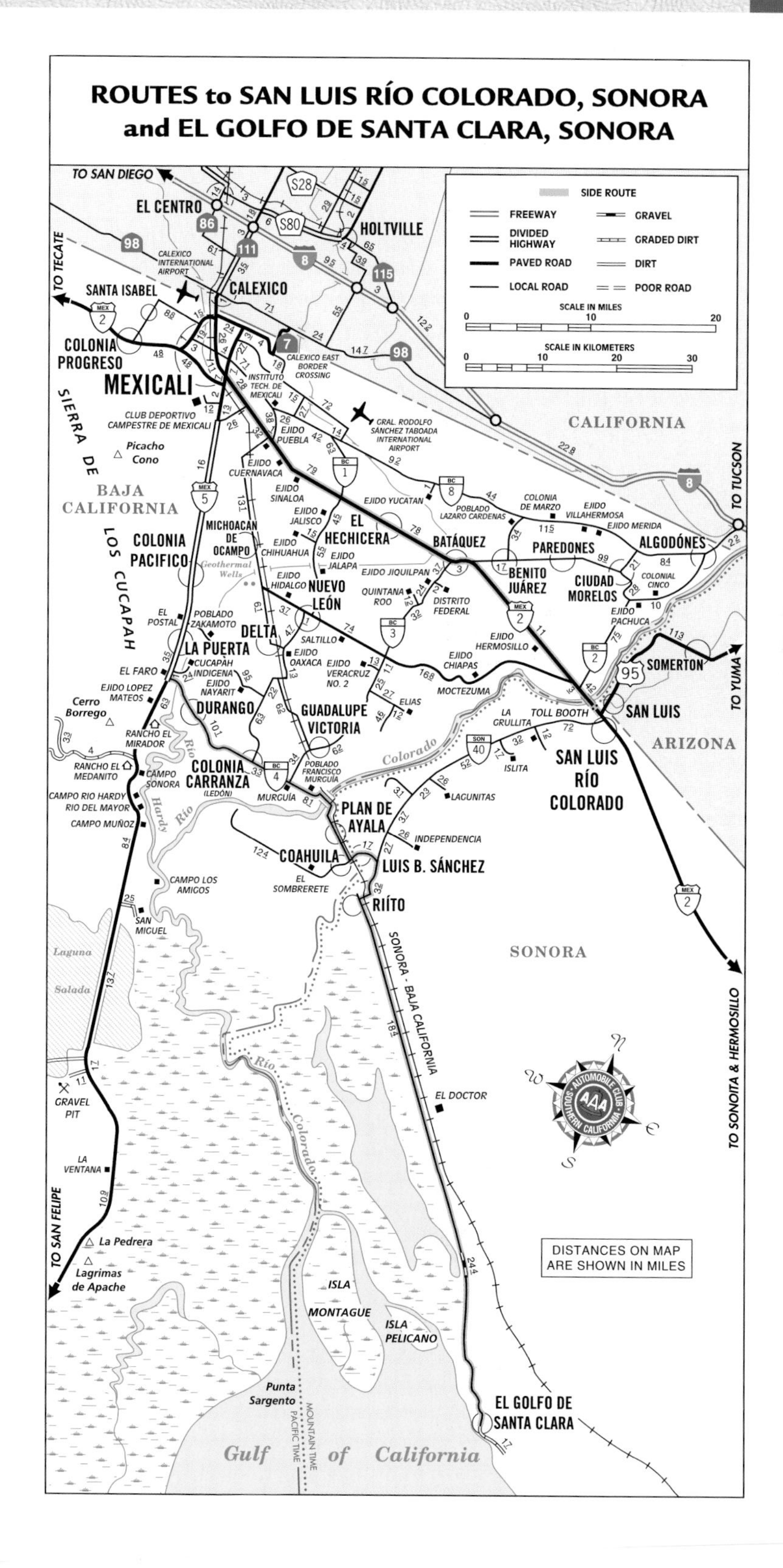
ROUTES to SAN LUIS RÍO COLORADO, SONORA and EL GOLFO DE SANTA CLARA, SONORA
SIDE ROUTE
FREEWAY
DIVIDED HIGHWAY
PAVED ROAD
LOCAL ROAD
GRAVEL
GRADED DIRT
DIRT
POOR ROAD
SCALE IN MILES
SCALE IN KILOMETERS
TO SAN DIEGO
EL CENTRO
HOLTVILLE
TO TECATE
CALEXICO INTERNATIONAL AIRPORT
SANTA ISABEL
CALEXICO
COLONIA PROGRESO
MEXICALI
CALEXICO EAST BORDER CROSSING
INSTITUTO TECH. DE MEXICALI
CLUB DEPORTIVO CAMPESTRE DE MEXICALI
GRAL. RODOLFO SÁNCHEZ TABOADA INTERNATIONAL AIRPORT
CALIFORNIA
SIERRA DE LOS CUCAPAH
Picacho Cono
EJIDO PUEBLA
EJIDO CUERNAVACA
BAJA CALIFORNIA
EJIDO SINALOA
EJIDO YUCATAN
POBLADO LAZARO CARDENAS
COLONIA DE MARZO
EJIDO VILLAHERMOSA
EJIDO MERIDA
TO TUCSON
EJIDO JALISCO
EL HECHICERA
BATÁQUEZ
PAREDONES
ALGODÓNES
COLONIA PACIFICO
MICHOACAN DE OCAMPO
EJIDO CHIHUAHUA
EJIDO JALAPA
Geothermal Wells
EJIDO JIQUILPAN
BENITO JUÁREZ
CIUDAD MORELOS
COLONIAL CINCO
EJIDO HIDALGO
NUEVO LEÓN
QUINTANA ROO
DISTRITO FEDERAL
EJIDO PACHUCA
EL POSTAL
POBLADO ZAKAMOTO
DELTA
SALTILLO
EJIDO HERMOSILLO
LA PUERTA
EJIDO OAXACA
EJIDO VERACRUZ NO. 2
EJIDO CHIAPAS
SOMERTON
TO YUMA
EL FARO
CUCAPAH INDIGENA
EJIDO NAYARIT
MOCTEZUMA
EJIDO LOPEZ MATEOS
ELIAS
Cerro Borrego
DURANGO
GUADALUPE VICTORIA
LA GRULLITA
TOLL BOOTH
SAN LUIS
RANCHO EL MIRADOR
ARIZONA
Río Colorado
ISLITA
SAN LUIS RÍO COLORADO
RANCHO EL MEDANITO
CAMPO SONORA
COLONIA CARRANZA (LEDÓN)
POBLADO FRANCISCO MURGUÍA
LAGUNITAS
CAMPO RIO HARDY
RIO DEL MAYOR
MURGUÍA
PLAN DE AYALA
CAMPO MUÑOZ
Río Hardy
INDEPENDENCIA
COAHUILA
LUIS B. SÁNCHEZ
CAMPO LOS AMIGOS
EL SOMBRERETE
RIÍTO
SAN MIGUEL
SONORA
Laguna Salada
SONORA - BAJA CALIFORNIA
TO SONOITA & HERMOSILLO
GRAVEL PIT
EL DOCTOR
AUTOMOBILE CLUB SOUTHERN CALIFORNIA AAA
LA VENTANA
TO SAN FELIPE
La Pedrera
Lagrimas de Apache
DISTANCES ON MAP ARE SHOWN IN MILES
ISLA MONTAGUE
ISLA PELICANO
Punta Sargento
PACIFIC TIME
MOUNTAIN TIME
EL GOLFO DE SANTA CLARA
Gulf of California

El Golfo, Via Highway 2

Mexico Highway 2 provides two alternate approaches that link up with the route to El Golfo. One approach heads south on BCN Highway 1 from its junction with Highway 2, 14 miles east of Mexicali. Passing through miles of cropland and skirting the towns of Nuevo León and Delta, BC 1 ends at a junction with BCN 4 in Colonia Carranza. Turn left at the junction and continue east on BCN 4 following the route described above. Driving distance from Highway 2 is 81 miles, but from Mexicali the total distance (95 miles) is just a mile more than the Highway 5 approach.

Another route starts in the city of San Luis Río Colorado, Sonora. From Highway 2, turn south on Calle 2, which becomes Sonora Highway 40 and continues to Riíto. From Riíto follow the previously described route to El Golfo. Total driving distance to San Luis Río Colorado is about 68 miles.

shoreline see-saws between sandy beaches at high tide and vast mud flats at low tide.

Fishing is the town's biggest business, with a packing plant and a harbor full of boats that head offshore for shrimp, clams and sierra, among other catches. Many more small fishing craft sit above the high-tide line along the beach. Visitors can sometimes make arrangements for sport fishing trips. Lodging is limited, but two RV parks can be found just south of town, and camping is allowed along the beach. El Golfo also has a Pemex station, a grocery store, a general store and several cafes.

State highways, such as BCN 4, are usually not indicated on signs, but the abbreviation does appear on occasional roadside posts.

The drive to El Golfo is an experience in its own right, passing through some of Baja's richest farmland, plus miles of desolate Sonoran Desert. The route leaves Highway 5 at a junction just south of El Faro and 26 miles south of Mexicali, with a sign pointing to Colonia Nuevas. Designated BCN Highway 4, the two-lane paved route heads east through miles of pastures and farmland, along with the towns of Ejido Durango, Colonia Carranza (Ledón) and Murguía. Four miles past Murguía the highway reaches the Colorado River—reduced to a shallow stream at this point by damming and irrigation demands on both sides of the border. The road takes an unlikely detour across the river, using a railroad trestle that doubles as a highway bridge. Police direct traffic across the narrow span, which is only wide enough to handle a one-way flow. Traffic grinds to a halt several times a day as police clear the bridge to make way for passing trains. (A new highway bridge is under construction.) Continuing east, the route passes through the dirt streets of Coahuila (also called Colonia Nuevas), the last town before leaving Baja California. Turn left, cross the railroad tracks and follow the signs that point to Sonora. There is no checkpoint at the state line, about 100 meters east of the tracks.

The state of Sonora is on Mountain Time, one hour ahead of Baja California.

Crossing into Sonora, you enter the town of Luis B. Sánchez, which together with Coahuila makes up a sizable farm market center, including Pemex stations, auto part shops, a clinic, and several markets and restaurants. After another mile, the road runs into state highway SON 40; a left turn leads north to San Luis Río Colorado, while a right turn leads southeast to El Golfo. Heading toward El Golfo, another three miles leads to Riíto, a hamlet at the southern edge of the farm belt, with the last services before the final destination. Beyond Riíto, the highway crosses 43 miles of barren Sonoran Desert to reach El Golfo. The only settlement along the way is El Doctor, a tiny railroad work station with a few buildings and a rustic cafe. Nearing El Golfo, the gulf pulls into view as the road curves and quickly descends to a small coastal basin. The pavement ends at the town entrance.

BEWARE OF THE SAND, MAN

El Golfo's sandy streets are usually OK for two-wheel drive vehicles, but even here, drifting sand can build up and trap your car or truck. If in doubt, deflate your tires for better traction, and refill them later at one of the shops advertising "*aire*/air."

Special Events & Holidays

Calendar Of Events

Each year thousands of race fans line the back roads of Baja to see their favorite off-road jockeys zoom by in a cloud of blinding dust. An armada of fishing boats takes to the seas off Cabo San Lucas as anglers vie to reel in a share of a $2 million purse. Towns of all sizes celebrate their birthdays or salute their patron saints with gala events. From big-name sporting events to homey small-town parades, Baja California has special events of all size and manner.

The list that follows is not exhaustive, and includes only those with a history of success and wide participation. For exact dates and more information on these and other events, contact the local tourism office.

January

VELA NEIL PRYDE BAJA CHAMPIONSHIPS

The Cape Region

Top windsurfers from around the world compete in a week of sailboard racing, sponsored in part by the Vela Windsurf Resort. *Los Barriles. (800) 223-5433.*

February

MEXICAN SURF FIESTA TODOS SANTOS

The Northern Triangle

Top big-wave riders from around the world compete in the surf off the Todos Santos Islands, home to some of the largest rideable waves in the world. *(858) 486-0370.*

CARNAVAL (MARDI GRAS)

Various Regions

In the days before Ash Wednesday, Mexico's version of Mardi Gras is a major happening in Ensenada, San Felipe and La Paz. Live entertainment, special events, midway rides and a rollicking parade are part of the celebrations in all three communities. Some years, the celebrations take place in March. *01152 (6) 178-29-88 or 178-39-09 (Ensenada), 01152 (6) 577-11-55 (San Felipe), 01152 (1) 124-01-00 or 124-01-03 (La Paz).*

March

SAN JOSÉ FIESTA

The Cape Region

Festivities lasting a week or longer celebrate the patron saint of San José del Cabo, climaxed by the saint's day, Día de San José on March 19. *San José del Cabo. 01152 (1) 142-29-60, ext 150.*

TECATE SCORE SAN FELIPE 250

The Desert Northeast

Off-road drivers and motorcyclists race across the desert and mountains of northern Baja in a 250-mile endurance test. *Starting and finish lines in San Felipe. (818) 225-8402. Website at www.score-international.com.*

April

BAJA PROG

The Desert Northeast

"Prog" is short for "progressive rock," which is the kind of music showcased in this annual concert series. Artists from around the world travel to Mexicali to perform, with the concert schedule often extending into May. *Teatro del Estado in Mexicali. (877) 700-2092, 01152 (6) 554-64-18.*

NEWPORT-ENSENADA REGATTA

The Northern Triangle

Held annually since 1947, this famed regatta sends hundreds of sailboats racing down 125 miles of Pacific coastline, leaving Newport Beach at noon, with the winner reaching Ensenada about 12 hours later. *(714) 771-0691. www.nosa.org.*

ROSARITO-ENSENADA BIKE RIDE

The Northern Triangle

Thousands of cyclists make the 50-mile fun ride from Rosarito Beach to Ensenada along the Highway 1 free road in this popular semiannual event. A party follows at the finish line. *(619) 583-3001.*

May

LA PAZ FOUNDING FAIR AND FESTIVAL

La Paz and Environs

Paceños mark the anniversary of Hernán Cortés' arrival at the shores of the modern-day La Paz in 1535 with a myriad of cultural and sporting events and other festivities in the first week of the month. *Various locations around La Paz. 01152 (1) 124-01-99.*

June

ESTERO BEACH VOLLEYBALL TOURNAMENT

The Northern Triangle

Nearly 2000 players from the United States and Mexico face off in two-on-two matches on the sand at this annual tournament. Live music, food and beverages are all there for the benefit of visitors. *Estero Beach, south of Ensenada. (858) 454-7166, 01152 (6) 176-62-25.*

TECATE SCORE BAJA 500

Various Regions

This legendary race takes off-road drivers and motorcyclists on a grueling 500-mile drive through northern Baja's backcountry. *Start and finish in El Sauzal, just north of Ensenada. (818) 225-8402. www.score-international.com.*

July

BAJA OPEN BEACH VOLLEYBALL TOURNAMENT

The Northern Triangle

Two-player teams from around the world compete on the sand near Ensenada in this two-day competition. A similar event takes place at the same location in August. *Playa Faro, south of Ensenada. (714) 432-5891, 01152 (6) 178-24-11.*

QUEEN OF THE CALIFORNIAS BEAUTY PAGEANT

The Northern Triangle

Señioritas from California and Baja California compete in Tijuana for the title of Queen of the Californias (Reyna de las Californias). *Grand Hotel Tijuana. 01152 (6) 634-63-30, 681-70-00.*

ROSARITO FAIR

The Northern Triangle

Carnival rides, traditional Mexican food, and concerts by Mexican and international stars are among the highlights of this month-long celebration. *Rosarito Beach. (800) 962-2252, 01152 (6) 612-03-96.*

SEAFOOD FESTIVAL

The Northern Triangle

Restaurants and individuals from northern Baja showcase their culinary skills, preparing all types of seafood dishes in this daylong gastronomic celebration. *Ave Revolución, Tijuana. 01152 (6) 634-63-30, 683-87-44.*

SUMMER EXPO FAIR

The Northern Triangle

Ensenada puts on a huge summer celebration with more than two weeks of live music, exhibitions, games, rides and regional fairs. *In Ensenada, on Blvd Costero next to Riviera del Pacífico. 01152 (6) 178-24-11 or 178-36-75.*

August

GRAPE HARVEST FESTIVAL

The Northern Triangle

A gastronomic, cultural and musical event all in one, this 10-day festival celebrates the beginning of the wine grape harvest in the Guadalupe and Santo Tomás valleys of northern Baja. *Events in Ensenada and neighboring grape-growing regions. 01152 (6) 174-08-36 or 174-08-29.*

September

FIESTAS DEL SOL

Mexicali celebrates the end of summer with an annual three-week fair that includes concerts, rides, business exhibitions, art shows, etc. The festivities start in late September and continue into mid-October. *Multiple locations, Mexicali. (877) 700-2092, 01152 (6) 557-23-76.*

The Desert Northeast

CABRILLO FESTIVAL

Ensenada celebrates the anniversary of Juán Rodriguez Cabrillo's arrival at Bahía de Todos Santos in 1542 with ceremonies and a reenactment of his landing. *Ensenada. 01152 (6) 176-19-01, 178-24-11.*

The Northern Triangle

ENSENADA CHILI COOK-OFF

Chili chefs from both sides of the border compete in this gastronomic competition, with judging done by spectators. The winner moves on to the international championships in Las Vegas. *Quintas Papagayo Hotel, Ensenada. 01152 (6) 174-45-75, 176-19-01.*

The Northern Triangle

ENSENADA INTERNATIONAL SEAFOOD FAIR

Restaurants from all over northern Baja and across the border in Southern California compete to produce the best seafood dishes, judged by a panel of professional chefs. *Ensenada. 01152 (6) 178-36-75 or 174-04-35.*

The Northern Triangle

DAY OF OUR LADY OF LORETO

Residents of Loreto spend three days celebrating their town's patron saint, for whom the local mission and town are named. Music, food, folkloric dancing and games are part of the celebration, with a series of masses held on the official saint's day, September 8. *Multiple locations, Loreto. 01152 (1) 135-04-11.*

San Ignacio and Down the Gulf

October

PUERTO NUEVO LOBSTER FESTIVAL

The spiny crustacean is the star of this culinary celebration as dozens of Puerto Nuevo restaurants prepare and serve a myriad of lobster dishes. There's also wine tasting, while mariachis and folkloric dancers provide the entertainment. *South of Rosarito Beach at Puerto Nuevo's Lobster Village, Rosarito Beach. (800) 962-2252, 01152 (6) 612-03-96.*

The Northern Triangle

ROSARITO-ENSENADA BIKE RIDE

Thousands of cyclists make the 50-mile fun ride from Rosarito Beach to Ensenada along the Highway 1 free

The Northern Triangle

road in this popular semiannual event. A party follows at the finish line. *(619) 583-3001.*

BISBEE'S BLACK & BLUE

The Cape Region

Billed as "the World's Richest Billfishing Tournament," this contest draws top anglers from around the world to Cabo San Lucas, where they compete for more than $2 million in prize money catching black marlin and blue marlin (hence the name), and sailfish from the offshore waters. A golf tournament and other events coincide. *Cabo San Lucas. (949) 650-8006. www.bisbees.com.*

TODOS SANTOS FESTIVAL

The Cape Region

A week of festivities celebrates the town's founding and fetes the saint's day for the patron saint of the local mission, Nuestra Señora de Pilar. *Todos Santos. 01152 (1) 145-00-03.*

LORETO CITY FOUNDERS DAY

San Ignacio and Down the Gulf

A week of music, art exhibitions and other cultural events celebrate the birth of the oldest city in the Californias, founded in 1697. *Various locations around Loreto. 01152 (1) 135-04-11.*

O'NEILL TECATE MEXICAN SURF FIESTA

The Northern Triangle

Top surfers from California and Mexico compete in this contest at San Miguel Beach, one of northern Baja's top surf spots. A barbecue takes place on the beach during the competition. *San Miguel Beach, 7 miles north of Ensenada. (858) 486-0370.*

TECATE FOUNDERS FIESTA

The Northern Triangle

Tecate residents and visitors celebrate the anniversary of the city's founding with a gala celebration. *Parque Hidalgo in Tecate. 01152 (6) 654-10-95.*

November

LOS CABOS BILLFISH TOURNAMENT

The Cape Region

Anglers cast their lines in the waters off Cabo San Lucas to catch marlin, tuna, wahoo and dorado in a tournament with a purse of more than $350,000. The tournament takes place the week following U.S. Thanksgiving. *Cabo San Lucas. (407) 571-4680. www.marlinmag.com.*

SAN FELIPE SHRIMP FESTIVAL

The Desert Northeast

A cookoff featuring shrimp dishes prepared by local restaurants and individuals is the main event of this festival, held in the first week of the month. Other attractions include a street bazaar, live music and fireworks. *San Felipe. (858) 454-7166, 01152 (6) 577-11-55.*

SAN FELIPE WELCOME SNOWBIRDS FIESTA

The Desert Northeast

The city rolls out the red carpet for its winter guests from the north with a gala celebration that includes mariachi music, folkloric dancing, gifts from local stores and more. *San Felipe. 01152 (6) 577-11-55.*

TECATE SCORE BAJA 1000

Various Regions

The most famous of all off-road races, this legendary event provides the ultimate challenge for drivers and motorcyclists, pitting their machines against some of Baja's most challenging terrain. *Start in Ensenada. (818) 225-8402. Website at www.score-international.com.*

December

TECATE ENSENADA-SAN FELIPE 250

Various Regions

Off-road drivers and motorcyclists race across the countryside from Ensenada to San Felipe in this annual test of speed and endurance. *01152 (6) 178-24-11, 176-16-37.*

Guide to Mexican Holidays

Pity the traveler who tries to cash a traveler's check, book a flight or find an open tourism office, say, on November 20, which they'll quickly learn is Mexican Revolution Day. The same goes for Independence Day (September 16), Day of the Dead (November 2) or one of the other holidays scattered throughout the year. Then again, these are also excellent times to join the festivities and immerse yourself in Mexico's culture. Some days, like Christmas and Easter, are familiar to most foreign tourists, while many others are uniquely Mexican. A list of major holidays and a brief description follows. Legal holidays are those in which government offices, banks and most businesses are closed.

New Year's Day, January 1, is a legal holiday.

Day of the Three Kings ***(Día de los Tres Reyes)***, January 6. See details under Christmas.

Constitution Day, February 5, is a legal holiday that marks the proclamation of the 1917 Constitution.

Flag Day, February 24, celebrates the designing of the Mexican flag, which debuted in the town of Iguala, Guerrero.

Benito Juárez's Birthday, March 21, is a legal holiday, commemorating the birth of one of Mexico's most revered presidents.

All-American Celebrations ... in Baja

They don't show up on any Mexican calendar, but spring break and several U.S. holidays spell fast times and throngs of revelers in much of Baja California. The weeks between mid-March and mid-April bring crowds of U.S. college students south for spring break in San Felipe, Rosarito Beach, Ensenada and Cabo San Lucas. Likewise, Americans by the thousands invade northern Baja on U.S. holiday weekends. In fact, many hotels and resorts plan special celebrations around U.S. holidays, especially Independence Day.

Holy Week ***(Semana Santa)***, during March or April, is the week preceding Easter Sunday. Schools are closed and millions of Mexicans take vacation. This is perhaps the busiest week of the year for tourist areas in Mexico, Baja included, as nearly all hotels and campgrounds fill to capacity. Good Friday is a legal holiday, although many businesses close Thursday as well.

Labor Day, May 1, is a legal holiday in Mexico, as it is in much of the world outside the United States.

Cinco de Mayo, May 5, is *not* a legal holiday and passes without great fanfare in much of Mexico, unlike the United States, where it has become a major celebration of Mexican culture. It marks the Mexican army's 1862 victory against invading French forces at Puebla.

Independence Day, September 16, is a legal holiday, celebrating Mexico's independence from Spain in 1810. Festivities begin the night of September 15, climaxed by the 11 p.m. *grito* (shout) as revelers throughout the country gather in public squares to join in cries of "*¡Viva México!*"

Columbus Day ***(Día de la Raza)***, October 12, marks Christopher Columbus' arrival in the New World.

Day of the Dead ***(Día de los Muertos)***, November 2, is a legal holiday in which Mexicans pay tribute to deceased loved ones. Gravestones and shrines nationwide are cleaned and often bedecked with fresh flowers. Many observe November 1 as well.

Revolution Day, November 20, is a legal holiday that marks the beginning of the Mexican Revolution in 1910, which overthrew the dictatorship of President Porfirio Díaz and led to establishment of the modern constitution.

Day of Our Lady of Guadalupe ***(Día de Nuestra Señora de Guadalupe)***, December 12, pays tribute to the Virgin of Guadalupe, Mexico's patron saint. Festivals and masses are held nationwide.

Christmas Day, December 25, is a legal holiday. Much government and business activity slows to a near halt starting December 16, however, as Mexicans begin a series of celebrations known as *posadas* feting the approaching birthday of Christ. The Christmas season officially continues until Day of the Three Kings on January 6, marked by a final round of exchanging gifts.

Other Holidays, observed nationwide, include Valentine's Day, February 14; Mother's Day, May 10; Teacher's Day, May 15; and Father's Day, third Sunday in June.

Itinerary Inspirations

If you're a seasoned Baja veteran with thousands of miles of peninsular travel to your credit, this chapter is probably not for you. But if you're a comparative newcomer and aren't sure where to begin, then consider one of these four itineraries as a starting point. Try a single day's outing, a weekend jaunt, or load your 4x4 for a multiweek trek, but whatever you do, take your time and enjoy the moment. Adventure waits in the least likely places, and you'll never see all of Baja in a single trip anyway.

On the Go in Tijuana

Time Frame: You'll spend a full day in this busy border city without seeing it all.

When a single day is all the time you've got, the wilds of central Baja will have to wait, but an exotic experience can still be yours less than 20 minutes south of downtown San Diego. Tijuana has been wooing Americans for decades, and every day thousands head south for shopping, eating, nightlife and more in a very foreign country.

You're usually better off not driving in Tijuana, but you'll want your own vehicle if you plan on doing much shopping. For more information on Tijuana, see *The Northern Triangle*, Chapter 4.

Assuming it's your first time here, the place to start is Avenida Revolución. This is not the real Baja, or even the

Avenida Revolución, Tijuana

real Tijuana, but Revolución is an experience not to be missed—a 10-block strip of nightclubs, drug stores, gift shops and restaurants that measures up to every border-town stereotype. "La Revo," as locals often call it, will take at least an hour to walk, longer if you plan to shop, and hardly anyone leaves without buying something. Time allowing, poke your head inside the Museo de Cero (Wax Museum) or go wine-tasting at L.A. Cetto Winery. They're in the neighborhood, and you can do them both for less than $5.

Mercado Hidalgo, Tijuana

After "La Revo," head over to the Zona Río, where you'll drive down Paseo de los Héroes, a verdant parkway known for its modern office buildings, shopping centers and huge traffic circle monuments. Your focal point will be the Tijuana Cultural Center, a government-supported complex designed to keep *tijuanenses* in touch with their nation's rich cultural heritage. Take an hour or two to enjoy the many exhibits and the Museo de los Californias (Museum of the Californias), a fine tribute to the history of Baja California.

Leaving the center, walk two blocks south and discover more Mexican culture at Mercado Hidalgo. Noisy, vibrant and never dull, it is typical of open-air markets all over the country, with dozens of food stands, produce stalls, bakeries, and craft shops with colorful piñatas dangling from the ceilings. Grab a bag, wade in with the locals and jawbone your best price on a kilo of mangos, or stand back and watch a pack of burly men unload another truck of melons from the farm.

By now you may be primed for dinner, in which case you're in a good part of town. Some of Tijuana's finest restaurants are in the Zona Río, and serve an outstanding assortment of seafood, steak and Mexican platters. La Espadaña, La Fogata and Cien Años are good picks for "fine dining," while the boisterous Guadalajara Grill is a great choice for a party atmosphere.

If dinner's done and you're still poised for adventure, head for the Caliente Racetrack on nearby Boulevard Caliente, where the greyhounds run nightly starting at 7:45. Admission is free, a program costs just a dollar and wagers start at less than $5. By the time the hounds are finished, the border traffic at San Ysidro should be easing up, at worst a 30-minute wait and somewhat less on most weeknights.

Heading north, it's hard to think you never strayed more than four miles from the border gate.

Northern Triangle Route

Time Frame: A two- or three-day weekend will give you a good introduction to the many sides of Baja's northwest corner. Driving distance from Tijuana to Ensenada to Tecate is about 140 miles. It's another 35 miles from Tecate to the center of San Diego via California SR 94.

Beyond the raucous streets of Tijuana, you'll catch a glimpse or two of the real Mexico as you head south to the seaside town of Ensenada, then inland on your way to the pleasant town of Tecate. There's beautiful coastline, unspoiled countryside and friendly towns that feel worlds removed from Southern California. Best of all, you'll skip the engine-boiling, temper-fraying border-crossing wait at Tijuana.

Tijuana is worth a separate outing in its own right, so skip the border town on your way south, taking the Highway 1 toll road, which meets the coastline six miles to the west before turning south to Ensenada. Plan a few stops along the way, however, starting at Rosarito Beach. Do some shopping if you like; there are literally hundreds of shops and craft stalls, with pricing and selection that rival any town in Baja. Then take a peek inside the Rosarito Beach Hotel, where ornate woodwork and beautiful murals fill the main lobby of this classic inn, opened in 1927. Make time to stroll the hotel pier, which opened in 2000 and is the only public pier on Baja's Pacific coast.

Remember to buy Mexican auto insurance before taking your car to Baja. It's available at the border or at any Auto Club district office.

If you're a movie buff or just liked the film *Titanic*, take note of Fox Studios, five miles south of town on the free road. The biggest moneymaking film of all time was shot here in 1997, although the huge scale model of the doomed ship is gone now. By now it may be lunchtime, in which case you'll head for Puerto Nuevo, a few miles farther down the free road. More than 30 seafood restaurants cram a few square blocks of this beachfront village, where the local specialty is Puerto Nuevo-style lobster served with beans, rice and oversized flour tortillas.

Back on the road, you're within an hour's drive of Ensenada, a town that can keep you busy for several days, especially if you like fishing, surfing, diving or other outdoor fun. At a minimum, stroll the bayside walkway known as the *malecón,* then head a block inland and do the same on Avenida López Mateos, the town's main tourist drag. If it's a weekday and there's no cruise ship in port, you may even find an empty barstool at Hussong's, the oldest cantina in Baja California. Afterward, check out the grounds at Riviera del Pacífico, a former casino and one of the loveliest buildings in northern Baja.

The next day, take the side route to La Bufadora, the famous blowhole at the western tip of Punta Banda, a three-hour round trip. The return route follows Highway 1, but only a short ways to El Sauzal, where Mexico Highway 3 heads inland, wandering northeast through rocky hills, fertile valleys and tiny farm towns to the border town of Tecate.

A pleasant burg of 50,000, Tecate—the border town for people who hate border towns—is set amid an inland valley that feels a thousand miles from the U.S. frontier. Tecate is best known for its namesake beer, produced at the huge Cuauhtémoc Brewery. Within its confines is a sunny beer garden (open Tuesday through Saturday), where your non-driving companions can enjoy a cold one on the house. Afterward, make the short walk over to Parque Hidalgo, the town's main square and a nice place to watch the world go by before returning to California.

Parque Hidalgo, Tecate

The square is only three blocks from the U.S. Customs gate (open 6 a.m. to midnight daily), where you'll seldom wait more than 10 minutes to cross the border. From here it's about an hour's drive to downtown San Diego, passing through some of the prettiest backcountry left in Southern California.

Northern Exposure

Time Frame: A week on the road will introduce you to the major towns of northern Baja. Plan on 10 days to two weeks if you want to see them in depth or unwind in one destination. Total driving distance, crossing the border at Tijuana and leaving at Tecate, is about 440 miles.

Unless you have a special fondness for 100-degree-plus weather, you'll enjoy this trip most during the non-summer months.

It's a long way from the border to the sunny shores of the Gulf of California ... if you're driving Mexico Highway 1. Otherwise, you don't need a three-week road trip to enjoy

San Felipe

the gulf side of Baja at its scenic best. A week will give you time to relax in the sunny gulfside town of San Felipe, with a night or two in Ensenada and Mexicali along the way. It's your own call as to where you spend the most time exploring this vast, mostly empty swath of northern Baja.

From Tijuana you'll take Mexico Highway 1 south to Ensenada, a good place to spend your first night. Arrive early and you'll have time to stroll the *malecón* walkway, shop on López Mateos and hoist a cold one at Hussong's. A second night here will give you time for more exploring, plus a side trip to the famous blowhole La Bufadora at the tipof Punta Banda.

Leaving Ensenada, you'll want a half-day to enjoy the drive to San Felipe. It's around 160 miles, heading southeast across rambling hills, ranchland and green farming valleys on Mexico Highway 3 before descending to the Colorado Desert, meeting Mexico Highway 5 about 30 miles north of San Felipe.

Odds are you'll find San Felipe a tranquil, low-key place where you'll wish to ease back, linger over breakfast, and admire the gleaming waters of the gulf—that is, unless it's spring break or a three-day U.S. weekend, when young gringos arrive by the thousands, buzzing the streets in their mechanized cycles and partying down till the small hours of the morning.

City Park, Mexicali

Departing San Felipe, it's 120 miles north past rugged mountains, salt flats and unworldly desert landscapes to Mexicali, a border city that most gringos blissfully overlook. A tourist resort it's not, but there's enough happening in this city of 800,000, the state capital of Baja California, to keep you here for a day or two at least. Museums, impressive monuments, and the biggest Chinatown in Mexico (with scores of Chinese restaurants) are a few of the highlights.

From Mexicali head north or, if time allows, stay in Baja a few hours more, driving west on Mexico Highway 2. The most scenic highway in northern Baja, this modern four-lane route climbs the east slope of the Sierra de Juárez. You'll have spectacular desert views, on clear days reaching north to California's Salton Sea. It's a 90-mile drive from Mexicali to Tecate, a peaceful border burg in a scenic inland valley, best known for its namesake beer. You'll seldom have a long wait at the border crossing here (open 6 a.m. to midnight), about one mile south of California SR 94. From the border, you're within an hour's drive of downtown San Diego.

The Highway 1 Experience

Time Frame: Plan two weeks for an unhurried round-trip drive from the border to the cape, with time allowed for sightseeing. Three weeks and some thoughtful planning will give you the trip of a lifetime. Without side routes, the total drive is about 2100 miles.

Call it the grand tour of Baja California, a 2000-mile-plus odyssey down Mexico Highway 1 from the border to Cabo San Lucas and back. En route you'll discover many sides of Baja—the rolling hills and temperate climes of the far north, the endless blue skies and strange foliage of the central desert, the barren desolation around Guerrero Negro, the grandeur of red rock peaks abruptly rising from turquoise waters along the gulf. Take your time, explore the major towns, make some side trips along the way, and this could be a trip you'll never forget.

Santiago, near the Tropic of Cancer

It's a long drive by any measure, and this is not some U.S.-style superhighway. The 1059-mile highway is two lanes nearly all the way, with no shoulders and many steep, winding sections. In theory you could drive it one way in three days, with only brief stops and no nighttime driving (a bad idea in most of Baja). A more measured pace would be four to five days (eight to 10 days round trip), but in reality you'll want at least two weeks to make this a truly rewarding experience.

How you approach this trip depends on your available time, interests and the vehicle you're driving. A well-maintained passenger car will take you from the border to Cabo and back in safety and comfort, and give you access to several side routes. A properly equipped truck or 4x4 offers many more possibilities, helping you take back roads to the remotest corners of the peninsula.

Southern Baja can be extremely hot and humid during late summer and early fall, with the possibility of heavy downpours.

Whatever your situation, consider driving south with all due speed, then taking your time on the return trip. Four days will take you from Tijuana to La Paz at a reasonable pace, with time to case the territory and decide what to focus on when you return north. San Quintín, Guerrero Negro and Loreto are ideally spaced for overnight stops on the southbound leg, giving you a maximum daily drive of around 260 miles.

La Paz is an excellent place to begin exploring in earnest, and deserves as much time as any city in Baja. The city and environs are worth three or four days alone, although the bay and gulf could keep the outdoor-lover busy for weeks. How long you spend here is up to you.

Lover's Beach, Cabo San Lucas

From La Paz, it's another 140 miles down Highway 1 to Baja's southern tip, Cabo San Lucas. It's a three- to four-hour drive at most, but the last 20 miles from San José del Cabo to Land's End are worth a few days in their own right, once more depending on your time and interests. Your own tastes will decide which town (if either) you choose to stay in—San José del Cabo, with its relaxed colonial ambiance, or Cabo San Lucas, party central for southern Baja.

All roads lead north from Cabo San Lucas, but the preferred route is Mexico Highway 19, which forms the western leg of an excellent loop trip around Baja's Cape Region. The scenic two-lane route follows the Pacific shoreline for 45 miles to reach the former sugar mill town-turned artist's colony of Todos Santos. Continuing north, it's another 32 miles to the junction of Highway 1, some 20 miles south of La Paz.

Heading north from La Paz, your own interests will again dictate where you spend the most time, although Loreto, with its historic mission and beautiful setting, will almost surely merit a stop. The mission towns of Mulegé and San Ignacio are worth a closer look as well, as is Santa Rosalía, with its famous French-designed iron church. If you plan a whale-watching trip, then a night in Ciudad Constitución or Guerrero Negro may also be in the cards.

As for side routes, there are more than 30 of them along Highway 1—so many you may not know where to start. Each one has its attributes, but if we had to pick a short list, it would include the East Cape Drive, Bahía de los Angeles and San Javier. All three feature superlative scenery, and the first two are important destinations for recreators. The East Cape and San Javier make excellent day outings, while the remote Bahía de los Angeles is best done as an overnighter. On the other hand, only the Bahía de los Angeles route is paved the entire way; a passenger car can negotiate the other routes, but they are better left to sturdy high-clearance vehicles.

Lodging & Campgrounds

Lodging and Campgrounds are organized alphabetically, first by city, then grouped individually with AAA-approved lodgings followed by non-rated properties, and lastly, campgrounds. Each property's location is given from either the center of town or the nearest major highway.

Ratings Baja California offers something for everyone, from seaside resorts to modest motels to rustic camping. Those lodging establishments with a diamond rating have been inspected by our trained staff, and bear a rating of one to five diamonds. One-diamond establishments have met AAA's minimum standards in specific areas of operation, including housekeeping, maintenance, service and quality of furnishings. The higher the quality of these facilities and services, the more diamonds are awarded, up to a maximum of five, which means it's the best there is, *anywhere.* Additionally, as a courtesy to our readers, for many communities we list such basic information as the name, location, phone number and approximate room rates of a number of lodging properties and campgrounds which have not been formally inspected. Bear in mind that the facilities and services at these operations may not be representative of AAA standards.

AAA-approved lodgings are classified accordingly: Motels typically offer a basic room and convenient parking, resorts have extensive recreational facilities, hotels usually cater to business travelers, and suite or apartment properties often appeal to families. While these classifications are somewhat more definable within the United States, there are some broad variations in Baja. Consider the type of property that meets your particular needs and inquire about specifics when making reservations.

All listings are complimentary. A discount may or may not be offered.

Reservations Reservations are always advisable and may be the only way to stay at the place you want. Deposits are often required, although most places accept a credit card number as a guarantee. If your plans change, be sure to cancel or change your reservation by the specified date; if you don't, you may find a cancellation fee on your charge card statement or lose your deposit. Communicate by phone or e-mail whenever possible. Due to the slowness of Baja California mail service, all correspondence should be sent at least six weeks in advance.

Rates Room rates were provided by each property's management. Rate ranges are shown in U.S. dollar equivalents from an off-season low to an in-season high for two people; the off-season low rate is typically for a room with one bed, and the in-season high is typically for a room with two beds. Some listings also include the rate for an additional person (XP) staying in the same room with existing equipment. Some hotels quote prices in pesos, others in dollars. Nearly all establishments accept dollars; however, you can sometimes get a better price by paying pesos. Ask for rates for special rooms, additional equipment (cribs, roll-aways, etc.), package plans or during events (careful, rates may be temporarily increased). Some rates may include breakfast or meal plans. A 10 percent sales tax is imposed on all hotel, restaurant and nightclub bills; it may or may not be included in the quoted price. Some establishments, particularly in the Los Cabos region, add a service charge of 10 to 20 percent to room bills; it is typically a gratuity fee used in lieu of tipping, but this may not always be the case.

All rates are subject to change.

In some smaller communities electricity is not always available 24 hours; even during times of scheduled availability there may be unexpected power outages.

Amenities Assume that in each AAA-rated establishment, each guest room has air conditioning, telephone and color TV; exceptions are noted. Outside of resort areas, you're likely to find shower baths rather than tub baths. Other guest room facilities and amenities may not be available in all units; upon reservation or registration ask for specifics. The ⊗ symbol indicates smoke-free rooms are available. There may be additional charges for some items (bars, microwaves, etc.).

As well, you may pay extra for some recreational facilities or activities (golf, bicycles, massage, etc.) and certain services (child care, laundry, transportation, etc.). Pools may or may not be heated, and outdoor pools may not be open in winter.

Most lodgings do not accept pets; the exceptions are noted.

Disabled Travelers Facilities accommodating handicapped travelers are largely unavailable in Baja California. Individuals with special needs should determine ahead of time an establishment's suitability by contacting the property directly.

Credit Cards Establishments typically accept credit cards. These abbreviations identify the cards accepted: AE=American Express, CB=Carte Blanche, DI=Diners Club, DS=Discover, MC=MasterCard, and VI=Visa.

Campgrounds Properties listed range from primitive beach camps to full-service RV parks. Reservations are a good idea where they are accepted. In campground listings these abbreviations are used: E=electricity hookup, W=water hookup, S=sewer hookup.

Bahía Concepción

Non-Rated Lodging

RESORT HOTEL SAN BUENAVENTURA

01152 (1) 153-04-08, 153-03-08; FAX 153-04-08. $50-60
At Km 94.5 on Bahía Concepción. Mail: Apdo Postal 56, Mulegé, BCS, Mexico.

Camping

BAHÍA EL COYOTE *Playa pública*

No phone. $3-4 per vehicle
17½ mi S of Mulegé off Hwy 1; just after "Rcho El Coyote," turn at sign with beach symbol and go S ½ mi.
On shore of the bay. **Facilities:** Pit toilets, cabañas.

EL REQUESÓN *Playa pública*

No phone.
$3 per vehicle
27 mi S of Mulegé via Hwy 1 and unpaved rd.
Attractive location on sand spit that links beach with offshore island. **Facilities:** Pit toilets, cabañas, *palapas*.

PLAYA EL BURRO *Playa pública*

No phone. $5 per day
17 mi S of Mulegé via Hwy 1 and unpaved rd.
Palapas ringing the shoreline along a lovely stretch of beach. **Facilities:** Pit toilets.

PLAYA SANTISPAC *Playa pública*

No phone. $4 per vehicle
13½ mi S of Mulegé via Hwy 1 and unpaved rd.
On Santispac Cove, part of Bahía Concepción. **Facilities:** Flush toilets, showers, *palapas*. **Dining:** 2 cafes.

POSADA CONCEPCIÓN

No phone. $10 for 2 persons
15 mi S of Mulegé on Hwy 1. Mail: Apdo Postal 14, Mulegé, BCS, Mexico.
XP $2. Overlooks the bay. **Sites:** 10 RV sites; area for tents. Hookups: EWS-10; electricity 10 am-10 pm. **Facilities:** Flush toilets, showers. **Recreation:** Tennis, beach, skin diving, fishing.

RESORT SAN BUENAVENTURA

01152 (1) 153-04-08, 153-03-08; FAX 153-04-08. $10 per vehicle
25 mi S of Mulegé via Hwy 1 at Km 94.5, on Bahía Concepción. Mail: Apdo Postal 56, Mulegé, BCS, Mexico.
Hotel adjacent. **Sites:** 16 tent/RV bayside sites. **Facilities:** Flush toilets; showers; 16 *palapas* on beach; 3 bungalows with 2 cots, $20. **Recreation:** Fishing and dive trips, boat tours arranged, kayaks, paved boat ramp. **Dining:** Restaurant; bar.

Bahía de los Angeles

Camping

GUILLERMO'S TRAILER PARK

No phone. $6 for 2 persons

On the shore of the bay. Mail: Montes de Oca No 190, Fraccionamiento Buenaventura, Ensenada, BC, Mexico.

XP $1. Gift shop. **Sites:** 40 RV sites. Hookups: EWS-15; electricity 7-11 am and 5-9:30 pm. **Facilities:** Flush toilets, showers. **Recreation:** Beach, fishing trips arranged, boat ramp, boat rental. **Dining:** Restaurant; bar.

LA PLAYA RV PARK

US Reservations: (760) 741-9583; FAX (760) 489-5687. $15 for 2 persons

On the shore of the bay. Mail: 509 Ross Dr, Escondido, CA 92029.

Sites: 30 RV sites; extensive area for tents. Hookups: E-30; electricity 7 am-9:30 pm. **Facilities:** Disposal station, flush toilets, showers. **Recreation:** Fishing trips arranged, boat launch. **Services:** Ice. **Dining:** Restaurant; bar.

Buena Vista

AAA-Approved Lodging

HOTEL BUENA VISTA BEACH RESORT

♦♦ Resort

01152 (1) 141-00-33; FAX 141-01-33. $75-150

US reservations: (619) 425-1551, (800) 752-3555.

On shore of Bahía de Palmas, ¼ mi E of Hwy 1. US reservations: 100 W 35th St, Ste V, National City, CA 91950.

XP $50. 10% service charge. 30-day refund notice. Meal plans available. DS, MC, VI. Pets allowed in designated rooms. Resort on hillside overlooking the sea. **Rooms:** 60. Shower baths, coffeemakers; no phones. **Recreation:** Beach, 2 pools, whirlpools, tennis, fishing trips arranged in cruisers and pangas, kayaking, scuba diving, horseback riding. **Dining:** Dining room; 6-11 am, noon-3, 7-9:30 pm; cocktails, bar.

Cabo San Lucas

AAA-Approved Lodging

FIESTA AMERICANA GRAND LOS CABOS

♦♦♦ Resort Hotel

01152 (1) 145-62-00; FAX 145-62-01. $265-381

US reservations: (800) 504-5000.

6 mi E on Hwy 1 at Cabo del Sol. Mail: Carr Transpen Km 10.3, Lote A-1 Cabo San Lucas, BCS 23410, Mexico.

XP $20. 10% service charge. AE, CB, DI, DS, MC, VI. Large complex terraced on hillside overlooking the bay. **Rooms:** 278. Combination baths, bars, cable TV, movies, radios, data ports. **Recreation:** Beach, pools, saunas, whirlpools, health facilities, steam rooms, tennis, golf, fishing trips arranged. **Services:** Valet parking, valet laundry, business center. **Dining:** 3 restaurants; 7 am-11 pm; 24-hr room service; cocktails, bar.

HOTEL FINISTERRA ♦♦♦ Resort Complex
01152 (1) 143-33-33; FAX 143-05-90. $99-195
US Reservations: (714) 476-5555, (714) 450-9000.
Located at southernmost tip of Baja California peninsula. Mail: Apdo Postal #1, Cabo San Lucas, BCS 23410, Mexico.
XP $20; ages 12 and under stay free. 10% service charge. 7-day refund notice, 30 days for holiday periods. AE, MC, VI. No pets. Spectacular location overlooking Land's End. Large pool area surrounded by tropical gardens. **Rooms:** 279; some efficiencies. Ocean/bay views, balconies, shower baths, coffeemakers, bars, cable TV, movies, data ports, ⊘. **Recreation:** Beach, 3 pools, sauna, whirlpools, health club, massage, tennis, fishing trips arranged. **Dining:** Dining room; 6:30 am-9:30 pm; cocktails, lounge, entertainment.

MARINA FIESTA RESORT HOTEL ♦♦♦ Condominium Hotel
01152 (1) 143-26-89; FAX 143-26-88. $180-450
US reservations: (888) 599-4334.
On E side of marina at Marina Lotes. Mail: Marina Lote 37, Cabo San Lucas, BCS 23410, Mexico.
XP $35-55; ages 12 and under stay free. 3-day refund notice. AE, MC, VI. No pets. Pueblo-style complex on the marina. 5 to 7 stories. **Rooms:** 155; luxury suites $480-650. Shower baths, kitchens & utensils, refrigerators, cable TV, movies, data ports. **Recreation:** 2 pools, whirlpools, exercise room, boat ramp, marina, playground. **Services:** Valet laundry. **Dining:** Restaurant; 6 am-10 pm; cocktails.

MELIÁ SAN LUCAS ♦♦♦ Resort Hotel
01152 (1) 143-44-44; FAX 143-04-20. $216-295
US Reservations: (800) 336-3542.
On the shore 2 blks E of Bl Marina (Hwy 1). Mail: El Médano s/n, Cabo San Lucas, BCS 23410, Mexico.
XP $40; ages 12 and under stay free. 10% service charge. 15-day refund notice. AE, MC, VI. No pets. Pueblo-style hotel overlooking the harbor and Land's End. Gift shop. **Rooms:** 187. Refrigerators, bars, cable TV, movies, safes. **Recreation:** 2 pools, beach, fishing trips arranged, scuba diving, snorkeling. **Services:** Business services. **Dining:** Restaurant; 7 am-11 pm; cocktails, entertainment.

PUEBLO BONITO RESORT ♦♦♦ Resort Hotel
01152 (1) 143-29-00; FAX 143-19-95. $180-300
US Reservations: (800) 937-9567.
3 blks S of Hwy 1 on Playa El Médano. Mail: Apdo Postal 460, Cabo San Lucas, BCS 23410, Mexico.
XP $30; ages 18 and under stay free. 10% service charge. 7-day refund notice. MC, VI. No pets. Beachfront hotel on Cabo San Lucas Bay. **Rooms:** 144. Efficiencies, cable TV, movies. **Recreation:** Beach, pool, exercise room, scuba diving, snorkeling, boating, fishing trips arranged. **Dining:** 2 restaurants; 7 am-10 pm; cocktails.

PUEBLO BONITO ROSE RESORT ♦♦♦ Resort Hotel
01152 (1) 143-55-00; FAX 143-55-22. $160-380
US Reservations: (800) 937-9567.
1 Km S of Hwy 1 at Playa El Médano. Mail: Apdo Postal 460, Cabo San Lucas, BCS 23410, Mexico.
XP $30; ages 18 and under stay free. 10% service charge. 7-day refund notice. MC, VI. No pets. Beachfront location with spacious grounds and gardens. **Rooms:** 260. Shower baths, efficiencies, cable TV, movies, safes. **Recreation:** Beach, pool, wading pool, whirlpools, health club, steam rooms, massage, tennis, boating, fishing trips arranged, sailing, scuba diving, snorkeling. **Services:** Valet laundry. **Dining:** 2 restaurants; 7 am-10 pm; cocktails, bar.

SHERATON HACIENDA DEL MAR RESORT & SPA ♦♦♦ Resort Hotel
01152 (1) 145-80-00; FAX 01152 (1) 145-80-01. $200-340
US reservations: (888) 672-7173.
6⅓ mi E on Hwy 1 at Cabo del Sol. Mail: Carr Turístico, Km 10, Lote D, Cabo San Lucas, BCS 23410, Mexico.
2% service charge. 7-day refund notice. AE, MC, VI. Expansive resort at the beach designed as a Mexican Colonial-style village. **Rooms:** 170. Shower baths, bars, cable TV, movies, data ports, safes. **Recreation:** Beach, pools, health club, massage, lighted tennis, golf, charter fishing. **Services:** Valet laundry, business services. **Dining:** 3 restaurants; 7 am-10 pm; 24-hr room service; cocktails, bar.

SIESTA SUITES HOTEL ♦ Motel
Phone & FAX 01152 (1) 143-27-73. $50
US reservations: (602) 331-1354.
Downtown on Calle E Zapata at Hidalgo. US reservations: Box 9416, Phoenix, AZ 85068.
XP $10. 15-day refund notice. No pets. **Rooms:** 20. Shower baths, kitchens with utensils, movies. **Recreation:** Fishing trips arranged.

SOLMAR SUITES RESORT ♦♦♦ Resort Complex
01152 (1) 143-35-35; FAX 143-04-10. $165-250
US reservations: (310) 459-9861, (800) 344-3349.
Located on the southernmost tip of the peninsula. US Reservations: Box 383, Pacific Palisades, CA 90272.
XP $28-40; discount for ages 12 and under. 10% service charge. 7-day refund notice. AE, MC, VI. No pets. All-suite hotel on the beach at Land's End. Expansive grounds and pool area. Most rooms face the Pacific Ocean. **Rooms:** 125; Roca suites and condominiums available. Patios or private balconies, some kitchens with utensils, bars, coffeemakers, cable TV, movies, safes. **Recreation:** Beach, 3 pools, whirlpool, tennis, fishing trips on cruisers, diving, snorkeling. **Dining:** Restaurant; 7 am-10 pm; cocktails, poolside bar.

Non-Rated Lodging

BAHÍA CONDO HOTEL
01152 (1) 143-18-88. $90 or more
US Reservations: (800) 932-5599.
Near E end of Playa El Médano.

THE BUNGALOWS BREAKFAST INN
01152 (1) 143-05-85. $60-$90
Calle Dorado, 4 blks N of Av Cabo San Lucas.

CABO INN HOTEL
01152 (1) 143-08-19. Up to $60
20 de Noviembre between Leona Vicario and Mendoza.

CHILE PEPPER INN
01152 (1) 143-86-11, 143-86-12. $60-$90
Corner of 16 de Septiembre and Abasolo.

CLUB CABO MOTEL RESORT
Phone & FAX 01152 (1) 143-33-48. $40-60
2 mi E of town center on old road; turn S off Hwy 1 on rd to Club Cascadas. Mail: Apdo Postal 463, Cabo San Lucas, BCS 23410, Mexico.

HACIENDA BEACH RESORT HOTEL
01152 (1) 143-01-22. $90 or more
W end of Playa El Médano.

HOTEL MAR DE CORTEZ
01152 (1) 143-00-32. $60-$90
US Reservations: (800) 347-8821.
Corner of Bl Lázaro Cárdenas and Vicente Guerrero.

HOTEL SANTA FÉ
01152 (1) 143-44-01, 143-44-02. $60-$90
Corner of Zaragoza and Obregón.

LAS MARGARITAS INN
01152 (1) 143-67-70. $60-$90
Corner of Bl Lázaro Cárdenas and Zaragoza.

MARINA CABO PLAZA
01152 (1) 143-18-33. $90 or more
On the NE corner of the Marina, Bl Marina 39.

MARINA HOTEL
01152 (1) 143-24-84. Up to $60
Corner of Bl Marina and Vicente Guerrero.

OLAS HOTEL
01152 (1) 143-17-80. Up to $60
Corner of Revolución and Gómez Farías.

PLAZA LAS GLORIAS
01152 (1) 143-12-20. $157-231
US reservations: (800) 342-2644.
Part of a large complex that includes condominiums and a shopping center, between Bl Marina and the harbor. Mail: Bl Marina s/n Lotes 9 y 10, Cabo San Lucas, BCS 23410, Mexico.

VILLA LA PALOMA
01152 (1) 143-11-57. $90 or more
Bl Lázaro Cárdenas near E entrance of town, just W of Hwy 19 turnoff.

Camping

CLUB CABO MOTEL & CAMPGROUND RESORT
Phone & FAX 01152 (1) 143-33-48. $7 per person
2 mi E of town center on the old road; turn S off Hwy 1 on rd to Club Cascadas. Mail: Apdo Postal 463, Cabo San Lucas, BCS, Mexico.
RV park and motel suites in open area; short walk to beach. **Sites:** 15 tent/RV. Hookups: EWS-10, EW-5. **Facilities:** Flush toilets, showers, pool, whirlpool. *Palapa* with TV, barbecue. **Recreation:** Fishing trips & horseback outings arranged, table tennis, trampoline. **Services:** Shuttle to town, ice.

EL ARCO TRAILER PARK
01152 (1) 143-16-86. $15 per site
2 mi E of town on Hwy 1. Mail: Km 5.5, Cabo San Lucas, BCS, Mexico.
Open area with view of Cabo San Lucas Bay. **Sites:** 85 tent/RV. EWS-65. **Facilities:** Flush toilets, showers. **Recreation:** Pool. **Services:** Laundry. **Dining:** Restaurant; bar.

EL FARO VIEJO TRAILER PARK
Phone & FAX 01152 (1) 143-42-11. $12 for 2 persons
¾ mi NW of town center near Hwy 19, at Matamoros and Mijares. Mail: Apdo Postal 64, Cabo San Lucas, BCS 23410, Mexico.
XP $3. 12% surcharge. AE, MC, VI. Curio shop. Partly shaded area surrounded by wall. **Sites:** 19 tent/RV. Hookups: EWS-19. **Facilities:** Flush toilets, showers. **Dining:** Restaurant; bar.

VAGABUNDOS DEL MAR RV PARK
01152 (1) 143-02-90; FAX 143-05-11. $16 for 2 persons
US reservations: (707) 374-5511; FAX (707) 374-6843.
1½ mi NE of town center on Hwy 1. Mail: 190 Main St, Rio Vista, CA 94571.
XP $3. 10-day cancellation notice. **Sites:** 65 RV. Hookups: EWS-65. **Facilities:** Flush toilets, showers. **Recreation:** Pool. **Services:** Laundry. **Dining:** Restaurant.

Cataviña

Non-Rated Lodging

HOTEL LA PINTA
No phone. $65
US reservations: (818) 275-4500, (800) 262-4500.
On Hwy 1, 1 mi N of Rancho Santa Inés. Mail: Apdo Postal 179, San Quintín, BC, Mexico. US reservations: Mexico Condo Reservations, 4420 Hotel Circle Ct, Ste 230, San Diego, CA 92108.

Camping

CATAVIÑA RV PARK
No phone. $5 per vehicle
On Hwy 1, ¼ mi N of Hotel La Pinta.
Open area with limited facilities. **Sites:** 66 tent/RV. Hookups: WS-66. **Facilities:** Flush toilets.

Ciudad Constitución

Non-Rated Lodging

HOTEL CONCHITA
01152 (1) 132-02-66.00 $12-37
E side of Bl Olachea, 3 blks S of town plaza.

HOTEL CONQUISTADOR
01152 (1) 132-27-45. $12-37
1 blk E of Bl Olachea on the S side of Nicolas Bravo near center of town.

HOTEL MARIBEL
01152 (1) 132-01-55. $12-37
On the E side of Bl Olachea at corner of Victoria.

HOTEL OASIS
01152 (1) 132-44-58. $12-37
In the N part of town, 3 blks W of Bl Olachea at Vicente Guerrero 284.

HOTEL REFORMA
01152 (1) 132-09-88. $12-37
1 blk E of Bl Olachea on the S side of main plaza at Obregón 125.

Camping

CAMPESTRE LA PILA
01152 (1) 132-05-62; FAX 132-02-29. $8.50 for 2 persons
1½ mi S of town center via Hwy 1 and ½ mi W on unpaved rd. Mail: Apdo Postal 261, Ciudad Constitución, BCS 23600, Mexico.

XP $3. Open area bordered by irrigated farmland. **Sites:** 44 tent/RV. Hookups: EW-44. **Facilities:** Disposal station, flush toilets, showers. **Recreation:** Pool, picnic area. **Dining:** Snack bar.

MANFRED'S RV PARK

Phone & FAX 01152 (1) 132-11-03. $6-14 for 2 persons

½ mi N of city center on Hwy 1. Mail: Apdo Postal 120, Ciudad Constitución, BCS 23600, Mexico.

RVs $12-15; tents $6; XP $1.50. Motel rooms. Nicely landscaped with flowering plants and trees. **Sites:** 80 RV. Hookups: EWS-50, EW-30. **Facilities:** Flush toilets, showers. **Recreation:** Pool. **Dining:** Restaurant.

Colonia Guerrero

Camping

MESÓN DE DON PEPE

01152 (6) 166-22-16; FAX 166-22-68. $5-8.50 for 2 persons

1 mi S via Hwy 1. Mail: Apdo Postal 7, Colonia Guerrero, BC 22920, Mexico.

RVs $8.50, tents $5; XP $1.50. Partly shaded area adjacent to highway. **Sites:** 35 RV, 20 tent. Hookups: EWS-35. **Facilities:** Flush toilets, showers. **Recreation:** Fishing. **Services:** Tourist information. **Dining:** Restaurant; bar.

POSADA DON DIEGO

01152 (6) 166-21-81; FAX 166-22-48. $10 for 3 persons

1 mi S via Hwy 1 and unpaved rd, past first RV park. Mail: Apdo Postal 126, Colonia Guerrero, BC 22920, Mexico.

XP $1.25. Pleasant area in rural setting. **Sites:** 80 tent/RV. Hookups: EW-80, S-60. **Facilities:** Disposal station, flush toilets, showers. **Recreation:** Playground. **Services:** Laundry, ice. **Dining:** Restaurant; bar.

El Pescadero

Camping

LOS CERRITOS RV PARK

No phone. $4 per vehicle

1½ mi S on Hwy 19, then 1½ mi SW via a dirt rd.

Wide beach on shore of the Pacific. **Sites:** 50 tent/RV. **Facilities:** Flush toilets.

Ensenada

AAA-Approved Lodging

BEST WESTERN CASA DEL SOL MOTEL ♦ Motel

01152 (6) 178-15-70; FAX 178-20-25. $70-85

US reservations: (800) 528-1234.

At avs López Mateos and Blancarte. Mail: Apdo Postal 557, Ensenada, BC 22800, Mexico.

XP $10; ages 12 and under stay free. 3-day refund notice. AE, MC, VI. Small pets. **Rooms:** 48. Kitchens, shower baths, cable TV, movies. **Recreation:** Pool. **Dining:** Restaurant; bar.

BEST WESTERN EL CID

♦ Motor Inn

01152 (6) 178-24-01; FAX 178-36-71. $47-99

US reservations: (800) 528-1234.

At Av López Mateos 993. Mail: PO Box 786, Chula Vista, CA 91910.

XP $8. AE, MC, VI. No pets. Attractive Spanish styling. **Rooms:** 52; suites available. Balconies, shower baths, cable TV, data ports. **Recreation:** Pool, fishing trips arranged. **Dining:** Restaurant; Mon 7 am-3 pm, Tue-Sun 7 am-10 pm; cocktails.

CORONA HOTEL

♦ Motor Inn

01152 (6) 176-09-01; FAX 246-40-23. $38-65

At Bl Costero No 1442 (Bl Lázaro Cárdenas) across from Riviera del Pacífico Building. Mail: 482 W San Ysidro Bl, Ste 303, San Ysidro, CA 92173.

XP $8-10; ages 13 and under stay free. 3-day refund notice. AE, MC, VI. No pets. 4 stories. **Rooms:** 92. Balconies, cable TV, movies, radios, data ports. **Recreation:** Pool. **Dining:** Restaurant; 7 am-11 pm; cocktails, bar.

DAYS INN VILLA FONTANA HOTEL

♦ Motel

Formerly DAYS INN.

Phone & FAX 01152 (6) 176-09-01. $46-50

US Reservations: (800) 432-9755.

Just W of Av Blancarte on Av López Mateos. Mail: Av López Mateos 1050, Ensenada, BC 22800, Mexico.

XP $10; ages 12 and under stay free. 3-day refund notice. AE, MC, VI. No pets. **Rooms:** 65. Shower baths, cable TV, movies. **Recreation:** Pool, whirlpool.

ESTERO BEACH RESORT HOTEL

♦♦ Resort Complex

01152 (6) 176-62-30; FAX 176-69-25. $55-130

8 mi S of city center via Hwy 1 and graded side rd. Mail: Box 1186, 482 W San Ysidro Bl, San Ysidro, CA 92173.

XP $5-10; ages 5 and under stay free. 3-day refund notice. MC, VI. No pets. Gift shop. Archaeological museum. Beach-front resort complex on attractive grounds. **Rooms:** 96; suites $250-285. Balconies/patios, shower/combination baths, cable TV, movies, ⊘. **Recreation:** Beach, pool, tennis, boat ramp, boat and personal watercraft rentals, water-skiing, fishing, horseback riding, bicycles, playground, recreation room. **Dining:** Restaurant; 7:30 am-11 pm; cocktails.

HACIENDA BAJAMAR

♦♦♦ Resort Complex

Formerly HACIENDA LAS GLORIAS.

01152 (6) 155-01-51; FAX 155-01-50. $65-85

At Bajamar Golf Resort, 21 mi N of Ensenada off Hwy 1. Mail: 416 W San Ysidro Bl, Ste #L-732, San Ysidro, CA 92173.

XP $35; ages 12 and under stay free. 2-night minimum stay on weekends. 8-day refund notice. AE, MC, VI. No pets. Mexican Colonial-style buildings. 2 stories. **Rooms:** 81; 1-bedroom suites with kitchens, $120-130. Cable TV, movies, safes. **Recreation:** Pool, whirlpool, tennis, golf, pro shop. **Dining:** Restaurant; 6 am-10:30 pm; cocktails, bar.

HOTEL CORAL & MARINA RESORT

♦♦♦ Resort Hotel

01152 (6) 175-00-00; FAX 175-00-05. $135-220

US reservations: (619) 523-0064, (800) 862-9020.

2 mi N of Ensenada on Hwy 1-D. Mail: Carr Tijuana-Ensenada, No 3421 Zona Playitas, Ensenada, BC 22860, Mexico.

AE, MC, VI. No pets. Gift shop. All-suite resort hotel overlooking the bay and marina. **Rooms:** 147; 11 efficiencies; wheelchair-accessible room. Balconies/patios, cable TV, movies, VCRs. **Recreation:** Pools (1 indoor), wading pool, sauna, whirlpools, health club, steam baths, lighted tennis, boating, sailing, marina, charter fishing. **Services:** Business services. **Dining:** Dining room; 7 am-11 pm; cocktails, bar.

HOTEL CORTEZ ♦♦ Motor Inn
01152 (6) 178-23-07; FAX 178-39-04. $60
US reservations: (800) 303-2684.
At Av Castillos and Av López Mateos No 1089. Mail: PO Box 5356, Chula Vista, CA 91912.
XP $7; ages 12 and under stay free. 12% service charge. 30-day refund notice. AE, MC, VI. **Rooms:** 82; 2 suites. Shower baths, coffeemakers, refrigerators, cable TV. **Recreation:** Pool. **Services:** Valet parking, business services. **Dining:** Restaurant; 7 am-11 pm.

HOTEL MISIÓN SANTA ISABEL ♦ Motor Inn
01152 (6) 178-36-16; FAX 178-33-45. $55-70
At Bl Costero (Bl Lázaro Cárdenas) and Av Castillo No 1100. Mail: Box 120-818, Chula Vista, CA 91912.
XP $10; ages 11 and under stay free. 3-day refund notice. AE, MC, VI. No pets. 3 stories. **Rooms:** 58. Colonial-style architecture. Shower baths, cable TV. **Recreation:** Pool. **Services:** Business services. **Dining:** Restaurant; Mon-Sat 7 am-11 pm, Sun 8 am-2 pm; cocktails, bar.

HOTEL PARAÍSO LAS PALMAS ♦ Motel
01152 (6) 177-17-01; FAX 177-17-01 ext 402. $58-71
In SE part on Calle Agustín Sanginés 206. Mail: 445 W San Ysidro Bl, Ste 2507, San Ysidro, CA 92173.
XP $5; ages 12 and under stay free. AE, MC, VI. No pets. 3 stories. **Rooms:** 67. Shower baths, cable TV. **Recreation:** Pool, whirlpool. **Dining:** Restaurant; 7 am-11 pm; cocktails, bar.

HOTEL SANTO TOMÁS ♦ Motel
01152 (6) 178-15-03; FAX 178-15-04. $60
US reservations: (800) 303-2684; FAX (619) 427-6523.
On Bl Lázaro Cárdenas (Costero) at Av Miramar. Mail: 1181 Broadway, Ste 2, Chula Vista, CA 91912.
XP $7. 30-day refund notice. AE, MC, VI. No pets. 3-story motel. **Rooms:** 80. Shower baths, cable TV, ⊗. **Dining:** Restaurant; 7 am-11 pm; bar.

LAS ROSAS HOTEL ♦♦♦ Motor Inn
01152 (6) 174-43-10; FAX 174-45-95. $126-154
4 mi N on Hwy 1. Mail: Apdo Postal No 316, Ensenada, BC 22800, Mexico.
XP $22; discount for ages 12 and under. 2-night minimum stay weekends. 3-day refund notice; handling fee. MC, VI. No pets. Located on a bluff with spectacular oceanfront view. 2 stories. **Rooms:** 48. Private balconies, shower baths, cable TV, movies. **Recreation:** Pool, sauna, whirlpool, gym, massage, tennis, racquetball. **Dining:** Restaurant; 6 am-10 pm; cocktails, bar.

POSADA EL REY SOL ♦♦ Motor Inn
Formerly ENSENADA TRAVELODGE.
01152 (6) 178-16-01; FAX 174-00-05. $64-110
US Reservations: (888) 315-2378.
At Av Blancarte 130, near Av López Mateos. Mail: 4492 Camino de la Plaza, Ste ESE-118, San Ysidro, CA 92173.
XP $12; ages 12 and under stay free. 8-day refund notice. No pets. **Rooms:** 52. Shower baths, coffeemakers, bar, cable TV, movies, radios. **Recreation:** Pool, whirlpool. **Services:** Business services. **Dining:** Restaurant; 7 am-11 pm; cocktails, bar. AE, MC, VI.

PUNTA MORRO HOTEL SUITES ♦♦♦ Suite Motor Inn
01152 (6) 178-35-07; FAX 174-44-90. $98-260
US reservations: (800) 526-6676.

On oceanfront, 3 mi N of town center off Hwy 1. Mail: Box 434263, San Diego, CA 92143.
XP $25; ages 12 and under stay free. 2-night minimum stay weekends. 7-day refund notice. AE, MC, VI. No pets. 3 stories. **Rooms:** 24; 2-bedroom suites for up to 4 persons, $105-145; 3-bedroom suites for up to 6 persons, $130-195; suites with kitchens and 3 studios with refrigerators. Fireplaces, balconies/patios, shower baths, cable TV, movies. **Recreation:** Pool, whirlpool. **Dining:** Restaurant; Mon-Fri noon-10 pm, Sat 8 am-10 pm, Sun 9 am-10 pm; cocktails, bar.

Non-Rated Lodging

CORONADO MOTEL
01152 (6) 176-14-16. $20-35
Av López Mateos between avs Espinoza and Floresta.

HOTEL BAHÍA
01152 (6) 178-21-03. $45-70
US Reservations: (888) 308-9048.
Av López Mateos between avs Riveroll and Alvarado.

HOTEL JOKER
01152 (6) 176-72-01. $45-70
5 mi S of downtown across from Ensenada Airport (El Ciprés).

HOTEL LA PINTA
01152 (6) 176-26-01. $40-65
US reservations: Mexico Condo Reservations, 4420 Hotel Circle Ct, Ste 230, San Diego, CA 92108. (800) 262-4500; (818) 275-4500.
At Av Floresta and Bl Bucaneros. Mail: Apdo Postal 929, Ensenada, BC 22800, Mexico.

HOTEL PLAZA
01152 (6) 178-27-15. $20-35
Av López Mateos between avs Miramar and Gastelum.

HOTEL RITZ
01152 (6) 174-05-01. $20-35
Corner of avs Ruíz and 3.

MOTEL AMÉRICA
01152 (6) 176-13-33. $20-35
Av López Mateos at Av Espinoza (behind Riviera del Pacífico).

MOTEL CARIBE
01152 (6) 178-34-81. $45-70
Av López Mateos between avs Macheros and Miramar.

QUINTAS PAPAGAYO
01152 (6) 174-45-75. $45-70
2 mi N of town on Hwy 1 at Km 108.

RUDI'S HOTEL
01152 (6) 176-32-45. $20-35
Av Hidalgo between calles 4 and 5.

SAN NICOLÁS RESORT HOTEL
01152 (6) 176-19-01. $95-115
Av López Mateos at Av Club Rotario.

VILLA MARINA HOTEL
01152 (6) 178-33-21. $95-115
Av Blancarte between Av López Mateos and Bl Costero.

Camping

CAMPO PLAYA RV PARK

Phone & FAX 01152 (6) 176-29-18. $13-20 for 2 persons

1 mi SE of downtown Ensenada, near intersection of Bl Costero and Calle Agustín Sanginés (Delante). Mail: Apdo Postal 789, Ensenada, BC 28600, Mexico.

XP $2. MC, VI. Fenced area near bay. **Sites:** 85 tent/RV. Hookups: E-60, WS-85. **Facilities:** Flush toilets, showers. **Recreation:** Recreation room.

ESTERO BEACH RV PARK

Formerly ESTERO BEACH TRAILER PARK.

01152 (6) 176-62-25. $16-25 for 2 persons

8 mi S via Hwy 1 and paved side rd (signs posted at turnoff). Mail: Box 1186, 482 San Ysidro Bl, San Ysidro, CA 92173.

XP $5. 3-day refund notice. MC, VI. Clubhouse. Large seaside resort adjacent to Estero Beach Hotel. **Sites:** 50 RV, 50 tent. Hookups: EWS-50. **Facilities:** Disposal station, flush toilets, showers. **Recreation:** Beach, tennis, fishing, boat launch, horseback riding, playground. **Dining:** Restaurant; bar.

PLAYA SALDAMANDO

US Reservations: (619) 582-8333. $8 for 4 persons

On beach 10½ mi N via Hwy 1 and steep, winding dirt rd. Mail: 3965 College Av, San Diego, CA 92115.

XP $1. No off-road vehicles. Trailers for rent, $25-35. **Sites:** 30 tent/RV. No hookups. **Facilities:** Disposal station, flush toilets, showers.

SAN MIGUEL VILLAGE (VILLA DE SAN MIGUEL)

Phone & FAX 01152 (6) 174-62-25. $8-10 per vehicle

In El Sauzal, 8 mi N via Hwy 1-D. On Bahía de Todos Santos, just S of toll gate. Mail: Apdo Postal 55, El Sauzal, BC 22760, Mexico.

MC, VI. **Sites:** 40 RV, 500 tent. Hookups: EWS-40. **Facilities:** Flush toilets, showers. **Recreation:** Beach. **Dining:** Restaurant; bar.

Guerrero Negro

Non-Rated Lodging

HOTEL EL MORRO

01152 (1) 157-13-01. $18-30

N side of Bl Zapata in the center of town.

HOTEL LA PINTA

01152 (1) 157-13-01. $73

US reservations: (800) 262-4500; (818) 275-4500.

Hwy 1 next to 28th parallel monument. US reservations: Mexico Condo Reservations, 4420 Hotel Circle Ct, Ste 230, San Diego, CA 92108.

HOTEL LAS BALLENAS

01152 (1) 157-01-16. $18-30

Off Bl Zapata just N of the Hotel El Morro.

MALARRIMO MOTEL

01152 (1) 157-02-50. $18-30

Near the E edge of town on the N side of Bl Zapata.

MOTEL SAN IGNACIO

01152 (1) 157-02-70. $18-30

N side of Bl Zapata in the center of town.

MOTEL SAN JOSÉ

01152 (1) 157-14-20. $18-30

N side of Bl Zapata across from the bus station.

Camping

MALARRIMO TRAILER PARK

01152 (1) 157-02-50; FAX 157-01-00. $10-14

1 mi W of Hwy 1 on E edge of town, next to Malarrimo Restaurant. Mail: Bl Zapata s/n, Col Fundo Legal, Guerrero Negro, BCS 23940, Mexico.

XP $5. Open area. **Sites:** 22 RV. Hookups: EWS-22. **Facilities:** Flush toilets, showers. **Services:** Whale-watching trips arranged, $40 per person. **Dining:** Restaurant; bar.

La Paz

AAA-Approved Lodging

ARAIZA INN PALMIRA ♦ Motor Inn

01152 (1) 121-62-00; FAX 121-62-27. $90

US reservations: (800) 927-2402.

1½ mi N on Carr Pichilingue. Mail: Apdo Postal 442, La Paz, BCS 23010, Mexico.

XP $7. AE, MC, VI. No pets. Gift shop. Across from bay, with tropical grounds. 3 stories. **Rooms:** 120. Shower baths, cable TV, movies. **Recreation:** Pool, wading pool, tennis, fishing/tour arrangements, playground. **Services:** Business services. **Dining:** Restaurant; 6:30 am-10:30 pm.

CABAÑAS DE LOS ARCOS ♦♦ Motel

01152 (1) 122-27-44; FAX 125-43-13. $60-75

US reservations: (800) 347-2252.

Opposite the malecón, *at Paseo Alvaro Obregón and Rosales. Mail: Apdo Postal 112, La Paz, BCS 23000, Mexico.*

XP $5-10; ages 12 and under stay free. 7-day refund notice. AE, MC, VI. No pets. 4-story hotel wing and 16 bungalows in tropical garden setting. **Rooms:** 52. Shower baths, coffeemakers, bars, cable TV, movies, radios. **Recreation:** Pool, fishing trips arranged. **Dining:** Restaurant and bar at Hotel Los Arcos, ½ blk away.

CLUB EL MORO ♦♦ Suite Motor Inn

01152 (1) 122-40-84; FAX 125-28-28. $40-70

1 mi N on Carr Pichilingue. Mail: Apdo Postal 357, La Paz, BCS 23010, Mexico.

3-day refund notice. AE, MC, VI. Pets allowed in designated rooms. Moorish-style buildings across from bay. 2 stories. **Rooms:** 21, most with kitchens. Shower baths. **Recreation:** Pool, whirlpool, kayaks, tour and diving arrangements, barbecue. **Dining:** Restaurant; 8 am-4 pm, closed Tue; cocktails, bar.

CROWNE PLAZA RESORT ♦♦♦ Suite Hotel

01152 (1) 124-08-30; FAX 124-08-37. $150-200

US reservations: Holiday Inn (800) 465-4329.

3½ mi W of town via Hwy 1 at Marina Fidepaz. Mail: Apdo Postal 482, La Paz, BCS 23096, Mexico.

XP $10; ages 12 and under stay free. 3-day refund notice. AE, MC, VI. No pets. Gift shop. On the bay. 2 stories. **Rooms:** 54; 2-bedroom suites $270 for 4 persons. Coffeemakers, refrigerators, bars, cable TV, movies, radios, data ports, safes. **Recreation:** Beach, 3 pools, whirlpool, exercise room, squash court; fishing trips, water sports and tours arranged. **Dining:** Restaurant; 7 am-11 pm; cocktails, bar, entertainment.

HOTEL LAS ARENAS
♦ Resort Hotel
$100-160

01152 (1) 122-31-46.
US reservations: (888) 644-7376.
44 mi SE of La Paz on Hwy 286 to Los Planes, then 11⅓ mi on gravel and dirt road to Bahía de la Ventana. Mail: 8080 La Mesa Bl, Suite 205, La Mesa, CA 91941.
XP $35. AE, MC, VI. **Rooms:** 40 units. Shower baths. **Recreation:** Pool, windsurfing, snorkeling, fishing, charter fishing. **Dining:** Dining room; 5-9 am, 1-3:30, 7-9:30 pm.

HOTEL LOS ARCOS
♦♦ Hotel
$75-80

01152 (1) 122-27-44; FAX 125-43-13.
Opposite the malecón, *facing La Paz Bay, at Paseo Alvaro Obregón and Allende. Mail: Apdo Postal 112, La Paz, BCS 23000, Mexico.*
US reservations: (800) 347-2252.
XP $10. 7-day refund notice. AE, MC, VI. No pets. Gift shop. Colonial-style hotel. **Rooms:** 130; suite $95-110. Shower baths, coffeemakers, cable TV, movies, radios. **Recreation:** Pool, sauna, fishing trips arranged. **Dining:** Restaurant; 7 am-11 pm; cocktails, bar.

HOTEL MARINA
♦♦ Hotel
$89

01152 (1) 121-62-54; FAX 121-61-77.
US reservations: (800) 826-1138.
1½ mi N on Carr Pichilingue. Mail: Apdo Postal 194, La Paz, BCS 23010, Mexico.
XP $16. 3-day refund notice. AE, MC, VI. No pets. On the bay and marina. 5 stories. **Rooms:** 92; suites with efficiencies and kitchens, $142-178, XP $26. Shower baths, cable TV, movies. **Recreation:** Pool, wading pool, whirlpool, lighted tennis, dock, marina, fishing/diving/snorkeling trips arranged. **Dining:** 2 restaurants; 7 am-11 pm; cocktails, bar.

LA CONCHA BEACH RESORT
♦♦ Resort Complex
$95

01152 (1) 121-61-61; FAX 121-62-18.
US Reservations: (800) 999-2252.
3 mi NE on Carr Pichilingue. Mail: Apdo Postal 607, La Paz, BCS 23010, Mexico.
XP $20. 3-day refund notice. AE, MC, VI. No pets. On tree-shaded grounds at the beach. 3-6 stories. **Rooms:** 119; condo units $125-219, downtown suites (near *malecón*) $125. Balconies, shower baths, refrigerators, cable TV, movies. **Recreation:** Swimming beach, pool, whirlpool, exercise room, boating, kayaks, windsurfing, scuba diving, snorkeling, charter fishing. **Services:** Business services. **Dining:** Restaurant; 7 am-10:30 pm; cocktails, bar.

Non-Rated Lodging

CASA LA PACEÑA BED & BREAKFAST
$50-65

01152 (1) 125-27-48.
On Calle Bravo, 2 blks from La Paz Bay. Mail: Apdo Postal 158, La Paz, BCS 23000, Mexico.

CLUB HOTEL CANTAMAR
$60-80

01152 (1) 122-18-26.
At Pichilingue marina, 9 mi N of town.

HOTEL LORIMAR
Up to $40

01152 (1) 125-38-22.
Calle Bravo, 1½ blks N of the malecón.

HOTEL MEDITERRANE

Phone & FAX 01152 (1) 125-11-95. $40-50

On Allende, ½ blk from Paseo Alvaro Obregón. Mail: Allende 36-B, La Paz, BCS 23000, Mexico.

HOTEL MIRAMAR

01152 (1) 122-88-85. Up to $40

Corner of calles 5 de Mayo and Dominguez.

HOTEL PERLA

01152 (1) 122-07-77. $60-80

On Paseo Obregón, between calles Arreola and La Paz.

HOTEL PLAZA REAL

01152 (1) 122-93-33. Up to $40

Corner of calles La Paz and Esquerro.

Camping

AQUAMARINA RV PARK

01152 (1) 122-37-61; FAX 125-62-28. $15 for 2 persons

1½ mi SW of city center, ½ mi off Hwy 1 on Calle Nayarit. Mail: Apdo Postal 133, La Paz, BCS 23094, Mexico.

XP $2. On the bay. **Sites:** 19 RV. EWS-19. **Facilities:** Flush toilets, showers. **Recreation:** Pool, fishing trips, boat ramp and storage, boat trips and scuba diving arranged. **Services:** Laundry.

CASA BLANCA RV PARK

Phone & FAX 01152 (1) 124-00-09. $10-15 for 2 persons

3 mi SW of town center on Hwy 1, corner of Av Delfines. Mail: Apdo Postal 681, La Paz, BCS 23094, Mexico.

RVs $15, tents $10, XP $3. Partly shaded area surrounded by wall. **Sites:** 46 RV sites. Hookups: EWS-46. Fee for air conditioning & heater. **Facilities:** Flush toilets, showers. **Recreation:** Pool, tennis. **Services:** Laundry, store.

EL CARDÓN TRAILER PARK

01152 (1) 124-02-61; FAX 124-00-78. $10-12 for 2 persons

2½ mi SW of city center on Hwy 1. Mail: Apdo Postal 104, La Paz, BCS 23000, Mexico.

XP $2. 3-day refund notice. Shaded area surrounded by wall. **Sites:** 80 RVs, 10 tents. Hookups: EWS-80. **Facilities:** Flush toilets, showers. **Recreation:** Pool, fishing trips. **Services:** Laundry, ice.

LA PAZ TRAILER PARK

01152 (1) 122-87-87; FAX 122-99-38. $11-15 for 2 persons

2 mi SW of city center off Hwy 1, on Brecha California, in residential area. Mail: Apdo Postal 482, La Paz, BCS 23094, Mexico.

XP $5. 3-day refund notice. AE, MC, VI. 35 RV sites. Hookups: EWS-35. **Facilities:** Flush toilets, showers. **Recreation:** Pool, wading pool, fishing trips arranged, boat ramp nearby. **Services:** Laundry.

OASIS LOS ARÍPEZ TRAILER PARK

No phone. $10 for 2 persons

On La Paz bay, 9½ mi before central La Paz when approaching from the N, in the town of El Centenario, on Hwy 1. Mail: Km 15 Transpeninsular Norte, La Paz, BCS, Mexico.

XP $2. 7-day refund notice. **Sites:** 22 tent/RV. Hookups: EWS-29. **Facilities:** Flush toilets, showers. **Recreation:** Beach, fishing. **Services:** Laundry. **Dining:** Restaurant; bar.

La Salina

Camping

BAJA SEASONS RV BEACH RESORT

01152 (6) 628-61-28; FAX 648-71-06. $32-48 for 4 persons

US Reservations: (800) 754-4190.

On beach facing Pacific Ocean, 14 mi N of Ensenada off Hwy 1-D. Mail: Apdo Postal 1492, La Salina, BC, Mexico.

XP $5. 14-day refund notice. MC, VI. **Sites:** 134 RV. Hookups: EWS-134. **Facilities:** Flush toilets, showers, cable TV. **Recreation:** Pool, whirlpool, saunas, steam room, tennis, horseback riding, recreation room. **Services:** Laundry, groceries. **Dining:** Restaurant; bar.

Loreto

AAA-Approved Lodging

EDEN LORETO RESORT—ALL INCLUSIVE ♦♦♦ Resort Hotel

01152 (1) 133-07-00; FAX 133-03-77. $170-310

US Reservations: (888) 282-3336.

At Nopoló, 8½ mi S via Hwy 1 and paved rd to beach. Mail: Bl Misión de Loreto, Loreto, BCS 23880, Mexico.

XP $80; age restriction, 18 years & older. Rates include all meals, beverages, taxes, gratuity & most recreational services. 14-day refund notice. AE, MC, VI. No pets. Modern 3-story hotel on beach. **Rooms:** 236. Patios, views, shower baths, cable TV, movies, safes. **Recreation:** Beach, 2 pools, exercise room, tennis, golf, fishing, scuba diving, snorkeling, sailboarding, bicycles. **Services:** Laundry. **Dining:** Restaurants; 7 am-10 pm; cocktails, bar.

Non-Rated Lodging

BAJA OUTPOST

01152 (1) 135-11-34. Up to $50

US reservations: (888) 649-5951. Website at www.bajaoutpost.com.

Near the S end of the malecón.

EL MORO MOTEL & RV PARK

01152 (1) 135-05-42. Up to $50

On Calle Robles between Calle Davis and the malecón.

HOTEL EL JUNÍPERO

01152 (1) 135-00-28. Up to $50

Paseo Hidalgo in front of the mission.

HOTEL LA PINTA

01152 (1) 135-00-25; FAX 135-00-26. $75-89

US reservations: (800) 262-4500, (818) 275-4500.

On beach, 1 mi N of town plaza. Mail: Apdo Postal 28, Loreto, BCS 23880, Mexico. US reservations: Mexico Condo Reservations, 4420 Hotel Circle Ct, Ste 230, San Diego, CA 92108.

HOTEL OASIS

01152 (1) 135-01-12. $52-115

On shore of Loreto Bay, ½ mi S of town plaza. Mail: Apdo Postal 17, Loreto, BCS 23880, Mexico.

HOTEL PLAZA LORETO

01152 (1) 135-02-80. Up to $50

Paseo Hidalgo near corner of Pino Suárez, 1 blk S of the mission.

HOTEL SALVATIERRA

01152 (1) 135-00-21. Up to $50

On Calle Salvatierra near the entrance to town, across from the Pemex station.

MOTEL BRENDA

01152 (1) 135-07-07. Up to $50

Calle Juárez between calles León and Ayuntamiento.

POSADA DE LAS FLORES

US Reservations: (877) 245-2860. $180

On the S side of Plaza Cívica.

VILLAS DE LORETO

Phone & Fax 01152 (1) 135-05-86. $50-60

On the beach, ½ mi S of town plaza. Mail: Apdo Postal 132, Loreto, BCS 23880, Mexico.

Camping

LORETO SHORES VILLAS & RV PARK

½ mi S of town plaza on beach. Mail: Apdo Postal 219, Loreto, BCS 23880, Mexico.

01152 (1) 135-06-29; FAX 135-07-11. $14 for 2 persons

RVs with hookups; sites without hookups $5 per person; XP $4; villas $65-120. **Sites:** 37 RV. Hookups: EWS-37. **Facilities:** Flush toilets, showers. **Recreation:** Beach, fishing. **Services:** Laundry.

PLAYA JUNCALITO

Playa pública

No phone. $2 per vehicle

13 mi S of Loreto via Hwy 1 and unpaved rd.

Attractive beach and view of mountains. **Facilities:** None.

TRIPUI RESORT RV PARK

01152 (1) 133-08-14; FAX 133-08-28. $10-14 for 2 persons

15 mi S of Loreto via Hwy 1 and paved side rd, 1 mi W of Puerto Escondido. Mail: Apdo Postal 100, Loreto, BCS 23880, Mexico.

XP $5. 3-day refund notice. Gift shop. Motel rooms $50, XP $5. **Sites:** 31 RV. Hookups: EWS-31. **Facilities:** Flush toilets, showers. **Recreation:** Pool, wading pool, playground. **Services:** Groceries. **Dining:** Restaurant; bar.

VILLAS DE LORETO

01152 (1) 135-05-86. $15 for 2 persons

½ mi S of town plaza on the beach. Mail: Apdo Postal 132, Loreto, BCS 23880, Mexico.

XP $5. No smoking on premises. **Sites:** 9 RV. Hookups: EWS-9. **Facilities:** Flush toilets, hot showers. 10 motel units, $50-60 for 2 persons; $15 for each additional person. **Recreation:** Fishing, kayaks, bicycles. **Services:** Laundry, local tours.

Los Barriles

Non-Rated Lodging

HOTEL LOS BARRILES
01152 (1) 141-00-24. $45-200
Reservations/information: (800) 700-7022 or (805) 493-5444.
1 blk from Playa del Sol near center of town.

HOTEL PALMAS DE CORTEZ
01152 (1) 141-00-50. $120-200
Reservations/information: (800) 368-4334.
Near the center of town on Playa del Sol.

HOTEL PLAYA DEL SOL
01152 (1) 141-00-50. $45-200
Reservations/information: (800) 368-4334.
On Playa del Sol, 300 yards N of Hotel Palmas de Cortez.

MARTÍN VERDUGO'S BEACH RESORT
01152 (1) 141-00-54. $45-200
On Playa del Sol, next to Hotel Playa del Sol.

RANCHO BUENA VISTA
01152 (1) 141-01-77. $45-200
Reservations: (800) 258-8200.
2 mi S of Los Barriles off Hwy 1.

Camping

JUANITO'S GARDEN RV PARK
Phone & FAX 01152 (1) 141-00-24. $10 for 2 persons
½ mi E of Hwy 1, 1 blk from the bay. Mail: Apdo Postal 50, Buena Vista, BCS 23580, Mexico.
XP $4. **Sites:** 10 RV. Hookups: EWS-10. **Facilities:** Flush toilets, showers. **Services:** Laundry, RV storage.

MARTÍN VERDUGO'S BEACH RESORT
Phone & FAX 01152 (1) 141-00-54. $11-13 for 2 persons
On beach of Bahía de Palmas, ½ mi E of Hwy 1. Mail: Apdo Postal 17, Los Barriles, BCS 23501, Mexico.
XP $3.50. Partially shaded area. Motel rooms $44-46. **Sites:** 69 RVs, 25 tents. Hookups: EWS-69. **Facilities:** Flush toilets, hot showers. **Recreation:** Pool, beach, boat launch, fishing trips arranged. **Services:** Laundry. **Dining:** Restaurant adjacent; bar.

Mexicali

AAA-Approved Lodging

ARAIZA INN CALAFIA ♦ Motor Inn
01152 (6) 568-33-11; FAX 568-20-10. $72
US reservations: (800) 927-2402.
2⅗ mi E of border crossing via Av Cristobal Colón, then 1⅕ mi S at Calzada Justo Sierra. Mail: Calzada Justo Sierra, No 1495, Mexicali, BC 21230, Mexico.
XP $8. 12% service charge. AE, MC, VI. **Rooms:** 171. Shower baths, refrigerators, cable TV, movies. **Recreation:** Pool. **Services:** Business services. **Dining:** Coffee shop; 6 am-11 pm; cocktails, bar.

ARAIZA INN MEXICALI ♦♦ Motor Inn
01152 (6) 564-11-00; FAX 01152 (6) 564-11-13. $104
US reservations: (800) 927-2402.
At Calzada Benito Juárez 2220, 5 mi SE of border crossing. Mail: 233 Pauline Av, #947, Calexico, CA 92231.
XP $5; ages 18 and under stay free. AE, MC, VI. No pets. Gift shop. **Rooms:** 172. Cable TV, radios, movies, ⊗. **Recreation:** Pool, exercise room, lighted tennis. **Services:** Business services. **Dining:** Restaurant; dining room; 7 am-11 pm; cocktails, entertainment.

CROWNE PLAZA HOTEL ♦♦♦ Hotel
Formerly HOLIDAY INN CROWNE PLAZA.
01152 (6) 557-36-00; FAX 557-05-55. $135-155
US reservations: (800) 465-4329.
5 mi SE of border crossing, at Av de Los Héroes #201, Mexicali, BC 21000, Mexico.
XP $40. 3-day refund notice. AE, MC, VI. No pets. Gift shop. 8 stories. 158 units. **Rooms:** Cable TV, movies, radios, data ports, ⊗. **Recreation:** Pool, exercise room. **Services:** Business services. **Dining:** Restaurant; 6:30 am-midnight; cocktails & bar.

HOTEL LUCERNA ♦♦♦ Hotel
01152 (6) 564-70-00; FAX 566-47-06. $130
US reservations: (800) 582-3762.
From the border crossing, 2½ mi E on Cristobal Colón, then 2 mi S on Calzada to 2151 Calzada Benito Juárez. Mail: PO Box 2300, Calexico, CA 92232.
XP $15. 12% service charge. AE, CB, DI, MC, VI. 3- and 6-story buildings among landscaped grounds with rooms in bungalows. **Rooms:** 175. Balconies/patios, shower baths, refrigerators, cable TV, movies, data ports. **Recreation:** 2 pools, sauna, exercise room. **Services:** Valet laundry, business services. **Dining:** Restaurant, coffee shop; 7 am-11:30 pm.

MOTEL COLONIAL LAS FUENTES ♦♦ Motel
01152 (6) 556-13-12; FAX 556-11-41. $94-104
US Reservations: (800) 437-2438.
5 mi SE of border crossing, at Bl López Mateos and Calle Calafia. Mail: PO Box 772, Ste 9, Calexico, CA 92232.
XP $10; ages 18 and under stay free. AE, MC, VI. No pets. **Rooms:** 144; suites with refrigerator, microwave and coffeemaker, $150 for up to 2 persons. Cable TV, movies. **Recreation:** Pool, wading pool. **Services:** Business services.

Non-Rated Lodging

CASA GRANDE
01152 (6) 553-57-71. Up to $50
Av Cristobal Colón, between calles Bravo and México.

HOTEL DEL NORTE
01152 (6) 552-81-01. Up to $50
Av Madero, next to the downtown border crossing.

HOTEL REGIS
01152 (6) 566-34-35, 566-88-01. Up to $50
On Calzada Juárez just S of Calzada Independencia (across from Hotel Lucerna).

HOTEL SAN JUÁN CAPISTRANO
01152 (6) 552-41-04. Up to $50
Av Reforma between calles Bravo and México.

MOTEL AZTECA DE ORO
01152 (6) 557-14-33. Up to $50
Calle de la Industria 600, just N of the train station.

MOTEL LIZ
01152 (6) 561-86-69. Up to $50
On the road to San Felipe, Hwy 5 at km 1.5.

SIESTA INN
01152 (6) 568-20-01. $75
Calzada Justo Sierra, just S of Calzada Cuauhtémoc.

Mulegé

Non-Rated Lodging

HOTEL HACIENDA
01152 (1) 153-00-21. $30-35
On Calle Madero in front of the town plaza.

HOTEL LAS CASITAS
01152 (1) 153-00-19. $30-35
Near town center at Calle Madero 50.

HOTEL MULEGÉ
01152 (1) 153-00-90. $30-35
At the W entrance to town next to the bus station.

HOTEL SERENIDAD
01152 (1) 153-01-11; FAX 153-03-11. $45-56
2½ mi S of town off Hwy 1 at mouth of river. Mail: Apdo Postal 9, Mulegé, BCS 23900, Mexico.

HOTEL TERRAZAS
01152 (1) 153-00-09. $30-35
N end of Calle Zaragoza.

Camping

THE ORCHARD RV PARK/HUERTA SAUCEDO
01152 (1) 153-03-00. $6.50-14.95 for 2 persons
½ mi S via Hwy 1. Mail: Apdo Postal 24, Mulegé, BCS 23900, Mexico.
RVs $14.95, tents $6.50; XP $2. Cottages & villas $55-250. Partly shaded area near river. **Sites:** 46 RV sites, 30 tent sites. Hookups: EWS-46. **Facilities:** Disposal station, flush toilets, showers. **Recreation:** Boat ramp, fishing. **Services:** Local tour arrangements.

VILLA MARÍA ISABEL RECREATIONAL PARK
01152 (1) 153-02-46. $14 for 2 persons
1¼ mi S via Hwy 1. Mail: Apdo Postal 5, Mulegé, BCS 23900, Mexico.
XP $2; tent site with palapa, $4.50 per person. Bakery. Partly shaded area on river. **Sites:** 33 RV, 25 tent. Hookups: EWS-33. **Facilities:** Disposal station, flush toilets, showers. **Recreation:** Pool, fishing, boat launch, recreation area. **Services:** Laundry, local tour arrangements.

Punta Banda

Camping

LA JOLLA BEACH CAMP

No phone. $6 for 2 persons

8 mi W of Maneadero on BCN 23, on shore of Bahía de Todos Santos. Mailing address: Apdo Postal 102, Punta Banda, BC 22791, Mexico.

XP $2. **Sites:** 120 RV, 80 tent. Hookups: E-20. Extension cords available. **Facilities:** Disposal station, flush toilets, showers. **Recreation:** Beach, tennis, boat launch, recreation room. **Services:** Groceries, propane.

VILLARINO CAMP

01152 (6) 154-20-45; FAX 154-20-44. $10 for 2 persons

8 mi W of Maneadero on BCN 23, on shore of Bahía de Todos Santos. Mail: PO Box 2746, Chula Vista, CA 91912

XP $5. **Sites:** 100 tent/RV. Hookups: E-50, W-100, S-50. **Facilities:** Flush toilets, showers. **Recreation:** Beach, boat ramp, fishing trips arranged. **Services:** Groceries, ice. **Dining:** Cafe; banquets arranged.

Punta Chivato

Camping

PUNTA CHIVATO CAMPGROUND

01152 (1) 153-01-88; FAX 152-03-95. $5 per vehicle

On Punta Chivato, 13 mi N of Mulegé via Hwy 1, then 13½ mi E on graded dirt rd. Mail: Apto Postal 18, Mulegé, BCS 23900, Mexico.

On the beach, open sites. Office nearby at Hotel Punta Chivato. **Sites:** 40 tent/RV. No hookups. **Facilities:** Disposal station, pit toilets, cold showers. **Recreation:** Fishing trips arranged in *pangas*. **Services:** Groceries, laundry. **Dining:** Restaurant; bar.

Rosarito

AAA-Approved Lodging

LAS ROCAS RESORT & SPA

♦♦ Motor Inn

Phone & FAX 01152 (6) 612-21-40. $65-169

US reservations: (888) 527-7622.

6 mi S of town on Hwy 1. Mail: Box 189003 HLR, Coronado, CA 92178.

XP $10; ages 10 and under stay free. 3-day refund notice. MC, VI. No pets. Hotel on a bluff overlooking the ocean. **Rooms:** 74. Fireplaces, ocean-view balconies, coffeemakers, microwaves, refrigerators, cable TV, movies, radios. **Recreation:** 2 pools, whirlpools, full-service spa, tennis. **Dining:** Restaurant; 7:30 am-10:30 pm; cocktails.

OASIS RESORT & CONVENTION CENTER

♦♦ Resort Motor Inn

Formerly OASIS RESORT SUITES.

01152 (6) 631-32-50; FAX 01152 (6) 631-32-52. $149-379

US reservations: (800) 818-3133.

On Hwy 1-D, 3 mi N of town; southbound exit El Oasis, northbound exit San Antonio. Mail: Box 158, Imperial Beach, CA 91933.

XP $15; ages 12 and under stay free. 3-day refund notice. AE, MC, VI. No pets.

All-suite resort and RV park on the beach. **Rooms:** 100. Refrigerators, cable TV, movies. **Recreation:** Beach, 2 pools, wading pool, sauna, whirlpools, tennis, putting green. **Services:** Business services. **Dining:** Dining room, restaurants; 7 am-11 pm; cocktails, bar.

RESIDENCE INN BY MARRIOTT/REAL DEL MAR ♦♦♦ Suite Hotel
01152 (6) 631-36-70; FAX 631-36-77. $119-149
US reservations: (800) 331-3131.
Off Hwy 1-D (toll rd), 5 mi N by Real del Mar Golf Club at Km 19.5. Mail: 4492 Camino de la Plaza, #1246, San Ysidro, CA 92173.
XP $10. Packages available. AE, MC, VI. Hotel/golf resort overlooking the ocean. **Rooms:** 75. Kitchens, cable TV, ⊗. **Recreation:** Pool, sauna, whirlpool, exercise room, steam room, tennis, golf, basketball, volleyball. **Dining:** 2 restaurants; 11 am-11 pm; cocktails, bar.

ROSARITO BEACH HOTEL & SPA ♦♦ Resort Complex
01152 (6) 612-01-44; FAX 612-11-25. $89-189
US reservations: (800) 343-8582.
In S part of town on Bl Benito Juárez, facing the Pacific Ocean. Mail: Box 430145, San Diego, CA 92143.
XP $15; ages 12 and under stay free. 3-day refund notice. MC, VI. No pets. Gift shop. **Rooms:** 275; suites. Balconies, shower baths, efficiencies, refrigerators, cable TV, movies, VCRs, ⊗. **Recreation:** Beach, 2 pools, 3 whirlpools, tennis, basketball. **Services:** Business services. **Dining:** 2 restaurants; 7:30 am-10:30 pm; buffet with live music Fri and Sat evenings; cocktails, 2 bars.

Non-Rated Lodging

BRISAS DEL MAR MOTEL
01152 (6) 612-25-47. $53-63
US Reservations: (800) 697-5223; FAX (619) 426-7873.
In center of town on Bl Benito Juárez 22. Mail: 311 Broadway Chula Vista, CA 91910.

CALAFIA OCEAN RESORT
01152 (6) 612-15-81. $60 or more
Overlooking the ocean 5 mi S of town.

HOTEL CALIFORNIA
01152 (6) 612-25-50. Up to $60
Corner of Bl Juárez and Calle Eucalipto.

HOTEL FESTIVAL PLAZA
01152 (6) 612-29-50. $60 or more
High-rise hotel on Bl Juárez near the S end of town.

HOTEL LOS PELÍCANOS
01152 (6) 612-04-45. Up to $60
Corner of Av Costa Azul and Calle Cedros.

MOTEL VILLA DE LIS
01152 (6) 612-23-20. Up to $60
Corner of Calle Alamo and Av Costa Azul.

QUINTA DEL MAR
01152 (6) 612-12-15. $60 or more
On Bl Juárez, just N of Quinta Plaza in the center of town.

Camping

OASIS RESORT

01152 (6) 631-32-50; FAX 631-32-52. $49-59 for up to 4 persons

US Reservations: (800) 818-3133.

On ocean beach, 3 mi N off Hwy 1-D, toll rd (northbound, San Antonio exit; southbound, Oasis exit). Mail: Box 158, Imperial Beach, CA 91933.

XP $10. 3-day refund notice. AE, MC, VI. Beachfront park with both concrete and grass sites, built-in barbecue. **Sites:** 53 RV. Hookups; EWS-53. **Facilities:** Flush toilets, showers. **Recreation:** Beach, 2 pools, wading pool, sauna, whirlpools, gym, tennis, playground. **Services:** Laundry, groceries. **Dining:** 2 restaurants; bar; entertainment.

San Bartolo

Camping

RANCHO VERDE RV PARK

Phone & FAX 01152 (1) 126-91-03. $11 for 4 persons

US Reservations: (888) 516-9462, (406) 889-3030.

8¼ mi N of town on Hwy 1 at Km 141. US Reservations: Box 1050, Eureka, MT 59917.

XP $2. Open sites. **Sites:** 26 RV. Hookups: WS-26. **Facilities:** Flush toilets, showers. **Recreation:** Fishing trips arranged.

San Carlos

Non-Rated Lodging

HOTEL ALCATRAZ

01152 (1) 136-00-17. $60-70

Calle Puerto La Paz.

HOTEL BRENNAN

01152 (1) 136-02-88. $40-60

US Reservations: (510) 428-5464.

Calle Puerto Acapulco.

HOTEL LAS BRISAS

01152 (1) 136-01-52. $13-65

Calle Puerto La Paz near the main plaza.

HOTEL PALMAR

01152 (1) 136-00-35. $13-65

Calle Puerto Acapulco.

San Felipe

AAA-Approved Lodging

SAN FELIPE MARINA RESORT ♦♦ Resort Motor Inn

01152 (6) 577-15-68; FAX 577-15-66. $105-145

US Reservations: (800) 291-5397.

3 mi S of town on rd to airport. Mail: 233 Pauline Av, #5574, Calexico, CA 92231.
XP $15; ages 15 and under stay free. 8-day refund notice. AE, MC, VI. No pets. Gift shop. On the beach overlooking the bay. **Rooms:** 59. Balconies/patios, walk-in showers, efficiencies/utensils, cable TV. **Recreation:** Beach, 2 pools (1 indoor, heated), saunas, exercise equipment, lighted tennis. **Services:** Business services. **Dining:** Restaurant; 7 am-10 pm, cocktails, lounge.

Non-Rated Lodging

HOTEL COSTA AZUL

01152 (6) 577-15-48. $40-90
Corner of Av Mar de Cortez and Calle Ensenada.

HOTEL LAS MISIÓNES

01152 (6) 577-12-80; FAX 577-12-83. $69
On road to airport, 1 mi S of town. Mail: 233 Pauline Av, #7544, Calexico, CA 92231.

HOTEL RIVIERA

01152 (6) 577-11-85. $40-90
Av Los Cedros, 1½ blks W of Av Mar de Cortez.

MOTEL EL CAPITÁN

01152 (6) 577-13-03. $36-45
On Av Mar de Cortez, corner of Manzanillo across from State Tourism Office. Mail: Box 1916, Calexico, CA 92232.

MOTEL EL CORTÉZ

01152 (6) 577-01-55, 577-01-56. $40-90
S end of Av Mar de Cortez, on the beach.

MOTEL VILLA LOS ARCOS

01152 (6) 577-15-88. $40-90
Near the entrance of town, just E of the arches.

PLAYA BONITA

01152 (6) 577-12-15. $65-80
US reservations: (626) 967-8977.
1 mi N of town center via Av Mar de Cortez. US Reservations: 475 E Badillo St, Covina, CA 91723.

VILLA DE LAS PALMAS

01152 (6) 577-13-33. $40-90
Av Los Cedros, 1½ blks W of Av Mar de Cortez (across from Hotel Riviera).

Camping

CAMPO SAN FELIPE TRAILER PARK

01152 (6) 577-10-12. $12-17 for 2 persons
In town on the bay shore. Mail: 301 Av Mar de Cortez, San Felipe, BC 21850, Mexico.
XP $2; tents $10. **Sites:** 34 tent/RV, 5 tent sites. Hookups: EWS-34. **Facilities:** Flush toilets, showers. **Recreation:** Beach, billiard room. **Services:** Ice.

CLUB DE PESCA TRAILER PARK

01152 (6) 577-11-80; FAX 577-18-88. $12-18 for 2 persons
1 mi S of town center at end of Av Mar de Cortez. Mail: Apdo Postal 90, San Felipe, BC 21850, Mexico.
XP $2. Large landscaped park on gulf shore. **Rooms:** 30 tent/RV; additional area on beach for large number of tents. Hookups: EW-30. **Facilities:** Disposal station, flush toilets. **Recreation:** Showers, boat launch and storage. **Services:** Groceries.

FARO BEACH TRAILER PARK

No phone. $25 per vehicle

On Punta Estrella, 10 mi SE of town via paved rd. Mail: Apdo Postal 107, San Felipe, BC 21850, Mexico.

Large, attractively landscaped park on terraced slope overlooking Gulf of California. **Sites:** 135 tent/RV. Hookups: EWS-135. **Facilities:** Flush toilets, showers. **Recreation:** Pool, tennis, recreation room. **Services:** Ice. **Dining:** Bar.

LA JOLLA TRAILER PARK

Phone & FAX 01152 (6) 577-12-22. $15 for 2 persons

½ mi W of town center at Manzanillo and Mar Bermejo in residential area. Mail: Box 978, El Centro, CA 92244.

XP $2.50. Sites with canopies. **Sites:** 55 tent/RV. Hookups: EWS-55. **Facilities:** Flush toilets, showers, fishing and boating trips arranged. **Recreation:** Pool, spa. **Services:** Laundry, ice.

MAR DEL SOL RV PARK

01152 (6) 577-10-88. $11-18 for 2 persons

US Reservations: (800) 336-5454, (619) 454-7166.

1½ mi S of town center on Misión de Loreto, adjacent to Hotel Las Misiónes. Mail: 7734 Herschel Av, Ste O, La Jolla, CA 92037.

XP $5. 12% service charge. 3-day refund notice. MC, VI. Unshaded sites on attractive beach. **Rooms:** 84 RV, 30 tent. Hookups: EWS-84. **Facilities:** Flush toilets, showers. **Recreation:** Pool. **Services:** Laundry.

PLAYA BONITA TRAILER PARK

01152 (6) 577-12-15. $10-20 for 5 persons

US Reservations: (626) 967-8977.

1 mi N of town center via Av Mar de Cortez. US Reservations: 475 E Badillo St, Covina, CA 91723.

XP $2. MC, VI. Condo suites available. Picturesque area on beach with rocky hills behind. **Sites:** 27 tent/RV. Hookups: EWS-27. **Facilities:** Flush toilets, showers. **Recreation:** Fishing trips arranged. **Services:** Laundry.

RUBEN'S TRAILER PARK

Phone & FAX 01152 (6) 577-14-42. $20

1 mi N of town center via Av Mar de Cortez. Mail: Golfo de California 703, San Felipe, BC 21850, Mexico.

MC, VI. Picturesque area on gulf shore with rocky hills behind. **Sites:** 58 tent/RV. Hookups: EWS-58. **Facilities:** Flush toilets, showers. **Recreation:** Beach, boat launch, fishing. **Services:** Groceries. **Dining:** Restaurant; bar.

SAN FELIPE MARINA RESORT RV PARK

01152 (6) 577-14-35; FAX 577-15-66. $22 for 4 persons

US Reservations: (800) 291-5397.

3 mi S of town on rd to airport. Mail: 233 Pauline Av, Box 8518, Calexico, CA 92231.

XP $5. 3-day refund notice. AE, MC, VI. Unshaded sites overlooking the marina. **Sites:** 136 RV sites (motorhomes and trailers only). Hookups: EWS-136. **Facilities:** Flush toilets, showers, TV hookups. **Recreation:** Beach, pool. **Services:** Laundry, groceries.

VISTA DEL MAR RV PARK

01152 (6) 577-12-52. $12 for 2 persons

¾ mi N of town center on Av Mar de Cortez overlooking the bay. Mail: 336 Av Mar de Cortez, San Felipe, BC 21850, Mexico.

XP $3. **Sites:** 21 tent/RV with shaded tables. Hookups: EWS-21. **Facilities:** Flush toilets, showers.

San Ignacio

Non-Rated Lodging

HOTEL LA PINTA

01152 (1) 154-03-00. $60-65

US reservations: (800) 262-4500; (818) 275-4500.

SE of the main plaza on Calle Carranza, 1 blk E of Callejón Ciprés. Mail: Apdo Postal 37, San Ignacio, BCS 23930, Mexico. US reservations: Mexico Condo Reservations, 4420 Hotel Circle Ct, Ste 230, San Diego, CA 92108.

LA POSADA

01152 (1) 154-03-13. $20-125

SE of the main plaza on Calle Carranza, 1 block E of Callejón Ciprés.

RICE & BEANS OASIS HOTEL

01152 (1) 154-02-83. $30-40

Turnoff ⅓ mi W of main entry rd to San Ignacio on Hwy 1, then ⅔ mi S.

Camping

RICE & BEANS OASIS RV PARK

01152 (1) 154-02-83. $30-40

Turnoff ⅓ mi W of main entry rd to San Ignacio on Hwy 1, then ⅔ mi S.

Sites: 28 RVs. Hookups: EW-28. **Facilities:** Showers. **Dining:** Restaurant; bar.

TRAILER PARK EL PADRINO

Phone & FAX 01152 (1) 154-00-89. $8-10 per site

1 mi S of Hwy 1 on entrance rd to San Ignacio, just beyond Hotel La Pinta. Mail: Ctra Transpeninsular Km 0.5, San Ignacio, BCS 23930, Mexico.

XP $2. **Sites:** 30 RVs. Hookups: E-10, W-30. **Facilities:** Dump station, flush toilets, showers. **Recreation:** Whale-watching trips arranged. **Services:** Tourist information. **Dining:** Restaurant; bar.

San José del Cabo

AAA-Approved Lodging

CASA DEL MAR GOLF RESORT & SPA ♦♦♦ Resort Motor Inn

01152 (1) 144-00-30; FAX 144-00-34. $225-375

US reservations: (800) 221-8808.

7 mi W of town at Cabo Real. Mail: Km 19.5 Carr Transpeninsular, San José del Cabo, BCS 23400, Mexico.

XP $25. 10% service charge. 3-day refund notice. AE, MC, VI. No pets. Gift shop. Attractive colonial-style building at the ocean. 2 stories. **Rooms:** 56. Whirlpool tubs, bars, cable TV, movies, safes. **Recreation:** Beach, 2 pools, wading pool, saunas, whirlpools, health club, steam rooms, lighted tennis, golf. **Services:** Business services. **Dining:** Restaurant, see listing in the *Cape Region*, Chapter 11; bar.

FIESTA INN ALL INCLUSIVE RESORT ♦♦ Motor Inn

Phone & FAX 01152 (1) 142-07-01; FAX 142-04-80. $89-132

US Reservations: (800) 343-7821.

On beach, 1½ mi W of town. Mail: Apdo Postal 124, San José del Cabo, BCS 23400, Mexico.

XP $49-66. AE, MC, VI. 3 stories. No pets. Gift shop. **Rooms:** 153. Patios/balconies, cable TV, movies, radios. **Recreation:** Beach, pool, scuba/snorkeling/fishing arrangements. **Services:** Business services. **Dining:** Restaurant; 7 am-11 pm.

HOWARD JOHNSON PLAZA SUITE HOTEL & RESORT

♦♦ Hotel
01152 (1) 142-09-99; FAX 142-08-06. $92-13
US reservations: (800) 446-4656.
¼ mi E of town, just off Hwy 1 on Paseo Finisterra. Mail: Apdo Postal 152, San José del Cabo, BCS 23400, Mexico.
7-day refund notice. AE, CB, DI, DS, MC, VI. No pets. Gift shop. Mexican Colonial and Moorish-style buildings surrounding courtyard and pool. 4 stories; no elevator. **Rooms:** 172; hotel rooms and 1- to 3-bedroom suites with kitchens. Cable TV, movies. **Recreation:** Pool, exercise room, tennis, golf, scuba/snorkeling/fishing arrangements. **Services:** Business services. **Dining:** Restaurant; 7 am-10:30 pm; cocktails, bar.

HUERTA VERDE

♦♦♦ Bed & Breakfast
Phone & FAX 01152 (1) 148-05-11. $115-140
US reservations: (303) 431-5162; FAX (303) 431-4455.
3 mi N of town along Hwy 1, then 1 mi E on Las Animas Altas. Mail: Las Animas Atlas, San José del Cabo, BCS 23400, Mexico.
XP $25. 10% service charge. DS, MC, VI. Tropical gardens in a secluded hillside setting. **Rooms:** 7 units; 2 suites with kitchenette, barbecue grill. Shower baths, refrigerators, radios. **Recreation:** Pool, hiking. **Dining:** Additional meals by arrangement.

LA JOLLA DE LOS CABOS

♦♦♦ Condominium Hotel
01152 (1) 142-30-00; FAX 142-05-46. $160-185
US reservations: (800) 524-5104.
3 mi W of town center on Hwy 1. Mail: Apdo Postal 127, San José del Cabo, BCS 23400, Mexico.
XP $15. 10% service charge. 3-day refund notice. AE, MC, VI. No pets. Gift shop. Beauty salon. On the beach. 3-6 stories. **Rooms:** 55 units; studios, 1- and 2-bedrooms with kitchens. Shower baths, coffeemakers, refrigerators, cable TV, movies. **Recreation:** Pools, whirlpools, saunas, spa, steam rooms, exercise room, lighted tennis courts. **Dining:** Restaurant; 7 am-10:30 pm; cocktails, bar.

LAS VENTANAS AL PARAÍSO

♦♦♦♦ Resort Complex
01152 (1) 144-03-00; FAX 144-03-01. $325-750
US reservations: (888) 767-3966.
Hwy 1 at Km 19.5, San José del Cabo, BCS 23400, Mexico.
XP $50. 15% service charge. 7-day refund notice. AE, DI, DS, MC, VI. Gift shop. Intimate oceanfront resort. **Rooms:** 60; 4 1-bedroom suites with private pool, $2000. Fireplaces, patios, whirlpool tubs, cable TV, movies, VCRs, data ports, safes. **Recreation:** Pools, whirlpool, saunas, health club, steam rooms, golf, sailing, arrangements for fishing, kayaking, horseback riding. **Services:** Business services. **Dining:** 2 restaurants; 6:30 am-10 pm; 24-hr room service; cocktails, bar.

MELIÁ CABO REAL BEACH & GOLF RESORT

♦♦♦ Resort Hotel
01152 (1) 144-00-00; FAX 144-01-01. $215-335
US reservations: (800) 336-3542.
On Hwy 1, 7 mi W of town. Mail: Carr a Cabo San Lucas, Km 19, San José del Cabo, BCS 23400, Mexico.
XP $45. 10% service charge. 15-day refund notice. AE, MC, VI. Spacious oceanfront grounds. **Rooms:** 309. Cable TV, movies. **Recreation:** Pool, wading pool, sauna, health club, tennis, golf, fishing trips arranged, scuba diving, snorkeling. **Dining:** 2 restaurants, 2 coffee shops; 7 am-11 pm; 24-hr room service; cocktails.

HOTEL PRESIDENTE INTERCONTINENTAL LOS CABOS ALL INCLUSIVE EXCLUSIVE RESORT ♦♦♦ Resort Hotel

Formerly PRESIDENTE INTERCONTINENTAL LOS CABOS ALL INCLUSIVE EXCLUSIVE RESORT.

01152 (1) 142-02-11; FAX 142-02-32. $270-410

US reservations: (800) 327-0200.

At beach 1¼ mi W of town. Mail: Apdo Postal 2, San José del Cabo, BCS 23400, Mexico.

XP $50; ages 12 and under stay free. 10% service charge. 3-day refund notice. Rates include all meals and beverages, and most recreational activities. AE, CB, DI, MC, VI. No pets. At the beach with spacious grounds. **Rooms:** 400; suite. Shower baths, cable TV, movies, ⊘. **Recreation:** 2 pools, wading pool, tennis, scuba diving, snorkeling, fishing trips arranged. **Services:** Business services. **Dining:** Dining room, 3 restaurants; 7 am-10 pm; 24-hr room service; cocktails, bar, disco.

MELIÁ LOS CABOS ♦♦♦ Resort Hotel

01152 (1) 144-02-02, FAX 144-02-16. $280-345

US reservations: (800) 336-3542.

7½ mi W on Hwy 1 at Cabo Real. Mail: Carr Transpeninsular Km 18.5, San José del Cabo, BCS 23400, Mexico.

XP $40. 10% service charge. 15-day refund notice. AE, MC, VI. Oceanfront resort with colonial style architecture. **Rooms:** 150 efficiencies. Combination baths, cable TV, movies, data ports, safes, **Recreation:** Pool, wading pool, sauna, whirlpools, full-service spa, exercise room, massage, steam room, lighted tennis, golf. **Services:** Valet laundry, business services. **Dining:** Restaurant; 7 am-10 pm; cocktails, poolside bar.

POSADA REAL LOS CABOS ♦♦ Motor Inn

01152 (1) 142-01-55; FAX 142-04-60. $84-120

US reservations: (800) 528-1234.

On beach, 1½ mi S of town. Mail: Apdo Postal 51, San José del Cabo, BCS 23400, Mexico.

XP $10. 3-day refund notice. AE, MC, VI. No pets. Gift shop. On the beach, most rooms with ocean view. 3 stories. **Rooms:** 150; suites, $150-200. Cable TV, movies. **Recreation:** Pool, wading pool, whirlpool, scuba/snorkeling/fishing arrangements, bicycles. **Services:** Business services. **Dining:** Restaurant; 7 am-10:30 pm; cocktails, bar.

TROPICANA INN ♦♦ Motor Inn

01152 (1) 142-09-07; FAX 2-15-90; FAX in USA (510) 939-2725. $69-86

On Bl Mijares just S of town plaza. Mail: Bl Mijares 30, San José del Cabo, BCS 23400, Mexico.

XP $10; ages 12 and under stay free. 7-day refund notice. AE, MC, VI. No pets. In-town location, attractive Mexican style with courtyard. 3-story motel. **Rooms:** 40. Shower baths, coffeemakers, cable TV, movies. **Recreation:** Pool.

WESTIN REGINA GOLF & BEACH RESORT—LOS CABOS ♦♦♦♦ Resort Complex

Formerly WESTIN REGINA RESORT—LOS CABOS.

01152 (1) 142-90-00; FAX 142-90-11. $240-450

US reservations: (800) 228-3000.

On Hwy 1, 6 mi SW of San José del Cabo. Mail: Apdo Postal 145, San José del Cabo, BCS 23400, Mexico.

XP $35-50. $2.50 daily service charge per room. AE, CB, DI, MC, VI. No pets. Gift shop. High-rise hotel, water-themed landscape, dramatic architecture. **Rooms:** 295; junior suites, $550. Balconies, whirlpool baths, bars, cable TV, movies, safes,

∅. **Recreation:** Beach, 3 pools, whirlpool, fitness center, saunas, steam rooms, lighted tennis, golf and fishing trips arranged. **Services:** Business services, children's programs. **Dining:** 3 restaurants; 7 am-11 pm; 24-hour rm service; cocktails, lounge.

Non-Rated Lodging

EL ENCANTO INN

01152 (1) 142-03-88. $30-70

Calle Morelos between calles Obregón and Comonfort.

HOTEL PALMITA

Phone & FAX 01152 (1) 142-04-34. $50-70

On Paseo San José, 1½ mi W of town. Mail: Paseo San José, San José del Cabo, BCS 23400, Mexico.

POSADA SEÑOR MAÑANA

01152 (1) 142-04-62. $30-70

Across from Plaza Mijares on Calle Obregón.

POSADA TERRANOVA HOTEL

01152 (1) 142-05-34. $30-70

On Calle Degollado between calles Zaragoza and Doblado.

SUITES LAS PALMAS

01152 (1) 142-21-31. $100 or more

1 mi W of town on Hwy 1, near Campo de Golf San José.

Camping

BRISA DEL MAR RV RESORT

No phone. $13.50-30 for 2 persons

2 mi SW of town center on Hwy 1. Mail: Apdo Postal 45, San José del Cabo, BCS 23400, Mexico.

XP $2. Fenced area on beautiful beach facing Gulf of California. **Sites:** 150 tent/RV. Hookups: EWS-150. **Facilities:** Flush toilets, showers. **Recreation:** Pool. **Services:** Laundry. **Dining:** Restaurant.

San Quintín

Non-Rated Lodging

HOTEL LA PINTA

01152 (6) 165-28-78. $65

US reservations: (800) 262-4500; (818) 275-4500.

2½ mi W of Hwy 1 via paved rd to outer San Quintín Bay. Mail: Apdo Postal 168, Valle de San Quintín, BC 22930, Mexico. US reservations: Mexico Condo Reservations, 4420 Hotel Circle Ct, Ste 230, San Diego, CA 92108.

MOTEL CHÁVEZ

01152 (6) 165-20-05. $20-30

On W side of Hwy 1 near Km 193.

OLD MILL HOTEL

US reservations: (619) 271-1304, (800) 479-7962; FAX (619) 271-0952. $30-60

On E shore of inner San Quintín Bay, 4 mi W of Hwy 1 via unpaved rd. Mail: 11217 Adriatic Place, San Diego, CA 92126-1109.

Camping

CIELITO LINDO

No phone. $5 per vehicle

Adjacent to Hotel Cielito Lindo, 3 mi W of Hwy 1 via paved rd to Hotel La Pinta and Outer San Quintín Bay.

Open area near the beach. Hotel adjacent. **Sites:** 13 RV; additional tent/RV sites on beach. Hookups: EW-8. **Facilities:** Flush toilets, showers. **Recreation:** Fishing trips arranged. **Dining:** Restaurant; bar.

ENRIQUE'S/EL PABELLÓN RV PARK

No phone. $5 per vehicle

9 mi S of Lázaro Cárdenas and 1 mi W of Hwy 1 via dirt rd.

Open area with access to beach. **Sites:** 15 tent/RV; additional tent sites on beach. Hookups: W-27. **Facilities:** Flush toilets, showers. **Recreation:** Fishing trips arranged.

MOTEL SAN CARLOS

01152 (6) 163-42-06. $2 per vehicle

Adjacent to Motel San Carlos, 2½ mi W of Hwy 1 via paved rd.

Overlooking inner San Quintín Bay. Hotel adjacent. **Sites:** 30 tent/RV. Hookups: none. **Facilities:** Flush toilets, showers. **Recreation:** Fishing trips arranged. **Dining:** Restaurant; bar.

Santa Rosalía

Non-Rated Lodging

HOTEL EL MORRO

01152 (1) 152-04-14. $23-25

On Hwy 1, 1 mi S of Santa Rosalía ferry terminal. Mail: Apdo Postal 76, Santa Rosalía, BCS, Mexico.

Camping

LAS PALMAS RV PARK

01152 (1) 152-01-09; FAX 152-22-70. $6-10 for 2 persons

2 mi S on Hwy 1. Mail: Apdo Postal 123, Santa Rosalía, BCS, Mexico.

$10 RVs, $6 tents, XP $2. Grass sites. **Sites:** 30 tent/RV. Hookups: EWS-30. **Facilities:** Flush toilets, showers. **Services:** Laundry. **Dining:** Restaurant; bar.

SAN LUCAS COVE RV PARK

No phone. $6 per vehicle

9 mi S via Hwy 1 and unpaved rd. Mail: Apdo Postal 50, Santa Rosalía, BCS, Mexico.

Open area adjacent to beach. **Sites:** 75 tent/RV. No hookups. **Facilities:** Disposal station, limited shower and toilet facilities. **Recreation:** Beach, fishing, boat ramp. **Dining:** Restaurant.

Santo Tomás

Camping

EL PALOMAR TRAILER PARK

Phone & FAX 01152 (6) 153-80-02. $12.50 for 2 persons

N edge of the village on Hwy 1 in olive tree-shaded area. Mail: PO Box 4492 Camino de la Plaza No 232, San Ysidro, CA 92173.

XP $2. 2-day cancellation notice. MC, VI. Motel adjacent. **Sites:** 50 RVs; large area for tents. Hookups: EWS-25. **Facilities:** Flush toilets, showers. **Recreation:** Pool, tennis, basketball, volleyball, hunting. **Services:** Groceries, curio shop, gas station. **Dining:** Restaurant; bar.

Tecate

Non-Rated Lodging

MOTEL EL DORADO
01152 (6) 654-10-84. $50-100
Av Juárez 1100, just W of Calle Estebán.

MOTEL EL PARAÍSO
01152 (6) 654-17-16. Up to $50
Corner of Av Juárez and Calle Aldrete.

MOTEL HACIENDA
01152 (6) 654-12-50. Up to $50
Hwy 2 at the W end of town.

OKAKOPA IWA HOTEL
01152 (6) 654-11-44. Up to $50
Callejón Madero, 1 blk W of the border crossing.

RANCHO TECATE RESORT
01152 (6) 654-00-11. $50-100
6 mi S of town off Hwy 3.

Camping

TECATE KOA ON RANCHO OJAI
Formerly RANCHO OJAI RV PARK & CAMPGROUND.
01152 (6) 653-30-14. $25-35 for 2 persons
13 mi E of town near Km 112 on Hwy 2. Mail: Box 280, Tecate, CA 91980.
XP $6. Log cabins available, $40-50 per night. **Sites:** 41 RV/tent. Hookups: EWS-41. **Facilities:** Flush toilets, showers, hiking trails, clubhouse. **Recreation:** Volleyball, horseshoes, bicycles, playground. **Services:** Laundry, groceries.

Tijuana

AAA-Approved Lodging

CAMINO REAL TIJUANA ♦♦♦ Hotel
01152 (6) 633-40-00; FAX 633-40-01. $140
US reservations: (800) 772-6466.
2 mi SE of border crossing; in Zona Río at Paseo de Los Héroes No 10305, Tijuana, BC 22320, Mexico.
XP $50. 12% service charge. AE, DI, MC, VI. **Rooms:** 241. Combination baths, bars, cable TV, movies, data ports. **Services:** Valet laundry, business services. **Dining:** Restaurant; 7 am-midnight; 24-hr room service, cocktails, bar.

EL CONQUISTADOR HOTEL ♦ Motel
01152 (6) 681-79-55; FAX 686-13-40. $50
Just E of Av Rodríguez at Bl Agua Caliente 10750. Mail: Box 5355, Chula Vista, CA 91912.
XP $5. AE, MC, VI. No pets. Near Tijuana Country Club. 2 stories. **Rooms:** 105

units. Shower baths, cable TV, data ports. **Recreation:** Pool, whirlpool, sauna. **Services:** Valet laundry, business services. **Dining:** Restaurant; 7 am-11 pm; cocktails, bar.

FIESTA INN

♦♦ Motel
$94

01152 (6) 634-69-01; FAX 634-69-12.
US reservations: (877) 767-3282.
2 mi SE of border crossing in Zona Río on Via Rápida Poniente at Paseo de Los Héroes. Mail: Paseo de Los Héroes No 18818, Tijuana, BC 22320, Mexico.
XP $14; ages 19 and under stay free. AE, MC, VI. **Rooms:** 127. Cable TV, movies, data ports, some shower baths. **Recreation:** Pool, natural hot springs whirlpool, full-service spa. **Services:** Valet laundry, business services. **Dining:** Dining room, 7 am-11 pm; cocktails, bar.

GRAND HOTEL TIJUANA

♦♦♦ Hotel
$100-135

01152 (6) 681-70-00; FAX 681-70-16.
US reservations: (800) 472-6385.
At Bl Agua Caliente No 4500, ¼ mi E of Av Rodríguez adjacent to Tijuana Country Club. Mail: Box BC, Chula Vista, CA 91912.
XP $10; ages 12 and under stay free. AE, CB, DI, DS, MC, VI. No pets. Gift shop. 25 stories. **Rooms:** 422. Bars, cable TV, movies, ⊗. **Recreation:** Pool, whirlpool, tennis. **Services:** Valet laundry, business services. **Dining:** 2 restaurants; coffee shop; 24 hrs; cocktails, bar.

HOTEL COUNTRY CLUB

♦ Motor Inn
$57

01152 (6) 681-77-33; FAX 681-76-92.
US reservations: (800) 303-2684.
3 mi E of border crossing via Bl Agua Caliente; between Tijuana Country Club and Caliente Race Track at Calle Tapachula No 1. Mail: PO Box 5536, Chula Vista, CA 91912.
XP $8. 12% service charge. 30-day refund notice. AE, MC, VI. **Rooms:** 135. Cable TV, movies. **Recreation:** Pool, whirlpool. **Services:** Business services. **Dining:** Restaurant; 7 am-10 pm; cocktails, bar.

HOTEL HACIENDA DEL RIO

♦♦♦ Resort Hotel
$71

01152 (6) 684-86-44; FAX 684-86-20.
US reservations: (800) 303-2684.
2 mi SE of the border crossing in Zona Río at Blvd Rodolfo Sánchez Taboada No 10606. Mail: PO Box 5356, Chula Vista, CA 91912.
XP $9; ages 12 and under stay free. 12% service charge. 30-day refund notice. AE, MC, VI. **Rooms:** 131; some suites. Cable TV. **Recreation:** Pool, exercise room. **Services:** Valet laundry, business services. **Dining:** Dining room; 7 am-10 pm; cocktails, bar.

HOTEL LA MESA INN

♦ Motor Inn
$57

01152 (6) 681-65-22; FAX 681-28-71.
US reservations: (800) 303-2684.
Via Blvd Agua Caliente at Blvd Díaz Ordaz 50, 2 blks E of Caliente Racetrack. Mail: PO Box 5356, Chula Vista, CA 91912.
XP $8; ages 12 and under stay free. 30-day refund notice. AE, MC, VI. **Rooms:** 122. Cable TV, movies. **Recreation:** Pool. **Services:** Business services. **Dining:** Restaurant; 7 am-10 pm; cocktails, bar.

HOTEL LUCERNA

♦♦♦ Hotel
$146-164

01152 (6) 633-39-00; FAX 01152 (6) 634-24-00.
US reservations: (800) 582-3762.
At Paseo de Los Héroes and Av Rodríguez in the Zona Río. Mail: Box 437910, San Ysidro, CA 92143.
XP $15; ages 12 and under stay free. AE, DI, MC, VI. No pets. Modern 6-story

hotel. **Rooms:** 167. Cable TV, data ports, ⊘. **Recreation:** Pool. **Services:** Valet laundry, business services. **Dining:** Restaurant, see listing in *Northern Triangle*, Chapter 4; dining room; 7 am-midnight; cocktails, bar.

HOTEL PLAZA LAS GLORIAS ♦♦ Hotel
01152 (6) 622-66-00; FAX 622-66-02. $92
US reservations: (800) 544-4686.
At Tijuana Country Club, Bl Agua Caliente No 11553. Mail: Box 43-1588, San Ysidro, CA 92173.
XP $10; ages 12 and under stay free. AE, MC, VI. No pets. 10 stories. **Rooms:** 200. Coffeemakers, refrigerators, cable TV, movies. **Recreation:** Pool, sun deck, whirlpool. **Services:** Valet laundry, business services. **Dining:** Restaurant; 7 am-11 pm; cocktails, bar.

HOTEL REAL DEL RIO ♦♦ Motor Inn
01152 (6) 634-31-00; FAX 634-30-53. $83-90
In the Zona Río, 2 blks W of Av Rodríguez on Calle Velasco. Mail: Calle Velasco 1409, Tijuana, BC 22320, Mexico.
XP $13; ages 11 and under stay free. AE, MC, VI. No pets. 5-story hotel. **Rooms:** 105. Cable TV, movies, data ports, safes, ⊘. **Dining:** Restaurant; 7 am-midnight; cocktails, bar.

PALACIO AZTECA HOTEL ♦ Hotel
Phone/FAX 01152 (6) 681-81-00. $55-73
½ mi S of Paseo de Los Héroes at Blvd Cuauhtémoc Sur No 213.
XP $10. AE, MC, VI. **Rooms:** 175; 2 suites. Cable TV. **Recreation:** Pool, exercise room. **Services:** Business services. **Dining:** Dining room; 7 am-11 pm; cocktails, bar.

PUEBLO AMIGO HOTEL ♦♦♦ Hotel
01152 (6) 683-50-30; FAX 683-50-32. $150-172
US reservations: (800) 386-6985.
At Via Oriente 9211 off Paseo de Tijuana in the Zona Río. Mail: Via Oriente 9211, Zona Río, Tijuana, BC 22320, Mexico.
XP $25; ages 12 and under stay free. AE, MC, VI. 6-story hotel. No pets. Gift shop. **Rooms:** 108. Coffeemakers, cable TV, movies, radios, safes, ⊘. **Recreation:** Pool, exercise room. **Services:** Valet parking, valet laundry, business services. **Dining:** Restaurant; 7 am-11 pm; cocktails.

Non-Rated Lodging

HACIENDA DEL MAR HOTEL
01152 (6) 630-86-03. $34
US reservations: (888) 676-2927.
At Playas de Tijuana, 5 mi W of the border crossing. Mail: Box 120578, Chula Vista, CA 91912.

HOTEL LAFAYETTE
01152 (6) 685-39-40. Up to $40
Av Revolución between calles 3 and 4.

HOTEL LA VILLA DE ZARAGOZA
01152 (6) 685-18-32. $45-80
Av Madero between calles 7 and 8.

HOTEL PARIS
01152 (6) 685-30-23. Up to $40
Calle 5 between avs Revolución and Constitución.

HOTEL PLAZA DE ORO
01152 (6) 685-14-37. Up to $40
Calle 2 at Av D.

MOTEL LEÓN
01152 (6) 685-63-20. $45-80
Calle 7 between avs Revolución and Constitución.

Todos Santos

Non-Rated Lodging

HOSTERÍA LAS CASITAS
01152 (1) 145-02-55. Up to $55
On Rangel between Hidalgo and Obregón.

HOTEL GULUARTE
01152 (1) 145-00-06. Up to $25
Corner of Juárez and Morelos.

HOTEL MIRAMAR
01152 (1) 145-03-41. Up to $25
Corner of Mutualismo at Pedrajo.

MISIÓN DEL PILAR HOTEL
01152 (1) 145-01-14. Up to $55
Corner of Hidalgo and Colegio Militar.

TODOS SANTOS INN
01152 (1) 145-00-40. $85-120
Corner of Legaspi and Topete.

Camping

EL MOLINO TRAILER PARK
01152 (1) 125-01-40. $10 for 4 persons
At S end of town near Hwy 19, behind Pemex station. Mail: Apdo Postal 209, La Paz, BCS 23000, Mexico.
Sites: 21 RV. Hookups: EWS-21. **Facilities:** Flush toilets, showers. **Services:** Laundry.

SAN PEDRITO RV PARK
01152 (1) 122-45-20; FAX 123-46-43. $3-13 for 2 persons
5 mi S on Hwy 19 and 2 mi SW via dirt rd. Mail: Apdo Postal 15, Todos Santos, BCS 23300, Mexico.
RV $13, tent $3, XP $3. Open area on the shore of the Pacific. **Sites:** 71 RV, 25 tent. Hookups: EWS-71. **Facilities:** Flush toilets, showers, 10 cabañas. **Recreation:** Pool, recreation area, playground. **Services:** Laundry. **Dining:** Restaurant; bar.

Appendix

The information included in this section is provided solely as a service to our readers, and no endorsement of any service by the Automobile Club of Southern California is implied or intended.

Transportation

Whether it's land, sea or sky, most travel operators change their schedules and fares on a frequent basis, so we've made no effort to provide these details. Air schedules and fares are available from the individual carriers or at any Auto Club Travel Agency. If you plan a bus trip to Baja California, contact the bus company or companies for information on departures.

AIR SERVICE

The listings below are not exhaustive, but do cover airlines that fly either within Baja California or between the southwestern United States and Baja. All flights noted are nonstop, and connecting flights to other cities are available. Current schedules and fares are available through the airlines or any Auto Club Travel Agency office. The Auto Club is not responsible for discontinuance of any flight or service.

Aerocalifornia Operates daily flights from Los Angeles to Loreto, La Paz and Los Cabos, and from Tijuana to La Paz. *(310) 322-2644, (800) 237-6225.*

Aerolitoral This affiliate of Aeromexico flies Monday through Saturday between Guerrero Negro and Hermosillo, Sonora, with connecting flights from Hermosillo to destinations throughout Mexico and the United States. *(800) 237-6639. www.aerolitoral.com.mx.*

Aeromexico Flies daily from Los Angeles to La Paz and from Tijuana to La Paz; it also flies daily from San Diego to Los Cabos. *(800) 237-6639. www.aeromexico.com.*

Alaska Airlines Flies daily from Los Angeles, San Diego and San Francisco to Los Cabos. Seasonal service (November through April) from Los Angeles to La Paz. *(800) 426-0333. www.alaska-air.com.*

America West Airlines Flies daily between Phoenix and Los Cabos. *(800) 235-9292. www.americawest.com.*

Mexicana Airlines Flies daily between Los Angeles and Los Cabos and once a week between Denver and Los Cabos. In addition, daily flights link the border cities of Tijuana and Mexicali with various cities in mainland Mexico. *(310) 646-7321, (800) 531-7921. www.mexicana.com.mx.*

BUS SERVICE

Intercity Service

Autotransportes de Baja California (ABC) is currently the only bus line linking Tijuana with destinations along Mexico Highway 1. The trip to La Paz lasts 24 to 27 hours and costs about $56 one way. Connecting service is available between La Paz and Los Cabos, with a fare of about $7 or $8. The trip to Ensenada takes about 90 minutes and costs about $8.50. ABC also operates buses from Tijuana to Mexicali and San Felipe. **Linea Elite** and **Norte de Sonora** also offer service between Tijuana and Mexicali. The trip takes about two hours and costs about $10 on any of these lines. In Mexicali, connections are available to Mexico City and other mainland cities.

Central de Autobuses (Central Bus Terminal) This is the main gateway for people traveling by bus from the United States to destinations in Baja California. Information on different bus lines, fares and schedules is available by calling the station at the phone number below. The old bus terminal located in downtown Tijuana at Calle Comercio and Avenida Madero serves some small local companies. Passengers arriving here by Greyhound bus can obtain inexpensive transportation on one of these small local buses to any business section of Tijuana. *01152 (6) 621-29-82. Located in the La Mesa district of Tijuana at the corner of blvds Lázaro Cárdenas and Alamar.*

Cross-Border Service

Five Star Tours San Diego pickups and drop-offs are available at San Diego International Airport and the Amtrak Depot at Broadway at Kettner Boulevard, with cross-border service to the Mexicoach Terminal at the corner of Avenida Revolución and Calle 7, and the Tijuana International Airport. Five Star Tours also provides bullfight trips. *(800) 553-8687 (California only), (619) 232-5049. Prices vary with number of passengers and destination. Van and bus service between San Diego and Tijuana.*

Greyhound Lines Frequent departures for Tijuana leave from downtown terminals in both Los Angeles and San Diego. Service from both cities to Calexico and Mexicali is less frequent but still available several times a day. Tijuana-bound buses let passengers off at different areas around the city, including Avenida Revolución, the Central Bus Terminal (see Intercity Service descriptions above) and the Tijuana airport. *In Los Angeles call (800) 231-2222 or (213) 629-8402; in San Diego call (619) 239-3266. From Los Angeles, fares to Tijuana are $15 one way, $24 round trip; to Calexico, $28 one way, $50 round trip; to Mexicali, $30 one way, $55 round trip. From San Diego, fares to Tijuana are $6.50 one way, $9.50 round trip; to Calexico, $19.50 one way, $33 round trip; to Mexicali, $33 one way, $64.50 round trip.*

Mexicoach Many buses run daily from the trolley station in San Ysidro to the Mexicoach Terminal in downtown Tijuana. Connecting service is available to Rosarito Beach. *Round-trip tickets are $2.*

San Diego Trolley Daily rail service runs between San Diego and the international border at San Ysidro. *(619) 233-3004. Trolleys operate from 5 am to 1 am, with 15-minute service most of the time; maximum 1-way fare is $2.*

CAR RENTALS

A few U.S. rental agencies allow customers to drive their vehicles into Mexico; others may arrange rentals with affiliated companies in Mexico. Check with individual companies for their policies. Fortunately, most of Baja's major cities and resorts have rental agencies. Alamo, Avis, Budget, Hertz, National and Thrifty offer rentals in Cabo San Lucas, San José del Cabo, La Paz and Tijuana. Alamo, Budget and Thrifty also have rentals in Mexicali. Dollar, meanwhile, has rentals in Cabo San Lucas, San José del Cabo and La Paz. In general, auto rentals in Mexico are considerably more expensive than in the United States. Toll-free numbers from the United States for major companies are as follows:

Alamo	(800) 327-9633	**Hertz**	(800) 654-3001
Avis	(800) 331-1084	**National**	(800) 227-7368
Budget	(800) 527-0700	**Thrifty**	(800) 847-4389
		Dollar	(800) 800-6000

FERRY SERVICE AND SCHEDULES

People, motor vehicles and all sorts of commercial goods cross the Sea of Cortez on the Baja California Ferry, a vital link between southern Baja and mainland Mexico. Owned and operated by Sematur, the formerly government-owned ferry has been in private hands for more than a decade now, with higher prices but improved service. Ferries operate between La Paz and the mainland ports of Mazatlán, Topolobampo and Guaymas, and between Santa Rosalía and Guaymas. Each ferry contains a telephone, cafeteria and medical assistance.

Pets are permitted on the ferries when accompanied by the appropriate health certificates that have been visaed by a Mexican Consul (see *Tourist Regulations & Travel Tips*, Chapter 2).

Motorists planning to ship their vehicle to the mainland must obtain a car permit. Permits are available at border crossings. **You must present the original current registration or a notarized bill of sale for each vehicle; copies and temporary papers are not accepted.** (See Automobile Requirements in *Tourist Regulations & Travel Tips*, Chapter 2.)

You may make reservations by telephone from the United States or within Mexico, but some knowledge of Spanish is necessary. Reservations via the Internet are also available. Many travelers prefer to make reservations in person at the ferry offices. Whatever method you choose, try to make reservations at least a week in advance, and a month in advance during holiday periods. Travelers unable to make reservations have sometimes secured a place on the ferry by discussing their needs with ferry officials on the day of sailing or shortly before. For complete information on the ferry system, visit the Sematur website,

www.ferrysematur.com. Within Mexico, ferry information is available by calling the toll-free number 01 (800) 696-96-00.

Ferry Ticket Offices

La Paz The ferry terminal is located at Pichilingue, the deepwater port for La Paz, 10 miles north of the city. *On Guillermo Prieto at Cinco de Mayo, 2 blocks southeast of Plaza Constitución. 01152 (1) 125-88-99, (1) 125-44-40. Open Mon-Fri 8 am-1 and 4 to 6 pm, Sat-Sun 8 am-1 pm. Ferry information may also be obtained at the State Tourism Office; 01152 (1) 122-59-39.*

Santa Rosalía *Located in the terminal building on Hwy 1 just south of the main entrance into the city. 01152 (1) 152-00-13 or 152-00-14.*

Ferry Routes

La Paz-Mazatlán *Ferries depart from both ports daily at 3 pm, some Sat excepted. Salón (general seating) class only is available on Wed sailings from La Paz and Thu sailings from Mazatlán. Travel time is about 18 hours.*

La Paz-Topolobampo (Los Mochis) *Ferries depart from both ports daily at 10 pm, some Sun excepted. Salón (general seating) class only is available all days except Wed and Fri. Sailing time is about 10 hours.*

La Paz-Guaymas *Service May-Aug and Dec only. Ferry departs from La Paz on Fri at 3 pm, from Guaymas on Sun at 9 pm. Sailing time is about 17 hours.*

Santa Rosalía-Guaymas *Ferries depart from Santa Rosalía on Wed and Fri at 9 am. They leave Guaymas Tue and Thu at 9 am. Sailing time is about 8 hours.*

FERRY RATES (shown in dollars)

ROUTE	PASSENGER CLASS				VEHICLE TYPE				
	Salon (Padded seats)	Tourist (Roomette with washbasin and bunks for four persons)	Cabin (Beds and bath for two persons)	**Special Cabin** (Beds, lounge and bath for two persons)	**Car, Small Truck, and Van** up to 16.4 feet (5 meters)	**Car, Small Truck, and Van** 16.5 to 21.3 feet (5 to 6.5 meters)	**Car or Truck with Trailer** up to 29.5 feet (9 meters)	**Car or Truck with Trailer** 29.5 to 55.8 feet (9 to 17 meters)	**Motor-home** over 16.4 feet (5 meters)
LA PAZ-MAZATLAN	32	64	96	128	303	393	550	1021	516
LA PAZ-TOPOLO-BAMPO	24	49	73	98	185	241	332	623	389
SANTA ROSALIA-GUAYMAS	32	64	96	128	303	393	550	1021	516

Distance Table

This table give distances between major points in Baja California both in miles and in kilometers; the italicized (upper) figures indicate miles, while the figures in regular type (lower) denote kilometers. All figures have been rounded off to the nearest whole mile or kilometer. To find the distance between two points, first find the northern point and read down the column below the name. Second, find the southern point and read across the column to the left of the name. The intersection of the two columns shows the distance. Note: Figures are based on the use of Mexico Highway 1-D (Toll Road) between Tijuana and Ensenada.

	Tijuana	Ensenada	Colonet	San Quintín	El Rosario	Cataviñá	Bahía de los Angeles Jct.	Guerrero Negro	San Ignacio	Santa Rosalía	Mulegé	Loreto	Ciudad Constitución	La Paz
Ensenada	*68* 109													
Colonet	*144* 232	*76* 123												
San Quintín	*187* 301	*119* 191	*43* 69											
El Rosario	*223* 359	*155* 249	*79* 127	*36* 58										
Cataviñá	*299* 481	*231* 372	*155* 249	*112* 180	*76* 122									
Bahía de los Angeles Jct.	*364* 586	*296* 476	*220* 354	*177* 285	*141* 227	*65* 105								
Guerrero Negro	*444* 714	*376* 605	*300* 483	*257* 414	*221* 356	*145* 234	*80* 129							
San Ignacio	*532* 856	*464* 747	*388* 624	*345* 555	*309* 497	*233* 376	*168* 271	*88* 142						
Santa Rosalía	*577* 928	*509* 819	*433* 697	*390* 628	*354* 570	*278* 449	*213* 344	*133* 215	*45* 73					
Mulegé	*615* 990	*547* 880	*471* 758	*428* 689	*392* 631	*316* 510	*251* 405	*171* 276	*83* 134	*38* 61				
Loreto	*699* 1125	*631* 1015	*555* 893	*512* 824	*476* 766	*400* 646	*335* 541	*255* 412	*167* 270	*122* 197	*84* 136			
Ciudad Constitución	*788* 1268	*720* 1158	*644* 1036	*601* 667	*565* 909	*489* 789	*424* 684	*344* 555	*256* 413	*211* 340	*173* 279	*89* 143		
La Paz	*922* 1483	*854* 1374	*778* 1252	*735* 1183	*699* 1125	*623* 1005	*558* 900	*478* 771	*390* 629	*345* 556	*307* 495	*223* 359	*134* 216	
Cabo San Lucas	*1059* 1704	*991* 1594	*915* 1472	*872* 1403	*836* 1345	*760* 1226	*695* 1121	*615* 992	*527* 850	*482* 777	*444* 716	*360* 580	*271* 437	*137** 221*

*Distance via Mexico Highway 19 is only 96 miles, 154 km.

ROAD SIGNS

Mexico has officially adopted a uniform traffic sign system in which many signs are pictorially self-explanatory. Some of the most common appear below with Spanish-English definitions.

STOP

ESCUELA
School

PUENTE ANGOSTO
Narrow Bridge

GANADO
Cattle

CRUCE F.C.
Railroad Crossing

YIELD RIGHT OF WAY

CURVA PELIGROSA
Dangerous Curve

CAMINO SINUOSO
Winding Road

HOMBRES TRABAJANDO
Men Working

VADO
Dip

VADO
Dip
(across arroyo)

ZONA DE DERRUMBRES
Slide Area

TOPE
Speed Bump

SPEED BUMP
100 Meters Ahead

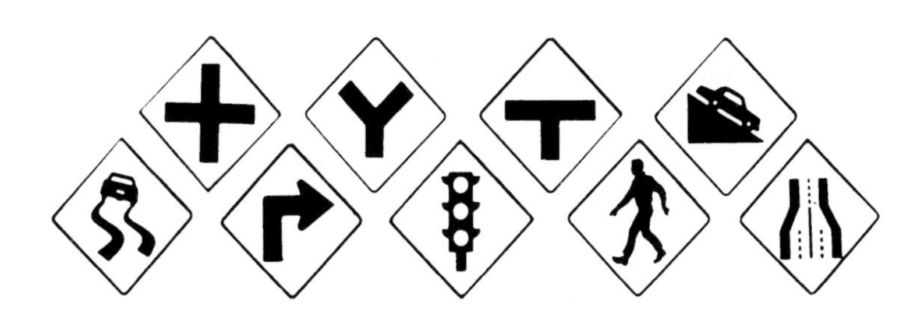

One Way

Two Way

Left Turn Only

Speed Limit

Keep to Right

No passing

NO VOLTEAR EN U
No U Turn

No parking
8 a.m. to 9 p.m.

PROHIBIDO ESTACIONARSE
No Parking

One Hour Parking

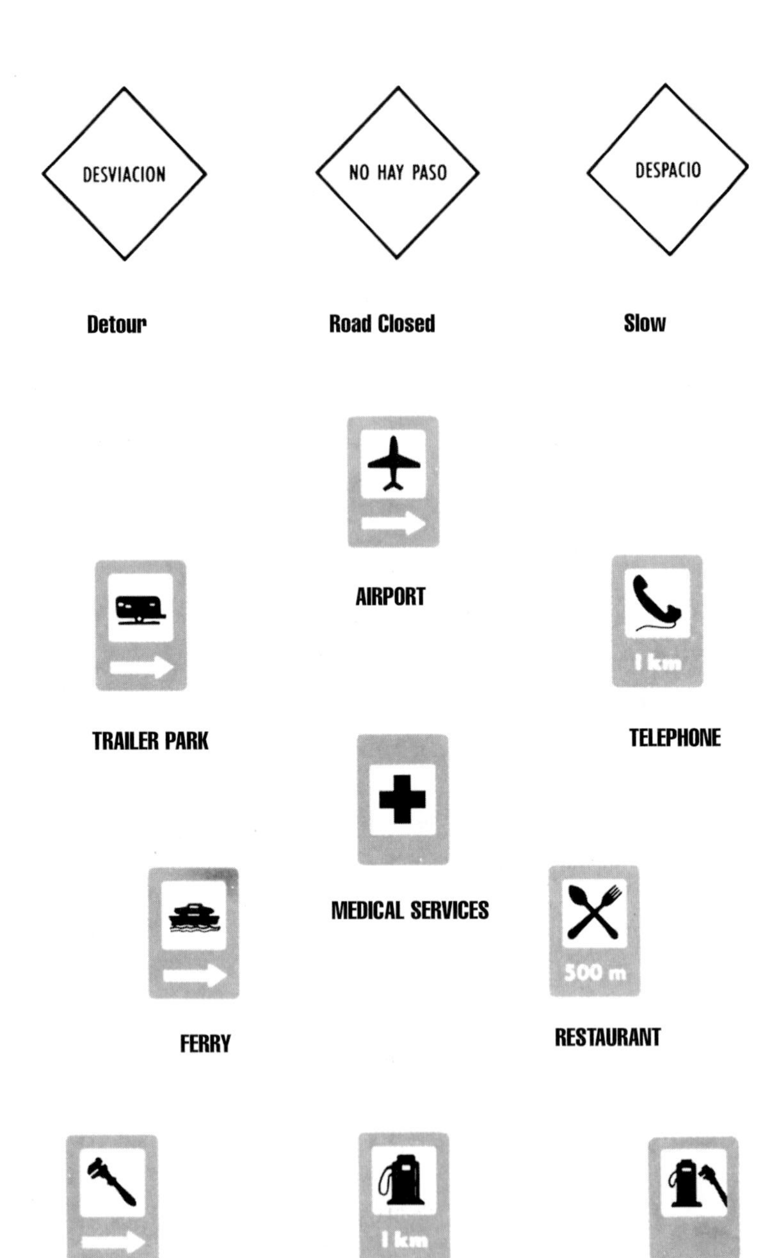

Detour

Road Closed

Slow

AIRPORT

TRAILER PARK

TELEPHONE

MEDICAL SERVICES

FERRY

RESTAURANT

GAS & MECHANICAL SERVICE

Recreation

HUNTING

Most of Baja's hunting is in the northern third of the peninsula. Several species of squirrel populate the region, as well as peccary, bobcat, fox, coyote, jackrabbit and cottontail. The Mexicali Valley is perhaps the most popular of the peninsula's hunting regions, having large quantities of mourning dove, white-wing dove, pheasant and quail. Ducks are found in the lagoons and marshes along both coasts, while quail, pheasant and dove are found in varying quantities throughout the state. San Quintín Bay is known for its large population of black brant, in addition to good shooting for quail.

Although mule deer and desert bighorn sheep inhabit some areas in Baja California, they are scarce and special permits are required to hunt them. Hunting seasons vary according to species, but most open seasons occur between September and the end of February.

Regulations

Hunting in Baja California requires a special-purpose visa, a consular certificate, a Military Gun Permit, a hunting permit, and during the hunt the presence of a licensed outfitter's assistant. In addition to the above, when hunting for mule deer or desert bighorn sheep, a contract with a licensed Mexican organizer must be purchased. It is advisable to contact an American organization that specializes in hunting in Mexico to obtain the necessary documents and to make arrangements with a Mexican contract organizer.

Weapons are forbidden in Mexico unless they are brought into the country during hunting seasons for the express purpose of hunting. Only two sporting firearms and 100 rounds of ammunition for each are permitted. Military and .22 caliber rimfire weapons and all pistols are prohibited. Bow and arrow hunting requires a special permit.

Standard Licensing Procedure

1. Consular Certificate This document is issued by all Mexican consulates. Applicants must present a letter of good conduct from their local police department or sheriff's office vouching for their moral character, plus two color, front-view, passport-size photographs. The consular certificate is not a hunting permit—it is merely an authorization for the hunter to enter Mexico in this capacity, and is also required when applying for a Military Gun Permit. It will contain a description of each firearm, including kind, make, serial number, caliber or gauge and number of cartridges. The hunter needs a consular certificate for each of the peninsula's states—Baja California and Baja California Sur.

2. Hunting Permits (Licenses) Hunters must purchase permits for each Mexican state in which they intend to hunt and for each species of bird or animal they intend to hunt. Hunting permits are issued in the names of individual hunters and are not transferable. Each permit is valid only for the current season and in the state for which it was issued. All the paperwork necessary for hunting in Baja California may be handled by the Mexican Hunting Association, information on which is provided below. The association also furnishes information on hunting conditions and government regulations (which are subject to change). Depending on the types of mammals or birds hunted, the total cost for permits ranges from about $400 to $600. For information about specific services, contact the Mexican Hunting Association, 3302 Josie Ave., Long Beach, CA 90808; phone (562) 421-6215; FAX (562) 496-2412. Or, contact their office in Mexicali; phone 01152 (6) 554-42-35 or 554-40-49; or by mail at P.O. Box 3598, Calexico, CA 92231. The Mexicali contact, Rafael Valle, speaks English and has more than 25 years' experience as a hunting guide in Baja California.

WATER RECREATION

Regulations

Boating Permits Anyone planning to operate a private boat in Mexican waters, regardless of size or construction, must first obtain a Mexican Boat Permit issued by the Mexico Department of Fisheries. Permits are sold on a yearly basis and are valid for 12 months from the date of issue. Fees for permits are based on the length of the craft: under 23 feet, $30.15; 23 feet to 29 feet-11 inches, $60.25; 30 feet and over, $90.30. For small auxiliary boats carried onboard vessels of 30 feet or longer, there is an additional fee of $30.15 per craft. These fees are subject to change; the Mexico Department of Fisheries office can provide current fees.

Obtain applications for Mexican Boat Permits and submit the completed forms to the Mexico Department of Fisheries at 2550 5th Ave., Suite 101, San Diego, CA 92103-6622; (619) 233-6956. The office is open Monday through Friday 8 a.m. to 2 p.m.

Boat permit applications must include a copy of the boat's registration document, which must be shown before applying for a permit. Fees must be paid by cash, or a cashier's check or money order (personal checks are not accepted) made payable to Oficina Recaudadora de Pesca for the exact amount due. For mail orders, include a stamped return envelope.

Prices are subject to change due to currency fluctuations.

Fishing Licenses Any nonresident alien must possess a valid Mexican Sportfishing License before fishing in Mexican waters. This license covers all types of fishing and is valid anywhere in Mexico. **Everyone aboard private boats in Mexican waters must have a fishing license regardless of age and whether or not they are fishing.** Licenses for people fishing on commercial sportfishing boats are normally provided by the boat operators. A fishing license is also officially required for underwater fishing and free diving.

Fishing licenses are issued for periods of one week, one month and one year, effective at 12:01 a.m. on the starting date specified on the license application. Fees for licenses are $21.20 for one week, $30.40 for one month and $39.50 for one year. (These fees

FISHING QUALITY PROFILE

Fish	PACIFIC				GULF							
	Ensenada	San Quintín	Bahía Tortugas	Los Cabos	San Felipe	Puertecitos	San Luis Gonzaga	Bahía de L.A.	Mulegé	Loreto	La Paz	East Cape
Albacore	6-10	6-10										
Barracuda	4-10	4-10	11-3									
Black sea bass		4-10										
Cabrilla							6-10	6-10	5-9	5-10	5-12	3-12
Corvina	7-9					5-8	3-9	2-6	6-9	4-10		
Dorado				5-12				4-11	1-12	6-9	5-11	5-12
Grouper				1-12		4-10	3-12	6-9		1-12	1-12	2-12
Jack Crevalle							4-10		5-7		1-10	4-10
Marlin	6-9	6-9		2-7				11-2		5-6	5-7	5-11
Needlefish								5-6			5-9	7-11
Rockfish	10-4	2-9										
Roosterfish						6-9			5-7	10-3	4-10	7-9
Sailfish				6-9					5-10	6-7	6-11	4-11
Sea bass							6-9	5-10	5-9			
Sierra			7-10	10-4	5-9	6-10			4-10	10-4	10-6	4 - 7
Skipjack				6-12						5-9		6-10
Snapper										4-10	4-10	4-10
Snook								4-5				
Tuna				5 -9						1-3		
Wahoo				9-1							4-12	6-10
White sea bass	4-10	4-10	4-10		11-4	11-3			11-3			
Yellowfin tuna			7-10	4-6, 10-12				7-10		10-6	4-12	4-5
Yellowtail	6-9	4-10	10-4	4-5		5-10					12-5	4-5

are subject to change; the Department of Fisheries office can provide current fees.) Mexican fishing licenses are not transferable, and each license must include the person's full legal name, home address and telephone number.

Obtain applications for Mexican Sportfishing Licenses and submit the completed forms to the Mexico Department of Fisheries at 2550 5th Ave., Suite 101, San Diego, CA 92103-6622; (619) 233-6956. The office is open Monday through Friday 8 a.m. to 2 p.m.

Applications must be accompanied by cash, a cashier's check or money order (no personal checks) for the exact amount due, payable to Oficina Recaudadora de Pesca. For mail orders, include a stamped return envelope. The Mexico Department of Fisheries also has offices in Mexico (Oficina de Pesca), but we recommend obtaining your license before crossing the border.

Fishing Bag Limits and Other Regulations

Each angler may catch up to 10 fish per day, with no more than five fish of the same species. In addition, anglers are subject to the following limits: no more than one billfish (marlin, sailfish or swordfish) and two tarpon, roosterfish, shad or halibut. Catching one of any of the above species counts as five of any other type of fish when calculating the day's limit. On inland bodies of water (rivers, lakes, etc.), the limit is five fish per day, whether of a single specie or a combination. Underwater fishing is limited to five fish per day, and only while skin diving. In all cases, once the permitted limit has been bagged, all further catches must be released.

Except when skin or scuba diving, fishing must be done with a hand-held line or a line attached to a rod. The use of nets (except handling nets), traps, poisons or explosives is prohibited. Skin divers may fish only with hand-held spears or band-powered spear guns. Selling, trading or exchanging fish caught is illegal. Fish can be eviscerated and filleted, but a patch of skin must be left to permit identification. Mexican law prohibits the taking of abalone, lobster, shrimp, Pismo clams, totuava, oysters and sea turtles. Anyone wishing to purchase any of these species to take into the United States must first obtain a form from the Mexico Department of Fisheries; available only through Oficinas de Pesca in Mexico. You must purchase these species at designated public markets or fishing cooperatives.

U. S. Customs Regulations

Anglers may enter the United States with only the fish they plan to use for personal consumption. Shellfish, except for lobster and shrimp, are prohibited. The number of fish must not exceed the Mexican bag limit. Fish transported across the border can be eviscerated but must be identifiable. The head, tail or a patch of skin left intact will usually suffice. Anyone bringing fish into the United States will be asked by Customs officials to present a valid Mexican fishing license or a Mexico Department of Fisheries form covering the purchase of the fish. For more information, contact the U.S. Fish and Wildlife Law Enforcement Agency at (619) 661-3130.

BAJA CALIFORNIA CLIMATE CHART

	January		February		March		April		May		June		July		August		September		October		November		December		Total Annual Rainfall
	Temp.*	Rainfall	Temp.	Rainfall	Temp.	Rainfall	Temp.	Rainfall	Temp.	Rainfall	Temp.	Rainfall	Temp.	Rainfall	Temp.	Rainfall	Temp.	Rainfall	Temp.	Rainfall	Temp.	Rainfall	Temp.	Rainfall	
Cabo San Lucas . . .	64	0.7	66	0.1	68	0.1	70	0.1	73	—	79	—	81	0.8	82	1.8	81	2.7	79	1.3	72	0.4	68	0.6	8.5
Ciudad Constitutión.	59	0.5	61	0.1	63	—	66	—	70	—	73	—	80	0.5	82	1.4	80	1.2	75	0.3	70	0.2	63	0.6	4.8
Colonia Guerrero . .	54	1.5	55	1.6	57	2.0	58	0.5	59	0.2	63	—	66	—	68	0.4	68	0.4	63	0.8	57	1.2	55	1.4	10.0
El Rosario	57	1.0	61	1.0	63	0.8	63	0.2	64	—	70	—	75	—	75	1.0	73	0.2	70	0.8	64	0.8	61	1.1	6.1
Ensenada	54	2.3	55	2.3	59	1.9	59	0.6	63	0.2	64	—	68	—	70	—	68	—	63	0.2	61	0.6	57	2.1	10.2
La Paz	64	0.4	66	—	68	—	72	—	75	—	80	—	84	0.2	85	1.2	84	2.4	79	0.8	73	0.8	67	0.4	6.2
Loreto	61	0.4	63	—	66	—	68	—	73	—	81	—	86	0.4	88	1.6	84	2.4	81	0.4	70	—	63	0.4	5.6
Mexicali	54	0.4	59	04	63	0.4	68	0.2	75	—	86	—	91	—	90	0.3	81	0.3	73	0.5	61	0.2	54	0.4	3.1
San Felipe	55	0.4	57	—	61	—	66	—	73	0.4	79	—	81	—	82	0.4	79	0.6	70	0.6	63	—	57	0.4	2.8
San Ignacio	57	0.4	61	0.4	63	0.4	64	—	72	—	75	0.4	81	0.4	82	0.4	79	0.8	73	0.4	64	0.4	57	0.4	4.4
San Vicente	54	2.4	55	2.4	55	1.9	57	0.2	63	—	68	—	72	—	73	—	70	0.1	64	0.1	59	0.7	54	2.1	9.9
Tecate	50	2.6	52	2	53	2.4	55	1.1	59	0.3	66	0.1	72	—	72	0.2	70	0.2	64	0.5	57	1.5	52	2.1	13.0
Tijuana	55	2	57	2.4	59	2	61	0.4	66	—	68	—	73	—	73	—	72	—	66	0.4	63	1.2	57	1.8	10.2

*Temperatures are expressed in degrees Fahrenheit - Rainfall in inches. Figures represent official monthly averages.

METRIC CONVERSION

Mexico uses the metric system of weights and measurements. Speed limits are posted in kilometers and gasoline is sold by the liter. Knowledge of simple conversions for kilometers/miles and liters/gallons is essential and may save you from a speeding ticket or being overcharged at the pump.

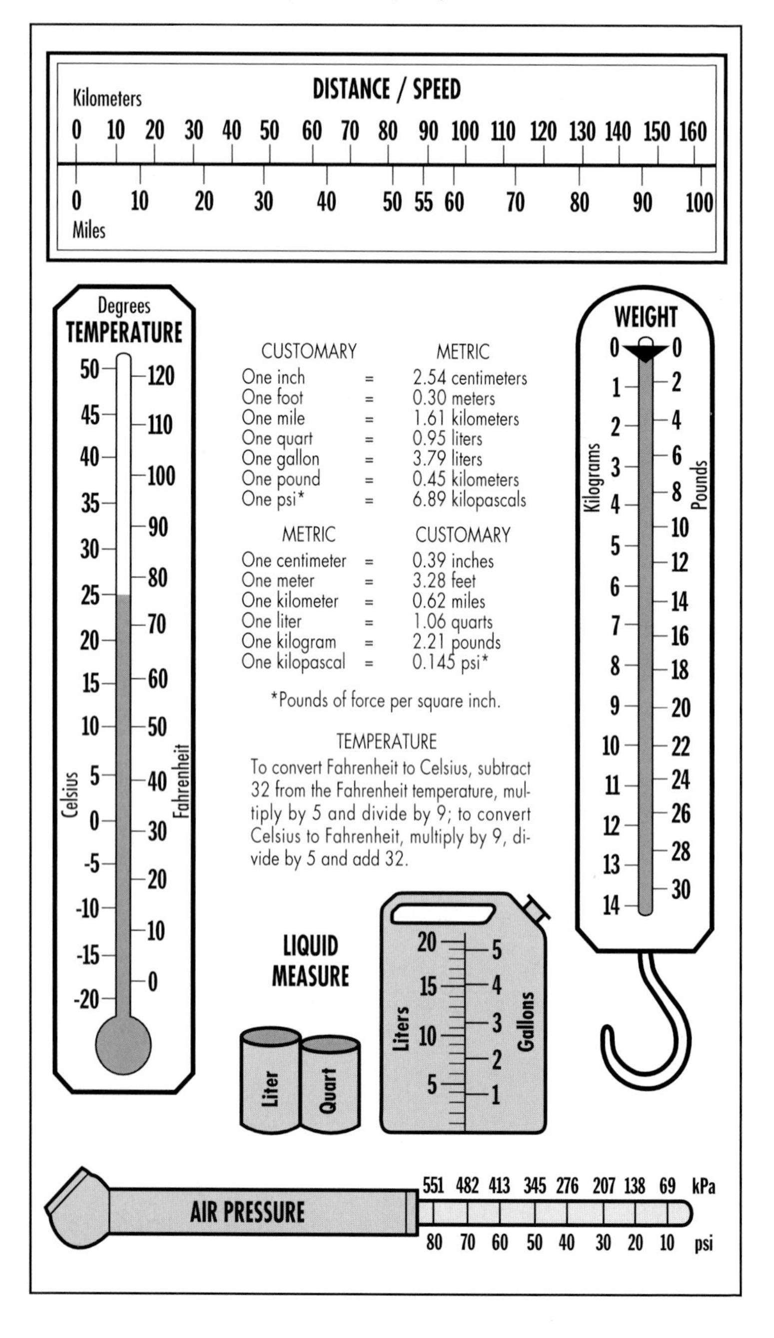

Speaking Spanish

Many Baja Californians speak at least some English—especially in the areas most frequented by tourists. Elsewhere, though, you may be hard-pressed to find someone who speaks fluent English. Very few gasoline stations beyond Ensenada have English-speaking employees. The same goes for most shops, stores, cafes, or even some hotels, trailer parks and government agencies. The tourist armed with a good English-Spanish dictionary, a basic Spanish phrase book and a little patience will do quite well in Baja California.

This section lists some of the Spanish phrases and sentences that are most useful to visitors in Baja. A basic knowledge of the language may be helpful. Many of the local residents who deal with tourists speak English; those who don't are glad to help you along with your attempts at their language. Spanish is not difficult to pronounce. A study of the following pronunciation rules will be sufficient to make yourself understood.

PRONUNCIATION

By and large, Spanish is an easy language to pronounce. The spelling is almost always phonetic; nearly every letter has one sound that it retains at all times.

Vowels

A	pronounced as in *father.*
E	pronounced as in *bed.*
I	pronounced as in *pizza.*
O	pronounced as in *hold*
U	pronounced as in *junior.*

Two-vowel combinations

Compared to English, Spanish does not use two-vowel combinations to produce different pronunciations. There are some notable exceptions, however, including those that follow:

au as in English ouch	*gaucho*
ay as in pie	*Mayan*
ue as in weh	*fuente*

Consonants

Consonants do not differ materially from the English. The few differences can be summarized as follows:

C is pronounced with a soft sound before *e* and *i*. Otherwise it has a *k* sound.

cinco SEEN-ko.

G is like a strong English *h* when it precedes *e* and *i*. In all other cases it is like the English *g* in go.

gente HEN-te.

H is always silent.

J is pronounced like a strong English *h*.

LL is pronounced like the English *y*.

caballo kah-BAH-yo

Ñ is pronounced like a combination of *n* and *y*.

niño NEEN-yo

Qu is pronounced like *k*.

Z is always pronounced like the English *s*.

Accent or Stress

1. When a word ends in a vowel, *n* or *s*, the stress falls on the next to the last syllable.
   hombre OM-bre
   hablan AH-blan
   estos ES-tos

2. When the word ends in a consonant other than *n* or *s*, the stress falls on the last syllable.
   hablar ah-BLAR

3. In some cases an accent mark will be found over a vowel. This does not change the pronunciation of that vowel, but indicates that the stress falls on that syllable.
   gramática gra-MAH-ti-ca
   corazón cor-a-SOWN

Words and Phrases

Nouns in Spanish are either masculine or feminine, and there are two words meaning "the": *el* is used before masculine nouns, *la* before feminine nouns. The plural of *el* is *los*, *la* is *las*. For instance, say *el hotel* and *los hoteles*; *la posada* and *las posadas*. After words given on these pages, the gender is indicated by (m.) for masculine, (f.) for feminine. The word "*usted*," meaning "you," is usually abbreviated *Ud*. An adjective also agrees in gender with the noun it modifies. For example, *el hombre pequeño*—the small man; *la camisa roja*—the red shirt. In most cases, the adjective follows the noun.

LANGUAGE

Do you understand English?
¿Entiende Ud. inglés?

I do not speak Spanish.
No hablo español.

Yes, sir; no, madam.
Sí, señor; no, señora.

Very little
Muy poco; (or) poquito

I do not understand.
No entiendo.

Do you understand me?
¿Me entiende Ud?

Please speak slowly.
Por favor hable despacio.

I wish to speak with an interpreter.
Me gustaría hablar con un intérprete.

What are you saying?
¿Qué dice?

POLITE PHRASES

Good morning.
Buenos días.

Good afternoon.
Buenas tardes.

Good night.
Buenas noches.

Goodbye.
Adiós; hasta la vista.

Thank you.
Gracias.

Yes; very good.
Sí; muy bueno.

Please.
Por favor.

Excuse me.
Perdóneme.

I am very sorry.
Lo siento mucho.

TO EXPLAIN YOUR NEEDS

I need; we need.
Necesito; necesitamos.

I would like to call.
Quisiera llamar.

I am hungry; we are hungry.
Tengo hambre; tenemos hambre.

I am thirsty; we are thirsty.
Tengo sed; tenemos sed.

I am cold; we are cold.
Tengo frío; tenemos frío.

I am warm; we are warm.
Tengo calor; tenemos calor.

I am tired; we are tired.
Estoy cansado(a); estamos cansados.

I am sick; we are sick.
Estoy enfermo(a); estamos enfermos.

The child is sick; tired.
El niño (la niña) está enfermo(a); cansado(a).

DIRECTIONS

north/**norte**
south/**sur**
east/**este**
west/**oeste**

(Note: In some addresses, east is **oriente**, abbreviated **Ote.**; west is **poniente**, abbreviated **Pte.**)

NUMERALS

1	**uno**	16	**dieciseis**
2	**dos**	17	**diecisiete**
3	**tres**	18	**dieciocho**
4	**cuatro**	20	**veinte**
5	**cinco**	21	**veinte y uno**
6	**seis**	30	**treinta**
7	**siete**	40	**cuarenta**
8	**ocho**	50	**incuenta**
9	**nueve**	60	**esenta**
10	**diez**	70	**setenta**
11	**once**	80	**ochenta**
12	**doce**	90	**noventa**
13	**trece**	100	**cien**
14	**catorce**	200	**doscientos**
15	**quince**		

DAYS AND TIME

Sunday/**domingo**
Monday/**lunes**
Tuesday/**martes**
Wednesday/**miércoles**
Thursday/**jueves**
Friday/**viernes**
Saturday/**sábado**
today/**hoy**
tomorrow/**mañana**
yesterday/**ayer**

morning/**la mañana**
noon/**el mediodía**
afternoon/**la tarde**
tonight/**esta noche**
night/**la noche**
last night/**anoche**
midnight/**a medianoche**

What time is it?
¿Qué horas son?

It is one o'clock.
Es la una.

It is two o'clock.
Son las dos.

It is ten minutes past two.
Son las dos y diez.

It is a quarter past three.
Son las tres y cuarto.

It is a quarter of five.
Son un cuarto para las cinco.

It is 25 minutes of six.
Son veintecinco para las seis.

It is half past four.
Son las cuatro y media.

USEFUL ADJECTIVES

bad/**malo**
beautiful/**hermoso**
cheap/**barato**
clean/**limpio**
cold/**frío**
difficult/**difícil**
dirty/**sucio**
early/**temprano**
easy/**fácil**
expensive/**caro**
fast/**rápido**
good/**bueno**
high/**alto**
hot/**caliente**
kind/**amable**
large/**grande**
low/**bajo**
late/**tarde**
long/**largo**
polite/**cortés**
sharp/**agudo**
short/**corto**
slow/**lento**
small/**pequeño, chico**
ugly/**feo**
unkind/**despiadado, duro**

COLORS

white/**blanco**
pink/**rosa**
black/**negro**
blue; dark blue/**azul; azul oscuro**
gray/**gris**
green; light green/**verde; verde claro**
brown/**café**
purple/**morado**
red/**rojo; colorado**
yellow/**amarillo**

AT THE BORDER

passport/**pasaporte**
tourist card/**tarjeta de turista**
age/**edad**
marital status/**estado civil**
single/**soltero (m.); soltera (f.)**
married/**casado (m.); casada (f.)**
widowed/**viudo (m.); viuda (f.)**
divorced/**divorciado (m.); divorciada (f.)**
profession; occupation/**profesión; ocupación**
vaccination card/**cartilla de vacunación**
driver's license/**licencia de manejar**
car owner's title (registration)/**título de propiedad (registro)**
year of car/**modelo (o año)**
make (Ford, Mazda, etc.)/**marca**
license plate and state/**placa y estado**
chassis and motor number/**número de chasis y motor**
number of doors/**número de puertas**
number of cylinders/**número de cilindros**
number of passengers/**número de pasajeros**

ON THE ROAD

kilometer/**kilómetro (m.)**
highway/**carretera (f.)**
road/**camino (m.)**
street/**calle (f.)**
avenue/**avenida (f.)**
boulevard/**bulevard (m.)**
block/**cuadra (f.)**
corner/**esquina (f.)**
left side/**lado izquierdo (m.)**
right side/**lado derecho (m.)**

Show me the road to...
Enséñeme el camino a...

How far is...?
¿Qué tan lejos está...?

Can we get to ...before dark?
¿Podemos llegar a ...antes del anochecer?

Is this road dangerous?
¿Es peligroso este camino?

Is that road in good condition?
¿Está en buen estado aquel camino?

Is it paved or is it a dirt road?
¿Está pavimentado o es de terracería?

Go straight ahead.
Siga derecho.

Turn to the right; left.
Vuelta a la derecha; izquierda.

What city, town, is this?
¿Qué ciudad, pueblo, es éste?

Where does this road lead?
¿A dónde conduce este camino?

IN CASE OF CAR TROUBLE

I want to ask you a favor.
Quiero pedirle un favor.

I need a tow truck.
Necesito una grua.

My car has broken down.
Se me ha descompuesto el carro.

My lights don't work.
Mis faros no funcionan.

The starter does not work.
El arranque no funciona.

I have run out of gasoline.
Se me acabó la gasolina.

Is there a gasoline station near here?
¿Hay una gasolinería cerca de aquí?

Is there a garage near here?
¿Hay un garage cerca?

Please send someone to repair my car.
Por favor mande a alguien a componer mi carro.

May I go with you to get a mechanic?
¿Puedo ir con usted a conseguir un mecánico?

Have you a rope to tow my car?
¿Tiene una cuerda para remolcar mi carro?

Do you want to help me push the car to one side of the road?
¿Quiere ayudarme a empujar el carro a un lado del camino?

Do you want to help me change a tire?
¿Quiere ayudarme a cambiar una llanta?

Do you want to be my witness?
¿Quiere ser mi testigo?

ARRIVING IN TOWN

Is English spoken here?
¿Se habla inglés aquí?

Where is the center of town?
¿Dónde está el centro de la ciudad?

Where is X Street, X Square, the X Hotel?
¿Dónde está la Calle X, la Plaza X, el Hotel X?

May I park here?
¿Puedo estacionarme aquí?

Please direct me to the nearest post office.
Por favor diríjame a la oficina de correos mascercana.

Where can I find a policeman, a hairdresser, a doctor, a drug store?
¿Dónde puedo hallar un policía, una estética, un médico, una farmacia?

Where is the police station, the chamber of commerce?
¿Dónde está la comisaría, la cámara de comercio?

Where can I find road maps, post cards, American newspapers?
¿Dónde se pueden hallar mapas de caminos, tarjetas postales, periódicos nortemericanos?

Please direct me to the railroad station, the bus station.
Por favor diríjame a la estación del ferrocarril, a la terminal del autobús.

How often does the bus go by?
¿Qué tan seguido pasa el autobús (camión)?

Does the bus stop here?
¿Para aquí el autobús?

Could you recommend a good restaurant; a good small hotel; a first class hotel?

¿Puede Ud. recomendar un buen restaurante; un buen hotel pequeño; un hotel de primera clase?

I wish to telephone, to telegraph, to cable.

Quiero telefonear, telegrafiar, cablegrafiar.

I wish to change some money.

Quiero cambiar dinero.

What is the rate of exchange?

¿Cuál es el tipo de cambio?

I want to cash a check.

Quiero cambiar un cheque.

AT THE HOTEL

hotel/**hotel (m.)**
inn/**posada (f.)**
apartments/**departamentos (m.)**
room/**cuarto (m.)**
furnished room/**cuarto amueblado**
bedroom/**recámara (f.)**
pillow/**almohada (f.)**
blanket/**cobija (f.), manta (f.)**
air conditioning/**aire acondicionado**
kitchen/**cocina (f.)**
bathroom/**cuarto de baño (m.)**
towel/**toalla (f.)**
wash cloth/**toalla chica (f.)**
soap/**jabón (m.)**
dining room/**comedor (m.)**
ice water/**agua con hielo (m.)**
hot water/**agua caliente (m.)**
elevator/**elevador (m.)**
stairway/**escalera (f.)**
key/**llave (f.)**
office/**oficina (f.)**
manager/**gerente (m.)**
maid/**recamarera (f.)**
office employee/**empleado de oficina (m.)**
bellboy/**maletero (m.)**
porter/**mozo de servicios (m.)**
guest/**huésped (m.)**

I want a single room, with bath.

Deseo un cuarto sencillo, con baño.

I want a room for two; with twin beds.

Deseo un cuarto para dos; con camas gemelas.

I want two connecting rooms.

Deseo dos cuartos comunicados.

A front room; a back room.

Un cuarto al frente; al fondo.

A quiet room.
Un cuarto tranquilo.

On the lower floor; upper floor.
En el piso bajo; piso alto.

Will you have the baggage brought up? ...down?
¿Quiere Ud. hacer subir ...bajar el equipaje?

We are leaving tomorrow.
Nos vamos mañana.

We are staying several days ...just tonight.
Nos quedaremos aquí unos pocos días ...
solamente esta noche.

What is the price (rate)?
¿Cuál es el precio (la tarifa)?

What is the minimum rate?
¿Cuál es el precio mínimo?

Do you accept checks in payment?
¿Acepta Ud. cheques en pago?

I want my bill, please.
Quiero la cuenta, por favor.

Have you hot running water?
¿Hay agua corriente y caliente?

The shower doesn't work.
La regadera no funciona.

Is there a garage?
¿Hay garage?

Where is the ladies' room, men's room?
¿Dónde está el baño (lavabo) de damas, de caballeros?

Where is the barber shop?
¿Dónde hay una peluquería?

Please send these clothes to the laundry.
Hágame el favor de mandar esta ropa a la lavandería.

Please clean and press this suit.
Hágame el favor de limpiar y planchar este traje.

I want it today; tomorrow.
Lo quiero hoy; mañana.

Please call me at six o'clock.
Hágame el favor de llamarme a las seis.

Please forward my correspondence to this address.
Por favor mande mi correspondencia a esta dirección.

Do you want to prepare a lunch for us to carry with us?
¿Quiere Ud. prepararnos un almuerzo para llevar?

AT THE GARAGE

How much is gasoline per liter?
¿Cuánto cuesta el litro de gasolina?

Fill up the gasoline tank; the radiator.
Llene el tanque de gasolina; el radiador.

Give me five, ten, fifteen, twenty liters.
Deme cinco, diez, quince, veinte litros.

Check the oil; change the oil.
Vea el aceite; cambie el aceite.

Please lubricate the car; wash the car.
Favor de lubricar el carro; lavar el carro.

Please tighten the brakes; adjust the brakes.
Favor de apretar los frenos; ajustar los frenos.

Please tune the engine; change the spark plugs.
Favor de poner a punto (afinar) el motor; cambiar las bujías.

My tire has a puncture. Can you repair the tube?
Mi llanta tiene un agujero. ¿Puede reparar la cámara?

The tire is flat.
La llanta está ponchada.

The horn is not working.
La claxón no funciona.

The battery needs charging.
La batería necesita carga.

Please put another bulb in this headlamp.
Favor de reemplazar el foco de este faro.

The gasoline tank is leaking.
El tanque de gasolina está goteando.

The gas line is clogged.
La manguera de gasolina está tapada.

The engine overheatsheats.
El motor se calienta.

The exhaust is choked.
Está obstruido el tubo de escape.

The steering gear is out of order.
La dirección está descompuesta.

The radiator leaks.
El radiador gotea.

The clutch slips.
El embrague resbala.

There is a short circuit.
Hay un corto circuito.

The windshield wiper does not work.
El limpia para brisas no funciona.

The taillight does not work.
El faro trasero no funciona.

Please clean the windshield.
Favor de limpiar el parabrisas.

When will the repairs be finished?
¿Cuándo terminará la reparación?

How much do I owe you?
¿Cuánto le debo?

AT THE RESTAURANT

Please bring me the menu.
Favor de traerme el menú.

I like my meat rare (well done).
Quiero la carne tierna (bien cocida).

Please bring me the check.
Favor de traerme la cuenta.

breakfast/**desayuno (m.)**
lunch/**almuerzo (m.)**
dinner/**comida (f.)**
supper/**cena (f.)**
knife/**cuchillo (m.)**
fork/**tenedor (m.)**
spoon/**cuchara (f.)**
cup/**taza (f.)**
glass/**vaso (f.)**
napkin/**servilleta (f.)**
bill/**cuenta (f.)**
tip/**propina (f.)**

BREAD

bread/**pan (m.)**
toast/**pan tostado (m.)**
crackers/**galletas saladas (f.)**

FRUIT

apple/**manzana (f.)**
avocado/**aguacate (m.)**
figs/**higos (m.)**
fruit/**fruta (f.)**
guava/**guayaba (f.)**
lemon/**lima (m.)**
lime/**limón (f.)**
banana/**plátano (m.)**
dates/**dátiles (m.)**
nuts/**nueces (f.)**
olives/**aceitunas (f.)**
orange/**naranja (f.)**
peach/**durazno (m.)**
pineapple/**piña (f.)**
strawberries/**fresas (f.)**

VEGETABLES

beans/**frijoles (m.)**
beets/**betabeles (f.)**
cabbage/**repollo (m.); col (f.)**
corn/**maíz (m.); elote (m.)**
lettuce/**lechuga (f.)**
onion/**cebolla (f.)**
peas/**chícharos (m.)**
vegetables/**verduras (f)**

MEAT, PORK, POULTRY, EGGS, FISH

sausage/**salchicha (f.)**
meat/**carne (f.)**
beef/**carne de res (f.)**
grilled meat/**carne asada (f.)**
pork/**carne de puerco (m.)**
pork chop/**chuleta (f.)**
ham/**jamón (m.)**
beefsteak/**bistec (m.); filete (m.)**
veal/**ternera (f.)**
lamb/**carne de carnero (m.)**
hard-boiled/**cocidos duro (m.)**
scrambled/**revueltos (m.)**
duck/**pato (m.)**
turkey/**pavo (m.)**

bacon/**tocino (m.)**
chicken/**pollo (m.)**
egg/**huevo (m.)**
fried/**frito (m.)**
soft-boiled/**tibio (m.)**
abalone/**abulón (m.)**
clam/**almeja (f.)**
fish/**pescado (m.)**
scallops/**callos (m.)**
shrimp/**camarónes (m.)**
lobster/**langosta (f.)**

BEVERAGES, LIQUORS

beer/**cerveza (f.)**
brandy/**brandy (m.)**
champagne/**champaña (m.)**
cocktail/**coctel (m.)**
coffee/**café (m.)**
with cream/**con crema (f.)**
without cream/**sin crema (f.)**
gin/**ginebra (f.)**
milk/**leche (f.)**
rum/**ron (m.)**
tea/**té (m.)**
water/**agua (m.)**
whiskey/**whiskey (m.)**
wine/**vino (m.)**

DESSERTS

cake/**pastel (m.)**
candies/**dulces (f.)**
custard/**flan (f.)**
ice cream/**helado (m.)**

MISCELLANEOUS

butter/**mantequilla (f.)**
cheese/**queso (m.)**
cookies/**galletas (f.)**
flour/**harina (f.)**
honey/**miel de abejas (f.)**
pepper/**pimienta (f.)**
salad/**ensalada (f.)**
salt/**sal (f.)**
sauce/**salsa (f.)**
soup/**sopa (f.); caldo (m.)**
sugar/**azúcar (m.)**

Supply Lists

The items in the following lists will help make a trip to Baja California safe and enjoyable. Two lists are shown: the first, for all trips, lists items that should be taken on any trip down the peninsula; the second, for backcountry travel, is more extensive and necessary only if you're planning an extended off-road or camping trip. Travelers should use their own discretion in deciding which items to include. It is better, however, to take along too much than too little, if there is room in the vehicle. All items on the first list should also be included in preparation for backcountry trips.

ALL TRIPS

For vehicles ...

Air filters
Brake fluid
Flares
Fuses (check amperage)
Motor oil
Power steering fluid
Tools
Water (5 gal. for radiator)
Window cleaner

For people ...

Can opener
Canteen
Drinking water and cups
First aid kit
Flashlight and batteries
Hat or other sunshade
Insect repellent
Keys (extra, for car)

Paper towels
Skin lotion
Spanish/English dictionary
Sun block
Salt tablets
Sunburn cream
Sunglasses
Toilet tissue
Trash bags

Auto Club personnel check out equipment and vehicles at Rancho Santa Inés during the 1973 research trip. (Auto Club Historical Photo)

BACKCOUNTRY TRIPS

For vehicles ...

Alternator brushes
Baling wire
Battery cables
Bolts and nuts (assorted sizes)
Chamois (for straining gasoline)
Duct tape
Electric fuel pump
Electric tape
Fire extinguisher
Fittings (gas lines)
Gaskets (head, fuel pump)
Gasoline cans (two, 5-gal.)
Gasoline filter (in-line)
Grease
GPS unit
Hammer (heavy)
Hoses and clamps (radiator)
Hydraulic jack (small sand-support board)
Ignition coil(s)
Ignition module
Lug wrench
Radiator sealant
Spare tires (extra)
Spark plugs
Tire inflator
Tow rope
Tube repair kit
Universal joints
Valve cores
Water cans (two, 5-gal.)
Wire (10-gauge electrical)
Wire connectors

For people and camps ...

Blankets
Camp cook set
Camp knives
Cell phone (populated areas only)
Chairs (folding)
Cleanser
Compass
Cots
Funnels (small and large)
Gloves (leather)
Grate (for cooking)
Hatchet
Lantern (extra mantles)
Matches (wooden)
Netting (mosquito)
Notebook
Pail or bucket
Pens and pencils
Portable toilet
Radio (portable, short-wave or CB)
Rags
Rope (small)
Crowbar
Detergent (liquid)
Dishes
Eating utensils
First aid kit (large)
Flashlight (large)
Fly swatter
Fuel (stove and lantern)
Scrub brush
Shovels (folding)
Signal mirror
Sleeping bags
Snake bite kit(s)
Soap (freshwater and saltwater)
Stove
Table (folding)
Tarpaulins
Tent
Toilet paper
Towels (bath, face)
Trash bags (large and small)
Wash cloths
Water purification tablets

~ General Index ~

For lodging, dining and maps, see separate indexes.

D

E

R

S

~ Recreation Index ~

~ Dining & Nightlife Index ~

~ Lodging & Campgrounds ~

H

J

L

M

~ Map Index ~

Regional Maps

City Maps

GreatestHits Maps

Route Maps

~ Side Routes Index ~

~ Photo Credits ~

David J. Brackney
Pages 8, 12, 13, 14, 15, 16 (both), 18, 19, 20 (both), 21, 22 (both), 23, 24, 25, 26, 29, 30, 42, 47, 49, 53, 63, 65, 67, 69, 71, 77, 79, 81, 83, 84, 89, 94, 95, 99, 100, 101, 104, 107, 112, 113, 115, 116 (both), 119, 120, 126, 128, 129, 131, 132, 138, 139, 140, 145, 152, 159, 161, 163, 172, 180, 181, 183, 184, 187, 189, 191, 193, 197, 198, 204, 207, 216, 220, 223, 225, 226, 229, 230, 233, 235, 236, 237, 241, 242, 246, 248, 261, 264, 266, 268, 269 (both), 273, 280, 284, 292, 299, 300, 302, 304, 316, 325, 330, 336, 344, 346, 349, 353, 357, 359, 361, 362, 371, 376, 380, 384, 387, 389, 390, 391, 395, 397, 401, 406, 409, 411, 414, 421, 423, 424, 425, 426, 429, 442, 445, 458, 459, 461, 462 (both), 463, 464

Bill Cory
Page 527

Todd Masinter
Cover, opening page, title page, pages 27, 50, 54, 73, 75, 88, 91, 98, 103, 121, 124, 136, 137, 141, 156, 164, 167, 168, 173, 174, 177, 202, 209, 217, 218, 224 (both), 251, 252, 254, 255, 258 (both), 286, 289, 290, 294, 297, 310, 313, 314, 315, 328, 332, 341, 343, 348, 366, 368, 370, 375, 386, 398, 402, 403, 413, 419, 434, 436, 441, 446

Alexander W. Kirkpatrick
Page 318

Auto Club Archives
Pages 28, 34, 37

John Skinner
Page 339